DOCUMENTS OF SOVIET HISTORY

Related Titles From

ACADEMIC INTERNATIONAL PRESS

USSR Calendar of Events, 1987–1991. Set of five volumes

Russia & Eurasia Facts & Figures Annual

Russia & Eurasia Documents Annual

Documents of Soviet-American Relations

INDEX
USSR Facts & Figures Annual, Volume 16
Index, Volumes 1–10, 1977–1986

DOCUMENTS

OF

SOVIET HISTORY

EDITED BY
ALEX G. CUMMINS

VOLUME 5

REVOLUTION FROM ABOVE

1929–1931

Academic International Press

2000

APPRECIATION

Special acknowledgment must be extended to
my wife REBECCA
who has supported me endlessly, patiently, and lovingly
and assisted in the preparation of this volume.
I am also indebted to my parents who instilled
in me the love of learning and curiosity.
Thanks are given to Professor Clifford Foust
for his support and encouragement,
Professor Rex Wade, and
to the University of Maryland, McKeldin Library,
and the Library of Congress
for access to resources and support.

DOCUMENTS OF SOVIET HISTORY, VOLUME 5, REVOLUTION FROM ABOVE, 1929-1931. Edited by Alex G. Cummins

ISBN: 0-87569-138-2

Composition by Peggy Pope

By direct subscription with the publisher

A list of Academic International Press publications is found at the end of this volume

ACADEMIC INTERNATIONAL PRESS
POB 1111 • GULF BREEZE FL 32562-1111 • USA

www.ai-press.com

CONTENTS

PREFACE

Documents of Soviet History attempts to meet the needs of researchers, be they scholars, students, journalists, government employees, or others who prefer a single source for documentary materials on the history of the Soviet Union. Previously researchers hunted through a large number of diverse works, usually specialized by time period, topic, or the organization which produced them. Success in this endeavor often requires considerable prior knowledge of the subject matter of the research conducted and about the particular document(s) needed. Even if researchers possess such knowledge, they may not have access to sources usually found only in the largest and most specialized libraries. If found, many of the documents are incomplete, while others lack the contextual information needed by most readers today. Some important documents, of course, are available only in Russian.

Documents of Soviet History brings together major documents of Soviet history in a multivolume set which eventually will cover the period from 1917 to 1986. Thereafter *USSR Documents Annual* and *Russia and Eurasia Documents Annual*, also published by Academic International Press, carry on the task of collecting and publishing primary source documents by and about the Soviet Union, Russia and Eurasian states. *Documents of Soviet History* seeks to select the most important documents, which best explain the development and policies of the Soviet Union. It includes not only those documents pertaining to politics, but those concerning culture and the arts, education, religion, the family, international relations, economics, military affairs, and other aspects of Soviet society and history. A distinct effort is made to include more than government and party pronouncements, which all too often represent the sole content of document collections. At the same time, such materials are recognizably an exceptionally important part of the documentary record and must be represented heavily. Given the nature of the Soviet system, certain leaders loom especially large and authoritative in some periods and their writings and statements are therefore heavily represented in the respective volumes. Both opposition and unofficial voices play a role at times, and they too are represented.

Only contemporary documents are used, that is, those originating at the time. Memoirs and other retrospective writings, including "diaries" which were rewritten, are not included. As editor of *Documents of Soviet History* I have continued the approach used by my predecessor, Rex A. Wade, and endeavored to select documents that (1) have lasting significance for understanding the Soviet Union in that they set forth fundamental policies and principles, (2) mark important events of Soviet development and history, (3) illustrate the debates on major issues, or (4) suggest the temper of the times. I acknowledge that no two people would make exactly the same selection from literally thousands of documents available, but I believe that the majority would agree on the inclusion of most of those found in this collection and hope that readers will find the selection reasonable as well as valuable.

Each volume in *Documents of Soviet History* covers a differing number of years. Some years and periods produced a larger number of important debates, decisions and documents than did others, and therefore the time span of each volume depends on the number and length of important documents in given years. This seems preferable to forcing the documents artificially into a uniform number of years for each volume. There are practical limitations on the size of such a collection and space imposes its own restraints on selection; "importance" is defined at least in part by the amount of space available. This collection will exceed the initially projected twelve volumes. Several future volumes will represent supplements to previous series of volumes, in order to include new sources as well as materials originally omitted because of the constraints of space. In any case, a compromise will be made between the effort to include a larger number and wider range of important documents than any general collection has done hitherto, and the exhaustion of both editor and users. For the sake of clarity and consistency, I have rendered the explanation and description of the presentation of documents that were used by my predecessor in the previous volumes.

The documents in this collection are arranged chronologically rather than grouping them by topic. While each method has advantages, the chronological approach is preferred here. It gives a better sense of historical development and in many instances clarifies how events and issues crowded in upon one another, influenced each other, and how the leaders grappled with many pressing problems simultaneously. Moreover, a single document often relates to several topics. For readers wanting material on a specific topic, the subject index will direct them to all documents on that subject as well as to shorter references within other documents. A listing of documents by main topics is also included for quick reference.

A headnote is provided for each document or series of documents for the purpose of placing the document in its historical framework, to indicate its significance and the more important issues it raises, and to make the necessary clarifications for readers. These headnotes are rather more extensive than in most document collections, on the assumption that most readers will have little knowledge of the historical context of the document.

One of the important principles guiding this collection is to publish each document in its entirety whenever possible. Deletion by editing for space can cause unintended shifts in meaning, and possibly exclude exactly those portions which a given reader needs. In some cases documents which simply are too long to be included in full, yet are too important to leave out, are edited in order to include them. Such instances are noted in the headnote to each document and marked in the text by standard ellipses (...). Readers should note some Soviet writers had a fondness for using ellipses for effect in their writings and so, in order to avoid confusing those with editor's omissions, the abridgment of a document is always noted in the headnote. Some peripheral matter, such as the names of signatories of formal decrees, laws and treaties, are not included unless there is a special reason to do so. These were generally a formality and take up a great deal of space better used for additional documents. When the signature of a particular official is of importance, it either is included or indicated in the headnote.

All parenthetical references in the documents are those of the original author. The few editorial clarifications I have made within texts are marked with my initials —[AGC] in brackets. All notes at the foot of the page are ones appearing in the original document. Many documents have passages in italics or bold print, and these are given as per the original. These were usually included in translations. I have attempted to reinstate them where they were dropped by the translator from the Russian original, keeping in mind that in some instances there are different Russian versions.

Within documents, the spelling and usage of the original translators generally were retained. There was little to gain in trying to force general stylistic uniformity on the translated documents. Some especially archaic or confusing usages, such as commissionary for commissar, workmen's for workers', etc., were replaced by the more common term. British and American spelling were retained according to the respective translators, except where the cold logic of the modern computer has homogenized them beyond the intent of the editor. Minor corrections—obvious grammatical and spelling errors, archaic or confusing terminology, a word or two of retranslation, etc.—were made "silently", that is to say, without noting it in every instance. All substantial modifications of translations are noted.

Russian names and words in the headnotes are given in the slightly simplified Library of Congress transliteration style familiar to readers of English, with diacritical marks and hard and soft sign usually omitted, and the *sky* rather than *skii* ending for family names (Trotsky, Lunacharsky). Within the documents they are given generally according to the translators' usage except in instances where names were transliterated in an unusual manner. To alleviate possible confusion, variant name spellings are listed in the index with cross–reference to the standard spelling.

For the benefit of those unfamiliar with Russian and the variations possible when it is transliterated into the Latin alphabet, introduction to the more common ones may help. One set of variations comes from two Russian letters, one of which is transliterated as *iu*, *yu*, or *ju*, and the other as *ia*, *ya*, or *ja*. Another common variation comes from the insertion of the letter *y*, most often before *e* to make *ye* or instead of *i* in connection with another vowel. Another common insertion is the letter *t* in front of *ch*. The apostrophe mark (') may be used to indicate the Russian soft sign or it may be omitted. Most readers are familiar with the three main sets of variations of name ending: the –sky, –skii or –ski; the –ov (ev), –of (ef) or –off (eff); the use of –a or –aya in some family names to indicate a woman (Stepanov/Stepanova, Krupskii/Krupskaia), which translators may or may not use. There are other variations, but these are the most common ones and the ones most likely to bother a reader of this volume.

The various party and government names used by different Russian authors and translators deserve special attention. The government formed in October 1917 was called the Council of People's Commissars, but is often referred to by the Russian acronym *Sovnarkom*. It was approved by the Second All–Russian Congress of Soviets of Workers' and Soldiers' Deputies, which also created an executive body to act for the Congress between its meetings—the Central Executive Committee, which is often referred to in documents by its initials, CEC (English) or TsIK (Russian). It is also important to keep these initials distinct from the initials sometimes used for the Central Committee of the Communist Party (C.C. or CC in English and TsK in Russian). The term "soviet" means in Russian "council"; many authors retain the Russian word soviet, now familiar to English readers, but some use council in the title of institutions containing that term. The Glossary will help readers unfamiliar with these and other Russian terms of the period, as will the headnote to documents containing them.

Sometimes there are variant dates for documents, among them the date when a resolution was introduced and when it was passed, the sending and receiving dates of a document, or the date when a law was passed by the Council of People's Commissars, when it was published in the newspapers, and when it was published in the official collection of laws. Thus readers may find a given document dated differently in different sources. In most cases the earliest verifiable date when action was taken or a document was created was used.

Soviet officials used the slash (/) between dates to refer to economic year, beginning on 1 October and ending on 30 September. For example, 1926/27 represented the economic year 1 October 1926—30 September 1927. The dash (—) refers to the calendar year.

Many of the documents given herein are being published for the first time in their complete form in English, and some for the first time in English at all, and yet others for the first time in a readily available source. The source for each document is given immediately following the document. A short form reference is used, and the reader who wishes can find the full citation in the list of sources cited. For some documents, both an English and a Russian language source are given. For a single document this means that an English translation existed but with some deletions and that the missing passages were added by the editor from the Russian source in order to make the document complete. In a few instances where two documents are given under one heading the two source references (of whatever language) refer to the different sources used for the respective documents.

Alex G. Cummins

INTRODUCTION

The disagreements between Stalin and Bukharin that receded by late 1928 re-emerged in the early months of 1929. Stalin and his followers were intent on accelerating the Five Year Plan at the expense of the peasantry, by focusing on means to extract grain and other products from the peasants and to eliminate the social and economic influence of the so-called kulaks in the countryside. They espoused the reintroduction of the "emergency measures," specifically the Urals-Siberian method, which proved relatively successful the preceding year. These measures consisted of sending government and party personnel into the countryside to seize grain and products, in many cases forcibly, from peasant holdings and storage bins. The Stalinists also wanted to accelerate the formation of state and collective farms as the basis of the marketable grain supply, thereby replacing reliance on market forces to acquire grain and other agricultural products to feed the cities and Red Army, and for export in exchange for the necessary equipment for industrialization.

Bukharin, Tomsky, Rykov, and their adherents, whom the Stalinists labeled the Right Opposition, Right Deviation, or Bukharin Group, preferred a gradual approach toward socialism. They believed the grain crisis of the previous year was temporal due to natural conditions and could be resolved by agricultural imports. They also believed the industrialization goals were too high for the country to support and would lead to a disastrous break in the alliance with the peasantry and the end of the New Economic Policy. Bukharin wrote an article, published in February 1929 on the eve of the anniversary of Lenin's death, in which he defended NEP and indirectly criticized Stalin's policies. Using excerpts from Lenin's later writings, he emphasized retaining ties with the peasantry so as to avoid a third revolution. The Bukharinites were not alone in their concern for the consequences of rapid and forced collectivization. Moderates, such as Lenin's wife, Nadezhda Krupskaia, urged caution. Krupskaia wrote that Lenin thought it would be foolish to establish and thrust collectivization from above.

The disagreements between Stalin and Bukharin turned acrimonious in late January and early February 1929 during the sessions of the Joint Plenum of the

Politburo and Central Control Commission. Stalin accused Bukharin of forming a secret bloc with Kamenev and other Trotskyists to remove Politburo members and reverse the party line. He learned recently of the secret meeting in July 1928 between Bukharin and Kamenev. He criticized Bukharin, Rykov, and Tomsky for threatening to resign their posts if their policies were not adopted. He called for a censure of the Bukharinites and expulsion from their posts. Bukharin, in turn, accused Stalin of the military-feudal exploitation of the peasantry and bureaucratism. A censure resolution against the Bukharinites was drafted but delayed until the meeting of a future full plenum. The full plenum convened in April and ratified the censure resolution against Bukharin, Rykov, and Tomsky, removed them from their posts, and threatened expulsion from the Politburo upon violation of the Party's Central Committee resolutions. With the Bukharinites cowed, the Stalinists were free to proceed with reintroducing the "emergency measures" in full force and devising measures to expand collectivization and attack the kulaks.

During the ensuing 18 months, the Stalinists introduced one improvised measure after another that literally transformed Soviet society, particularly the countryside, all to overfulfill the ambitious goals of the Five Year Plan. Rationing was introduced to prevent hoarding and to control the distribution of goods. Thousands of workers from the major urban areas, the so-called "25,000-ers", volunteered to go to the countryside to assist in the "emergency measures" and collectivization drive. Early in November 1929, Stalin proclaimed the collectivization drive successful and a significant breakthrough, signaling a year of great change, because collective and state farms, in his view, had achieved more than fifty percent of the agricultural output. By the end of the year, he called for rapid collectivization and liquidation of the kulaks as a class. In the interim, the Central Committee created a special commission to develop a resolution for general collectivization. After several revisions, originated by Stalin, a resolution finally was published on 5 January 1930 that called for the collectivization of the majority of peasant farms; however, it stopped short of providing specific guidance to party, government, and security officials concerning the formation and organization of kolkhozes, and especially how to deal with the kulaks in the process.

By late February the countryside was in turmoil. Public speeches by party leaders, including Stalin, decrees issued by local party and government officials and implementation of the policy and decrees by workers, and Red Army and security units raised tensions in the countryside and led to the forceful formation of kolkhozes and the arrest and deportation of thousands of peasants who were correctly or incorrectly identified as kulaks. Abuse, vendettas, and opportunities for sordid gain were prevalent. Peasants resisted in many ways, from demonstrations to the killing of livestock. The Stalinists believed that a civil war was imminent in the countryside.

The Politburo instructed Stalin to draft a resolution to stop the collectivization drive. Instead, Stalin went over the heads of the Politburo and published an article in *Pravda,* entitled "Dizzy with Success," in which he declared collectivization a success and claimed there were many mistakes made by overzealous officials. He announced that these local officials, drunk with previous successes in overcoming obstacles, did not adhere to the voluntary principle of forming kolkhozes, and that peasants could leave the kolkhozes if they chose to do so. Peasants left kolkhozes en masse. The total number of collectivized farms went from more than fifty to less than twenty-five percent. Stalin suddenly became a hero to the peasants and most likely saved his political power by this cynical maneuver of blaming local officials for the chaos in the countryside. His amassing of personal and political power was laying the basis for the Stalin cult.

For all intents and purposes, the old Russian village was destroyed. By late July 1930 it was replaced by the kolkhoz and village soviet, becoming the economic and political link between the State and countryside. The Soviet government formed associations to unify kolkhozes and cooperatives, and centralized all agricultural affairs in the newly created People's Commissariat for Agriculture. It established Machine Tractor Stations to provide kolkhozes with tractors and machine and farm implements. Party and State gradually organized their forces to reinstitute the collectivization drive. It was not lost on the Stalinists that the kolkhozes provided about forty percent of the marketable grain supply. The Central Committee declared in August 1931 that collectivization was basically completed, depending on the goals for each region, and predicted total collectivization by 1933.

Party and State instituted measures to maximize resources and improve efficiency and labor productivity. The main administrations, the Glavki, were abolished and replaced by associations of enterprises, which became the basic unit of industry. These organizations were held accountable by the so-called economic accounting, called khozraschet. Long plagued by confusion and diffusion of managerial responsibility in the factory, the manager was given sole responsibility for the performance of the factory; the party leader and trade union official were now tasked with advisory, motivational, and monitoring responsibilities. The continuous work week was introduced to sustain production as well as to reduce the influence of religion by eliminating workbreaks for worship on Sundays. Unemployment insurance was abolished to move more workers into industry to meet the increasing labor shortage. Thousands of displaced peasants and deported kulaks worked in remote industrial and mining regions, particularly in the building of gigantic construction projects such as the Magnitogorsk iron and steel complex. Corrective labor camps were organized and expanded in the remotest areas to harness the labor of counterrevolutionaries, exiled kulaks, and criminals. Party and State encouraged and supported the formation of shock brigades and socialist competition within and among factories and plants. The need to motivate and expand the technical workforce led to the differentiation of wages, which was anathema to Marxists.

Propaganda was used to promote the ambitious goals of the Five Year Plan. Slogans were an important ingredient in the propaganda campaigns. For example,

Stalin called for the Five Year Plan in three years and catching up with the capitalist powers. Maxim Gorky called for a civil war against all domestic capitalist elements. Artists and writers were induced to conform to party policies. Vladimir Maiakovsky's suicide in April 1930 symbolized the knell of avant-garde culture ushered in by the October Revolution. The censorship statute of 1921 was updated and extended to all media.

The resignation of A.V. Lunacharsky as People's Commissar for Education paved the way for major educational reforms. Compulsory education was introduced. Primary and secondary schools were ordered to eliminate progressive education and introduce traditional subject and methodology. Factories and plants assumed greater responsibility for preparing and training the technical workforce. The Academy of Sciences, long a bastion of independence, was expanded and brought in line with party policies.

Party and State pursued a policy of eliminating opposition. Trotsky was exiled to Turkey in January 1929. The party initiated a purge in April 1929, the second such purge since 1921, aimed at eliminating those who supported Bukharinist policies. The famous show trials of the "Industrial Party" and "Menshevik Party" were intended to cower the technical intelligentsia the Soviets inherited from the Tsarist period. The party uncovered the "Syrtsov-Lominadze Plot" to demonstrate to party officials that any criticism of the party line bore grave consequences.

The Soviet government pursued a nonrevolutionary foreign policy to support the Five Year Plan. It sought contacts with Western powers to support industrialization through trade and credits, and downplayed international revolution. Maxim Litvinov's appointment in 1930 as People's Commissar for Foreign Affairs symbolized the shift toward a nonrevolutionary foreign policy. Anglo-Soviet relations were restored after the Labor Party defeated the Conservatives in parliamentary elections. In Germany, the German Communist Party and the rise of the Nazis created political instability at the expense of the ruling Social Democrats. Soviet and German diplomats continued to find ways to continue the spirit of Rapallo and reaffirmed the 1926 Treaty of Berlin. They also supported each other at international organizations sponsored by the League of Nations. In the Far East, Chinese forces of the Mukden Government seized sections of the Chinese Eastern Railway in May 1929. Threats, protracted negotiations and delays, and the counterattack of Soviet military troops against Chinese forces on the Soviet-Chinese border in Manchuria resulted in the restoration of the joint Soviet and Chinese management of the railway. When Japanese troops occupied Manchuria in 1931 the Soviet Government maintained strict neutrality and did not object to the occupation, hoping for reaction by the world community and anticipating a Sino-Japanese conflict. The party believed the Red Army was making progress toward modernization. The new Far Eastern Army proved successful in Manchuria. The Red Army published the first formal Soviet view of modern warfare in its Field Service Regulations of 1929.

The Communist International underwent a change in policy following its congress of 1928, from collaboration with foreign socialist parties to activities aimed at attacking and undermining them. The Stalinists believed the stabilization of world capitalism was coming to a close. Bukharinist supporters of the previous policy were ousted from the foreign communist parties. At the onset of the Great Depression, many foreign communist parties, especially the German Communist Party, became more militant.

Although the ambitious goals of industrialization in the Five Year Plan went unmet, economic growth was phenomenal. This growth contrasted sharply with the decline in economic growth among the capitalist nations because of the depression. Unemployment, a major feature of the depression, was also nonexistent in the Soviet Union. Soviet propaganda exploited the phenomenal growth and low unemployment in contrasting the benefits of socialism versus capitalism. The depression nevertheless affected the fulfillment of the Five Year Plan. The Five Year Plan did not predict the drastic fall in the world price for grain, the export of which the Soviets needed to pay for rapid industrialization. Increased Soviet exports at low prices led to accusations of selling below cost.

The Stalinists expanded the State's involvement in Soviet society. The expansion represented a transformation of society emanating from the hierarchical centers of party and Government, a revolution from above. The mixed market and socialist economy of NEP came to an ignominious end. The tolerant NEP ground under the Stalinists' need for rapid, massive industrialization and to retain their line and power through ruthless elimination of entrenched, and potential, opposition.

1 THE YEAR 1929

PARTY DOMINATES ACADEMY OF SCIENCES
NEWS REPORT
17 January 1929

Pravda published information from the Russian News Agency on 25 January 1929 that showed how the Academy of Sciences, meeting in a special general session in Leningrad, finally acceded to the wishes of the Communist Party to increase the number of Marxists in an institution which was resisting Party interference. Under pressure from the Party, the Academy revised its charter, which was continued from the Tsarist period, in 1927 and 1928 to expand its membership to eighty-five and establish detailed procedures for advertising vacancies, receiving nominations from public organizations of all kinds, and considering the nominations by eleven special election commissions. The USSR Council of People's Commissars assumed responsibility for the Academy. The Academy met on 12 January 1929 and rejected three of the Party's nominees: the Marxist philosopher A.M. Deborin; the Marxist literary critic V.M. Friche; and N.M. Lukin, a Marxist historian. Frightened by the resulting criticism and fury in the Party and press, it met in a special session on 17 January and, after heated debate, submitted a petition to Sovnarkom to deviate from the existing charter and bring the three Party nominees to a second vote. Following Sovnarkom's approval, the Academy met on 13 February and elected the three nominees as new members.

EXTRAORDINARY SESSION OF ACADEMICS

On 17 January there took place at the Academy of Sciences the extraordinary general session of academics in its new expanded form in which 41 individuals participated. Academic Karpinsky chaired the session. Part of the new academics attended the session.

The acting Vice President, Academic Fersman, delivered a report on the financial situation of the Academy of Sciences. He presented a series of figures which represented the allocation for the scientific work of the Academy. Thus, the Academy of Sciences was allocated 1,500,000 rubles in 1924, and for 1929 the sum of the allocation for the work of all 39 academic institutes, laboratories, and commissions has already reached 3,200,000 rubles. In connection with the fact that the actual number of Academy members has doubled, it is necessary to increase significantly the allocation to individual academics for the work of the institutes and laboratories which they direct, as well as to increase the allocation to academics for business trips abroad. The doubling of academic personnel calls for the necessity of allocating larger amounts for the printing of their scientific works.

The permanent secretary of the Academy, Academic Oldenburg, focused his report on the work of academic institutions. In view of the joining of the Academy by a series of new prominent Soviet scientists, Oldenburg considers it necessary to expand still further the work of academic institutions for which it is necessary to acquire new equipment for laboratories and institutes.

Then the question was raised for discussion by the general session about the reballoting of three candidates who did not receive the required two-thirds majority of votes at the general session of the Academy of Sciences on 12 January.

The decision of the Academy presidium of 12 January was presented to the general session for examination. The vacancies for the three chairs would not be declared, the three candidates would be submitted to a vote by the general session of the Academy in its new form, all the preparations for election procedures would not be repeated, and a petition would be sent to the Council of People's Commissars of the USSR to authorize this deviation from the charter.

The following academics engaged in discussions about the last question: I.P. Pavlov, Borodin, Prianishnikov, Oldenburg, Uspensky, Platonov, Levinson-Lessing, Arkhangelsky, Chichibabin, Petrushevsky, Liapunov, Karpinsky, et. al.

Academic Pavlov sharply spoke against the proposal of the Academy's presidium, declaring that elections had proceeded on the basis of the charter and were formally correct, although they were undertaken in a very complex situation because of the mass of candidates, shortness of time for the elections, and in view of attracting the attention of public organizations to the elections. Academic Pavlov was shocked that this was the first time in the history of the Academy that public and scientific organizations participated in the elections, and, as it is known, this did not take place in prerevolutionary times.

In Academic Pavlov's opinion, in spite of the complexity of this situation, the elections proceeded normally, and the fact of the balloting of the three candidates does not represent anything exceptional or extraordinary.

Academic Platonov declared that in his opinion the balloting of the three candidates, which took place almost unanimously in the election commissions and by secret ballot in the humanities section, is an unusual fact.

Objecting to Academic Pavlov, Academic Platonov noted that due to continual illness Academic Pavlov could not attend and personally participate in all of the election work in which the academics participated, each individually in the section and in the general session as a whole. Therefore, in the words of Academic Platonov, Academic Pavlov was forced in this whole question to rely on rumors and conversations, because as such his behavior bore the nature of an outsider.

Concluding his speech, Academic Platonov declared that he is able to count on his point of view as that of this colleagues in the humanities section, and therefore he with complete responsibility put his signature, along with other chairmen of the election commissions, to the resolution of the Academy's presidium.

Academics Borodin, Levinson-Lessing, and Petrushevsky proposed voting against the resolution of the presidium, since it contradicted the charter and did not call for any necessity. Academic Arkhangelsky proposed raising the question about reexamining the charter in its entirety.

Academics Uspensky and Chichibabin underscored the desire to repeat the balloting of the three candidates in the humanities section so that the latter could once again express its relationship to this.

In the opinion of Academic Liapunov, the humanities section rests on its initial view, but it cannot answer for the results of the joint voting of the section of mathematics and physics.

After lively debates, the resolution of the presidium was put to vote, the result of which was that it was adopted by the majority of 28 votes to 9 (Academics Pavlov, Levinson-Lessing, Karsky, Borodin, Liapunov, Lavrov, Petrushevsky, Vladimirtsev, and Sakulin) with four abstaining (including Academics Lazarev and Vinogradov).

The general session authorized the presidium of the Academy of Sciences to submit a petition before the USSR Council of People's Commissars about the reballoting.

Pravda, 25 January 1929, 2.

KRUPSKAIA'S COURAGEOUS ARTICLE AGAINST RAPID AND FORCED COLLECTIVIZATION

20 January 1929

On the eve of the anniversary of Lenin's death, Nadezhda Krupskaia published an article which supported the formation of collectives, but cautioned against the coercion of small farmers to form and join collective farms. At the time, a Central Committee commission was preparing a plan to collectivize farms. Stalin was strongly encouraging the commission to adopt a faster rate of collectivization. Krupskaia, using the occasion of the anniversary of her late husband's death and his last writing about Russian agricultural policy, publicly argued for a gradual approach to collectivization. She pointed out that a noncoercive approach to collectivization was central to Lenin's legacy in agrarian policy, and it could not be imagined that the confiscation of small peasant farms and other methods could be established and conducted from above. Without being specific about individuals, she explained that Lenin's article on cooperatives was being interpreted in highly different ways and she wanted to set straight the record. Stalin and others were claiming that their collectivization project and Lenin's policy concerning cooperatives were one and the same. Krupskaia risked future retaliation for her action.

NADEZHDA KRUPSKAIA
IL'ICH ON KOLKHOZ CONSTRUCTION

Our kolkhoz construction is growing at a rapid rate. The communes are growing, and they are giving birth to a new way of life. And, it is necessary often to speak with commune members about what Il'ich wrote on this question.

The question about uniting small peasant farmers into large public farms was raised even in the 90s, when there were sharp arguments between the narodniks and marxists. The narodniks accused the marxists of wanting to deprive the peasants of their land and to transform them into workers.

The best answer could be served by Engels' article "The Peasant Question in France and Germany," which was published in 1891 in "Neue Zeit". Engels writes that when the communists possess state power, they will not confiscate the farms of the small peasant, but will by the example of state assistance promote their unification, organization into cooperatives, large farms, and will help them gradually to make the transition to the higher form of unified farms, the communes.

I do not know if Vladimir Il'ich knew this article at the time of these arguments with the narodniks. This article was first published in Russian only in 1905. Vladimir Il'ich never cited this article anywhere, although he later reread it many times. In any case, he then knew what Marx wrote in connection with this. The entire polemic at the time with the narodniks, with the "friends of the people," revolved around the question: Is it possible under Russian conditions, under autocracy, under the complete political deprivation of the masses' rights under the conditions of growing capitalism, to grow in easy stages and slowly into socialism, without any kind of political struggle, by way of artels, associations, cooperatives of small producers? Vladimir Il'ich proved that this is a naive and harmful utopia. He said that he was not against artels and associations, not against the cooperatives of small producers, but about the necessary preconditions for this cooperative process to make sense, and about the necessity of political struggle, of the struggle for power. After conquering power, there will be a different argument. Il'ich typically wrote on this question in his "The Development of Capitalism", which finally buried the legal narodniks on principle. There he cited a quotation from the third volume of Marx' "Capitalism": "Small land property, by its very own nature, prevents the development of public productive labor, a public form of labor, the public concentration of capital, cattle-breeding on a large scale, and the progressive application of science." (Volume III, Lenin's Works, p. 261—old edition).

And in keeping with this, Il'ich writes: "The systematic use of machines in agriculture displaces the patriarchal 'middle' peasant with the same implacability that the steam-powered loom displaces the hand-weaving of the handicraftsman." (Volume III, Lenin's Works, p. 176). Furthermore: "Large machine industry in agriculture, as in industry, advances with tremendous force the demand for public control and regulation of production." (op. cit., p. 181). "The Development of Capitalism" was written for the legal press. Therefore, it was impossible then to speak openly. Under capitalism the industrialization of agriculture leads to the destruction of the peasantry, to proletarization; then, when power will be in the hands of the proletariat, industrialization will lead inevitably to the collectivization of agriculture. Everything had to be said, with hints, between the lines. In addition to what was said above, Il'ich adds: "'Under our conditions' only agricultural entrepreneurs are in position to advance technology. 'Under our conditions' this progress of agricultural entrepreneurs, small and large, are indissolubly connected with the destruction of the peasantry and creation of the agricultural proletariat" (op. cit., p. 181). "Under our conditions", in quotations, meant "under capitalism".

This was all written 30 years ago. "The Development of Capitalism", as it is known, was written while in prison and modified in exile. This was followed by about 20 years of intensive political struggle. Il'ich did not speak or write about the process of forming cooperatives, about collectivization. But then came the February Revolution, radically changing the conditions of political life. And so, when returning from abroad and delivering a speech on 14 April at the Petrograd city-wide party conference, Il'ich said: "The nationalization of land, this is a measure which does not emanate from the framework of the bourgeois order, but nationalization can change this, if the peasants will take the land. We, as a proletarian party, must say that some of the land will not provide grain. To work the land, it will be necessary, consequently, to establish the commune." In "An Open Letter to the Delegates of the First All-Russian Congress of Peasant Deputies in May 1917," he writes in detail about the organization of large model farms, with the general farming of the land under the leadership of agricultural workers. "Without this general farming under the leadership of soviets of agricultural workers, it will not turn out that the entire land will belong to the workers. Of course, general farming, of course, is a difficult theory, if anyone would imagine that it could be possible to establish and thrust such general farming from above. This would be crazy, because a century of the customs of individual farms cannot be eliminated at once, because this would require money, and require adapting to new conditions of life."

Il'ich writes further that the transfer of land into the hands of the workers is not at all the way out: "We know that the slave owners were defeated in America in 1865 and then hundreds of millions of desiatins were distributed to peasants as a gift, or partially as a gift. Nevertheless, capitalism prevails there, as no where else, and likewise tramples the working masses, even if it is more difficult than in other countries. So, it is socialist teaching as well as observation of other peoples which led us to the strong conviction that without this general farming of land by agricultural workers, using the best machines and under the leadership of scientific-educated agronomists, there is no way out from under the yoke of capitalism" (Ibid.).

On 25 October the proletarian revolution was victorious, and power transferred into the hands of the soviets. On 26 October at the Second Congress of Soviets, the decree on land was adopted, long anticipated by the peasants. By itself, the decree did not eliminate the class struggle in the countryside. The class struggle proceeded to its utmost. The soviets, in the true sense of the word, did not exist at all in the countryside. In the spring of 1918 "committees of the poor" were organized by a decree of the VTsIK. On 13 November 1918 the Sixth Congress of Soviets decreed to disband the committees of the poor, having organized village and volost soviets as true organs of Soviet power in the countryside and elected by the entire population, not by those who exploit someone else's labor. In December convened the First

All-Russian Congress of Land Departments, Committees of the Poor, and Communes. At this congress Il'ich passionately called for the restructure of all bases of the economy and spoke about the necessity of the struggle for the public farming of the land. "To live as in the old days, as we lived before the war, is impossible, and such misappropriation of human resources and labor which are connected with small individual peasant farms cannot continue any longer. Labor productivity would increase two-fold and three-fold, a two-fold and three-fold savings could be made in human labor for agriculture and human economy, if the transition from these elaborated small farms to public farming can be completed" (Volume XV, pp. 589-590).

Communes began to be formed with relative intensity. But cultural backwardness hampered the matter, as well as the backwardness of production capability and the inability to undertake the matter. In March 1919 at the Eighth RKP Congress, Il'ich, speaking about work in the countryside, revealed all the difficulties of this work. "You know—he said—that the countryside was condemned to darkness even in the leading countries. Of course, the culture of the countryside will be improved by us, but this matter takes years and years. And so there are comrades among us who forget, that there are so graphically depicted before us every word of the people from the provinces." And he spoke about another difficulty: "Up to the present time, they (peasants—N.K.) remained biased against large farms. The peasant thinks: "If there is a large farm, that means I am hired labor again." Of course this is incorrect. But the peasant has the idea that connected with the large farm are hatred and the memory about how the landowners oppressed the people. This feeling remains, it still has not died." Il'ich pointed out how our poverty makes our work difficult in the countryside. "If we could not tomorrow give 400,000 first-class tractors, supply them with petroleum, supply them with mechanics (you know very well that for the time being this is fantasy), for the middle peasant would say: 'I am for the commune' (i.e., for communism). But to do this, it is necessary first to defeat the international bourgeoisie, necessary to force them to give us these tractors, or even necessary to raise our productivity so much that we can deliver them ourselves." The matter of restructuring all the bases of agriculture—it is a long drawn-out matter. It is impossible to conduct the revolution in agriculture "from above". "There is nothing more stupid than the very thought of force in the economic relations of the middle peasant." And Il'ich remembers Engels' article of 1894 and says that it is necessary not to command, but persuade and propagandize by demonstration. Il'ich speaks about the tremendous role of urban workers in this matter. In November 1919 at the All-Russian Conference on Work in the Countryside, he again repeats: "Only with the help of general, artel, and association labor can we exit that blind alley to which the imperialist war has driven us" (Volume XVI, p. 374).

In December 1919 convened the First Congress of Agricultural Communes and Artels. In his speech at this congress, Vladimir Il'ich devoted his speech to the question that communes, artels, and all kinds of organizations directed toward transforming, gradually assisting their transformation, the small, individual peasant farm into the public farm, must not isolate but must help the neighboring peasant population. He spoke about the tremendous significance of communes in that they must conquer the trust of the neighboring peasantry. "We must avoid the fact that the peasant would say that members of communes, artels, and associations are state parasites and differ from peasants only in that they get privileges." During the transition to the new economic policy, in the article "On the Tax in Kind," Vladimir Il'ich dwelled on the question of cooperatives (he uses Engels' term "forming cooperatives, and not collectivization). "The transition from cooperatives of small farms to socialism is the transition from small to large-scale production, i.e., a more complex transition, but therefore capable of involving, for success, broader masses of the population, capable of extracting the deeper and more tenacious roots of old, even precapitalist relationships, the most stubborn in the sense of opposition to all kinds of 'newness'.... The policy of forming cooperatives, for success, will give you a rise in small farming and the facilitation of its transition in an indefinite period of time to large-scale production on the basis of voluntary unification" (Volume XVIII, Part 1, p. 220).

In 1922, having examined the theses about work in the countryside at the Eleventh Party Congress, Il'ich in a letter to Politburo members remarks that it is now impossible to speak purely and abstractly about the formation of cooperatives. "It is necessary to state something completely different,—he writes—not repeating the empty slogan 'form cooperatives', but **showing concretely** what is **PRACTICAL EXPERIENCE** in forming cooperatives and **HOW** to assist this." He speaks about the necessity of collecting material on this question and develop it practically. It is harmful to repeat platitudes,—he writes. Instead of this, it is really better to take on a **uezd** and show through **business-like** analysis how it is necessary to assist the "formation of cooperatives". He warns against "playing games with the cooperative", against overestimating the acumen of sovkhoz workers (Leninskii Sbornik, Volume IV, p. 390). At the Eleventh Congress Il'ich especially underscored the necessity in all work to get much closer with the peasant masses, the common working peasantry, and lead them. And in his last article "On Cooperatives", he speaks once again about the complete importance of forming cooperatives, how to lead the peasantry along the path of forming cooperatives toward restructuring all bases of agriculture, and how to lead them toward socialism.

I took the liberty of citing certain of Il'ich's many quotes, because I needed to observe that Il'ich's article "On Cooperatives" is interpreted in highly different ways that often do not have any connection with what Il'ich says and what he wrote or said previously about this question. And now, six years later since the writing of this article, when kolkhoz construction involves even more of the general public, this article has tremendous and namely practical significance.

Pravda, 20 January 1929, 1.

BUKHARIN CRITICIZES STALIN'S POLICIES

24 January 1929

In a long speech commemorating the fifth anniversary of Lenin's death, Bukharin used the later writings of Lenin on party policy as a way to present an antiStalinist manifesto in defense of the philosophy and policies of NEP. Quoting and paraphrasing Lenin's words, he showed that Stalin, without mentioning him by name, was violating Lenin's legacy and directives, and distorting and revising the dead leader's principles of conciliating and avoiding a split with the peasantry, and preventing a third revolution. The speech, which was published in Pravda and Bednota, represented the last explicit statement of Bukharin's thinking and policies to be published in the Soviet Union. The title of his speech made readers aware of Lenin's other testament, though unpublished, yet known, that called for Stalin's removal as Party general secretary.

NIKOLAI BUKHARIN
LENIN'S POLITICAL TESTAMENT

Comrades! Creativity of great people—and one of the greatest people was our deceased teacher and leader—represents a marvelous treasure-house of ideas. It is necessary to select from this remarkable variety in this treasure-house. It is necessary to limit the topic, for the wealth of the progessive heritage is inexhaustible and immense. I am limiting therefore the topic of my speech to *Lenin's Political Testament*, that is, the total sum of ideas which Vladimir Il'ich left as his last wisest, most weighted word, as his last most well-thought-out directive. I shall speak about the penetrating and brilliant plan left to the party, which Lenin created, which he led, which he brought to victory, which he led in the heroic difficult days of the civil war, which he rebuilt and led again to battle at the beginning epoch of *great economic work.*

The most important of these that comrade Lenin willed to us is contained in five of his articles, remarkable and most profound by their content: "Pages from a Diary", "On Our Revolution", "How Do We Reorganize Rabkrin?", "Better Less and Better", "On Cooperatives". All these articles, if closer attention were given to them, represent not individual, uncoordinated pieces, but organic parts of one *large whole*, one large plan of Leninist strategy and tactics, and a plan developed on the basis of a completely definite *perspective* which was foreseen by the brilliant and sharp vision of the commander of the world revolutionary forces.

I know very well that all these articles have been subjected to study. But up to the present time there is one gap which I want to fill at this current funeral ceremony. This gap consists of the fact that up to now there have not been—as far as I know—attempts to analyze all these articles *in their mutual connection*, to understand them namely as a small part of a large perspective plan of all our communist work.

In passing to the sixth year since the agonizing end of our teacher, apprehension may indeed be appearing: Can we not philosophize here too much, are we associating ourselves with after the fact, and besides that with the artificial, and that Vladimir Il'ich had only individual, though brilliant remarks? Is there indeed commonality between the evaluation of our entire revolution and remarks about how to reorganize Rabkrin? Nevertheless, the author of these articles himself looked at them as the extension of a certain integral plan.

Right in the article about Rabkrin,—it would seem, there is here "only" a "personal" question!—Lenin writes: "Well, I link the general plan of our work, our policy, our tactics, our strategy with the tasks of a reorganized Rabkrin" (p. 405).

If we attentively look closely at Lenin's articles written before his death, we will see that there are in them a general evaluation of our revolution from the point of view of the possibility of constructing socialism in our country, the sharply outlined general lines of our development, very deep, though very brief analysis of the international situation, and the basis of our strategy and tactics, questions about our economic construction, questions about the cultural revolution, and questions about fundamental class relationships, about the *state bureaucracy*, about the *organization of the masses*, and, finally, about the organization of our party and its leadership. Really and truly, it is impossible to name any *single* large question about policy, the analysis of which would find its place in this general plan developed by comrade Lenin in his last directives. Lenin developed these most important questions of policy not from the point of view of the momentary and rapidly transient state of the market; he presented them from the point of view of a "large policy", the widest perspectives, general pathos, high road of our development. His analysis is not a narrowly pedantic analysis of a small area, but a vast painting, on which with unusual power, convincing simplicity, and expressiveness is portrayed the difficult step of the historical process. From this analysis, Lenin makes huge conclusions, but on this very analysis he coordinates comparatively minor organized details. To depict Il'ich's entire plan is the task which I have placed on myself today.

I. GENERAL EVALUATION OF OUR REVOLUTION FROM THE POINT OF VIEW OF THE POSSIBILITY OF THE SOCIALIST REVOLUTION

I shall begin first of all with the question about *the general evaluation of our revolution from the point of view of the possibility of socialist construction in our country*. To this is devoted the article which is the so-called: *"On Our Revolution"*. From the first (superficial) glance we can consider this article as a casual, almost reviewed "remark". This, however, is glaringly incorrect. In my view the "remark" "On Our Revolution" is one of the most original and most daring of Vladimir Il'ich's works. He, of course, did not by chance select the topic "On Our Revolution", that is, about the evaluation of this revolution and its possibility *as a whole*. He foresaw that what can arise are various doubts related to the construction of socialism in our country; he knew that our working class would need, perhaps, to survive numerous waves of various "attacks" from the side of the party which sometimes acted in the capacity of active political enemies within our country, from their successors, and from the renegades of our own party. He knew perfectly well that various difficulties of construction can again and again be presented before wavering intellectuals, the question about the possibility of socialism in our country. Secret admirers of "normal", capitalist relationships will be found, old wives' tales of fellow-travelers about the great benefit of the October Revolution, from the point of view of destroying the old gentry coat-of-arms, feudal stables, and tsarist middle ages, will from time to time warm up, but at *the very same* time from the point of view of prosperity and future victory of the nepman. We know perfectly that there will be such doubts, that they are here and there and in all probability *will be* around for a known period of time.

So, that is why Lenin once more raised the *fundamental* question "about our revolution", about the *nature* of our revolution, and its evaluation as a whole.

Comrade Lenin raises the fundamental question: They assert that we did not have sufficient objective economic and cultural preconditions for the transition to socialism. Fine. But this does not resolve the matter. What do the Kautsky pedants not understand? They do not understand basically that if developed countries from the point of view of world history must make the proletarian revolution, countries with an extremely developed economic base quite "sufficient" for the transition to socialism (although no one can say at what stage of development this sufficiency begins), then *special exceptions* can be determined by the *peculiarity* of the domestic and foreign situation. This peculiarity of the situation has now taken place, for our revolution was linked, first, with the world war, second, with the beginning of the gigantic revolutionary fermentation among the hundreds of millions of eastern peoples, and, third, with the specially favorable combination of class forces within the country, a combination which Marx back in the fifties of the past century considered the most advantageous, namely: The combination of *peasant warfare and the proletarian revolution*. And so these are the very circumstances, this completely peculiar and original situation was the basis for the entire development of our revolution. Such an original situation became possible, that we from the beginning took for ourselves "worker-peasant power", and then we really must "on the basis of worker-peasant power and soviet structure move to catch up with and surpass other nations." Vladimir Il'ich found these extremely daring reasons necessary to extend from here the thread for the future. If our socialist revolution to a considerable degree is supported by that *special* combination of class forces, which were taken into account even by Marx, then this "combination of proletarian revolution and peasant warfare" (that is, the union of the working class with the peasantry under the leadership of the working class) must be extended and retained at all costs. For if this specially favorable combination of class forces is *lost*, then the entire basis for expanding the *socialist* revolution in our country collapses.

Evaluating again "our revolution" as socialist, having repulsed the most basic arguments of people who flirt with a return to "healthy capitalism", to bourgeois restoration, and having characterized "our revolution" in all its capacity, Lenin, with uncommon thoughtfulness, raises the most general question *about the nature of the development of "our revolution"*, and consequently, *about the bases, about the direction of our tactics*. Lenin foresees the danger that people who take refuge in a revolutionary phrase will not understand the entire *great*, decisive, principal change which occurs in the entire development of society after the taking of power by the proletariat.

II. GENERAL DIRECTION OF OUR DEVELOPMENT AND GENERAL ESTABLISHMENT OF POLICY

From this is again an unusually bold, clear, precise and exceptionally energetic formulation of this question. Vladimir Il'ich gave it in his remarkable article "On Cooperatives".

In this article comrade Lenin writes:

"...We are forced to recognize the radical change in our entire point of view to socialism" (p. 376).

When and where was this thesis formulated with such harshness? I argue that of all the writings with the most precisely, sternly and passionate political energy is this thesis formulated namely in the article "On Cooperatives".

"...We are forced to recognize the radical change in our entire point of view of socialism",—writes comrade Lenin.

"This radical change consists of the fact that previously we placed and had to place the center of gravity on the political struggle, taking of power, etc. Now the very center of gravity has changed to moving to peaceful organized "cultural" work. I am ready to say that the center of gravity for us is moving to culture-mongering, if there are not to be international relationships, not the responsibility to struggle for our position on an international scale. But, if we put this to the side, then we shall now definitely take the center of gravity of work to culture-mongering" (Ibid.).

This does not at all mean that Lenin here disclaims the class struggle, for "peaceful organized" "cultural" work is also a *special form* of the class struggle. This means that the proletariat leads the "entire" working nation, that it answers to the development of the *entire society* as a whole, that it becomes a great collective organizer of the *entire "economy"*, that the direction of development *does not* proceed along the line of splitting the precipice between the basic classes (working class and peasantry), that the matter leads by all means *not* to a "third revolution", etc.

Of course, there is the actual progress of life, according to the Mephistopheles dictum: "Theory, my friend, is sulphur, but green is the eternal wood of life." It is actually more complex: Objective conditions can be more complex, and our tactics cannot be quite ideal. Therefore, in reality there can be periods of exacerbating the class struggle and whose form is connected with the regroupings of social classes. We are now surviving one ofsuch periods of exacerbating the class struggle, when we cannot say that our work "is heading" toward "culture-mongering". It would be, of course, absolutely incorrect if we cannot consider the special characteristics of each individual stage of our struggle. At the same time, comrade Lenin's basic positions about the nature of our development remain profoundly correct. *And this must remain as a theoretical foundation under the determination of our great tactical road.*

III. THE INTERNATIONAL SITUATION AND ITS EVALUATION

In his political testament, Lenin in no way limits himself to these general questions. From the general, he goes to the specific, to the most concrete and with the hand of the master he sketches the most lively and clearest paintings, presenting the most stirring problems. Vladimir Il'ich was an international revolutionary, a first-class theoretical Marxist, and, it goes without saying, he understood the greatest difficulties, the most perfidious threats and dangers connected with our *international* situation. We sometimes forget that Vladimir Il'ich wrote in his political testament about our international situation, but in the meantime the analysis is given that, with several exceptions, it has been confirmed by the entire further course of world events. On one point life introduced the greatest correction to the point which

I raise first: Comrade Lenin sketched so the international situation: 1) In Western Europe the schism of the imperialist states: Germany lies on the bottom, the victor countries slander Germany and do not let her rise up. This point has been "cancelled" to a great degree. Germany, as is known, rose up under the life-giving American golden rain, although she is running into the greatest difficulties. 2) On the other hand, Lenin analyzes the situation, in that the victors, that is, France, England, United States, Japan, on the basis of their victory, can strengthen their power, can make concessions to the working class that "always" delay the revolutionary movement in them and create a certain likeness of "social peace" (p. 402). This formulation is exact, correct and in proper measure cautious. 3) At this same time, the revolutionary movement is ripening in the East (India, China, etc.)—the majority of mankind is entering the revolutionary maelstrom. 4) International conflicts are ripening, as Lenin writes, between the "prosperous imperialist states of the West and the prosperous imperialist states of the East..." (p. 403). 5) Contradictions and conflicts are ripening between the counterrevolutionary imperialists and the national revolutionary movement in the East, the material resources of which are still small. 6) Conflict is ripening between imperialism and the Country of the Soviets.

Then, when Vladimir Il'ich wrote these lines, we did not raise the question relative to the stabilization of capitalism—there was not a characteristic of this stabilization. But Vladimir Il'ich as a matter of fact gave on the whole the analysis which we developed with the greatest difficulty only in the course of a whole series of subsequent years. Vladimir Il'ich was not a bit afraid of being suspicious of opportunism or of any similar deadly sin and wrote that the victorious states will "prosper", and on the other hand, he noted those very *contradictions* to which capitalist stabilization gives birth. And what is especially interesting is that Vladimir Il'ich linked the next revolutionary explosion with the *coming war*.

As regards the great national movements, he first looked for them in the East, where he saw the revolutionary situation and the possibility of the immediate explosion of the great national masses. Did history not really prove this prognosis completely correct?

IV. BASES OF OUR STRATEGY AND TACTICS FROM THE POINT OF VIEW OF THE INTERNATIONAL SITUATION

In light of this analysis of the international situation Vladimir Il'ich determined the bases of both our strategy and our tactics.

Comrade Lenin examined our international situation in the first instance from the point of view of the *military danger*.

Indeed, *how* did he raise the question? How did he formulate it?

"What kind of tactics is prescribed by such a situation of affairs for our country?

"Can we be spared the coming conflict with these imperialist states?" (p. 403).

What kind of tactics must we maintain "to prevent the West-European counterrevolutionary states from crushing us?" (p. 404).

Who knows the preciseness of Vladimir Il'ich's expression, who knows how much Vladimir Il'ich was chaste in his treatment of "great" words, and who remembers the matter about his *political testament*, cannot in raising these questions but read the most serious alarm (alarm of the serious thinker and wise strategist) for the fate of the entire socialist construction, for the fate of the entire revolution. Lenin was not at all a flippant "jingoist", he seriously took into account the enemies' powerful forces. He *openly* spoke even about our weaknesses, called upon the *masses* to overcome them. He above all pointed to the *low productivity of national labor*. He remarked that the imperialists were not successful in destroying the Soviet state, but were successful in ruining it, making its development difficult, and slowing down its development, that is, they were successful in accomplishing half the task ("half accomplishment of the task").

It is necessary to recognize that although we made a great leap forward in the area of economic and cultural development, we live also in a situation of a *semi-blockade*. As regards the "low productivity of national labor", although we here have made a tremendous leap forward, but, in comparison with Western Europe and America, we still find ourselves in an extremely low, semi-barbaric stage of development.

But how did Vladimir Il'ich himself answer the questions raised above? He answered extremely carefully. He said: Solving the *general* question about the outcome of the gigantic struggle depends on the "many circumstances" which it is impossible to consider beforehand. *In the final analysis*, however, our victory is based on the power of the gigantic *masses*. The basic masses of mankind (USSR, India, China, etc.) decide the outcome of the struggle. However, this outcome presupposes the specific tactics.

Thus: "What kind of tactics is prescribed by such a situation of affairs for our country? It is obvious for the following: We must to the greatest extent be careful to preserve our workers' power, to hold under its authority and its leadership our small and smallest peasantry" (p. 403).

Thus, when Lenin raised the question about the *basic domestic guarantee* in the struggle against the assault of the imperialists, the *basic tactical rule* necessary for the proletarian revolution to be victorious in the struggle against the counterrevolutionary West-European governments, he answered: *The greatest caution on those points of policy that concern the relationship of the workers' power to the peasantry*. In another place in the same article, he clearly, precisely and with the least sparring of words gave formulas which are more expressive than they are concise.

"We need to keep such tactics or adopt the following policy for our salvation.

We must try to construct a state in which workers would preserve their leadership over the peasants, trust of peasants in relation to them, and with the greatest economy distill from our social relationships all kinds of traces of whatever excesses there would be.

We must maintain our state bureaucracy at the maximum economy" (pp. 404-405).

At first glance, this would seem not very much for "our salvation" under assault from the West-European capitalist powers. But further on comrade Lenin along all directions develops from these apparently "poor" directives the richest chain of the most concrete instructions, despite the fact that one link is fastened to another and what increases is the entire complex and living practice of the revolutionary struggle and construction. The thought which Lenin emphasized so powerfully, bringing it down like a heavy block, as if it is meager: Leadership over the peasantry, the "greatest caution", trust of the peasantry, streamlining the bureaucracy to the minimum—this is apparently very little, all of this is apparently very simple.

But simplicity has a two-fold nature: There is "simplicity" which is *worse than theft*, and there is *genius* simplicity, such a simplicity which represents the product of the most extensive penetration of a subject and most extensive knowledge of this subject. In the area of literature, Leo Tolstoi had such genius simplicity. In the area of politics, Vladimir Il'ich had such genius simplicity.

From this, as I have already said, follows that Vladimir Il'ich considered military conflict early or later inevitable, and established that our revolution can come out of this victorious only when the peasants will trust workers' power. According to Lenin's testament, this is the *deciding precondition*, without which the entire revolution will not be able to exist. This, in turn, presupposes the greatest economy in our management. Why? Here comrade Lenin expresses the most internal richness of these slogans: The thought of the "greatest economy" appears much more extensive than it appears at first glance.

V. BASES OF ECONOMIC POLICY

In his well known article "Better Less And Better", Lenin develops his plan along two directions, which are coordinated with the directive of the union of workers and peasants and with the directive of economy. These are the plan of *industrialization* and the plan to *form cooperatives of the population.* Having raised the question that we need to maintain the trust of peasants, expel the most superfluous from our public relationships, maintain the state bureaucracy to the minimum, and accumulate gradually, comrade Lenin asks: But "would there be the kingdom of peasant narrow-mindedness?" (p. 405).

Vladimir Il'ich knew our people well, he knew perfectly that there would be an assault of this sort, when he preached about the "kingdom of peasant narrow-mindedness", when he spoke many times about the peasantry, etc. In answer to this, Vladimir Il'ich says:

"No. If we maintain the leadership by the workers' class over the peasantry, we shall get the possibility at the greatest value and greatest economy in our state, so that the smallest savings can be achieved for the development of our large-scale machine industry, for the development of electrification, peat, or building Volkhovstroi and others".

"In this and only in this will be our hope" (Ibid.).

Then we hold on *for sure* and by this "not on the level of a small peasant country..., but on the level rising steadily forward and forward toward large-scale machine industry" (pp. 405-406).

What is the "crux" here? What is there here so special that distinguishes Lenin's aim from anything else? First, on the basis of the entire plan rests the union of workers and peasants and the "greatest caution" on this point, caution that so sharply separates Lenin's "earth" from Trotsky's "heaven". Second, here is given a completely definite answer *on what* we need to construct the matter of the industrialization of the country, where the *sources* of that *additional sum* which we must in increasing measure spend on the matter of industrializing the country. These sources can be various. They can consist of *spending the reserves*, which we had (the increasing passive balance), *issuing paper currency* with the risk of inflation and the goods famine; they can consist of overtaxing the peasantry. But all this is not a healthy basis for industrialization. This is not at all solid, not sound; all this can threaten a break with the peasantry. Comrade Lenin shows other sources. These sources are above all *the maximum streamlining of all nonproductive expenditures* which we in truth have in large amounts, and increasing the qualitative indicators, in the first place *increasing the productivity of national labor.* Not emission, not the eating up of reserves (gold, goods, currency), not overtaxing the peasantry, but *qualitatively increasing the productivity of all-national labor and the decisive struggle with nonproductive expenditures—these are all really the main sources of accumulation.* This is the definite directive, definite political line, and its wisdom consists of the one and only line under which economic construction, socialist accumulation, etc. affect the *economic* side and which an *actual, strong, healthy base* affects the *socialist-class* side. The path to industrialization, the answer to the question about the sources of accumulation, the directive that the policy *should not make a break with the peasantry but, on the contrary, unite with the peasantry*, and the general evaluation of the question about industrialization as the deciding question ("in this and only in this will be our hope"—wrote Lenin about the *large-scale machine industry*),—so these are the directives from Lenin that flow from all the socialist-economic conditions and analysis of the international situation.

Giving concrete expression to the question *on what kind of organizational base* must be achieved the alliance between growing industry and the small and smallest peasant farms, Lenin develops his "cooperative plan", the plan of alliance through the "cooperative turn" (p. 371). Why through the cooperative must their alliance take place? Why is the cooperative proposed as the deciding matter? Because this is the transition, as Lenin very carefully expresses, toward "a new order by means of possibly *simpler, easier, and more approachable way for the peasant*" (p. 370), when the population moves toward socialism through the cooperative, *while being guided by its own interests.*

The question about the alliance between the workers' class and peasantry (from the economic and social-class point of view) can, of course, be raised in different ways. It can be raised that the *workers' class* will build socialism, the peasantry just cannot build any socialism, such as the petty bourgeoisie (property owners), which *under any kind of condition* is incapable of this at all in this relationship. Vladimir Il'ich *wrongly* raised this question. Having noted that the cooperative is the simplest and easiest method of drawing in the peasantry, he continues:

"And as you know in this, however, is the main thing. One matter is to fantasize about all kinds of workers' associations for building socialism, another matter is to learn how practically to build this socialism so that *all kinds* of small peasants could participate in this building. We have now reached this stage. And it is beyond question that, having achieved it, we are profiting by it very little" (pp. 370-371).

The latter is true up to the present day.

It is known to everyone how comrade Lenin always valued the cooperative; he said that the universal process for forming the population into cooperatives under our conditions is socialism, and we need "only" this.

We do not now need any other wisdom to make the transition toward socialism. But to complete this "only", what is needed is total overturn, an entire period of the cultural development of the national masses. Therefore our rule must be: Less philosophizing as possible and less idiosyncracies as possible. NEP in this relationship produces from itself a process that adapts itself to the level of the most ordinary peasantry, that it demands from it nothing higher" (p. 372).

When we are now surviving a whole series of new difficulties with the peasantry, it is not harmful for us to remember this very simple and at the same time very wise rule. *We need to catch hold of the peasant for his interests, not philosophize, be without any kind of idiocyncracy, we need to search for the simplest approaches to him.* To realize the cooperative plan, a *cultural revolution* is needed, for what is needed to realize the universal forming of cooperatives in the first instance is that cooperative members *trade in a civilized manner.* Our cooperative member, comrade Lenin wrote literally: "now trades like Asiatics, but to be a trader, he needs to trade like Europeans" (p. 373).

So, the position is based on the fact that it is necessary to proceed *from methods which are simple and intelligible to the peasant*: To hook "our matter" onto the personal interests of the peasant. In another place in the same article, Vladimir Il'ich raises this question in extremely sharp form: NEP, he writes, is the "stage of uniting the personal interests, personal trade interests, their checking and control by the state, the stage of subordinating them to the general interests, that previously constituted a stumbling block to so many socialists" (p. 370). Lenin teaches: To hook the peasant onto his own interests and on this basis, through the cooperative breakthrough, through the cooperative to lead him toward socialism. And so that the cooperative would bring him toward socialism, the *civilized cooperative* is necessary, for which it is necessary to trade *not as Asiatics*, but *as Europeans.*

VI. QUESTIONS OF FUNDAMENTAL CLASS RELATIONSHIPS

Vladimir Il'ich approached all economic questions not from the point of view of any nonclass economics. He coordinated any large question in one way with the international situation, in another way with the class struggle in our country. His economics develop together with the constant movement and interweaving in the area of class construction in our society. Under this, our *main guarantee of a SOCIALIST* structure *is the concern about the most advantageous combination of class forces which would secure for us the possibility of the further construction of socialism... the concern about the combination of the "proletaian revolution" with "peasant warfare" in a new form, this time in a "building" form.* This is the *MAIN THING.* This is what Marx points out, that, despite the LaSalle traditions, despite all kinds of Kautskyites, mensheviks, and others, *Marxist views* are continuing. The necessity of the strongest union of workers and peasants is particularly underscored by the serious and difficult international situation. In connection with this central position of Lenin's is found that remarkable place for which it is impossible for each of us to waste *not a minute*. This place is known to everyone, but I consider it my duty to remind you of it here once again:

"Of course, in our Soviet republic social structure is based on the collaboration of two classes: Workers and peasants, to whom is now added the "nepmen" based on known conditions, i.e., the bourgeoisie. If there arise serious massive disagreements between these classes, then a split will be inevitable. But, in our social structure there is no reason for the inevitability of such a split, and the main task of our TsK and TsKK as in our party as a whole consists of watching attentively over the circumstances from which a split can flow, and to anticipate them. For in the final analysis, the fate of our republic will depend on whether or not the peasant masses will go with the workers' class, maintaining with them loyalty to the union, or they will enable the "nepmen", i.e., the new bourgeoisie, to cut them off from the workers, thus breaking with them. The clearer all our workers and peasants will understand this, the greater the chances that we shall successfully avoid the split, which would be ruinous for the Soviet republic" (pp. 387-388).

I draw your attention to certain things, which, for Marxists, it would seem to be "miraculous". Everyone knows that the workers' class is not the same as the peasantry. The peasantry, even if to speak about the middle and poor peasant, is the village petty bourgeoisie (Vladimir Il'ich did not once mention the kulak in these articles). It is understandable to anyone that if two classes exist, then there are class differences between these two classes, but Vladimir Il'ich gives such a formulation, in which it is said that if serious class disagreements arise between these classes, then a split is inevitable and then the ruin of the Soviet republic is inevitable. What does this mean? Did Lenin deviate from Marxism or did Lenin stop considering the peasantry as a special class? It is in no way impossible to understand this "matter" if you stand on the trivial, vulgar, antiLeninist point of view, if you do not understand the entire actual dialectic of original "soviet" development. Before the workers' class now stands the task constantly to remake the peasantry, remake them "in its own image", not separating itself from them, but merging with and leading the masses. A completely different relationship exists between the proletariat and peasantry in a capitalist society. Our Red Army, which consists to a large degree of peasants, is the greatest cultural machine for remaking the peasant, who emerges from this with a new psychology.

Vladimir Il'ich is completely correct: The split between these two classes, that is, the appearance between them of *serious class disagreements*, which would destroy this mechanism of remaking one class by another, *means the ruin of the Soviet republic*. And therefore it is completely understandable that Vladimir Il'ich examined many of his positions from the point of view of the relationship of the workers' class with the peasantry. And namely from this follows his general directive: *The MAIN task of our entire party, of all its organs, consists of examining from what the split can result, and, having noted the danger at the proper time, liquidate it.*

VII. QUESTIONS OF CULTURAL CONSTRUCTION

So, industrialization plus the formation of cooperatives. But the formation of cooperatives presupposes a cultural revolution. There Lenin, while putting forward the slogan of cultural revolution, does not at all confine himself to this unadorned slogan. Here he exposes his concrete substance, he says what needs *to be done*, to what the most special attention needs to be rendered, here where the "link" is. To this is devoted specifically his article entitled "Pages from a Diary". And Lenin raises this question, of course, from the point of view of the relationship between the workers' class and peasantry: "There is the basic political question in the relationship of the city toward the countryside that has a deciding importance for our entire revolution" (p. 366). The *general* purpose is clear. We are not doing the "main thing": *We did not establish a national teacher for the required level.* And Lenin right away goes further: Taking the structure of our state budget, he says: If you want to conduct a cultural revolution, then my directive to you is: The necessary rearrangement of *our entire state budget on the side of primary education.* Well, Lenin not only advanced the slogan of cultural revolution, he immediately made practical instructions from this, and besides, the instructions are of a very wide range. No one will say that this can be carried out right away or in the current year, but the directive is bold, revolutionary, profoundly correct. You will see what this really means: To expel all excesses from our social relationships, all gentry toys, all unnecessary things; to shift the state budget to primary education, to raise our national teacher to the required level. This, of course, is a complete "revolution". This revolution *can* be conducted, but against it stand spontaneous forces of habit, ways of life, prejudices, bureaucratic routine, like monkeys swinging from bars. Vladimir Il'ich was not inhibited to say that we "are not doing almost anything for the countryside besides our official budget or our official relationships" (p. 367). Proceeding from the tasks of the cultural revolution, he proposes the idea of *mass workers' organizations* which would penetrate the countryside, raises the question about state societies, gives the formula that leader-workers must carry communism to the countryside. But now comrade Lenin deciphers the substance of this understanding, once again knowing how in our country they love the phrase and drum-beating instead of deed. He clarifies his idea:

It is impossible "to carry right away purely narrow communist ideas to the countryside. Til that time, while we do not have the material base for communism in the countryside, til that time it will be, it is possible to say, harmful, it will be, it is possible to say, ruinous for communism.

No. It should begin by establishing a link between the city and countryside by no means not taking up the preconcluded goal of introducing communism into the countryside. Such a goal cannot now be achieved. Such a goal is inopportune. Setting up such a goal will bring harm to the matter instead of benefit" (Ibid.).

It is the wisdom of the organizer who organizes not a cell of young people from among Soviet employees, but organizes dozens and hundreds of millions and knows how to approach these dozens of millions. Discussing the question about the forms of linking the countryside with the city (government sponsors, etc.), he insists: Do not do this bureaucratically,—and promote the slogan of *all possible unification of work, while avoiding with all means their bureaucraticization.*

So this is the question raised by Lenin about the cultural revolution and especially the question about the countryside and besides this it is characteristic how highly Vladimir Il'ich appreciated this work. In the article "On Cooperatives" he says: Before us stand two main tasks: 1) Remaking the state bureaucracy and 2) cultural work for the peasantry (p. 376). This cultural work among the peasantry he estimated in another place as *a worldwide historical cultural concern.*

You see, thusly, what kind of plan Vladimir Il'ich expressed related to cultural work and how it is closely linked, how it is, perhaps to say, "rubbed in lightly" to his other positions: On the cooperative organization, industrialization of the country, struggle with international capitalism, and others.

VIII. QUESTIONS OF THE STATE BUREAUCRACY STATE AND PARTY LEADERSHIP

Vladimir Il'ich approaches the fact that one of the most important components of the cultural revolution, one of the greatest levers of socialist accumulation and the involvement of the masses in construction,—every small peasant must construct socialism!—is the condition of the state bureaucracy and the quality of leadership.

This question is developed in two articles: "How to Reorganize Rabkrin" and "Better Less and Better". Vladimir Il'ich's very same approach is interesting:

"Need to come to one's senses at the proper time. Need to penetrate with life-saving distrust into hastily rapid movement in advance, all sorts of boasts, etc. Need to ponder checking those steps in advance, that we proclaim every hour, we do every minute, and then every second we prove their precariousness, instability, and misunderstanding. It would be more harmful above all to be in a hurry" (p. 390).

Proceeding from setting up such that presupposes "stability", "preciseness", "understanding"—things quite simple, Vladimir Il'ich approaches the questions about our bureaucracy.

You remember what kind of preconditions Vladimir Il'ich had on the question about our bureaucracy: Economy is necessary because only then is it possible to carry out industrialization. Simplification is needed because only then can we involve *the masses*. It is necessary to achieve the general increase of *labor productivity*. Thus, the question about the state bureaucracy, from the point of view of involving the masses, economy, labor productivity, is connected to all questions. On the question about the state bureaucracy are connected, as in a trick, all questions—from the economic to the cultural.

And this is understood. Finally, the state bureaucracy is that same lever, that same machine through which our party, the victorious leader of the proletariat, directs its entire policy. In the final analysis, if examined from the point of view of perspective, our state bureaucracy is that same bureaucracy which then must, while involving millions, involving to a man all laborers, constitute the well-known stage in the transition to the state-commune, from which we are still unfortunately far away. So, comrades, Vladimir Il'ich asks: If the question arises about the state bureaucracy, then how do we carry it out, where must we turn, what kind of levers must we seize? And he gives a remarkable formulation. He says: We must turn to the deepest source of the dictatorship—and this deepest source is the "leading workers".

So, first, we must turn to the *leading workers*, and, second, to "the actually enlightened elements in our country! It is necessary to be concerned about the concentration in Rabkrin the best "that is in our social structure" (p. 391), "human material of real contemporary quality, i.e., not distant from the best West European models" (p. 389).

From this end it is necessary to purge the state bureaucracy.

The elements, the "real enlightened", must have such qualities: First, they will not take any words on faith; second, they will not speak any words against conscience (conscience does not change, as some think, in politics); third, they will not be afraid to admit to any kind of difficulty, and, fourth, they will not be afraid of any struggle to meet a goal seriously established by them.

So these are the kinds of requirements Vladimir Il'ich showed these people.

But this is not enough. To rennovate the state bureaucracy and begin with Rabkrin, by uniting it with the TsKK, Lenin proposed the introduction of special tests, "examinations" (*examination* for candidate employees to the RKI, and *examination* for candidate members to the TsKK). These examinations must consist of checking the knowledge of the structure of our state bureaucracy, theory of the organization of that branch of labor in which they wish to work, and so forth.

Having made of RKI such a power battery for improving production methods, it is necessary to make its lever, which determines all other people's commissariats, remakes the entire structure of our work, and improves labor productivity. But why did Vladimir Il'ich propose the unification with the TsKK, how is this linked with the entire plan? This, comrades, will become very simple and understandable upon the attentive study of Vladimir Il'ich's plan *as a whole*. He has two main axis: First is the best work, economy, industrialization, improvement in labor productivity, improvement in quality indicators, second is the correct relationship between the workers' class and peasantry, and concern about how not to begin the split between these two classes through our party, through a split in our party. From here is the unification of RKI and TsKK, an organization of this dually unified body which must examine the two most important tasks and which consists of the best elements of the country. This organizational plan is connected thus entirely with all preceding things, beginning with international policy. And, finally, in this very plan are developed the corresponding requirements *about the masses.* Vladimir Il'ich brought together these requirements in one extremely short, but expressive formula: "*True participation of the true masses*". For it is possible to assemble lots of people, but this will not be the true masses. It is possible to assemble them as if they would "participate", but they actually do not participate. So here is the formula: "True participation of the true masses".

So, if we now bring together the entire plan, then we see that besides the general evaluation of our revolution there is the evaluation of the international situation. From this international situation comes the problem of *establishing power, its strengthening* and the main directive to the workers' class *to establish power over the small and smallest peasantry.* From here, in turn, comes the development of the course for the industrialization of the country based on savings, based on improving the quality of work through the formation of peasant cooperatives, this being the easiest, simplest, and voluntary means to involve the peasantry in socialist construction. From here once again flows the slogans about cultural revolution, restructuring the bureaucracy in business, excellent working bureaucracy which involves the masses. From the concern about the correct relationship of the classes comes the concern about the party line, about our party unity. From here is built the plan for a dually unified organ (Rabkrin plus TsKK) that looks after, on the one hand, the quality of work, combines in itself the control, practical activities and scientific and theoretical activities in the area of the organization of labor, and, on the other hand, looks after party unity—and through the party—after the friendly realization of the worker-peasant union.

The entire plan is grandiose, the entire plan is calculated for many years. The entire plan proceeds from the widest perspective. The entire plan stands on the solid foundation of fundamental Leninist positions. And the entire plan at the very same time is rendered concrete, that is, it gives a whole series of indications of truly practical properties.

Comrades, I attempted here not to omit a single important view of Lenin's and did not add absolutely anything from him, except for certain commentary which flow from Vladimir Il'ich's corresponding articles. I tried to present them as something as a whole, as Vladimir Il'ich's *political testament.* It is indeed understandable that the great historical period through which we have lived since his end brought in significant changes in objective conditions of development, international class relationships, relations between imperialist states and the Soviet Union, economic construction, relationships among the classes (here is related the growing activity of the kulaks), and the regrouping within our party, etc., etc. But we have actually established a whole series of recorded figures, we have many achievements in the area of rationalization of our industry, scientific fertilization of the farm, direct technical reorganization, increasing production, etc., etc. We have economically made a tremendous step forward.

We have to a well known extent strengthened ourselves in the international arena, although contradictions of development enable us here to have the most acute knowledge. However, our growth has gone extremely uneveningly, bringing forth a whole series of difficulties about which we are now speaking so much. Raised before our party recently are a whole series of new tasks which are literally not written in the texts of Vladimir Il'ich's testament.

We raised questions about kolkhoz construction (that is connected with the cooperative on which we are now stressing), sovkhoz construction, tasks on technical reconstruction—questions and tasks which Vladimir Il'ich raised only in general outline. In our country many problems arose rather in a different way. But the basic outline of our policy, our strategy, and our tactics are brilliantly anticipated and predetermined by Vladimir Il'ich. And those difficulties which our country and party are now enduring, still again compel us to turn to one of the inexhaustible sources of political wisdom, to Vladimir Il'ich's testament, and still again by the most attentive model examine the basic question: About the relationship of the workers' class with the peasantry. For the questions about industrialization, bread, goods famine, defense—these are all questions about the worker and peasantry. It is not without reason that our party at the most recent conference raises this question on the agenda.

Comrades, five years ago on a quiet winter day the genius of the proletarian revolution left us. Many of us were indebted for the chance to work together with this man, this solid "Old Man", as we called him, leader, revolutionary, teacher.

In the five years since his end, after checking his testament with the brutal experience of life we more than it could ever be, with great pride, great persistence, great knowledge of the conditions, raise our red banners to go *forward and forward*! (Continuous applause. Orchestra plays "The Internationale").

Kommunist, 2 (1318) January 1988, 93-102.

SOVIET-GERMAN AGREEMENT ON CONCILIATION COMMISSION
25 January 1929

Concerned about the potential for allowing any dispute to hamper Soviet-German relations, the two governments agreed to form a commission to resolve any differences of opinion. An agreement was signed in Moscow on 25 January 1929 and several months later in Berlin. Both parties were concerned about the actions of the German Communist Party and how these would affect diplomatic relations, particularly the 1926 Treaty of Berlin.

CONCILIATION CONVENTION WITH PROTOCOL OF SIGNATURE
Moscow, 25 January 1929; Berlin, 12 April 1929

The Central Executive Committee of USSR and the President of the German Reich, animated by a desire further to strengthen the friendly relations which exist between the two countries, have decided, in execution of the Agreement reached in the Exchange of Notes of 24 April 1926, to conclude an Agreement for a procedure of conciliation, and with this object have appointed their plenipotentiaries:

The Central Executive Committee of USSR: Maxim Litvinov, Member of the Central Executive Committee of USSR, People's Commissar ad interim for Foreign Affairs; and

The President of the German Reich: Dr. Herbert von Dirksen, German Ambassador in Moscow;

Who...have agreed upon the following terms:

I. Disputes of all kinds, particularly differences of opinion which arise regarding the interpretation of the bilateral treaties which exist between the two Contracting Parties or regarding past or future agreements concerning their elucidation or execution, shall, in the event of difficulties arising over their solution through diplomatic channels, be submitted to a procedure of conciliation in accordance with the following provisions.

II. The procedure of conciliation shall be before a conciliation commission.

The conciliation commission shall not be permanent, but shall be formed expressly for each meeting. It shall meet once a year in the middle of the year, in ordinary session, the exact date of which shall be arranged each year by agreement between the two Governments.

There shall be extraordinary sessions whenever in the opinion of the two special need arises.

The meetings of the conciliation commission shall be held alternately in Moscow and Berlin. The place of the first meeting shall be decided by lot.

A session shall ordinarily last not longer than fourteen days.

III. For each meeting each Government shall appoint two members of the conciliation commission.

At each meeting the chair shall be taken by one of the members of that country in whose territory the meeting is taking place.

Either Party shall have the right on occasion to send experts to discuss one or other of the questions on the agenda, who shall be empowered to speak during the session of the conciliation commission.

IV. Not later than fourteen days before the date of the meeting of the ordinary session of the conciliation commission, each of the two Parties shall communicate to the other, through the ordinary diplomatic channels, a list of the questions which it wishes discussed at that session.

In the event of a proposal to convene an extraordinary session, the Government shall communicate to the other, through the ordinary diplomatic channels, a list of the questions which it wishes discussed at that session.

In the event of a proposal to convene an extraordinary session, the Government which shall have made the proposal shall explain to the other Government the special circumstances underlying the proposal. The commission shall meet at the latest within one month of the communication of the proposal.

V. The task of the conciliation commission shall be to submit to the two Governments a solution of the questions laid before it which shall be fair and acceptable to both Parties, with special regard to the avoidance of possible future differences of opinion between the two Parties on the same question.

Should the conciliation commission in the course of a session fail to agree upon a recommendation regarding any question on the agenda, the question shall be laid before an extraordinary session of the conciliation commission, which must, however, meet not later than four months after the first meeting. Otherwise the matter shall be dealt with through diplomatic channels.

The results of each session of the conciliation commission shall be submitted to the two Governments for approval in the form of a report.

The report, or parts of it, shall be published only by agreement between the two Governments.

VI. The conciliation commission itself shall settle the further details of the procedure in so far as may be necessary.

VII. Both Parties undertake to furnish the commission with all the necessary data and to give it every assistance in accomplishing its task.

VIII. Both Parties undertake to refrain from any measure which might prejudicially affect the deliberations of the conciliation commission on any particular question. They declare their readiness more especially to take into consideration precautionary measures for this purpose.

IX. This Convention shall be ratified. The exchange of the instruments of ratification shall take place in Berlin.

The Convention shall come into force on the day on which the instruments of ratification are exchanged. It shall remain in force for three years.

X. This Convention is drawn up in German and in Russian, both texts being authentic.

PROTOCOL OF SIGNATURE

The undersigned met in the People's Commissariat for Foreign Affairs to sign an Agreement for a procedure of conciliation between USSR and Germany.

It was declared that, at the time of the negotiation for the conclusion of the Agreement with regard to the formation of the conciliation commission, the question of the appointment of a chairman of the work of the commission was carefully discussed.

The representative of USSR at that time clearly explained his point of view, namely, that he did not consider possible the acceptance of a provision in the Agreement concerning the appointment of a chairman. He was, further, of the opinion that between USSR and Germany, he did not consider the appointment of a chairman necessary.

The two Contracting Parties were, however, agreed at the time of the preliminary negotiations that the omission from the text of the Agreement did not exclude the possibility of the appointment of a chairman in special cases, and that in special cases they would submit proposals on this question from the conciliation commission for careful consideration.

Soviet Treaty Series, II, 1-2.

STALIN CRITICIZES THE BUKHARIN GROUP AND RECOMMENDS PUNISHMENT

Late January 1929

Taking advantage of the clandestine circulation of the description of the conversation held between Bukharin and Kamenev in July 1928, Stalin called upon the Politburo and Presidium of the Central Control Commission to stop the crimes and opposition activities of Bukharin, Rykov, and Tomsky, and punish them accordingly. He accused the Bukharinites of criticizing and violating party decisions, and conducting secret negotiations with the Trotskyites to form an opposition bloc against the party and its Central Committee.

JOSEPH STALIN

BUKHARIN'S GROUP AND THE RIGHT DEVIATION IN OUR PARTY

From Speeches Delivered at a Joint Meeting of the Political Bureau of the CC and the Presidium of the CCC, CPSU (B) at the End of January and the Beginning of February 1929

(Brief Record)

Comrades, sad though it is, we have to record the fact that within our Party a separate Bukharin group has been formed, consisting of Bukharin, Tomsky and Rykov. The Party knew nothing of the existence of this group before—the Bukharinites carefully concealed its existence from the Party. But now the fact is known and evident.

This group, as is seen from their statement, has its own separate platform, which it counterposes to the Party's policy. It demands, firstly—in opposition to the existing policy of the Party—a slower rate of development of our industry, asserting that the present rate of industrial development is "fatal". It demands, secondly—also in opposition to the policy of the Party—curtailment of the formation of state and collective farms, asserting that they do not and cannot play any serious part in the development of our agriculture. It demands, thirdly—also in opposition to the policy of the Party—the granting of full freedom to private trade and renunciation of the regulating function of the state in the sphere of trade, asserting that the regulating function of the state renders the development of trade impossible.

In other words, Bukharin's group opposes the emergency measures against the kulaks and "excessive" taxation of the kulaks, and unceremoniously levels against the Party the accusation that, in applying such measures, it is in point of fact conducting a policy of "military and feudal exploitation of the peasantry". Bukharin needed this ludicrous accusation in order to take the kulaks under his protection, and in doing so he confused and lumped together the laboring peasants and the kulaks.

Bukharin's group demands that the Party radically change its policy along the lines of the group's platform. They declare further that if the Party's policy is not changed, Bukharin, Rykov and Tomsky will resign.

Such are the facts which have been established in the course of the discussion at this joint meeting of the Political Bureau of the CC and the Presidium of the CCC.

It has been established, furthermore, that on the instructions of this group, Bukharin conducted secret negotiations with Kamenev with a view to forming a bloc of the Bukharinites and the Trotskyites against the Party and its Central Committee. Evidently, having no hope that their platform would carry the day in the Central Committee of our Party, the Bukharinites thought it necessary to form such a bloc behind the back of the Party's Central Committee.

Were there disagreements between us before? There were. The first outbreak occurred prior to the July plenum of the CC (1928). The disagreements concerned these same questions: The rate of industrial development, the state and collective farms, full freedom for private trade, emergency measures against the kulaks. At the plenum, however, the matter ended with the adoption of a united and common resolution on all these questions. We all believed at that time that Bukharin and his followers had renounced their errors, and that the disagreements had been resolved by the adoption of a common resolution. This was the basis which gave rise to the statement on the unity of the Political Bureau and the absence of disagreements within it, which was signed by all the members of the Political Bureau (July 1928).

A second outbreak of disagreements among us occurred prior to the November plenum of the CC. Bukharin's article, "Notes of an Economist", clearly indicated that all was not well in the Political Bureau, that one of the members of the Political Bureau at any rate was trying to revise or "correct" the CC's line. At any rate we, the majority of the members of the Political Bureau, had no doubt that the "Notes of an Economist" was an eclectic antiParty article, designed to slow down the rate of industrial development and to change our policy in the countryside along the lines of Frumkin's well known letter. To this must be added the question of the resignation of Rykov, Bukharin and Tomsky. The fact is that at that time Rykov, Bukharin and Tomsky came to the commission which was drafting the resolution on the control figures and declared that they were resigning. However, in the course of the work on the commission on the control figures all disagreements were smoothed over in one way or another: The present rate of industrial development was preserved, the further development of state and collective farms was approved, maximum taxation of the kulaks was preserved, the regulating function of the state in the sphere of trade was also preserved, the ludicrous accusation that the Party was conducting a policy of "military and feudal exploitation of the peasantry" was repudiated amid the general laughter of the members of the commission, and the three withdrew their resignation. As a result, we had a common resolution on the control figures adopted by all the members of the Political Bureau. As a result, we had the Political Bureau's decision to the effect that all its members should declare both at the November plenum of the CC and outside it that the Political Bureau was united and that there were no disagreements within the Political Bureau.

Could we have known at that time that Bukharin, Rykov and Tomsky were voting for the joint resolution only for appearance's sake, that they were keeping their specific points of difference with the Party to themselves, that Bukharin and Tomsky would in reality practice what amounted to a refusal to work in the AUCCTU, in the Comintern and on

Pravda, that Kamenev had among his private papers a certain "memorandum" which makes it clear that we have within the CC a separate group with its own platform, a group which is trying to form a bloc with the Trotskyists against the Party?

Obviously, we could not have known that.

It is now clear to all that disagreements exist and that they are serious. Bukharin is apparently envious of the laurels of Frumkin. Lenin was a thousand times right when he said in a letter to Shliapnikov as far back as 1916 that Bukharin was "devilishly unstable in politics". Now this instability has been communicated by Bukharin to the members of his group.

The principal misfortune of the Bukharinites is that they have a faith, a conviction that making things easier for the kulak and untying his hands is the way to solve our grain and other difficulties. They think that if we make things easier for the kulak, if we do not restrict his exploiting tendencies, if we let him have his own way, and so on, the difficulties will disappear and the political state of the country will improve. It goes without saying that this naive faith of the Bukharinites in the saving power of the kulak is such ludicrous nonsense as not even to be worth criticizing. The Bukharinites' misfortune is that they do not understand the mechanics of the class struggle, do not understand that the kulak is an inveterate enemy of the working people, an inveterate enemy of our whole system. They do not understand that a policy of making things easier for the kulak and untying his hands would worsen the entire political state of the country, improve the chances of the capitalist elements in the country, lose us the poor peasants, demoralize the middle peasants, and bring about a rupture with the working class of our country. They do not understand that no untying of the hands of the kulak is capable of easing our grain difficulties in any way, for the kulak will not voluntarily give us grain anyhow so long as there exists the policy of procurement prices and state regulation of the grain market—and we cannot abandon the policy of state regulation of trade if we do not want to undermine the Soviet system, the dictatorship of the proletariat. The Bukharinites' misfortune is that they do not understand these simple and elementary things. That is apart from the fact that the policy of untying the hands of the capitalist elements is absolutely incompatible, theoretically and politically, with the principles of Lenin's policy and of Leninism.

That is all very well, comrades may say, but what is the way out, what must be done in connection with the appearance on the scene of Bukharin's group? As to the way out of the situation, the majority of the comrades have already expressed their opinion. The majority of the comrades demand that this meeting should be firm and categorically reject Bukharin's and Tomsky's resignation (Rykov has already withdrawn his). The majority of the comrades demand that this joint meeting of the Political Bureau of the CC and Presidium of the CCC should condemn the Right-opportunist, capitulatory platform of Bukharin, Tomsky and Rykov, that it should condemn the attempt of Bukharin and his group to form an antiParty bloc with the Trotskyists. I fully subscribe to these proposals.

The Bukharinites disagree with this decision. They would like to be allowed freedom of factional grouping—in defiance of the Party Rules. They would like to be allowed freedom to violate decisions of the Party and the CC—in defiance of the vital interests of the Party. On what grounds, it may be asked.

According to them, if rank-and-file Party members do not obey CC decisions, they must be punished with all the severity of Party law; but if so-called leaders, members of the Political Bureau, say, violate CC decisions, not only must they not be punished, they must simply not even be criticized, for criticism in such a case is qualified by them as "being put through the mill".

Obviously, the Party cannot accept this false view. If we were to proclaim one law for the leaders and another or the "common" people in the Party, there would be nothing left either of the Party or of Party discipline.

They complain of "being put through the mill". But the hollowness of this complaint is apparent. If Bukharin has the right to write such a crassly antiParty article as the "Notes of an Economist", then all the more have Party members the right to criticize such an article. If Bukharin and Tomsky allow themselves the right to violate a CC decision by stubbornly refusing to work in the posts entrusted to them, then all the more have Party members the right to criticize them for such conduct. If this is what they call "being put through the mill", then let them explain what they understand by the slogan of self-criticism, inner-Party democracy, and so on.

It is said that Lenin would certainly have acted more mildly than the CC is now acting towards Tomsky and Bukharin. That is absolutely untrue. The situation now is that two members of the Political Bureau systematically violate CC decisions, stubbornly refuse to remain in posts assigned to them by the Party, yet, instead of punishing them, the Central Committee of the Party has for two months already been trying to persuade them to remain in their posts. And—just recall—how did Lenin act in such cases? You surely remember that just for one small error committed by Tomsky, Comrade Lenin packed him off to Turkestan.

Tomsky. With Zinoviev's benevolent assistance, and partly yours.

Stalin. If what you mean to say is that Lenin could be persuaded to do anything of which he was not himself convinced, that can only arouse laughter.... Recall another fact, for example, the case of Shliapnikov, whose expulsion from the CC Lenin recommended because he had criticized some draft decision of the Supreme Council of the National Economy in the Party unit of that body.

Who can deny that Bukharin's and Tomsky's present crimes in grossly violating CC decisions and openly creating a new opportunist platform against the Party are far graver than were the offense of Tomsky and Shliapnikov in the cases mentioned? Yet, not only is the Central Committee not demanding that either of them should be excluded from the CC or be assigned to somewhere in Turkestan, but it is confining itself to attempts to persuade them to remain in their posts, while at the same time, of course, exposing their nonParty, and at times downright antiParty, line. What greater mildness do you want?

Would it not be truer to say that we, the CC majority, are treating the Bukharinites too liberally and tolerantly, and that we are thereby, perhaps, involuntarily encouraging their factional antiParty "work"?

Has not the time come to stop this liberalism?

I recommend that the proposal of the majority of the members of this meeting be approved, and that we pass to the next business.

Stalin, *Works*, XI, 332-340.

PARTY RESOLUTION. PARTY CONDEMNS BUKHARIN GROUP

9 February 1929

On 30 January at the Joint Plenum of the Politburo and Central Control Commission Presidium Bukharin defended his activities, particularly the discussion with Kamenev in July 1928, and criticized Stalin's behavior and policies. By 7 February a compromise was reached, in which Bukharin participated in drafting. Bukharin refused to denounce himself, as part of the compromise, and presented at the final session of the plenum on 9 February a detailed indictment of Stalin for bureaucratism, abuses of power, and disastrous economic policies.

The Stalinist majority on the Politburo responded with a harsh resolution which instructed Bukharin, Tomsky and Rykov to obey party decisions. This resolution of censure, which was not published at the time, was reviewed and approved two months later by a full plenum of the Central Committee and Central Control Commission. At this time, the full plenum was dominated by Stalinists who were eager to crush the Bukharinite opposition.

RESOLUTION ON THE BUKHARIN FACTION

Ratified 23 April 1929

Having become acquainted with the documents of, and taking account of the exchange of opinions at the 30 January 1929 joint session of the Politburo of the Central Committee and Presidium of the Central Control Commission, the joint session of the Politburo and Central Control Commission Presidium has come to the following conclusion.

I. COMRADE BUKHARIN'S BEHIND-THE-SCENES ATTEMPTS TO ORGANIZE A FACTIONAL BLOC IN OPPOSITION TO THE CENTRAL COMMITTEE

The joint session of the Politburo and Central Control Commission Presidium asserts that:
1) During the July Central Committee Plenum (1928), unknown and contrary to the wishes of the Central Committee and Central Control Commission, Comrade Bukharin, together with Comrade Sokolnikov, conducted behind-the-scenes factional discussions with Comrade Kamenev on questions of changing the policy of the Central Committee and the composition of the Politburo;
2) Comrade Bukharin conducted these talks with the knowledge, if not the agreement, of Comrades Rykov and Tomsky, and these comrades, knowing of the talks in question and understanding their impermissibility, kept this knowledge from the Central Committee and the Central Control Commission;
3) the aim of Comrade Bukharin's talks was to demonstrate to Comrade Kamenev that the Central Committee's policy on economic questions is incorrect, to reach agreement on changing that policy, to reach agreement on corresponding changes in the composition of the Politburo and in this way to substantiate the need for organizing a factional bloc of Comrade Bukharin and others together with Comrade Kamenev's group;
4) these factional talks took place at a time when there was already in existence a resolution on the economic situation and the policy for grain procurements that had been unanimously adopted by the Politburo (2 July) and the Central Committee (10 July);
5) these factional talks with Comrade Bukharin took place at a time when the Politburo, at the initiative of Comrades Bukharin, Rykov, and Stalin, was working out the declaration of the Central Committee for the Sixth Comintern Congress on the absence of differences of opinion within the Politburo in which (i.e., in the declaration) there is the following categorical statement by all members of the Politburo: "The undersigned members of the Central Committee Politburo of the VKP(b) declare to the senoren konvent of the Congress that they protest in the most resolute fashion against the dissemination of any and all rumors whatsoever concerning differences of opinion among members of the Central Committee Politburo of the VKP(b)."

On the basis of the facts set forth, the joint session of the Politburo and Central Control Commission presidium resolves:

a) *to condemn the conduct of Comrades Bukharin and Sokolnikov (the talks with Comrade Kamenev) as a factional act that attests to the total lack of principle on the part of Comrades Bukharin and Sokolnikov and that runs contrary to the elementary requirements of honesty and simple decency;*

b) *to declare the conduct of Comrades Rykov and Tomsky, who concealed from the Central Committee and the Central Control Commission their knowledge of the behind-the-scenes talks between Comrades Bukharin and Kamenev, to be absolutely impermissible.*

II. WHERE COMRADE BUKHARIN'S FACTIONAL ACTIVITIES LEAD

The joint session of the Politburo and Central Control Commission Presidium asserts that Comrade Bukharin's factional activities did not end with his behind-the-scene talks with Comrade Kamenev's group but, on the contrary, they did not cease in the period since the July Plenum of the Central Committee but have continued, unfortunately, in one form or another, down to the present day. Such events as Comrade Bukharin's refusal to work in the Comintern; his refusal to work on the editorial board of *Pravda*; Bukharin's publication, without the knowledge of the Central Committee, of his "Notes of an Economist", which are an eclectic muddle impermissible of a marxist and which created a danger of discussion within the Party; submission of their resignations prior to the November Plenum by Comrades Bukharin, Rykov and Tomsky; Comrade Bukharin's 30 January 1929 statement confirming by and large the substance of his talks with Comrade Kamenev in July 1928; Comrade Tomsky's resignation in December 1928; the refusal of Comrades Bukharin and Tomsky to submit to repeated Politburo resolutions demanding that they withdraw their resignations; all these events and others of a similar sort show that Comrade Bukharin continues to desire secretly to struggle against the Central Committee.

To justify his factional activities Comrade Bukharin is resorting to a series of highly impermissible slanders against the Central Committee, its domestic and foreign policy, and its organizational leadership, slanders whose aim is to discredit the party and its Central Committee. And while seeking to discredit party policy, Comrade Bukharin is slipping to a position of diplomatic defense of the rightist elements in the VKP (Comrade Frumkin and Co.), which are demanding the unleashing of the capitalist elements of town and countryside, and defense of the conciliatory elements in the Comintern (Humbert-Droz and Co.), that deny the precariousness of the capitalist stabilization, that are revising the decisions of the Sixth Comintern Congress on the struggle against rightist and conciliatory views, and that are opposing the decisions of the Presidium of the ECCI on the expulsion of rightists from the German Communist Party.

In this connection the joint session of the Politburo and Central Control Commission Presidium establishes the following facts:

1) Comrade Bukharin's statement to the effect that party policy since the July Plenum has allegedly been determined by the slogan set forth by Comrade Stalin in his speech to the plenum, "the slogan of tribute, i.e., of the military-feudal exploitation of the peasantry," is an intrinsically mendacious and thoroughly false statement. The party as a whole, as well as Comrade Stalin, have always combatted and will combat the trotskyite theory of the "military-feudal exploitation of the peasantry." This is as well known to Comrade Bukharin as it is to the entire party. The party as a whole, as well as Comrade Stalin, proceed from the fact that the peasantry is still overpaying for manufactured goods and is being underpaid for agricultural produce, but that this surtax ("tribute") cannot be eliminated at once unless we wish to forego industrialization, that it must be reduced step by step, with a view of eliminating it completely in a few years. If this point is indeed a point of divergence between Comrade Bukharin and the party, then why did not Comrade Bukharin make a statement to this effect to the Politburo or the Central Committee plenum? It is a known fact that immediately after the July Plenum all members of the Politburo, including Comrade Bukharin, signed the 30 July 1928 declaration of the members of the Politburo to the Sixth Comintern Congress to the effect that "the undersigned members of the Central Committee Politburo of the VKP(b) declare to the senoren konvent of the Congress that they protest in the most resolute fashion against the dissemination of any and all rumors whatsoever concerning differences of opinion among members of the Central Committee Politburo of the VKP(b)." How could Comrade Bukharin have signed that declaration if, in fact, he felt that his views differed fundamentally from those of Comrade Stalin or of the Politburo on the question of the "military-feudal exploitation of the peasantry"? Is it possible that he was deceiving the party at that time? It is known that all members of the Politburo, including

Comrade Bukharin, adopted in November 1928, during the November Plenum, a unanimous resolution to affirm, both at the plenum and in reports, the unity of the Politburo and the absence of differences of opinion within it. How could Comrade Bukharin have voted for such a resolution if, in fact, he feels that his views differ fundamentally from those of Comrade Stalin or of the Politburo on the question of policy with respect to the peasantry? Is it possible he was deceiving the party at that time? Is it not clear that Comrade Bukharin himself does not believe in the twaddle about "tribute", and if he now resorts to such slander, it is to justify his factional activities, even if with fabricated tales and slander against the party.

Incidentally, this is not the first time that Comrade Bukharin has resorted to slander against the party. The history of our party knows instances from the period of the Treaty of Brest-Litovsk when Comrade Bukharin, himself bogged down in the petty bourgeois, opportunistic swamp, accused Lenin and his party of opportunism and petty bourgeois views, when he wrote in his theses of the "Left" communists, which were presented to the Seventh Party Congress, that *"the policy of the party's leading institutions was a policy of waverings and compromises,"* and that *"the social basis of such a policy was the process of our party's degeneration from a purely proletarian party to a party of the entire people,"* and that *"the party, instead of raising the peasant masses to its own level, itself sank to their level, was transformed from the vanguard of the revolution into a middle peasant"*...

2) Bukharin's statement to the effect that the "overtaxation" of peasantry is an integral part of party policy and that the party and Central Committee are allegedly not carrying out the decisions of the Central Committee plenum on providing incentives for the individual peasant holding and for increasing its yields is incorrect and false. The entire party as a whole recognized last year that taxes are insufficient, that the agricultural tax is low and must be increased. In this connection the Central Committee last year unanimously adopted a decision to increase taxes to 400,000,000 rubles. Practice this year has shown, however, that such an increase in taxes, with 35 percent of holdings, places excessive burdens on certain strata of the middle peasants. On this basis the Politburo, at the suggestion of Comrades Kalinin and Stalin, set up a commission as far back as December of last year to work out measures to relieve the tax burden of the middle peasant. On the same basis the Politburo, at the initiative of Comrade Stalin, has placed the question of tax relief for the middle peasant on the agenda of the forthcoming party conference. On the very same basis the Politburo on the strength of a report by Comrade Kalinin, has adopted a decision to reduce taxes to 375,000,000 rubles and to offer tax advantages to poor and middle peasant holdings that are expanding their sown areas.

These facts cannot be unknown to Comrade Bukharin.

As concerns the work of the party to raise the yields of the poor and middle peasant holdings, it is enough to note such instances as the extensive campaign by the entire party to raise yields, a campaign that has been particularly stepped up since the last session of the USSR Central Executive Committee, or the local and oblast conferences being convened in all the grain-growing regions to discuss grain problems, or the fact of the extremely widespread application of contractual methods, in order to understand the full intensity of the attention that the party is devoting to the grain problem, to the raising of crop yields, and to the provision of incentives for the individual peasant holding.

These facts must also be known to Comrade Bukharin.

The same must be said about supplying the villages with goods and about the state of affairs of grain procurements this year. It would be quite correct to deny that we have been able to improve both qualitatively and quantitatively on last year's results in supplying the countryside with consumer and production goods. It would be equally incorrect to deny that the party has been able to avoid application of extraordinary measures this year and that by and large it has been able to maintain what, for the USSR is a good rate of grain procurement if one takes into consideration such unfavorable circumstances as the very poor harvest in the Ukraine, the partial crop failure in the North Caucasus and in the Central Black-Earth raion, and the serious crop failure in the Northwestern raion. One can scarcely doubt that had it not been for these instances of poor harvests, particularly in wheat and rye, we would have had an even higher rate of grain procurements and would not have to resort to a certain reduction in the norm under which grain is supplied.

These facts must also be known to Comrade Bukharin.

If, despite the existence of these facts, Comrade Bukharin none the less considers it necessary to discredit the work of the Central Committee and to wage a struggle against its policy on the peasant question by asserting unjustly that the Central Committee resolves to do one thing but carries out another, then this means that Comrade Bukharin does not subscribe to the party line and that he is developing a different line, distinct from that of the party.

But there cannot be two lines in the party. Either the party line is incorrect, in which case Comrade Bukharin is right, in standing apart from the Central Committee. Or the party line is correct, in which case Comrade Bukharin's "new" line on the peasant question can be nothing other than an approximation of Comrade Frumkin's line, which is predicated upon an unleashing of the capitalist elements. One cannot endlessly shuttle back and forth between the slogans "enrich yourselves" and "attack the kulaks". The fact of the matter is that Comrade Bukharin has sunk to Comrade Frumkin's position.

3) Comrade Bukharin's statement to the effect that our currency situation is hopeless, that he "predicted" that this would be the case, that no heed was paid him, etc., is completely incorrect. This statement of Comrade Bukharin is nothing but vainglory. In actual fact it was Comrade Rudzutak who spoke more than, and before, anyone else about currency difficulties. Comrade Bukharin evidently does not understand that this is an area in which not everything depends on us, that a great deal depends in this matter on the covert financial blockade imposed by Britain and France with a certain collaboration on the part of Germany and that has only in recent times begun to weaken. Comrade Bukharin does not understand that the situation cannot be helped through talk and exhortations, that to accumulate foreign currency reserves requires that very stern measures be taken to reduce imports of secondary importance, to increase exports of lumber, oil, etc., and to reduce foreign currency expenditures, etc., measures that are already being taken by the party without, incidentally, the slightest help on Comrade Bukharin's part. Comrade Bukharin cannot but know that these measures have already yielded their result, and that we now have certain foreign currency reserves at our disposal.

If, despite this fact, Comrade Bukharin none the less continues to bemoan the hopelessness of our foreign currency situation, this can only mean that he has succumbed to panic and is, in fact, demanding reduction in our imports of equipment—that is a reduction in the rate of our industrial development.

4) Comrade Bukharin's statement to the effect that we have no intraparty democracy, that the party is being "bureaucratized", that "we are spreading bureaucratism," that there are no elected secretaries in the party, that we have allegedly established a system of political commissars in *Pravda*, in the Comintern and in the All-Union Central Council of Trade Unions, that the present party regime has become unbearable, etc., is a completely incorrect and thoroughly false statement. One cannot but note that Comrade Bukharin has sunk in this matter to Trotsky's position in his notorious letter of 8 October 1923. One has only to compare Trotksy's words in that letter on the "intraparty regime", on "the bureaucratism of the secretariat", on the fact that "the bureaucratization of the party apparatus has reached an unprecedented development with the application of the secretarial selection"—one has only to compare these words of Trotsky's with Comrade Bukharin's statement to understand the full depth of Comrade Bukharin's fall. Only people who are dissatisfied with the existence

of an iron intraparty discipline, only people who are dissatisfied with the fact that the party majority is not in agreement with these panicky "platforms" and "theses", only people who are dissatisfied with the present composition of the leading organs of our party—only such people are capable of levelling a charge of bureaucratism and bureaucratization of our party, with its method of self-criticism. Lenin was right when he called such comrades people afflicted with "lordly anarchism". Lenin was right when he said of such people: "It seems clear that outcries concerning notorious bureaucratism are a simple cover-up for unhappiness with the staffs at the various centers, that they are a fig leaf..."

Comrade Bukharin believes that if the party promoted him to the post of editor-in-chief of *Pravda* and secretary of the ECCI, and Tomsky to the position of chairman of the All-Union Central Council of Trade Unions, then that means that the Party has turned *Pravda*, the ECCI, and the All-Union Central Council of Trade Unions over to them to be run as a mandate, and has surrendered the right to any supervision whatsover over their day-to-day work by the organs of the Central Committee. This is absolutely incorrect. If that were the case, then we would have no unified, centralized party, but a formless conglomerate made up of feudal principalities, which would include a *Pravda* principality, an All-Union Central Council of Trade Union principality, an ECCI secretariat principality, a People's Commissariat for Transport principality, a Supreme Council of the National Economy principality, etc., etc. This would signify a breakup of the unified party and the triumph of "party feudalism". Therefore, Bukharin's howls about the political commissars merely betray the intrinsic unsoundness of his organizational position.

In his attacks on the "intraparty regime", Comrade Bukharin is, as a matter of fact, slipping to the very same position of "freedom of ideological groupings" that was held by the trotskyite opposition in the initial stage of its development.

5) Bukharin's assertion to the effect that the policy of the ECCI, for which he is responsible, comes down to replacing conviction with shouts, that it has resulted in a disintegration of the Comintern sections, in defections and splits, etc., is completely incorrect. By this he means to say that he is opposed to the expulsion of the opportunists Thalheimer and Brandler from the German Communist Party. But he cannot muster the resolve to state this outright, since he knows that to defend Thalheimer and Brandler against the German Communist Party and the ECCI would mean to testify to his own opportunism. By this he means to say that he is opposed to the recall of the conciliators Ewert and Gerhardt from Germany. But he cannot muster the resolve to state this outright, since he knows that to defend Ewert and Gerhardt against the German Communist Party and the ECCI would mean to testify to his own waverings. In fact, what we are witnessing in the Comintern is a beneficial process of cleansing such parties as the German and Czechoslovak ones of social democratic filth and of opportunistic elements. Bukharin evidently does not understand that the Comintern sections cannot be strengthened and bolshevized without cleansing themselves of social democratic elements. Comrade Bukharin does not understand that the present time of intensification of the class struggle in Europe and of growth in the conditions for a new revolutionary upsurge demand of the Comintern that it select for leading positions in communist parties the most steadfast and consistent revolutionary marxists, who are free of opportunistic waverings and unworthy panicking, that only leaders of this type are capable of preparing the working class for the coming battles with international capital and of leading it into battle for the dictatorship of the proletariat.

In fact, Comrade Bukharin has slipped to the position of diplomatic defense of the "carriers" of the right deviation and conciliatory views within the Comintern.

Comrade Bukharin's statement to the effect that he accepts the decisions of the Sixth [Comintern] Congress on combatting rightists and conciliators is merely a fig leaf to avert the eye, for he accepts these decisions only in so far as they are not offensive to Brandler and Thalheimer, Ewert, and Gerhardt, Humbert-Droz and Serra. But not to offend them is

impossible, for it is they, and they above all, who are keeping the ECCI from isolating the rightists and overcoming the conciliators in the Comintern sections.
6) There is no substance whatsoever in Comrades Bukharin and Tomsky's statements to the effect that they are being "picked to pieces" in the party, that they are the object of an "organizational encirclement" and that as a result they are forced to insist on their right to resign, that the appointment of Comrade Kaganovich to the Presidium of the All-Union Central Council of Trade Unions creates "bicentrism", that in such circumstances Comrade Tomsky is forced not to submit to the decisions of the Politburo rejecting his resignation, and that the resignation of Comrades Tomsky and Bukharin is allegedly the best way out of the situation...

On the basis of the materials set forth, the joint session of the Central Committee Politburo and the Central Control Commission Presidium finds that:
1) Comrade Bukharin's completely incorrect criticism of the activities of the Central Committee, which found expression in such documents as Comrade Kamenev's "record", the article "Notes of an Economist", and Comrade Bukharin's 30 January 1929 statement, have as their aim to discredit the line of the Central Committee both in the field of domestic policy and in the field of Comintern policy;
2) in seeking to discredit the line of the Central Committee and in using all and sundry slanders against the Central Committee for that purpose, Comrade Bukharin is clearly leaning in the direction of working out a "new" line, distinct from the party line, that can only mean drawing near the line of Comrade Frumkin (in the field of domestic policy), which is predicated on unleashing capitalist elements, and a duplication of the line of Humbert-Droz (in the field of Comintern policy) predicated on a diplomatic defense of the rightist elements in the Comintern;
3) Comrade Bukharin's waverings in the direction of a "new" line could be intensified in the near future in view of the difficulties confronting our party and in view of Comrade Bukharin's political instability, and this is not the first time in the history of our party that he has shown such instability, if the party does not take all measures incumbent upon it for Bukharin's preservation. Lenin was right when he said of Comrade Bukharin in a letter to Comrade Shliapnikov in 1916 that "Nikolai Ivanovich is a working economist, and *in this* we have always supported him. But he is 1) credulous of slanders and 2) devilishly *unstable* in politics;"
4) Comrade Bukharin's waverings could be given new impetus if the party sanctions his and Comrade Tomsky's resignations.

Proceeding from the above, and with the aim of unconditionally maintaining party unity, the joint session of the Central Committee Politburo and Central Control Commission Presidium resolves:
a) to declare Comrade Bukharin's criticism of the activities of the Central Committee to be absolutely groundless;
b) to advise Comrade Bukharin to resolutely renounce Comrade Frumkin's line in the field of domestic policy and Comrade Humbert-Droz' line in the field of Comintern policy;
c) to refuse to accept Comrades Bukharin and Tomsky's resignations;
d) to advise Comrades Bukharin and Tomsky to carry out loyally all decisions of the ECCI and of the party and its Central Committee...

McNeal/Gregor, Vol. 2, 349-357.
KPSS v rezoliutsiiakh, Vol. 4, 188-197.

TROTSKY DEFENDS HIS ACTIONS AND BLAMES STALIN FOR EXILE. LETTER TO WORKERS
29 March 1929

The Politburo decided in January 1929, with objections from Bukharin, that Trotsky must be deported from his exile in Alma-Ata. Trotsky was shipped to Turkey, where he eventually found a suitable place for the next four years on the Island of Prinkipo. When he arrived at Constantinople on 12 February, he presented a Turkish official with a letter addressed to President Kemal of Turkey, expressing his deportation under duress. From his base in Turkey flowed a series of writings, which were critical of Stalin and his regime. He also received substantial advances for books and articles yet unwritten. In June 1929, the first issue of Trotsky's Bulletin of the Opposition, based in Paris, was published. It contained what was purported to be a brief communique from Moscow about the secret session which decided Trotsky's exile. It also included the letter below in which Trotsky refuted Stalin's criticisms of him, accused Stalin of distorting Bolshevism-Leninism, and defended his receiving of substantial sums of money for his writings. Trotsky reminded readers of Lenin's testament which characterized Stalin as disloyal.

LETTER TO THE WORKERS OF THE USSR

I am writing you to tell you once again that the Stalins, Iaroslavskys, and brothers are deceiving you. They tell you that I have turned to the bourgeois press to conduct the struggle against the Soviet Republic, the creation and defense of which I worked hand in hand with Lenin. They are deceiving you. I turned to the bourgeois press to defend the interests of the Soviet Republic against the lies, perfidy, and treachery of Stalin and Co.

They call upon you to discuss my articles. Have you read them? No, you have not read them. They give you the false, forged translations of individual, small excerpts. My articles were published in Russian as an individual brochure in the very same form that I wrote them. Demand that Stalin reprint them without abridgements and forgeries! He will not dare. He above all is afraid of the truth. Here I want to lay out the fundamental content of my articles.

1. In the GPU's decree about my exile it is said that I am leading the preparation for armed struggle against the Soviet Republic. In "Pravda" the words about the armed struggle were cut out. Why? Because Stalin did not decide in "Pravda" (No. 14 of 19 February 1929) to repeat what is said in GPU's decree. Because he knew that no one will believe him. After the history with the Wrangel officer, after the exposed agent-provocateur who was sent by Stalin to the opposition with a proposal of a military conspiracy, after all this no one will believe that bolshevik-leninists, who wish to convince the party of the innocence of their views, are preparing an armed struggle. So this is why Stalin was not able to print in "Pravda" what is said in the GPU decree of 18 January. So why in this such case was this obvious lie introduced in the GPU decree? Not for the USSR, but for Europe, and for the entire world. Through the TASS agency Stalin systematically contributes daily to the bourgeois press of the entire world, spreading his slander against bolshevik-leninists. Stalin could not otherwise explain the exile and innumerable arrests, as an indication of the opposition's armed struggle. By this enormous lie he caused the greatest harm to the Soviet Republic. The entire bourgeois press said that Trotsky, Rakovsky, Smilga, Radek, I. N. Smirnov, Beloborodov, Muralov, Mrachkovskii and many others, who built the Republic and defended it, are now preparing armed struggle against the Soviet Republic. It is clear to what extent such a view must weaken the Soviet Republic in the eyes of the whole world! In order to justify the repression, Stalin is forced to create enormous legends which inflict incalculable harm to Soviet power. So why did I consider it necessary to publish in the bourgeois press and tell the whole world: It is not true that the opposition is trying to conduct armed struggle with Soviet power. The

opposition conducted and will conduct the relentless struggle for Soviet power against all its enemies. This is my declaration that is printed in dozens of millions of copies in languages of the entire world. It serves the strengthening of the Soviet Republic. Stalin wants to strengthen his own position, while weakening the Soviet Republic. I want to strengthen the Soviet Republic by exposing the lies of the stalinists.

2. Stalin and his press are spreading information throughout the entire world that I declared that the Soviet Republic has become a bourgeois state, that proletarian power has perished and so forth. Many workers in Russia know that this is malicious slander, that it is based on forged citations. I exposed this forgery dozens of times in letters which were passed from hand to hand. But the world bourgeois press believes this or pretends that it believes. All the forged stalinist citations are all over the columns of newspapers of the entire world, as proof that Trotsky acknowledged the inevitable ruin of Soviet power. Thanks to the large interest of world public opinion, above all the widespread masses of people, added to what goes on in the Soviet Republic, bourgeois newspapers, induced by their market interests, concern about circulation, pressure by readers, had to print my articles. In these articles I told the entire world that Soviet power, despite the incorrect policy of the stalinist leadership, has the deepest roots among the masses, is very strong and will survive its enemies.

It is necessary not to forget that the overwhelming majority of workers in Europe, especially in America, are still fed by the bourgeois press. I stipulated that my articles would be printed without any changes whatsoever. It is true that individual newspapers in certain countries violated this condition, but the majority carried it out. In any case all the newspapers had to print that Trotsky, despite the lies and slander of the stalinists, is convinced of the deep internal power of the Soviet regime and strongly believes that the workers will succeed by peaceful means in changing the lying policy of the TsK.

In the spring of 1917 Lenin, shut up in a Swiss cage, used the "sealed" railroad car of the Hohenzollern's to fall upon the Russian workers. The chauvinistic press persecuted Il'ich, calling him none other than a German mercenary and Herr Lenin. Shut up by thermidorians in a Constantinople cage, I used the sealed car of the bourgeois press to tell the truth to the entire world. The unbridled stupid persecution by the stalinists against "mister Trotsky" represents only the repeating of the bourgeois and SR persecution against "Herr Lenin". Together with Lenin I with quiet contempt have to be concerned with the public opinion of the petty bourgeoisie and bureaucrats whose spirit Stalin expresses.

3. I discussed in my articles, distorted and falsified by Iaroslavsky, how, why, and under what conditions they exiled me from the USSR. The stalinists spread the rumor in the European press that they let me go abroad because of my pleading. I exposed this very lie. I said that they forcibly exiled me abroad by way of a prior agreement between Stalin and the Turkish police. And here I acted not only in the interests of protecting myself personally from slander, but above all in the interests of the Soviet Republic. If the oppositionists tried to leave the boundaries of the Soviet Union, this would be understood by the entire world that we consider the situation of the Soviet Union as hopeless. Meanwhile, there is not a trace of this. Stalinist policy inflicted terrible blows not only to the Chinese revolution, English workers' movement, and the entire Comintern, but also to the domestic stability of the Soviet regime. This is indisputable. However, the matter is not at all hopeless. The opposition is not in any case trying to flee the Soviet Republic. I categorically refused to go abroad, proposing that I be put in jail. The stalinists were not able to pass to this means, they were afraid that the workers will urgently strive for liberation. They preferred to come to an understanding with the Turkish police and forced me to settle in Constantinople. I am laying this out to the whole world. All kinds of reasoning workers will say that if Stalin through TASS daily feeds the bourgeois press with slander against the opposition, then I was obligated to publish in order to refute this slander.

4. I told the whole world in dozens of millions of copies that I was not exiled by the Russian workers, not by the Russian peasantry, not by the Soviet Red Army solders, not by those with whom we conquered power and fought shoulder to shoulder on all the fronts in the civil war,—I was exiled by the apparatchiks who put power in their hands, turned into a bureaucratic caste which is connected with a collective guarantee. I told the whole world the truth about Stalin and the stalinists in order to defend the October revolution, Soviet Republic, and the revolutionary name of bolshevik-leninists. I still remember that Lenin's mature carefully thought-out "Testament" called Stalin **disloyal**. This word is understandable in all languages of the world. It means an unscrupulous or dishonorable person who in his actions is led by evil motives, a person whom it is impossible to trust. So this is how Lenin characterized Stalin, and we again see how correct was Lenin's warning. There is no greater crime for the revolutionary, than deceiving his own party, poison with lies the consciousness of the workers' class. Meanwhile, this is what occupies Stalin. He deceives the Comintern and the world workers' class, attributing the opposition to counterrevolutionary purposes and activities in relation to Soviet power. Namely for internal penchant to such a manner of behavior, Lenin even called Stalin disloyal, and namely for this reason he proposed to remove Stalin from his post. Moreover it is necessary now after all that has happened, to explain before the face of the whole world what is expressed by disloyalty, i.e., Stalin's unscrupulousness and dishonesty in relation to the opposition.

5. The slanderers (Iaroslavsky and Stalin's other agents) raised noise on the issue of American dollars. It was hardly worth it under other conditions to bend down to such rubbish. But the most malicious bourgeois press spread with satisfaction Iaroslavsky's filth. So as not to leave anything unclear, I shall therefore speak about the dollars.

I sent my articles to the American newspaper agency in Paris. It is with such type of agencies that both Lenin and I dozens of times held interviews and gave written explanations of our views on this and other questions. Thanks to my exile and its mysterious situation, interest in this matter was colossal in the entire world. The agency counted on excellent profits. It proposed to me half of the profits. I answered them that I personally shall not take a single cent, but that the agency will have to transfer per my instruction half of the proceeds from my articles and that with this money I shall publish in Russian and in foreign languages a whole series of Lenin's works (his speeches, articles, letters) which are prohibited in the Soviet Republic by stalinist censorship. Likewise, I shall publish with this money a whole series of the most important documents (protocols of conferences, congresses, letters, articles, etc.) which have been hidden from the party only because they clearly show Stalin's theoretical and political bankruptcy. And this is the counterrevolutionary literature (in the words of Stalin and Iaroslavsky) that I plan to publish. The exact amount expended with this money will be published in due course. All kinds of workers will say that it is immeasurably better to publish Lenin's works with the money received in the form of casual tribute from the bourgeoisie, than it is with money collected from Russian workers and peasants to spread slander against bolshevik-leninists. Do not forget comrades: Lenin's "Testament" remains in the USSR as before counterrevolutionary literature for the spreading of which they arrest and exile. And this is not by accident. Stalin conducts the struggle against Leninism on an international scale. There does not remain a single country in the world where there stand today at the head of the communist party those revolutionaries who led the party during Lenin's time. Almost all of these are excluded from the Communist International. Lenin led the first four congresses of the Comintern. Together with Lenin I developed all the fundamental Comintern documents. At the Fourth Congress (1922) Lenin and I shared half-and-half in reporting on the new economic policy and the perspectives of the international revolution. After Lenin's death almost all the participants, in any case, without exception all the influential participants in the first four congresses have been excluded from the Comintern. Here, there, and everywhere there stand at the head of the communist party new, casual people who came yesterday from the camps of the enemies. In order to conduct antileninist policy, it is necessary first of all to overthrow the leninist leadership. Stalin did this, relying on the bureaucracy, on the new petty bourgeois circles, on the state apparatus, on the GPU, on the material means of the state. This took place not only in the USSR, but in Germany, in France, in Italy, in Belgium, in the United States, in Scandanavia, in short, almost in all countries without exception. Only a blind man cannot understand the sense that Lenin's closest associates in the VKP and in the entire Comintern, all the participants and leaders of the communist party in the first difficult years, all the participants and leaders of the first four congresses, almost all, to a man, have been removed from their posts, slandered, and excluded. This mad struggle with the leninist leadership is needed by the stalinists in order to conduct an antileninist policy. When they destroyed the bolshevik-leninists, they soothed the party with the idea that the party will henceforth be monolithic. You know that the party is now more broken-up than it ever was. And this is still not the end. On the stalinist path there is no salvation. One can conduct either the Ustrialov policy, i.e., consequent thermidorian policy, or the leninist. Stalin's centric position inevitably leads to the accumulation of the greatest economic and political difficulty and to the permanent devastation and destruction of the party.

It is still not too late to change course. It is necessary clearly to change policy and the party regime in the spirit of the opposition's platform. It is necessary to stop the shameful persecution of the best revolutionary-leninists in the VKP and in the entire world. It is necessary to establish leninist leadership. It is necessary to condemn and eradicate the disloyal, i.e., the unscrupulous and dishonest methods of the stalinist apparatus. The opposition with all its forces is ready to help the proletarian core of the party to carry out this vital task. Mad persecution, disgraceful slander and state repression cannot darken our relationship to the October revolution and to the international party of Lenin. By both we remain true to the end—in stalinist prisons, exile and banishment.

With bolshevik greetings
L. Trotsky

Biulleten' Oppozitsii, I, 3-5.

DECREE. STATE INCREASES CONTROL OVER RELIGION
8 April 1929

In the drive toward industrialization, the Soviet State increased its control over cultural and educational organizations and activities, particularly religion. The decree below clarified several articles from the decree of 1918 on the separation of church and state, for example, on the collection of funding to support a religious society (see Volume 1, p. 96). It established in great detail the limits of property usage and the compulsory registration of the religious society by its members, and approved and prohibited specific religious activities. I am indebted to Dr. John Bunyan of the Hoover Institution for making me aware of the US Senate source below.

LAW ON RELIGIOUS ASSOCIATIONS OF 8 APRIL 1929
(as amended 1 January 1932)

1. Churches, religious groups, sects, religious movements, and other cultic associations of all appellations come under the decree of the Council of People's Commissars of the RSFSR

of 23 January 1918 concerning the separation of the Church from the State and the School from the Church (Collection of Laws of 1918, No. 18, Article 203).
2. Religious associations of believing citizens of all cults shall be registered as religious societies or groups of believers.

A citizen may be a member of only one religious association (society or group).
3. A religious society is a local association of not less than 20 believing citizens who are at least 18 years of age, who belong to the same cult, orientation or sect, and who are united for the common satisfaction of their religious needs.

Believing citizens who do not constitute a sufficient number to form a religious society have the right to form a group of believers.

Religious societies and groups do not enjoy the rights of a legal entity.
4. A religious society or group of believers may begin its activities only after the registration of the society or group by the committee for religious affairs at the proper city or raion soviet.
5. In order to register a religious society, at least 20 of its initiators must submit to the agencies mentioned in the previous Article an application in accordance with the form determined by the Permanent Committee for Religious Affairs of the [Council of Ministers].
6. In order to register a group of believers, the representative of the group (Article 13 above) must submit an application to the agencies mentioned in Article 4 of the city or raion where the group is located in accordance with the form determined by the Permanent Committee for Religious Affairs of the [Council of Ministers].
7. The registration agencies shall register the society or group within one month, or inform the initiators of the denial of the registration.
8. The registration agencies shall be informed on the composition of the society, as well as on their executive and accounting bodies and on the clergy, within the period and in accordance with the forms determined by the Permanent Committee for Religious Affairs of the [Council of Ministers].
9. Only believers who expressed consent thereto may be included in the list of members of religious societies or groups.
10. For the satisfaction of their religious needs, the believers who have formed a religious society may receive from the city or raion soviet by contract, free of charge, special edifices to be used for prayer and objects intended exclusively for the cult.

Moreover, believers who have formed a society or group of believers may use for prayer meetings other premises left to them by private persons or leased to them by local soviets. Such premises shall be subject to all regulations provided for in the present Law relating to prayer buildings; the contracts for use of such premises shall be concluded by individual believers on their personal responsibility. Such premises shall be subject to technical and sanitary regulations.

Each religious society or group of believers may use only one prayer building or [complex of] premises.
11. Transactions relating to the management and use of property, such as the hiring of watchmen, the purchase of fuel, repair of the prayer building and of objects used in the cult, the acquisition of products or property necessary for religious rites and ceremonies and similar transactions closely and directly connected with the doctrines and ritual of a given religious cult, as well as the renting of premises of prayer meetings, may be made by individual citizens who are members of the executive bodies of religious societies or are representatives of groups of believers.

No contract embodying such arrangements may contain in its text any reference to commercial or industrial transactions, even if these are of a kind directly connected with the affairs of the cult, such as the renting of a candle factory or of printing works for the purpose of printing religious books, etc.

12. For each general assembly of a religious society or group of believers, permission shall be obtained: in cities from committees for religious affairs of the city soviets, and in rural areas from the executive committees of the raion.
13. For the carrying out of functions connected with the management and use of religious property (Article 11 above), as well as for outside representation, religious associations elect executive bodies at their general meetings from among their members, by open ballot. In religious societies, an executive body consists of three persons, in a group of believers, of one representative.
14. Registration agencies have the right to remove individual members from the executive body of a religious society or group or the representative elected by a group of believers.
15. The general assembly may elect an auditing committee of no more than three members for the examination of religious property and money collected by religious associations from their members as donations or voluntary offerings.
16. No permission of the government authorities is necessary for the meetings of the executive and auditing organs.
17. Religious associations may not: (a) Create mutual aid funds, cooperative or commercial enterprises or, in general, use property at their disposal for other than religious purposes; (b) give material assistance to their members; (c) organize for children, young people and women special prayer or other meetings, or generally meetings, circles, groups, or departments for biblical or literary study, sewing, working or the teaching of religion, etc., or organize excursions, children's playgrounds, public libraries, or reading rooms, or organize sanatoria and medical assistance.

Only books necessary for the purpose of the cult may be kept in the buildings and premises of worship.
18. The teaching of any kind of religious cult in schools, boarding schools, or preschool establishments maintained by the State, public institutions or private persons is prohibited. Such teaching may be given exclusively in religious courses created by the citizens of the USSR with the special permission of the Permanent Committee for Religious Affairs of the [Council of Ministers].
19. The activities of clergymen, preachers, preceptors and the like shall be restricted to the area in which the members of the religious association reside and to the area where the prayer building or premises are situated.
20. Religious societies and groups of believers may organize local, All-Russian or All-Union religious conventions or conferences by special permission issued separately for each case by

a. the Permanent Committee for Religious Affairs of the [Council of Ministers] if an All-Russian or All-Union convention or congress on the territory of the RSFSR is supposed to be convoked;

b. the local Committee for Religious Affairs, if a local convention is supposed to be convoked.

The permission for convocation of republican conventions and conferences shall be granted by the Committee for Religious Affairs of the appropriate republic.
21. Local, All-Russian and All-Union religious conventions and conferences may elect from among their members executive bodies in implementation of the decisions of the convention or conference. The list of members of the elected executive bodies shall be submitted simultaneously with the materials of the convention or conference to the authority which granted the permission for organizing the convention or conference in two copies in accordance with the form determined by the Permanent Committee for Religious Affairs of the [Council of Ministers].
22. Religious congresses and executive bodies elected by them do not possess the rights of a legal entity and, in addition, may not:

a. form any kind of central fund for the collection of voluntary gifts from believers;

b. make any form of obligatory collection;

c. own religious property, receive the same by contract, obtain the same by purchase, or hire premises for religious meetings;

d. conclude any kind of contract or legal transaction.

23. Executive bodies of religious societies and groups, as well as religious conferences, may use stamps, seals and stationery bearing the imprint of their names exclusively in religious matters. Such stamps, seals and stationery must not include emblems or slogans used by Soviet governmental agencies.

24. Religious conventions and conferences may be initiated and convoked by religious societies and groups of believers, their executive bodies and executive bodies of religious conferences or conventions.

25. Property necessary for the rites of the cult, whether handed over under contract to the believers forming the religious society or newly purchased by them, or given to them for the purposes of the cult, is nationalized and shall be under the control of the city or raion Committee for Religious Affairs.

26. Premises used for the residence of a watchman which are located near the prayer building shall be leased, together with other religious property, to believers by contract, free of charge.

27. Prayer buildings with objects shall be leased to believers who form religious associations for use by the Committee for Religious Affairs of the city or raion soviet.

28. Prayer buildings with objects in these buildings shall be received by contract from the representatives of the raion or city soviet by no less than 20 members of a religious society for use by all believers.

29. In the contract concluded between believers and the city or raion soviet [it] shall be required that the persons who receive a prayer building and religious objects for use (Article 28 above) shall:

a. keep and take care of it as State property entrusted to them;

b. repair the prayer building, as well as pay expenses connected with the possession and use of the building, such as heating, insurance, guarding, taxes, [state and] local, etc.;

c. use the property exclusively for the satisfaction of religious needs;

d. compensate for any damage to the State caused by deterioration or defects of the property;

e. keep an inventory of all religious objects, in which [inventory] shall be entered all newly obtained objects for the religious cult either by purchase, donation, transfer from other prayer buildings, etc., which are not owned by individual citizens. Objects which become unfit for use shall be excluded from the inventory with the consent of the authority which concluded the contract;

f. admit, without any hindrance, representatives of the city or raion soviet to exercise control over the property with the exception of the time when religious ceremonies are performed.

30. Prayer buildings of historical or artistic value registered as such in the Ministry of Education may be leased to believers on the same conditions, however, with the obligation to observe the regulations prescribed for registration and maintenance and the guarding of monuments of art and antiquity.

31. All local inhabitants of a corresponding faith have the right to sign the contract upon the receipt of buildings and religious objects for use and to obtain by this, after the leasing of property, similar rights of management over the property with persons who signed the original document.

32. Whoever has signed a contract may cancel his signature on the above-mentioned contract by filing the corresponding application to the agencies enumerated in Article 4; this, however, does not free him from the responsibility for the good condition and safekeeping of the property during the period of the time prior to the filing of the above-mentioned application.

33. Prayer buildings shall be subject to compulsory insurance at the expense of the persons who signed the contract. In case of fire, the insurance payment may be used for the reconstruction of the prayer building destroyed by fire or upon decision of the appropriate local government for social and cultural needs of a given locality in full accordance with the Decree of 24 August 1925, on the Utilization of Insurance Payments Acquired for Prayer Buildings Destroyed by Fire.

34. If there are no persons who wish to use a prayer building for the satisfaction of religious needs under the conditions provided for in Articles 27-33, the city or raion soviet puts up a notice of this fact on the doors of the prayer building.

35. If, after the lapse of a week from the date of notice, no applications are submitted, the city or raion soviet informs the higher authority. This information supplies data giving the date of the construction of the building and its condition, and the purpose for which the building is supposed to be used. The higher authority decides the further destination of the building in accordance with the provision of Articles 40-42.

36. The transfer of a prayer building leased for the use of believers for other purposes (liquidation of the prayer building) may take place only according to a decision of the [Council of Ministers] of the autonomous republic or oblast which must be supported by reasons, in case where the building is needed for government or public purposes. The believers who formed the religious society shall be informed regarding such decision.

37. If the believers who formed the religious society appeal to the [Council of Ministers] within two weeks from the date of the announcement of the decision, the case on the liquidation of the prayer building shall be conveyed to the Council. If the [Council] confirms the decision, the contract with the believers becomes null and void, and the property shall be taken away from them.

38. The lease of nationalized or private houses for the needs of religious associations (Article 10, para. 2 above) may be broken by a court decision in accordance with the general provisions of court procedure.

39. The liquidation of prayer buildings may be carried out in some instances by the Council for Religious Affairs by order of the city or raion soviet in the presence of representatives of the local finance department and other interested departments as well as the representative of the religious association.

40. The religious property of the liquidated prayer building shall be distributed as follows:

a. all objects of platinum, gold, silver and brocade, as well as jewels, shall be included in the account of the State fund and transmitted for disposal by local financial agencies or of agencies of the Ministry of Education, if the objects were registered there;

b. all objects of historical, artistic or museum value shall be transferred to the agencies of the Ministry of Education;

c. other objects, such as icons, priestly vestments, banners, veils and the like, which have special significance for the performance of religious rites, shall be entrusted to believers for use in other prayer buildings or premises; they shall be included in the inventory of religious property in accordance with the general rules;

d. such everyday objects as bells, furniture, carpets, chandeliers and the like shall be included in the account of the State fund and transmitted for disposal by local financial agencies or agencies of education if the objects were registered with these agencies;

e. so-called expendable property, such as money, frankincense, candles, oil, wine, wax, wood and coal, shall not be taken away if the religious association will continue to exist after the liquidation of the prayer building.

41. Prayer buildings and wayside shrines subject to liquidation, which are registered in special local agencies for State funds, may be transferred for use free of charge to proper executive committees or city soviets under the condition that they will be continuously considered as nationalized property and their use for other purposes than stipulated may not take place without the consent of the Ministry of Finance.

42. Special local agencies for State funds shall register only such liquidated prayer buildings as are not included in the register of the Ministry of Education, such as monuments of art, or [those which] may not be used by local soviets as cultural or educational establishments (schools, clubs, reading halls, etc.) or dwelling houses.
43. When the religious association does not observe the terms of the contract or orders of the Committee for Religious Affairs (on reregistration, repair, etc.) or dwelling houses.

The contract may also be annulled upon the presentation of lower executive committees by the [Council of Ministers] of the autonomous republic, oblast, etc.
44. When the decision of the authorities mentioned in Article 43 is appealed to the [Council of Ministers] within two weeks, the prayer building and property may actually be taken from the believers only after the final decision of [the Council].
45. The construction of new prayer buildings may take place upon the request of religious societies under the observance of the general regulations pertaining to construction and technical rules as well as the special conditions stipulated by the Permanent Committee for Religious Affairs of the [Council of Ministers].
46. If the prayer building, because of dilapidation, threatens to fall apart completely or partly, the Committee for Religious Affairs of the city or raion soviet may request the executive body of the religious society or the representative of the group of believers to discontinue temporarily the holding of divine services and meetings of believers in such building until examined by the technical committee.
47. Simultaneously with the requirement on the closing of the prayer building, the officials exacting such requirement shall ask the appropriate agency of construction control to make a technical examination of the building. A copy of the letter shall be given to the agency which concluded the contract upon the leasing of the building and property to believers.

If the building is registered by the Ministry of Education, a copy shall be given to the appropriate agency of the Ministry.
48. The [following persons] shall be invited with the right of deliberative vote to the examination procedure by the technical committee:

a. the local representative of the Ministry of Education, if the building is registered by the Ministry;

b. the representative of the Committee for Religious Affairs at the appropriate city or raion soviet;

c. the representative of the religious association.
49. The decision of the technical committee stated in the examination document is binding and subject to execution.
50. If the technical committee decides that the building threatens to collapse, the committee must also indicate whether the building should be demolished or made safe if appropriate repairs are made. In such case, the [examination] document shall describe in detail the necessary repairs for the prayer building and the date of completion. The religious association may not hold prayer or other meetings in the building until the repair work has been completed.
51. If the believers refuse to carry out the repairs as indicated in the [examination] document of the technical committee, the contract for the use of the building and religious property shall be annulled according to the decision of the [Council of Ministers] of the autonomous republic or oblast.
52. If, as required by the decision of the technical committee, the building shall be demolished, the contract for the use of the building and religious property shall be annulled according to the decision of the [Council of Ministers] of the autonomous republic or oblast.
53. [Any decision for the demolition of the prayer building] shall be carried out by the Committee for Religious Affairs at the raion or city soviet and the expenses defrayed from the sale of the building material remaining after the demolition of the building. Any money left over shall be transferred to the Treasury.

54. Members of a group of believers or religious society may pool money together and collect voluntary donations in the building of the church or outside of it, but only among members of their religious association and only for the purposes connected with the upkeep of the church building and property incidental to the cult and with hiring of the clergy and maintenance of the executive bodies.

Any form of obligatory contribution in aid of religious associations is punishable under the Criminal Code of the RSFSR.

55. It is compulsory to enter in the inventory of religious property any kind of religious property, whether donated, or purchased with the money received through voluntary donations.

The donations made for the purpose of beautifying the prayer building or religious property shall be entered in the general inventory of the religious property which is in use by the religious association free of charge.

All other donations in kind made for indefinite purposes, as well as donations in money to cover the upkeep of prayer buildings (renovation, heating, etc.), or for the benefit of the clergy shall not be subject to entry in the inventory. The donations in money shall be entered by the cashier in the account book.

56. Expenditures of donated money may be carried out by the members of the executive body in connection with the purposes for which they are donated.

57. Prayer meetings of believers who formed a group or society may be held, without the notification to or permission of the authorities, in prayer buildings or in specially adapted premises which comply with technical and sanitary regulations.

Divine services may be performed in the premises not specially adapted for these purposes, if notification [is made] to the Committee for Religious Affairs.

58. Any kind of religious ceremonies or rites or display of objects of the cult in the buildings belonging to the State, public, cooperative or private institutions or enterprises is prohibited.

Such prohibition does not apply to the performance of religious rites in hospitals and prisons, in specially isolated rooms, if requested by dangerously ill or dying persons, or to the performance of religious ceremonies in cemeteries and in crematoria.

59. Special permission [granted] for each case separately by the Committee for Religious Affairs is required for the performance of religious rites in the open air. An application for such permission must be submitted at least two weeks prior to the ceremony.

Such permission is not required for religious processions connected with funerals.

60. Permission is not required for religious processions which are an inevitable part of the divine service and are made only around the prayer building, provided they do not disturb normal street traffic.

61. Permission of the agency which concluded the contract for the use of property is necessary for each religious procession as well as the performance of religious ceremonies outside the place where the religious association is situated. Such permission may be granted only with the agreement of the executive committee of the place where the procession or performance of ceremonies is supposed to take place.

62. A record of religious societies and groups of believers shall be kept by the agencies which register the religious association (Article 6 above).

63. The registration agencies of religious associations (Article 6 above) submit data to the Committee for Religious Affairs at the city and raion soviets in accordance with the forms and within the period established by the Permanent Committee for Religious Affairs of the [Council of Ministers].

64. Surveillance over the activities of religious associations, as well as over the maintenance of prayer buildings and property leased to religious associations, shall be exercised by registration agencies, and in rural areas by village soviets.

U.S. Senate, *The Church and State Under Communism*, 12-17.
Gsovski, 330-332.
Matthews, 298-304.

STALIN ATTACKS BUKHARIN AND HIS GROUP
22 April 1929

Stalin delivered an extensive condemnation of Bukharin, Rykov, and Tomsky at the meeting of the full plenum of the Central Committee and Central Control Commission. He accused the Bukharinites of forming a disloyal and factional bloc against the party's line of industrialization, collectivization, and destablization in the capitalist system, and grossly violating Party discipline. He used Lenin's "Testament" and remarks to show that Bukharin considered himself a greater theoretician than Lenin and that he was not a Marxist theoretician. Stopping short of calling for expulsion from the Politburo, he asked the plenum to censure Bukharin's group, remove Bukharin and Tomsky from their posts, and warn them of expulsion if they deviated in any way from the party line and decisions.

JOSEPH STALIN

THE RIGHT DEVIATION IN THE CPSU(B)

Speech Delivered at the Plenum of the Central Committee and Central Control Commission of the CPSU(B)
(Verbatim Report)

Comrades, I shall not touch on the personal factor, although it played a rather conspicuous part in the speeches of some of the comrades of Bukharin's group. I shall not touch on it because it is a trivial matter, and it is not worthwhile dwelling on trivial matters. Bukharin spoke of his private correspondence with me. He read some letters and it can be seen from them that although we were still on terms of personal friendship quite recently, now we differ politically. The same note could be detected in the speeches of Uglanov and Tomsky. How does it happen, they say: We are old Bolsheviks, and suddenly we are at odds and unable to respect one another.

I think that all these moans and lamentations are not worth a brass farthing. Our organization is not a family circle, nor an association of personal friends; it is the political party of the working class. We cannot allow interests of personal friendship to be placed above the interests of our cause.

Things have come to a sorry pass, comrades, if the only reason why we are called old Bolsheviks is that we are *old*. Old Bolsheviks are respected not because they are *old*, but because they are at the same time eternally fresh, never-aging revolutionaries. If an old Bolshevik swerves from the path of the revolution, or degenerates and fails politically, then, even if he is a hundred years old, he has no right to call himself an old Bolshevik; he has no right to demand that the Party should respect him.

Further, questions of personal friendship cannot be put on a par with political questions, for, as the saying goes—friendship is all very well, but duty comes first. We all serve the working class, and if the interests of personal friendship clash with the interests of the revolution, then personal friendship must come second. As Bolsheviks we cannot have any other attitude.

I shall not touch either on the insinuations and veiled accusations of a personal nature that were contained in the speeches of comrades of the Bukharin opposition. Evidently these comrades are attempting to cover up the underlying political basis of our disagreements with insinuations and equivocations. They want to substitute petty political scheming or politics. Tomsky's speech is especially noteworthy in this respect. His was the typical speech of a trade-union politician who attempts to substitute petty political scheming or politics. However, that trick of theirs won't work.

Let us get down to business.

I
ONE LINE OR TWO LINES?

Have we a single, common, general line or have we two lines? That, comrades, is the basic question.

In his speech here, Rykov said that we have a single general line and that if we do not have some "insignificant" disagreements, it is because there are "shades of difference" in the interpretation of the general line.

Is that correct? Unfortunately, it is not. And it is not merely incorrect, but it is absolutely contrary to the truth. If we really have only one line, and there are only shades of difference between us, then why did Bukharin run off to yesterday's Trotskyists led by Kamenev, in an effort to set up with them a factional bloc directed against the Central Committee and its Political Bureau? Is it not a fact that Bukharin spoke there of a "fatal" line of the Central Committee, of Bukharin's, Tomsky's and Rykov's disagreements in principle with the Central Committee of the Party, of the need for a drastic change in the composition of the Political Bureau of the Central Committee?

If there is only one line, why did Bukharin conspire with yesterday's Trotskyists against the Central Committee, and why did Rykov and Tomsky aid him in this undertaking?

If there is only one general line, how can one part of the Political Bureau, which supports the single, common, general line, be allowed to undermine the other part, which supports the same general line?

Can such a fluctuating policy be allowed if we have a single, common, general line?

If there is only one line, how are we to account for Bukharin's declaration of 30 January, which was wholly and solely aimed against the Central Committee and its general line?

If there is only one line, how are we to account for the declaration of the trio (Bukharin, Rykov, Tomsky) of 9 February, in which, in a brazen and grossly slanderous manner, they accuse the Party: a) of a policy of military-feudal exploitation of the peasantry, b) of a policy of fostering bureaucracy, c) of a policy of disintegrating the Comintern?

Perhaps these declarations are just ancient history? Perhaps it is now considered that these declarations were a mistake? Perhaps Rykov, Bukharin and Tomsky are prepared to take back these undoubtedly mistaken and antiParty declarations? If that is the case, let them say so frankly and honestly. Then everyone will understand that we have only one line and that there are only shades of difference between us. But, as is evident from the speeches of Bukharin, Rykov and Tomsky, they would not do that. And not only would they not do that, but they have no intention of repudiating these declarations of theirs in the future, and they state that they adhere to their views as set forth in the declarations.

Where then is the single, common, general line?

If there is only one line, and, in the opinion of Bukharin's group, the Party line consists in pursuing a policy of military-feudal exploitation of the peasantry, then do Bukharin, Rykov and Tomsky really wish to join us in pursuing this fatal policy, instead of combating it? That is indeed absurd.

If there is only one line, and, in the opinion of the Bukharin opposition, the Party line consists in fostering bureaucracy, then do Rykov, Bukharin and Tomsky really wish to join us in fostering bureaucracy within the Party, instead of combating it? That is indeed nonsense.

If there is only one line, and, in the opinion of the Bukharin opposition, the Party line consists in disintegrating the Comintern, then do Rykov, Bukharin and Tomsky really wish to join us in disintegrating the Comintern, instead of combating this policy? How are we to believe such nonsense?

No, comrades, there must be something wrong with Rykov's assertion that we have a single, common line. Whichever way you look at it, if we bear in mind the facts just set forth regarding the declarations and conduct of Bukharin's group, there is something amiss with the business of one, common line.

If there is only one line, then how are we to account for the policy of resigning adopted by Bukharin, Rykov and Tomsky? Is it conceivable that where there is a common general line, one part of the Political Bureau would systematically refuse to implement the repeated decisions of the Central Committee of the Party and continue to sabotage Party work for six months? If we really have a single, common, general line, how are we to account for this disruptive policy of resigning that is being methodically pursued by one part of the Political Bureau?

From the history of our Party we know of examples of the policy of resigning. We know, for instance, that on the day after the October Revolution some comrades, led by Kamenev and Zinoviev, refused the posts assigned to them and demanded that the policy of the Party should be changed. We know that at that time they sought to justify the policy of resigning by demanding the creation of a coalition government that would include Mensheviks and Socialist-Revolutionaries, in opposition to the Central Committee of our Party whose policy was to form a purely Bolshevik government. But at that time there was some sense in the policy of resigning, because it was based on the existence of two different lines, one of which was for forming a purely Bolshevik government, and the other for forming a coalition government jointly with the Mensheviks and Socialist-Revolutionaries. That was clear and comprehensible. But we see no logic, no logic whatsoever, when the Bukharin opposition, on the one hand, proclaims the unity of the general line, and, on the other hand, pursues a policy of resigning, adopted from that of Zinoviev and Kamenev in the period of the October Revolution.

One thing or the other—either there is only one line, in which case Bukharin and his friends' policy of resigning is incomprehensible and inexplicable; or we have two lines, in which case the policy of resigning is perfectly comprehensible and explicable.

If there is only one line, how are we to explain the fact that the trio of the Political Bureau—Rykov, Bukharin and Tomsky—deemed it possible, during the voting in the Political Bureau, to *abstain* when the main theses on the five year plan and on the peasant question were being adopted? Does it ever happen that there is a single general line but that one section of the comrades abstains from voting on the main questions of our economic policy? No, comrades, such wonders do not occur.

Finally, if there is only one line, and there are only shades of difference between us, why did the comrades of the Bukharin opposition—Bukharin, Rykov and Tomsky—reject the compromise proposed by a commission of the Political Bureau on 7 February of this year? Is it not a fact that this compromise gave Bukharin's group a perfectly acceptable way out of the impasse in which it had landed itself?

Here is the text of the compromise proposed by the majority of the Central Committee on *7 February* of this year:

"After an exchange of views in the commission it was ascertained that:

"1) Bukharin admits that his negotiations with Kamenev were a political error;

"2) Bukharin admits that the assertions contained in his 'declaration' of 30 January 1929, alleging that the Central Committee is in fact pursuing a policy of 'military-feudal exploitation of the peasantry,' that the Central Committee is disintegrating the Comintern and is fostering bureaucracy within the Party—that all these assertions were made in the heat of the moment, during passionate polemics, that he does not maintain these assertions any longer, and considers that there are no differences between him and the Central Committee on these questions;

"3) Bukharin recognizes, therefore, that harmonious work in the Political Bureau is possible and necessary;

"4) Bukharin withdraws his resignation both as regards *Pravda* and as regards the Comintern;

"5) Consequently, Bukharin withdraws his declaration of 30 January.

"On the basis of the above, the commission considers it possible not to submit its draft resolution containing a political appraisal of Bukharin's errors to the joint meeting of the Political Bureau and the Presidium of the Central Control Commission, and requests the joint meeting of the Political Bureau and the Presidium of the Central Control Commission to withdraw from the circulation all existing documents (verbatim reports of speeches, etc.).

"The commission requests the Political Bureau and the Presidium of the CCC to provide Bukharin with all the conditions necessary for his normal work as editor-in-chief of *Pravda* and Secretary of the Executive Committee of the Comintern."

Why did Bukharin and his friends reject this compromise if we really have only one line, and if there are only shades of difference between us? Is it not perfectly obvious that Bukharin and his friends should have been extremely eager to accept the compromise proposed by the Political Bureau, so as to put an end to the tension existing within the Party and create an atmosphere conducive to unanimity and harmony in the work of the Political Bureau?

There is talk of the unity of the Party, of collective work in the Political Bureau. But is it not obvious that anyone who wants genuine unity and values the collective principle in work should have accepted the compromise? Why then did Bukharin and his friends reject this compromise?

Is it not obvious that if we had only one line, then there would never have been either the trio's declaration of February 9 or Bukharin and his friends' refusal to accept the compromise proposed by the Political Bureau of the Central Committee?

No, comrades, if we bear in mind the facts set forth above, there must be something amiss with the business of your one, common line.

It turns out that in reality we have not one line, but two lines; one of them being the line of the Central Committee and the other the line of Bukharin's group.

In his speech, Rykov did not tell the truth when he declared that we have only one general line. He sought thereby to disguise his own line, which differs from the Party line, for the purpose of stealthily undermining the Party line. The policy of opportunism consists precisely in attempting to slur over disagreements, to gloss over the actual situation within the Party, to disguise one's own position and to make it impossible for the Party to attain complete clarity.

Why does opportunism need such a policy? Because it enables opportunists to carry out in effect their own line, which differs from the Party line, behind a smoke screen of talk about the unity of the line. In his speech at the present plenum of the Central Committee and Central Control Commission Rykov adopted this opportunist standpoint.

Here is what Lenin says about the specific features of opportunism and of opportunists:

"When we speak of fighting opportunism, we must never forget the feature characteristic of the whole of present-day opportunism in every sphere, namely, its indefiniteness, diffuseness, elusiveness. An opportunist, by his very nature, always evades formulating an issue definitely and decisively, he seeks a middle course, he wriggles like a snake between two mutually exclusive points of view, trying to 'agree' with both and to reduce his differences of opinion to petty amendments, doubts, righteous and innocent suggestions, and so forth" (Volume VI, p. 320).

There you have a portrait of the opportunist, who dreads clearness and definiteness and who strives to gloss over the actual state of affairs, to slur over the actual disagreements in the Party.

Yes, comrades, one must be able to face the facts no matter how unpleasant they may be. God forbid that we should become infected with the disease of fear of the truth. Bolsheviks, incidentally, are different from all other parties because they do not fear the truth and are not afraid of facing the truth no matter how bitter it may be. And in the present case the truth is that in fact we do not have a single, common line. There is one line, the Party line, the revolutionary, Leninist line. But side by side with it there is another line, the line of Bukharin's group, which is combating the Party line by means of antiParty declarations, by means of resignations, by means of slander and camouflaged undermining activities against the Party, by means of backstairs negotiations with yesterday's Trotskyists for the purpose of setting up an antiParty bloc. This second line is the opportunist line.

There you have a fact that no amount of diplomatic verbiage or artful statements about the existence of a single line, etc., etc., can disguise.

II
CLASS CHANGES AND OUR DISAGREEMENTS

What are our disagreements? What are they connected with?

They are connected, first of all, with the class changes that have been taking place recently in our country and in capitalist countries. Some comrades think that the disagreements in our Party are of an accidental nature. That is wrong, comrades. That is quite wrong. The disagreements in our Party have their roots in the class changes, in the intensification of the class struggle which has been taking place lately and which marks a turning point in development.

The chief mistake of Bukharin's group is that it fails to see these changes and this turning point; it does not see them, and does not want to notice them. That, in fact, explains the failure to understand the new tasks of the Party and of the Comintern which is the characteristic feature of the Bukharin opposition.

Have you noticed, comrades, that the leaders of the Bukharin opposition, in their speeches at the plenum of the Central Committee and Central Control Commission, completely evaded the question of the class changes in our country, that they did not say a single word about the intensification of the class struggle and did not even remotely hint at the fact that our disagreements are connected with this very intensification of the class struggle? They talked about everything, about philosophy and about theory, but they did not say a single word about the class changes which determine the orientation and the practical activity of our Party at the present moment.

How is this strange fact to be explained? Is it forgetfulness, perhaps? Of course not! Political leaders cannot forget the chief thing. The explanation is that they neither see nor understand the new revolutionary processes now going on both here, in our country, and in the capitalist countries. The explanation is that they have overlooked the chief thing, they have overlooked those class changes, which a political leader has no right to overlook. This is the real explanation for the confusion and unpreparedness displayed by the Bukharin opposition in face of the new tasks of our Party.

Recall the recent events in our Party. Recall the slogans our Party has issued lately in connection with the new class changes in our country. I refer to such slogans as the slogan of *self-criticism*, the slogan of intensifying *the fight against bureaucracy and of purging the Soviet apparatus*, the slogan of *training new economic cadres and Red experts*, the slogan of strengthening *the collective- and state-farm movement*, the slogan of *purging the Party*, etc. To some comrades these slogans seemed staggering and dizzying. Yet it is obvious that these slogans are the most necessary and urgent slogans of the Party at the present moment.

The whole thing began when, as a result of the Shakhty affair, we raised in a new way the question of new economic cadres, of training Red experts from the ranks of the working class to take the place of the old experts.

What did the Shakhty affair reveal? It revealed that the bourgeoisie was still far from being crushed; that it was organizing and would continue to organize wrecking activities to hamper our work of economic construction; that our economic, trade-union and, to a certain extent, our Party organizations had failed to notice the undermining operations of our class enemies, and that it was therefore necessary to exert all efforts and employ all resources to reinforce and improve our organizations, to develop and heighten their class vigilance.

In this connection the slogan of *self-criticism* became sharply stressed. Why? Because we cannot improve our economic, trade-union and Party organizations, we cannot advance the cause of building socialism and of curbing the wrecking activities of the bourgeoisie, unless we develop criticism and self-criticism to the utmost, unless we place the work of our organizations under the control of the masses. It is indeed a fact that wrecking has been and is going on not only in the coal-fields, but also in the metallurgical industries, in the war industries, in the People's Commissariat of Transport, in the gold and platinum industries, etc., etc. Hence the slogan of self-criticism.

Further, in connection with the grain-procurement difficulties, in connection with the opposition of the kulaks to the Soviet price policy, we stressed the question of developing collective and state farms to the utmost, of launching an offensive against the kulaks, of organizing grain procurements by means of pressure on the kulak and well-to-do elements.

What did the grain-procurement difficulties reveal? They revealed that the kulak was not asleep, that the kulak was growing, that he was busy undermining the policy of the Soviet government, while our Party, Soviet and cooperative organizations—at all events, some of them—either failed to see the enemy, or adapted themselves to him instead of fighting him.

Hence the new stress laid on the slogan of self-criticism, on the slogan of checking and improving our Party, cooperative and procurement organizations generally.

Further, in connection with the new tasks of reconstructing industry and agriculture on the basis of socialism, there arose the slogan of systematically reducing production costs, of strengthening labor discipline, of developing socialist competition, etc. These tasks called for a revision of the entire activities of the trade unions and Soviet apparatus, for radical measures to put new life into these organizations and for purging them of bureaucratic elements.

Hence the stress laid on the slogan of fighting bureaucracy in the trade unions and in the Soviet apparatus.

Finally, the slogan of purging the Party. It would be ridiculous to think that it is possible to strengthen our Soviet-economic, trade-union and cooperative organizations, that it is possible to purge them of the dross of bureaucracy, without giving a sharp edge to the Party itself. There can be no doubt that bureaucratic elements exist not only in the economic and cooperative, trade-union and Soviet organizations, but in the organizations of the Party itself. Since the Party is the guiding force of all these organizations, it is obvious that purging the Party is the essential condition for thoroughly revitalizing and improving all the other organizations of the working class. Hence the slogan of purging the Party.

Are these slogans a matter of accident? No, they are not. You see yourselves that they are not accidental. *They are necessary links in the single continuous chain which is called the offensive of socialism against the elements of capitalism.*

They are connected, primarily, with the period of the reconstruction of our industry and agriculture on the basis of socialism. And what is the reconstruction of the national economy on the basis of socialism? It is the offensive of socialism against the capitalist elements of the national economy along the whole front. It is a most important advance of the working class of our country towards the complete building of socialism. But in order to carry out this reconstruction we must first of all improve and strengthen the cadres of socialist construction—the economic-Soviet and trade-union cadres, and also Party and cooperative cadres; we must give a sharp edge to all our organizations, purge them of dross; we must stimulate the activity of the vast masses of the working class and peasantry.

Further, these slogans are connected with the fact of the resistance of the capitalist elements of the national economy to the offensive of socialism. The so-called Shakhty affair cannot be regarded as something accidental. "Shakhtyists" are at present entrenched in every branch of our industry. Many of them have been caught, but by no means all of them. The wrecking activities of the bourgeois intelligentsia are one of the most dangerous forms of resistance to developing socialism. The wrecking activities are all the more dangerous because they are connected with international capital. Bourgeois wrecking is undoubtedly an indication of the fact that the capitalist elements have by no means laid down their arms, that they are gathering strength for fresh attacks on the Soviet regime.

As for the capitalist elements in the countryside, there is still less reason to regard as accidental the opposition of the kulaks to the Soviet price policy, which has been going on for over a year already. Many people are still unable to understand why it is that until 1927 the kulak gave his grain of his own accord, whereas since 1927 he has ceased to do so. But there is nothing surprising in it. Formerly the kulak was still relatively weak; he was unable to organize his farming properly; he lacked sufficient capital to improve his farm and so he was obliged to bring all, or nearly all, his surplus grain to the market. Now, however, after a number of good harvests, since he has been able to build up his farm, since he has succeeded in accumulating the necessary capital, he is in a position to maneuver on the market, he is able to set aside grain, this currency of currencies, as a reserve for himself, and prefers to bring to the market meat, oats, barley and other, secondary crops. It would be ridiculous now to hope that the kulak can be made to part with his grain voluntarily.

There you have the root of the resistance which the kulak is now offering to the policy of the Soviet regime.

And what does the resistance offered by the capitalist elements of town and country to the socialist offensive represent? It represents a regrouping of the forces of the class enemies of the proletariat for the purpose of defending the old against the new. It is not difficult to understand that these circumstances cannot but lead to an intensification of the class struggle. But if we are to break the resistance of the class enemies and clear the way for the advance of socialism, we must, besides everything else, give a sharp edge to all our organizations, purge them of bureaucracy, improve their cadres and mobilize the vast masses of the working class and laboring strata of the countryside against the capitalist elements of town and country.

It was on the basis of these class changes that our Party's present slogans arose.

The same must be said about the class changes in capitalist countries. It would be ridiculous to think that the stabilization of capitalism has remained unchanged. Still more ridiculous would it be to assert that the stabilization is gaining strength, that it is becoming secure. As a matter of fact, capitalist stabilization is being undermined and shaken month by month and day by day. The intensification of the struggle for foreign markets and raw materials, the growth of armaments, the growing antagonism between America and Britain, the growth of socialism in the USSR, the swing to the left of the working class in the capitalist countries, the wave of strikes and class conflicts in the European countries, the growing revolutionary movement in the colonies, including India, the growth of communism in all countries of the world—all these are facts which indicate beyond a doubt that the elements of a new revolutionary upsurge are accumulating in the capitalist countries.

Hence the task of intensifying the fight against Social Democracy, and, above all, against its "Left" wing, as being the social buttress of capitalism.

Hence the task of intensifying the fight in the Communist Parties against the Right elements, as being the agents of Social-Democratic influence.

Hence the task of intensifying the fight against conciliation towards the Right deviation, as being the refuge of opportunism in the Communist Parties.

Hence the slogan of purging the Communist Parties of Social-Democratic traditions.

Hence the so-called new tactics of communism in the trade unions.

Some comrades do not understand the significance and importance of these slogans. But a Marxist will always understand that, unless these slogans are put into effect, the preparation of the proletarian masses for new class battles is unthinkable, victory over Social Democracy is unthinkable, and the selection of real leaders of the communist movement, capable of leading the working class into the fight against capitalism, is impossible.

Such, comrades, are the class changes in our country and in the capitalist countries, on the basis of which the present slogans of our Party both in its internal policy and in relation to the Comintern, have arisen.

Our Party sees these class changes. It understands the significance of the new tasks and it mobilizes forces for their fulfillment. That is why it is facing events fully armed. That is why it does not fear the difficulties confronting it, for it is prepared to overcome them.

The misfortune of Bukharin's group is that it does not see these class changes and does not understand the new tasks of the Party. And it is precisely because it does not understand them that it is in a state of complete bewilderment, is ready to flee from difficulties, to retreat in the face of the difficulties, to surrender the positions.

Have you ever seen fishermen when a storm is brewing on a big river—such as the Yenisei? I have seen them many a time. In the face of a storm one group of fishermen will muster all their forces, encourage their fellows and boldly guide the boat to meet the storm: "Cheer up, lads, keep a tight hold of the tiller, cut the waves, we'll win through!"

But there is another type of fishermen—those who, on sensing a storm, lose heart, begin to snivel and demoralize their own ranks: "It's terrible, a storm is brewing: lie down, lads, in the bottom of the boat, shut your eyes, let's hope she'll make the shore somehow." (*General laughter.*)

Does it still need proof that the line and conduct of Bukharin's group exactly resembles the line and conduct of the second group of fishermen, who retreat in panic in the face of difficulties?

We say that in Europe the conditions are maturing for a new revolutionary upsurge, that this circumstance dictates to us new tasks along the line of intensifying the fight against the Right deviation in the Communist Parties and of driving the Right deviators out of the Party, of intensifying the fight against conciliation, which screens the Right deviation; of intensifying the fight against Social-Democratic traditions in the Communist Parties, etc., etc. But Bukharin answers us that all this is nonsense, that no such new tasks confront us, that the whole fact of the matter is that the majority in the Central Committee wants to "haul" him, i.e., Bukharin, "over the coals".

We say that the class changes in our country dictate to us new tasks which call for a systematic reduction of costs of production and improvement of labor discipline in industry; that these tasks cannot be carried out without radical change in the methods of work of the trade unions. But Tomsky answers us that all this is nonsense, that no such new tasks confront us, that the whole fact of the matter is that the majority in the Central Committee wants to "haul" him, i.e., Tomsky, "over the coals".

We say that the reconstruction of the national economy dictates to us new tasks along the line of intensifying the fight against bureaucracy in the Soviet and economic apparatus, of purging this apparatus of rotten and alien elements, of wreckers, etc., etc. But Rykov answers us that all this is nonsense, that no such new tasks confront us, that the whole fact of the matter is that the majority in the Central Committee wants to "haul" him, i.e., Rykov, "over the coals".

Now, is this not ridiculous, comrades? Is it not obvious that Bukharin, Rykov and Tomsky see nothing but their own navels?

The misfortune of Bukharin's group is that it does not see the new class changes and does not understand the new tasks of the Party. And it is precisely because it does not understand them that it is compelled to drag in the wake of events and to yield to difficulties.

There you have the root of our disagreements.

III
DISAGREEMENTS IN REGARD TO THE COMINTERN

I have already said that Bukharin does not see and does not understand the new tasks of the Comintern along the line of driving the Rights out of the Communist Parties, of curbing conciliation, and of purging the Communist Parties of Social-Democratic traditions—tasks which are dictated by the maturing conditions for a new revolutionary upsurge. This thesis is fully confirmed by our disagreements on Comintern questions.

How did the disagreements in this sphere begin?

They began with Bukharin's theses at the Sixth Congress on the international situation. As a rule, theses are first examined by the delegation of the CPSU(B). In this case, however, that condition was not observed. What happened was that the theses, signed by Bukharin, were sent to the delegation of the CPSU(B) at the same time as they were distributed to the foreign delegations at the Sixth Congress. But the theses proved to be unsatisfactory on a number of points. The delegation of the CPSU(B) was obliged to introduce about twenty amendments to the theses.

This created a rather awkward situation for Bukharin. But who was to blame for that? Why was it necessary for Bukharin to distribute the theses to the foreign delegations before they had been examined by the delegation of the CPSU(B)? Could the delegation of the CPSU(B) refrain from introducing amendments if the theses proved to be unsatisfactory? And so it came about that the delegation of the CPSU(B) issued what were practically new theses on the international situation, which the foreign delegations began to counterpose to the old theses signed by Bukharin. Obviously, this awkward situation would not have arisen if Bukharin had not been in a hurry to distribute his theses to the foreign delegations.

I should like to draw attention to four principle amendments which the delegation of the CPSU(B) introduced into Bukharin's theses. I should like to draw attention to these principal amendments in order to illustrate more clearly the character of the disagreements on Comintern questions.

The first question is that of the character of the stabilization of capitalism. According to Bukharin's theses it appeared that nothing new is taking place at the present time to shake capitalist stabilization, but that, on the contrary, capitalism is *reconstructing itself* and that, on the whole, it is maintaining itself more or less *securely*. Obviously, the delegation of the CPSU(B) could not agree with such a characterization of what is called the third period, i.e., the period through which we are now passing. The delegation could not agree with it because to retain such a characterization of the third period might give our critics grounds for saying that we have adopted the point of view of so-called capitalist "recovery", i.e., the point of view of Hilferding, a point of view which we Communists cannot adopt. Owing to this, the delegation of the CPSU(B) introduced an amendment which makes it evident that capitalist stabilization is not and cannot be secure, that it is being shaken and will continue to be shaken by the march of events, owing to the aggravation of the crisis of world capitalism.

The question, comrades, is of decisive importance for the Sections of the Comintern. Is capitalist stabilization being shaken or is it becoming more secure? It is on this that the whole line of the Communist Parties in their day-to-day political work depends. Are we passing through a period of the mere gathering of forces, or are we passing through a period when the conditions are maturing for a new revolutionary upsurge, a period of preparation of the working class for future class battles? It is on this that the tactical line of the Communist Parties depends. The amendment of the delegation of the CPSU(B), subsequently adopted by the congress, is a good one for the very reason that it gives a clear line based on the latter prospect, the prospect of maturing conditions for a new revolutionary upsurge.

The second question is that of the fight against Social Democracy. In Bukharin's theses it was stated that the fight against Social Democracy is one of the fundamental tasks of the Sections of the Comintern. That, of course, is true. But it is not enough. In order that the fight against Social Democracy may be waged successfully, stress must be laid on the fight against the so-called "Left" wing of Social Democracy, that "Left" wing which, by playing with "Left" phrases and thus adroitly deceiving the workers, is retarding their mass defection from Social Democracy. It is obvious that unless the "Left" Social Democrats are routed it will be impossible to overcome Social Democracy in general. Yet in Bukharin's theses the question of "Left" Social Democracy was entirely ignored. That, of course, was a great defect. The delegation of the CPSU(B) was therefore obliged to introduce into Bukharin's theses an appropriate amendment, which was subsequently adopted by the congress.

The third question is that of the conciliatory tendency in the Sections of the Comintern. Bukharin's theses spoke of the necessity of fighting the Right deviation, but not a word was said there about fighting conciliation towards the Right deviation. That, of course, was a great defect. The point is that when war is declared on the Right deviation, the Right deviators usually disguise themselves as conciliators and place the Party in an awkward position. To forestall this maneuver of the Right deviators we must insist on a determined fight against conciliation. That is why the delegation of the CPSU(B) considered it necessary to introduce into Bukharin's theses an appropriate amendment, which was subsequently adopted by the congress.

The fourth question is that of Party discipline. In Bukharin's theses no mention was made of the necessity of maintaining iron discipline in the Communist Parties. That also was a defect of no little importance. Why? Because in a period when the fight against the Right deviation is being intensified, in a period when the slogan of purging the Communist Parties of opportunist elements is being put into effect, the Right deviators usually organize themselves as a faction, set up their own factional discipline and disrupt and destroy the discipline of the Party. To protect the Party from the factional sorties of the Right deviators we must insist on iron discipline in the Party and on the unconditional subordination of Party members to this discipline. Without that there can be no question of waging a serious fight against the Right deviation. That is why the delegation of the CPSU(B) introduced into Bukharin's theses an appropriate amendment, which was subsequently adopted by the Sixth Congress.

Could we refrain from introducing these amendments into Bukharin's theses? Of course not. In olden times it was said about the philosopher Plato: We love Plato, but we love truth even more. The same must be said about Bukharin: We love Bukharin, but we love truth, the Party and the Comintern even more. That is why the delegation to the CPSU(B) found itself obliged to introduce these amendments into Bukharin's theses.

That, so to speak, was *the first stage of our disagreements* on Comintern questions.

The second stage of our disagreements is connected with what is known as the Wittorf and Thaelmann case. Wittorf was formerly secretary of the Hamburg organization, and was accused of embezzling Party funds. For this he was expelled from the Party. The conciliators in the Central Committee of the German Communist Party, taking advantage of the fact that Wittorf had been close to Comrade Thaelmann, although Comrade Thaelmann was in no way implicated in Wittorf's crime, converted the Wittorf case into a Thaelmann case, and set out to overthrow the leadership of the German Communist Party. No doubt you know from the press that at that time the conciliators Ewert and Gerhardt succeeded temporarily in winning over a majority of the Central Committee of the German Communist Party against Comrade Thaelmann. And what followed? They removed Thaelmann from the leadership, began to accuse him of corruption and published a "corresponding" resolution without the knowledge and sanction of the Executive Committee of the Comintern.

Thus, instead of the directive of the Sixth Congress of the Comintern about fighting conciliation being carried out, instead of a fight against the Right deviation and against conciliation, there was, in fact, a most gross violation of this directive, there was a fight against the revolutionary leadership of the German Communist Party, a fight against Comrade Thaelmann, with the object of covering up the Right deviation and of consolidating the conciliatory tendency in the ranks of the German Communists.

And so, instead of swinging the tiller over and correcting the situation, instead of restoring the validity of the violated directive of the Sixth Congress in calling the conciliators to order,

Bukharin proposed in his well known letter to sanction the conciliators' coup, to hand over the German Communist Party to the conciliators, and to revile Comrade Thaelmann in the press again by issuing another statement declaring him to be guilty. And this is supposed to be a "leader" of the Comintern! Can there really be such "leaders"?

The Central Committee discussed Bukharin's proposal and rejected it. Bukharin, of course, did not like that. But who is to blame? The decisions of the Sixth Congress were adopted not in order that they should be violated but in order that they should be carried out. If the Sixth Congress decided to declare war on the Right deviation and conciliation towards it by keeping the leadership in the hands of the main core of the German Communist Party, headed by Comrade Thaelmann, and if it occurred to the conciliators Ewert and Gerhardt to upset that decision, it was Bukharin's duty to call the conciliators to order and not to leave in their hands the leadership of the German Communist Party. It is Bukharin, who "forgot" the decisions of the Sixth Congress, who is to blame.

The third stage of our disagreements is connected with the question of the fight against the Rights in the German Communist Party, with the question of routing the Brandler and Thalheimer faction, and of expelling the leaders of that faction from the German Communist Party. The "position" taken by Bukharin and his friends on that cardinal question was that they persistently avoided taking part in settling it. At bottom, it was the fate of the German Communist Party that was being decided. Yet Bukharin and his friends, knowing this, nevertheless continually hindered matters by systematically keeping away from the meetings of the bodies which had the question under consideration. For the sake of what? Presumably, for the sake of remaining "clean" in the eyes of both the Comintern and the Rights in the German Communist Party. For the sake of being able subsequently to say: "It was not we, the Bukharinites, who carried out the expulsion of Brandler and Thalheimer from the Communist Party, but they, the majority in the Central Committee." And that is what is called fighting the Right danger!

Finally, *the fourth stage of our disagreements*. It is connected with Bukharin's demand prior to the November plenum of the Central Committee that Neumann be recalled from Germany and that Comrade Thaelmann, who, it was alleged, had criticized in one of his speeches Bukharin's report at the Sixth Congress, be called to order. We, of course, could not agree with Bukharin, since there was not a single document in our possession supporting his demand. Bukharin promised to submit documents against Neumann and Thaelmann but never submitted a single one. Instead of documents, he distributed to the members of the delegation of the CPSU(B) copies of the speech delivered by Humbert-Droz at the Political Secretariat of the ECCI, the very speech which was subsequently qualified by the Presidium of the ECCI as an opportunist speech. By distributing Humbert-Droz' speech to the members of the delegation of the CPSU(B), and by recommending it as material against Thaelmann, Bukharin wanted to prove the justice of his demand for the recall of Neumann and for calling Comrade Thaelmann to order. In fact, however, he thereby showed that he identified himself with the position taken up by Humbert-Droz, a position which the ECCI regards as opportunist.

Those, comrades, are the main points of our disagreements on Comintern questions.

Bukharin thinks that by conducting a struggle against the Right deviation and conciliation towards it in the Sections of the Comintern, by purging the German and Czechoslovak Communist Parties of Social-Democratic elements and the Thalheimers from the Communist Parties, we are "disintegrating" the Comintern, "ruining" the Comintern. We, on the contrary, think that by carrying out such a policy and by laying stress on the fight against the Right deviation and conciliation towards it, we are strengthening the Comintern, purging it of opportunists, bolshevizing its Sections and helping the Communist Parties to prepare the working class for the future revolutionary battles, for the Party is strengthened by purging itself of dross.

You see that these are not merely shades of difference in the ranks of the Central Committee of the CPSU(B), but quite serious disagreements on fundamental questions of Comintern policy.

IV
DISAGREEMENTS IN REGARD TO INTERNAL POLICY

I have spoken above on the class changes and the class struggle in our country. I said that Bukharin's group is afflicted with blindness and does not see these changes, does not understand the new tasks of the Party. I said that this has caused bewilderment among the Bukharin opposition, has made it fearful of difficulties and ready to yield to them.

It cannot be said that these mistakes of the Bukharinites are purely accidental. On the contrary, they are connected with the stage of development we have already passed through and which is known as the period of *restoration* of the national economy, a period during which construction proceeded peacefully, automatically, so to speak; during which the class changes now taking place did not yet exist; and during which the intensification of the class struggle that we now observe was not yet in evidence.

But we are now at a new stage of development, distinct from the old period, from the period of restoration. We are now in a new period of construction, the period of the *reconstruction* of the whole national economy on the basis of socialism. This new period is giving rise to new class changes, to an intensification of the class struggle. It demands new methods of struggle, the regrouping of our forces, the improvement and strengthening of all our organizations.

The misfortune of Bukharin's group is that it is living in the past, that it fails to see the specific features of this new period and does not understand the need for new methods of struggle. Hence its blindness, its bewilderment, its panic in the face of difficulties.

a) THE CLASS STRUGGLE

What is the theoretical basis of this blindness and bewilderment of Bukharin's group?

I think that the theoretical basis of this blindness and bewilderment is Bukharin's incorrect, nonMarxist approach to the question of the class struggle in our country. I have in mind Bukharin's nonMarxist theory of the kulaks growing into socialism, his failure to understand the mechanics of the class struggle under the dictatorship of the proletariat.

The passage from Bukharin's book, *The Path to Socialism*, on the kulaks growing into socialism has been quoted several times here. But it has been quoted here with some omissions. Permit me to quote it in full. This is necessary, comrades, in order to demonstrate the full extent of Bukharin's departure from the Marxist theory of the class struggle.

Listen:

"The main network of our cooperative peasant organizations will consist of cooperative units, not of a kulak, but of a 'toiler' type, units that grow into the system of our general state organs and thus become *links in the single chain of socialist economy*. On the other hand, *the kulak cooperative nests will, similarly*, through the banks, etc., *grow into the same system*; but they will be *to a certain extent an alien body, similar, for instance, to the concession enterprises*." (My italics—*J. Stalin*.)

In quoting this passage from Bukharin's pamphlet, some comrades, for some reason or other, omitted the last phrase about the concessionaires. Rosit, apparently desiring to help Bukharin, took advantage of this and shouted here from his seat that Bukharin was being misquoted. And yet, the crux of this whole passage lies precisely in the last phrase about the concessionaires. For if concessionaires are put on a par with the kulaks, and the kulaks are growing into socialism—what follows from that? The only thing that follows is that the concessionaires are also growing into socialism; that not only the kulaks, but the concessionaires too, are growing into socialism. (*General laughter.*)

That is what follows.

Rosit. Bukharin says, "an alien body."

Stalin. Bukharin says not "an alien body," but "to a certain extent an alien body." Consequently, the kulaks and concessionaires are "to a certain extent" an alien body in the system of socialism. But Bukharin's mistake is precisely that, according to him, kulaks and concessionaires, while being "to a certain extent" an alien body, nevertheless grow into socialism.

Such is the nonsense to which Bukharin's theory leads.

Capitalists in town and country, kulaks and concessionaires, growing into socialism—such is the absurdity Bukharin has arrived at.

No, comrades, that is not the kind of "socialism" we want. Let Bukharin keep it for himself.

Until now, we Marxist-Leninists were of the opinion that between the capitalists of town and country, on the one hand, and the working class, on the other hand, there is an *irreconcilable* antagonism of interests. That is what the Marxist theory of the class struggle rests on. But now, according to Bukharin's theory of the capitalists' *peaceful growth* into socialism, all this is turned upside down, the irreconcilable antagonism of class interests between the exploiters and the exploited disappears, the exploiters grow into socialism.

Rosit. That is not true, the dictatorship of the proletariat is presumed.

Stalin. But the dictatorship of the proletariat is the sharpest form of the class struggle.

Rosit. Yes, that is the whole point.

Stalin. But, according to Bukharin, the capitalists grow into this very dictatorship of the proletariat. How is it that you cannot understand this, Rosit? Against whom must we fight, against whom must we wage the sharpest form of the class struggle, if the capitalists of town and country grow into the system of the dictatorship of the proletariat?

The dictatorship of the proletariat is needed for the purpose of waging a relentless struggle against the capitalist elements, for the purpose of suppressing the bourgeoisie and of uprooting capitalism. But if the capitalists of town and country, if the kulak and the concessionaires are growing into socialism, is the dictatorship of the proletariat needed at all? If it is, then for the suppression of what class is it needed?

Rosit. The whole point is that, according to Bukharin, the growing into presumes the class struggle.

Stalin. I see that Rosit has sworn to be of service to Bukharin. But his service is really like that of the bear in the fable; for in his eagerness to save Bukharin he is actually hugging him to death. It is not without reason that it is said, "An obliging fool is more dangerous than an enemy." (*General laughter.*)

One thing or the other: either there is an irreconcilable antagonism of interests between the capitalist class and the class of the workers who have come to power and have organized their dictatorship, or there is no such antagonism of interests, in which case only one thing remains—namely, to proclaim the harmony of class interests.

One thing or the other:

Either Marx' theory of the class struggle, *or* the theory of the capitalists growing into socialism;

either an irreconcilable antagonism of class interests, or the theory of harmony *of* class interests.

We can understand "Socialists" of the type of Brentano or Sydney Webb preaching about socialism growing into capitalism and capitalism into socialism, for these "Socialists" are really antiSocialists, bourgeois liberals.

In his speech Bukharin tried to reinforce the theory of the kulaks growing into socialism by referring to a well known passage from Lenin. He asserted that Lenin says the *same thing* as Bukharin.

That is not true, comrades. It is a gross and unpardonable slander against Lenin.

Here is the text of the passage from Lenin:

"Of course, in our Soviet Republic the social order is based on the collaboration of two classes: the workers and peasants, in which the "Nepmen", i.e., the bourgeoisie, are now permitted to participate on certain conditions" (Volume XXVII, p. 405).

You see that there is not a word here about the capitalist class growing into socialism. All that is said is that we have "permitted" the Nepmen, i.e., the bourgeoisie, "on certain conditions" to participate in the collaboration between the workers and the peasants.

What does this mean? Does it mean that we have thereby admitted the possibility of the Nepmen growing into socialism? Of course not. Only people who have lost all sense of shame can interpret the quotation from Lenin in that way. All that it means is that *at present* we do not destroy the bourgeoisie, that *at present* we do not confiscate their property, but permit them to exist on certain conditions, i.e., provided they unconditionally submit to the laws of the dictatorship of the proletariat, which lead to increasingly restricting the capitalists and gradually ousting them from national-economic life.

Can the capitalists be ousted and the roots of capitalism destroyed without a fierce class struggle? No, they cannot.

Can classes be abolished if the theory and practice of the capitalists growing into socialism prevails? No, they cannot. Such theory and practice can only cultivate and perpetuate classes, for this theory contradicts the Marxist theory of the class struggle.

But the passage from Lenin is wholly and entirely based on the Marxist theory of the class struggle under the dictatorship of the proletariat.

What can there be in common between Bukharin's theory of the kulaks growing into socialism and Lenin's theory of the dictatorship as a fierce class struggle? Obviously, there is not, and cannot be, anything in common between them.

Bukharin thinks that under the dictatorship of the proletariat the class struggle must *die down* and *come to an end* so that the abolition of classes may be brought about. Lenin, on the contrary, teaches us that classes can be abolished only by means of a stubborn class struggle, which under the dictatorship of the proletariat becomes *even fiercer* than it was before the dictatorship of the proletariat.

"The abolition of classes," says Lenin, "requires a long, difficult and stubborn *class struggle*, which, *after* the overthrow of the power of capital, *after* the destruction of the bourgeois state, *after* the establishment of the dictatorship of the proletariat, *does not disappear* (as the vulgar representatives of the old socialism and the old Social-Democracy imagine), but merely changes its forms and in many respects becomes even fiercer" (Volume XXIV, p. 315).

That is what Lenin says about the abolition of classes.

The abolition of classes *by means of the fierce class struggle of the proletariat*—such is Lenin's formula.

The abolition of classes *by means of the extinction of the class struggle and by the capitalists growing into socialism*—such is Bukharin's formula.

What can there be in common between these two formulas?

Bukharin's theory of the kulaks growing into socialism is therefore a departure from the Marxist-Leninist theory of the class struggle. It comes close to the theory propounded by Katheder-Socialism.

That is the basis of all the errors committed by Bukharin and his friends.

It may be said that it is not worthwhile dwelling at length on Bukharin's theory of the kulaks growing into socialism, since it itself speaks, and only speaks, but cries out, against Bukharin. That is wrong, comrades! As long as that theory was kept hidden it was possible not only to pay attention to it—there are plenty of such stupid things in what various comrades write. Such has been our attitude until quite lately. But recently the situation has changed.

The petty-bourgeois elemental forces, which have been breaking out in recent years, have begun to encourage this antiMarxist theory and made it topical. Now it cannot be said that it is being kept hidden. Now this strange theory of Bukharin's is aspiring to become the banner of the Right deviation in our Party, the banner of opportunism. That is why we cannot now ignore this theory. That is why we must demolish it as a wrong and harmful theory, so as to help our Party comrades to fight the Right deviation.

b) THE INTENSIFICATION OF THE CLASS STRUGGLE

Bukharin's second mistake, which follows from his first one, consists in a wrong, nonMarxist approach to the question of the intensification of the class struggle, of the increasing resistance of the capitalist elements to the socialist policy of the Soviet government.

What is the point at issue here? Is it that the capitalist elements are growing faster than the socialist sector of our economy, and that, because of this, they are increasing their resistance, undermining socialist construction? No, that is not the point. Moreover, it is not true that the capitalist elements are growing faster than the socialist sector. If that were true, socialist construction would already be on the verge of collapse.

The point is that socialism is successfully attacking the capitalist elements, socialism is growing *faster* than the capitalist elements; as a result the relative importance of the capitalist elements is *declining*, and for the very reason that the relative importance of the capitalist elements is *declining* the capitalist elements realize that they are in mortal danger and are increasing their resistance.

And they are still able to increase their resistance not only because world capitalism is supporting them, but also because, in spite of the decline in their relative importance, in spite of the decline in their relative growth as compared with the growth of socialism, there is still taking place an absolute growth of the capitalist elements, and this, to a certain extent, enables them to accumulate forces to resist the growth of socialism.

It is on this basis that, *at the present stage of development and under the present conditions of the relation of forces*, the intensification of the class struggle and the increase in the resistance of the capitalist elements of town and country are taking place.

The mistake of Bukharin and his friends lies in failing to understand this simple and obvious truth. Their mistake lies in approaching the matter not in a Marxist, but in a philistine way, and trying to explain the intensification of the class struggle by all kinds of accidental causes: The "incompetence" of the Soviet apparatus, the "imprudent" policy of local comrades, the "absence" of flexibility, "excesses", etc., etc.

Here, for instance, is a quotation from Bukharin's pamphlet, *The Path to Socialism*, which demonstrates an absolutely nonMarxist approach to the question of the intensification of the class struggle:

"Here and there the class struggle in the countryside breaks out in its former manifestations, and, as a rule, this intensification is provoked by the kulak elements. When, for instance, kulaks, or people who are growing rich at the expense of others and have wormed their way into the organs of Soviet power, begin to shoot village correspondents, that is a manifestation of the class struggle in its most acute form. (This is not true, for the most acute form of the struggle is rebellion. *J. Stalin.*) However, such incidents, as a rule, occur in those places where the local Soviet apparatus is weak. *As this apparatus improves*, as all the lower units of Soviet power become stronger, as the local, village, Party and Young Communist League organizations improve and become stronger, *such phenomena*, it is perfectly obvious, will become more and more rare and will finally disappear without a trace." (My italics—*J. Stalin.*)

It follows, therefore, that the intensification of the class struggle is to be explained by causes connected with the character of the apparatus, the competence or incompetence, the strength or weakness of our lower organizations.

It follows, for instance, that the wrecking activities of the bourgeois intellectuals in Shakhty, which are a form of resistance of the bourgeois elements to the Soviet government and a form of intensification of the class struggle, are to be explained, not by the relation of class forces, not by the growth of socialism, but by the incompetence of our apparatus.

It follows that before the wholesale wrecking occurred in the Shakhty area, our apparatus was a good one, but that later, the moment wholesale wrecking occurred, the apparatus, for some unspecified reason, suddenly became utterly incompetent.

It follows that until last year, when grain procurements proceeded automatically and there was not particular intensification of the class struggle, our local organizations were good, even ideal; but that from last year, when the resistance of the kulaks assumed particularly acute forms, our organizations have suddenly become bad and utterly incompetent.

That is not an explanation, but a mockery of an explanation. That is not science, but quackery.

What then is the actual reason for this intensification of the class struggle?

There are two reasons.

Firstly, our advance, our offensive, the growth of socialist forms of economy both in industry and in agriculture, a growth which is accompanied by a corresponding ousting of certain sections of capitalists in town and country. The fact is that we are living according to Lenin's formula: "Who will beat whom?" Will we overpower them, the capitalists—engage them, as Lenin put it, in the last and decisive fight—or will they overpower us?

Secondly, the fact that the capitalist elements have no desire to depart from the scene voluntarily; they are resisting, and will continue to resist socialism, for they realize that their last days are approaching. And they are still able to resist because, in spite of the decline of their relative importance, they are nevertheless growing in absolute numbers; the petty bourgeoisie in town and country, as Lenin said, daily and hourly produce from their midst capitalists, big and small, and these capitalist elements go to all lengths to preserve their existence.

There have been no cases in history where dying classes have voluntarily departed from the scene. There have been no cases in history where the dying bourgeoisie have not exerted all their remaining strength to preserve its existence. Whether our lower Soviet apparatus is good or bad, our advance, our offensive will diminish the capitalist elements and oust them, and they, the dying classes, will carry on their resistance at all costs.

That is the basis for the intensification of the class struggle in our country.

The mistake of Bukharin and his friends is that they identify the growing resistance of the capitalists with the growth of the latter's relative importance. But there are absolutely no grounds for this identification. There are no grounds because the fact that the capitalists are resisting by no means implies that they have become stronger than we are. The very opposite is the case. The dying classes are resisting, not because they have become stronger than we are, but because socialism is growing faster than they are, and they are becoming weaker than we are. And precisely because they are becoming weaker, they feel that their last days are approaching and are compelled to resist with all the forces and all the means in their power.

Such is the mechanics of the intensification of the class struggle and of the resistance of the capitalists at the present moment of history.

What should be the policy of the Party in view of this state of affairs?

The policy should be to arouse the working class and the exploited masses of the countryside, to increase their fighting capacity and develop their mobilized preparedness for the fight against the capitalist elements in town and country, for the fight against the resisting class enemies.

The Marxist-Leninist theory of the class struggle is valuable, among other reasons, because it facilitates the mobilization of the working class against the enemies of the dictatorship of the proletariat.

Wherein lies the harm of the Bukharin theory of the capitalists growing into socialism and of the Bukharin conception of the intensification of the class struggle?

It lies in the fact that it lulls the working class to sleep, undermines the mobilized preparedness of the revolutionary forces of our country, demobilizes the working class and facilitates the attack of the capitalist elements against the Soviet regime.

c) THE PEASANTRY

Bukharin's third mistake is on the question of the peasantry. As you know, this question is one of the most important questions of our policy. In the conditions prevailing in our country, the peasantry consists of various social groups, namely, the poor peasants, the middle peasants and the kulaks. It is obvious that our attitude to these various groups cannot be the same. The poor peasant as the *support* of the working class, the middle peasant as the *ally*, the kulak as the *class enemy*—such is our attitude to these social groups. All this is clear and generally known.

Bukharin, however, regards the matter somewhat differently. In his description of the peasantry this differentiation is omitted, the existence of social groups disappears, and there remains but a singe drab patch, called the countryside. According to him, the kulak is not a kulak, and the middle peasant is not a middle peasant, but there is a sort of uniform poverty in the countryside. That is what he said in his speech here: Can our kulak really be called a kulak? Why, he is a pauper! And our middle peasant, is he really like a middle peasant? Why, he is a pauper, living on the verge of starvation. Obviously, such a view of the peasantry is a radically wrong view, incompatible with Leninism.

Lenin said that the individual peasantry is the last capitalist class. Is that thesis correct? Yes, it is absolutely correct. Why is the individual peasantry defined as *the last capitalist class*? Because, of the two main classes of which our society is composed, the peasantry is the class whose economy is based on private property and small commodity production. Because the peasantry, as long as it remains an individual peasantry carrying on small commodity production, produces capitalists from its midst, and cannot help producing them, constantly and continuously.

This fact is of decisive importance for us in the question of our Marxist attitude to the problem of the alliance between the working class and the peasantry. This means that we need, not *just any kind* of alliance with the peasantry, but only *such an alliance* as is based on the struggle against the capitalist elements of the peasantry.

As you see, Lenin's thesis about the peasantry being the last capitalist class not only does not contradict the idea of an alliance between the working class and the peasantry, but, on the contrary, supplies the basis for this alliance as an alliance between the working class and the majority of peasantry directed against capitalist elements in general and against the capitalist elements of the peasantry in the countryside in particular.

Lenin advanced this thesis in order to show that the alliance between the working class and the peasantry can be stable only if it is based on the struggle against those capitalist elements which the peasantry produces from its midst.

Bukharin's mistake is that he does not understand and does not accept this simple thing, he forgets about the social groups in the countryside, he loses sight of the kulaks and the poor peasants, and all that remains is one uniform mass of middle peasants.

This is undoubtedly a deviation to the Right on the part of Bukharin, in contradistinction to the "Left", Trotskyist, deviation, which sees no other social groups in the countryside than the poor peasants and the kulaks, and which loses sight of the middle peasants.

Wherein lies the difference between Trotskyism and Bukharin's group on the question of the alliance with the peasantry? It lies in the fact that Trotskyism is *opposed* to the policy of a *stable* alliance with the middle-peasant masses, while Bukharin's group is in favor of *any kind* of alliance with the peasantry in general. There is no need to prove that both these positions are wrong and that they are equally worthless.

Leninism unquestionably stands for a stable alliance with the main mass of the peasantry, for an alliance with the middle peasants; but not just any kind of alliance, however, but such an alliance with the middle peasants ensures the *leading role* of the working class, *consolidates* the dictatorship of the proletariat and *facilitates the abolition of classes.*

"Agreement between the working class and the peasantry," says Lenin, "may be taken to mean anything. If we do not bear in mind that, from the point of view of the working class, agreement is permissible, correct and possible in principle only if it supports the dictatorship of the working class and is one of the measures aimed at the abolition of classes, then the formula of agreement between the working class and the peasantry remains, of course, a formula to which all the enemies of the Soviet regime and all the enemies of the dictatorship subscribe" (Volume XXVI, p. 387).

And further:

"At present," says Lenin, "the proletariat holds power and guides the state. It guides the peasantry. What does guiding the peasantry mean? It means, in the first place, pursuing a course towards the abolition of classes, and not towards the small producer. If we wandered away from the radical and main course we should cease to be Socialists and should find ourselves in the camp of the petty bourgeoisie, in the camp of the Socialist-Revolutionaries and Mensheviks, who are now the most bitter enemies of the proletariat" (*Ibid*, pp. 399-400).

There you have Lenin's point of view on the question of the alliance with the main masses of the peasantry, of the alliance with the middle peasants.

The mistake of Bukharin's group on the question of the middle peasant is that it does not see the dual nature, the dual position of the middle peasant between the working class and the capitalists. "The middle peasantry is a vacillating class," said Lenin. Why? Because, on the one hand, the middle peasant is a toiler, which brings him close to the working class, but, on the other hand, he is a property owner, which brings him close to the kulak. Hence the vacillations of the middle peasant. And this is true not only theoretically. These vacillations manifest themselves also in practice, daily and hourly.

"As a toiler," says Lenin, "the peasant gravitates towards socialism, preferring the dictatorship of the workers to the dictatorship of the bourgeoisie. As a seller of grain, the peasant gravitates towards the bourgeoisie, toward freedom of trade, i.e., back to the 'habitual', old, "time-hallowed' capitalism" (Volume XXIV, p. 314).

That is why the alliance with the middle peasant can be stable only if it is directed against the capitalist elements, against capitalism in general, if it guarantees the leading role of the working class in this alliance, if it facilitates the abolition of classes.

Bukharin's group forgets these simple and obvious things.

d) NEP AND MARKET RELATIONS

Bukharin's fourth mistake is on the question of NEP (the New Economic Policy). Bukharin's mistake is that he fails to see the two-fold character of NEP, he sees only one aspect of NEP. When we introduced NEP in 1921, we directed its spearhead against War Communism, against a regime and system which excluded *any and every form* of freedom for private trade. We considered, and still consider, that NEP implies a *certain* freedom for private trade. Bukharin remembers this aspect of the matter. That is very good.

But Bukharin is mistaken in supposing that this is the only aspect of NEP. Bukharin forgets that NEP has also another aspect. The point is that NEP by no means implies *complete* freedom for private trade, the *free* play of prices in the market. NEP is freedom for private trade within *certain* limits, within *certain* boundaries, *with the proviso that the role of the state as the regulator of the market is guaranteed.* That, precisely, is the second aspect of NEP. Moreover, this aspect of NEP is more important for us than the first. In our country there is no free play of prices in the market, such as is usually the case in capitalist countries. We, in the main, determine the price of grain. We determine the price of manufactured goods. We try to carry out a policy of reducing production costs and reducing prices of manufactured goods, while striving to stabilize the prices of agricultural produce. Is it not obvious that such special and specific market conditions do not exist in capitalist countries?

From this it follows that as long as NEP exists, both its aspects must be retained: The first aspect, which is directed against the regime of War Communism and aims at ensuring a *certain* freedom for private trade, and the second aspect, which is directed against *complete* freedom for private trade, and aims at ensuring the role of the state as the regulator of the market. Destroy one of these aspects, and the New Economic Policy disappears.

Bukharin thinks that danger can threaten NEP only "from the Left", from people who want to abolish *all* freedom of trade. It is a gross error. Moreover, such a danger is the least real at the present moment, since there is nobody, or hardly anybody, in our local and central organizations now who does not understand the necessity and expediency of preserving a *certain measure* of freedom of trade.

The danger from the Right, from those who want to abolish the role of state as regulator of the market, who want to "emancipate" the market and thereby open up an era of complete freedom for private trade, is much more real. There cannot be the slightest doubt that the danger of disrupting NEP from the Right is much more real at the present time.

It should not be forgotten that the petty-bourgeois elemental forces are working precisely in this direction, in the direction of disrupting NEP from the Right. It should also be born in mind that the outcries of the kulaks and the well-to-do elements, the outcries of the speculators and profiteers, to which many of our comrades often yield, bombard NEP from precisely this quarter. The fact that Bukharin does not see this second, and very real, danger of NEP being disrupted undoubtedly shows that he has yielded to the pressure of the petty-bourgeois elemental forces.

Bukharin proposes to "normalize" the market and to "maneuver" with grain-procurement prices according to areas, i.e., to raise the price of grain. What does this mean? It means that he is not satisfied with Soviet market conditions, he wants to put a brake on the role of the state as the regulator of the market and proposes that concessions be made to the petty-bourgeois elemental forces, which are disrupting NEP from the Right.

Let us assume for a moment that we followed Bukharin's advice. What would be the result? We raise the price of grain in the autumn, let us say, at the beginning of the grain-purchasing period. But since there are always people on the market, all sorts of speculators and profiteers, who can pay three times as much for grain, and since we cannot keep up with the speculators, for they buy some ten million puds in all while we have to buy hundreds of millions of puds, those who hold grain will all the same continue to hold it in expectation of a further rise in price. Consequently, towards the spring, when the state's real need for grain mainly begins, we should again have to raise the price of grain. But what would raising the price of grain in the spring mean? It would mean ruining the poor and economically weaker strata of the rural population, who are themselves obliged to buy grain in the spring, partly for need and partly for food—the very grain which they sold in the autumn at a lower price. Can we by such operations obtain any really useful results in the way of securing a sufficient quantity of grain? Most probably not, for there will always be speculators and profiteers able to pay twice and three times as much for the same grain. Consequently, we would have to be prepared to raise the price of grain once again in a vain effort to catch up with the speculators and profiteers.

From this, however, it follows that once having started on the path of raising grain prices we should have to continue down the slippery slope without any guarantee of securing a sufficient quantity of grain.

But the matter does not end there.

Firstly, having raised grain-*procurement* prices, we should next have to raise the prices of agricultural raw materials as well, in order to maintain a certain proportion in the prices of agricultural produce.

Secondly, having raised grain-procurement prices, we should not be able to maintain low retail prices of bread in the towns—consequently, we should have to raise the *selling* price of bread. And since we cannot and must not injure the workers, we should have to increase wages at an accelerated pace. But this is bound to lead to a rise in the prices of manufactured goods, for, otherwise, there could be a diversion of resources from the towns into the countryside to the detriment of industrialization.

As a result, we should have to adjust the prices of manufactured goods and of agricultural produce not on the basis of *falling* or, at any rate, stabilized prices, but on the basis of *rising* prices, both of grain and of manufactured goods.

In other words, we should have to pursue a policy of *raising the prices* of manufactured goods and agricultural produce.

It is not difficult to understand that such "maneuvering" with prices can only lead to the complete nullification of the Soviet price policy, to the nullification of the role of the state as the regulator of the market, and to giving a free rein to the petty-bourgeois elemental forces.

Who would profit by this?

Only the well-to-do strata of the urban and rural population, for expensive manufactured goods and agricultural produce would necessarily become out of the reach both of the working class and of the poor and economically weaker strata of the rural population. It would profit the kulaks and the well-to-do, the Nepmen and other prosperous classes.

That, too, would be a bond, but a peculiar one, a bond with the wealthy strata of the rural and urban population. The workers and the economically weaker strata of the rural population would have every right to ask us: Whose government are you: A workers' and peasants' government or a kulak and Nepmen's government?

A rupture with the working class and the economically weaker strata of the rural population, and a bond with the wealthy strata of the urban and rural population—that is what Bukharin's "normalization" of the market and "maneuvering" with grain prices according to areas must lead to.

Obviously, the Party cannot take this fatal path.

The extent to which all conceptions of NEP in Bukharin's mind have become muddled and the extent to which he is firmly held captive by the petty-bourgeois elemental forces is shown, among other things, by the more than negative attitude he displays to the question of the new forms of trade turnover between town and country, between the state and the peasantry. He is indignant and cries out against the fact that the state has become the supplier of goods to the peasantry and that the peasantry is becoming the supplier of grain for the state. He regards this as a violation of all the rules of NEP, as almost the disruption of NEP. Why? On what grounds?

What can there be objectionable in the fact that the state, state industry, is the supplier, without middlemen, of goods for the peasantry, and that the peasantry is the supplier of grain for industry, for the state, also without middlemen?

What can there be objectionable, from the point of view of Marxism and a Marxist policy, in the fact that the peasantry *has already become* the supplier of cotton, beet and flax for the needs of state industry, and that state industry has become the supplier of urban goods, seed and instruments of production for these branches of agriculture?

The contract system is here the principal method of establishing these new forms of trade turnover between town and country. But is the contract system contrary to the principles of NEP?

What can there be objectionable in the fact that, thanks to this contract system, the peasantry *is becoming* the state's supplier not only of cotton, beet and flax, but also of grain?

If trade in small consignments, petty trade, can be termed trade turnover, why cannot trade in large consignments, conducted by means of agreements concluded in advance (contracts) as to price and quality of goods be regarded as trade turnover?

Is it difficult to understand that it is on the basis of NEP that these new, mass forms of trade turnover between town and country based on the contract system have arisen, that they mark a very big step forward on the part of our organizations as regards strengthening the planned, socialist direction of our national economy?

Bukharin has lost the capacity to understand these simple and obvious things.

e) THE SO-CALLED "TRIBUTE"

Bukharin's fifth mistake (I am speaking of his principal mistakes) is his opportunist distortion of the Party line on the question of the "scissors" between town and country, on the question of the so-called "tribute".

What is the point dealt with in the well known resolution of the joint meeting of the Political Bureau and the Presidium of the Central Control Commission (February 1929) on the question of the "scissors"? What is said there is that, in addition to the usual taxes, direct and indirect, which the peasantry pays to the state, the peasantry also pays a certain supertax in the form of an overpayment for manufactured goods, and in the form of an underpayment received for agricultural produce.

Is it true that this supertax paid by the peasantry actually exists? Yes, it is. What other name have we for this supertax? We also call it the" scissors", the "diversion" of resources from agriculture into industry for the purpose of speeding up our industrial development.

Is this "diversion" necessary? We all agree that, as a temporary measure, it is necessary if we really wish to maintain a speedy rate of industrial development. Indeed, we must at all costs maintain a rapid growth of our industry, for this growth is necessary not only for our industry itself, but primarily for agriculture, for the peasantry, which at the present time needs most of all tractors, agricultural machinery and fertilizers.

Can we abolish this supertax at the present time? Unfortunately, we cannot. We must abolish it at the first opportunity, in the next few years. But we cannot abolish it at the present moment.

Now, as you see, this supertax obtained as a result of the "scissors" does not constitute "something in the nature of a tribute." It is "something in the nature of a tribute" on account of our backwardness. We need this supertax to stimulate the development of our industry and to do away with our backwardness.

But does this mean that by levying this additional tax we are thereby exploiting the peasantry? No, it does not. The very nature of the Soviet regime precludes any sort of exploitation of the peasantry by the state. It was plainly stated in the speeches of our comrades at the July plenum that under the Soviet regime exploitation of the peasantry by the socialist state is *ruled out*, for a constant rise in the well-being of the laboring peasantry is a law of development of Soviet society, and this rules out any possibility of exploiting the peasantry.

Is the peasantry capable of paying this additional tax? Yes, it is. Why?

Firstly, because the levying of this additional tax is effected under conditions of a constant improvement of the material position of the peasantry.

Secondly, because the peasants have their own private husbandry, the income from which enables them to meet the additional tax, and in this they differ from the industrial workers, who have no private husbandry, but who nonetheless devote all their energies to the cause of industrialization.

Thirdly, because the amount of this additional tax is being reduced year by year.

Are we right in calling this additional tax "something in the nature of a tribute"? Unquestionably, we are. By our choice of words we are pointing out to our comrades that this additional tax is detestable and undesirable, and that its continuance for any considerable period is impermissible. By giving this name to the additional tax on the peasantry we intend to convey that we are levying it not because we want to, but because we are forced to, and that we, Bolsheviks, must take all measures to abolish this additional tax at the first opportunity, as soon as possible.

Such is the essence of the question of the "scissors", the "diversion", the "supertax", of what the above-mentioned documents designate as "something in the nature of a tribute."

At first, Bukharin, Rykov and Tomsky tried to wrangle over the word "tribute", and accused the Party of pursuing a policy of military-feudal exploitation of the peasantry. But now even the blind can see that this was just an unscrupulous attempt of the Bukharinites at gross slander against our Party. Now, even they themselves are compelled tacitly to acknowledge that their chatter about military-feudal exploitation was a resounding failure.

One thing or the other:

Either the Bukharinites recognize the inevitability, at the present time, of the "scissors" and "diversion" of resources from agriculture into industry—in which case they are forced to admit that their accusations are of a slanderous nature, and that the Party is entirely right;

or they deny the inevitability, at the present time, of the "scissors" and "diversion", but in that case let them say it frankly, so that the Party may class them as opponents of the industrialization of our country.

I could, incidentally, refer to a number of speeches of Bukharin, Rykov and Tomsky, in which they recognize without any reservations the inevitability, at the present time, of the "scissors" and "diversion" of resources from agriculture into industry. And this, indeed, is equivalent to an acceptance of the formula "something in the nature of a tribute."

Well then, do they continue to uphold the point of view with regard to the "diversion", and the preservation of the "scissors" at the present time, or not? Let them say it frankly.

Bukharin. The diversion is necessary, but "tribute" is an unfortunate word. (*General laughter.*)

Stalin. Consequently, we do not differ on the essence of the question; consequently, the "diversion" of resources from agriculture into industry, the so-called "scissors", the additional tax, "something in the nature of a tribute"—is a necessary though temporary means for industrializing our country at the present time.

Very well. Then what is the point at issue? Why all the tumult? They do not like the *word* "tribute" or the words "something in the nature of a tribute," because they believe that this expression is not commonly used in Marxist literature?

Well then, let us discuss the *word* "tribute".

I assert, comrades, that this word has long been in use in our Marxist literature, in Comrade Lenin's writings, for example. This may surprise some people who do not read Lenin's works, but it is a fact, comrades. Bukharin vehemently asserted here that "tribute" is an unfitting word to use in Marxist literature. He was indignant and surprised at the fact that the Central Committee of the Party, and Marxists in general, take the liberty of using the word "tribute". But what is surprising in this, if there is proof that this word has long been in use in the writings of such a Marxist as Comrade Lenin. Or perhaps, from Bukharin's viewpoint, Lenin does not qualify as a Marxist? Well, you should be straightforward about it, dear comrades.

Take for example the article "'Left-Wing' Childishness and Petty-Bourgeois Mentality" (May 1918), which was written by no less a Marxist than Lenin, and read the following passage:

"The petty bourgeois who hoards his thousands is an enemy of state capitalism; he wants to employ these thousands just for himself, against the poor, in opposition to any kind of state control; yet the sum total of these thousands amounts to many thousands of millions that supply a base for speculation, which undermines our socialist construction. Let us assume that a certain number of workers produce in a few days values equal to 1,000. Let us then assume that 200 out of this total vanishes owing to petty speculation, all kinds of pilfering and of "dodging" Soviet decrees and regulations by small property owners. Every class-conscious worker would say: If I could give up 300 out of the 1,000 for the sake of achieving better order and organization, I would willingly give up 300 instead of 200, because to reduce this "tribute" later on, to, say, 100 or 50, will be quite an easy matter under the Soviet regime, once we have achieved order and organization and once we have completely overcome the disruption of all state monopoly by small property owners" (Volume XXII, p. 515).

That is clear, I think. Should Lenin on this account be declared an advocate of the policy of military-feudal exploitation of the working class? Just try, dear comrades!

A voice. Nevertheless, the term "tribute" has never been used in relation to the middle peasant.

Stalin. Do you believe by any chance that the middle peasant is closer to the Party than the working class? You are some Marxist! (*General laughter.*) If we, the Party of the working class, can speak of "tribute" when it concerns the working class, why cannot we do so when it concerns the middle peasantry, which is only our ally?

Some of the fault-finding people may imagine that the word "tribute" in Lenin's article "'Left-Wing' Childishness" is just a slip of the pen, accidental slip. A checkup on this point, however, will show that the suspicions of those fault-finding people are entirely groundless. Take another article, or rather a pamphlet, written by Lenin: *The Tax in Kind* (April 1921) and read page 324 (Volume XXVI, p. 324). You will see that the above-quoted passage regarding "tribute" is repeated by Lenin word for word. Finally, take Lenin's article "The Immediate Tasks of Soviet Power" (Volume XXII, p. 448, March-April 1918), and you will see that in it, too, Lenin speaks of the "tribute (without quotation marks) which we are paying for our backwardness in the matter of organizing accounting and control from below on a nation-widescale."

It turns out that the *word* "tribute" is very far from being a fortuitous element in Lenin's writings. Comrade Lenin uses this *word* to stress the temporary nature of the "tribute", to stimulate the energy of the Bolsheviks and to direct it so as, at the first opportunity, to abolish this "tribute", the price the working class has to pay for our backwardness and our "muddling".

It turns out that when I use the expression "something in the nature of a tribute" I find myself in quite good Marxist company, that of Comrade Lenin.

Bukharin said here that Marxists should not tolerate the word "tribute" in their writings. What kind of Marxists was he speaking about? If he had in mind such Marxists, if they may be so called, as Slepkov, Maretsky, Petrovsky, Rosit, et. al., who are more like liberals than Marxists, then his indignation is perfectly justified. If, on the other hand, he has in mind real Marxists, Comrade Lenin, for example, then it must be admitted that among them the word "tribute" has been in use for a long time, while Bukharin, who is not well-acquainted with Lenin's writings, is wide of the mark.

But this does not fully dispose of the question of the "tribute". The point is that it was no accident that Bukharin and his friends took exception to the word "tribute" and began to speak of a policy of military-feudal exploitation of the peasantry. Their outcry about military-feudal exploitation was undoubtedly meant to express their extreme dissatisfaction with the Party policy toward the kulaks that is being applied by our organizations. Dissatisfaction with the Leninist policy of the Party in its leadership of the peasantry, dissatisfaction with our grain-procurement policy, with our policy of developing collective and state farms to the utmost, and lastly, the desire to "emancipate" the market and to establish complete freedom for private trade—that is what was expressed in Bukharin's howling about a policy of military-feudal exploitation of the peasantry.

In the history of our Party I cannot recall any other instance of the Party being accused of pursuing a policy of military-feudal exploitation. That weapon against the Party was not borrowed from the arsenal of Marxists. Where, then, was it borrowed from? From the arsenal of Miliukov, the leader of the Cadets. When the Cadets wish to sow dissension between the working class and the peasantry, they usually say: You, Messieurs the Bolsheviks, are building socialism on the corpses of the peasants. When Bukharin raises an outcry about the "tribute", he is singing to the tune of Messieurs the Miliukovs, and is following in the wake of the enemies of the people.

f) THE RATE OF DEVELOPMENT OF INDUSTRY AND THE NEW FORMS OF THE BOND

Finally, the question of the rate of development of industry and of the new forms of the bond between town and country. This is one of the most important questions of our disagreements. Its importance lies in the fact that it is the converging point of all the threads of our practical disagreements about the economic policy of the Party.

What are the new forms of the bond, what do they signify from the point of view of our economic policy?

They signify, first of all, that besides the old forms of the bond between town and country, whereby industry chiefly satisfied the *personal* requirements of the peasant (cotton fabrics, footwear, and textiles in general, etc.), we now need new forms of the bond, whereby industry will satisfy the *productive* requirements of peasant economy (agricultural machinery, tractors, improved seed, fertilizers, etc.).

Whereas formerly we satisfied *mainly* the personal requirements of the peasant, hardly touching the productive requirements of his economy, now, while continuing to satisfy the personal requirements of the peasant, we must do our utmost to supply agricultural machinery, tractors, fertilizers, etc., which have a direct bearing on the reconstruction of agricultural production on a new technical basis.

As long as it was a question of restoring agriculture and of the peasants putting into use the land formerly belonging to the landlords and kulaks, we could be content with the old forms of the bond. But now, when it is a question of reconstructing agriculture, that is not enough. Now we must go further and help the peasantry to reorganize agricultural production on the basis of new technique and collective labor.

Secondly, they signify that simultaneously with the reequipment of our industry, we must begin seriously reequipping agriculture too. We are reequipping, and have already partly reequipped our industry, placing it on a new technical basis, supplying it with new, improved machinery and new, improved cadres. We are building new mills and factories and are reconstructing and extending the old ones; we are developing the iron and steel, chemical and machine-building industries. On this basis new towns are springing up, new industrial centers are multiplying and the old ones are expanding. On this basis the demand for food products and for raw materials for industry is growing. But agriculture continues to employ the old equipment, the old methods of tillage practiced by our forefathers, the old, primitive, now useless, or nearly useless technique, the old, small-peasant, individual forms of farming and labor.

Consider, for example, the fact that before the Revolution, we had nearly 16,000,000 peasant households, while now there are no less than 25,000,000. What does this indicate if not that agriculture is becoming more and more scattered and disunited. And the characteristic feature of scattered small farms is that they are unable properly to employ technique, machines, tractors and scientific agronomic knowledge, that they are farms with a small marketable surplus.

Hence the insufficient output of agricultural produce for the market.

Hence the danger of a rift between town and country, between industry and agriculture.

Hence the necessity for increasing the rate of development of agriculture, bringing it up to that of our industry.

And so, in order to eliminate this danger of a rift, we must begin seriously reequipping agriculture on the basis of new technique. But in order to reequip it we must gradually unite the scattered individual peasant farms into large farms, into collective farms; we must build up agriculture on the basis of collective labor, we must enlarge the collectives, we must develop the old and new state farms, we must systematically employ the contract system on a mass scale in all the principal branches of agriculture, we must develop the system of machine and tractor stations which help the peasantry to master the new technique and to collectivize labor—in a word, we must gradually transfer the small individual peasant farms to the basis of large-scale collective production, for only large-scale production of a socially-conducted type is capable of making full use of scientific knowledge and modern technique, and of advancing the development of our agriculture with giant strides.

This, of course, does not mean that we must neglect individual poor- and middle-peasant farming. Not at all. Individual poor- and middle-peasant farming plays a predominant part in supplying industry with food and raw materials, and will continue to do so in the immediate future. For that very reason we must continue to assist individual poor- and middle-peasant farms which have not yet united into collective farms.

But this does mean that individual peasant farming alone is *no longer* adequate. That is shown by our grain-procurement difficulties. That is why the development of individual poor- and middle-peasant farming must be *supplemented* by the widest possible development of collective forms of farming and of state farms.

That is why we must make a bridge between individual poor- and middle-peasant farming and collective, socially-conducted forms of farming by means of machine and tractor stations and by the fullest development of a cooperative communal life in order to help the peasants to transfer their small, individual farming on to the lines of collective labor.

Failing this it will be impossible to develop agriculture to any extent. Failing this it will be impossible to solve the grain problem. Failing this it will be impossible to save the economically weaker strata of the peasantry from poverty and ruin.

Finally, they signify that we must develop our industry to the utmost as the principal source from which agriculture will be supplied with the means required for its reconstruction; we must develop our iron and steel, chemical and machine-building industries; we must build tractor works, agricultural-machinery works, etc.

There is no need to prove that it is impossible to develop collective farms, that it is impossible to develop machine and tractor stations without drawing the main mass of the peasantry into collective forms of farming, with the aid of the contract system on a mass scale, without supplying agriculture with a fairly large quantity of tractors, agricultural machinery, etc.

But it will be impossible to supply the countryside with machines and tractors unless we accelerate the development of our industry. Hence, rapid development of our industry is the key to the reconstruction of agriculture on the basis of collectivism.

Such is the significance and importance of the new forms of the bond.

Bukharin's group is obliged to admit, in words, the necessity of the new forms of the bond. But it is an admission only *in words*, with the intention, under cover of a verbal recognition of the new forms of the bond, of smuggling in something which is the very *opposite*. Actually, Bukharin is opposed to the new forms of the bond. Bukharin's starting point is not a rapid rate of development of industry as the lever for the reconstruction of agriculture, but the development of individual peasant farming. He puts in the foreground the "normalization" of the market and permission for the free play of prices on the agricultural produce market, complete freedom for private trade. Hence his distrustful attitude to the collective farms which manifested itself in his speech at the July plenum of the Central Committee and in his theses prior to that July plenum. Hence his disapproval of any form of emergency measures against the kulaks during grain procurement.

We know that Bukharin shuns emergency measures as the devil shuns holy water.

We know that Bukharin is still unable to understand that under present conditions the kulak will not supply a sufficient quantity of grain voluntarily, of his own accord.

That has been proved by our two years' experience of grain-procurement work.

But what if, in spite of everything, there is not enough marketable grain? To this Bukharin replies: Do not worry the kulaks with emergency measures, import grain from abroad. Not long ago he proposed that we import about 50,000,000 puds of grain, i.e., to the value of about 100,000,000 rubles in foreign currency. But what if foreign currency is required to import equipment for industry? To this Bukharin replies: Preference must be given to grain imports—thus, evidently, relegating imports of equipment for industry to the background.

It follows, therefore, that the basis for the solution of the grain problem and for the reconstruction of agriculture is not a rapid rate of development of industry, but the development of individual peasant farming, including kulak farming, on the basis of a free market and the free play of prices in the market.

Thus we have two different plans of economic policy.

The Party's plan:

1. We are reequipping industry (reconstruction).
2. We are beginning seriously to reequip agriculture (reconstruction).
3. For this we must expand the development of collective and state farms, employ on a mass scale the contract system and machine and tractor stations as means of establishing a *bond* between industry and agriculture *in the sphere of production*.
4. As for the present grain-procurement difficulties, we must admit the permissibility of temporary emergency measures that are backed by the popular support of the middle- and poor-peasant masses, as one of the means of breaking the resistance of the kulaks and of obtaining from them the maximum grain surpluses necessary for dispensing with imported grain and saving foreign currency for the development of industry.
5. Individual poor- and middle-peasant farming plays, and will continue to play, a predominant part in supplying the country with food and raw materials; but alone it is no longer adequate—the development of individual poor- and middle-peasant farming must be *supplemented* by the development of collective farms and state farms, by the contract system on a mass scale, by accelerating the development of machine and tractor stations, in order to facilitate the ousting of the capitalist elements from agriculture and the gradual transfer of the individual peasant farms on to the lines of large-scale collective farming, on to the lines of collective labor.
6. But in order to achieve this, it is necessary first of all to accelerate the development of industry, of the metallurgical, chemical and machine-building industries, tractor works, agricultural-machinery works, etc. Failing this it will be impossible to solve the grain problem just as it will be impossible to reconstruct agriculture.

Conclusion: *The key to the reconstruction of agriculture is a rapid rate of development of our industry*.

Bukharin's plan:

1. "Normalize" the market; permit the free play of prices on the market and a rise in the price of grain, undeterred by the fact that this may lead to a rise in the price of manufactured goods, raw materials and bread.
2. The utmost development of individual peasant farming accompanied by a certain reduction of the rate of development of collective and state farms (Bukharin's theses in July and his speech at the July plenum).
3. Grain procurements to proceed automatically, excluding at any time or under any circumstances even a partial use of emergency measures against the kulaks, even though such measures are supported by the middle- and poor-peasant masses.
4. In the event of shortage of grain, to import about 100 million rubles' worth of grain.
5. And if there is not enough foreign currency to pay for grain imports and imports of equipment for industry, to reduce imports of equipment and, consequently, the rate of development of our industry—otherwise our agriculture will simply "mark time", or even "directly decline".

Conclusion: *The key to the reconstruction of agriculture is the development of individual peasant farming*.

That is how it works out, comrades!

Bukharin's plan is a plan to *reduce* the rate of development of industry and to *undermine* the new forms of the bond.

Such are our disagreements.

Sometimes the question is asked: Have we not been late in developing the new forms of the bond, in developing collective farms, state farms, etc.?

Some people assert that the Party was at least about two years late in starting with this work. That is wrong, comrades. It is absolutely wrong. Only noisy "Lefts", who have no conception of the economy of the USSR, can talk like that.

What is meant by being late in this matter? If it is a question of foreseeing the need for collective and state farms, then we can say that we began that at the time of the October Revolution. There cannot be the slightest doubt that already then—at the time of the October Revolution—the Party foresaw the need for collective and state farms. Lastly, one can take our program, adopted at the Eighth Congress of the Party (March 1919). The need for collective and state farms is recognized there quite clearly.

But the mere fact that the top leadership of our Party foresaw the need for collective and state farms was not enough for carrying into effect and organizing a *mass movement* for collective and state farms. Consequently, it is not a matter of foreseeing, but of *carrying out* a plan of collective- and state-farm development. But in order to carry out such a plan a number of conditions are required which did not exist before, and which came into existence only recently.

That is the point, comrades.

In order to carry out the plan for a mass movement in favor of collective and state farms, it is necessary, first of all, that the Party's top leadership should be supported in this matter by the mass of the Party membership. As you know, ours is a Party of a million members. It was therefore necessary to convince the mass of the Party membership of the correctness of the policy of the top leadership. That is the first point.

Further, it is necessary that a mass movement in favor of collective farms should arise within the peasantry, that the peasants—far from fearing the collective farms—should themselves join the collective farms and become convinced by experience of the advantage of collective farming over individual farming. This is a serious matter, requiring a certain amount of time. That is the second point.

Further, it is necessary that the state should possess the material resources required to finance collective-farm development, to finance the collective and state farms. And this, dear comrades, is a matter that requires hundreds of millions of rubles. That is the third point.

Finally, it is necessary that industry should be fairly adequately developed so as to be able to supply agriculture with machinery, tractors, fertilizers, etc. That is the fourth point.

Can it be asserted that all these conditions existed here two or three years ago? No, it cannot.

It must not be forgotten that we are a party *in power, not in opposition*. An opposition party can issue slogans—I am speaking of fundamental practical slogans of the movement—in order to carry them into effect after coming into power. Nobody can accuse an opposition party of not carrying out its fundamental slogans immediately, for everybody knows that it is not the opposition party which is at the helm, but other parties.

In the case of a party in power, however, such as our Bolshevik Party is, the matter is entirely different. The slogans of such a party are not mere agitational slogans, but something much more than that, for they have the force of *practical decision*, the *force of law*, and must be carried out immediately. Our Party cannot issue a practical slogan and then defer its implementation. That would be deceiving the masses. For a practical slogan to be issued, especially so serious a slogan as transferring the vast masses of the peasantry on to the lines of collectivism, the conditions must exist that will enable the slogan to be carried out directly; finally, these conditions must be created, organized. That is why it is not enough for the Party's top leadership merely to foresee the need for collective and state farms. That is why we also need the conditions to enable us *to realize*, to *carry out*, our slogans immediately.

Was the *mass* of our Party membership ready for the utmost development of collective and state farms, say, some two or three years ago? No, it was not ready. The serious turn of the mass of the Party membership towards the new forms of the bond began only with the first serious grain-procurement difficulties. It required those difficulties for the mass of the Party membership to become conscious of the full necessity of accelerating the adoption of the new forms of the bond, and primarily, of the collective and state farms, and resolutely to support its Central Committee in this matter. This is one condition which did not exist before, but which does exist now.

Was there any serious movement among the vast masses of the peasantry in favor of collective or state farms some two or three years ago? No, there was not. Everybody knows that two or three years ago the peasantry was with hostility disposed to the state farms, while they contemptuously called the collective farms the "kommunia", regarding them as something utterly useless. And now? Now, the situation is different. Now we have entire strata of the peasantry who regard the state and collective farms as a source of assistance to peasant farming in the way of seed, pedigree cattle, machines and tractors. Now we have only to supply machines and tractors, and collective farms will develop at an accelerated pace.

What was the cause of this change of attitude among certain, fairly considerable, strata of the peasantry? What helped to bring it about?

In the first place, the development of the cooperatives and a cooperative communal life. There can be no doubt that without the powerful development of the cooperatives, particularly the agricultural cooperatives, which produced among the peasantry a psychological background in favor of the collective farms, we would not have that urge towards the collective farms which is now displayed by whole strata of the peasantry.

An important part in this was also played by the existence of well-organized collective farms, which set the peasants good examples of how agriculture can be improved by uniting small peasant farms into large, collective farms.

The existence of well-organized state farms, which helped the peasants to improve their methods of farming, also played its part here. I need not mention other facts with which you are all familiar. There you have another condition which did not exist before, but which does exist now.

Further, can it be asserted that we were able some two or three years ago to give substantial financial aid to the collective and state farms, to assign hundreds of millions of rubles for this purpose? No, it cannot be asserted. You know very well that we even lacked sufficient means for developing that minimum of industry without which no industrialization at all is possible, let alone the reconstruction of agriculture. Could we take those means from industry, which is the basis for the industrialization of the country, and transfer them to the collective and state farms? Obviously, we could not. But now? Now we have the means for developing the collective and state farms.

Finally, can it be asserted that some two or three years ago our industry was an adequate basis for supplying agriculture with large quantities of machines, tractors, etc.? No, it cannot be asserted. At that time our task was to create the minimum industrial basis required for supplying machines and tractors to agriculture in the future. It was on the creation of such a basis that our scanty financial resources were then spent. And now? Now we have the industrial basis for agriculture. At all events, this industrial basis is being created at a very rapid rate.

It follows that the conditions required for the mass development of the collective and state farms were created only recently.

That is how matters stand, comrades.

That is why it cannot be said that we were late in developing the new forms of the bond.

g) BUKHARIN AS A THEORETICIAN

Such, in the main, are the principal mistakes committed by the theoretician of the Right opposition, Bukharin, on the fundamental questions of our policy.

It is said that Bukharin is one of the theoreticians of our Party. This is true, of course. But the point is that not all is well with his theorizing. This is evident if only from the fact that on questions of Party theory and policy he has piled up the heap of mistakes which I have just described. These mistakes, mistakes on Comintern questions, mistakes on questions of the class struggle, the intensification of the class struggle, the peasantry, NEP, the new forms of the bond—these mistakes could not possibly have occurred accidentally. No, these mistakes are not accidental. These mistakes of Bukharin's followed from his wrong theoretical line, from the defects in his theories. Yes, Bukharin is a theoretician, but he is not altogether a Marxist theoretician; he is a theoretician who has much to learn before he can become a Marxist theoretician.

Reference has been made to the letter in which Comrade Lenin speaks of Bukharin as a theoretician. Let us read this letter:

"Of the younger members of the Central Committee," says Lenin, "I should like to say a few words about Bukharin and Piatakov. In my opinion, they are the most outstanding forces (of the youngest ones), and regarding them the following should be born in mind: Bukharin is not only a very valuable and important theoretician in our Party, he is also legitimately regarded as the favorite of the whole Party; but *it is very doubtful whether his theoretical views can be classed as fully Marxist, for there is something scholastic in him (he has never studied and, I think, has never fully understood dialectics)* (My italics,—*J. Stalin.*) (Verbatim report of the July plenum, 1926, Part IV, p. 66).

Thus, he is a theoretician without dialectics. A scholastic theoretician. A theoretician about whom it was said: "It is very doubtful whether his theoretical views can be classed as fully Marxist." That is how Lenin characterized Bukharin's theoretical complexion.

You can well understand, comrades, that such a theoretician has still much to learn. And if Bukharin understood that he is not yet a full-fledged theoretician, that he still has much to learn, that he is a theoretician who has not mastered dialectics—and dialectics is the soul of Marxism—if he understood that, he would be more modest, and the Party would only benefit thereby. But the trouble is that Bukharin is wanting in modesty. The trouble is that not only is he wanting in modesty, but he even presumes to teach our teacher Lenin on a number of questions and, above all, on the question of the state. And that is Bukharin's misfortune.

Allow me in this connection to refer to the well known theoretical controversy which flared up in 1916 between Lenin and Bukharin on the question of the state. This is important for us in order to expose both Bukharin's inordinate pretensions to teach Lenin and the roots of his theoretical weaknesses on such important questions as the dictatorship of the proletariat, the class struggle, etc.

As you know, an article by Bukharin appeared in 1916 in the journal *International Molodezhy*, signed Nota Bene; this article was in point of fact directed against Comrade Lenin. In this article Bukharin wrote:

"...It is quite a mistake to seek the difference between the Socialists and the Anarchists in the fact that the former are in favor of the state while the latter are against it. The real difference is that revolutionary Social-Democracy desires to organize the new social production as centralized production, i.e., technically the most advanced production; whereas decentralized anarchist production would mean only retrogression to old technique, to the old form of enterprises...."

"...Social-Democracy, which is, or at least should be, the educator of the masses, must now more than ever emphasize its hostility in principal to the state.... The present war has shown how deeply the roots of the state idea have penetrated the souls of the workers."

Criticizing these views of Bukharin's, Lenin says in a well known article, published in 1916:

"This is wrong. The author raises the question of the difference in the attitude of Socialists and Anarchists *towards the state*. But he replies *not* to this question, but to *another*, namely the difference in the attitude of Socialists and Anarchists towards the economic foundation of future society. That, of course, is a very important and necessary question. But it does not follow that the *main* point of difference in the attitude of the Socialists and Anarchists towards the state can be ignored. The Socialists are in favor of utilizing the modern state and its institutions in the struggle for the emancipation of the working class, and they also urge the necessity of utilizing the state for the peculiar transitional form from capitalism to socialism. This transitional form, which is *also* a state, is the dictatorship of the proletariat. The Anarchists want to 'abolish' the state, to 'blow it up' ('sprengen'), as Comrade Nota Bene expresses it in one place, erroneously ascribing this view to the Socialists. The Socialists—unfortunately the author quotes the words of Engels relevant to this subject, rather incompletely—hold that the state will 'wither away', will gradually 'fall asleep' *after* the bourgeoisie has been expropriated...."

"In order to 'emphasize' our 'hostility in principle' to the state, we must indeed understand it 'clearly'. This clarity, however, our author lacks. His phrase about the 'roots of the state idea' is entirely muddled, nonMarxist and nonsocialist. It is not 'the state idea' that has clashed with the repudiation of the idea of the state, but opportunist policy (i.e., an opportunist, reformist, bourgeois attitude towards the state) that has clashed with revolutionary Social-Democratic policy (i.e., with the revolutionary Social-Democratic attitude to the bourgeois state and towards utilizing the state against the bourgeoisie in order to overthrow it). These are entirely different things" (Volume XIX, p. 296).

I think it is clear what the point at issue is, and what a semianarchist mess Bukharin has got into!

Sten. At that time Lenin had not yet fully formulated the necessity for "blowing up" the state. Bukharin, while committing anarchist mistakes, was approaching formulation of the question.

Stalin. No, that is now what we are concerned with at present. What we are concerned with is the attitude towards the state in general. The point is that in Bukharin's opinion the working class should be hostile *in principle* to *any kind* of state, including the working-class state.

Sten. Lenin then only spoke about utilizing the state; he said nothing in his criticism of Bukharin regarding the "blowing up" of the state.

Stalin. You are mistaken, the "blowing up" of the state is not a Marxist formula, it is an anarchist formula. Let me assure you that the point here is that, in the opinion of Bukharin (and of the Anarchists), the workers should emphasize their hostility in principle to any kind of state, and, therefore, also to the state of the transition period, to the working-class state.

Just try to explain to our workers that the working class must become imbued with hostility in principle to the proletarian dictatorship, which, of course, is also a state.

Bukharin's position, as set forth in his article in *International Molodezhy*, is one of repudiating the state in the period of transition from capitalism to socialism.

Bukharin overlooked a "trifle" here, namely, the whole transition period, during which the working class cannot do without its own state if it really wants to suppress the bourgeoisie and build socialism. That is the first point.

Secondly, it is not true that at the time Comrade Lenin in his criticism did not deal with the theory of "blowing up", of "abolishing" the state in general. Lenin not only dealt with this theory, as is evident from the passages I have quoted, but he criticized and demolished it as an anarchist theory, and counterposed to it the theory of *forming* and *utilizing* a new state after the overthrow of the bourgeoisie, namely, the state of the proletarian dictatorship.

Finally, the anarchist theory of "blowing-up" and "abolishing" the state must not be confused with the Marxist theory of the "withering away" of the *proletarian* state or the "breaking up", the "smashing" of the *bourgeois* state machine. There are persons who are inclined to confuse these two different concepts in the belief that they express one and the same idea. But that is wrong. Lenin proceeded precisely from the Marxist theory of "smashing" the *bourgeois* state machine and the "withering away" of the *proletarian* state when he criticized the anarchist theory of "blowing up" and "abolishing" the state in general.

Perhaps it will not be superfluous if, for the sake of greater clarity, I quote here one of Comrade Lenin's manuscripts on the state, apparently written at the end of 1916, or the beginning of 1917 (before the February Revolution of 1917). From this manuscript it is easily seen that:

a) In criticizing Bukharin's semianarchist errors on the question of the state, Lenin proceeded from the Marxist theory of the "withering away" of the proletarian state and the "smashing" of the bourgeois state machine,

b) although Bukharin, as Lenin expressed it, "is nearer to the truth than Kautsky," nevertheless, "instead of exposing the Kautskyites, he helps them with his mistakes."

Here is the text of this manuscript.

"Of *extremely* great importance on the question of the state is the letter of *Engels* to *Bebel* dated 18-28 March 1875.

"Here is the most important passage in full:

"...'The free people's state is transformed into the free state. Taken in its grammatical sense, a free state is one where the state is free in relation to its citizens, hence a state with a despotic government. *The whole talk about the state should be dropped*, especially *since the Commune, which was no longer a state in the proper sense of the word.* The "people's state" has been thrown in our faces by the Anarchists to the point of disgust, although already Marx' book against Proudhon and later the *Communist Manifesto* directly declare that *with the introduction of the socialist order of society the state will dissolve of itself* (sich aufloest) *and disappear*. As, therefore, the state is only a transitional institution which is used in the struggle, in the revolution, in order to hold down one's adversaries by force, it is pure nonsense to talk of a free people's state: so long as the proletariat still *uses* (Engels' italics) the state, it does *not use it in the interests of freedom but in order to hold down its adversaries, and as soon as it becomes possible to speak of freedom the state as such ceases to exist.* We would therefore propose to replace the word *state* (Engels' italics) everywhere by the word "*community*" (Gemeinwesen), a good old German word which can very well represent the French word "*commune*".'

"This is, perhaps, the most remarkable, and certainly, the most pronounced passage, so to speak, in the works of Marx and Engels '*against* the state'.

"(1) 'The whole talk about the state should be dropped.'

"(2) 'The Commune was *no longer* a state in the proper sense of the word.' (What was it, then? A transitional form from the state to no state, obviously!)

"(3) The 'people's state' has been 'thrown in our faces' (in die Zaehne geworfen, literally—thrown in our teeth) by the Anarchists too long (that is, Marx and Engels were ashamed of the obvious mistake made by their German friends; but they regarded it, and of course, *in the circumstances that then existed*, correctly regarded it as a far less serious mistake than that made by the Anarchists. This NB!!).

"(4) The state will 'disintegrate ("dissolve") (Nota Bene) of itself and disappear'... (compare later "will wither away") 'with the introduction of the socialist order of society'...

"(5) The state is a 'temporary institution', which is used 'in the struggle, in the revolution'... (used by the *proletariat*, of course)...

"(6) The State is needed *not for freedom*, but for *holding down* (Niederhaltung is not suppression in the proper sense of the word, but preventing restoration, keeping in submission) the *adversaries of the proletariat*.

"(7) When there will be freedom, there will be no state.

"(8) 'We' (i.e., Engels and *Marx*) would propose to replace the word 'state' *everywhere* (in the program) by the word 'community' (Gemeinwesen), 'commune'!!!

"This shows how Marx and Engels were vulgarized and defiled not only by the opportunists, but also by Kautsky.

"The opportunists *have not* understood a single one of these *eight* rich ideas!!

"They have taken *only* what is practically necessary for the present time: To utilize the political struggle, to utilize the *present* state to educate, to train the proletariat, to 'wrest concessions'. That is correct (as against the Anarchists), but that is only 1/100 part of Marxism, if one can thus express it arithmetically.

"In his propagandist works, and publications generally, Kautsky has completely slurred over (or forgotten? or not understood?) points 1, 2, 5, 6, 7, 8, and the 'Zerbrechen' of Marx (in his controversy with Pannekoek in 1912 or 1913, Kautsky (see below, pp. 45-47) completely dropped into opportunism on this question).

"What distinguishes us from the Anarchists is (a) the use of the state *now* and (b) during the proletarian *revolution* (the 'dictatorship of the proletariat')—points of very great importance in the practice at this moment. (But it is these very points Bukharin *forgot*!)

"What distinguishes us from the opportunists is the more profound, 'more permanent' truths regarding (aa) the 'temporary' nature of the state, (bb) the *harm* of 'chatter' about it now, (cc) the not entirely state character of the dictatorship of the proletariat, (dd) the contradiction between the state and freedom, (ee) the more correct idea (concept, programmatic term) 'community' instead of state, (ff) 'smashing' (Zerbrechen) of the bureaucratic-military machine.

"It must not be forgotten also that the avowed opportunists in Germany (Bernstein, Kolb, et. al.) directly repudiate the *dictatorship of the proletariat*, while the official program and Kautsky *indirectly* repudiate it, by not saying anything about it in their day-to-day agitation and *tolerating* the renegacy of Kolb and Co.

In August 1916, Bukharin was written to: 'allow your ideas about the state *to mature*.' *Without*, however, allowing them to mature, he broke into print, as 'Nota Bene', and did it in such a way that, instead of exposing the Kautskyites, he *helped them* with his mistakes!! Yet, as a matter of fact, Bukharin is nearer to the truth than Kautsky."

Such is the brief history of the theoretical controversy on the question of the state.

It would seem that the matter is clear: Bukharin made semianarchist mistakes—it is time to correct these mistakes and proceed further in the footsteps of Lenin. But only Leninists can think like that. Bukharin, it appears, does not agree. On the contrary, he asserts that it was not he who was mistaken, but Lenin; that it was not he who followed, or ought to have followed, in the footsteps of Lenin, but, on the contrary, that it was Lenin who found himself compelled to follow in the footsteps of Bukharin.

You do not believe this, comrades? In that case, listen further. After the controversy in 1916, nine years later, during which interval Bukharin maintained silence, and *a year after the death of Lenin*—namely, in 1925—Bukharin published an article in the symposium *Revoliutsiia Prava*, entitled "Concerning the Theory of the Imperialist State", which previously had been rejected by the editors of *Sbornik Sotsial-Demokrata* (i.e., by Lenin). In a *footnote* to this article Bukharin bluntly declares that it was not Lenin but he, Bukharin, who was right in this controversy. That may seem incredible, comrades, but it is a fact.

Listen to the text of this footnote:

"V.I. (i.e., Lenin) wrote a short article containing criticism of the article in *Internatsional Molodezhy*. The reader will easily see that I had not made the mistake attributed to me, for I clearly saw the need for the dictatorship of the proletariat; on the other hand, from Il'ich's article it will be seen that at that time he was *wrong about the thesis on 'blowing up' the state* (bourgeois state, of course), *and confused that question with the question of the withering away of the dictatorship of the proletariat*. (My italics—*J. Stalin*) Perhaps I should have enlarged on the subject of the dictatorship at that time. But in justification I may say that *at that time* there was such a wholesale exaltation of the bourgeois state by the Social-Democrats that it was natural to concentrate all attention on the question of *blowing up* that machine.

"When I arrived in Russia from America and saw Nadezhda Konstantinovna [Krupskaia—AGC] (that was at our illegal Sixth Congress and at that time V.I. was in hiding) her first words were: 'V.I. asked me to tell you that he has no disagreements with you now over the question of the state.' Studying this question, *Il'ich came to the same conclusions* (My italics—*J. Stalin.*) regarding 'blowing up', but he developed this theme, and later the theory of the dictatorship, to such an extent as to create a whole epoch in the development of theoretical thought in this field."

That is how Bukharin writes about Lenin *a year after* Lenin's death.

There you have a pretty example of the hypertrophied pretentiousness of a half-educated theoretician!

Quite possibly, Nadezhda Konstantinovna did tell Bukharin what he writes here. But what conclusions can be drawn from this fact? The only conclusion that can be drawn is that Lenin had certain grounds for believing that Bukharin had renounced or was ready to renounce his mistakes. That is all. But Bukharin thought differently. He decided that henceforth, not Lenin, but he, i.e., Bukharin must be regarded as the creator, or, at least, the inspirer of the Marxist theory of the state.

Hitherto we have regarded ourselves as Leninists, and we continue to do so. But it now appears that both Lenin and we, his disciples, are Bukharinites. Rather funny, comrades. But that's what happens when one has to deal with Bukharin's puffed-up pretentiousness.

It might be thought that Bukharin's footnote to the above-mentioned article was a slip of the pen, that he wrote something silly, and then forgot about it. But it turns out that that is not the case. Bukharin, it turns out, spoke in all seriousness. That is evident, for example, from the fact that the statement he made in this footnote regarding Lenin's *mistakes* and Bukharin's *correctness* was republished recently, namely, in 1927, i.e., two years after Bukharin's first attack on Lenin, in a biographical sketch of Bukharin written by Maretsky, and it never occurred to Bukharin to protest against this... boldness of Maretsky. Obviously Bukharin's attack on Lenin cannot be regarded as accidental.

It appears, therefore, that Bukharin is right, and not Lenin, that the inspirer of the Marxist theory of the state is not Lenin, but Bukharin.

Such, comrades, is the picture of the theoretical distortions and the theoretical pretensions of Bukharin.

And this man, after all this, has the presumption to say in his speech here that there is "something rotten" in the theoretical line of our Party, that there is a deviation towards Trotskyism in the theoretical line of our Party!

And this is said by that same Bukharin who is making (and has made in the past) a number of gross theoretical and practical mistakes, who only recently was a pupil of Trotsky's, and who only the other day was seeking to form a bloc with the Trotskyists against the Leninists and was paying them visits by the backdoor.

Is that not funny, comrades?

h) A FIVE YEAR PLAN OR A TWO YEAR PLAN

Permit me now to pass to Rykov's speech. While Bukharin tried to provide a theoretical basis for the Right deviation, Rykov attempted in his speech to provide it with a basis of practical proposals and to frighten us with "horrors" drawn from our difficulties in the sphere of agriculture. That does not mean that Rykov did not touch upon theoretical questions. He did touch upon them. But in doing so he made at least two serious mistakes.

In his draft resolution on the five year plan, which was rejected by the commission of the Political Bureau, Rykov says that "the central idea of the five year plan is to increase the productivity of labor of the people." In spite of the fact that the commission of the Political Bureau rejected this absolutely false line, Rykov defended it here in his speech.

Is it true that the central idea of the five year plan in the *Soviet country* is to increase the productivity of labor? No, it is not true. It is not *just any kind* of increase in the productivity of labor of the people that we need. What we need is a specific increase in the productivity of labor of the people, namely, an increase that will guarantee the *systematic supremacy of the socialist sector of the national economy over the capitalist sector*. A five year plan which overlooks this central idea is not a five year plan, but five year rubbish.

Every society, capitalist and precapitalist society included, is interested in increasing the productivity of labor in general. The difference between *Soviet* society and every other society lies in the very fact that it is interested not in just any kind of increase of the productivity of labor, but in such an increase as will ensure the supremacy of socialist forms of economy over other forms, and primarily over capitalist forms of economy, and will thus ensure that the capitalist forms of economy are overcome and ousted. But Rykov forgot this really central idea of the five year plan of development of *Soviet society*. This is his first theoretical mistake.

His second mistake is that he does not distinguish, or does not want to understand the distinction—from the point of view of trade turnover—between, let us say, a collective farm and all kinds of individual enterprises, including individual capitalist enterprises. Rykov assures us that from the point of view of trade turnover on the grain market, from the point of view of obtaining grain, he does not see any difference between a collective farm and a private holder of grain; to him, therefore, it is a matter of indifference whether we buy grain from a collective farm, a private holder, or an Argentinian grain merchant. That is absolutely wrong. It is a repetition of the statement of Frumkin, who at one time used to assure us that it was a matter of indifference to him where and from whom we bought grain, whether from a private dealer or from a collective farm.

That is a masked form of defense, of rehabilitation, of justification of the kulak's machinations on the grain market. That this defense is conducted from the point of view of trade turnover does not alter the fact that it is, nevertheless, a justification of the kulak's machinations on the grain market. If from the viewpoint of trade turnover there is no difference between collective and noncollective forms of economy, is it worthwhile developing collective farms, granting them privileges and devoting ourselves to the difficult task of overcoming the capitalist elements in agriculture? It is obvious that Rykov has taken a wrong line. That is his second theoretical mistake.

But this is by the way. Let us pass to the practical questions raised in Rykov's speech.

Rykov said here that in addition to the five year plan we need another, a parallel plan, namely, a two year plan for the development of agriculture. He justified this proposal for a parallel two year plan on the grounds of the difficulties experienced in agriculture. He said: The five year plan was a good thing and he was in favor of it; but if at the same time we drew up a two year plan for agriculture it would be still better—otherwise agriculture would get into a fix.

On the face of it there appears to be nothing wrong with this proposal. But upon closer scrutiny we find that the two year plan for agriculture was invented in order to emphasize that the five year plan is unreal, a plan merely on paper. Could we agree to that? No, we could not. We said to Rykov: If you are dissatisfied with the five year plan with regard to agriculture, if you think that the funds we are assigning in the five year plan for developing agriculture are inadequate, then tell us plainly what your supplementary proposals are, what additional investments you propose—we are ready to include these additional investments in agriculture into the five year plan. And what happened? We found that Rykov had no supplementary proposals to make about additional investments in agriculture. The question arises: Why then a parallel two year plan for agriculture?

We said to him further: In addition to the five year plan there are yearly plans which are part of the five year plan. Let us include into the first two of the yearly plans the concrete additional proposal for developing agriculture that you have, that is, if you have any at all. And what happened? We found that Rykov had no such concrete plans for additional assignments to propose.

We then realized that Rykov's proposal for a two year plan was not made for the purpose of developing agriculture, but arose from a desire to emphasize that the five year plan was unreal, a plan merely on paper, from a desire to discredit the five year plan. For "conscience" sake, for appearance's sake, a five year plan; but for work, for practical purposes, a two year plan—that was Rykov's strategy. Rykov brought the two year plan on the scene in order subsequently, during the practical work of carrying out the five year plan, to counterpose it to the five year plan, reconstruct the five year plan and adapt it to the two year plan by paring down and curtailing the assignments for industry.

It was on these grounds that we rejected Rykov's proposal for a parallel two year plan.

i) THE QUESTION OF THE CROP AREA

Rykov tried here to frighten the Party by asserting that the crop area throughout the USSR is showing a steady tendency to diminish. Moreover, he threw out the hint that the policy of the Party was to blame for the diminution of the crop area. He did not say outright that we are faced with a retrogression of agriculture, but the impression left by his speech is that something like retrogression is taking place.

Is it true that the crop area is showing a steady tendency to diminish? No, it is not true. Rykov made use of average figures of the crop area throughout the country. But the method of average figures, if it is not corrected by data for individual districts, cannot be regarded as a scientific method.

Rykov has, perhaps, read Lenin's *Development of Capitalism in Russia*. If he has read it he ought to remember how Lenin inveighed against the bourgeois economists for using the method of average figures showing the expansion of the crop area and ignoring the data for individual districts. It is strange that Rykov should repeat the mistake of the bourgeois economists. Now, if we examine the changes in the crop area according to districts, i.e., if we approach the matter scientifically, it will be seen that in certain districts the crop area is expanding *steadily*, while in others it *sometimes* diminishes, depending chiefly on meteorological conditions; moreover, there are no facts to indicate that there is a *steady* diminution of the crop area anywhere, even in a single important grain-growing district.

Indeed, there has recently been a decrease in the crop area in districts which have been affected by frost or drought, in certain regions of the Ukraine, for instance....

A voice. Not the whole Ukraine.

Schlichter. In the Ukraine the crop area has increased by 2.7 percent.

Stalin. I am referring to the steppe regions of the Ukraine. In other districts, for instance in Siberia, the Volga region, Kazakhstan, and Bashkiria, which were not affected by unfavorable weather conditions, the crop area has been steadily expanding.

How is it that in certain districts the crop area is steadily expanding, while in others it sometimes diminishes? It cannot really be asserted that the Party has one policy in the Ukraine and another in the east or in the central area of the USSR. That would be absurd, comrades. Obviously weather conditions are of no little importance here.

It is true that the kulaks are reducing their crop areas irrespective of weather conditions. For that, if you like, the policy of the Party, which is to support the poor- and middle-peasant masses *against* the kulaks, is "to blame". But what if it is? Did we ever pledge ourselves to pursue a policy which would satisfy all social groups in the countryside, including the kulaks? And, moreover, how can we pursue a policy which would satisfy both the exploiters and the exploited—if we desire at all to pursue a Marxist policy? What is there strange in the fact that, as a result of our Leninist policy, which is intended to restrict and overcome the capitalist elements in the countryside, the kulaks begin partly to reduce the area of their crops? What else would you expect?

Perhaps this policy is wrong? Then let them tell us so plainly. Is it not strange that people who call themselves Marxists are so frightened as to try to make out that the partial reduction of crop areas by the kulaks is a decrease of the crop area *as a whole*, forgetting that besides the kulaks there are also the poor and middle peasants, whose crop area is expanding, that there are the collective and state farms, whose crop area is growing at an increasing rate?

Finally, one more error in Rykov's speech regarding the crop area. Rykov complained here that in certain places, namely, where there has been the greatest development of collective farms, the tillage of the individual poor and middle peasants is beginning to diminish. That is true. But what is wrong with that? How could it be otherwise? If the poor- and middle-peasant farms are beginning to abandon individual tillage and are going over to collective farming, is it not obvious that the growth in size and numbers of the collective farms is bound to result in a decrease of the tillage of the individual poor and middle peasants? But what would you expect?

The collective farms now have something over two million hectares of land. At the end of the five year plan period, the collective farms will have more than 25,000,000 hectares. At whose expense does the tillage of the collective farms expand? At the expense of the tillage of the individual poor and middle peasants. But what would you expect? How else is the individual farming of the poor and middle peasants to be transferred on to the lines of collective farming? Is it not obvious that in a large number of areas the tillage of the collective farms will expand at the expense of individual tillage?

It is strange that people refuse to understand these elementary things.

j) GRAIN PROCUREMENTS

A lot of fairy-tales have been told here about our grain difficulties. But the main features of our current difficulties have been overlooked.

First of all, it has been forgotten that this year we harvested about 500-600 million puds of rye and wheat—I refer to the gross harvest—less than last year. Could this fail to affect our grain procurements? Of course it was bound to affect them.

Perhaps the policy of the Central Committee is responsible for this? No, the policy of the Central Committee has nothing to do with it. The explanation lies in the serious crop failure in the steppe regions of the Ukraine (frost and drought), and the partial crop failure in the North Caucasus, the Central Black Earth region, and the North-Western region.

That also explains the drop in wheat and rye procurements in the Central Black Earth region to about one-eighth and in the North Caucasus to one-fourth.

In certain regions in the East, grain procurements this year almost doubled. But this could not compensate, and, of course, did not compensate, for our grain deficit in the Ukraine, the North Cauacasus and the Central Black Earth region.

It must not be forgotten that in normal harvest years the Ukraine and the North Caucasus provide about one-half of the total grain procurements in the USSR.

It is strange that Rykov lost sight of this fact.

Finally, the second circumstance, which constitutes the chief feature of our current grain-procurement difficulties. I refer to the resistance of the kulak elements in the countryside to the grain-procurement policy of the Soviet government. Rykov ignored the circumstance. But to ignore it means to ignore the chief factor in grain procurements. What does the experience of the past two years as regard grain procurements show? It shows that the well-to-do strata of the countryside, who hold considerable grain surpluses and play an important role in the grain market, refuse to deliver voluntarily the necessary quantity of grain at the prices fixed by the Soviet government. In order to provide bread for the towns and industrial centers, for the Red Army and the regions growing industrial crops, we require about 500,000,000 puds of grain annually. We are able to procure 300-350 million puds coming in automatically. The remaining 150,000,000 puds have to be secured through organized pressure on the kulaks and the well-to-do strata of the rural population. That is what our experience of grain procurements during the past two years shows.

What has happened during these two years? Why these changes? Why were automatic deliveries adequate before, and why are they inadequate now? What has happened is that during these years the kulak and well-to-do elements have grown, the series of good harvests have not been without benefit to them, they have become stronger economically; they have accumulated a little capital and now are in a position to maneuver in the market; they hold back their grain surpluses in expectation of high prices, and get a living from other crops.

Grain should not be regarded as an ordinary commodity. Grain is not like cotton, which cannot be eaten and which cannot be sold to everybody. Unlike cotton, grain, under our present conditions, is a commodity which everybody will take and without which it is impossible to exist. The kulak takes this into account and holds back his grain, infecting the grain holders in general by his example. The kulak knows that grain is the currency of currencies. The kulak knows that a surplus of grain is not only a means of self-enrichment, but also a means of enslaving the poor peasant. Under present conditions, grain surpluses in the hands of the kulak is a means of economically and politically strengthening the kulak element. Therefore, by taking these grain surpluses from the kulaks, we not only facilitate the supply of grain to the towns and the Red Army, but we also destroy a means of strengthening the kulaks economically and politically.

What must be done to obtain these grain surpluses? We must, first of all, abolish the harmful and dangerous mentality of letting matters take their own course. Grain procurements must be organized. The poor- and middle-peasant masses must be mobilized against the kulaks, and their public support organized for the measures of the Soviet government to increase grain procurements. The significance of the Urals-Siberian method of grain procurement, which is based on the principle of self-imposed obligations, lies precisely in the fact that it makes it possible to mobilize the laboring strata of the rural population against the kulaks for the purpose of increasing grain procurements. Experience has shown that this method gives us good results. Experience has shown that these good results are obtained in two directions: Firstly, we extract the grain surpluses from the well-to-do strata of the rural population and thereby help to supply the country; secondly, we mobilize on this basis the poor- and middle-peasant masses against the kulaks, educate them politically and organize them into a vast, powerful, political army supporting us in the countryside. Certain comrades fail to realize the importance of this latter factor. Yet it is one of the important results, if not the most important result, of the Urals-Siberian method of grain procurement.

It is true that this method is sometimes coupled with the employment of emergency measures against the kulaks, which evokes comical howls from Bukharin and Rykov. But what is wrong with it? Why should we not, sometimes, under certain conditions, employ emergency measures against our class enemy, against the kulaks? Why is it regarded as permissible to take the grain surpluses from the kulaks—who are speculating in grain and trying to seize the Soviet government by the throat and to enslave the poor peasants—by methods of public compulsion and at prices at which the poor and middle peasants sell their grain to our procurement organizations? Where is the logic in this? Has our Party ever declared that it is opposed *in principle* to the employment of emergency measures against speculators and kulaks? Have we no laws against speculators?

Evidently, Rykov and Bukharin are opposed *in principle* to any employment of emergency measures against the kulaks. But that is bourgeois-liberal policy, not Marxist policy. Surely you know that, after the introduction of the New Economic Policy, Lenin even expressed himself in favor of a return to the policy of Poor Peasants' Committees, under certain conditions of course. And what indeed is the partial employment of emergency measures against the kulaks? Not even a drop of the ocean compared with the policy of Poor Peasants' Committees.

The adherents of Bukharin's group hope to persuade the class enemy voluntarily to forego his interests and voluntarily to deliver his grain surpluses to us. They hope that the kulak, who has grown stronger, who is speculating, who is able to hold out by selling other products and who conceals his grain surpluses—they hope that this kulak will give us his grain surpluses voluntarily at our procurement prices. Have they lost their senses? Is it not obvious that they do not understand the mechanics of the class struggle, that they do not know what classes are?

Do they know how the kulaks jeer at our officials and the Soviet government at village meetings called to promote grain procurements? Have they heard of such facts as, for instance, what happened in Kazakhstan, when one of our agitators tried for two hours to persuade the holders of grain to deliver grain for suppling the country, and a kulak stepped forward with a pipe in his mouth and said: "Do us a little dance, young fellow, and I will let you have a couple of puds of grain."

Voices. The swine!

Stalin. Try to persuade people like that.

Class is class, comrades. You cannot get away from that truth. The Urals-Siberian method is a good one for the very reason that it helps to rouse the poor- and middle-peasant strata against the kulaks, it helps to smash the resistance of the kulaks and compels them to deliver the grain surpluses to the Soviet government bodies.

The most fashionable word just now among Bukharin's group is the word "excesses" in grain procurements. That word is the most current commodity among them, since it helps them to mask their opportunist line. When they want to mask their own line they usually say: "We, of course, are not opposed to pressure being brought to bear upon the kulak, but we are opposed to the excesses which are being committed in this sphere and which hurt the middle peasant. They then go on to relate stories of the "horrors" of those excesses; they read letters from "peasants", panic-stricken letters from comrades, such as Markov, and then draw the conclusion: The policy of bringing pressure to bear upon the kulaks must be abandoned.

How do you like that? *Because* excesses are committed in carrying out a correct policy, *that correct policy*, it seems, *must be abandoned*. That is the usual trick of the opportunists: On the pretext that excesses are committed in carrying out a correct line, abolish that line and replace it by an opportunist line. Moreover, the supporters of Bukharin's group very carefully hush up the fact that there is another kind of excesses, more dangerous and more harmful—namely, excesses in the direction of merging with the kulak, in the direction of adaptation to the well-to-do strata of the rural population, in the direction of abandoning the revolutionary policy of the Party for the opportunist policy of the Right deviators.

Of course, we are all opposed to those excesses. None of us wants the blows directed against the kulaks to hurt the middle peasants. That is obvious, and there can be no doubt about it. But we are most emphatically opposed to the chatter about excesses, in which Bukharin's group so zealously indulges, being used to settle the revolutionary policy of our Party and replace it by the opportunist policy of Bukharin's group. No, that trick of theirs won't work.

Point out at least one political measure taken by the Party that has not been accompanied by excesses of one kind or another. The conclusion to be drawn from this is that we must combat excesses. But can one *on these grounds* decry the line itself, which is the only correct line?

Take a measure like the introduction of the seven-hour day. There can be no doubt that this is one of the most revolutionary measures carried out by our Party in the recent period.

Who does not know that this measure, which by its nature is a profoundly revolutionary one, is frequently accompanied by excesses, sometimes of a most objectionable kind? Does that mean that we ought to abandon the policy of introducing the seven-hour day?

Do the supporters of the Bukharin opposition understand what a mess they are getting into in playing up the excesses committed during the grain-procurement campaign?

k) FOREIGN CURRENCY RESERVES AND GRAIN IMPORTS

Lastly, a few words about grain imports and our reserves of foreign currency. I have already mentioned the fact that Rykov and his close friends several times raised the question of importing grain from abroad. At first Rykov spoke of the need to import some 80-100 million puds of grain. This would require about 200 million rubles' worth of foreign currency. Later, he raised the question of importing 50,000,000 puds, that is, for 100 million rubles' worth of foreign currency. We rejected this suggestion, as we had come to the conclusion that it was preferable to bring pressure to bear upon the kulaks and wring out of them their quite substantial grain surpluses, rather than expend foreign currency ear-marked for imports of equipment for our industry.

Now Rykov makes a change of front. Now he asserts that capitalists are offering us grain on credit, but that we refuse to take it. He said that several telegrams had passed through his hands, telegrams showing that the capitalists are willing to let us have grain on credit. Moreover, he tried to make it appear that there are people in our ranks who refuse to accept grain on credit either owing to a whim or for some other inexplicable reasons.

That is all nonsense, comrades. It would be absurd to imagine that the capitalists in the West have suddenly begun to take pity on us, that they are willing to give us some tens of millions of puds of grain practically free of charge or on long-term credit. That is nonsense, comrades.

What is the point then? The point is that for the past six months various capitalist groups have been probing us, probing our financial possibilities, our financial standing, our endurance. They approach our trade representatives in Paris, Czechoslovakia, America and the Argentine with offers of grain on very short-term credit, not exceeding three, or, at the most, six months. Their object is not so much to sell us grain on credit, as to find out whether our position is really very difficult, whether our financial possibilities are really exhausted, or, whether our financial position is strong, and whether we will snatch at the bait that they have thrown out.

There are big disputes going on now in the capitalist world on the subject of our financial possibilities. Some say that we are already bankrupt, and that the fall of Soviet power is a matter of a few months, if not weeks. Others say that this is not true, that Soviet power is firmly rooted, has financial possibilities and sufficient grain.

At the present time our task is to display the requisite firmness and stamina, not to succumb to mendacious promises of grain on credit, and to show the capitalist world that we shall manage without importing grain. That is not just my personal opinion. That is the opinion of the majority of the Political Bureau.

For this reason we decided to decline the offer of philanthropists of the Nansen type to import into the USSR a million dollars' worth of grain on credit.

For the same reason we gave a negative answer to all those intelligence agents of the capitalist world in Paris, America and Czechoslovakia, who were offering us a small quantity of grain on credit.

For the same reason we decided to exercise the utmost economy in grain consumption, and the maximum degree of organizing efficiency in grain procurement.

By doing so, we sought to achieve two aims: On the one hand to do without importing grain and thus keep our foreign currency for importing equipment, and, on the other hand, to show all our enemies that we stand on firm ground and have no intention of succumbing to promises of alms.

Was this policy correct? I believe that it was the only correct policy. It was correct not only because we found here, within our own country, new possibilities of obtaining grain. It was correct, too, because by managing without grain imports and by sweeping aside the intelligence agents of the capitalist world, we have strengthened our international position, improved our financial standing and exploded all idle chatter about "the impending collapse" of Soviet power.

Some days ago we held preliminary talks with representatives of German capitalists. They are promising us a 500,000,000 rubles credit, and it looks as though they in fact consider it necessary to grant us this credit so as to ensure Soviet orders for their industry.

A few days ago we had the visit of a delegation of British conservatives, who also consider it necessary to recognize the stability of Soviet power and the expediency of granting us credits so as to ensure Soviet orders for their industry.

I believe that we would not have had these new possibilities of obtaining credits, in the first place from the Germans, and then from one group of British capitalists, if we had not displayed the necessary firmness that I spoke of earlier.

Consequently, the point is not that we are refusing some imaginary grain or imaginary long-term credit because of an alleged whim. The point is that we must be able to size up our enemies, to discern their real desires, and to display the stamina necessary for consolidating our international position.

That, comrades, is the reason why we have refused to import grain.

As you see, the question of grain imports is far from being as simple as Rykov would have us believe. The question of grain imports is one that concerns our international position.

V
QUESTIONS OF PARTY LEADERSHIP

Thus we have reviewed all the principal questions relating to our disagreements in the sphere of theory as well as in the sphere of the policy of the Comintern and the internal policy of our Party. From what has been said it is apparent that Rykov's statement about the existence of a *single* line does not correspond to the real state of affairs. From what has been said it is apparent that we have in fact *two* lines. One line is the general line of the Party, the revolutionary Leninist line of our Party. The other line is the general line of Bukharin's group. This second line has not quite crystallized yet, partly because of the incredible confusion of views within the ranks of Bukharin's group, and partly because this second line, being of little importance in the Party, tries to disguise itself in one way or another. Nevertheless, as you have seen, this line exists, and it exists as a line which is *distinct* from the Party line, as a line *opposed* to the general Party line on almost all questions of our policy. This second line is that of the *Right* deviation.

Let us pass now to questions of Party leadership.

a) THE FACTIONALISM OF BUKHARIN'S GROUP

Bukharin said that there is no opposition within our Party, that Bukharin's group is not an opposition. That is not true, comrades. The discussion at the plenum showed quite clearly that Bukharin's group constitutes a new opposition. The oppositional work of this group consists of attempts to revise the Party line; it seeks to revise the Party line by another line, the line of the opposition, which can be nothing but a line of the Right deviation.

Bukharin said that the group of three does not constitute a factional group. That is not true, comrades. Bukharin's group has all the characteristics of a faction. There is the platform, the factional secrecy, the policy of resigning, the organized struggle against the Central Committee. What more is required? Why hide the truth about the factionalism of Bukharin's group, when it is self-evident? The very reason why the plenum of the Central Committee and Central Control Commission has met is to tell all the truth here about our disagreements. And the truth is that Bukharin's group is a factional group. And it is not merely a factional group, but—I would say—the most repulsive and the pettiest of all the factional groups that ever existed in our Party.

This is evident if only from the fact that it is now attempting to use for its factional aims such an insignificant and petty affair as the disturbances in Adzharia. In point of fact, what does the so-called "revolt" in Adzharia amount to in comparison with such revolts as the Kronstadt revolt? I believe that in comparison with this the so-called "revolt" in Adzharia is not even a drop in the ocean. Were there any instances of Trotskyists or Zinovievites attempting to make use of the serious revolt which occurred in Kronstadt to combat the Central Committee, the Party? It must be admitted, comrades, that there were no such instances. On the contrary, the opposition groups which existed in our Party at the time of the serious revolt helped the Party in suppressing it, and they did not dare to make use of it against the Party.

Well, and how is Bukharin's group acting now? You have already had evidence that it is attempting in the pettiest and most offensive way to utilize against the Party the microscopic "revolt" in Adzharia. What is this if not an extreme degree of factional blindness and factional degeneration?

Apparently, it is being demanded of us that no disturbances should occur in our border regions which have common frontiers with capitalist countries. Apparently, it is being demanded of us that we should carry out a policy which would satisfy all classes of our society, the rich and the poor, the workers and the capitalists. Apparently, it is being demanded of us that there should be no discontented elements. Have not these comrades from Bukharin's group gone out of their minds?

How can anybody demand of us, people of the proletarian dictatorship who are waging a struggle against the capitalist world, both inside and outside our country, that there should be no discontented elements in our country, and that disturbances should not sometimes occur in certain border regions which have common frontiers with hostile countries? For what purpose then does the capitalist encirclement exist, if not to enable international capital to apply all its efforts to organize actions by discontented elements in our border regions against the Soviet regime? Who, except empty-headed liberals, would raise such demands? Is it not obvious that factional pettiness can sometimes produce in people a typically liberal blindness and narrow-mindedness?

b) LOYALTY AND COLLECTIVE LEADERSHIP

Rykov assured us there that Bukharin is one of the most "irreproachable" and "loyal" Party members in his attitude towards the Central Committee of our Party.

I am inclined to doubt it. We cannot take Rykov's word for it. We demand facts. And Rykov is unable to supply facts.

Take, for example, such a fact as the negotiations Bukharin conducted behind the scenes with Kamenev's group, which is connected with the Trotskyists; the negotiations about setting up a factional bloc, about changing the policy of the Central Committee, about changing the composition of the Political Bureau, about using the grain-procurement crisis for attacking the Central Committee. The question arises: Where is Bukharin's "loyal" and "irreproachable" attitude towards the Central Committee?

Is not such behavior, on the contrary, a violation of *any kind of* loyalty to his Central Committee, to his Party, on the part of a member of the Political Bureau? If this is called loyalty to the Central Committee, then what is the word for betrayal of one's Central Committee?

Bukharin likes to talk about loyalty and honesty, but why does he not try to examine his own conscience and ask himself whether he is not violating the most dishonest manner the elementary requirements of loyalty to his Central Committee when he conducts secret negotiations with Trotskyists against his Central Committee and thereby betrays his Central Committee?

Bukharin spoke here about the lack of collective leadership in the Central Committee of the Party, and assured us that the requirements of collective leadership were being violated by the majority of the Political Bureau of the Central Committee.

Our plenum, of course, has to put up with everything. It can even tolerate this shameless and hypocritical assertion of Bukharin's. But one must have really lost all sense of shame to make so bold as to speak in this way at the plenum against the majority of the Central Committee.

In truth, how can we speak of collective leadership if the majority of the Central Committee, having harnessed itself to the chariot of state, is straining all its forces to move it forward and is urging Bukharin's group to give a helping hand in this arduous task, while Bukharin's group is not only not helping its Central Committee but, on the contrary, is hampering it in every way, is putting a spoke in its wheels, is threatening to resign, and comes to terms with enemies of the Party, with Trotskyists, against the Central Committee of our Party?

Who, indeed, but hypocrites can deny that Bukharin, who is setting up a bloc with the Trotskyists against the Party, and is betraying his Central Committee, does not want to and will not implement collective leadership in the Central Committee of our Party?

Who, indeed, but the blind can fail to see that if Bukharin nevertheless chatters about collective leadership in the Central Committee, he is doing so with the object of disguising his treacherous conduct?

It should be noted that this not the first time that Bukharin has violated the elementary requirements of loyalty and collective leadership in relation to the Central Committee of the Party. The history of our Party knows of instances when, in Lenin's lifetime, in the period of the Brest Peace, Bukharin, being in the minority on the question of peace, rushed to the Left Socialist-Revolutionaries, who were the enemies of our Party, conducted backstairs negotiations with them, and attempted to set up a bloc with them against Lenin and the Central Committee. What agreement he was trying to reach at the time with the Left Socialist-Revolutionaries—we, unfortunately, do not yet know. But we do know that at the time the Left Socialist-Revolutionaries were planning to imprison Lenin and carry out an antiSoviet coup d'etat.... But the most amazing thing is that, while rushing to the Left Socialist-Revolutionaries and conspiring with them against the Central Committee, Bukharin continued, just as he is doing now, to clamor about the necessity of collective leadership.

The history of our Party knows, too, of instances when, in Lenin's lifetime, Bukharin, who had a majority in the Moscow Regional Bureau of our Party and the support of a group of "Left" Communists, called on all Party members to express lack of confidence in the Central Committee of the Party, to refuse to submit to its decisions and to raise the question of splitting our Party. That was during the period of the Brest Peace, after the Central Committee had already decided that it was necessary to accept the conditions of the Brest Peace.

Such is the character of Bukharin's loyalty and collective leadership.

Rykov spoke here about the necessity of collective work. At the same time he pointed an accusing finger at the majority of the Political Bureau, asserting that he and his close friends were in favor of collective work, while the majority of the Political Bureau, consequently, was against it. However, Rykov was unable to cite a single fact in support of his assertion.

In order to expose this fable of Rykov's, let me cite a few facts, a few examples which will show you how Rykov carries out collective work.

First example. You have heard the story about the export of gold to America. Many of you may believe that the gold was shipped to America by decision of the Council of People's Commissars or the Central Committee, or with the consent of the Central Committee, or with its knowledge. But that is not true, comrades. The Central Committee and the Council of People's Commissars have had nothing to do with this matter. There is a ruling which prohibits the export of gold without the approval of the Central Committee. But this ruling was violated. Who was it that authorized the export? It turns out that the shipment of gold was authorized by one of Rykov's deputies with Rykov's knowledge and consent.

Is that collective work?

Second example. This concerns negotiations with one of the big private banks in America, whose property was nationalized after the October Revolution, and which is now demanding compensation for its losses. The Central Committee has learned that an official of our State Bank has been discussing terms of compensation with that bank.

Settlement of private claims is, as you are aware, a very important question inseparably connected with our foreign policy. One might think that these negotiations were conducted with the approval of the Council of People's Commissars or the Central Committee. However, that is not the case, comrades. The Central Committee and the Council of People's Commissars have had nothing to do with this matter. Subsequently, upon learning about these negotiations, the Central Committee decided to stop them. But the question arises: Who authorized these negotiations? It turns out that they were authorized by one of Rykov's deputies with Rykov's knowledge and consent.

Is that collective work?

Third example. This concerns the supplying of agricultural machinery to kulaks and middle peasants. The point is that the EKOSO of the RSFSR, which is presided over by one of Rykov's deputies for matters concerning the RSFSR, decided to *reduce* the supply of agricultural machines to the middle peasants and *increase* the supply of machines to the upper strata of the peasantry, i.e., to the kulaks. Here is the text of this antiParty, antiSoviet ruling of the EKOSO of the RSFSR:

"In the Kazakh and Bashkir ASSR, the Siberian and Lower Volga territories, the Middle Volga and Urals regions, the proportion of sales of farm machines and implements set forth in this paragraph shall be *increased* to 20 percent for the upper strata of the peasantry and *decreased* to 30 percent for the middle strata."

How do you like that? At a time when the Party is intensifying the offensive against the kulaks and is organizing the masses of the poor and middle peasants against the kulaks, the EKOSO of the RSFSR adopts a decision to *reduce* the level of deliveries of farm machinery to the middle peasants and *increase* the level of deliveries to the upper strata of the peasantry.

And it is suggested that this is a Leninist, communist policy.

Subsequently, when the Central Committee learned about this incident, it annulled the decision of the EKOSO. But who was it that authorized this antiSoviet ruling? It was authorized by one of Rykov's deputies, with Rykov's knowledge and consent.

Is that collective work?

I believe that these examples are sufficient to show how Rykov and his deputies practice collective work.

c) THE FIGHT AGAINST THE RIGHT DEVIATION

Bukharin spoke here of the "civil execution" of three members of the Political Bureau, who, he says, "were being hauled over the coals" by the organizations of our Party. He said that the Party had subjected these three members of the Political Bureau—Bukharin, Rykov and Tomsky—to "civil execution" by criticizing their errors in the press and at meetings, while they, the three members of the Political Bureau, were "compelled" to keep silent.

All that is nonsense, comrades. Those are the false words of a Communist gone liberal who is trying to weaken the Party in its fight against the Right deviation. According to Bukharin, if he and his friends have become entangled in Right deviationist mistakes, the Party must stop fighting the Right deviation and wait until it shall please Bukharin and his friends to renounce their mistakes.

Is not Bukharin asking too much from us? Is he not under the impression that the Party exists for him and not he for the Party? Who is compelling him to keep silent, to remain in a state of inaction when the whole Party is mobilized against the Right deviation and is conducting determined attacks against difficulties? Why should not he, Bukharin, and his close friends come forward now and engage in a determined fight against the Right deviation and conciliation towards it? Can anyone doubt that the Party would welcome Bukharin and his close friends if they decided to take this not so difficult step? Why do they not decide to take this step, which, after all, is their duty? Is it not because they place the interests of their group above the interests of the Party and its general line? Whose fault is it that Bukharin, Rykov and Tomsky are missing in the fight against the Right deviation? Is it not obvious that talk about the "civil execution" of the three members of the Political Bureau is a poorly camouflaged attempt on the part of the three members of the Political Bureau to compel the Party to keep silent and to stop fighting against the Right deviation?

The fight against the Right deviation must not be regarded as a secondary task of our Party. The fight against the Right deviation is one of the most decisive tasks of our Party. If we, in our own ranks, in our own Party, in the political General Staff of the proletariat, which is directing the movement and is leading the proletariat forward—if we in this General Staff should allow the free existence and the free functioning of the Right deviators, who are trying to demobilize the Party, demoralize the working class, adapt our policy to the tastes of the "Soviet" bourgeoisie, and thus yield to the difficulties of our socialist construction—if we should allow all this, what would it mean? Would it not mean that we are ready to put a brake on the revolution, disrupt our socialist construction, flee from difficulties, and surrender our positions to the capitalist elements?

Does Bukharin's group understand that unless we overcome the Right deviation and conciliation towards it, it will be impossible to overcome the difficulties facing us, and unless we overcome these difficulties it will be impossible to achieve decisive successes in socialist construction?

In view of this, what is the worth of this pitiful talk about the "civil execution" of three members of the Political Bureau?

No, comrades, the Bukharinites will not frighten the Party with liberal chatter about "civil execution". The Party demands that they should wage a determined fight against the Right deviation and conciliation towards it side by side with all the members of the Central Committee of our Party. It demands this of Bukharin's group in order to help to mobilize the working class, to break down the resistance of the class enemies and to organize decisive victory over the difficulties of our socialist construction.

Either the Bukharinites will fulfil this demand of the Party, in which case the Party will welcome them, or they will not do so, in which case they will have only themselves to blame.

VI
CONCLUSIONS

I pass to the conclusions.

I submit the following proposals:

1) We must first of all condemn the views of Bukharin's group. We must condemn the views of this group as set forth in its declarations and in the speeches of its representatives, and state that these views are incompatible with the Party line and fully coincide with the position of the Right deviation.

2) We must condemn Bukharin's secret negotiations with Kamenev's group as the most flagrant expression of the disloyalty and factionalism of Bukharin's group.

3) We must condemn the policy of resigning that was being practiced by Bukharin and Tomsky, as a gross violation of the elementary requirements of Party discipline.

4) Bukharin and Tomsky must be removed from their posts and warned that in the event of the slightest attempt at insubordination to the decisions of the Central Committee, the latter will be forced to exclude both of them from the Political Bureau.

5) We must take appropriate measures forbidding members and candidate members of the Political Bureau, when speaking publicly, to deviate in any way from the line of the Party and the decisions of the Central Committee or of its bodies.

6) We must take appropriate measures so that press organs, both Party and Soviet, newspapers as well as periodicals, should fully conform to the line of the Party and the decisions of its leading bodies.

7) We must adopt special provisions, including even expulsion from the Central Committee and from the Party, for persons who attempt to violate the confidential nature of the decisions of the Party, its Central Committee and Political Bureau.

8) We must distribute the text of the resolution of the joint plenum of the Central Committee and Central Control Commission on inner-Party questions to all the local Party organizations and to the delegates to the Sixteenth Party Conference, without publishing it in the press for the time being.

That, in my opinion, is the way out of this situation.

Some comrades insist that Bukharin and Tomsky should be immediately expelled from the Political Bureau of the Central Committee. I do not agree with these comrades. In my opinion, for the time being we can do without resorting to such an extreme measure.

Stalin, *Works*, XII, 1-113.

PARTY RESOLUTION. PARTY PLENUM CENSURES BUKHARIN'S GROUP AND TAKES MEASURES TO PREVENT DEVIATION FROM THE PARTY LINE

23 April 1929

The full plenum of the Central Committee and Central Control Commission approved the 9 February resolution of the Politburo and Presidium of the Central Control Commission, and adopted Stalin's proposal of 22 April. It drafted and approved a resolution that condemned Bukharin's group and reiterated the party line on the international revolutionary movement, socialist reconstruction of the economy, and the class struggle in the countryside. It instructed the Politburo to ensure conformity with the party line and decisions in the press and among individual members and candidate members of the Politburo.

JOINT PLENUM OF THE CENTRAL COMMITTEE AND THE CENTRAL CONTROL COMMISSION

On Intraparty Affairs

The joint plenum of the TsK and TsKK of the VKP(b) approves the 9 February 1929 resolution of the joint session of the Central Committee Politburo and the Central Control Commission Presidium on intraparty affairs.

Considering that the joint session of the Politburo of the TsK and the Presidium of the TsKK did not have an opportunity to evaluate the 9 February 1929 statement of Bukharin, Tomsky and Rykov, which in itself introduced a factionalist platform; that in their interventions at the joint plenum of the TsK and TsKK of the VKP(b) Bukharin, Rykov and Tomsky continued to develop and defend their views, which run contrary to the party line and that Bukharin and Tomsky refused to submit to the decisions of the joint session of the TsK

Politburo and the TsKK Presidium on the repudiation of their resignations, the joint plenum of the TsK and TsKK of the VKP(b), considers it necessary to adopt the following resolution:

1. The growth and formation of the right deviation in the party is very closely linked with features that are specific to the present stage in the development of the international proletarian revolution. The Fifteenth Congress of the VKP(b) and the Sixth Comintern Congress have already noted signs of a serious turning point in the situation of world capitalism and in the international revolutionary movement. The characteristic features of this turning point are: A sharpening of internal contradictions in the capitalist camp that is increasingly impairing and undermining its temporary and precarious stabilization and a growth of elements of a new revolutionary upsurge (the wave of strikes in a number of European countries, the radicalization of the working class and communist successes in parliamentary elections, the important victories in the elections to factory committees in Germany, the development of a revolutionary crisis in India, and the continuing revolutionary ferment in other colonies, the growth of contradictions and the danger of war both in the imperialist camp and between the capitalist world and the USSR).

In these conditions the most important tasks of communist parties are: Further bolshevization of communist parties, freeing those parties of social democratic traditions, securing the leading role of the party in the growing revolutionary movement, and preparation of the broad masses for the approaching, decisive class battles.

Hence the need to intensify across the entire front the struggle of communist parties against social democracy, and in particular against its "left" wing, and against reformist and bureaucratic leadership in the trade unions; hence the need for a broader and more energetic mobilization of organized, and in particular disorganized, workers behind the slogans of the Comintern.

The reality of partial capitalist stabilization, the presence of a strong social democratic movement that exercises influence on certain elements of communist parties and, finally, the survivals of social democratic traditions in the communist parties themselves, feed right opportunist trends in the ranks of the Comintern sections, trends that, at the present time, represent the principal danger in the international communist movement.

In questions of international politics, the right deviation tends toward a social democratic appraisal of the stabilization of capitalism (the theory of capitalism's "normalization"), which takes the form of papering over the constantly intensifying crisis of capitalism, of denying the fact of the unsteadiness of capitalist stabilization, of concealing the features of the "third period". Thus the rightists and the conciliators, who are their hangers-on, have arrived at the point of revising the leninist evaluation of the present era as a period of crisis for capitalism, as the era of wars and the world proletarian revolution. They underestimate elements of the growth of a new revolutionary upsurge and in this connection deny the tasks of mobilizing the working masses (particularly the disorganized working masses) for an independent struggle against the reformist trade union bureaucracy.

The link between the right deviation in the VKP(b) and these opportunistic trends in the ranks of the Comintern is quite apparent. Comrade Bukharin has, in fact, made common cause with the opportunistic position of the conciliators Humbert-Droz, Ewert, Gerhardt, and others. Comrades Bukharin, Rykov and Tomsky are impeding the struggle of the Comintern against the right deviation and against conciliation within the Comintern. The statement of these three comrades to the effect that the policy of our party "demoralizes" the Comintern, weakens its ranks and leads to schisms and defections in foreign communist parties, not only signifies a philistine, opportunistic misunderstanding of the tasks of cleansing communist parties of the elements of social democracy, but also actual support for the rightist renegades. Thus, objectively, Comrades Bukharin, Rykov and Tomsky are increasingly becoming a center of attraction for all the opportunistic and conciliatory groups in the Comintern sections.

2. The political position of the right deviation in the party means capitulation in the face of difficulties connected with the socialist reconstruction of the economy and the sharpening of the class struggle in the USSR. The reconstruction period signifies a serious turning point in the economic and political development of the USSR. The necessity to catch up with and surpass the advanced capitalist countries technically and economically in a brief historical period commits the party to conduct a policy of rapid industrial development. In implementing socialist industrialization, the proletariat has at present undertaken the difficult job of destroying the roots of capitalism in the country's economy, the job of socialist reorganization of agriculture, which is our central task in the countryside for the period ahead. The union of the working class with the basic peasant masses has entered a new stage and is taking new forms, more and more assuming a production character (sovkhozes and kolkhozes, equipping of the farms with machinery, contractual arrangements, etc.). The task of eliminating the technical and economic backwardness of our country in rapid order under conditions of hostile capitalist encirclement and of a predominantly small holding peasant agriculture, and setting directly to work on a fundamental, socialist reorganization of agriculture inevitably involves great difficulties. The party openly puts to the working masses the question of thenecessity of overcoming these inevitable difficulties, as opposed to a policy of capitulating before them. The socialist and capitalist paths for the development of agriculture are in sharper opposition today than ever before. The growth of socialist forms of the economy, the exclusion of capitalist elements, and connected with it the growth of opposition from class forces that are hostile to us, inevitably give rise to a sharpening of the class struggle at the present stage, which represents a turning point in socialist construction. At the given stage, proletarian dictatorship means a continuation and sharpening (and not slackening) of the class struggle.

The capitalist elite in the countryside, which has been growing in strength over the years of the NEP, has at its disposal greater possibilities of economic character for manuever today than it did during the early years of the NEP (grain reserves, means of production). The kulaks are taking advantage of these possibilities for manuever in a fierce struggle against the advance of socialism, in attempts to thwart state regulation of the market and Soviet state price policy. These attempts to thwart the policy of Soviet authorities represent one of the most acute forms of the struggle of the basic demands of the country's capitalist elements, and above all for the path of a free capitalist development of agriculture.

The joint plenum of the TsK and the TsKK states that in recent times the Bukharin group has gone over from a position of vacillation between the party line and the line of the right deviation in the basic questions of our policy to what is, in fact, a defense of the positions of the right deviation. Both Bukharin's "Notes of an Economist" and, in particular, the platform of the three as enunciated at the 9 February joint session of the Politburo and the TsKK Presidium, as well as the statements of these comrades at the plenum of the TsK and the TsKK are clearly directed toward a reduction in the rate of industrialization. The liberal interpretation of the NEP, which leads in fact to renunciation of regulation of market relations by the proletarian state, failure to attach proper significance to the new forms of the alliance of socialist industry with agriculture, failure to attach proper significance to the role of the sovkhozes and kolkhozes, while at the same time clearly overestimating the possibilities for the development of an individual, smallholding peasant economy—all this amounts, objectively, to a line of thwarting the advance of socialism and weakening the positions of the proletariat in the struggle against the capitalist forms of economy. Contrary to the party line, the Bukharin group, following in the footsteps of Frumkin, is in fact, counting on greater possibilities for the development of kulak economy. In line with this are the proposals to abolish individual taxation of kulaks, to further raise grain prices, and to put an end to pressure on the kulaks with regard to grain collection. In coming out against party measures to mobilize the poor and middle strata of the rural population for struggle against the kulaks' malicious concealment of, and speculation in, grain, the rightists are objectively assisting kulak attempts to thwart grain collections and the supply of grain to the working class and the poor peasants. Basic to this political line of the rightists is a theory of constant concessions to the peasantry, which attests to the fact that the rightists have forgotten and signifies an obvious revision of Lenin's teachings on the alliance with the middle peasants. The same political meaning attaches to the denial by Bukharin, Rykov and Tomsky of the inevitable sharpening of the class struggle under present conditions of the reconstruction period and to their attempts to explain the fact of a sharpening of the class struggle not by socioeconomic conditions, but by so-called planning oversights and by shortcomings in the local apparatus, etc.

3. Fulfillment of the highly complex tasks of the reconstruction period, surmounting the difficulties connected with this period, intensification of the class struggle in the country require reorganization of the ranks and work methods of all organs of the proletarian dictatorship and of all organizations of the working class along the following lines: Broadest mobilization of the activism of the proletarian and semiproletarian masses, strengthening proletarian leadership of the peasantry, rallying and inciting the entire poor and middle peasantry against the kulaks, and assurance of consistent rebuffs to the pressures from petty bourgeois elements. Continued development of mass proletarian self-criticism, which is encountering resistance from bureaucratic elements in our apparatus, is the basis of this reorganization. In its struggle for socialism, the vanguard of the working class must be strengthened by a general party *purge* of elements of degeneration and by the development of *self-criticism* and intraparty democracy. Reorganization of the state apparatus and its continued improvement must be promoted by *purifying soviet institutions* of hostile class elements and bureaucratic distortions, by revitalization of the soviets, by a decisive strengthening of the control of the masses from below over the work of all organizations of the working class, and by adapting the management system to the tasks of the reconstruction period. The *trade unions*, which are called upon to play a decisive role in the building of socialist industry, in increasing labor productivity and discipline, in organizing the production initiative of the working class and of socialist competition, and also in instilling class values in the new strata of the proletariat, must resolutely rid themselves of all remnants of guild exclusiveness and bourgeois trade-unionism, as well as of bureaucratic lack of concern for the masses and disregard for the tasks of defending the day-to-day needs and interests of the working class. *Stimulation of the cooperative movement* and the complete freeing of certain of its organizations from the influences of the well-to-do and kulak elite in the villages, and strengthening of the proletarian direction of the movement are necessary to assure the socialist development of the most important mass organizations of the peasantry.

The solution of these tasks is impossible unless the right deviation is decisively overcome. The slanderous statement of the Bukharin group to the effect that the party is spreading bureaucratism means discrediting the immense job that the party has done in combatting bureaucratism. The philistine denigration of self-criticism on the part of this group can have no other meaning than a direct struggle against the slogan of self-criticism. On the trade union question, Comrades Bukharin, Rykov and Tomsky have taken the highly dangerous course of setting off the trade unions against the party, they are, in fact, pursuing a policy of weakening party leadership of the trade union movement, they are concealing the shortcomings in trade union work, covering up bourgeois trade-unionist tendencies and instances of bureaucratic petrification in a part of the trade union apparatus and representing the party struggle against these shortcomings as a trotskyite "shake-up" of the trade unions. But it is in the question of the role of the party apparatus and of the intraparty regime that the position of the Bukharin group completely reproduces the most malicious accusations that were ever levelled against our party by the trotskyite opposition. The party is fighting and will continue to fight for continued development of intraparty democracy and proletarian self-criticism within its ranks, "without regard to individuals". The party, however, resolutely rejects the sort of "freedom" of criticism that the rightist elements seek in order to defend their antileninist political line. The leninist party resolutely repudiates the sort of "democracy" that legalizes deviations and factional groupings within the party. Intraparty democracy serves the interests of strengthening the leninist unity of the party, it serves to rally the party behind the general line of the Fifteenth Congress of the VKP.

4. The right deviation has its roots in the petty bourgeois elements that surround the working class. The right deviation has as its basis within the party the least stable elements, the elements in the nonproletarian sector of the party that are most subject to petty bourgeois influence and to the danger of degeneration; it has as its basis the most backward strata of workers, the strata that have not undergone a prolonged schooling in the factories and that have ties with the petty bourgeoisie in the countryside and the towns. The 9 February platform of the Bukharin group and the views defended by members of the group at the plenum of the TsK and TsKK are an appeal to these unstable elements and objectively are an aid to the formation of a right deviation within the party.

Insofar as the party has achieved a decisive success in exposing trotskyism both within its ranks as well as among the broad masses of the working class, the main task of intraparty policy in the present conditions must be to overcome fully the right deviation and conciliatory attitudes toward it. This task is to be solved both by systematically exposing the antileninist theory and policy of the right deviation and by mercilessly combatting manifestations of the right deviation in the everyday practical work of party, trade union, soviet, economic, cooperative, and other organizations. In the ranks of the leninist party, whose basic cadres have been strengthened by many years of struggle against opportunism, the openly opportunistic right deviation cannot hope to encounter any sort of extensive or open support. The greater the danger, then, of a covert form of the right deviation in which, hiding themselves behind public agreements with the decisions of the party, the opportunistic elements distort its class line in practice. Therefore, exposing the right deviation in practical work is, of necessity, an integral part of the struggle against opportunism within the party.

5. The joint plenum of the TsK and TsKK states that the Bukharin group has already begun a factional struggle against the party leadership. It is resorting to the most impermissible violation of party discipline (the refusal of Comrades Bukharin and Tomsky to carry out repeated decisions by the Politburo concerning their work). It is attempting to impose its line on the party by means of resignations. It has instigated factional work against the TsK within the Moscow organization, attempted to set off against the Central Committee, the party faction at the Eighth Trade Union Congress, resorted to attempts to form an unprincipled, high-level bloc in opposition to the Central Committee (Comrade Bukharin's proposal to Comrade Kamenev to form a bloc against the TsK), etc. The unprecedented slander against the party concerning the alleged slipping to trotskyite positions, the slanderous attack on the party concerning a "military-feudal exploitation" of the peasantry, which was borrowed from the arsenal of Miliukov's party [the prerevolutionary liberals], the accusation that the party is spreading bureaucratism and demoralizing the Communist International—all this unquestionably attests to the factional character of the Bukharin group and its deviation from the general line of the party. In so doing, the Bukharin group flagrantly violates leninist party unity, breaks bolshevik discipline, and subverts collective leadership in the TsK.

6. Guiding itself by the will of all party organizations, which unanimously support the line of the TsK and have decisively condemned the conduct and views of Comrades Bukharin, Rykov and Tomsky as basically reflecting right deviation; considering the fact that Comrades Bukharin, Rykov and Tomsky have not admitted their mistakes; finally, proceeding from the interests of party unity, which is particularly necessary under the present conditions, the plenum of the TsK and TsKK of the VKP(b) resolves:

a) to condemn the views of Comrade Bukharin's group set forth in Comrade Bukharin's statement of 30 January, in the 9 February statement of Comrades Bukharin, Rykov and Tomsky, and in the speeches of these comrades at the plenum of the TsK and TsKK, as incompatible with the general line of the party and as basically in accord with the position of the right deviation, and to bind them to carry out unquestioningly the decisions of the party and its organs;

b) to condemn Comrade Bukharin's behind-the-scenes talks with Comrade Kamenev as the most striking expression of Comrade Bukharin group's factionalism;

c) to condemn Comrades Bukharin and Tomsky's policy of resignation as a gross violation of party discipline;

d) to remove Bukharin and Tomsky from their present positions (*Pravda*, the Comintern, the All-Union Central Council of Trade Unions) and to warn them that should they make the slightest attempt to violate the resolutions of the TsK and its organs, they will be immediately removed from the Politburo as violators of party discipline;

e) that the Politburo must take steps to see to it that no divergences whatsoever from the party line and from the decisions of the leading party organs are permitted in statements by individual members and candidate members of the Politburo;

f) to take all necessary measures to see to it that the party line and the decisions of the TsK are fully carried out in the press organs, both party and Soviet, in newspapers as well as in journals;

g) to establish special procedures—up to and including exclusion from the TsK and from the party—capable of guaranteeing the secrecy of the decisions of the TsK and the Politburo and ruling out all possibility of informing the trotskyites about the affairs of the TsK and the Politburo;

h) to disseminate the present resolution to all local party organizations and to members of the Sixteenth Party conference, without publishing it in the press.

McNeal/Gregor, Vol. 2, 342-349.
KPSS v rezoliutsiiakh, Vol. 4, 180-187.

PARTY RESOLUTION. SIXTEENTH PARTY CONFERENCE APPROVES FIVE YEAR PLAN FOR RAPID DEVELOPMENT OF NATIONAL ECONOMY

25 April 1929

The first Five Year Plan of the Soviet national economy actually went into operation in October 1928; its official approval was not consummated until its adoption by the Sixteenth Party Conference in April 1929. The Conference approved what was called the "maximum" variant, which projected the annual rise in industrial output at over 20 percent by 1933. It rejected the "minimal" variant, which projected a relatively moderate rise in industrial output. This variant was advocated by the professional planners in the State Planning Commission. The "maximum" variant, strongly supported by Stalin, was predicated on favorable conditions prevailing throughout the period of the plan. Stalin and his supporters wanted to use the approval by the Party Conference as a mandate for the rapid development of the national economy.

RESOLUTION OF THE SIXTEENTH CONFERENCE OF THE VKP(B) ON THE FIVE YEAR PLAN FOR THE DEVELOPMENT OF THE NATIONAL ECONOMY

I

1. Having heard the reports about the five year plan for the development of the national economy of the Union of Soviet Socialist Republics, the Sixteenth All-Union party conference decrees, first, that the five year plan in relation to the *general rise* of the national economy foresees the following achievements:

a) While the total sum of capital investment in the five years 1923/24-1927/28 consisted of 26.5 billion rubles, for the five years 1928/29-1932/33 the amount of capital investment for the entire national economy is determined at the sum of 64.6 million rubles. While the capital investment in industry for the preceding five years consisted of 4.4 billion rubles, it is determined for the projected five years at 16.4 billion rubles; the corresponding figures for agriculture consists of 15 and 23.2 billion rubles; for transport it is 2.7 and 10 million rubles and for electrification, 0.9 and 3.1 billion rubles.

b) As a result of these investments the total sum of the basic funds of the country grows from 70 billion rubles in 1927/28 to 128 billion rubles in 1932/33, which include the basic funds for all of industry growing from 9.2 to 23.1 billion rubles, for electrification from 1 to 5 billion rubles, i.e., a five-fold increase, for railroads from 10 to 17 billions rubles, i.e., a 70 percent increase, and for agriculture from 28.7 to 38.9 billion rubles, i.e., a 35 percent increase.

c) The large size of capital investment accompanies the corresponding rise in production in all of industry from 18.3 billion rubles in 1927/28 to 43.2 in 1932/33, which signifies more than triple the prewar size of industrial production; in agriculture, from 16.6 to 25.8 billion rubles, signifying an increase of more than one-half times over prewar agricultural production. Railroads increase from 88 billion to 163 tons per kilometer; the net output of the entire national economy (in manual capacity) is from 24.4 to 49.7 billion rubles.

d) Proceeding from the general idea of industrializing the country, the strengthening of the Union's defense capability and being free in dependence on relations with capitalist countries are directed chiefly at industry which produces the means of production (78 percent of all capital investment to industry), in accordance with the fact that the output of these branches of industry grows significantly faster: during the rise of the entire gross output of industry planned at 2.8 times, the gross output of the branches which produce the means of production increases 3.3 times.

For the construction of electric power stations the plan foresees the construction of 42 central power stations (Dnieper hydroelectric station, Svir' hydroelectric station, peat power station at M. Visher, brown-coal station in Bobriki, Zuevsk power station in the Donbas, etc.). This enormous construction must increase the quantity of producing electric power from 5 billion kilowatts per hour to 22 billion kilowatts per hour at the end of the five year plan.

For ferrous metallurgy construction is proposed for new powerful metallurgical plants (Magnitogorsk, Tel'bes, Dnieper, Krivoi Rog, etc.). The construction of new plants and reconstruction of existing ones must bring the output of iron from 3.5 billion tons to 10 billion tons in 1932/33.

For coal large mine construction is projected in such places as the Donbas, Urals, Kuzbas and the Moscow basin, and coal extraction must be brought from 35 billion tons in 1927/28 to 75 billion tons in 1932/33.

Reconstruction and the construction of new plants in the area of *machine building* (automobile plant, tractor plants in Stalingrad and in the Urals, Sverdlovsk heavy machine building plant, Rostov agricultural machine building plant, tool-making plants, etc.) give the possibility of making the 3.5 increase in the gross output of the machine building industry, and a fourfold increase in the output of agricultural machine building.

For the chemical industry projected is the construction of chemical combines (Berezniki, Moscow phosphate combine, in the Donbas, etc.), and the production of chemical fertilizers in 1932/33 reaches more than 8 million tons versus 175,000 tons in 1927/28.

e) The significant increase in the projected rate of economic development of the Soviet Union in comparison with all capitalist countries will by the end of the five year plan change definitely the place of the USSR in world production: In iron the USSR will move from sixth to third place (after Germany and the United States), in coal, from fifth to fourth place (after the United States, England and Germany).

2. The conference decrees, secondly, that the general growth of the national economy is foreseen by the five year plan in the direction of the *decisive growth of the socialist sector* in town and countryside at the expense of the capitalist elements of the national economy, that is apparent from the following data:

a) Changes in the structure of the basic funding (in percentage of the total at the end of the year):

Sectors	1927/28	1932/33
State—Socialist	51.0	63.6
Cooperative—Socialist	1.7	5.3
Private	47.3	31.1

b) Corresponding to this, changes in the percentages of gross output in the socialist sector (in percentage):

	1927/28	1932/33
For industry	80	90
For agriculture	2	15
For retail turnover	75	91

Special shift is given to the construction program of the socialist sector (sovkhozes and kolkhozes) in agriculture. The growth of sown area of the socialist sector in agriculture reaches 26 million hectares of sown area in 1933, consisting of 17.5 percent of the total sown area, and secures by 1933 (from the harvest of 1932 when the socialist sector consists of 13 percent of the entire sown area) 15.5 percent of the gross output and 43 percent of the commodity output of grain. The individual sector in agriculture ends its numerical growth as a consequence of the projected population increase, drawn into the socialist sector, to 20 million souls, and the state sovkhozes (old and new) will give from the harvest of 1932 the output of no less than 34 million centners of commodity grain, and the kolkhozes, no less than 50 million centners, comprising 84 million centners, i.e., more than 500 million puds of commodity grain.

c) The most important indicators of the growth of forming cooperatives are given in the comparisons below:

	1927/28	1932/33
Share of the gross output of kolkhozes	1.0%	11.4%
Share of output of small cooperative industry in the entire output of small industry	19.4%	53.8%
Cooperatives of commodity turnover	60.2%	78.9%
Number of farms united into agricultural cooperatives	9.5 mil. (37.5% of all farms)	23.58 mil. (85% of all farms)
Number (in millions of shareholders) of consumers in cooperative population		
In the town	8.7 mil.	16.5 mil.
In the village	13.7 mil.	31.8 mil.

This significant increase of the socialist elements in the entire national economy, in production and commodity trade during the development of the network of machine tractor stations and the extensive practice of contracts, which brings in 85 percent of the grain by the end of the five year plan, means the strengthening of the leading role of the workers' class and creates a new form of alliance between town and country, leading to the massive restructuring of agriculture on the basis of the highest technology and collectivization.

3. The conference decrees, thirdly, that:

a) national income grows at current prices from 24.4 billion rubles in 1927/28 to 49.7 billion rubles, i.e., at 103 percent. This gives an annual growth in national income at more than 12 percent, i.e., at a rate of four times the prewar growth of the national economy and sharply surpassing the rate of any capitalist country.

b) *the social structure* of the national income is characterized above all by the rise of the real wages of industrial workers at 71 percent by the end of the five year plan, and the percentages in income of the entire workers' class, in relation to the entire income of the national economy, rises from 32.1 to 37 percent. The incomes of the entire rural population grow to 67 percent at the end of the five year plan with a decrease, in connection with the increased growth of industry, from 49.8 to 42.5 percent in the percentages of these incomes in the entire national income.

c) *the growth of the total budget* (net) is characterized by the fact that the total sum of the budget in the upcoming five year plan consisted of 51 billion rubles versus 19 billion in the previous five years (a growth of 166.7 percent). In relation to the national income in 1932/33 the budget consists of 30.9 percent versus 25.9 percent in 1928/29. This budget growth gives the possibility, side by side with the strengthening of defense capability, to increase fourfold (393 percent) the financing of the national economy for the upcoming five year plan in comparison with the previous five years, the possibility to raise the social-cultural expenditures almost threefold (276 percent).

d) the five year plan foresees a significant rise in both *commodity* and *currency reserves.*

II

Proceeding from the above-enumerated data on the five year plan and taking account of the fact that the plan makes complete provision for:

a) maximum development of production of the means of production as the basis for the industrialization of the country;

b) decisive strengthening of the socialist sector in town and countryside at the expense of capitalist elements in the economy, involving the millions-strong peasant masses in socialist construction on the basis of cooperative community and collective labor, and aid of every sort to the individual holdings of poor and middle peasants in the struggle against kulak exploitation.

c) overcoming the excessive backwardness of agriculture with respect to industry and a basic solution of the grain problem;

d) a significant rise in the material and cultural level of the working class and the toiling masses in the countryside;

e) strengthening the leading role of the working class on the basis of the development of new forms of union with the basic masses of the peasantry;

f) strengthening of the economic and political positions of the proletarian dictatorship in its struggle against class enemies both inside and outside the country;

g) an economic and cultural advance in the national republics and in backward raions and oblasts;

h) a significant strengthening of the country's defense capability;

i) a major step forward in realizing the party slogan: Overtake and surpass the advanced capitalist countries in the technological and economic spheres,

The conference resolves to approve the five year plan of the State Planning Commission in its optimal version, as confirmed by the Council of People's Commissars of the USSR, as a plan that fully accords with the directives of the Fifteenth Party Congress.

III

The execution of the five year plan, which represents a program of large-scale socialist advance, entails the overcoming of immense difficulties of both an internal and external character. These difficulties result from the strenuous goals of the plan itself, which are conditioned by the country's technical and economic backwardness, from the complexity of the task of reconstructing the many millions of scattered peasant holdings on the basis of collective labor, and finally, from the circumstances of the capitalist encirclement of our country. These difficulties are compounded by the intensification of the class struggle and the resistance of the capitalist elements that are inevitably being squeezed out by the growing advance of the socialist proletariat.

It is possible to overcome these difficulties only by decisively improving work quality and labor discipline in all branches of the economy. Reducing the cost of industrial production by 35 percent over the course of the next five years; reducing the cost of construction by 50 percent; raising the productivity of industrial labor by 110 percent; raising agricultural crop yields by 35 percent; expanding the sown area by 22 percent; unfailing fulfillment of the program for kolkhoz and sovkhoz construction; a resolute struggle against absenteeism and laxity in production; providing industry and agriculture with the necessary managerial cadres and the creation of new cadres of red specialists from among the ranks of the working class; finally, reinforcement of the planning and regulatory principle in the economic system—such are the elementary conditions of a general economic nature that are necessary for overcoming the difficulties in fulfilling the five year plan.

The conference considers it necessary to point out that it will be possible to overcome these difficulties and carry out the five year plan only on the basis of a vast increase in the activism and organization of the toiling masses in general and of the working class in particular, on the basis of involving by all possible means the millions-strong masses of the working class in socialist construction and in managing the economy, on the basis of the development by all possible means of socialist competition and of a powerful development of self-criticism from below, by the millions-strong masses, directed against bureaucratic distortions in the state apparatus.

The difficulties of the period of socialist reconstruction, particularly in conditions of intensification of the class struggle, inevitably give rise to waverings among the petty bourgeois strata of the population, which are reflected among certain segments of the working class and even in the ranks of the party. These waverings, which reflect the influence of petty bourgeois elements, find expression in departures from the general party line in fundamental questions, and above all in the question of the rate of socialist industrialization, in the question of unleashing a socialist advance against the kulaks and against capitalist elements in general, and in the question of strengthening in every way the socialist forms of economic organization in the countryside.

In this connection, the greatest danger within the party in the given circumstances is the right deviation, as the expression of an outright repudiation of the leninist policy of the party, as the expression of a frankly opportunistic surrender of leninist positions under pressure from the class enemy. Only a merciless rebuff to all manner of waverings in the carrying out of the general bolshevik line, whose implementation signifies strengthening the leading role of the working class, can assure the solution of the tasks of socialist construction posed by the five year plan.

The conference expresses its firm conviction that the party will deliver a crushing rebuff not only to the right deviation, but also to any other conciliatory sentiments with respect to deviation from the leninist line.

The party, at the head of the working masses, is moving ahead with confidence along the path of accomplishing the tasks of socialist reconstruction of the entire economy and is mobilizing the broadest masses of toilers under the leadership of the working class in order to surmount difficulties and implement the five year plan for economic construction.

McNeal/Gregor, Vol. 2, 359-361.
Resheniia, 21-26.

PARTY RESOLUTION. PARTY INITIATES SECOND PURGE

29 April 1929

The Sixteenth Party Conference issued a resolution to purge the party of all alien and corrupt elements. The last party purge was conducted in 1921 at the end of the Civil War. The 1929 purge ended in May 1930 and resulted in the expulsion of a reputed eleven percent of the party membership. It intended to make way for the recruitment of workers and supporters of the party line, and to expel careerists, immoral members, and, to a lesser extent, those who participated in "fractional" activities, namely those supporters of Bukharinist policies.

ON THE PURGE AND VERIFICATION OF MEMBERS AND CANDIDATE MEMBERS OF THE VKP(B)

1. Throughout its existence, the VKP(b) has conducted only one general purge, and that in 1921, at the beginning of the period of the restoration of the economy, after the Civil War had ended, a time when the party, having set itself the task of "clearing the party of noncommunist elements by means of a careful review of each member of the RKP both in terms of work performance in his given capacity and as concerns his comportment as a member of the Russian Communist Party," freed itself to a considerable extent of alien and corrupted elements, reinforced party ranks, and adopted a number of measures limiting the acceptance into the party of nonproletarian elements and assuring a more careful selection of those joining the party from the ranks of the working class and the peasantry.

2. Eight years have passed since that purge, a period during which the party has trebled in number. During this period a verification of the party members and candidates of party cells that were not associated with productive bodies was held between the Thirteenth and Fourteenth party congresses; the task of this review was above all to "clear the party of socially alien and corrupted elements, and also to clear the party of those nonworker elements that during their period of membership in the party failed to comport themselves like communists in the matter of improving the work of one or another state, economic, or other organization and who had no direct ties with the worker and peasant masses. In all, about 25 percent of the party membership was subjected to review, and of those checked, some 6 percent were dismissed from the party. A partial check of rural party cells was conducted in 1926, and an all-union census (registration) of party members and candidate members was held in 1927. So the VKP(b) fulfilled one of the conditions (point 13) belonging to the Comintern that requires:

"Communist parties of those countries where communists can conduct their work legally must produce periodic purges (reregistrations) of personnel of party organs, so as systematically to clear the party of petty bourgeois elements who are unavoidably attached to it."

Moreover, during the reconstruction period the party regularly, on a day-to-day basis, kept a check on its ranks through the work of the control commissions and by means of calling to account members of the party who had violated the party program or party discipline as well as corrupt and alien elements; as a result, 260,144 members and candidates were expelled from the VKP(b) by the control commissions or voluntarily resigned and did not figure in the reregistration between 1922 and 1 July 1928.

3. In the period of reconstruction of the country's national economy, connected with the socialist attack on the capitalist elements in town and countryside and the sharpening of class warfare, the party must quite carefully reexamine its ranks to strengthen resistance to the influence of petty bourgeois elements and to make the party more homogeneous, more battle-worthy to overcome the difficulties of the socialist reconstruction of the national economy.

The decision of the November plenum of 1928 about the most decisive purging "of alien, self-seeking, bureaucratized, and corrupt elements,"—"of elements who are using residence in the ruling party for their own mercenary and careerist aims, of elements of bourgeois-philistine degeneration that have merged with the kulaks," also has in mind the requirement adopted by the Comintern for the periodic purging (reregistration) of all members and candidates of the VKP(b) with the aim of improving the social composition, raising the political and moral level of party organizations at local levels and in the party as a whole for the most difficult stage in the struggle for socialism, at the beginning of the period of the radical socialist restructuring of the USSR national economy.

4. In addition to the unquestionable improvement in the social make-up of the VKP(b) and the reinforcement of its proletarian core (44 percent at the time of Lenin's death and 62 percent as of 1 July 1928) and in addition to the fact that the number of workers in the party more than trebled in the same period, while the number and relative importance of worker party cells also increased, the social composition of the party is still not commensurate with the demands made on the party by the tasks of the socialist reorganization of the USSR economy. Nevertheless, the existence at almost all levels of the state, economic, trade union, and even party apparatus of bureaucratized elements, and in places, particularly at the lowest levels of the apparatus in the countryside, of elements of bourgeois-philistine degeneration, elements that have merged with the kulaks and that are distorting the party class line, is slowing down the enlistment of the best proletarian elements of town and countryside into the party, is weakening the scope of socialist reconstruction, and at times sows distrust among the broad masses of workers and peasants with respect to the measures of the party and Soviet power. Alongside the hundreds of thousands of proletarians that form the firm basis of the leninist party, there has been a penetration of party ranks by petty bourgeois elements, by carriers of rot in everyday life, people who are bringing corruption to the party ranks by the example of their personal and public life, people who hold the public opinion of the workers and toiling peasants in contempt, self-seeking and careerist elements of which the party is not sufficiently ridding itself through the regular, day-to-day work by the control commissions.

The purge presently being undertaken is to clear the ranks of the VKP(b) of those elements and in so doing to improve its mobilization readiness for the socialist offensive, to further strengthen the party's authority and faith in the party, and to attract new urban proletarian and rural labor strata to its cause.

5. In posing the question of a *general purge of the party*, it is necessary to keep in mind the fact that the make-up of the working class has considerably changed in recent years. Lenin considered it necessary to prevent this soon after the purge of 1921, when he wrote:

"It is undoubtable that we constantly consider as workers those people who had the least serious schooling, in the sense of large-scale industry. More often than not the most genuine petty bourgeoisie fall into the category of workers and they suddenly are transformed into workers in the shortest amount of time. All the wise whiteguardists quite definitely take into account those circumstances that apparently the proletarian nature of our party actually does not guarantee it at all from the possible superiority, and by this in the shortest period of time, over the small-proprietary elements."

Lenin considered it necessary also to prevent the fact that "joining the workers will not offer under our conditions absolutely any difficulties for the highly intellectual and semiintellectual elements."

He insisted on the necessity of "defining the concept 'worker' thusly, so that approaching this concept are only those who indeed must in their own living conditions master the proletarian psychology. And this is impossible without many years of residence in the factory, without any kind of outside aims, and in accordance with the general conditions of economic and social life" (*Lenin*, 1922).

While the party considers its factory cells the soundest, it must, nonetheless, check not only its cells outside the production sphere and its cells in the village; it is necessary to take account of the fact that the factory party cells have also been penetrated, although to a much lesser extent than the others, by elements that are incapable of fulfilling the role of a communist vanguard, elements that are in league with the kulak sector in the village and that are propagators of petty bourgeois influence on the proletariat, elements that consider work at a factory nothing more than a means for enriching their own, individual holdings, self-seeking elements who take no active part in increasing labor discipline, elements that take an indifferent view of such counterrevolutionary phenomena as antisemitism, elements that have not made a final break with religious observances, etc.

Without a purge of the entire party, *production cells* included, the party will be unable to attract to its ranks the best elements from among the significant number of nonparty proletarian activists in order to strengthen the basic proletarian core of the party. Without such a purge of their ranks, while at the same time making a systematic effort to recruit the best proletarian elements, the factory party cells will be unable to fulfil the large and complex tasks of the new stage, tasks that require maximum homogeneity, unity, consciousness, and proletarian leninist tenacity.

6. The party must review the composition of its *village cells* with particular care and resolutely cleanse them of the alien class elements that have penetrated their ranks or of those who have identified themselves with kulak elements—with merchant, *bai* [rich Central Asian landowner] and clergy—of party members conducting a policy that repels farm laborers and poor peasants from the party, of party members who do not participate in implementing measures for the socialist reorganization of agriculture, of functionaries who are not carrying out the party's directives concerning reliance on support by the poor peasants in alliance with the mass of middle peasants, of party members for whom personal aggrandizement has taken precedence over the task of communist propaganda and organization in the village, of inveterate violators of revolutionary legality and of those who abuse power for personal gain....

7. The verification of *nonproduction party cells* following the Thirteenth Congress showed, in general, that their social composition had considerably improved. The composition of nonproduction cells by social origin proved to be: 39.4 percent workers, 36.7 percent peasants and 23.9 percent employees and others. Although the nonproduction cells are continually being reinforced with new proletarian strata that the party is promoting from the working ranks, the nonproduction cells are often the most subject to the influence of nonproletarian elements and the most cluttered with them.

Lenin repeatedly pointed out that careerists and rogues inevitably try to attach themselves to the government party. "Attaching themselves to us here and there are the careerists, adventurers who called themselves communists and swell us up, who made their way to us stealthily because the communists are now in power...." Lenin advised to clear the party of "self-seekers, adventurers", of "ostentatious party members", "of those who want only to enjoy the benefits of membership in the government party of communism, who does not want to bear the weight of selfless work on behalf of communism," "so that those who remain in the party are those politically conscious and sincerely devoted to communism," so that those who join the party are only "those conscientiously devoted to the workers' state, only the honest toilers, only the genuine representatives of the masses oppressed under capitalism" (*Lenin*). It is precisely in the nonproduction cells that the broadest possibilities exist for exploiting one's party position for mercenary motives—for speculation, protectionism, careerism, and a bureaucratic attitude toward the masses; it is precisely here that one finds cases of "rot in everyday life" that are particularly repellent to the masses; it is precisely in these cells that socially alien, bureaucratized and corrupt elements and hangers-on are doing the greatest harm to the party, it is precisely in the nonproduction cells that one finds the greatest number of former members of other parties, of people who have not adjusted in the Bolshevik Party and who have retained their ideologically alien views.

However, the faith of the broad masses of party and nonparty workers and peasants in the apparatus of the Soviet state, the economic organs, the trade unions, and the party, as well as the success of their communist work depend on the composition of these cells, on the quality of their work, on the degree of their steadfastness as party members and on their ties with the masses.

Therefore there must be a particularly thoroughgoing purge of all noncommunist, corrupted, alien, bureaucratized and self-seeking elements and hangers-on who take a functionary's view of their duties.

In so doing, it is necessary to exercise particular care with respect to those who have been advanced from the ranks of the workers, to take into account their difficulties during the initial period in mastering what are for them new forms of work, and to link the purge of nonproduction cells with a more energetic and carefully considered promotion of workers and women workers to the economic, party, and administrative apparatus.

8. In this way the verification and purge of the party ranks that is being undertaken is to make the party more homogeneous and to free it from everything noncommunist. It goes without saying that such a verification is bound to entail immense difficulties and must be carried out in a most painstaking fashion, after a comprehensive explanation of the tasks of the purge and the verification both to party members and candidate members as concerns their moral level, their ties with the masses, their active participation in the party's work, in the building of communism, etc. The party warns against turning the review into a petty and carping investigation into the personal lives of party members, against a vulgarization of the review itself, and against conducting it from a standpoint other than that of the *class tasks* of the Communist Party. The purge must pitilessly eject from party ranks all elements that are alien to the party, that constitute a danger to its successes and that are indifferent to its struggle; it must eject incurable bureaucrats and hangers-on, those who are in league with the class enemy and are helping him, those who are cut off from the party by virtue of economic and personal aggrandizement, antisemites, and covert adherents of religious cults; it must expose covert trotskyites, adherents of Miasnikov, and Democratic Centralists, and adherents of other antiparty groups and cleanse the party of them. But the purge must at the same time strengthen the work of organization, check the work of the cell, create more comradely relations between party members, increase each man's sense of responsibility for the policy and for the fate of the entire party, give impetus to raising the level of political knowledge, intensify the struggle against bureaucratism, increase the activism of all members of the organization, strengthen their ties with the masses of workers and peasants, intensify active participation in the socialist reorganization of the countryside, in the rationalization of production and management, in increasing labor discipline, in the elimination of all manner of excess, etc. Thus the verification must not assume either a narrowly inquisitorial or judicial-investigatory character. In cases where a party member qualifies for

membership in all respects except for a lack of political literacy, this circumstance must in no case serve as a basis for expelling him from the party, but must be taken into consideration with a view toward creating conditions that would enable the given party member to make good this shortcoming. While clarifying the fitness of each party member and candidate member for fulfilling party obligations, while helping to remedy their mistakes and shortcomings, and leaving within the ranks of the party all elements that are devoted to communism, the verification must at the same time determine the extent to which the leadership of the given party cell is being correctly exercised and the extent to which the mistakes and shortcomings of the party members are a reflection of that leadership.

9. The verification and purge can be successful only in case if they will be accompanied by the most extensive development of criticism and self-criticism in the local and general press, on wall newspapers, in party and open meetings with the participation of the workers and peasants. It is necessary to adopt measures to attract nonparty workers and peasants to the verification and purge. It is necessary to be led by the instruction of Lenin, who wrote:

"There are places where they purge the party, relying primarily on experience, on the directives of nonparty workers, leading their directives, taking into consideration the representatives of the nonparty proletariat. So this is the most valuable, most important thing. If we actually would *thusly* succeed in clearing the party from top to bottom, 'without respect of persons,' the victory of the revolution would indeed be large" (*Lenin*, Volume XVII, Part 1, p. 360).

"Of course, we are subordinating ourselves not to all the instructions of the masses, for the masses also sometimes yield—especially in the years of extreme backwardness, over-straining by extreme burdens and torture—they yield to moods that are not at all advanced. But in the estimation of people, in the negative relationships with "hangers-on", "commissar" and "bureaucratized elements", the instructions of the nonparty proletarian masses, and in many cases even of the nonparty peasant masses, are valuable in the highest degree. The toiling masses detect with the greatest keenness the difference between honest and devoted communists, and those who instill disgust with the person getting grain himself with the sweat of his brow and the person not having any privileges, "any path to command".

"To clear the party, taking into consideration the instructions of nonparty laborers, is a great deed. It will give us significant results. It will make the party a much stronger vanguard of the class, than before, make it the vanguard that is more closely linked with the class, and more capable of carrying it to victory over the difficulties and dangers among the masses" (*Lenin*, Volume XVIII, part 1, p. 360).

However, while enlisting nonparty workers and peasants in the extensive participation in the verification of party ranks, it is necessary:

1) not to turn open meetings in any way into an arena of demagogic discrediting of the party by elements alien to the proletariat and not to allow nonlabor and alien class elements to attend such meetings;

2) not in any way to lag behind the nonparty masses where the matter concerns the determination of the correct party line of that or another party member;

3) to use such open meetings to clarify the party line and enlist into the party ranks the best elements of the nonparty workers, farm laborer, and poor peasants.

All instructions for the necessity of careful, cautious approach to the valuable communist elements in the party and for the necessity of observing the principal approach to the purge and creating the completely comradely condition for the purge and verification, are especially related to the open meetings in which the nonparty workers and peasants attend.

10. An especially important task during the period of verification of party ranks falls to the party press. It is necessary to be concerned about the fact that the information provided about the tasks of the purge are from the very beginning completely consistent, that definite political level of discussion about purge issues is maintained the entire time, and that along with information about the facts on the merciless expulsion of all unsuitable from the party

ranks, all valuable, positive information on the work of the organization being verified is sufficiently recorded in the press. While castigating all the unsuitable elements, the press must not in any way terrorize and persecute comrades who accidently made these or other mistakes because of their lack of experience. Local control commissions must manage this information in the press about everything that appears on the verification, not tolerating the discrediting of the party because of the unsuitability and faults of its individual members.

11. The party must devote *attention to the most painstaking preparation for the purge* so that the actual process of the purge and review can be conducted in the shortest possible time. This requires the most painstaking preparatory work, elucidation of the purge's tasks in the press and at meetings, and the explanation of the demands that the party is making during the purge on every party member and candidate and, above and beyond the party mass, on those nonparty members as well who will be enlisted to help the party in the verification of, and purge of, its ranks.

Bearing in mind the mistakes made during former verifications and the fact that the checkup applies to about 1,500,000 party members and candidates scattered across an immense territory and working under the most varied conditions, the party must be particularly painstaking in preparations for this verification. The party devotes exceptional attention to the *composition of the verification commissions*, to whose ranks it must attract, side by side with the most steadfast and irreproachable party members from the Bolshevik old guard, those party members who entered the party in 1917 and during the Civil War; the party must assure the most steadfast proletarian composition of these commissions, and the composition of these verification commissions must be made widely known to the working masses ahead of time so that workers and party members can rectify in good time the composition of the verification commissions in cases where they have been made up in an unsatisfactory fashion. These commissions must painstakingly prepare for their work; they must define precisely the tasks of the verification in each separate cell, depending on its composition, work conditions, level of development, etc.

12. The present verification will only avoid committing numerous mistakes if the party approaches each party member and candidate carefully, if derogatory accusations are thoroughly checked on, if the verifying commissions are able to prevent the settling of personal accounts during the verification, to prevent group struggles and to spot squabbles, intrigues, and intentional discrediting, and if the verification is conducted on a certain principled level, avoiding pettiness and callousness of approach and stereotypes. In particular, the party considers it necessary to warn against a formal attitude toward those who are the object of the verification. It is the job of the verification commissions to take into account all features peculiar to the work of party members and candidates in production work and in institutions, the everyday and material conditions in the life of party members, features peculiar to the nationalities, and the particular work conditions of comrades who are ill, of women, agricultural workers, peasants, young people, et. al. The TsKK must constantly oversee the progress of the verification and correct mistakes as they occur in the work of the local control commissions or of the individual verification commissions.

13. Proceeding from these considerations, the joint plenum of the TsK and TsKK resolves:

1) to conduct a general purge of the party such that the verification of party ranks will be completed by the time of the Sixteenth Congress of the VKP(b). The calendar dates for the verification of particular categories of party cells (villages, production, teaching, etc.) must be set up with regard for features peculiar to their work (for the village party cells, at a time between the periods of the most important farm work; for the higher educational institutions, at times other than the examination periods, etc.). These dates must be set for each individual organization;

2) to assign to the TsKK the job of working out highly detailed guidelines for the local control commissions on procedures for selecting the verification commissions, on procedures for conducting the actual verification and purge, for registering the work experience

of the verification commissions, and for supervising their work, and to establish procedures for appealing the decisions of the local verification and control commissions, while assuring the most painstaking selection of the verification commissions and constant supervision of them on the part of the TsKK and the responsible control commissions locally (the republic, krai, and oblast commissions);

3) to conduct the purge of the party openly with respect to nonparty workers and farm labor and poor and middle peasant masses in the village;

4) to conduct an extensive preparatory campaign both in the press and at party meetings, to acquaint all party members and candidate members—as well as nonparty workers and peasants—with the tasks of the verification and purge.

McNeal/Gregor, Vol. 2, 361-367.
KPSS v rezoliutsiiakh, Vol. 4, 238-248.

PARTY REORIENTS WORK OF TRADE UNIONS THROUGH RESOLUTION ON SOCIALIST COMPETITION

9 May 1929

The Stalin leadership saw competition among workers as a way to improve labor productivity and challenge weak and inefficient management and the existing trade-union bureaucracy. The Central Committee's resolution on socialist competition was an attempt to stimulate greater worker participation in production activities and to reorient the trade unions toward directing the cause of competition instead of resisting it, and focusing on production.

RESOLUTION OF THE TSK VKP(B) ON SOCIALIST COMPETITION IN FACTORIES AND PLANTS

1. The resolution of tasks for the socialist reconstruction of the entire national economy requires the mobilization of all working class forces in the struggle for the rapid rate of industrialization of the country.

One of the most important methods of socialist education of the proletariat and the involvement of the broadest working masses in economic management must be the further and most extensive development of socialist competition in factories and plants, mines and shops, on the basis of which the most thorough development must be obtained by the creative initiative of the masses, the involvement of the more backward strata of workers in socialist construction and the advancement of the broadest cadres of new organizational forces from the proletarian ranks.

The leninist idea about the organization of competition on socialist foundations practically embodied the working class and embodies under our conditions the organization of communist subbotniks, production inspections, exchanging of views, competitive vacancies, etc., which have already played a large role in the rise of the USSR's national economy.

The Lenin komsomol lately began the successful competition of young workers, who are finding more and more active and wide support among the working masses. Begun also are the competitions expanded by "Pravda" (inspection of production meetings, exchanging of views at the "Krasnyi vyborzhets" and Kamensk paper factory and others), "Rabochaia Gazeta" (all-union coal competition), and other newspapers. It is necessary to develop also competition in factories, plants, mines and transportation enterprises that draw in the broadest masses of workers, having linked this matter with carrying out the basic practical tasks of socialist industry to reduce cost, increase labor productivity and strengthen labor discipline.

The practical tasks of competition must be: Fulfillment and exceeding of industrial financial plans, fulfillment and exceeding of planned norms to reduce cost and raise labor productivity, improving product quality, struggle with absenteeism and waste, reducing overhead expenditures, achieving exemplary production discipline, and active carrying out of technical refinement and rationalization of production with the extensive attraction of worker inventiveness.

2. The decisive condition for achieving these tasks and real economic results of competition is the conscious and active participation of the working masses, as well as the most active participation of specialists in competition at the enterprise and in the shop. For this, all the calls and decisions about participating in competition must proceed without fail through general meetings of the shop and enterprise. Important is especially the initiative of the workers themselves in the organization, development and consolidation of the results of competition. It is necessary decisively to fight against any attempts to regulate bureaucratically and to introduce into diagrams, established from above, the various forms of competition advanced by the experience of the masses. It is also necessary to warn all organizations against the danger of turning competition into a ceremonial exchange of views of organizations without the active participation of the masses. Leadership of competition must be accomplished by trade union organizations.

From the side of trade unions and all factory and plant organizations must be rendered all kinds of support to the initiative of workers in the development of socialist competition. All cultural work of the masses in clubs, red corners, communities, etc. must be brought to bear to competition. It is necessary to consolidate the results of the all-union inspection of production meetings, to use to the maximum those forms of mass involvement of workers in increasing labor productivity that are advanced by life and experience (exemplary brigades, improvement groups, interplant and intershop exchange of views, etc.), and to make them wait for all other factories and plants.

The basic standard for the success of competition at each enterprise is the achievement of practical results in the area of increasing labor productivity and reducing production cost in a given shop, enterprise, trust, etc., and also such consolidation of these achievements through rational measures and technical completion that secures the further increase in labor productivity.

3. It is necessary to introduce encouraging measures for the best enterprises, shops, groups of workers, specialists, and individual workers. The VSNkh and NKPS proposes in agreement with the VTsSPS to allocate a special fund to reward for the best satisfaction of the material and cultural needs of male and female workers, and to establish various forms of public encouragement: Outstanding list, honorary certificate, labor banner, transfer from one shop to another shop and from one enterprise to another, etc.

4. The Soviet and party press must organize extensive and thorough illumination of competition in factories and plants, mobilizing the attention of the masses on the vital experience of the best enterprises, pushing those who lag behind, and organizing public accounting and control of achieved results. The entire press, especially the factory and plant press, must place questions about the organization of socialist competition in the center of its work.

5. On the basis of experience of competition in industrial enterprises what must be widely shown is competition in sovkhozes and kolkhozes, cooperatives and soviet institutions, schools and hospitals, etc. Party organizations with the active participation of trade unions and komsomols must render support to the development of these types of competition, having secured the general leadership of this matter while taking into account those who here have the peculiarities and mass practice in socialist competition.

KPSS v rezoliutsiiakh, Vol. 4, 264-266.

DECREE. MACHINE TRACTOR STATIONS AS MAJOR FORCE IN COLLECTIVIZATION

5 June 1929

Machine Tractor Stations were seen as a means of introducing modem technology in the countryside and linking this technology with large collective farms. They also represented a means of exercising control over the kolkhozes. The state-run MTSs received 20 percent of the harvest for their services and prevented concealment of harvests from MTS personnel. The MTS concept originated in the Shevchenko state farm in the Ukraine, where its founder, Markevich, publicized its successes and equated large-scale agriculture to industrial production.

RESOLUTION OF THE COUNCIL FOR LABOR AND DEFENSE ON THE ORGANIZATION OF MACHINE TRACTOR STATIONS

While noting the positive results of the work of the machine tractor station in the Shevchenko sovkhoz, which amounts to intensifying the collectivization of peasant farms and increasing their productivity with the maximum use of tractors, the Council for Labor and Defense resolves:

1. To acknowledge the timely approach to the extensive construction of machine tractor stations as one of the fundamental paths to restructuring individual peasant farms into large collective farms.

2. To approach immediately the organization of machine tractor stations so that by the end of 1929/30 their network would occupy an area of peasant plowed field at no less than one million hectares.

3. To acknowledge the necessity of providing machine tractor stations with skilled repairmen who answer all the requirements of contemporary technology, and supplying them with materials needed for uninterrupted work.

4. To provide machine tractor stations with the needed means of automotive transportation with the goal of carrying out the complete mechanization of all the work of the machine tractor stations, and of freeing fodder, which is expended for the sustenance of working cattle, and using this fodder for the expansion of productive cattle breeding.

5. To link closely the organization of machine tractor stations with the plan to construct soviet and collective farms and carrying out this organization as the first priority in those regions where significant expansion of sown area is taking shape and where the lack of draught animals and peasant inventories delays the development of agriculture. Under this machine tractor stations must be organized as the first priority in the regions of the most developed construction of collective farms.

6. To reserve for the newly organized machine tractor stations in the plan for the supply of tractors in 1929/30 not less than 5,000 tractors with the total power capacity of 100,000 horsepower per pulley.

7. To establish that in the region of the activity of the machine tractor stations that credit be permitted only for those peasant farming activities and those agricultural operations which cannot be served by machine tractor stations.

8. To acknowledge the necessity to organize a joint-stock company under the name of "All-Union Center of Machine Tractor Stations" (VTsMTS) for carrying out the planned program to construct machine tractor stations and operating them.

The basic task of the named company along with the farming of the land of the surrounding population is the application of all measures necessary to increase the general level of agronomy in the operating regions of the machine tractor stations and the extensive transformation of individual peasant farms into large socialist mechanized farms.

9. To include in the composition of the founders of the named joint-stock company the people's commissars for agriculture of the union republics, USSR Supreme Council of the

National Economy, USSR People's commissariat for foreign and domestic trade, All-Union council and republic centers of collective farms, All-Union council of cooperative farms, Union of unions of agricultural cooperatives, Sel'skii gospodar', Khlebotsentr, Sel'skosoiuz, the joint-stock company "Sel'khozsnabzhenie", Sakharotrest, Zernotrest, Ukrsovkhozob' edinenie, Gossel'sindikat, and the joint-stock company "Soiuzkhleb".

10. To determine 50 million rubles as the prescribed capital for the joint-stock company "All-Union center of machine tractor stations".

11. To acknowledge it absolutely compulsory to attract, along with the means of the state and cooperatives issued for the establishment of machine tractor stations, the means of the peasant population being served by these stations. The forms and scale of attracting the means of the peasants must be determined simultaneously with the development of a plan to expand the network of stations. Under this must be established a different scale for the participation of individual groups of peasant farms, depending on their economic capacity.

12. In cases when machine tractor stations are being worked out at soviet farms, the fundamental task of which is the farming of peasant fields, the corresponding soviet farms are subject to transfer to the All-Union center of machine tractor stations.

13. To establish the composition of the bureau for organizing the All-Union Center of machine tractor stations at five members.

14. To commit the organizational bureau of the All-Union center of machine tractor stations, together with representatives from the union republics under the USSR government, All-Union council of collective farms and All-Union council of agricultural cooperatives, to develop in two weeks' time on the basis of the present resolution a draft statute on the All-Union center of machine tractor stations and to introduce it for approval by the Council for Labor and Defense.

15. To commit the organizational bureau of the All-Union center of machine tractor stations to offer the Soviets of the largest proletarian centers (Moscow, Leningrad, Khar'kov, Rostov, etc.) a proposal to join the staff of companies of the All-Union center of machine tractor stations.

Resheniia, 74-75.

MILITANT GODLESS LEAGUE REINVIGORATED
E.M. IAROSLAVSKY'S SPEECH AT SECOND ALL-UNION CONGRESS
11 June 1929

The first congress of the League of the Militant Godless was held in 1924. By 1929, the Party considered religion and the church as an obstacle to the building of socialism during the Five Year Plan, and lent encouragement to the League. The League grew from less than half a million in 1929 to more than five million within the following three years. E.M. Iaroslavsky, the league's founder and a highly visible party leader, gave the league the party's endorsement in his speech at the opening session of the second congress.

COMRADE IAROSLAVSKY'S SPEECH AT THE OPENING OF THE SECOND ALL-UNION CONGRESS OF THE MILITANT GODLESS

Comrades. Four years ago several dozens of people of the active of the militant godless met in Moscow for the first congress of the league of the militant godless. This was not really the first congress of the league because the league had not yet been formally organized. These were primarily the so-called friends of the newspaper "Militant Godless". Since that time, we worked on this most difficult field of the ideological front, in this most difficult field of the class struggle, in the environment of restoring the national economy.

Now we are beginning to work in another environment. We began to work in the environment when the entire country, the entire conscious masses of workers and peasants, are transferring to the socialist restructuring of our entire economy. We need to glance back to correct these mistakes which we made. We cannot boast of very great success on the antireligious front. There are many reasons for this: Here is that obstacle that we ourselves do not have much systematic experience for such a struggle, because our struggle, the struggle of communists in the country of the proletarian dictatorship against church and religion, is being waged for the first time, and to a significant degree it differs from the antireligious struggle in the West. Our struggle also differs from the antireligious struggle which the enlightened revolutionaries of the Great French Revolution waged against the pope and church. Our struggle is waged in a different environment, in other forms, and by different methods of struggle. We also did not have many trained antireligious cadre. In the period of the underground struggle, we devoted least attention to this field of the front. Before us stood more urgent tasks, requiring more urgent expenditure of resources and therefore to a significant degree place this aspect of the work to the side.

It was another matter when the working class in the Soviet state became the ruling class, when it had to take a hand itself in separating schools from the church and in uprooting the ideological and social roots of religion.

So it was at this difficult stage that we made a whole series of mistakes. One of these mistakes is of organizational procedure. On this we will need to work in detail at the congress. We did not decide to create a centralized league, and due to the weakness of leadership in the local areas, and organizations acted in a disunified manner. Among the antireligious there was little of any kind of wavering of ideas and organizations that weakened the scope of work. But we undoubtedly had mistakes in the application of methods and form of antireligious propaganda.

Our congress will have to discuss all these questions and it will have to correct all these. We must keep in mind that we are entering a period, a period which is an assault against capitalist elements, and we will have violent resistance from the exploiting elements of the country. We know from the experience of the history of all countries and nations, that these capitalist elements find their own support, also their ideological expression in the activity of church and sectarian organizations. In our country there exist a whole series of survivors and remnants of different economic relationships, not socialist, there exist remnants of the undefeated exploiting classes, there exists the obscurantism of religious ideology rooted in centuries. This ideology is tenacious, and we will need to expend no small amount of resources in the struggle to overcome it. This is work that is not just for one decade. Those who think that this can be done by any suggestion, by any measures or administrative pressure, does not understand neither the essence of this religious ideology nor any way of uprooting this ideology.

Our league, the league of the militant godless, this is a somewhat special organization, a somewhat voluntary society. This is an organization which places before itself the task of antireligious propaganda, the struggle on the ideological front. Here without a strong marxist purpose, without strong scientifically proven marxist methods of the struggle, one can make a whole series of mistakes, can fall into both anarchic radicalism and liberal enlightenment, can fall into such a situation which will not have anything at all to do with scientifically presented antireligious propaganda. Therefore we need to consider all those comrades whom we are uniting in the league of the militant godless, and we are uniting primarily workers and peasants, so as to educate these comrades in scientific, marxist-leninist, scientific-materialist understanding of socialist relationships, of relationships among people, among classes. This is one of the most difficult tasks. Of course, we do not at all think that antireligious propaganda can be conducted only by highly educated people, by people who have graduated from a large learned school. We need, on the contrary, to make the masses our agitators and propagandists—the masses of workers and peasants. But any kind of antireligious propaganda requires a definite amount of knowledge, definite study of the questions. There are certain comrades who think that all this can be successful by feeling, impulse, special pressure and such comrades can easily make and will make a whole series of mistakes. Therefore our task consists of so directing the work of the league of the militant godless, so that each understands that he is not at all a member of some self-sufficient organization. It is necessary that none of the members of our society breaks away from these general tasks of socialist reconstruction, that advance our party, Soviet power, the entire working class to the conscious part of the laboring peasantry.

Comrades, we will have to pull out from these masses new cadre of workers. This is very difficult, but we will achieve this. We have very few people trained for this, and we lost many during this period. We recently lost one of the most educated antireligious marxists—Comrade Skvortsov-Stepanov, who possessed extensive educated knowledge and keen agitation talent, and the talent of a publicist. His scientific articles are valuable, as are his small brochures and pamphlets, and his heated, interesting, deeply penetrating revolutionary speeches. We lost such a profound expert in religious ideology in professor Reismer, we lost two serious experts on the East, profoundly educated people who knew the East like none of us—Narimanov and Vol'tman-Pavlovich. We lost the most educated natural scientist, the dear lecturer of Moscow and other lecture-halls, Comrade Poniatskii. We lost and recently are losing almost every week, each month on the front of the antireligious struggle, many rank-and-file, workers, peasants, communists, komsomol members, whom the kulaks and other elements, undoubtedly connected in one way or another with various white-guard, monarchist, and other antisoviet organizations, killed because of antireligious propaganda. We lost in the East where the woman tries to free herself from the yoke of century-old religious traditions, where she tries to throw off the iashmak, which hides her from the sunlight and public light of the woman-worker, social-peasant, who severs the paths of religious and family slavery in order to join free public life.

Comrades, I propose to honor and remember these comrades, let's stand. (All stand. The orchestra plays "You Fall Victim To").

There is no doubt, comrades, that our congress will devote attention not only to the laborers of our country, but it will concern itself with great attention to our class enemies not only in our country but in other countries. We are really stepping forward as the bearers of a special antireligious, godless morality. Of course, some of our class enemies will laugh at such a comparison: Godless morality, even perhaps godless morality! Can even the godless speak about morality? Are they really not the destroyers of all morality? But it is worth comparing the two worlds—the godless world of the USSR and other countries—the world of the religious leaders of the capitalist classes, reactionary organizations which now rule five-sixths of the earth's globe, in order to see that such a combination of "godless morality" is better than legitimate. As a matter of fact, do we have in capitalist countries what transpires on five-sixths of the earth's globe where there are not soviets, where the red banner does not wave? In the past years after the imperialist war, we see all the more worsening position of the broad masses of the working class, even taking away those minimal victories which were achieved by the bloody struggle of the workers. We see that such a victory of the working class as the eight-hour work day is being taken away. The laboring masses are being condemned to a starving existence. In a whole series of countries defenseless people are being killed—workers and peasants are spilling their blood in Morocco and Syria and in a whole series of other countries—in China, Indonesia, India, on the streets of Berlin, Warsaw and in other cities, blood being spilled for the defense of capitalist morality—so this is what we have on five-sixths of the earth's globe.

If we compare this with the fact that in such a democratic country as the USA there is being revived the process of the middle ages against the adherents of Darwin; if we take the fact that in Italy Mussolini is reestablishing the authority of the pope, that the current inquisitors of the workers—the fascists—are fraternizing with the descendants of the inquisitors of the middle ages, the pope, and his servants; if we take the fact that the social-democrats are supporting the concordat in Germany, that the social-democrats are competing with others in the elections to the church council; if we take the fact that trade unions are opening and closing their congresses with holy prayer services; if we compare all these and take the Country of the Soviets, where the working class and toling masses are constructing a bright world of labor fraternity literally from filth and blood, where they are uprooting the roots of inequality and where they are struggling against all kinds of possibilities for a blood-spilling war, where they are the pioneers of total universal disarmament. If we compare these two countries—the country of the godless and the countries where religion, kings, presidents, and others rule—then I think it will be clear to each on whose side is justice, whither must we strive to achieve the attention, the sympathies of the broadest masses of workers and peasants. Such morality as is the morality of workers and peasants is for us, for the godless, in a country where is forged new moral values, which have nothing in common with religious morality, saying that the law of this morality is that which is good for laborers, defends the interests of the working class, the interests of which in the final analysis are the general interests of all mankind.

Comrades, we are cultivating among our godless the sense of internationalism, the deep international fraternal union among laborers, at a time when our class enemies who strut their own morality, stir up one nation against another, at a time when they are ready to lynch a negro on the streets of any American city, shoot a working negro because he entered a railroad car, a compartment which is created only for while rulers.

We are cultivating this deep sense of international solidarity and we are proud that our league is gaining greater and greater influence in other countries. Through these comrades attending from other countries, we extend our brotherly ardent greetings to all the workers and laborers of all countries who are leading the struggle. (*Applause*). We ask them to tell workers in all countries that our internationalism is not internationalism in the platonic sense, we are ready actually to show that the interests of the laborers of all countries are our interests, that their suffering, their pain are our suffering and our pain, that their happiness is our happiness. We ask them to say that our tasks consist of uniting millions of laborers, independently of their nation, their race, into one worldwide fraternal union.

We together with them will storm the land strongholds of capitalism and stronghold of heaven.

We are against god, we are against capitalism. (*Applause*). We are for socialism, for the worldwide union of laborers, we are for the Communist International. We are for such a structure that destroys the possibility of any kind of war, that puts an end to all kinds of exploitation of man by man. We are for the socialist revolution. (*Applause*).

Pravda, 12 June 1929, 1.

★

FIRST FORMAL SOVIET VIEW OF MODERN WARFARE. ORDER OF THE REVOLUTIONARY MILITARY COUNCIL OF THE USSR. FIELD SERVICE REGULATIONS OF 1929. FIRST SECTION, CHAPTER I

21 June 1929

The Soviet military published on 21 June 1929 its first formal codification of the role of the military in modern warfare. It published its views in the Field Service Regulations of 1929 to replace the provisional regulations of 1925, which merely expanded upon Tsarist military precepts. The new regulations emphasized the necessity of the offensive maneuver, to include outflanking the enemy and attacking with large concentrations in many directions. They also emphasized the role of political education and indoctrination, and the importance of coordination among all service arms. Each service arm had a defined role, primarily in support of the infantry. Chemicals were to be used only if the enemy used them first. The two documents below are the order, signed under the signature of Konstantin Voroshilov, the People's Commissar for Military and Naval Affairs, that established the Field Service Regulations, and the first of 20 chapters of the Regulations.

ORDER OF THE REVOLUTIONARY MILITARY COUNCIL OF THE USSR

21 June 1929

No. 154, Moscow

I. To put into operation the announced "Field Service Regulations of the RKKA" (PU 29). To cancel the "Temporary Field Service Regulations of the RKKA, Part II" published in 1925.

II. The Field Regulations consist of instructions about the leading and fighting of military formations (regiment, division, corps).

III. The Regulations do not give templates and it is necessary to apply them, while firmly adapting to the situation.

IV. The contemporary battle requires of the Red Army:

1) class political education, which is the foundation of the healthy political state and morale of a unit and a token of the revolutionary steadfastness of the army and its soldiers;

2) the attempt to concentrate all forces and means for an attack in the decisive sector;

3) construction of a battle plan that takes material possibilities into account;

4) operational and tactical mobility of forces, which are the main quality of the fighting capacity of the army; on the training of mobility and flexibility of the forces must be rendered the most intent attention of the entire command staff during army training;

5) bold, swift assault and expert maneuver; advancing operations of forces must be distinguished by rapidity, pressure, and fearlessness;

6) sustained and active defense; wide enveloping movements and breakthroughs of the enemy are opposed by energetic and sustained resistance of firepower which secures the decisive counterattack of attack groups;

7) preciseness and rapidity of given orders, clarity in the presentation of battle tasks and undeviating decision in putting the adopted decision into practice;

8) courage and decisiveness of each commander and soldier, based on extensive initiative, in uniting with revolutionary activity and constant readiness to assume the responsibility for a bold decision;

9) constant work of the command staff in the area of training in the army of extensive independence, persistence, and undeviating confidence in its own weapons.

V. The means of chemical attack, the instructions for which are in the Field Service Regulations, will be used by the Worker and Peasant Red Army (RKKA) only in that case when our class enemies use them first.

VI. While carrying out their battle tasks, commanders and soldiers—the conscious sons of the Worker and Peasant state—must remember their responsibility before the laborers for entrusting them with the great deed of defending the worker and peasant state.

Polevoi Ustav RKKA (1929), 7-8.

FIELD SERVICE REGULATIONS

FIRST SECTION

MANAGEMENT OF SERVICES

CHAPTER I.

GENERAL FUNDAMENTALS

1. *The Red Army* is the instrument of the proletarian state—the first and only fatherland of laborers in the world.

It is called upon to secure and defend from all attempts from enemies against socialism and the proletarian revolution the independence of the USSR and to protect socialist construction, peaceful labor, and the freedom of workers and peasants.

While defending the USSR, it, by the very fact of its existence, furthers the struggle of the oppressed laboring masses of the entire world for their liberation.

The Red Army is powerful by its class consciousness, selfless devotion to communism, connection with and support of the widespread worker and peasant masses, constant combat readiness, discipline, and the ability to use completely its arms for the crippling, crushing defeat of the armed forces of the enemies of the Soviet Union.

2. *The Red Army*, while defending the interests of laborers, *must be ready for bold and decisive actions* directed against the destruction of the armed forces of class enemies. These actions, arising from a series of operations, by way of engaging on the wide front army masses to inflict defeat on the enemy by a series of battles of individual military formations and units.

3. *The battle* is the most decisive means for achieving the objective of an operation. The battle is achieved by the defeat and destruction of the enemy by way of its physical extermination or taking prisoners and seizure and extermination of its technical means of war. In addition, the battle, during the energetic deployment of operations, is achieved by the disintegration of the organizational unity of the enemy's army and moral steadfastness.

Any battle has the goal of inflicting defeat on the enemy, but *only a decisive offensive in a decisive sector*, completed by persistent pursuit, *brings the complete destruction of its forces and means.*

Defense can only weaken the enemy, but not destroy it. To inflict a decisive defeat on the enemy, it is necessary to attempt to end the defensive battle by passing, at the appropriate moment, to the offensive.

4. *Military cohesion and the political steadfastness of its units, disorganization (disintegration) of the military might of the enemy and attracting to the side of the proletarian revolution the worker and peasant masses of its army the population in the theater of operations, are the most important conditions for the victory over the enemy.* This is achieved by tireless political work, being organized and led both in the army and outside it by the political departments of the military formations.

The entire command staff at all levels and all organs of military management are obligated to secure all the necessary conditions for the extensive and continuous expansion of political work in the RKKA and to leave at the disposal of the political organs and bureaucracy all the necessary means for the successful strengthening of the army's combat readiness.

5. *Success in battle* is best secured:

a) by the political training of the forces, firm decisiveness of all soldiers, based on revolutionary will and victory;

b) by the correct determination of the nature of operations and deployment of the enemy's forces along the front and in depth;

c) *by the clear presentation of the battle's objective and expedient organization of operations*, based on the careful calculation of the technical means and men, corresponding to their characteristics and situation;

d) *by the readiness to bear responsibility for bold decision*; the threat merits not those who in attempting to destroy the enemy suffer failure, but those who, fearing responsibility, at the necessary moment do not throw all their forces and means for achieving victory;

e) by the training of troops in the use of technical means and by the rapid mastery of new methods of war that are caused by the improvement of technical means or the appearance of new ones;

f) by the careful guarantee of operations by reconnaissance, by observation, and by protection in order to determine at the same time changes in the situation during the course of the battle;

g) by the uninterrupted work of the rear directed toward the satisfaction of the needs of the troops for all types of allowances and both the evacuation of the sick and wounded and property not needed by the troops.

6. *It is impossible to be powerful equally everywhere; for ensuring success it is necessary*, by way of the appropriate regrouping of forces and means, *to achieve decisive superiority over the enemy in the decisive sector*, while leaving to secondary areas fewer forces sufficient only for containing the enemy. The activity of units, which are operating in secondary sectors, above all contains the enemy and can bring the enemy to make an error relative to the sector of the main attack and by this contribute to the freedom of operation of the units in the main sector.

7. *Surprise* has a stunning affect on the enemy. Therefore all operations of troops must be completed with the greatest secrecy and rapidity. *The rapidity of operations*, in combination with organization, *is the basic token of success in battle*. Troops, capable of reacting quickly to orders received and changes in situation, able to get up quickly from rest, complete quickly field operations, deploy quickly in battle formation, and quickly attack and pursue the enemy, can always count on success.

Surprise achieves the unexpected, for the enemy, use of new means and new methods of war.

8. It is not enough simply to concentrate superior forces and means to crush the enemy. *What is necessary in depth of the developing battle are the cooperation of the arms of the services* operating in one sector and the *coordination of the operations* of units in different sectors.

Under contemporary means of firepower and in depth of the battle formation, success is achieved by the intensive exertion of units operating logically from the depth of the battle formation in full cooperation and coordination and inflicting the defeat on the enemy's units, by way of the logical neutralization of the deployment of its battle formation. Achieved success develops up to the complete destruction of the enemy. The personal initiative of commanders at all levels and rank-and-file soldiers, appearing in the sector of the general target of operations, has decisive importance during this. The greatest exertion of all the forces in pursuing the beaten enemy up to its complete destruction, does not give the enemy the possibility of recovering for new resistance. Success is decisively used also in that case when it is achieved not in that sector where it is intended.

9. *While organizing operations of the troops for battle, the commander studies the attributes and possibilities of each arm of the services* individually and, corresponding to their attributes and possibilities, uses the nature of their task and their situation.

Infantry is the fundamental arm of the services whose victory or defeat is determined to a significant degree by the fate of the battle. All the remaining arms of the services contribute to the infantry in fulfilling its military objectives. The infantry possesses the capability of finishing the battle by hand-to-hand fighting, while preparing it with its own means of firepower, of seizing the military means of the enemy, and of holding on to the terrain, while arranging for it with its own forces. The combination of movement and the attack of men with the powerful firepower of all the means of firepower is the fundamental contemporary operation of the infantry.

Artillery is by the fact of its firepower the most powerful arm of the services. By defeating men, destroying or suppressing the firepower means of the enemy, both in the open and under cover, and warfare with the enemy's air forces, artillery assists infantry (and calvary) in fulfilling the military objectives with the least amount of casualties.

Strategic calvary is by the fact of its mobility is most adaptable to the combination of firepower with the surprise attack of masses in calvary formation on the flank and in the rear of the enemy. The contemporary weapons of the calvary allow it independently to prepare an attack and fulfill military objectives. The attack and pursuit by the calvary of the enemy's disordered infantry bring the complete destruction of the latter.

The basic assignment of the calvary is reconnaissance.

Armored forces, which can approach the enemy in earnest, assists the infantry (and calvary), while increasing its firepower. The dependency of *armored vehicles* and *armored trains* on roads and their condition limits their use. *Tanks*, capable of moving without roads and smash artificial barriers, are by the use of large numbers the most powerful means of destroying the firepower means of the enemy and men; they operate with the infantry and calvary.

Aviation assists land arms in fulfilling military objectives, while attacking the enemy's men from the air and protecting the land arms from air attack in fighting the enemy's aviation; it paralyzes the enemy's rear; it hinders the enemy's air reconnaissance; it serves the command and troops with reconnaissance, artillery spotting, and communication services; it carries out independent operational objectives.

Chemical means in contemporary warfare serves as a powerful means of defeating the enemy's men and sharply constraining its military effectiveness both on the offensive and defensive, and is used by the basic arms of services and especially the chemical arms.

Engineer troops assist the other arms of services in carrying out their objectives by equipping the terrain (such as: construction and repair of roads and bridges, technical organization of crossings, technical camouflage, carrying out especially complex fortification work, etc.) and making a situation more difficult for the enemy to use (damaging and destroying bridges and roads and constructing other obstacles).

Communications troops serve as the organizer of communications and safeguard management.

Military communication and various types of services provide for the organization of uninterrupted feeding and services to the troops.

10. The success of managing military operations of troops is achieved:

a) by the technical training of military formations in peacetime and by accomplishing such in wartime, in the spirit of single and mutual understanding;

b) by the high discipline of the troops;

c) by the constant studying of the situation and the correct evaluation of it; by a decision adopted boldly and without vacillation, and clearly expressed;

d) by the ability to study correctly the political situation;

e) by the independence of all commanders, by firmness in carrying out their assigned objectives, and by their initiative in adopting independent decisions;

f) by the cooperation of military and political leadership;

g) by the precision and rapidity of management organs and by the maintenance of uninterrupted communications;

h) by personal relations.

11. *The development of existing means of warfare proceed at a rapid rate, and new fighting means appear.* All these change the form and capability of military operations, and that is why commanders and Red Army soldiers are obligated to study carefully the appearance of new fighting means and tactical methods used by the enemy and to report through the command structure their conclusions and observations.

Commanders and political workers are obligated to use the respite between operations to produce an understanding in their units about the goal: training them in the ownership of their weapons, studying the methods of battle, political training and education.

12. The complexity and pressure of the contemporary battle, the dispersal and smashing of contemporary battle formations makes management difficult, but together with this what is persistently required is the planning and firmness of battle leadership. Under such conditions real planned leadership is carried out only upon revelation by the entire battle formation, all of the component units, right up to individual soldier, of the most strict discipline, greatest independence in achieving the established targets, and initiative.

Strong will and unbending decisiveness to achieve the established goal are the truest token of success. However upon *radical* change in the situation the previously established goal of operations can even be changed. In this case, if there is not time or not communications with the senior commander, *the commander is obligated, proceeding from* the general goal of the higher formation or the local situation and in connection with operations of neighboring units, *to adopt the bold decision in accordance with one's own starting point* (initiative).

13. *What is required from the commander for the correct accounting of the political situation in the entire work for leading the military activity of troops is*:

a) class consciousness and political preparedness, which are developed by practical leadership and the training of red army soldiers and active participation in social and political life;

b) ability to use correctly upon adopting a decision the evaluation of the political situation of party and political organs of the Red Army.

14. *The command supports combat readiness of its formation*, while achieving:

a) class consciousness of all personnel, constant readiness to sacrifice itself for Soviet power and communism, clear understanding of the goals of war, the revolutionary will for victory, courage, and persistence;

b) direct contact with and influence on subordinates; internal cohesion, discipline, and trust in commanders and political leaders;

c) the order and expertise of battle leadership; victories above all strengthen the battle readiness of the unit and trust in the commander;

d) care about provisions and maintaining the freshness of troops, existence of military reserves just before the battle and the expedient use of them in battle.

15. The most important means of strengthening discipline are: political work, training and development of the feeling of revolutionary duty, the firm observance of military order in the units, undeviating and firm requirement for observing the rules for performing military service, and the personal example of the commander and political worker.

The commander is obligated with all means to support in subordinates success, energy, and good spirits in work, to summon in them initiative and decisiveness. This is necessary both at the moment of victories and particularly in cases of military failures. In relation to those to whom befall failure, which is the consequence of occurrences unavoidable in war, the commander must show special restraint.

Polevoi Ustav RKKA (1929), 9-17.

DECREE. SOVIET GOVERNMENT EMPOWERS LOCAL COLLECTIVE FARMS WITH EXECUTIVE POWERS
21 June 1929

The Central Executive Committee and the Council of People's Commissars decreed that the republican, regional and okrug associations of collective farms should have executive powers, such as the right to distribute among their subordinate kolkhozes tractors, credits, and other resources. Prior to this, the associations played more of an advisory role in respect to local governments.

ON MEASURES TO STRENGTHEN THE KOLKHOZ SYSTEM

In connection with the growing significance of collective farming and with the aim of increasing the planning management of the industrial work of the kolkhozes and improving their economic and financial services, particularly servicing large kolkhozes, the Central Executive Committee and the Council of People's Commissars of the USSR resolve:

1. To propose to the union republic governments to reexamine the existing legislation on kolkhozes and charters for associations of kolkhozes, having taken this into account:

a) granting the right of operational and economic activity to both a group of associations and unions of kolkhozes (republic, krai, oblast, and okrug);

b) formation in kolkhoz associations of fundamental and other forms of capital at the expense of both the deposits of the members being united into the associations and special allocations in the state and local budgets, as well as at the expense of the resources of the agricultural cooperatives.

2. To establish the following procedures for supplying kolkhozes with the means of production:

a) in all-union and republic plans supplying agricultural machinery (in particular, tractors), tools and fertilizers, from both domestic production and imports, reserving the necessary amount for kolkhozes;

b) republic centers of collective farms organize supply to kolkhozes with the means of production by way of concluding contracts and agreements with the corresponding cooperative organizations and state enterprises on the basis being established by the legislation of union republics;

c) kolkhoz associations construct supply plans on the basis of requests of lower-level associations and kolkhozes; the requests must be in full conformity with production plans.

3. To establish the following procedure for the sale of kolkhoz products:

Contracts for the sale of kolkhoz products must, as a general rule, be coordinated with contracts for the supply to kolkhozes of means of production and consumer goods.

The sale of kolkhoz products must be made on the basis of contracts being concluded with cooperative organizations and state enterprises being established by legislation of union republics.

4. Production and financial plans of the kolkhoz system are formed on the basis of control figures of the national economy and are included as a component of agricultural plans. The combined production and financial plans of the kolkhoz system are entered by the All-Union Council of Collective Farms through the USSR State Planning Commission to the Council for Labor and Defense for approval.

5. While increasing the special significance for establishing the organization and management of large kolkhozes, to propose to the union republic governments to concentrate management of large kolkhozes (with 2,000 hectares and more of sown land), organization and their financing in the republic centers of collective farms. Annual production and financial plans and construction plans of these kolkhozes must especially be approved by union republic governments no later than 1 May of the preceding year. The combined

production and financial plan of these kolkhozes must be entered by the All-Union of Collective Farms through the USSR State Planning Commission to the Council for Labor and Defense no later than 1 June of the preceding year.

Comment. Plans for 1929/1930 must be approved by union republic governments no later than 1 July 1929, and a combined plan must be presented for approval by the Council for Labor and Defense no later than 1 August 1929.

6. The Council for Labor and Defense allocates a total sum of production credits for the union republics in conformity with the production plans of the system of kolkhozes. The procedure and conditions for using these credits are determined by the general contracts of the republic associations of kolkhozes with the system of agricultural credit.

7. To order the USSR People's Commissariat for Finance with the participation of the USSR Central Agricultural Bank and the All-Union Council of Collective Farms to develop a system of production credits for kolkhozes and their associations on the following bases:

a) the right to establish amounts and designation of credits for individual kolkhozes and groups of associations, as well as to shut off credits it is granted: To the republic centers in relation to the largest kolkhozes, to the krai, oblast, and okrug unions of kolkhozes in relation to the remaining kolkhozes and groups of associations, through the proper channels;

b) the amounts and time periods for credits must correspond to the production plans of the kolkhozes and their associations;

c) must be established the strictest credit discipline both in relation to the procedures for using credits and, particularly, in relation to their timely repayment.

8. With the aim of securing the stability of kolkhozes, as a socialist form of economy, by way of increasing the indivisible capital in kolkhozes, to order the USSR State Planning Commission, with the participation of union republic governments and the All-Union Council of Collective Farms, to develop no later than 15 July 1929 regulations on funds for collective farming and on indivisible capital of kolkhozes and present them to the USSR Council of People's Commissars.

9. With the aim of improving the training for kolkhozes of special cadres of qualified agronomists and technicians, to propose to the union republic governments to organize, beginning with 1929/1930, faculties of collective farming in the basic higher education agricultural institutions and branches of collective farming in the remaining higher education agricultural institutions, as well as technical colleges of collective farming.

10. While increasing special significance to raising the cultural level of members of kolkhozes and while pointing to its backwardness in comparison with the economic successes of kolkhozes, to propose to the union republic governments:

a) to develop no later than two months' time a system of measures that provides by 1929/1930 a significant growth of cultural work in kolkhozes;

b) to present in six months' time to the USSR Council of People's Commissars a report on the results of measures taken in this area.

II

11. To draft sections II and VIII of the resolution of the Central Executive Committee and Council of People's Commissars of the USSR of 16 March 1927 on collective farms (Collection of Laws of the USSR 1927, No. 15, article 161) in the following version:

"II. To acknowledge the necessity, along with the existence of the All-Union Council of Collective Farms, of organizing in the established order special republic centers of collective farms, that are endowed with the rights of organizational management, spokesmen for collective farms, and the planned coordination of their development with the general system of agricultural cooperatives and the state economy.

With the aim of increasing the significance of republic centers of collective farms, to grant them also the right of carrying out operational and economic activity".

"VIII. To acknowledge the necessity of organizing everywhere groups and higher-level associations of kolkhozes. Associations of kolkhozes have as their goal both the organizational and agricultural and production services of their own members and the carrying out of operational and economic activity for their supply and the sale of their products.

Associations of kolkhozes act on the bases of a charter, have capital, and use the rights of a legal person.

Large kolkhozes are directly subordinate to republic unions of kolkhozes".

Sobranie Zakonov i Rasporiazhenii, No. 40 (8 July 1929), Article 359, 748-750.

MIKOIAN, BREAD RATIONING INTRODUCED

27 June 1929

Bread rationing was introduced initially in February 1929 by decree and eventually extended to other goods. On 27 June 1929, A. Mikoian, People's Commissar for Trade, gave the rationale for introducing bread rationing as well as a detailed description of the status of domestic trade and supply. The editors of International Press Correspondence published extracts from the speech that are presented below. Mikoian explained that bread rationing was so successful in effecting savings in bread consumption and eliminating bread lines, that rationing would be continued. Rationing continued until 1935.

A. MIKOIAN

THE BREAD SUPPLY AND THE SOCIALIZATION OF AGRICULTURE

12 July 1929

The Causes of the Grain Difficulties

The chief cause of the difficulties is that the development of agriculture lags behind the growing demands of the towns. The basis of this phenomenon is the excessive individualism of the peasant farms and the low level of agricultural commodity production. Apart from these general causes, the present grain difficulties are a result of two elementary catastrophes: The destruction of the autumn sowings of last year over an area of six million hectares in the Ukraine and in the North Caucasus, and a drought immediately prior to the last harvest considerably reduced the results of the spring sowings. These two natural catastrophes had a considerable effect upon the course of this year's grain purchase campaign. The prospects for the bread supply in the coming year will depend upon the result of this year's harvest, which will on its part depend upon the extent of the area under seed and upon climatic conditions.

The Prospects of the New Harvest

The control figures for the present year provided for an increase of the area under grain by seven percent. The autumn and spring sowings will, in all probability, show an increase of from five to six percent, i.e., they will almost be up to standard, despite the pessimistic prophesies of the right-wingers and of the theory about the "decline of agriculture".

In this year also certain damage was done to the autumn sowings in the Ukraine. This referred to certain sorts of wheat. The extent of the damage is, however, incomparably less than it was last year. On the whole the autumn sowings have suffered very little damage. Climatic conditions in the spring and at the beginning of summer were favorable to the harvest. According to the latest report, the prospects are good. This is to be seen not only from the information of the Statistical Bureau and of the experimental stations of the Agricultural Commissariat but also from the situation of the grain market. In consequence of the good prospects, the grain prices have begun to fall rapidly in all districts recently. Unless the harvest prospects become less favorable, the new harvest will be considerably larger than that of last year and will considerably facilitate the bread supply.

The Success of the Organized Bread Distribution

The favorable influence of the system of bread purchase cards upon the bread supplies must be especially mentioned. Before the introduction of the bread cards and although at that time there was more bread on the market than at present, we had large queues before the bakers' shops. Speculators set various provocative rumors in circulation and the proletarian consumers fell into the trap. In consequence of these rumors they hoarded unnecessarily large supplies. The system of bread cards represents a guarantee that the working population will under all circumstances obtain the necessary amount of bread. Before the introduction of the new system, it was possible to argue whether it was necessary and desirable, but today the positive results of the introduction of the bread card system are that we have been able to effect considerable savings in the consumption of bread and we have abolished the queues. The opinion of the broad masses of the workers is that the system is absolutely necessary and correct. It must be pointed out that not all the owners of bread cards use them to the full, and every day there remain about from 131 to 148 tons of bread over from the supplies set aside for sale upon the bread cards. These successes have determined us to maintain the system of bread cards for the coming period, and we intend to improve the quality of the bread after the new harvest.

The Objective Role of the Difficulties is to Speed up the Socialization of Agriculture

If we analyze the grain and other food difficulties, we come to the conclusion that the pressure of these difficulties of the food supply, raises the necessity of creating a stable socialist basis for agricultural production. I fear that my statement may be interpreted as heresy, but I am convinced that if there had been no grain difficulties, we would never had raised the question of powerful collective agricultural undertakings, Soviet farms and machine and tractor stations to the same extent as we do today. Of course, in time we would have arrived at this task anyhow, but not so quickly. If we had had bread in plenty, we would never have raised so energetically the question of creating collective and Soviet agricultural undertakings. The powerful growth of our industry makes it possible for us to approach the solution of the gigantic tasks of the socialization of agriculture.

The food supply difficulties were caused by the resistance of the capitalist elements in the village and by the excessive backwardness of agriculture as compared with industry. These difficulties, however, were only intensified when the growth of industry had already created the preliminary basis for tackling the socialization of our individualized agriculture.

We often tend to underestimate the forces at the disposal of our working class. Take what questions you like, it always turns out that when we set to work with Bolshevik energy and determination, we can always accomplish more than the wildest optimists imagine possible. Remember, for instance, that at the Fifteenth Party Conference we all declared than an annual growth of industrial production from 30 to 35 percent was only possible because we were in the period of the reconstruction of our existing industries and that, afterwards, the growth would be approximately from 6 to 8 percent annually. We pointed out that the growth of production in the United States was only from 3 to 4 percent annually.

We are now three years away from the close of the period of reconstruction, and the growth of our production is still over 20 percent annually. The hidden internal reserves of our socialist system are opening up ever new possibilities of development for us.

At the end of the five year period, the Soviet agricultural undertakings alone will supply from 6 to 6 1/2 million tons of commodity grain, i.e., just about the amount we require this year in order to supply our industrial centers with bread. When we consider that the area tilled by the new Soviet undertakings of the grain trust will be from 11 to 12 million hectares by the end of the five year period and that the old Soviet farms will work an area of 7 1/2 million hectares, and when we remember that the newly formed cattle breeding association "Skotovod" will use about 4 to 5 million hectares of land for cattle breeding, then we see that our state agricultural sector (not including the numerous collective agricultural undertakings and other cooperative forms of agricultural production) alone will work 20 million hectares, the half of which will be under seed. For the moment, whilst we are about to carry out this magnificent program of the socialist organization of grain production, we are in a period of grain difficulties. When we have carried out only one half of our program, then we need not fear any difficulties.

International Press Correspondence, Vol. 9, No. 33 (12 July 1929), 721.

SOVIET GOVERNMENT WARNS OF CONSEQUENCES FOLLOWING CHINESE RAID AND SEIZURE OF CHINESE EASTERN RAILWAY

13 July 1929

Conflict with China resurfaced when forces of the Mukden Government seized sections of the Chinese Eastern Railway and arrested Soviet officials. Upon learning of the seizure by Chinese forces of the CER, Leonid Karakhan, Vice-Commissar for Foreign Affairs, warned the Mukden Government that the Soviet Union would take the appropriate action unless the forces were withdrawn, arrested officials released, order restored, and a conference convened to settle all questions. He described in great detail how the Mukden Government violated the mutual agreements of 1924. Protracted negotiations and delays ended when Soviet troops led a successful counterattack against Mukden forces in November 1929 and restoration of the status quo followed within a month.

NOTE FROM USSR PEOPLE'S COMMISSARIAT FOR FOREIGN AFFAIRS TO CHARGE D'AFFAIRES OF THE CHINESE REPUBLIC IN MOSCOW

Mr. Charge d'Affaires.

I am instructed by my government of the Union of Soviet Socialist Republics to request you to communicate the following to the Mukden government and to the national government of the Chinese Republic in Nanking:

According to reports received by the government of the USSR, on the morning of 10 July the Chinese authorities raided the Chinese Eastern Railway and seized the railway telegraph along the entire line, thus cutting telegraphic communication with the USSR; closed and sealed, without offering any reason, the Soviet trade delegation's premises and also the offices of the State trading department, the textile syndicate, the oil syndicate, and the merchant shipping department. Then the taipan of the railway (the chairman of the board of directors of the CER), Lin Yung-huan, presented to Mr. Emshanov, manager of the CER, the demand that the management of the railway be handed over to a person appointed by the taipan. When the manager of the railway, Mr. Emshanov, refused to accede to this illegal demand as a gross violation of the agreement on the provisional administration of the CER signed in Peking on 31 May 1924 and also of the agreement between the USSR government and the autonomous government of the Three Eastern Provinces of the Chinese Republic signed in Mukden on 20 September 1924, both he and the assistant manager of the railway, Mr. Eismont, were removed from their posts. They were replaced by persons appointed by the taipan. The heads of the traction and traffic departments, as well as other persons, were removed at the taipan's orders and replaced in the main by Russian white guards. Throughout the CER, the trade union and cooperative organizations of the CER workers and employees were closed and sacked, and searches and arrests carried out, more than 200 Soviet citizens in the employ of the railway being arrested. About 60 Soviet citizens, including Mr. Emshanov and Mr. Eismont, have already been expelled from China.

At the same time news was received of the concentration along the Soviet borders of Manchurian troops which have been brought into a state of combat readiness and moved right up to the border. It is reported that in addition to the Manchurian troops, Russian white guard detachments are positioned along the Soviet border that the Manchurian command intend to send across into Soviet territory.

The said actions are a most glaring and flagrant violation of the direct and unambiguous provisions of the treaties in force between the USSR and China. and these violations do not become less glaring because the taipan of the railway in his declaration himself cited the responsibility of the CER representatives as rigidly observing the treaties, while trying to mask by this citation his own clearly illegal actions.

As it is clear from the first article of the agreement on the provisional management of the CER of 31 May 1924 and from a similar first article, paragraph 6 of the Mukden agreement, all questions related to the CER are discussed and resolved by the 10-member board and the "decisions of the board enter into force if they are approved by no less than six members of the board", and the chairman of the Board is a Chinese citizen and the deputy chairman is a Soviet citizen and "together they manage the board's affairs and both sign all board documents".

Thus, the very fact the taipan published the unilateral order under his own signature alone and without the agreement of both the board and his deputy, a Soviet citizen, adds to this his act as a clear illegal nature, not to mention that this act at the root violates the principle of parity established by the treaties.

According to the third article of the same Peking agreement and article 1, paragraph 8 of the Mukden agreement, "Management of the railway lies with the manager, a citizen of the USSR and two assistant managers, from whom one must be a citizen of the USSR, and the other a citizen of the Chinese Republic. The said responsible persons are appointed by the Board and approved by the governments through proper channels".

Their rights and responsibilities are determined by the Board, which also appoints the manager and assistant managers of the various departments of the railway.

Thus, the removal of the railway manager and his replacement by the taipan's order, although temporarily, with a Chinese citizen, as well as the unilateral removal of the assistant and a series of official people of the railway violate the fundamental statutes of the 1924 agreement and at the root change the conditions for managing the railway, that were established in accordance with the agreement of the governments of the USSR and China and recorded in the existing treaties between them. This violation which in no way is justified bears a more glaring nature than that which is evident in the articles of the treaties cited above, the appointment, and, consequently, the dismissal of the said official people is the prerogative of the Board totally and it cannot be carried out by another procedure and particularly by unilateral, personal orders of the taipan. The taipan in his declaration cites the order given by him to the manager Mr. Emshanov related to putting into practice a whole series of demands from the Chinese side concerning the procedure for managing the railway. However, the manager of the railway is the executive organ of the entire Board totally and cannot execute the orders of the taipan or his deputy if they do not proceed from the Board itself under the signature of the chairman and his deputy, as it is required by article one, paragraph 8 in the Mukden agreement of 1924. The citation itself on the nonfulfillment by the manager of any unilateral orders by the taipan only confirms the illegal nature of the actions of the latter.

According to the spirit and letter of the Peking and Mukden agreements of 1924, the CER is to be jointly administered by the USSR and China; it may become Chinese property either upon the expiration of the term fixed in the treaties, or, prior to that date, by China purchasing the railway by agreement of the two parties; the illegal actions of the taipan of the CER noted above, sanctioned by the Chinese government, amount in fact to the seizure of the CER and are an attempt at the unilateral abrogation of existing treaties.

The 1924 agreements provide a quite explicit procedure for the settlement of all disputed questions concerning the railway. Under Article 6 of the agreement of 31 May 1924, and article 1, paragraph 11 of the Mukden agreement "all questions on which the management cannot agree must be submitted to the governments for a just and friendly settlement". Each party therefore has the fullest opportunity of placing any question before the other party in a perfectly legal and normal manner and of trying to get its demands satisfied. The Chinese side, however, both in this instance and in several preceding instances, such as the seizure of the telephone station, has preferred to act in a unilateral and illegal manner which not merely violates the treaties in force between the USSR and China, but throws them completely overboard.

In noting the above-mentioned actions of the taipan of the CER as a gross violation of the treaties between the USSR and China, the government of the USSR enters a most emphatic protest against them and calls the attention of the Mukden government and the national government of the Chinese Republic to the extreme seriousness of the situation which has been thereby created.

The USSR government gave repeated proof of its peaceloving and friendly relations to China in that struggle which the Chinese people waged and are waging for the destruction of the unequal treaties and the reestablishment of the sovereignty of China. The government of the USSR was the first government which concluded a treaty with China on the foundations of equality and respect for the sovereignty of China. The government of the USSR itself, on its own initiative, back in 1919 made a declaration to the Chinese people in which it declared its readiness to destroy all the unequal treaties concluded between China and tsarist Russia. In the treaty of 1924 the declarations of the government of the USSR have been realized. The government of the USSR voluntarily rejected in favor of China the concessions in Tiantsin and Khankou. It voluntarily rejected the consulate jurisdiction and extraterritoriality for its citizens in China. It, on its very own initiative, rejected the boxer contribution, transferring it to the matter of enlightenment of the Chinese people. Finally, it also voluntarily rejected all those privileges which were established by Russia on the CER, and namely the right to have in China its own forces, police, court and other military and administrative functions that were prior to this the prerogative of Russian authorities on the CER and in the entire area along the railway. This rejection of all the privileges, which are used up to the present by foreign states with whom China has normal relations, was a display of the socialist nature of the foreign policy of the Soviet state. The conclusion of the treaty of 1924 between the USSR and China was met with the greatest sympathy in all parts of China, for this treaty is the first to carry out the principle of the equality of sides and the full sovereignty of China.

If the Chinese authorities had any complaints about the regime established for the CER or about the actions of individual Soviet representatives on the railway, or even about the rights on the CER established by treaty, including the duration of the treaty and the purchase of the CER before the designated date, they had under the provisions of the treaties every opportunity of putting any such complaint before the government of the USSR in a legal manner.

The Soviet government observes that in regard to the CER it has always shown its willingness to settle any disputed point in a friendly manner. As recently as 2 February in a note delivered by the Soviet consul-general in Mukden to the central diplomatic office of the Three Eastern Provinces of China, the Soviet government declared that it "considers it highly desirable that all disputed questions, and in particular questions regarding the railway, which have not been settled in the past years and have created misunderstandings and complications in the normal working of the railway should be examined and settled in order to avoid possible misunderstandings and conflicts". This proposal, which shows how ready the Soviet government is to meet the reasonable wishes of the Chinese side, gave the Chinese government the opportunity of having any of the questions in which it was interested examined. It did not, however, wish to take the opportunity offered by the Soviet government and the proposal remained unanswered. Neither was there any reply to the telegram sent on the 11th of this month by the People's Commissar for Transport to the chairman of the board of directors of the CER declaring Soviet willingness to examine all disputed questions immediately and stating that the conduct of these negotiations had been entrusted by the Transport Commissariat to Mr. Serebriakov, a member of its collegium.

The present Chinese authorities are apparently inclined to interpret this policy of the peaceful and friendly settlement of all disputed questions, and the policy of respect for China's sovereign rights, which is a fundamental negation of the principles of the imperialist policy of bourgeois states, not as one arising from the very nature of Soviet power, but as a manifestation of its weakness. This clearly is the reason why the Chinese authorities allow themselves to commit a series of grossly violent and provocative acts against the USSR, abusing its pacific attitude. The Soviet government is therefore compelled to remind the Chinese authorities that it disposes of the means required to defend the legal rights of the peoples of the USSR from any violent encroachments whatever.

Remaining true to its policy of peace the Soviet government, despite the violence and provocation of the Chinese authorities, again declares its readiness to enter into negotiation with China on all the questions connected with the CER. Such negotiations are, however, possible only on condition that the arrested Soviet citizens are immediately set free and all the illegal actions of the Chinese authorities abrogated.

In accordance with the foregoing the Soviet government proposes:

1. To convene immediately a conference to settle all questions connected with the CER;

2. The Chinese authorities to cancel immediately all the illegal actions concerning the CER;

3. All arrested Soviet citizens to be released immediately, and the Chinese authorities to put a stop to all prosecutions and persecutions of Soviet citizens and Soviet institutions.

The Soviet government suggests that the Mukden government and the national government of the Chinese Republic ponder the serious consequences which the rejection of the Soviet proposal might have.

The Soviet government declares that it will expect an answer to this proposal within three days and gives notice that if a satisfactory answer should not be received, it will be compelled to resort to other means to defend the legal rights of the USSR.

Degras, II, 384-387.
Sovetsko-Kitaiskie Otnosheniia, 126-130.

★

PARTY RESOLUTION. PARTY CONSIDERS MILITARY FORCES STABLE AND MOVING TOWARD MODERNIZATION

15 July 1929

The Party Central Committee gave its evaluation of the state of the Soviet military in its resolution, most of which is translated below. It was pleased that the military officer corps was purged of alien and antisoviet elements, and that the Armed Forces were increasing their emphasis on technical arms while decreasing emphasis on auxiliary troops. It singled out the need to develop the aviation defense industry, particularly engine-building, to the level of the leading bourgeois powers. It considered the Armed Forces stable and reliable, indicating that the military previously was subjected to confusion resulting from the political struggles among the Party leadership. The military was also to increase its involvement in collectivization activities.

ON THE STATE OF DEFENSE OF THE USSR

1. The TsK VKP(b) resolves that the evaluation of the state of the Armed Forces of the USSR and the perspectives of development given by the previous resolution (May 1927) were completely correct, that finds its expression in the continuous growth of the fighting efficiency of the Red Army for the past two years. The internal structure of the army changed on the side of increasing the technical forces. Combat readiness of the forces made further successes in mastering contemporary methods of warfare. Territorial construction, in spite of intensifying class relationships within the country, grew quite normally, having shown once again the expediency of the territorial system as one of the organizational forms in the construction of the Red Army. The strengthening of command and political cadres proceeded along the line of increasing workers and peasants, growth of party strata, and the improvement in the quality of political education and military qualifications. The economic and social position of the Red Army generally improved. The political and moral position, in spite of the complicating domestic political situation, remained strong and quite stable.

The basic result of the past five years (1924-1929) of the planned construction of the armed forces is the creation of a strong, fighting-efficient army, in the political relationship is quite reliable, in the technical relationship stands on the level of increasing the country's labor productivity.

2. In the area of preparing the country for defense on the basis of the previous decisions of the TsK VKP(b), what has also been achieved are the first real results which provide for the normal conduct of measures for preparing the country for defense in peacetime.

3. The five year plan for developing the national economy creates favorable conditions for the significant qualitative and quantitative improvement of the defense of the USSR. Just as much as the preceding five years gave the possibility in the construction of the armed forces to lay the solid foundation for organizing the army, so in the second five years must be created the contemporary military and technical basis for defense. In connection with this the TsK VKP(b) resolves:

4. In relation to the organization of the army to consider that the course for the further increase of technical forces and for the decrease of auxiliary and service units must be continued. It is necessary to achieve the correlation among the arms of the contemporary army.

To complete completely all measures of the RVS of the USSR directed for the past two years toward the general improvement in the quality of combat readiness and, in particular, toward the decisive improvement in the tactical training of the forces. Education in the forces of extensive military initiative, courage in operations, persistence in achieving established goals, and maneuvering mobility must proceed first through the education of the field capacities of the command staff.

5. To acknowledge that the economic and social position of the Red Army still continues to serve as a brake on the normal training and education of the forces. To confirm the previous resolution of the TsK VKP(b) on the necessity of the complete liquidation in the course of three years (by 1930-1931) of the fundamental economic and social deficits of the Red Army.

6. To acknowledge as correct and timely the extensive development of work for strengthening and improving the technical arms of the army.

To propose:

The RVS of the USSR to strengthen the concluded rate of work to improve the technology of the Red Army;

alongside the modernization of existing armaments to receive within the course of the next two years experimental models, and then introducing these into the army, of contemporary types of artillery, all contemporary types of tanks, armored vehicles, etc.

7. One of the most important results of the past five years is to acknowledge the creation of the red air force. To consider that the most important task for the upcoming years in the construction of red aviation is the most speedy leading of it to the level of the leading bourgeois countries, and with all resources it is necessary to inculcate, culturalize, and develop our own soviet, scientific and design forces, especially in engine-building.

8....

9. At the present time the Red Army is reliable, politically stable, class-mature, and has a command staff of excellent military quality. This was the result of a careful purge of the command staff of alien, politically unstable, and antisoviet elements, but also thanks to the intense work of class selection, education, retraining, and the raising of its political level.

To consider that as a result of the firm carrying out of the principle of single-management what took place was the general strengthening of units of the Red Army, the strengthening of discipline in it, and the increase of the responsibility of the command staff in the state of units and increase of its authority among the red army masses.

The RVS to continue the course of the further strengthening of single-management, while not allowing any wavering in this relationship.

To acknowledge the economic and social position of the command staff as insufficiently satisfactory and as not corresponding to its service obligation. To propose in the five year plan to provide for the gradual improvement in the economic and social conditions of the command staff.

10. To establish the unconditional political growth of the Red Army and the strengthening of its political and morale condition, the indicators of which are:

the qualitative and quantitative growth of party and komsomol organizations;

the continuous growth of the political activity of all masses of military personnel not only in the scope of general army questions, but also in the social and political life of the country.

However, the difficulties, which accompany socialist construction, call for in the army a series of negative phenomena: Cases of kulak moods, antisemitism, perversions in the practice of discipline, and the existence of certain bureaucratism in the work of the military apparatus and command staff.

To confirm the measures being carried out by the RVS for the liquidation of the above negative phenomena. Furthermore, to carry out the work, while eliminating conflicts among the command staff and stopping all kinds of attempts to violate its unity and cohesion.

KPSS o Vooruzhennykh Silakh, 1981, 258-260.
KPSS o Vooruzhennykh Silakh, 1958, 318-321.

★

DECREE. SUNDAYS ELIMINATED AND THE CONTINUOUS WORK WEEK INTRODUCED

26 August 1929

The Council of People's Commissars and Council for Labor and Defense introduced the continuous work week, thus eliminating Sundays as a day of rest. Although the measure was intended to keep industrial production on an uninterrupted pace, it represented another attempt to undermine religion. As a general rule, the new system amounted to four work days followed by a day of rest. The system continued until 1940.

ON THE TRANSITION TO THE CONTINUOUS WORK WEEK IN ENTERPRISES AND INSTITUTIONS OF THE USSR

Before the working masses and poor- and middle-peasant masses stand the major tasks of economic construction and socialist restructuring of the USSR. These tasks have been established in the five year plan of the national economy and approved by the Fifth Congress of Soviets. At the present time what stands out are the possibilities of completing this plan in many of its parts. These possibilities are created by the growth of the creative initiative of the masses that find expression in the socialist competition of laborers and the further strengthening of planning principles in the economic construction of the country.

The growth of the socialist consciousness of the working class and the successes already achieved along with the introduction of the seven-hour work day now makes it possible to make a new large step in socialist construction by way of introducing continuous production in enterprises and institutions of the USSR. Considering that the introduction of continuous production, while guaranteeing the existing norms of rest days, will strengthen the economic might of the country, provide for better use of existing equipment, shorten the time for new construction and the time for reconstructing old factories and plants, give additional possibilities for developing industry, and, hereby, bring about the additional and significant increase of the number of workers engaged in industry.

Considering further that what is hereby created are new significant possibilities for the extensive satisfaction of the needs of workers and peasants in industrial goods, as well as the further improvement in the economic and social level of life of the working class, the Council of People's Commissars of the USSR resolves:

1. To acknowledge it necessary beginning with the economic year 1929/1930 to start the planned and consequential transition of enterprises and institutions to continuous production.

2. Continuous production in enterprises and institutions must be introduced with the full observation of the interests of workers and employees engaged in them. In particular after the transition of enterprises and institutions to continuous production for each worker and employee, the total number of rest days must not be decreased and the total annual number of work days must not be increased.

3. To order the State Planning Commission of the USSR:

a) In agreement with the USSR Supreme Council of the National Economy, USSR People's Commissariat for Foreign and Domestic Trade, People's Commissariat for Transport, USSR People's Commissariat for Labor, People's Commissariat for Posts and Telegraph, union republic governments, and cooperative centers, with the attraction of the appropriate trade unions, to establish a plan for the transition of enterprises and institutions to continuous production in 1929/1930, while keeping in mind during this in the first instance:

1) of enterprises for the extraction of fuel, iron ore, construction materials, for energy production, and all construction (state, cooperative and public), particularly construction of new railroads, waterways, and highways;

2) of those enterprises of the processing industry that can be provided by additional raw materials and fuel, particularly at the expense of increasing in 1929/1930 the output of enterprises indicated in point 1) as a result of the transition of the latter to the continuous work week;

3) of individual shops and departments of other enterprises the rapid expansion of which are especially necessary;

4) of loading and unloading work and commercial operations in transportation;

5) of logging;

6) of wholesale and retail trade in cities and workers' settlements, that are being produced by state and cooperative enterprises;

b) To make provision in the draft control figures of the national economy for 1929/1930 the changes being called for by the introduction of the continuous work week corresponding to the plan indicated in point "a" of the present article.

4. In view of the fact that the more equitable distribution of rest days in the course of the year, connected with the introduction of the continuous work week, the wider possibilities are for using rest days to satisfy the cultural and social needs of the working class, to propose to the union republic governments, USSR People's Commissariat for Labor, and All-Union Central Council of Trade Unions to present in a timely manner to the USSR Council of People's Commissar their proposals to organize further the work of institutions which serve the cultural and social needs of workers engaged in enterprises and institutions being transferred to continuous production and on the means for carrying out these proposals.

5. To order the USSR People's Commissariat for Labor and the All-Union Central Council of Trade Unions to present on 20 September 1929 proposals to the USSR Council of People's Commissars:

a) on establishing both the number of rest days and their distribution, while providing in this the best satisfaction of the cultural and social needs of workers;

b) changes in the existing labor legislation stipulated by the transition of enterprises and institutions to continuous production.

6. To order the USSR Supreme Council of the National Economy to develop measures to strengthen the providing of engineering and technical cadre for enterprises being transferred to continuous production, especially by way of moving them from institutions to production and present to the USSR Supreme Council of the National Economy proposals necessary for legislative approval.

7. In view of the special complexity and difficulty in the transition to continuous production and the necessity of constant observation and inspection of the carrying out of this most important measure, and to establish within the Council for Labor and Defense under the chairmanship of one of the deputies of the USSR Council of People's Commissars and Council for Labor and Defense a government commission for the transition of enterprises and institutions to continuous production that consists of representatives from: USSR State Planning Commission, USSR Supreme Council of the National Economy, USSR People's Commissariat for Labor, People's Commissariat for Transport, USSR People's Commissariat for Finance, USSR People's Commissariat for Foreign and Domestic Trade, All-Union Central Council of Trade Unions, Communist Academy, and people's commissariats for education of the union republics per their agreement among themselves of the Moscow and Leningrad soviets.

Sobranie Zakonov i Rasporiazhenii, No. 8 (10 September 1929), Article 502, 1080-1082.

★

PARTY RESOLUTION. PARTY ESTABLISHES ONE-MAN MANAGEMENT IN INDUSTRY

5 September 1929

Managers in industry long complained about the interference of trade unions and party in factory decisions. The Party Central Committee responded by prohibiting party and trade-union organizations from intervening in managerial issues. It found it necessary to eliminate ambiguity and conflict, and institute managerial efficiency and accountability for the goal of rapid industrialization. The resolution below established the one-man management system in industry and described the roles of party and trade-union organizations in aiding and monitoring management.

ON MEASURES FOR REGULATING MANAGEMENT OF PRODUCTION AND ESTABLISHING ONE-MAN MANAGEMENT

TO ALL PARTY ORGANIZATIONS, ALL PARTY MEMBERS

The successful conduct of the party's course for industrialization, successful development of industry, especially under the complex conditions of its technical reconstruction, depend on the correct organization of production and its management, i.e., on securing specified order and firm internal discipline in production. Meanwhile the TsK VKP(b) is compelled to certify that, despite the great achievements in the area of the development of industry, until now we have still not achieved the necessary order in the management of enterprises: There is not a clear and sufficiently strict demarcation of functions and responsibilities among factory organizations—among the director, plant committee, and party cell; at enterprises there still takes place the direct interference of party and trade-union organs in the operational and production work of plant management. As a result of this, there is an incidental and sometimes incorrect resolution of economic questions, factual hiding of various mistakes and shortcomings in the management of production by decisions of cells and plant committees and the weakening of the production responsibility of directors. On the other hand, there take place facts of completely intolerable relationships of plant administration with party and trade union organizations, of ignoring completely correct decisions by party cells and plant committees based on party directives.

The complexity of economic work in the present period, the introduction of new production methods and processes, and tremendous development of production and construction require the decisive elimination of these abnormalities, since without this it would be impossible to secure the strengthening of labor discipline, raising of labor productivity, improvement of production management, and carrying out of economic policy—of these most important tasks of the working class. It is necessary to understand that each mistake, each disorder in an enterprise finally strikes against the interests of the working class, against the interests of the proletarian dictatorship. Therefore it is necessary to establish the kind of order of production management that would guarantee the subordination and responsibility of each person engaged in production—from director to rank-and-file worker—for the matter charged to him and that would eliminate irresponsibility, confusion, and factual anarchy in production flowing from the interference of one organ in the function of another.

It is namely in these aims that the party many times decided to carry through one-man management of production. It is more possible and necessary at the present time to concentrate in the hands of managers of factories and plants the threads of managing the economic life of enterprises, when we have the undoubted growth of economic cadre from among workers and the improvement of their business qualifications for practical work.

Carrying through of party directives on one-man management in enterprises under the condition of the growth of organizational forms for the participation of workers in the management of production must be in the closest way linked with the further development of creativity, activity and initiative of the masses in the organization of production and the management of them. "It is necessary to learn to link together the raging, beating spring flood, bursting from all shores, mass-meeting democraticism of the laboring masses with the *iron* discipline during labor, with *unquestioning obedience*—for the freedom of one person, the soviet manager, during labor" (*Lenin*, Immediate tasks of Soviet power, Volume XV).

In view of the fact that not all party organizations, communists and workers understand this most important principle of production management for the successful development of socialist industry, the TsK considers it necessary to give the following instructions:

1. In the organization of production management it is necessary to proceed from the fact that the administration (director) directly answers for the fulfillment of the industrial plan and all production tasks. The administration directs both the management apparatus and the organizational and technical processes of production at an enterprise. All of his operational and economic instructions are absolutely obligatory for both the lower administration and workers whatever position they hold in party, trade union, and other organizations. The administration of an enterprise directly appoints all the administrative and technical personnel of an enterprise, and in the interrelation between the enterprise director and shop administration it is necessary to proceed from the extension of the rights and granting the greatest independence of the shop administration, to include the selection of administrative and technical resources in the shop (foreman, brigade, etc.). During the appointment and dismissal of this or that worker, the administration is obligated to consider the opinion of the party and trade-union organization, for which in the case of disagreement with the appointment or dismissal remains the right of appeal to higher party, trade-union, and economic organs, that, however, does not suspend bringing into practice administration decisions.

The administration of an enterprise and shop, while conducting all the necessary measures for strengthening and introducing production discipline in the enterprise, must at the same time be able to combine methods of its own organizational and administrative activity with the necessity of developing the creative initiative of the working masses, with the attraction of them to production management, with the obligatory calculation of their proposals and realization of adopted proposals, while encouraging by all means rational initiative and worker invention, etc., and with the maximum sensitivity to the needs of workers and their indications of both technical and management deficiencies. "The more decisive must we stand now for relentlessly strong authority, for the dictatorship of individuals *for definite work processes*, at definite moments *purely executive* functions, the more varied must be the forms and capability of control from below..." (*Lenin*, Immediate tasks of Soviet power, Volume XV).

2. Trade union organizations in enterprises, while directly vindicating and defending the daily cultural and social needs of workers, must at the same time be energetic organizers of the production activity and independence of the working masses. Factory and plant committees must actively participate, particularly through production meetings, in discussing and developing basic questions about the production of industrial financial plans and reconstruction measures at enterprises, and supervise bringing into practice various proposals by workers, further the rationalization of production, improvement in the organization of labor, etc. Having listened regularly to administration reports, studying materials on production and submitting their own proposals, trade union organizations must not, however, interfere directly in plant management and moreso substitute themselves for the administration, while with all means at their disposal furthering the actual carrying out and strengthening of one-man management, growth of production, development of the enterprise, and hereby improving the material condition of the working class.

3. Party cells, being the foundation of the party, especially at enterprises, must by their own work, lead the social, political, and economic life of enterprises thus to provide for the

fulfillment by professional and economic organs of the basic directives of the party, while not interfering during this in the work details of the plant committee and director, particularly in the operative orders of the administration. Party cells must actively further the execution in the entire management system of production the principle of one-man management. Party cells must not in any case substitute themselves as the enterprise administration in the appointment of lower-level administration; it is more intolerable to interfere in the orders of the administration for the distribution of workers in shops. During the appointment and dismissal of basic officials at enterprises below director (those who manage large shops, etc.) cells and factory and plant committees discuss these appointments and dismissals, however in the case of disagreement with this or other candidate cannot delay the orders of the administration, relaying disputed issues to higher-level party, trade-union, and economic organs.

The cells likewise must not substitute themselves as a plant committee. In particular, the cells must not substitute themselves as a plant committee and administration in examining the submission of complaints from workers and in resolving individual production conflicts. While receiving workers' complaints, investigating thoroughly the content of these complaints, observing that they are not ignored, the cells must at the same time present the possibility to the corresponding organs and to the same organizations to exhaust all existing possibilities for resolving conflicts. After listening to reports by directors of enterprises and managers of large shops about the fundamental issues of production, about the perspectives for fulfilling industrial financial plans and the most important production tasks, about reconstruction measures, the cells must during this not permit petty harassment of the economists, while sticking to planning in the raising of these issues. While not being distracted by petty questions about the life of the enterprise, the cells hereby will receive a greater possibility of carrying out the most important task of the political leadership of the masses and their organizations and educating them in class vigilance and conscious relationships to the interests of the socialist enterprise, alleviate the struggle with wrecking in industry and transportation, and will further the fulfillment of industrial financial plans.

4. These bases for dividing the functions among party, professional, and administrative organs not only will not deny, but, on the contrary, presuppose the closest link, mutual assistance, and the creation of the actual comradely atmosphere in work, while excluding the possibility of nepotism and mutual covering up of one for another. The closest cooperation and enrichment by experience are especially necessary for developing and carrying out the industrial financial plan. Party, professional, and economic organs must raise the activity of the masses in all stages of the development and fulfillment of the industrial financial plan. During the development of the industrial financial plan, it is necessary to provide for the business discussion of it at production conferences, shop meetings, and general plan conferences, while furthering the fulfillment of all the enterprise's possibilities for establishing higher tasks in the production program, improving the condition of the working masses, increasing labor productivity, reducing cost, improving the quality of output, etc., while waging the most decisive struggle with all cases of the violation of established rules of internal regulation and with the violations of labor production discipline. After the adoption of the industrial financial plan, party and professional organizations must in every way possible assist the administration in carrying it out. During this work, Party and professional organs at enterprises must be reconstructed thus to lead the creative enthusiasm of the masses, quickly catch up with initiative coming from the side of workers in the area of improving the organization of production, actively lead socialist competition and direct the activity of production commissions, conferences and temporary inspection commissions in the first instance of fulfilling industrial financial plans.

Party and professional organizations must systematically introduce into the consciousness of the working masses the measures that are being carried out by enterprise leaders directed toward strengthening production discipline, raising labor productivity, and rationalizing production, are measures which flow from party directives, Soviet authority, and trade unions, and directed toward improving the condition of workers and strengthening the proletarian dictatorship.

5. With the aims of the most complete use of initiative of the working masses and carrying out the proposals of workers, decisions of production commissions and conferences, and with the aim of establishing greater communication of the enterprise administrations with these organs of workers' independence, the TsK considers it expedient from experience to appoint at several enterprises chairmen of production conferences for the period of their appointment as directors' assistants specially for realizing decisions of production conferences and commissions and workers' proposals. This must not at all mean that the enterprise director himself does not bear responsibility for putting into practice the resolutions of production conferences being adopted for completion by the administration. The director is obligated by all means to further the work of the production conferences and raise the initiative of workers, while attracting the attention of participants in production conferences to the most important deficiencies in the work of the enterprise, while developing and carefully preparing issues being submitted for examination by the production conferences.

Together with this, the TsK of the Party proposes to all Party organizations, trade-union fractions, and economic organs more decisively and more actively to advance workers to administrative posts, while regularly advancing them from one level of management to another and selecting workers, who demonstrate a conscious relationship to production, have the ability to lead the working masses and technical personnel, particularly these qualities revealed in the work in production and inspection commissions. Candidates nominated by workers are listed by Party and trade-union organizations in reserve, from which resources are drawn for appointment to the appropriate administrative and economic posts.

6. Since the tasks of enterprise management are becoming complicated and enterprise directors must possess not only issues of general administration but also knowledge of all production processes, while at the same time strengthening communication with the masses, the TsK proposes to Party organizations to create a favorable condition for the work of administrators and provide them with the possibility of the further improvement in their technical and political qualifications.

In connection with this it is necessary: a) to provide for assigning longer periods of time for enterprise directors. The replacement of a director is made by those organs which appointed him, and during discussion at Party cells or in raion committees of the issue about the director's leaving it, cells and raion committees must make it known in timely fashion and summon a meeting of the chairman of the higher-level economic organ, which appointed this director, and the higher-level trade-union organization; b) while attracting by all means economists to the appropriate Party organs, local Party organizations are obligated to the maximum to relieve directors of enterprises from work not connected with their direct responsibilities at the plant; c) except for established regular leave, the VSNKh must grant enterprise directors additional leave approximately for 1 1/2-2 months for increasing their theoretical qualifications.

7. Applying new experiments and methods in the area of rationalizing production and unavoidable risk, connected with these experiments, requires deep study and knowledge of production processes and especially serious approaches. During the disclosure of these or other mistakes and deficiencies, it is necessary to separate actual mistakes from conscious wrecking. It is necessary to direct the effort of workers, their vigilance, their active creative criticism for the positive correction of mistakes and deficiencies and for the decisive struggle with the class enemy and wrecker at enterprises.

The increasing activity of the working masses on the basis of raising the economy and the difficulties in reconstructing industry require still greater intensification of the attention of professional, party, and soviet organizations to the life and work of the basic lower sections of factory and plant organizations, which must reconstruct their own work in conformity with directives issued by higher organizations.

To obligate the present resolution to be made public and discussed at all party, general plant and shop cells.

To order the Orgburo of the TsK in three months' time to begin a systematic review of putting the present resolution into practice in the local areas, after hearing the appropriate reports.

To propose to local party, professional, and economic organizations to observe the procedure established by the nomenclature of the TsK VKP(b) for appointing and approving enterprise directors.

To propose to the USSR VSNKh to change the formulation of the VSNKh order of 4 October 1927.

Resheniia, 125-131.

STALIN LAUNCHES SOCIALIST OFFENSIVE AGAINST CAPITALIST ELEMENTS: "YEAR OF THE GREAT CHANGE"

3 November 1929

On the eve of the twelfth anniversary of the October Revolution, Stalin launched the campaign against the kulaks and other capitalist elements in an article in Pravda. Based on data showing the enormous success of collectivization, he argued that the middle peasants were flocking to collective farms in large numbers and that whole villages were joining the collectives. He predicted that the Soviet Union would become a leading grain producer, if not the world's leading grain producer, in the next three years. Industrialization would enable the Soviet Union to leave its backwardness behind and overtake the advanced capitalist countries. Stalin's article represented a clarion call to encourage the party to prepare for the upcoming plenum of the Central Committee. Stalin described the past year as one of great change, a breakthrough, in the development of socialism.

A YEAR OF GREAT CHANGE
On the Occasion of the Twelfth
Anniversary of the October Revolution

The past year was a year of great *change* on all the fronts of socialist construction. The keynote of this change has been, and continues to be, a determined *offensive* of socialism against the capitalist elements in town and countryside. The characteristic feature of this offensive is that it has already brought us a number of decisive *successes* in the principal spheres of the socialist reconstruction of our national economy.

We may, therefore, conclude that our Party succeeded in making good use of our retreat during the first stages of the New Economic Policy in order, in the subsequent stages, to organize the *change* and to launch a *successful offensive* against the capitalist elements.

When NEP was introduced Lenin said:

"We are now retreating, going back as it were; but we are doing this in order, by retreating first, afterwards to take a run and make a more powerful leap forward. It was on this condition alone that we retreated in pursuing our New Economic Policy... in order to start a most persistent advance after our retreat" (Volume XXVII, pp. 361-62).

The results of the past year show beyond a doubt that in its work the Party is successfully carrying out this decisive directive of Lenin's.

If we take the results of the past year in the sphere of economic construction, which is of decisive importance for us, we shall find that the successes of our offensive on this front, our achievements during the past year, can be summed up under three main headings.

I
IN THE SPHERE OF LABOR PRODUCTIVITY

There can scarcely be any doubt that one of the most important facts in our work of construction during the past year is that we have succeeded in bringing about a *decisive* change in the sphere of labor productivity. This change has found expression in a growth of the *creative initiative* and intense *labor enthusiasm* of the vast masses of the working class on the front of socialist construction. This is our first fundamental achievement during the past year.

The growth of the creative initiative and labor enthusiasm of the masses has been stimulated in three main directions:

a) the fight—by means of self-criticism—against bureaucracy, which shackles the labor initiative and labor activity of the masses;

b) the fight—by means of *socialist competition*-against the labor-shirkers and disrupters of proletarian labor discipline;

c) the fight—by the introduction of the *continuous workweek*—against routine and inertia in industry.

As a result we have a tremendous achievement on the labor front in the form of labor enthusiasm and competition among the vast masses of the working class in all parts of our boundless country. The significance of this achievement is truly inestimable, for only the labor enthusiasm and zeal of the vast masses can guarantee that progressive increase of labor productivity without which the final victory of socialism over capitalism in our country is inconceivable.

"In the last analysis," says Lenin, "productivity of labor is the most important, the principal thing for the victory of a new social system. Capitalism created a productivity of labor unknown under serfdom. Capitalism can be utterly vanquished, and will be utterly vanquished, by the fact that socialism creates a new and much higher productivity of labor" (Volume XXIV, p. 342).

Proceeding from this, Lenin considered that:

"We must become imbued with the labor enthusiasm, the will to work, the persistence upon which the speedy salvation of the workers and peasants, the salvation of the national economy now depends" (Volume XXV, p. 477).

That is the task Lenin set for our Party.

The past year has shown that the Party is successfully carrying out this task and is resolutely overcoming the obstacles that stand in its path.

Such is the position regarding the Party's first important achievement during the past year.

II
IN THE SPHERE OF INDUSTRIAL CONSTRUCTION

In separately connected with the first achievement of the Party is its second achievement. This second achievement of the Party consists in the fact that during the past year we have in the main successfully solved the *problem of accumulation* for capital construction in heavy industry, we have *accelerated* the development of the production of means of production and have created the prerequisites for transforming our country into a *metal* country.

That is our second fundamental *achievement* during the past year.

The problem of light industry presents no special difficulties. We solved that problem several years ago. The problem of heavy industry is more difficult and more important.

It is *more difficult* because this solution demands colossal investments, and, as the history of industrially backward countries has shown, heavy industry cannot manage without huge long-term loans.

It is *more important* because, unless we develop heavy industry, we cannot build any industry at all, we cannot carry out any industrialization.

And as we have not received, and are not receiving, either long-term loans or credits of any long-term character, the acuteness of the problem for us becomes more than obvious.

It is precisely for this reason that the capitalists of all countries refuse us loans and credits, for they assume that we cannot by our own efforts cope with the problem of accumulation, that we shall suffer shipwreck in the task of constructing our heavy industry, and be compelled to come to them cap in hand, for enslavement.

But what do the results of our work during the past year show in this connection? The significance of the results of the past year is that they shatter to bits the anticipations of Messieurs the capitalists.

The past year has shown that, in spite of the overt and covert financial blockade of the USSR, we did not sell ourselves into bondage to the capitalists, that by our own efforts we have successfully solved the problem of accumulation and laid the foundation for heavy industry. Even the most inveterate enemies of the working class cannot deny this now.

Indeed, since, in the first place, capital investments in large-scale industry last year amounted to over 1,600,000,000 rubles, of which about 1,300,000,000 rubles were invested in heavy industry, while capital investment in large-scale industry this year will amount to over 3,400,000,000 rubles, of which over 2,500,000,000 rubles will be invested in heavy industry; and since, in the second place, the gross output of large-scale industry last year showed an increase of 23 percent, including a 30 percent increase in the output of heavy industry, while the increase in the gross output of large-scale industry this year should be 32 percent, including a 46 percent increase in the output of heavy industry—is it not clear that the problem of accumulation for the building up of heavy industry no longer presents insuperable difficulties for us?

How can anyone doubt that we are advancing at an accelerated pace in the direction of developing our heavy industry, exceeding our former speed and leaving behind our "age-old" backwardness?

Is it surprising after this that the targets of the five year plan were exceeded during the past year, and that the *optimum* variant of the five year plan, which the bourgeois scribes regard as "wild fantasy", and which horrifies our Right opportunists (Bukharin's group), has actually turned out to be a *minimum* variant?

"The salvation of Russia," says Lenin. "lies not only in a good harvest on the peasant farms—that is not enough; and not only in the good condition of light industry, which provides the peasantry with consumer goods—that, too, is not enough; we also need *heavy* industry.... Unless we save heavy industry, unless we restore it, we shall not be able to build up any industry; and without it we shall be doomed altogether as an independent country.... Heavy industry needs state subsidies. If we do not provide them, then we are doomed as a civilized state—let alone as a socialist state" (Volume XXVII, p. 349).

That is how sharply Lenin formulated the problem of accumulation and the task of the Party in building up heavy industry.

The past year has shown that our Party is successfully coping with this task, resolutely overcoming all obstacles in its path.

This does not mean, of course, that industry will not encounter any more serious difficulties. The task of building up heavy industry involves not only the problem of accumulation. It also involves the problem of cadres, the problem:

a) of *enlisting* tens of thousands of Soviet-minded technicians and experts for the work of socialist construction, and

b) of *training* new Red technicians and Red experts from among the working class.

While the problem of accumulation may in the main be regarded as solved, the problem of cadres still awaits solution. And the problem of cadres is now—when we are engaged in the technical reconstruction of industry—the key problem of socialist construction.

"The chief thing we lack," says Lenin, "is culture, ability to administer.... Economically and politically, NEP fully ensures us the possibility of laying the foundation of a socialist economy. It is 'only' a matter of the cultural forces of the proletariat and of its vanguard" (Volume XXVI, p. 207).

It is obvious that Lenin refers here primarily to the problem of "cultural forces", the problem of the cadres for economic construction in general, and for building and managing industry in particular.

But from this it follows that, in spite of important achievements in the sphere of accumulation, which are of vital significance for heavy industry, the problem of building heavy industry cannot be regarded as fully solved until we have solved the problem of cadres.

Hence the task of the Party is to tackle the problem of cadres in all seriousness and to conquer this fortress at all costs.

Such is the position regarding our Party's second achievement during the past year.

III
IN THE SPHERE OF AGRICULTURAL DEVELOPMENT

Finally, about the Party's third achievement during the past year, an achievement organically connected with the two previous ones. I am referring to the *radical change* in the development of our agriculture from small, backward, *individual* farming to large-scale, advanced, *collective* agriculture, to joint cultivation of the land, to machine and tractor stations, to artels, collective farms, based on modern technology, and, finally, to giant state farms, equipped with hundreds of tractors and harvester combines.

The Party's achievement here consists in the fact that in a whole number of areas we have succeeded in *turning* the main mass of the peasantry away from the old, *capitalist* path of development—which benefits only a small group of the rich, the capitalists, while the vast majority of the peasants are doomed to ruin and utter poverty—to the new, *socialist* path of development, which ousts the rich and the capitalists, and reequips the middle and poor peasants along new lines, equipping them with modern implements, with tractors and agricultural machinery, so as to enable them to climb out of poverty and enslavement to the kulaks on to the high road of cooperative, collective cultivation of the land.

The achievement of the Party consists in the fact that we have succeeded in bringing about this *radical change* deep down in the peasantry itself, and in securing the following of the broad masses of the poor and middle peasants in spite of incredible difficulties, in spite of the desperate resistance of retrograde forces of every kind, from kulaks and priests to philistines and Right opportunists.

Here are some figures.

In 1928, the crop area of the state farms amounted to 1,425,000 hectares with a marketable grain output of more than 6,000,000 centners (over 36,000,000 puds), and the crop area of the collective farms amounted to 1,390,000 hectares with a marketable grain output of about 3,500,000 centners (over 20,000,000 puds).

In 1929, the crop area of the state farms amounted to 1,816,000 hectares with a marketable grain output of about 8,000,000 centners (nearly 47,000,000 puds), and the crop area of the collective farms amounted to 4,262,000 hectares with a marketable grain output of about 13,000,000 centners (nearly 78,000,000 puds).

In the coming year, 1930, the crop area of the state farms, according to the plan, will probably amount to 3,280,000 hectares with a marketable grain output of 18,000,000 centners (approximately 110,000,000 puds), and the crop area of the collective farms will certainly amount to 15,000,000 hectares with a marketable grain output of about 49,000,000 centners (approximately 300,000,000 puds).

In other words, in the coming year, 1930, the marketable grain output of the state and collective farms will amount to over 400,000,000 puds or more than 50 percent of the marketable grain output of the *whole* of agriculture (grain sold outside the rural districts).

It must be admitted that such an impetuous speed of development is *unequalled* even by our socialized, large-scale industry, which in general is marked by the outstanding speed of its development.

It is clear that our young large-scale socialist agriculture (the collective and state farms) has a great future before it and that its development will be truly miraculous.

This unprecedented success in the development of collective farming is due to a variety of causes, of which the following at least should be mentioned.

It is due, *first of all*, to the fact that the Party carried out Lenin's policy of educating the masses by consistently leading the masses of the peasantry to collective farming through implanting a cooperative communal life. It is due to the fact that the Party waged a successful struggle against those who tried to run ahead of the movement and force the development of collective farming by means of decrees (the "Left" phrasemongers) and remain in the wake of the movement (the Right blockheads). Had it not pursued such a policy the Party would not have been able to transform the collective-farm movement into a real mass movement of the peasants themselves.

"When the Petrograd proletariat and the soldiers of the Petrograd garrison took power," says Lenin, "they truly realized that our constructive work in the countryside would encounter great difficulties; that there it was necessary to proceed more gradually; that to attempt to introduce collective cultivation of the land by decrees, by legislation, would be the height of folly; that an insignificant number of enlightened peasants might agree to this, but that the vast majority of the peasants had no such object in view. We, therefore, confined ourselves to what was absolutely essential in the interests of the development of the revolution; in no case to run ahead of the development of the masses, but to wait until, as a result of their own experience and their own struggle, a progressive movement grew up" (Volume XXIII, p. 252).

The reason why the Party achieved a great victory on the front of collective-farm development is that it exactly carried out this tactical directive of Lenin's.

Secondly, this unprecedented success in agricultural development is due to the fact that the Soviet government correctly recognized the growing needs of the peasants for new implements, for modern technology; it correctly recognized that the old forms of cultivation leave the peasantry in a hopeless position and, taking all this into account, it came to their aid in good time by organizing machine-hiring stations, tractor columns and machine and tractor stations; by organizing collective cultivation of the land, by establishing collective farms, and finally, by having the state farms give every assistance to peasant farming.

For the first time in the history of mankind there has appeared a government, that of the Soviets, which has proved by deeds its readiness and ability to give the laboring masses of the peasantry systematic and lasting assistance in the sphere of *production*.

It is not obvious that the laboring masses of the peasantry, suffering from age-long lack of agricultural equipment were bound to reach out eagerly for this assistance and join the collective-farm movement?

And can one be surprised if henceforth the old slogan of the workers, "face to the countryside," is supplemented, as seems likely, by the new slogan of the collective-farm peasants, "face to the town"?

Lastly, this unprecedented success in collective-farm development is due to the fact that the matter was taken in hand by the advanced workers of our country. I am referring to the workers' brigades, tens and hundreds of which are scattered in the principal regions of our country. It must be acknowledged that of all existing and potential propagandists of the collective-farm movement among the peasant masses, the worker propagandists are the best. What can there be surprising in the fact that the workers have succeeded in convincing the peasants of the advantages of large-scale collective farming over individual small farming, the moreso as the existing collective and state farms are striking examples of these advantages?

Such was the basis for our achievement in collective-farm development, an achievement which, in my opinion, is the most important and decisive of all our achievements in recent years.

All the objections raised by "science" against the possibility and expediency of organizing large grain factories of 40,00 to 50,000 hectares each have collapsed and crumbled to dust. Practice has refuted the objections of "science", and has once again shown that not only has practice to learn from "science" but that "science" also would do well to learn from practice.

Large grain factories do not take root in capitalist countries. But ours is a socialist country. This "slight" difference must not be overlooked.

In capitalist countries large grain factories cannot be organized without previously buying a number of plots of land or without the payment of absolute ground rent, which cannot fail to burden production with colossal expenses, for private ownership of land exists there. In our country, on the other hand, neither absolute ground rent, nor the sale and purchase of land exist, which cannot fail to create favorable conditions for the development of large grain farms, for in our country there is no private ownership of land.

In capitalist countries the large grain farms aim at obtaining the maximum profit, or, at all events, a profit equal to the so-called average rate of profit, failing which, generally speaking, there would be no incentive to invest capital in grain production. In our country, on the contrary, the large grain farms, being state undertakings, need neither the maximum profit, nor the average rate of profit for their development; they can limit themselves to a minimum profit, and sometimes even manage without any profit, which again creates favorable conditions for the development of large grain farms.

Finally, under capitalism large grain farms do not enjoy special credit privileges or special tax privileges, whereas under the Soviet system, which is designed to support the socialist sector, such privileges exist and will continue to exist.

Esteemed "science" forgot all this.

There have collapsed and crumbled to dust the assertions of the Right opportunists (Bukharin's group) that:

a) the peasants would not join the collective farms,

b) the accelerated development of collective farms could only cause mass discontent and estrangement between the peasantry and the working class,

c) the "high road" of socialist development in the countryside is *not* the collective farms, *but* the cooperatives,

d) the development of collective farms and the offensive against the capitalist elements in the countryside might deprive the country of grain altogether.

All that has collapsed and crumbled to dust as old bourgeois-liberal rubbish.

Firstly, the peasants are joining the collective farms; they are joining by whole villages, volosts, districts.

Secondly, the mass collective-farm movement is not weakening the bond, but strengthening it, by putting it on a new, production basis. Now even the blind can see that if there is any serious dissatisfaction among the main mass of the peasantry it is not because of the collective-farm policy of the Soviet government, but because the Soviet government is unable to keep pace with the growth of the collective-farm movement as regards supplying the peasants with machines and tractors.

Thirdly, the controversy about the "high road" of socialist development in the countryside is a scholastic controversy, worthy of young petty-bourgeois liberals of the type of Eichenwald and Slepkov. It is obvious that, as long as there was no mass collective-farm movement, the "high road" was the lower forms of the cooperative movement—supply and marketing cooperatives; but when the higher form of the cooperative movement—the collective farm—appeared, the latter became the "high road" of development.

The high road (without quotation marks) of socialist development in the countryside is Lenin's cooperative plan, which embraces all forms of agricultural cooperation, from the lowest (supply and marketing cooperatives) to the highest (producers' and collective-farm cooperatives). To *counterpose* collective farms to cooperatives is to make a mockery of Leninism and to acknowledge one's own ignorance.

Fourthly, now even the blind can see that without the offensive against the capitalist elements in the countryside, and without the development of the collective farm and state-farm movement, we would not have achieved the decisive successes of this year in the matter of grain procurements, nor could the state have accumulated, as it has already done, an emergency reserve of grain totalling tens of millions of puds.

More than that, it can now be confidently asserted that, thanks to the growth of the collective- and state-farm movement, we are definitely emerging, or have already emerged, from the grain crisis. And if the development of the collective and state farms is accelerated, there is no reason to doubt that in about three years' time our country will be one of the world's largest grain producers, if not the largest.

What is the *new* feature of the present collective farm movement? The new and decisive feature of the present collective-farm movement is that the peasants are joining the collective farms not in separate groups, as was formerly the case, but by whole villages, volosts, districts, and even okrugs.

And what does this mean? It means that *the middle peasant is joining the collective farm.* And that is the basis of the radical change in the development of agriculture that constitutes the most important achievement of the Soviet government during the past year.

Trotskyism's Menshevik "conception" that the working class is incapable of securing the following of the main mass of the peasantry in the work of socialist construction is collapsing and being smashed to smithereens. Now even the blind can see that the middle peasant has turned towards the collective farm. Now it is obvious to all that the five year plan of industry and agriculture is a five year plan of building a socialist society, that those who do not believe in the possibility of completely building socialism in our country have no right to greet our five year plan.

The last hope of the capitalists of all countries, who are dreaming of restoring capitalism in the USSR—"the sacred principle of private property"—is collapsing and crumbling to dust. The peasants, whom they regarded as material that fertilizes the soil for capitalism, are abandoning en masse the lauded banner of "private property" and are going over to the lines of collectivism, of socialism. The last hope for the restoration of capitalism is collapsing.

This, by the way, explains the desperate efforts of the capitalist elements in our country to rouse all the forces of the old world against advancing socialism—efforts which are leading to an intensification of the class struggle. Capital does not want "to grow into" socialism.

This also explains the furious howl against Bolshevism which has been raised recently by the watchdogs of capital, by the Struves and Hessens, the Miliukovs and Kerenskys, the Dans and Abramoviches and their like. The last hope for the restoration of capitalism is disappearing—that is no joke for them.

What other explanation for the violent rage of our class enemies and this frenzied howling of the lackeys of capital can there be except the fact that our Party has actually achieved a decisive victory on the most difficult front of socialist construction?

"Only if we succeed," says Lenin, "in practice in showing the peasants the advantages of common, collective, cooperative, artel cultivation of the soil, only if we succeed in helping the peasant by means of cooperative, artel farming, will the working class, which holds state power in its hands, actually prove to the peasant the correctness of its policy and actually secure the real and durable following of the vast masses of the peasantry" (Volume XXIV, p. 579).

That is how Lenin put the question of the ways of winning the vast masses of the peasantry to the side of the working class, of the ways of transferring the peasants on to the lines of collective-farm development.

The past year has shown that our Party is successfully coping with this task and is resolutely overcoming every obstacle standing in its path.

"In a communist society," says Lenin, "the middle peasants will be on our side only when we alleviate and improve their economic conditions. If tomorrow we could supply 100,000 first-class tractors, provide them with fuel, provide them with drivers (you know very well that at present this is fantasy), the middle peasant would say: 'I am for the kommunia' (i.e., for communism). But in order to do that we must first defeat the international bourgeoisie, we must compel it to give us these tractors, or we must so develop our productivity as to be able to provide them ourselves. That is the only correct way to pose this question" (Volume XXIV, p. 170).

That is how Lenin put the question of the ways of technically reequipping the middle peasant, of the ways of winning him to the side of communism.

The past year has shown that the Party is successfully coping with this task too. We know that by the spring of the coming year, 1930, we shall have over 60,000 tractors in the fields, a year later we shall have over 100,000 tractors, and two years after that, over 250,000 tractors. We are now able to accomplish and even to exceed what was considered "fantasy" several years ago.

And that is why the middle peasant has turned towards the "kommunia".

Such is the position regarding our Party's third achievement.

Such are the fundamental achievements of our Party during the past year.

CONCLUSIONS

We are advancing full steam ahead along the path of industrialization—to socialism, leaving behind the age-old "Russian" backwardness.

We are becoming a country of metal, a country of automobiles, a country of tractors.

And when we have put the USSR on an automobile, and the muzhik on a tractor, let the worthy capitalists, who boast so much of their "civilization", try to overtake us! We shall yet see which countries may then be "classified" as backward and which as advanced.

Stalin, *Works*, XII, 124-141.

SOVIET MILITARY FORCES LAUNCH SUCCESSFUL COUNTERATTACK AGAINST CHINESE FORCES IN MANCHURIA. PRESS COMMUNIQUE

17 November 1929

Growing conflict in the Far East led Soviet leaders to strengthen military forces on the eastern borders. These military forces, the Special Far Eastern Army, demonstrated the success of the build-up in responding to attacks from the Chinese military under the command of the Mukden Government in Manchuria. As a result of the counterattack, Chinese military action along the eastern borders of the USSR came to an end. The document below is a press communique from Khabarovsk about the successful counterattack.

COUNTERATTACK OF THE SPECIAL FAR EASTERN ARMY IN ANSWER TO THE ATTEMPTS OF CHINESE FORCES TO PENETRATE USSR TERRITORY

From the first days of November of this year, Chinese forces, positioned in the area of Manchuria and town of Shveisian (east of Nerchinsk plant on the Argun river), began the systematic shelling with artillery, machine guns, and rifle fire of our border sections and the peaceful inhabitants who live along the Chinese border on the Argun river. As a result of this shelling the inhabitants of the stanitsas Olochinsk and Abagaituev were forced to end their grain threshing and evacuate. Among the inhabitants of these stanitsas there are dead and wounded. However, the Chinese forces were not limited to this. Beginning on 13 November of this year, the Chinese command with intensity sent across into our territory white guard detachments that it formed in the Trekhrech'e area. White guards whom we captured show that they received the goal of destroying our rear.

On 15 November of this year, Chinese forces in the area of station No. 86 attempted with a force of about a battalion renewed their attack. The attack was beaten back by the arms of our border guards. On the night of 16-17 November Chinese forces, with significant forces under artillery support, ›ttacked stanitsa Abagaituev and station No. 86.

Provocative actions by the Chinese forces took place during this time not only in Zabaikal, but in Primor'e, where they shelled daily our border guards and peaceful inhabitants in the area of Poltavsk, Pogranichnii, and Turii Rog, and beginning on 10 November forced the peaceful inhabitants in the border area to quit their field work and evacuate.

At the same time as this, in Primor'e an attack was made on our territory by white guard bands from the area of Mishan'fu (25 km northwest of Turii Rog), which is the place where the white guards were formed for action in our rear.

Beginning on 15 November, the Chinese command with intensity threw its forces again on stanitas Pogranichnii and Mishan'fu. On this same day the Chinese forces, with a force of about a battalion, unsuccessfully attempted to attack in the area of the stanitsa Pogranichnii.

Beginning on the morning of 17 November, Chinese calvary crossed our border in the area of Turii Rog and the settlement of Pervomaisk, and began to mass on our border sections.

Considering the situation created in the Far East, the command of the Special Far Eastern Army was forced to adopt, from its side, countermeasures to defend our borders and for securing the safety of the border population and our rear.

As a result, units of the Special Far Eastern Army, both in Zabaikal and in Primor'e, having beaten back the attack of the Chinese forces on 17 November, pursued them into Chinese territory and drove them farther away from our borders. More than 8000 Chinese soldiers and 300 officers were disarmed; seized were up to 10,000 rifles, a significant quantity of field artillery, ammunition, and other field equipment.

Sovetsko-Kitaiskie Otnosheniia, 308-309.

PARTY RESOLUTION. PARTY PLENUM CALLS FOR DECISIVE OFFENSIVE AGAINST KULAKS

17 November 1929

The Central Committee Plenum met between 10 and 17 November 1929 and heard reports from G.N. Kaminsky, head of Kolkhoztsentr, V.M. Molotov, and others about successes of collectivization resulting from the middle peasants' joining the kolkhozes. The reports by Kaminsky and Molotov called for rapid and comprehensive collectivization and stressed the urgency of massive collectivization. The party resolution, based primarily on Kaminsky's report, took a more cautious tone, calling for a decisive offensive against the kulak, stopping short of expelling him from the village, and muting the urgent pace expressed by Kaminsky and Molotov. It also called for sending 25,000 workers, the so-called 25,000-ers, to the countryside to assist in collectivization.

PLENUM OF THE CENTRAL COMMITTEE
On the Results and Coming Tasks of Kolkhoz Construction

I

1. The Fifteenth Party Congress set as the party's basic task in the countryside the "gradual transition of dispersed peasant holdings to large-scale production". In the past two years the party has scored major successes in carrying out this directive of the Fifteenth Party Congress.

The USSR has entered the period of extensive socialist reorganization of the village and construction of large-scale socialist agriculture.

On the basis of the development of joint production work, of mass contractual growing, etc., there is a growth of production cooperation between peasant households that is increasingly making the transition to a higher stage and is growing into the kolkhoz movement. Following in the footsteps of the poor peasants, the mass of *middle peasants* has also moved into the kolkhozes. With the recruitment of rural masses numbering in the millions, the kolkhoz movement is assuming decisive importance in the realization of the leninist cooperative plan.

In summing up the results of kolkhoz construction, one would have to note: The speed with which the kolkhozes have absorbed peasant holdings; the realization of new organizational forms and methods of collectivization, particularly on the basis of experience with the machine tractor stations; the construction of large-scale kolkhozes and the fact that they now play a greater role; the fact that kolkhozes have encompassed entire settlements; and the transition to complete collectivization of entire raions and okrugs. The kolkhoz movement is already posing the task of collectivization of entire oblasts.

These significant successes of the kolkhoz movement are a direct result of the consistent implementation of the general party line, which has secured a powerful growth of industry, a strengthening of the alliance of the working class with the basic masses of the peasantry, the formation of a cooperative community, the strengthening of the masses' political activism, and the growth of the material and cultural resources of the proletarian state.

In addition, this turbulent growth of the kolkhoz movement confronts the party with a number of new and highly complex tasks; it brings to light new difficulties and shortcomings in kolkhoz construction, of which the most important at the present time are: The low level of the kolkhozes' technical base; the inadequate standards of organization and low labor productivity at kolkhozes; the acute shortage of kolkhoz cadre and the near total lack of the needed specialists; the blighted social make-up at a portion of the kolkhoz; the fact that the forms of management are poorly adapted to the scale of the kolkhoz movement, that direction lags behind the rate and scope of the movement, and the fact that the agencies directing the kolkhoz movement are often patently unsatisfactory.

2. The widespread development of the kolkhoz movement is taking place in a situation of intensified class struggle in the countryside and of a change in its forms and methods. Along with the kulaks' intensification of their direct and open struggle against collectivization, which has gone to the point of outright terror (murder, arson, and wrecking), they are increasingly going over to camouflaged and covert forms of struggle and exploitation, penetrating the kolkhozes and even the kolkhoz management bodies in order to corrupt and explode them from the inside.

In conditions of intensified class struggle, it is a matter of particular importance to consistently combat pseudokolkhozes, which are a means of camouflage and a weapon of the kulak elements in the countryside.

While continuing and intensifying the struggle against capitalist elements in the countryside, deploying a decisive advance against the kulak, and in every way blocking and heading off attempts by kulaks to penetrate the kolkhozes, the party must assure through persistent and regular work the rallying of a farm laborer and poor peasant nucleus on the kolkhozes. This is all the more necessary since in the kolkhozes themselves a considerable danger of kulak influence remains, particularly in kolkhozes of the more rudimentary type, in view of the fact that as yet they have by no means communalized all the means of production, and the interests of petty owners are generally strong. In this connection it is particularly necessary to strengthen in every possible way the communalized property of the kolkhozes as the bases for the growth of the kolkhoz movement, and also to assure a firm connection between the kolkhozes and the entire Soviet economic system.

A most important task of party organizations is to strengthen in every way the participation and leading influence of urban proletarian elements and of rural proletarian and semiproletarian strata in the kolkhoz movement. In this matter, particular importance attaches to the organization of farm laborer and poor peasant groups in the simpler cooperative productive associations and in the primary form of collective farming (the TOZ).

3. The achieved scope of kolkhoz construction has surpassed all plan assumptions and is revealing ever more clearly that gigantic acceleration in the rate of development of socialist construction that Lenin foresaw.

The party is enjoying constantly growing success in solving the tasks of building a large-scale communalized agriculture, and in so doing is laying bare the capitulatory nature of the right opportunists' views that are opposed to party policy in the area of collectivization of agriculture.

The party and the working class, while fighting relentlessly against opportunistic elements and conciliatoriness toward such elements within its ranks, and while deploying an energetic attack against the class forces hostile to the proletarian dictatorship, have resolutely led the poor and middle peasant masses forward along the path of the socialist reconstruction of agriculture.

Despite the false "theories" of the leaders of the right opposition concerning the 'degradation' of agriculture, we are enjoying, in fact, an accelerating growth of productive forces in agriculture on the basis of the rapid development of the communalized sector and the massive increase in individual poor and middle peasant holdings.

Despite the capitulatory "theories" concerning the kulaks' "growing into" socialism, despite the panicky demands of the right opportunists to unleash "free trade" for the capitalistic elements and to reduce the rate of industrialization and communalization of agriculture, the party is conducting and will continue to conduct a course of resolute struggle against the kulaks, a policy of uprooting capitalism in agriculture, of uniting individual poor and middle peasant holdings as quickly as possible into large-scale kolkhozes, and of preparing conditions for the development of a planned exchange of products between town and countryside.

The results of the collective construction that is underway show the gigantic possibilities for a rise in agricultural productive forces that are implicit in the Soviet system. We are marking the beginning of a *new historical stage* in the socialist transformation of agriculture along the lines of strengthening the production union of the proletarian state with the basic masses of poor and middle peasants in the countryside.

II

4. The basic difficulty in kolkhoz construction in the present period is one of backwardness of the *technical base*. Large-scale, highly productive and truly socialist production in

agriculture can only be built on the basis of modern machine technology and electrification. Therefore the creation of the material and technical base for the socialist transformation of the countryside is a question of primary importance.

The Central Committee plenum approves the Politburo resolution augmenting the plan for the production of tractors and machinery, and providing for an immediate start on the construction of two new tractor plants with a production capacity of 50,000 tractors (caterpillars) each, on the construction of two harvester combine plants, on expansion of plants manufacturing complex farm machinery, chemical industry plants, etc.. It is also necessary to develop the construction of electric power stations and electric machinery for agriculture and for processing agricultural produce. The all-out development of this construction will create the necessary technical base for a large-scale socialist agriculture and the necessary prerequisites for effecting a fundamental technical revolution in agriculture and for the communalization of it.

The Central Committee plenum considers it necessary to begin marshalling the funds of the peasant population to finance this construction, and specifically to do so by arranging at tractor and complex machinery plants for the taking of advance orders—secured by a down payment—directly from individual kolkhozes and from kolkhoz associations for the purchase of tractors, harvester combines, and complex farm machinery. It is necessary to conduct a large-scale campaign at kolkhozes to form a special export fund to offset the cost of imported tractors.

In conditions of a mass development of kolkhoz construction, it is necessary to devote ever greater attention to the construction of large-scale mechanized kolkhozes that would utilize the experience of sovkhozes in their technical organization, gradually becoming true socialist enterprises built on a basis of modern machine technology and the latest achievements of science.

The intervillage machine tractor stations are particularly important to the construction of large-scale kolkhozes. In creating widespread possibilities for reaping the benefits of modern technology on peasant holdings, the machine tractor stations must become centers for the total collectivization of entire raions.

The Central Committee plenum approves the creation of an All-Union Center of Machine Tractor Stations (Traktorotsentr) and its inclusion in the overall system of kolkhoz construction (the All-Union Kolkhoztsentr) as a special autonomous center.

Given the existence of a high percentage of peasant holdings without significant quantities of equipment and livestock and given the acute shortage of tractors and complex machinery, it is a most important task of kolkhoz construction in the present period—apart from the question of creating the higher forms of collectivization on an advanced technical base—to also help the millions of peasant holdings to make more effective use of the simpler production implements within the bounds of the rudimentary kolkhozes and cooperative production associations. An important role belongs to the regional kolkhoz associations, which have been formed at the initiative of the kolkhozes themselves and have completely justified themselves in the practical work of kolkhoz construction. By organizing joint use of complex machinery and tractors on small kolkhozes and by uniting the small kolkhozes for the joint construction of enterprises, tractor pools, and large-scale machine stations with horse or mixed traction (in particular by reorganizing the existing rental centers), the regional associations must become production centers preparing the necessary material and technical prerequisites for strengthening the small kolkhozes and for inducing the surrounding peasant holdings to join them.

Thus the construction of large-scale kolkhozes must develop in various ways and in differing forms, with continuous strengthening of the organizing influence of socialist industry and of the large sovkhozes, under the direction of the proletarian state.

In view of the degree of complexity and the variety of paths for the transition of tens of millions of peasant households to large-scale socialist agriculture, the task of the party consists in developing in every way the masses' own initiative and independent action in kolkhoz construction, while at the same time strengthening the party's leadership of the kolkhoz movement and developing new forms of ties and assistance from the working class to the basic masses in the countryside in the matter of reorganizing agriculture. At the same time, the role of state—and above all of land—agencies in directing kolkhoz construction must be considerably increased.

5. A fundamental shortcoming in the kolkhoz movement is the relatively low *labor productivity*, insufficient production discipline, and the lack of requisite attention by the directing bodies of the kolkhoz movement to the matter of labor organization on kolkhozes. Therefore, a persistent and systematic struggle is needed at each kolkhoz to increase labor productivity, to raise yields, and to augment commodity production.

To these ends it is necessary above all to achieve a decisive breakthrough in increasing labor discipline on kolkhozes on the basis of a truly conscious attitude on the part of kolkhoz members toward their obligations, while at the same time applying the principle of responsibility for work assigned and creating personal material incentives for each kolkhoz to raise labor productivity (piecework payment, work norms, bonus systems, etc.). To increase labor productivity, all possible use must be made of the methods of socialist competition, of developing the work of production meetings, and of widespread development of self-criticism.

An essential matter in strengthening kolkhozes is to organize operations in such a way as to guarantee—depending on the conditions in the region—maximum utilization of the kolkhozes' labor force (animal husbandry, intensive farming, auxiliary enterprises, cottage industry, etc.). The management of the kolkhozes must necessarily keep this in mind in working out their organizational plans.

6. The particular attention of the party, the soviets and the kolkhoz system must be directed toward the problem of *cadres*. The kolkhoz movement has assumed proportions that make necessary a decisive, revolutionary reorganization of the entire system, program, and methods of training organizers, agronomists, engineers, land utilization specialists, technicians, finance and accounting personnel, etc., for kolkhoz construction. Provision must be made for a decisive increase in the number of kolkhoz farmers—particularly those of landless farm labor and poor peasant origins—admitted to higher educational institutions and technicums for the coming school year.

The Central Committee plenum recognizes a need to organize under the Kolkhoztsentr a central school for training the organizers of large-scale kolkhozes.

Besides this it is necessary to organize on a broad scale the training of kolkhoz cadres at sovkhozes and major kolkhozes, which are to serve as a mass school for those who are the builders of the large-scale farms in practice, schools where they are to learn from the experience of state and kolkhoz work the application of the latest machinery, of the new forms of farm production and labor organization, and of improved agronomic methods, the utilization of chemicals, etc.

Industrial workers form a powerful reserve from which to draw managerial cadres for the building of socialist agriculture. The Central Committee considers it necessary in the months immediately ahead—apart from regularly reinforcing the kolkhoz movement with party leadership—to send not less than 25,000 workers with sufficient organizational and political experience into the countryside to work on kolkhozes, at machine tractor stations, in regional associations, etc. The trade unions are to play a most active part in the selection of these workers, putting forward the most advanced workers.

Kolkhoz construction is unthinkable without a rigorous improvement in the cultural standards of the kolkhoz populace. The agencies of the soviets, the kolkhoz system itself, agricultural and consumer cooperatives, and the Soviet public as a whole must develop extensive work in serving the cultural needs of the kolkhoz populace, above all at large kolkhozes and in the areas of complete collectivization. An advance in the work of the societies to liquidate illiteracy and in the work of libraries, an intensification in the work of kolkhoz courses and various types of study by correspondence; maximum enrollment of children in the schools; intensification of cultural and political work among women; widespread development of the schools for peasant young people; mass dissemination of agronomic knowledge, and improvement in the social and everyday services to the kolkhoz populace—and in particular to women (the organizing of creches, public catering, etc.)—are necessary conditions for the successful development of kolkhoz construction. It is also particularly important to set up cultural centers at the intervillage machine tractor stations. Consumer cooperatives are to play a most active role in this work. Particular attention must be devoted to radio and motion pictures, and also to organizing means of communications (telephone, postal service) and to developing road construction at kolkhozes. There must be considerable advance in the servicing of kolkhozes by the general and specialized press.

7. The development of mass kolkhoz construction and lasting success in such construction are unrealizable unless the kolkhoz movement's *communal holdings* are systematically strengthened and increased in every way. The growth and strengthening of the communal sector—and in this connection of the indivisible funds [assets that cannot be distributed to individual peasants] as well—is the basis for creating the necessary production assets on the kolkhozes. All-out enlargement of this kolkhoz base and combatting the squandering of inventory (both animate and inanimate) on the part of new members joining the kolkhozes, are necessary conditions for the development of the kolkhoz movement. It should be taken as a rule, and applied firmly and decisively, that state aid is given to kolkhozes only on condition that the peasantry itself is making growing investments in the kolkhozes, and in particular, that the kolkhozes fulfill the requirements established by farm rules and by agreements on the internal accumulation of farm assets. This aim is to be served by establishing obligatory allocations to the kolkhozes' indivisible funds, by assessing members on the basis of shares, and by setting up special funds for specific purposes (the collection of down payments for the purchase of tractors and for setting up industrial undertakings, the creation of a special export fund in order to increase the import of tractors, farm machinery, etc.).

8. One form of *production and economic regulation* of kolkhozes on the part of the proletarian state should be the signing of contracts with kolkhozes for set amounts of output, the aim being to increase the commodity output of the kolkhozes and to assure planned sales of kolkhoz commodity surpluses to the state on the basis of improved production and development of the kolkhozes' communal sector.

Kolkhozes are to be granted credits, supplied with means of production and provided agronomic and animal husbandry services on condition that they bind themselves to deliver commodity output at set times and in quantities stipulated by contracts covering grain products, livestock, poultry, raw materials, and special crops, etc., in accordance with their operations.

In this connection it is necessary to wage a resolute struggle against kolkhozes that do not fulfil their obligations with respect to the state, preferring instead to sell their surplus to private parties.

9. The kolkhoz movement, which is developing primarily along the line of collectivization of grain growing, must be assigned the task of speeding up in every way the process of communalizing the remaining branches of agriculture on the basis of the *specialization* of kolkhozes in accordance with regional farming characteristics.

Noting the inadequate performance of the kolkhoz system in this area and the inadequate attention to this most important task on the part of the special centers of the agricultural cooperatives, the Central Committee plenum considers it necessary to force the pace in building kolkhozes specializing in livestock, dairy, grain, truck gardening, industrial crops, etc., kolkhozes that are to become a most important base for meeting the country's growing food, raw materials, and export requirements.

Kolkhoz construction, being an integral part of Lenin's cooperative plan and the highest form of cooperation, can only develop successfully by basing itself on the entire system of agricultural cooperatives, which is increasingly evolving from sales and supply cooperatives and the rudimentary forms of production partnership into the kolkhoz movement proper. It is therefore a most important organizational task to establish correct relations between the kolkhoz system and the special systems of agricultural cooperatives.

The Central Committee plenum considers it necessary—in addition to organizational reinforcement of the special systems of agricultural cooperatives and the strengthening of their material and technical base—to organize *autonomous kolkhoz centers* at the basic special centers and special unions of agricultural cooperatives in the various localities, on a basis established by agreement with the All-Union Kolkhoztsentr and basing themselves directly on the kolkhozes and their associations (or regional groupings) and serving their organizational and cooperative needs. The special centers of agricultural cooperatives are to carry out the construction of kolkhozes in the branches of agriculture that they serve, and to do so under the direct supervision of the kolkhoz centers and unions of kolkhozes, and in close coordination with the appropriate branches of industry.

In view of the rapid growth of kolkhoz construction and the need to strengthen the direction of this construction and render technical assistance to it (in particular in connection with the development of enterprises to process agricultural products), the Central Committee plenum considers it expedient to set up special organizations to serve the needs of kolkhozes for capital construction (kolkhoz trusts) attached to the All-Union Kolkhoztsentr and to certain of the major oblast kolkhoz associations.

At the present time particular importance attaches to the union of associations of agricultural cooperatives as a center that unites all agricultural cooperatives, including the kolkhoz system.

10. It should be particularly stressed that in the *national regions* as well, where the remnants of feudal and tribal relations are still strong in the village (aul), and where the transition from a nomadic or seminomadic economy to settled farming is in progress, collectivization and the introduction of advanced machine technology in agriculture play a decisive role in effecting the rise in the material and cultural level of the masses and in drawing them into socialist construction.

The plenum advises the All-Union Kolkhoztsentr and the organizations supplying machinery to devote sufficient attention to collectivization in the national regions of the East and to promote this cause in every way.

11. *Sovkhozes*, being agricultural enterprises of a consistently socialist type, must, to an even greater extent than previously, serve as an example in their practical work as to how a large-scale operation is to be organized and how high technology is to be utilized in agriculture. In addition, these sovkhozes, with a powerful material and technical apparatus at their command must in every way increase their role as levers, which throw the switch to put individual peasant holdings on the track of collectivization.

It is necessary to encourage initiative in the matter of establishing direct economic ties between state industrial enterprises (sugar, flax processing, cotton-ginning mills, etc.) and the sovkhozes, on the one hand, and the surrounding kolkhozes on the other, and wherever possible to create mixed sovkhoz-kolkhoz associations under the overall direction of these industrial enterprises and sovkhozes, with a coordinated economic plan, with a common technical base (tractor teams, repair shops, etc.), and with common enterprises to process their agricultural products (butter, oil, cheese, flax-processing plants, flour mills, etc.).

III

12. In connection with the turbulent growth of the kolkhoz movement and the task confronting the working class and peasant masses of raising the movement to a still higher level, the Central Committee plenum warns against underestimating the difficulties of

kolkhoz construction and in particular against a formal and bureaucratic approach to it and to the evaluation of its results.

The Central Committee plenum considers it a most important task of the *Soviets*—particularly in the countryside—to strengthen in every way their attention to the matter of collectivization. The attention of the Soviets must be directed toward serving the kolkhoz populace as fully as possible on a priority basis, toward making them into bases for an upsurge in, and the socialist reconstruction of, agricultural production, into bases for the soviets' agricultural, social, and cultural measures. It is necessary to strengthen the directing role of the Soviets with respect to the collectives, to raise Soviet responsibility for kolkhoz construction, and to introduce a system whereby the kolkhozes report regularly to the Soviets, but without permitting petty tutelage and administrative interference in the direction of the collectives.

Collectivization of the countryside must occupy a most important place in the work of the *trade unions*. The leading role of the working class in the kolkhoz movement must be consolidated by resolutely assigning workers to the jobs of organizers and executives at kolkhozes and in the kolkhoz system at all levels, which would make it possible to raise the kolkhoz movement to a higher level and to achieve the earliest possible transition to a truly socialist agriculture.

The Central Committee plenum takes note of a growing desire on the part of *industrial workers* to participate actively in the collectivization of the countryside, a desire expressed in the mass organization of worker brigades, in the putting forward of initiators and organizers of kolkhoz construction, in the participation of workers in the production meetings of kolkhozes, in the holding of the "Day of the Harvest and Collectivization", etc. This mass initiative on the part of factory workers must be supported and developed in every way, particularly on the basis of creating a mutual interest in one another's production results. The work of the societies for the patronage of collectivization must be strengthened, and the setting up of new societies to promote collectivization of agriculture must be speeded up; there must be a strengthening of worker participation in passing contracts with kolkhozes for supplying industry with raw materials and the worker centers with food, and the practice of presenting collective farm reports at enterprises, sending worker brigades to the kolkhozes, etc. must be expanded.

The plenum calls attention to the need to intensify in every way the work of enlisting the masses of farm laborers in the kolkhozes and to the special role to be played in this respect by the Agriculture and Timber Workers' Union.

In connection with the new tasks, the immense increase in the scope of the kolkhoz movement and the intensification of the class struggle in the countryside, it is necessary to strengthen in every way the *party direction* of the kolkhoz movement. This requires that all village party cells play a most active part in kolkhoz construction; it also requires that assistance to the kolkhoz movement on the part of all party organizations be increased in every way.

It is necessary to note the inadequacy of the work of Komsomol organizations in the matter of collectivization. It is a most important duty of the Komsomol in the countryside to march in the front ranks of the kolkhoz movement and to regularly assign thousands and thousands of kolkhoz organizers from among their own ranks.

In stepping up the work of implementing the directives of the Sixteenth Party Conference on enlisting the Komsomol and the Communist Party the most conscious members of the kolkhozes and those most devoted to the socialist cause, it is necessary to devote particular attention to organizing the strengthening of party cells in the major kolkhozes. Party organizations must head up the kolkhoz movement in actual fact; by their direction of the kolkhoz movement they must assure the reinforcement of it as the mainstream for enlisting the broad masses of the peasantry in the cause of building socialism.

The change that has taken place among the broad masses of the peasantry with respect to the collectivization of agriculture must, in the forthcoming spring sowing season, become the point of departure for a *new move forward* in the improvement of poor and middle peasant farming and in the socialist reorganization of the countryside. In deploying an attack against capitalist elements across the entire front and in strengthening in every way the production union between socialist industry and agriculture, party organizations must mobilize forces in good time for conducting the forthcoming spring sowing; they must give first priority to the task of further developing mass production cooperation, collectivization of peasant holdings, and development of sovkhoz construction.

The successful progress of grain procurements and the fact that they will be completed by the first of the year frees the forces of the party, soviets, and cooperatives and creates favorable conditions for the conduct of spring sowing. While mobilizing the forces of the working class and striving for highly organized and active worker participation in preparatory work for the spring sowing, the party is to rally the decisive masses of the peasantry to accomplish the tasks of an economic advance and of the transition to collective forms of agriculture. Only in this way—by uniting the masses of poor and middle peasantry behind the party and soviets—can the working class assure a decisive strengthening of the agricultural base of the socialist industrialization of the country and in so doing assure a consolidation in the entire cause of building socialism.

McNeal/Gregor, Vol. 3, 28-38.

PARTY PLENUM APPROVES COLLECTIVIZATION AND INDUSTRIALIZATION GOALS AND REMOVES BUKHARIN FROM POLITBURO. NEWSPAPER SUMMARY.

18 November 1929

Pravda *published a summary of the results of the sessions of the Central Committee Plenum. Readers saw that the Plenum approved the control figures for the national economy, and expected industrial output to exceed the goals of the Five Year Plan and the prewar level by 100 percent, except for the chemical industry. They read that the Plenum approved the accelerated collectivization of farms, that Bukharin was removed from the Politburo, and that other members of the so-called Bukharin group recanted.*

AFTER THE PLENARY SESSION OF THE CC OF THE CPSU

(Lead Article in "Pravda")

The recently held CC Plenum of the CPSU drew a number of important conclusions from the results of the past economic year and showed the broad perspectives of the new phase of socialist construction on which the Party is entering.

The Plenum approved the control figures for the current year. Especially worthy of note in these control figures is the enormous rate of development of the socialist economy, which not only does not lag behind the provisions of the five year plan, but considerably surpasses them. Lenin's slogan—that we must catch up with and get ahead of the capitalist countries is being practically realized by us. At the end of the present economic year the industrial output must have exceeded the prewar output by 100 percent. In the control figures the leading role of heavy industry is especially emphasized. In all the main branches (electroeconomy, fuel industry, metal industry, machine construction, etc.) the control figures considerably exceed the limits laid down for in the five year plan. The only exception is the chemical industry, in which we lag somewhat behind the realization of the five year plan. The enormous importance of this industry, especially for the socialist construction of agriculture, needs no special emphasis. The Party must devote special attention to all the questions connected with the development of the chemical industry and bring about a decisive change in the shortest possible time in this important section of socialist construction.

The great success of the Party in the development of socialist industry can before all be explained by the powerful development of the activity of the working masses, which found particularly clear expression in the spread of socialist competition. The increasing activity, the fact that the working class and the broad masses of the middle peasantry are to a growing extent rallying more closely around the Party on the basis of its general line, form the firm basis of the record rate of development prescribed in the control figures. The most urgent prerequisite for the realization of this rate in the current year is the lowering of prime costs of industrial production by eleven percent. It will not only enable the Party to realize the plan in the sphere of building construction, of the reconstruction of industry and the growth of its production, but also to increase considerably the real wages of the workers (on an average by twelve percent). Our party organizations must without waiting a minute, set about with the greatest energy the work for lowering prime costs.

The decisive results which the Party achieved in the development of heavy industry, and which increased the leading role of industry in the improvement and the socialist reconstruction of agriculture along with a correct general policy of the Party in the village, created the preconditions for the solution of the grain problem, which has caused us great difficulties in the last two years. Grain provisioning, which in the very important districts has been carried out before the fixed term, the collection of numerous grain reserves by means of the ever extending process of raising the level of and reconstructing agriculture on a socialist basis, incontestably prove, in spite of the pessimistic prophesies of the Rights, that we have emerged from the grain crisis. The Party is now confronted by the problem of cattle-breeding. A successful solution of this question not only means a radical solution of all the questions connected with the food supply of the masses, but also the creation of a firm raw material basis for numerous industries.

The Plenum discussed with particular care and attention the questions of collectivization of the peasant economy. The magnificent results achieved in this sphere by the Party and which even surpass the most optimistic calculations and estimates, already now render possible the complete collectivization of enormous districts of the Soviet Union with a population of several dozens of millions (Northern Caucasus, steppe district of the Ukraine, etc.) as a real task for the next eighteen months or two years. The follow-in-the-rear and panic-spreading policy of the Rights, who recently maintained that the peasants would not join the collective undertakings, has suffered an annihilating defeat. The accelerated rate of the collectivization of peasant undertakings renders the leadership of this movement by the Party a very complicated and difficult task. Precisely now there arises in its whole acuteness the question of socialist transformation of the millions of peasant undertakings which are linked up in the collective undertakings, with which question there is bound up the thorough overcoming of the mentality of the peasant as a petty proprietor, a mentality which he brings with him when joining the collective undertaking. The supplying of machines, especially tractors, and the organization of labor are becoming the decisive questions of collective construction. The Party must also clearly realize that the kulak who failed in his attempt to keep back the small and middle peasants from mass affiliation to the collective undertakings, is now striving, and will continue to strive to exert his antiSoviet disintegrating activity inside the collective undertakings in order to create for himself points of support for his struggle against the Party. To accept the kulak into the collective undertaking is quite out of the question. The local Party organizations must make it their immediate and urgent task to purge the collective undertakings of the kulak elements. The Party must make use of the mass process of collectivization which has seized the village in order finally and completely to isolate the kulak politically.

In connection with the general tasks of the socialist transformation of agriculture the Plenum dealt with the work of the Ukrainian Party organization as a special item of the agenda. The Ukrainian steppe land forms a powerful basis for the development of agricultural export which will be able already in the next few years to glut the world market with hundreds of millions of puds of wheat. Those portions of the Ukraine situated on the right bank of the Dnieper with their reserves of labor power, form the basis for an intensive agriculture. In the socialist transformation of agriculture the Party in the Ukraine is encountering the specially bitter resistance of the kulak who possesses considerable economic power and political experience. The difficulties of the struggle against the kulak are being complicated by the national question. The Plenum approved the work of the Ukrainian Party organization in the village, which is characterized by the successful conclusion of the grain provision campaign before the fixed time.

The decision of the Plenum regarding the establishment of a People's Commissariat for Agriculture for the whole Soviet Union is of very great importance for the further activity of the Party in the sphere of agriculture. The main task of this commissariat is to accelerate the socialist reconstruction of agriculture in the backward republics, with the assistance of the advanced proletarian districts of the Soviet Union.

The Plenum then dealt with the question of the economic cadres which is especially acute today. The pace of socialist construction makes great claims upon the experts, whereby it must be taken into account that a certain portion of the old specialists has gone over into the camp of the active enemies of socialist construction and must be replaced by new forces. Up to now we have not made much progress towards the solution of the question of cadres. The practical realization of the measures indicated by the Plenum for the preparation of the necessary cadres, is at present one of the most urgent tasks of the Party. Special importance attaches to the training of engineers for the smelting and chemical industry, of agronomists for the socialized portion of agriculture and of medium technical forces.

The period between the Sixteenth Party Conference and the November Plenum has clearly confirmed the correctness of the general line of the Party. It is therefore no mere chance that in this period there took place the disintegration of Trotskyism, which for many years has been conducting an unrelenting fight against the policy of our Party. In this same period there was exposed before the Party the antiLeninist, antiBolshevik and bourgeois-liberal nature of the Right deviation led by Comrade Bukharin, a deviation which since the April Plenum of the Party has crystallized into a definite system of conceptions fundamentally differing from the general line of the Party. Therefore, the last Plenum declared propaganda for the conceptions of Right opportunism and conciliatory tendencies to be incompatible with membership in the Party.

The best elements of the Bukharin group have realized the antiBolshevik and antiLeninist character of Bukharin's opposition and the complete bankruptcy of their policy in face of the strict test of facts. Already during the discussion on the first item of the agenda Comrade Kotov, the former second secretary of the Moscow district committee, declared his renouncement of the opposition. At the same time, Comrade Mikhailov submitted a declaration in which he unconditionally recognized the general line of the Party. Immediately before the conclusion of the Plenum, Comrades Uglanov and Kulikov decisively dissociated themselves from the Bukharin opposition. Thus the nucleus of the old Moscow leadership has separated from the Opposition.

The leaders of the Right are clinging to their conceptions which have been rejected by the Party. The Right leaders, headed by Comrade Bukharin, who hypocritically declare their agreement with the general line of the Party and who grudgingly admit, along with the bourgeois correspondents and the bourgeois national economists, the successes of the Party, at the same time dare to reproach the Party with the fact that the plans for the extension of the area under seed have not been fulfilled, etc.; they defend the "recipe" which they proposed in the spring of this year (importing of grain, increase in prices for agricultural products) and demand the abandonment of the emergency measures and of the offensive against the kulak. The leaders of the Rights not only do not withdraw their former accusations against the Party (military-feudal exploitation, degeneration to Trotskyism, growth of bureaucratism), but they also add to them new accusations which in their mendacity place everything hitherto in the shade. They declare, for instance, that the Party and the Comintern had advocated the theory of the growing of the kulak into socialism.

The two-faced tactic of the Right leaders cannot be estimated otherwise than the Trotskyist maneuvers: As a temporary retreat in order to renew the attacks upon the Party as soon as fresh difficulties arise. The Plenum of the CC which declared propaganda of Right opportunism and conciliatory tendencies to be incompatible with membership of the CPSU, decided to recall from the Politburo the chief leader and spiritual father of the Rights, Comrade Bukharin. The least attempt of the Rights to continue the fight against the Party line will immediately be answered by organizational measures. The Plenum, which recognized the continuation of the most ruthless struggle against the Right opposition to be necessary, at the same time advocated a determined overcoming of Left tendencies, which are becoming noticeable in various strata of the Party as well as of the conciliatory attitude towards them.

The decisions of the November Plenum, which give a clear answer to the most important questions of present politics, will play a great role in the further closer rallying together of the Party on the basis of the Leninist general line and in the solution of the tremendous tasks by which the Party is confronted in the present stage of the socialist offensive.

International Press Correspondence, Vol. 9, No. 66 (29 November 1929), 1408-1410.

LITVINOV REPORTS THAT USSR MAINTAINED INTERNATIONAL POSITION

4 December 1929

Maxim Litvinov, as Deputy Commissar for Foreign Affairs, delivered a report to the USSR Central Executive Committee on the successes and failures of Soviet foreign policy, and on the current international situation. He said that the USSR had on the whole maintained its positions. The bulk of the report consisted of disarmament, conflict in China, and Anglo-Soviet relations. He said that the USSR was surrounded by capitalist enemies who looked for any opportunity to vilify and encircle the workers' state and that Soviet foreign policy, in advocating peace through disarmament and nonaggression pacts, and its growing economic and military power prevented intervention and reduced hostility from the capitalist states. He pointed to successes in the resumption of Anglo-Soviet diplomatic relations, in the counter-attack of the Far Eastern Army in Manchuria, in increasing relations with Italy, and in stabilizing relations with Japan. He said that amicable relations with Germany were being maintained, but that there were groups which were advocating a radical change in relations with the USSR. He explained the illegal loss of control of the Chinese Eastern Railway and accused the imperialist powers of encouraging and supporting China in this quarrel over the CER.

MAXIM LITVINOV
THE INTERNATIONAL SITUATION OF THE SOVIET UNION
Our Five Year Plan of Peace

In contradiction to the other, the economic commissariats, the Commissariat for Foreign Affairs is unfortunately not in a position to submit a five year plan of its work, showing the development of its foreign policy. Why this is so, should not be hard to explain. Whereas in submitting the control figures and setting up a plan of economic development in regard to the Soviet Union we can start altogether from our own wishes and endeavors, from a consideration of our own possibilities and requirements, and from the firmly established principles of our own policy, we are faced in our consideration of the development of international politics with numerous factors which can hardly be estimated, with numerous elements beyond our control and our influence.

International life consists not only of our own endeavors and actions, but of those of a number of other countries which are built up on a system different from that of the Soviet Union, which pursue other aims and employ other means to attain them than those which are permissible in our case. In these countries the capitalist order of society still prevails, with no less anarchy and no less chaos in foreign politics as in economy. The economic differences existing between these countries create political differences. The ruin called forth by the imperialist war and the incisive alterations it brought about have underlined and deepened these differences.

If it proves possible by means of political arrangements and combinations temporarily to eliminate the one or other differences within a group of states, it is only to make way for new differences between this group and other groups. The geographic seat of these differences may be changed, but neither their extent, volume nor quality is altered.

If we also take into consideration the instability of the inner political systems in the majority of these states (which in most cases has developed since the war), the frequent changes of the so-called democratic Parliamentary system into Fascist, semiFascist, and into such other forms of government for which not even a general designation has yet been found, the continual internal struggle of the classes and of the political parties representing their interests, and the kaleidoscope of changes of government and the overthrow of governments whose policy was in many instances diametrically opposed to that of their predecessors, it will be apparent that there can be no question of system in international politics. In such circumstances, the lack of success attending most of the international economic and political congresses and conferences during the last few years is not to be wondered at.

In contradistinction to the aspect I have just shown of international life, we need to exercise no unique modesty in understanding the invariable consistency and systematic character of the foreign policy of the Soviet Union. The cornerstone of this policy is what it was at the inception of the Soviet Government 12 years ago, the defense of the achievements of the October Revolution against all attacks from the outside, the endeavor to secure peaceful conditions for the internal development of Socialism and, as far as lies in our power, to preserve the workers of the world from the sufferings and burdens of a further war. The power in the hands of the proletariat, which has always stood for the cause of international peace, strict adherence to the principles of the October Revolution and to the heritage of Lenin, nonparticipation in political groupings and combinations of some States against others, the absence of all imperialist desires and efforts for the subjugation of other nations, the solution of national questions on the basis of a maximum of toleration and respect for the national culture even of the smallest nationality—such are the factors which lend special stability to the foreign policy of the Soviet Union.

The fact that on one-sixth of the earth's surface there exists so stable and peace-imbued a State, which is far from cherishing aggressive plans of any kind, is in itself a powerful factor of peace.

I shall not discuss all the concrete steps taken by the Soviet Government for the sake of ensuring universal peace, having already reported on the subject to the preceding session of the Central Executive Committee of the Soviet Union.

A new, increased, and absolutely impartial proof of our peaceful tendencies lies in our five year plan, the realization of which presumes that we aspire to a state of inviolable peace. It ought to be apparent to all that it would be madness to start this plan, which calls for no slight exertion of all our resources, if we were not determined at the same time not to allow any breach of the peace, in so far as it depends upon us. Nor is the realization of the five year plan our final and only aim, but merely the foundation of the gigantic Socialist structure at which we are at work and which we intend to erect. The first five year plan will be followed by other similar plans, for the realization of which peaceful conditions will be just as necessary as in the present case.

The Capitalist Sabotage of Disarmament

Important as the contribution of the Soviet Union is to the cause of peace, it cannot be guaranteed by the efforts of our country alone. Therefore the Soviet Union, besides coming forward actively and independently with peace proposals of its own, is ready to meet any action of peace from whatever nation it emanates and by whatever considerations it is prompted.

The Soviet Union, which looks upon the complete liquidation or the restriction of armaments as the surest guarantee of peace, made a point in the current year of continuing its participation in the Preparatory Commission of the Disarmament Conference, although this commission had throughout the previous sessions given convincing proof of its inability and unwillingness to engage seriously in discussing the problem of disarmament. At its sixth session in the course of this year, the Preparatory Commission almost wholly completed its "activities", which unfortunately ended in the final turning down of the Soviet Government's suggestions, both of total disarmament and of an essential reduction in the present status of armaments. The Commission, which rejected both draft conventions submitted by the Soviet Union and insisted on the discussion of the project worked out by itself, persistently declined all the Soviet Government's amendments to this project and deleted from it everything that hinted at even a partial disarmament.

By reciprocal concessions the delegations managed to secure the removal of all such items in the project as had reference to the armaments in their respective countries. Thus the Commission deleted from the draft convention all mention of war reserves, whether of men or of material. It is sufficiently characteristic of the work of the last session of the Preparatory Commission that it should determinedly and persistently have denied my repeated suggestion that the project of the convention should make mention of the "reduction of armaments". The Commission thus determined to recommend to the upcoming Conference of Disarmament not a reduction but a restriction of armaments, which will allow not only of a maintenance of the present status but even of its augmentation.

As I have already remarked, the Commission has almost completed its activity, not having dealt at all at its last three sessions with the problem of naval disarmament. In this regard certain naval Powers, which will meet at the London Conference in January next, have been carrying on separate negotiations which have led to little result so far.

It is to be seen that the capitalist countries manifest consistency, uniformity, unanimity, and even a certain system in their sabotage of disarmament and of other measures for peace, in spite of all modifications and oscillations of their foreign policies.

The Soviet Union Surrounded by Enemies

It would, however, be unjust, were we not also to record another uniform characteristic in the policy of these countries. I am referring to their consistent animosity towards the Soviet

Union. This unfriendly attitude naturally assumes different aspects at different moments and in different States, being sometimes stronger and sometimes temporarily weaker, but at the very least always remains latent. This, of course, does not apply absolutely to all countries, but to the majority of States. I am not forgetting either that in all these countries there are millions and dozens of millions of proletarians who follow with warm sympathy and affection all happenings in the land in which Socialism is being built up, taking moral part in its development and lending it their moral support. What we are up against is the hostility of the reactionary elements of the big and petty bourgeoisie, the ruling circles, and the majority of the press organs, in these countries. The main agency lending expression and realization to this policy of hostility, is the capitalist and the so-called Social-Democratic press, which for the last twelve years has never ceased throwing mud at the Soviet Union and its statesmen, inventing impossible occurrences, distorting the true state of affairs in the Soviet Union, making the most of the inevitable difficulties encountered in the execution of our gigantic tasks, passing over our achievements and successes in silence, and charging us with "sins" we never committed with the employment of the alleged revelations of false witnesses, forged documents, and other equally dirty means. Not only the press, however, but many Governments are anything but fastidious in regard to the obviously inferior productions of forgers from the scum of the "white guard" emigrant circles.

The forgers of antiSoviet documents continue to enjoy the hospitality and sometimes also the protection of the authorities in instances which are on friendly terms with us and this even in instances in which the activities of the forgers in question harm the interests of the countries in which they have found refuge.

The unfriendly attitude and the hostility to which I have referred are inter alia, also fostered by the policy of nonrecognition of the Soviet Union on the part of certain States and by the attempts of other States to injure the prestige of the Soviet Union. The resulting atmosphere of enmity and ill will can very naturally not only not be conducive to the consolidation of peace, on the contrary it fosters an increase of distrust and unrest in regard to international relations. Nay, more than this, for such an atmosphere is at times a positive encouragement of the most adventurous and irresponsible of governments, inducing them to take steps which may occasion an immediate jeopardization of peace.

The Conflict with China

In outlining the present position, reference must also be made to the differences with China which have arisen in the current year. I need not dwell here on the merits of the Soviet Union in the interest of the Chinese people and of the Chinese national government, which found their main utterance in the renunciation of the unequal treaties, extraterritorial rights, and other privileges. On the other hand, the Chinese people are still burdened by unequal treaties with other States, which guard their concessions, jurisdiction, and privileges with troops and warships. How is it then that in relation to these States the Nanking rulers have recourse to the most slavishly abject petitions and put up with all sorts of abuse and humiliation, whereas in relation to the one State which has recognized the equal rights of the Chinese nation and its unrestricted authority on its own territory, and which has concluded with China an equitable treaty highly favorable to Chinese interests, the Nanking and Mukden generals have not observed the usual diplomatic forms but have decided in favor of impudent and provocative actions, measures of violence, and armed attacks? How is it that in the last few years the history of the relations between the ruling men of China and the Soviet Union has been replete with the systematic violation on the part of the former of voluntarily concluded treaties, and with assaults, arbitrary occupations, and the bestial treatment of official representatives of the Soviet Union?

How is it to be explained that, after completing this policy of violence by the occupation of the Chinese Eastern Railway (jointly administered by the two Governments on the basis of a treaty), the Chinese generals impudently flung a challenge in the face of the Soviet Union, a step which would undoubtedly have led to war at once but for the patience and love of peace of the Soviet Government? How can such a striking contrast in the conduct of Nanking, in relation to the imperialist States and to the Soviet Union, respectively, be explained? A partial explanation, certainly, is to be found in the fact that they reckon on our love of peace and on our well known lack of imperialist desires. To provoke a quarrel with the imperialist Powers means to incur danger, seeing that in spite of the Kellogg agreement and the League of Nations it could give rise to fresh conquests in China, to an extension of the privileges of foreigners, to the imposition of heavy contributions on the Chinese, and the like. Of the Soviet Union, the Nanking Government obviously does not expect any such reprisals. It has therefore entered upon this adventure in the persuasion that at the worst the Soviet Union will make use of its forces merely for the restitution of its illegally violated rights. But this only partly explains the procedure of the Nanking Government, which would hardly have risked an action of such far-reaching consequences to itself had it not reckoned with the general antiSoviet atmosphere and therefore with the sympathies, or possibly even the help, of the capitalist States. Even if, therefore, we eliminate the very probable presumption of some other Power or group of Powers having egged China on in this quarrel, it must be recognized that in any case the responsibility for the conflict on the Russo-Chinese frontier lies with the capitalist States collectively, seeing that by their antiSoviet policy they encouraged the hope that they would support any action undertaken against the Soviet Union. There can be no doubt but that without tacit, or possible active, support on the part of the other Powers in the early stages of the conflict and without the hope engendered by the universal hostility towards the Soviet Union, Nanking would never have resolved to adopt the provocative policy which has led to the present state of affairs.

The situation became so serious that we were forced to equip the Special Army of the Far East, being that we had no guarantee that the Nanking Government would not be induced by the same unseen hand to undertake further hostile steps and that no attacks would be made on our frontiers by Chinese or White Guard bandits. Our misgivings proved to be well founded. During the last few months there were not a few cases of military provocation on the part of the Chinese, which naturally met with firm resistance by the Army of the Far East. At each new attack of the aggressors, this resistance became more deadly. Our troops would have placed themselves in too disadvantageous a position if, after driving back the bands and military units which had invaded our territory, they had halted at the frontier, thus affording them the possibility of reoccupying their former positions for the purpose of fresh attacks. Our troops had thus in some instances to destroy the "nests" in which the most frequent and most troublesome attacks on our frontiers were prepared, since this way of proceeding was the only possible one in the interests of the border population. Such countermeasures are of an exclusively defensive character and pursue no political aims.

At the same time we cannot forget that the Soviet citizens remaining in Manchuria, workers and employees of the Chinese Eastern Railway, are constantly exposed to preposterous insults, cruelties, tortures, and even to execution, without any fault on their part. The rumors spread by the Chinese as to the conspiracies and propaganda on the part of our citizens which they profess to have discovered, are naturally no more than childish fairy-tales, which no serious person in China or outside China would believe. We are far from holding the Chinese people responsible for these actions; we blame only those who are really guilty of the antiSoviet policy, the present rulers of China, all the more so as this policy is highly detrimental to China itself, since it impedes the fight of the Chinese people for emancipation from the unequal treaties and for the renunciation of extraterritoriality by the foreigners. Only recently I was asked not without malice by a foreign diplomat in Moscow whether I did not recognize the mistake we had made in waiving our right to extraterritoriality in China.

"Just see", he said, "what liberties the Chinese are taking with your citizens." I replied that in spite of what had happened we had no reason to regret our policy of friendship towards the Chinese people. It was not in our renunciation of extraterritoriality that the mistake lay;

it is the policy of the Governments of Nanking and Mukden that is mistaken and mad, inasmuch that their policy of forcing China to submit with an excuse to declare that their policy of forcing China to submit to extraterritoriality and refusing to recognize the sovereignty of the Chinese people on their own territory was just and right.

We know that the Chinese people are longing for as speedy as possible a solution of the conflict, which is confirmed by the fact that the Nanking and Mukden Governments again and again publish reports of negotiations having been entered into with the Soviet Government. These reports are obviously intended to pacify the Chinese people. As a matter of fact, Nanking sought and still seeks to avoid negotiations. True, a short while ago the Nanking Government made us a suggestion through the German Government for the signing of a common declaration. But when, in accepting their drafted formula and in order to test their sincerity and procure a guarantee that they would really fulfil their obligations, we suggested the immediate reinstatement of the Soviet director of the Chinese Eastern Railway and his assistant according to the Nanking and Mukden treaties, our proposals were declined. We submitted minimum preconditions for the solution of the conflict, from which we were not willing to depart. This we had declared so often and so categorically that the Nanking and Mukden Governments must have been absolutely aware of the fact that the quarrel could only be settled by an acceptance of our conditions. If they nevertheless hesitated and delayed a settlement, this is again to be explained by their hope of an intervention on the part of a third Power of the League of Nations.

It was only in the last few days, when the Chinese and White Guard bands had received a serious lesson at the hands of the Army of the Far East, that Chang-Hsuch-Liang, commander-in-chief and governor of the provinces mainly affected by the economic and military results of the greatly protracted operations, officially announced the acceptance of our conditions, a step now confirmed by the recently published protocol, signed by his diplomatic commissar Tsai.

In this connection I should like to point out that the situation on the Chinese Eastern Railway was based prior to the quarrel not only on the Peking agreement but also on the Mukden agreement concluded with the father of Chang-Hsuch-Liang, that we have never formally recognized the Nanking Government, and that the relations into which we had entered with Nanking were interrupted through its own fault. And just as we are about to prepare a peaceful settlement of the conflict with Mukden, the Nanking Government, on its own initiative or else at the instigation of some outside agency, makes a fresh attempt to obtain the help of the imperialist Powers and of the League of Nations for the purpose of upsetting the peaceful and speedy solution of the dispute.

The Intervention of the Imperialist Powers

It is probably well known from press reports that the Governments of the United States, France, and Great Britain have declared their willingness to grant Nanking the "help" demanded. They are said to be anxious as to the preservation of peace and therefore consider it their duty to interfere and to prevent a peaceful settlement of the quarrel. When Nanking was planning and preparing the occupation of the Chinese Eastern Railway, when subsequently it effected the occupation, and when we brought the Chinese attacks on our territory to the knowledge of the public, these "peace-loving" Powers did not think that such provocative actions could disturb the peaceable and amicable relations between the Soviet Union and China and prove a menace to peace. They did nothing to prevent China from undertaking these steps, they did not hasten to intervene, nor did they draw the attention of the Nanking Government to the illegality and senselessness of this mode of procedure and to the justice and acceptable character of our conditions. Only now that the Mukden Government has convinced itself that the situation on the Chinese Eastern Railway not only promises no advantages for China but entails great damage and sacrifices to that country now that the Mukden Government has taken the only possible step under the circumstances for the purpose of putting an end to this state of affairs, the Powers begin to get busy and confer together to find means of prompting China to further obstinacy and procrastination. And all this is done in the name of peace, in the name of the Kellogg Agreement.

No fewer than 55 nations signed this agreement, and three of them, without any authorization of the part of others, consider themselves called upon to safeguard its stipulations.

In this connection they probably had need of a special mental effort so as to forget for the time being their own detachments of troops at Peking, Tientsin, Shanghai, and Weihawei, their cruisers and torpedo boats, their submarines and minesweepers in the Chinese harbors and on the Yangtse River, their troops in Egypt and on the Rhine, and the fairly recent occurrence in Central America, besides numerous other facts which greatly encumber their past and even their present. The American Government even forgot that our Soviet Government, which is after all only twelve years old, is a "negligible" factor the existence of which they had made up their minds not to notice and not to recognize. Their declaration says that they are following the development of events with anxiety. To our knowledge, however, there is not in this country no representative of the American Government in a position to follow, from the Russian side, the events on the Russo-Manchurian border, while we, without any representative in the United States, are also not in a position to inform the American Government of the matters in which Americans could really follow the events in question and are really informed in this regard. True, the representative of Nanking, that well known Soviet-hater U-Tsao-Tsu, has free access to the State Department in Washington. He is probably also Mr. Stimson's main informant. But does Mr. Stimson never consider that such information can be neither exhaustive nor unprejudiced, and that, at the very least, it might be called one-sided? We therefore think it particularly strange that just the American Government should appear to be the initiator of the collective intervention of the three Powers.

However badly and one-sidedly the participants in this intervention are or desired to be informed, there is one fact which they cannot overlook. The last repulsion of the Chinese bands by our troops has apparently convinced the Chinese generals concerned that they cannot resist the Red Army with any chance of success. In case of a further advance, our Far Eastern Army is not likely to meet with any serious resistance.

We are thus in a position in which the imperialist Powers generally prefer not to negotiate but simply to dictate their conditions. And how about ourselves? Are we forcing China to accept any new conditions? The protocol we signed yesterday together with Mr. Tsai proves that we are not. Our conditions have remained the same as at the commencement of the conflict. This fact alone proves most unquestionably that the countermeasures of the Far Eastern Army have no political aims in view and can therefore in no sense be said to infringe the Kellogg Pact.

What results are likely to arise from the intervention of the Powers? In my opinion not at all. At the very worst, the originators of this intervention will be able to look to the credit of the cause of peace a certain delay or complication in the negotiations already begun and to increase the pressure exercised by Nanking on Mukden. But I am rather of the opinion that Mukden, and possibly also Nanking, will understand that we shall not allow ourselves to be dissuaded by an intervention from the standpoint we have occupied from the very beginning, and that a delay can merely enhance the disadvantages accruing for China. We believe that we are on the way to a definite settlement of the quarrel in regard to the Chinese Eastern Railway and also to the elimination of all possibility of a further artificial spread of enmity and distrust between the people of the Soviet Union and of China, who are anxious to live not only at peace but in relations of sincere friendship and mutual respect.

Be this as it may, whether the immediate contact now reestablished between Mukden and ourselves leads to a speedy settlement of the points at issue or whether the Powers hostile both to the Soviet Union and to China succeed temporarily in preventing this settlement, we are inspired with the conviction that, relying on the general sympathy our policy meets with among the workers and peasants of the Soviet Union, on the consciousness of our rights which are not even contested by our enemies, and on the strength of our Far Eastern Army, which has already given so much proof of its steadfastness, unbounded devotion, and courage, we shall attain an acceptance of our equitable conditions and the restoration of the violated rights of our Workers' and Peasants' Republic.

Adjustment of the Differences between
Great Britain and the Soviet Union

By means of Bolshevik persistence, discipline, and consistency, we recently succeeded in terminating another serious difference, a difference which greatly encumbered the international position and represented perhaps an even more serious menace to peace than the events on the Russo-Chinese border. I am referring to the Anglo-Soviet difference now eliminated. Both these conflicts, it will be remembered, gave rise to illegal and provocative attacks on Soviet institutions. In both cases much was based on forged documents and on a malicious distortion of the character of Soviet policy. Apart from this purely outward analogy, the two quarrels arose from the same far spread hostility towards the Soviet Union of which I have already made mention. Both the British initiative at the rupture of relations and the Chinese adventure started from an expectation of sympathy, support, and even imitation on the part of the other Powers.

It was temporarily believed at the Commissariat for Foreign Affairs that the questions arising in connection with the termination of the Anglo-Soviet differences would have to be submitted for solution to the Central Executive Committee. I trust I may be permitted to dwell upon this matter in greater detail and to point out how an appeal to the Central Executive Committee might have been occasioned and why such a necessity no longer obtained. It is a well known fact that the chief sources of conflict between ourselves and the British lie in the so-called financial claims of the British bourgeoisie, resulting from our enactments in regard to the cancellation of the Tsarist debts and the nationalization of the banks and factories. These claims were in part the cause of the intervention which fostered civil war and protracted it for several years, while at the same time they called forth our counterclaims in respect of the severe material damage inflicted on our country and our citizens. Great Britain, which spent hundreds of millions on intervention only to suffer defeat, continued its endeavors to obtain a satisfaction of its claims by peaceful means, which consisted in the economic blockade of the Soviet Union and subsequently for many years in a refusal to recognize the Soviet Government and to resume diplomatic relations. When these means also failed and the Soviet Union persistently declined negotiations of any kind whatever in regard to the proffered claims pending the resumption of normal diplomatic relations, Great Britain, personified by the Labor Government, recognized the Soviet Union and thus rendered negotiations possible.

These negotiations led to the draft of a commercial treaty and a provisional general treaty, embodying certain foundations for the solution of the problems of the British claims and of our counterdemands.

With the aid of a document opportunely prepared and known in history as the "Zinoviev Letter", the Conservatives defeated the Labor Party and immediately refused the ratification of the treaties just mentioned. The question of British claims was again left pending, since with characteristic steadfastness the Soviet Government refused to go beyond the concessions it had agreed to at the time when the treaties were first drawn up. After two years and a half of fruitless endeavors, the Conservative Government resorted to new "heroic" means—to the breaking off of diplomatic relations, hoping in this way to force the Soviet Government to agree to such conditions for a solution of the matter of claims as the most irreconcilable and reactionary circles of the British bourgeoisie were endeavoring to force upon it. The Conservatives would not have resolved on a step of such moment if they had not reckoned on finding allies and imitators in the other leading European Powers. In this they were destined to be disappointed.

For a resumption of relations, the Conservative Government made it an ultimative condition that all points at issue should first be discussed and settled in the manner it desired. Negotiations within the limits of ordinary diplomatic intercourse, on the basis of equality did not appear opportune to the British Conservatives. They preferred to decline normal relations, hoping thus to bring pressure to bear upon us and to force us to accept their conditions. But we did not beg pardon or profess penitence, nor yet did we apply with suggestions to the Conservative Government. In British industrial circles, including the Conservatives, serious doubts arose as to the correctness of the tactics chosen by the British Government, which not only did not accelerate the solution of questions in which these circles were interested but obviously harmed the British economy. One of the results of these doubts and on the attempts undertaken in the City to find new ways of solving the problems of interest to the British economy was the sending of a delegation of industrialists to Moscow this year. It was apparent that the ace of the Conservative Government in its antiSoviet game had been trumped.

Along with other failures in foreign politics, the rupture of diplomatic relations with the Soviet Union played a part in bringing about the defeat of the Conservative Party at the last British elections. It was not hard for their opponents to exploit the failure of the breach for election purposes by setting up an opposite program of an immediate and unconditional resumption of diplomatic relations with the Soviet Union.

The promises made by the Labor Party during the election campaign are naturally a domestic affair of Great Britain's and impose no obligations on the British Government in its relations to ourselves. But since they were made quite openly there was no possibility for us to ignore them or to pretend we did not know of them. Apart from these promises and pledges, however, it was not to be expected that the party that had issued victoriously from the elections and that had severely criticized the Conservative policy towards the Soviet Union, would not, on coming to power, seriously decide in favor of an opposite course to the Conservative policy.

We must once more call to mind that this policy consisted in the endeavor to force us to settle the questions at issue prior to the resumption of normal relations. We were therefore not a little surprised when, instead of immediately informing us of their readiness to resume normal relations without further delay, the new British Government suggested that we should send a representative to England for the purpose of negotiating. True, according to the wording of the formal proposal, the negotiations were merely to refer to the nature of the deliberations to take place once normal relations had been resumed. It seemed to us, however, that this point might also have been discussed when the main negotiations themselves were started, all the more so seeing that the volume and nature of the questions at issue were very well known to both parties concerned and that the Soviet Government had never been averse to attempting the solution of these questions in normal circumstances. Seeing, however, that our policy consists in a firm representation of our decisive standpoint and our essential interests without quarrelling over trifles of a technical nature, we sent Comrade Dovgalevsky to London as our representative, at the same time carefully informing the British Government that the discussions should refer only to the form of negotiations and not to their contents. When Comrade Dovgalevsky reached London, however, he found himself faced with the following proposal on the part of Henderson: Since the first session of the new British Parliament is over and the next session will not begin for about three months, and since the Government cannot well resolve on the resumption of relations without the sanction of Parliament, it would perhaps be advisable to make use of the interim for discussing and solving the points at issue.

It was thus suggested that, pending the resumption of normal relations, and therefore in a situation in which normal relations did not exist between the two Governments, we should enter into negotiations for the sake of satisfying the pretensions of the British bourgeoisie. In its actual substance, therefore, this suggestion does not differ from the proposal which for several years the Conservative Government tried in vain to coerce us into accepting. This suggestion was by no means in accordance with the purpose for which Comrade Dovgalevsky had been invited to London and had been delegated thither by us. His further sojourn in London was thus useless. We had no choice but to recall him and to declare to Henderson that his suggestion would be submitted to the Central Executive Committee or its presidium.

Why did the People's Commissariat for Foreign Affairs resolve to submit the matter to the Central Executive Committee? Naturally not because it considered it necessary or possible to abandon the standpoint it had occupied for many years or because it expected to receive new directives from the Committee. The decision of the Committee was not hard to foresee. In view of the lack of understanding evinced not only by the Conservative Government but also by the new British Government for our standpoint and for its irrevocability it seemed to us to be right that the highest legislative institution of the Soviet Union should be enabled to declare once and for all that no Government and no means of coercion would succeed in ousting the Soviet Government from the positions it occupied in defense of the most essential interests of the Soviet Union.

It was necessary that all doubt should once and for all be dispelled and all hope destroyed of the possibility of concessions on our part, concessions which we had more than once declared to be impossible.

Mr. Henderson understood that our reference to the Central Executive Committee constituted a more decisive refusal of his suggestion than a simple "No". He once more invited our representative to London thereby giving us to understand that this time he would limit himself exclusively to matters of procedure.

The second meeting between Dovgalevsky and Henderson really ended with the signing of the protocol regarding the agenda of the coming negotiations. And this protocol, which embodied the obligation of an immediate complete resumption of normal diplomatic relations and the exchange of ambassadors, Mr. Henderson promised to submit to Parliament. In due course, the House of Commons sanctioned the protocol by the votes of the Labor and Liberal members against those of the Conservatives, among whom there were, however, some apostates, whereupon the Governments of the Soviet Union and Great Britain appointed their ambassadors with the observance of all the customary forms.

Old Claims and Propaganda

We have pleasure in recording the fact of the resumption of normal relations with Great Britain which, we do not doubt, also fully and wholly corresponds to the interests of the British people. All sincere friends of peace must rejoice that the state of discord between two such powerful States as the Soviet Union and Great Britain is now at an end. The adjustment of the Anglo-Soviet differences must be considered as the removal of one of the greatest anomalies of international life. But what actually happened? Is not the existence of diplomatic relations between any two capitalist States looked upon as an altogether normal and ordinary phenomenon, not deserving of any particular degree of attention? Why, then, is the resumption of relations in this instance looked upon as anything extraordinary? There is no satisfactory answer to this question, unless we realize the atmosphere to which I have already referred, the atmosphere of general hostility towards the Soviet Union. In spite of numerous declarations on the part of statesmen of the capitalist countries as to their alleged endeavors to include the Soviet Union in the so-called "family of nations" on the basis of full equality and their readiness to concede to the people of the Soviet Union the right to construct their own social and political system, they are in fact of the opinion that the absence of diplomatic relations between the Soviet Union and capitalist countries is altogether a normal state of affairs. The resumption of relations with the Soviet Union is looked upon as something out of the ordinary, something calling for explanation and justification. If any European State makes an exchange of diplomatic representatives with the most distant transoceanic country, with which it has hardly any political or economic interests in common, no one thinks it necessary to ask for an explanation.

But if it is a question of establishing diplomatic and economic relations with the Soviet Union, a country of 140 million inhabitants, the question is raised as to why and wherefore, as to the interests at stake and the nature and extent of the advantage to accrue therefrom, as to whether the trade balance between the two countries will be favorable and whether any guarantee of a favorable balance can be given.

It is definitely pointed out that a connection with the Soviet State is bound to stimulate trade and industry, to diminish unemployment, to cheapen raw materials and articles of consumption, and, in a word, that this connection will prove highly advantageous to the entire economy and thus also to the entire population, fresh questions are put forward; will such a connection benefit a certain factory owner, a certain bank, a certain insurance company, or a certain group of persons that suffered losses twelve years ago at a historical moment during the October Revolution? And if no absolutely satisfactory answer can be given to this question, the interests of the country in its entirety are sacrificed to the apparent interests of individuals or individual groups. I say, to the apparent interests, since in reality even these persons and groups fall prey to profit by the absence of a connection between their countries and the Soviet Union. The defenders of these apparent interests, whose plans are bound up with the long past facts of debt-annulment and the nationalization of factories, ought to remember the incidents of a yet more recent past, e.g., the time of the intervention, from which claims likewise arise in favor of our State and of numerous private persons. We do not, however, consider the existence of these pretensions an obstacle to the maintenance of normal relations with other countries.

The refusal to resume normal relations with the Soviet Union or the rupture of such relations is not always openly substantiated by a reference to the prosaic interests of certain persons or groups. If there is a need of an explanation based on "superior" considerations and more comprehensible to the broader bourgeois class and particularly to politically less matured circles, the "bogey" known as **Propaganda** is trotted out.

In the capitalist countries, be it remembered, contentment, tranquility and social peace prevail. All classes of the population—proletarians, peasants, officials, and petty bourgeoisie, are extremely content with the state of affairs, aspire to no improvement, and find no reason to protest. There are no street demonstrations, no strikes, no peasant revolts, no Communist movement, no one knows anything of the country that is engaged in building up Socialism or of the dictatorship of the proletariat, not a word penetrates regarding the Comintern. In short, there is nothing to menace the foundations of the country. But if in such a country an embassy or trade delegation of the Soviet Union makes its appearance, the aspect of things changes immediately. Suddenly the workers' movement grows, suddenly, as through magic, it adopts violent forms of development; the appeals of the Comintern have quite a different sound and are differently interpreted by the proletariat, the hitherto quiet and peaceable colonial peoples begin to rise against the mother country, and the revolutionary movement and discontent start drawing ever wider circles.

This is generally how the consequences of an initiation of relations with the Soviet Union are described whenever some bourgeois group or other political party representing it does not desire such relations for some entirely different reason. It is useless to prove that a workers' movement of a substantially revolutionary nature existed long before the October Revolution and now exists everywhere irrespective of the existence or absence of a Soviet representation in the country in question, that there is not only a simple workers' movement but a Communist movement, that this movement develops differently even in two countries in which there is a Soviet representation and consequently has altogether different roots, that its development is affected by absolutely different and unchangeable causes of capitalist society, which is based on the exploitation of the workers, and that there has never been any proof of the existence of a formal or actual connection between the Soviet organs abroad and the local labor movements. It is useless to point to the simple truth that in every country and every colony there are plenty of people well acquainted with the local conditions, vernacular, and mentality of their compatriots, who are better in a position to rally and guide the existing economic or national discontent than are the legendary ubiquitous "emissaries" from Moscow.

It is useless to argue because those who scare their fellow countrymen with the bogey of propaganda do not themselves seriously believe in the existence or significance of such propaganda. They merely rely on the ignorance and backwardness of their hearers or readers, who can be served up with any nonsense without regard to facts or documents.

The question broached by me has, however, also a reverse side. What is it that is really wanted of us when we are accused of propaganda?

An authentic reply is to be found in the formulation of those obligations which were suggested by Mr. Henderson and which we agreed to accept in a reciprocal relation with the British Government. This formula, to which we agreed on the basis of the agreement of 1924, runs as follows:

"The contracting parties formally declare their resolution and intention to live in peace and friendship with one another, carefully to observe the incontestable right of a State to arrange its existence according to its own desires within the limits of its own jurisdiction, and to keep themselves and all persons and organizations directly or indirectly under their control—including the organizations receiving any form of financial help from them—from any overt or covert act which might in any way constitute a danger to the peace and safety of any part of the Union of Soviet Socialist Republics or the British Empire, or which aims at undermining the relations of the USSR or of the British Empire with a neighboring or any other State."

The preceding paragraph obviously refers to the indisputable principles by which the States must be guided in their reciprocal relations but which in the past were obviously not adhered to by someone or other.

Let us inquire into these principles. In making use of our unassailable right to fashion our lives as we choose, we have established the irrevocable principle of a foreign trade monopoly. Do the capitalist States show respect for our rights in again and again attacking our foreign trade monopoly and attempting, by an albeit futile pressure exercised upon us, to attain an abolition thereof by all the economic means at their disposal? Do they respect our jurisdiction if foreigners and their governments are not ashamed of openly protesting against the one or other judicial or administrative measure of the Soviet authorities? Can analogous instances of a pressure on our part on other States be cited, for the purpose of attaining a renunciation in our favor of one or other system of their internal institutions? There are no instances of this sort.

Who is it that violates the relative principle of international life, we or they? And furthermore, did the intervention of the Powers in 1918-20 create a danger for the peace and prosperity of the Soviet territory? Did the military help rendered to Poland in its attack on the Ukraine in 1920 constitute a danger for the peace and prosperity of any part of Soviet territory? And the relations of official personages and even of governments with the monarchist and terrorist organizations of emigrants and their Ukrainian and Georgian "pseudogovernments"—are they perhaps kept up in the interest of the welfare of the Soviet Union? The confirmation of the so-called Bessarabian protocol by Great Britain, France, and Italy with the object of an apparent legalization of the military occupation of Bessarabia—did it not constitute a danger to the peace and welfare of Soviet territory? And this same fact of the confirmation of the Bessarabian protocol—did it not aggravate the relations between the Soviet Union and its Rumanian neighbor by creating a lengthy and very serious conflict? The conclusion of military conventions by numerous States with Poland and Rumania, their constant provision with war material and instructors, the delegation of military missions or generals to Poland and Rumania for the advancement of their war preparations, and finally the favoring of various combinations for the purpose of surrounding the Soviet Union with a ring of alliances among the Baltic and other States—does all this improve or spoil the Soviet Union's relations with its neighbors? Did the attitude of certain States during the present dispute with Manchuria, particularly in the last few days, aim at an improvement or at a deterioration of our relations with our Chinese neighbor? Can analogous or even approximately similar actions on our part to the damage of other countries be cited? It will not be possible, since no such instances exist. And if the facts enumerated by me stand for "propaganda", are they not for the most part committed by those States which raise the greatest hue and cry at our alleged propaganda and demand of us guarantees for the future?

If we look more closely at the "propaganda" which is not mentioned but obviously meant in the formula I had occasion to speak of, what is the general impression we shall gain? Hundreds and thousands of press organs in almost all countries have for the last twelve years been daily libelling the Soviet Union, attacking the Soviet system, and insulting the Soviet Government in its entirety and especially certain members thereof, without any squeamishness in the choice of epithets, inveighing, besmirching, trying to prove the bankruptcy of our aims and methods, forecasting our inevitable ruin and praising the capitalist system at the expense of the Communist.

But it is not only press organs that occupy themselves with this matter; many highly esteemed statesmen do so too—Ministers past, present, and future. AntiSoviet speeches are delivered from Parliamentary benches in anything but Parliamentary language. Such speeches, indeed, are to be found in the inferences and substantiations of the findings of foreign courts of law, which are well known to distinguish themselves by their "impartiality". Is not all of this a form of propaganda directed against the Soviet Union? This propaganda the severe political public prosecutors on the other side of our borders effect not to see. But when "Izvestiia" or "Pravda" or any other of the numerous newspapers in the Soviet Union dares to speak disrespectfully of the capitalist regime or of some foreign statesman or other, at the same time extolling the advantages of the Communist system, there is a storm throughout the international press, questions are asked in the different Parliaments, there is a rain of diplomatic notes and protests, and rumors arise of so-called Soviet propaganda which must be countered by special measures and which even represents an obstacle to the initiation or maintenance of normal relations with the Soviet Union.

If Socialism, which is for the present only being built up in one—albeit a large and powerful—country, is not a prey to misgivings, and fears no breakdown as a result of the spoken and written utterances in Parliamentary speeches, sermons, and thousands of newspapers and periodicals distributed in various countries in millions of copies, why must the capitalist system, which exists in almost all the rest of the world, "tremble" at the literary productions of some Moscow papers or the speeches of Soviet functionaries? All this would be ridiculous if it did not cloud the international atmosphere.

In this connection, I cannot refrain from citing a remark made by Mr. Lloyd George on 5 November in the British Parliament in discussing the question of propaganda. Lloyd George, who is not a man likely to be suspected of friendly partiality towards the Soviet Union, spoke as follows: "As regards propaganda in the East, I must say that I have been a member of the House longer than the leader of the Opposition (Baldwin). I can tell him how we were formerly wont to judge of the propaganda of imperialist Russian in the East. I remember very well how the Russians at times—and in my opinion rightly—were accused of propaganda in India and plans on that country. I remember one speech delivered by the father of the last Foreign Secretary (Chamberlain), in which he declared that not one word of the Russian Foreign Secretary was to be trusted and that whoever supped with the devil would need a long spoon. No one, and least of all Mr. Joseph Chamberlain then thought of a rupture of relations with Russia and of the expulsion of the Russian Ambassador. If anyone in Parliament had suggested it, he would have been considered crazy." Going on to speak of the Soviet Union, Mr. Lloyd George made the following utterances: "It has possibly not quite the table manners of the older Governments which have more practice in the methods of reservation, in hiding their thoughts, and in the management of propaganda. The thing is, to be prepared to deny everything. That is how it was in the past and that is how it will be in the future. The Soviet Government is slightly cruder, but the old Russian finesse of intercourse will return and then it will probably excel even past masters in the art. It will manage its affairs in such a way that no one will be able to point a finger at the one or other Minister concerned. This is almost inevitable as long as the nations do not learn to understand each other better and as long as there is no greater degree of goodwill among them."

Mr. Lloyd George is not without humor and takes care to distinguish between himself and other statesmen who make themselves ridiculous when they speak with serious faces of the so-called propaganda. What is of importance, however, is the fact that we now possess the authoritative declaration of Lloyd George, who has occupied a great variety of offices in British Cabinets, including those of Foreign Secretary and Prime Minister. He publicly announced that the British Government, like the other Governments, carries on propaganda against all foreign States. It may be imagined that they make no exception in favor of the Soviet Union. Are further proofs needed of the hypocrisy of the pathetic accusations of propaganda on the part of the Soviet Union?

We ourselves demand of all countries represented at Moscow noninterference in our internal affairs, and this same policy of noninterference we loyally observe, and shall continue to observe towards other countries. We must declare, however, that the unfounded general accusation of so-called propaganda or the attempt to make the Soviet Government responsible for persons and organizations over which it neither formally nor actually, neither directly nor indirectly, exercises any control, cannot be regarded by us save as an intentionally trumped-up substantiation of the nonresumption or the rupture of normal relations or of yet more serious antiSoviet machinations.

The Economic Cooperation of Great Britain and the Soviet Union

In returning to speak of the significance of a resumption of diplomatic relations with Great Britain, I must expressly point out that there can be no doubt as to the resulting economic advantage for both countries, which is hardly denied by anyone in England either. The British delegation of industrialists that visited us this year was convinced by reliable data of the enormous possibilities which in our opinion attach to the cooperation of the two countries. It will be on the British business world and not least on the British Government that the extent to which these possibilities are exploited will depend. This is in our opinion a complete and separate task, independent of the solution of one or the other question at issue from former times. We hold that the liquidation of the past, which in view of the complicated nature of the matters at issue may take a considerable time, need not necessarily precede such measures as are occasioned by the interests of the present and the future. We hope that a way will be found for the satisfactory solution of these questions, provided the other interested party does not make fruitless attempts to force ideas and principles upon us to which we are strangers, rather joining us in seeking such a solution of the problem as will prove advantageous to both parties. On our side there is no lack of goodwill or of earnest endeavor to observe friendly relations with the British people and to remove the misunderstanding hitherto created by certain circles with the intention of entailing a mutual estrangement of the two States.

I have occupied myself mainly with our relations with two foreign countries, China and Great Britain, since the adjustment of our differences with them has constituted the essential part of our foreign policy of late. In our relations with other countries no material changes have come about since my last report at the session of the Central Executive Committee.

Our Relations with Germany

We continue to entertain the most amicable relations with Germany. We continue to watch with the greatest sympathy Germany's attempts to liberate itself from the fetters imposed upon it by the Treaty of Versailles, under which the working classes suffer most acutely. We should be heartily glad to see these attempts lead to a removal or at any rate a loosening of these fetters. Our own interests are not affected by Germany's endeavors towards better relations with other countries—in so far, of course, as Germany is not inveigled into antiSoviet combinations or induced to depart from the basis of the Rapallo agreement, which was so beneficial both to Germany and to ourselves. During the last twelve months, we have we have had fresh proof that there are persons, groups, organizations, and even parties in Germany that advocate a radical change of the entire German policy in the direction of antiSoviet machinations for the sake of illusory political or economic advantages. Such attempts must be carefully watched, few and unimportant as their initiators may be. But we must not draw conclusions from them in the sense of a fundamental change in Soviet-German relations, which must also not be thought to be affected by a few inevitable misunderstandings and differences of opinion on questions of secondary importance. The circumstances which dictated the Rapallo agreement and laid the foundations of our long friendship, are to a great extent still in existence and must long continue to determine our mutual relations. The presumptions still exist which enabled Germany to occupy the first place in our mutual economic relations with the west. By the conclusion of a number of treaties and agreements, a broad basis has been created for the elaboration of our relations with Germany. Our connection with the Western countries has naturally increased and will continue to do so. This will obviously tend to enhance the competition of foreign countries for our market. At the same time, the tremendous rate of development of our industry and agriculture has caused our requirements to grow enormously.

It is on Germany itself that its share in the satisfaction of these requirements will primarily depend.

Our Relations with Other Countries

It is not without regret that we contemplate our somewhat rusty though undoubtedly normal relations with France. Though the French bourgeois press in its entirety reflects the attitude of the French Government towards us in no more than a very slight degree, this attitude cannot but be considered very unsatisfactory. It is obvious that France is not inclined to occupy the least important place in the international action against the Soviet Union. On our part there are no obstacles in the way of an improvement of relations both political and economic. But we have no cause to assume that any possible steps in this direction on our part would meet with the necessary welcome in France.

Our relations with Italy are quite unimpeachable. During the last twelve months, an Italian air-flotilla was received at Odessa and Soviet warships visited Naples, a spirit of hospitality being evinced in both cases. The economic relations between the two countries are likewise developing satisfactorily with the support and promotion of the respective Governments. We are glad to be able to establish the total absence of any misunderstandings between the two States.

I have just received a short communication from the Italian ambassador at Moscow to the effect that his Government has resolved to join the action initiated by the United States. I should be glad to assume that the tardy arrival of this information points to hesitation on the part of the Italian Government and to its recognition of the fact that this step is not altogether in keeping with the relations which the two countries have been endeavoring to develop.

By signing the Moscow Protocol in regard to an accelerated operation of the Kellogg Agreement, we furnished an undeniable proof of our anxiety to ensure peace in general and peace with our immediate neighbors in the West in particular. Quite especially we had hoped that the Moscow Protocol would exercise a restraining influence on those Polish circles which are always endeavoring to sow and perpetuate discord between the two States. Unfortunately these hopes have been disappointed and our relations have from time to time been vacillating by reason of attacks on the part of certain representatives of the Polish State or of the Polish press.

The Polish Government apparently considers the present relations to be sufficient and altogether in order. We have rather a different opinion of what relations should be like and should greatly welcome an improvement; indeed, we once made suggestions to the Polish Government in this sense and it was by no means our fault that they remained abortive. We are glad, meanwhile, to observe a successful development of commercial relations of late.

It is with great satisfaction that we can record an uninterrupted development of friendly relations between the Soviet and the Free City of Danzig, a development which recently found utterance in the visit to Russia of Herr Saam, President of the Free City. The Danzig Government, moreover, recently gave us proof of its sincere endeavors to maintain friendly relations with the Soviet Union.

In our mutual relations with the Baltic States, no particular changes have come about of late. I am very glad to be able to record that in our relations with Estonia, with whom we concluded a commercial agreement in May last, undoubted progress has been made. It is my conviction that the better mutual understanding that has arisen between ourselves and Estonia in the last few months will serve as the basis of further development of the relations between the two States.

We entertain normal relations with all the Scandinavian States, though attention is called for in regard to certain imperialist aspirations of some Swedish circles in an Eastern direction.

The new Austrian Government has declared its readiness to promote the maintenance and further development of economic relations.

With Greece we have concluded a provisional commercial treaty guaranteeing the development of mutually advantageous economic relations.

In surveying our relations with Western countries, we cannot help remembering that on our South-Western frontier a province is under foreign domination. This occupation does not seem to worry the self-appointed guardians of the Kellogg Pact. I refer to Bessarabia, the population of which has never ceased to desire a reunion with the Soviet Union, a fact we can never forget.

In passing over to extra European countries, I must in the first place underline the uninterrupted and unimpaired maintenance of friendly relations with the great Turkish Republic. Friendship with the Soviet Union has the great advantage over friendly relations with other countries in that, in the latter case, a party temporarily in authority may sometimes enter into an amicable relationship which is perhaps immediately afterwards abandoned by the contrary policy of its successor. The friendship of the Soviet Union, on the other hand, is not dependent on transient conjunctions and casual combinations. It is backed up by a hundred million workers and all the peoples of a vast territory. This fact is bound to make itself felt in international politics. We know that Turkey appreciates our friendship just as much as we for the same reason appreciate that of the Turkish people. Comrade Karakhan will shortly betake himself to the Turkish capital to transmit in person the assurance of our unchanged friendly attitude. Very shortly, too, there will be negotiations at Moscow in regard to some alterations of the Turkish-Soviet agreement of 1927. In view of the experience gained in the two years during which this agreement has been in operation, I do not doubt that we shall speedily bring these discussions to a satisfactory termination, thus creating a yet better basis for our further economic cooperation.

We are glad to be able to underline the fact that our relations with our great Far Eastern neighbor Japan have become essentially stabilized and that there are proofs of mutual loyalty in our intercourse. In Japan, as in other countries, there are certain groups that seek to bring about a deterioration of our relations and have recourse to all the methods customary in such a connection. In one instance these endeavors led to an action which was altogether incompatible with mutual loyalty. I venture to express the conviction that the endeavors of these elements will continue to fail as they have failed hitherto in view of the earnest desire of the Japanese Government and the Japanese people to extend and consolidate our friendly relations.

Our relations with Persia remain undisturbedly amicable. Persia's aspirations towards economic independence and a consolidation of its international position will at all times meet with our understanding and sympathy.

Both countries are taking all possible steps to ensure an unhindered development of the mutual economic relations which are of great importance toboth of them.

Our South–Eastern neighbors, the people of Afghanistan, have been through severe trials during the last twelve months. The occurrences in Afghanistan awakened apprehensions among us, who are interested in a continuation of the absolute independence of that country. Faithful to the fundamental principles of our policy, we refrained from any interference in the violent internal struggles of Afghanistan and from the support of one party against the other, at the same time paying attention lest interference should ensue from any other neighboring country of Afghanistan. The troubles in Afghanistan appear to be at an end. Just as in 1919, when Afghanistan first appeared in the international arena as an independent State, the Soviet Government which was interested in a speedy pacification and stabilization of the inner situation of Afghanistan, lost no time in officially recognizing the new government. In reply to the announcement of the Afghan Foreign Minister on 15 October in regard to the formation of a new Government under Mahomet Nadir Khan, the Commissariat for Foreign Affairs stated on 19 October in the name of the Soviet Government that the amicable relations between the two States had not ceased to exist and assured the Afghan Government of its readiness to develop these relations on the basis of such agreements as were already in force and in the interest of a consolidation of the independence and cultural progress of Afghanistan.

As regards the transAtlantic countries, there are unfortunately no diplomatic relations between this country and the United States. At the same time, our relations with the American business world have been greatly stabilized and extended. The industry of the United States is particularly well suited to the rate of development in the industry of the Soviet Union. Under given circumstances further important steps can be taken towards an economic approach. We can quietly wait, until this economic necessity is also recognized by those on whose part the steps in question depend, as has already been recognized by wide circles of the American business world. The reception recently accorded to our airplane "Land of the Soviets", speaks, along with many other facts, of the existence and growth of interest and sympathy for our country in the United States.

Suddenly the independent Republic of Panama seems to have remembered the existence of the Soviet Union, and expresses apprehensions as to the safety of the Kellogg Agreement. We can only express the wish that the agreement in question may also protect Panama itself and consolidate its independence.

We Must Continue to Consolidate our Power

From this short survey of our foreign relations, it appears that on the whole we have maintained our positions, apart from our loss in connection with the Chinese Eastern Railway, a loss I am certain we shall soon make up for. An undoubted asset lies in the resumption of the normal relations with Great Britain broken off two years and a half ago. It would, however, be naive and frivolous if we were to content ourselves with the stabilization and improvement achieved and believe we had secured ourselves against all dangers from without. The disturbances affecting the capitalist world, its attempts to settle by violence the differences by which it is rent, and the complete failure of the pseudopacifist suggestions of disarmament, which betray the spirit of militarism and imperialism permeating international politics—all these are factors which do not permit us to relax our vigilance. The greatest menace, meanwhile, lies in the unrelenting hostility and ill will towards the Soviet Union evinced by the capitalist world, which serves as a hotbed for intervention as in the case of Manchuria, for a policy of nonrecognition and the rupture of diplomatic relations, and even more serious complications. There is no need to point out when and where warlike actions are prepared against us. It is sufficient to establish the existence of the hostility and the unwillingness of the capitalist States to put up with the existence of the Soviet Union—a fact which we cannot but regard as a continual menace to our country. By diplomatic means alone we cannot neutralize this menace and render it ineffective. A real balance of the situation can only be attained by a further strengthening of our internal power, by a successful realization of our economic plans, by the promotion and development of the rise and the enthusiasm of the workers and small and middle peasants, by a further uniform consolidation of our Party, and—inasmuch as all our peaceful suggestions are consistently declined—by untiring efforts to strengthen the defensive forces of our country.

It cannot be expected that the hostility towards our country will materially decline, not to speak of ceasing altogether.

While strictly adhering to a policy of peace, it will be necessary to prepare for the possibility of a deepening of the said hostility into acts of violence against the Soviet Union. By economic measures we must render our country so strong and capable of defense that such acts of violence are altogether without prospect of success and that the hopelessness and risk of all such actions become apparent to all our possible opponents. But as long as the capitalist world with its imperialist tendencies continues to exist, obstinately declining all our suggestions of general disarmament and even increasing its armaments, there can naturally be no full guarantee that no violence will be practiced on the Soviet Union. In view of that the army and navy of the workers and peasants are always ready to answer to a sudden provocation. Our brilliant repulsion of the Chinese bands and of the efforts at conquest is a sufficient guarantee that we may be absolutely tranquil in this respect too. (Long and vociferous applause.)

International Press Correspondence, Vol. 9, No. 70 (20 December 1929), 1471-1476; No. 71 (27 December 1929), 1487-1491.

DECREE. PARTY CENTRAL COMMITTEE ESTABLISHES THE ENTERPRISE AS BASIC UNIT OF INDUSTRIAL MANAGEMENT

5 December 1929

The Party Central Committee issued a decree to establish the enterprise as the basic unit in the operation and management of industry. The enterprise was to be independent in setting plans for production, supply, and accounting. It was endowed with autonomy in economic accounting, called khozraschet. Depending on location and production specialization, enterprises were to be part of associations or trusts, which in turn were to be part of associations. Associations were formed, as a general rule, from the merger of main administrations, or "glavki," which were part of the Supreme Council of the National Economy. The Supreme Council of the National Economy was limited to planning, modernization through technology, coordinating the various branches of industry, and preparing the directives for current planning. The decree amounted to setting limits on the one-man management of enterprises.

ON THE REORGANIZATION OF INDUSTRIAL MANAGEMENT

I. PRODUCTION ENTERPRISE

1. The enterprise is the fundamental section of industrial management. Therefore the technical services of the enterprise, correct organization of supply, the most complete organization of labor within the enterprise, the complete carrying out of one-man management in production, the creation of the most favorable conditions for the maximum activity of the workers' collective and technical personnel of the enterprise, the selection of qualified administration, and the necessary degree of enterprise independence are the basis for the further improvement in the system of management of socialist industry.

2. The transition of enterprises to economic accounting [khozraschet—AGC] is completely justified. Economic accounting reveals the person of the enterprise, furthers the rationalization of production and the correct organization of sales and supply, and stimulates at the same time opposition to elements of bureaucratism and red tape.

At the same time the transition of enterprises to economic accounting furthers the rational establishment of the calculation of production activity and acquaints the masses with this activity.

Up to the present time the transition to economic accounting has by far not been accomplished in all enterprises. This measure must be decisively carried out within the shortest time in all enterprises of state industry without exception.

3. During the strictest observation of production, financial, and planning discipline in the range of set limits, the enterprise must be independent. Its administration bears full responsibility for fulfilling the program.

The enterprise is granted under instruction a definite sum of means, the scale of which is determined annually by the industrial financial plan. On the basis of the industrial financial plan what is agreed to in the order request is the production budget cost being established for the enterprise for the year, and a reciprocal additional sum upon violation of the conditions established by the order request.

4. The logical carrying out of khozraschet of enterprises requires adopting measures to reveal the successes and deficiencies of individual shops and departments of enterprises. With this aim the enterprise must establish planned tasking for its individual sections (shop, department). For shops and departments of the enterprise what must be taken stock of are the expenditures produced for the month (to include the expenditures which both overhead and those falling in their allotted portion of amortization). Expenditures of individual sections of the enterprise must compare with the results of their production activity.

The results of the activity of enterprises and their sections must be discussed at periodic production conferences, and on the basis of this professional organizations must organize their own mass economic work in enterprises.

5. The enterprise has an independent balance. The basis of the enterprise's monthly balance must be the given cost of production. The difference between the set and factual cost during the permanent condition of fulfilling the demands for quality of production being developed is the basic indicator of the successful work of the enterprise.

Part of this difference in scale, preordained by law, remains under the direction of the enterprise and, upon the approval of the annual balance, is spent following review of the latter on production and social needs.

With the aim of providing for the fulfillment of tasks for cost it is necessary to guarantee for the enterprise the receiving of raw materials in accordance with prices established beforehand.

6. The establishment of inventory and accounting must be improved at the enterprise. The full balance with the necessary supplement and the accounting for the cost of the main types of products being manufactured must be formed by enterprises no later than the 15-17th day in accordance with the expiration of the operational month. Accounting of cost must become the basic material for technical management and measures for the rationalization with the absolute responsibility of technical inspection of the quality of production.

7. The tasks presented before industry for increasing production, reducing cost, and the quality of production require the decisive carrying out of the specialization of enterprises.

8. For the improvement of the technical management of the enterprise, to propose to the USSR VSNKh to pay special attention to the development of a network of factory and plant laboratories and the increase in the number of specialists engaged directly in production, as well as to introduce into the composition of technical conferences at enterprises representatives of the best workers, plant inventors, and junior engineers.

II. ASSOCIATION OF ENTERPRISES

1. The present existing system of main administrations does not correspond to the tasks of the reconstruction period, especially in the area of technical management.

At the same time the syndicates concentrated in their hands the factual management of the corresponding branches of industry and the majority of them were forced to occupy themselves with issues of production programs, capital construction, planning, supply, distribution, etc.

As a result of this in a whole series of syndicates it was observed to a significant degree that their work was being duplicated by VSNKh glavki.

In view of this it is necessary to liquidate the main administrations and create organizations based on khozraschet to manage the branches of industry on the basis of syndicates (for example this was carried out in the textile industry).

2. The main functions of these khozraschet organizations must be the following:

planning of production,
planning and management of capital construction,
technical management,
organization of sales and supply,
management of commercial and financial activity,
issues of labor,
training and distribution of cadre,
appointment and dismissal of management personnel.

3. There are created three types of associations of individual branches of industry:

a) Association which has *enterprises and trusts only of union significance.* In this case the association manages all aspects of the industrial enterprises united in it corresponding to the functions laid out in point 2.

b) Association which has *enterprises and trusts of union as well as republic and local industry.* In this case in relation to enterprises and trusts of a union significance the association carries out all functions laid out in point 2 of the present section.

In relation to the enterprises and trusts of republic significance the association carries out syndicate functions, to which is added the planning of production and capital construction, general technical management in the area of rationalization and reconstruction, and general management in the training of cadre.

c) Association of the syndicate type has enterprises and trusts *only of republic and local significance*. In this case the association carries out only syndicate functions, to which are added general interrepublic planning of production and capital construction and observing the carrying out of rationalization and especially technical reconstruction. The mutual relationships of trusts of republic and local significance with associations are constructed on the foundations of economic accounting.

4. Associations are created not only of union but republic significance.

5. Being a khozraschet organ, the association has its own balance. In this balance what is meant are all the means and property of enterprises and trusts of union significance in a given branch of industry. The association's profit is formed from the difference between the selling prices and production cost of the association.

For trusts of republic and local significance that are part of an association, the latter (association) operates a special account of profits and losses with the deduction of them at the expense of these trusts in correlation with products yielded by these trusts.

The association makes its calculation with trusts of republic and local significance, that are part of it, on those very bases which are now adopted for syndicates.

The creation of a single khozraschet organization requires a decisive simplification of the system to tax industry; to order the USSR NKF and VSNKh to develop a system of taxation of state industry on the principle of a single deduction from the profits.

6. The central place in the work of the association must be assigned to the management of technical and production work of the enterprises and trusts which are part of it.

In correlation with this in each enterprise must be selected a group of highly qualified specialists who are freed from all kinds of current work, excluding their direct responsibilities for technical management.

This group must develop general lines for the reconstruction of a given branch of industry and must be responsible for the dissemination of foreign technical experience and achievements of the best USSR enterprises to other existing and newly constructed enterprises which are part of the association's administration.

Technical management in the association must be organized mainly along a functional basis.

7. With the aim of drawing in the activity of scientific and research institutes closer to the practical tasks of production associations are getting scientific and research institutes which occupy themselves with issues related principally to a given branch of industry.

8. The association organizes the supply to its enterprises of the basic materials both directly and by way of concluding general contracts with the appropriate supply organizations.

9. With the aim of strengthening the operational rights and responsibility of the association of industrial enterprises, it is necessary during the planning of commodities for the VSNKh and NKT to give only general directives for the reduction of sales prices, while indicating the average limit of this reduction, so that further operational work in the area of establishing prices would be to a maximum degree granted to the associations themselves.

III. TRUST

1. During the creation of associations, enterprises can enter them directly or through trusts.

Trusts must concentrate their work on issues of technical management, rationalization, reconstruction, and, as a rule, lose the functions of sales and supply.

There can be also cases when the trust retains all the functions given to it by the current existing statute.

2. To provide for the use of contemporary achievements of science and technology in the production life of industrial enterprises, the following major tasks must be raised before the trusts:

a) organization of the exchange of technical experience among enterprises;

b) providing for the timely use of industrial achievements of scientific and research institutes, laboratories, and other research organizations;

c) timely acquainting of enterprises with contemporary achievements in technical thought at foreign enterprises; adopting measures so that these achievements could be applied in a short period of time at enterprises of the USSR;

d) inspecting the mobilization of internal resources of enterprises and correctly arranging warehouse matters;

e) timely application of standards in industrial enterprises developed by special organs;

f) formation of special organs for rationalization.

3. Technical management of enterprises and trusts must be carried out by a specially selected cell of highly qualified specialists who are freed from all kinds of other work.

Technical management is carried out by the trust primarily along a functional basis.

With the aim of resolving tasks raised above, the trust must widely practice the organization of temporary technical commissions from among the practical workers of an enterprise, to include outstanding workers, plant inventors, most experienced masters, and young engineers, instructing them to work out issues about new technical innovations and the dissemination of achievements of one enterprise to the remaining.

4. Technical management of enterprises on the side of the trust must be based on cost.

5. As a general rule, trusts must be constructed on the principles of enterprises of similar production and their specialization.

Parallel trusts, which have enterprises of a similar nature of production within the borders of the same economic region, must not be organized.

IV. SUPREME COUNCIL OF THE NATIONAL ECONOMY OF THE USSR

1. The VSNKh, while reducing the area of its operational interference in relation to lower instances, must concentrate its basic attention on establishing production and financial plans for the development of industry and its technical reconstruction, on coordinating the work of individualbranches of industry, on developing the main directives in the area of current planning and regulation of industry, on inspecting their fulfillment, and on bringing economic organs up to strength and providing them with instructions.

2. The mutual relationships of the USSR VSNKh with republic VSNKhs is determined by the existing statute currently established.

3. The work of the USSR VSNKh in managing associations must basically consist of developing the fundamental directives for establishing plans for the reconstruction of a given branch of industry, approval of control figures and plans for capital, appointment and dismissal of the governing body of the association, approval of balances and reports, distribution of profits and losses, resolution of expenditures of special capital, auditing and investigation of the activity of the association, approval of charters and prescribed capital, and the setting of sales prices.

4. The strengthening of technical features both in perspective and current planning of industry requires the creation in the USSR VSNKh a single organ for technical and economic planning.

5. The single technical and economic planning directorate of VSNKh carries out the following basic functions:

a) planning of industry, development of perspective plans and control figures, planning of the geographical distribution of enterprises and regionalization of industry, development of questions on industrial policy and legislation, and approval of the work of individual associations;

b) management of the technical reconstruction of industry, development of general lines of the technical growth of industry, organization of new production, specialization, etc.;

general management of scientific and research work and scientific and research institutes directly subordinate to it; management of work for the transference of foreign experience, for the exchange of experience among enterprises for standardization and rationalization.

6. The basic task of chief inspection must be the review of the fulfillment by all organs of industry of the most important directives of the government and the VSNKh presidium.

The chief inspection must widely practice the use of republic and local VSNKh organs for the inspection of industry, as well as the attraction of the working masses and social organizations to investigations.

7. The VSNKh is obligated to manage the training, selection, inventory, and use of cadre in industry. During this must be provided the extensive participation of professional organizations in the selection of managerial cadre of organs to manage all sections of industry.

During the putting into practice of the reorganization of industrial management, trade unions and economic organs must provide for the active participation of workers in resolving all the most important issues of managing the enterprise and corresponding branches of industry, in setting up the study of production plans and tasks, and in inspecting their fulfillment.

All professional organizations, beginning with the factory and plant committee and ending with the VTsSPS, must take part in the entire process to develop control figures and industrial financial plans, and to allot tasks for trusts, enterprises, and shops. With this aim party professional organs must daily collect, study, and systematize proposals of workers, shock brigades, production conferences, and production commissions, while preparing on the basis of these proposals their own corrections and additions to the production and financial plans of enterprises and economic organs.

Trade unions and economic organizations must organize work for planning in such a way that the preparatory discussion of planning proposals (control figures, industrial financial plans, etc.) are achieved at extensive meetings of the working masses: Production conferences, shop and group meetings of workers.

Economic organs and professional organizations must devote special attention to supporting shock brigades and creating all the necessary conditions for the expansion of socialist competition.

Economic organs are obligated to organize permanent business studies of the experience of socialist competition and shock brigades, proposals of individual workers, production conferences, temporary inspection commissions, etc., with the aim of the most rapid advancement and dissemination to all of industry or to its individual branches of the inventions and improvements proposed by workers.

Resheniia, 136-142.

DECREE. CENTRAL EXECUTIVE COMMITTEE UNIFIES AND CENTRALIZES AGRICULTURAL AFFAIRS

7 December 1929

The USSR Central Executive Committee created the People's Commissariat for Agriculture to unify and centralize all agriculture affairs, which previously had been relegated to the union republics. The Commissariat, the Narkomzem, also absorbed various all-union organizations, such as the Collective Farm Center, the Kolkhoztsentr. I.A. Iakovlev, former deputy commissar of the Workers' and Peasants' Inspectorate, was appointed commissar, thus guaranteeing the subordination of agriculture to the party's needs for industrialization.

ON THE FORMATION OF THE PEOPLE'S
COMMISSARIAT FOR AGRICULTURE OF THE USSR

The tasks, which stand at the present time before Soviet power, in the area of the decisive acceleration in the rise of agriculture and its socialist reconstruction can be solved only on the basis of the union of petty small-producing farms into large collective farms that are armed with all the contemporary means of production, during simultaneous creation of an extensive network of soviet farms in unfamiliar lands. The rapid process growing from below of forming individual poor- and middle-peasant farms, that is uniting millions of such farms, has already entered on the path of creating large kolkhozes and even on the path of the complete collectivization of entire raions and okrugs, supplanting large kulak farms and uprooting the roots of capitalism in the countryside.

The area, being simultaneously prepared for crops, that is under nothing but only new grain sovkhozes, will achieve in the current year 4 million hectares of crops. Together with this has been decided the beginning of the development of a wide network of sovkhozes for cattle-breeding, sheep-breeding, etc. and sovkhozes under industrial crops.

For carrying out these tasks the USSR government has already created a series of all-union organizations: "Zernotrest", "Skotovod", "Ovtsevod", "Sel'khozsnabzhenie", Lenin Academy of Agricultural Sciences, and others.

That achieved at the present time in connection with the growth of sovkhozes and kolkhozes and by greater inclusion of agricultural cooperatives of individual poor- and middle-peasant farms, the degree of organization of agricultural production, the growing demands which industry makes in correlation with the rate of industrialization of the country on raw materials and goods, and the growing role of industry in the reconstruction of agriculture make it necessary to introduce unity in the planning and management of agricultural production on the scale of the USSR and the concentration in a single center the direct management of large agricultural enterprises.

This single management must be carried out in such a manner that in a significant degree there will be achieved the development of initiative in the independence of union republics in the expansion of productive forces and socialist reconstruction of the countryside.

With the aim of creating such a single management and with the aim of uniting the work of people's commissariats for agriculture of union republics, the Central Executive Committee of the USSR resolves:

1. To form the united People's Commissariat for Agriculture of the USSR.

2. To place on the People's Commissariat for Agriculture of the USSR:

1) Organization and management of agricultural enterprises of union significance.

2) Management and unification of the work of agricultural cooperatives and a system of agricultural credit.

3) Organization of agricultural services along the line of supplying of machines, tractors, and fertilizers, meteorological services, irrigation, resettlement, struggle with wreckers and plant diseases, veterinary science, struggle with epizotics, and the creation of a needed network of design and construction enterprises.

4) Management of agricultural electrification and arrangement of the first processing of agricultural products.

5) Organization and management of resettlement affairs.

6) Organization and management of scientific and experimental work in the area of agriculture.

7) Observation of the conduct of timber harvesting.

8) Management of the creation and retraining of cadre for reorganizing agriculture.

9) Development of a general plan for the development of agriculture, a perspective plan, and annual control figures.

10) Management of the conduct of sowing campaigns.

3. To propose to the central executive committees of union republics to transform the people's commissariats for agriculture of union republics into unified people's commissariats.

4. To order the People's Commissar for Agriculture of the USSR:

1) To introduce in two months' time through the USSR Council of People's Commissars for approval by the Presidium of the USSR Central Executive Committee a decree on the People's Commissariat for Agriculture of the USSR.

2) To introduce in six months' time for approval by legislative organs the drafts of resolutions to change the existing legislation of the USSR, in connection with the formation of the People's Commissariat for Agriculture of the USSR.

Sobranie Zakonov i Rasporiazhenii, No. 75 (21 December 1929), Article 718, 1415-1416.

THE SHOCK BRIGADE MOVEMENT FIRST CONGRESS
7 December 1929

The Party political leadership found a convenient tool in promoting socialist competition, which developed spontaneously throughout the 1920s among young workers who felt materially disadvantaged and discriminated against by traditional workers and the existing industrial system. Factories and individual workers competed for increased production, labor discipline, and cost reduction. Workers formed shock brigades to promote and foster socialist competition and other social and political goals. The document below illustrates the degree to which the movement achieved formal status and organizational exposure in the convening of the first congress of shock brigades. Note the enthusiasm for the goals of the Central Committee.

GREETINGS OF THE FIRST ALL-UNION CONGRESS OF SHOCK BRIGADES TO THE CENTRAL COMMITTEE OF THE VKP(B)

The all-union congress of shock brigades sends ardent greetings to the steadfast fighter and leader of socialist construction—the Leninist Central Committee of the VKP(b).

Before the face of the imperialists, who in violent anger and bestial hatred for the state of workers and peasants are preparing an attack and who are sending to our territory detachments of Chinese white-guard bandits pillaging the peaceful population and disrupting the peaceful labor of peasants and workers of the USSR, shock workers promise full and unconditional support to all the steps of the Central Committee of the Communist Party to accelerate socialist construction and to strengthen with all means possible the defensive capability of the Soviet Union. The congress of shock workers follows with admiration the steadfast and heroic operations of the Special Far Eastern Army.

The congress decisively protests against the insolent and provocative interference of the imperialists in the affairs of the USSR, which is fighting against the bandit raid of Chinese mercenaries.

The congress of shock workers calls upon the entire working class and laboring peasants to rally around the Communist Party and with still greater enthusiasm, vigor, and urgency to move forward the business of the construction of socialism, the business of the relentless tearing out of the roots of capitalism.

We together with the entire working class are straining every effort to carry out the five year plan of the national economy in four years. The working class in alliance with poor and middle peasants is fulfilling at a rapid rate the plan for industrialization and the collectivization of the countryside.

Together with the entire party we are decisively rejecting the waverings and line of the right opportunists, who are retreating before the pressure of the kulak and capitalist elements and are surrendering the position of socialism to the class enemy.

The congress calls upon all shock workers, the entire working class to select the best among them as representatives, amounting to 25 thousand workers, to be sent to the countryside to assist the peasantry in the most rapid construction of kolkhozes.

With the aim of the most rapid carrying out of the five year plan, with the aim of carrying out and increasing the control figures for the current year, the shock workers assume the responsibility for the more energetic, more extensive expansion of the front of the struggle, a continual and intense struggle, for new, socialist labor discipline.

The congress sets up the tasks for the still wider expansion of socialist competition and for drawing into it with the participation of trade unions the entire working class, to a man.

The shock workers assume the responsibility for the still more energetic and wider expansion of education work among the masses of workers and laborers and make them steadfast fighters for socialism.

The shock worker assumes the responsibility not to give mercy to self-seekers and absentees, the disorganizers of socialist production.

The shock worker must become and will become actually the peredovik of the working class in work, in way of life, and in study.

Wave high the banner of Lenin!

Wave high the banner of the struggle for new, socialist labor discipline!

Sbornik Dokumentov, 263-264.

RESUMPTION OF ANGLO-SOVIET RELATIONS. EXCHANGE OF NOTES

20 December 1929

Great Britain severed relations with the Soviet Union in 1927 because of Soviet interference in British domestic affairs, particularly in the area of propaganda and espionage. After the victory of the Labor Party over the Conservatives, the British Government cautiously initiated negotiations for the resumption of diplomatic relations. The bone of contention was the interpretation of the propaganda clause in the Treaty of 1924, which established diplomatic relations between Great Britain and the USSR. Below is the exchange of notes between Arthur Henderson, British Secretary of State for Foreign Affairs, and the designated Soviet Ambassador to London, G. Sokolnikov, that reestablished diplomatic relations between the two countries.

RESUMPTION OF DIPLOMATIC RELATIONS BETWEEN GREAT BRITAIN AND SOVIET UNION

Sir, London, 20 December 1929

By Clause 7 of the Protocol signed on 3rd October last by the Soviet Ambassador in Paris on behalf of the Government of the USSR, and His Majesty's Principal Secretary of State for Foreign Affairs on behalf of his Majesty's Government in the United Kingdom of Great Britain and Northern Ireland, both Governments engaged themselves to confirm the pledge with regard to propaganda contained in Article XVI of the General Treaty signed on the 8th August 1924, between USSR and Great Britain and Northern Ireland.

The terms of that Article were as follows:

"The Contracting Parties solemnly affirm their desire and intention to live in peace and amity with each other, scrupulously to respect the undoubted right of a state to order its own life within its own jurisdiction in its own way, to refrain and to restrain all persons and organizations under their direct or indirect control, including organizations in receipt of financial assistance from them, from any act overt or covert liable in any way whatsoever to endanger the tranquility or prosperity of any part of the territory of the British Empire or USSR, or intended to embitter the relations of the British Empire or the Union with their neighbors or any other countries."

It was further agreed that effect should be given to this clause of the aforesaid Protocol not later than the day on which the respective ambassadors presented their credentials.

Having this day presented to His Royal Highness the Prince of Wales the letters accrediting me as Ambassador of the USSR to His Majesty the King, I have the honor, by the direction of the People's Commissar for Foreign Affairs and on behalf of the Government of USSR, to confirm the undertaking contained in the Article quoted above, and to inform you that the Government of USSR regard that undertaking as having full force and effect as between themselves and His Majesty's Government in the United Kingdom of Great Britain and Northern Ireland and the Government of India.

I am instructed to add that the Government of USSR will be happy to receive, in accordance with Clause 7 of the Protocol of the 3rd October, a corresponding declaration from His Majesty's Government in the United Kingdom of Great Britain and Northern Ireland and the Government of India.

I have....

Secretary of State
for Foreign Affairs

G. Sokolnikov
Ambassador of USSR in London

Your Excellency, London 20 December 1929

I have the honor to acknowledge the receipt of the Note dated today, in which your excellency confirms, on behalf of the Government of USSR, the pledge regarding propaganda contained in Article XVI of the General Treaty signed on the 8th August 1924 between Great Britain and Northern Ireland and USSR.

2. In taking due note of this declaration, I have the honor to inform your Excellency that, in accordance with the understanding between His Majesty's Government in the United Kingdom and the Government of USSR, as recorded in the Protocol of the 3rd October 1929, His Majesty's Ambassador in Moscow has been instructed to inform the Government of USSR that His Majesty's Government in the United Kingdom and the Government of India, for their part, also regard the undertaking contained in Article XVI of the Treaty signed on the 8th August 1924 as having full force and effect as between themselves and the Government of USSR.

I have....

Ambassador of
USSR in London

Arthur Henderson
Secretary of State for Foreign Affairs

Soviet Treaty Series, II, 16.

PRAVDA GLORIFIES STALIN ON HIS FIFTIETH BIRTHDAY

21 December 1929

Soviet readers learned on 21 December 1929 that Stalin was the great leader and closest follower of Lenin. Praises permeated the Soviet Union, in Pravda *and other newspapers, pamphlets, etc., all glorifying Stalin's contributions, though exaggerated, and attributes. Unlike Lenin, Stalin appreciated all the proceedings and the homage paid to him. In retrospect, the birthday glorifications represented the beginning of the Stalin cult.*

TO THE TRUE CONTINUER OF MARX AND LENIN, THE STEADFAST FIGHTER FOR THE PURITY OF MARXISM-LENINISM, THE UNITY OF THE RANK AND FILE OF THE ALL-UNION COMMUNIST PARTY (BOLSHEVIKS) AND THE COMMUNIST INTERNATIONAL, AND THE NATIONAL PROLETARIAN REVOLUTION; TO THE ORGANIZER AND LEADER OF SOCIALIST INDUSTRIALIZATION AND COLLECTIVIZATION OF THE SOVIET COUNTRY; TO THE LEADER OF THE PARTY OF THE PROLETARIAT, WHICH IS BUILDING SOCIALISM IN ONE-SIXTH OF THE WORLD; TO THE OLDEST PRAVDA EMPLOYEE—TO COMRADE IOSIF VISSARIONOVICH STALIN FROM "PRAVDA", A MILITANT BOLSHEVIK GREETING

The communist party, working class, and world revolutionary movement celebrate today the fiftieth birthday of their leader, friend, and militant comrade, comrade Stalin.

The name of Stalin is included among the closest and true students and associates of Lenin, among the truest sons of the revolution. This name became a synonym for bolshevik firmness, steadfastness, and irreconcilability. It is the banner of the relentless struggle for bolshevism, for Leninism.

Difficult is the path of the bolshevik party. Overcoming all obstacles, destroying all the roadblocks erected by the vilest of the vile bloody regime of the tsar, in spite of the savage persecution by the landowner-bourgeois monarchy, our party at the dawn of its existence carved its way to the workers and was transformed into the party of the revolutionary working class. Under the brilliant leadership of Lenin, our party endured the long and heavy path through the revolution of 1905, through the consequent wild outburst of reaction, through the new revolutionary uprising of 1912-1914 and the period of the imperialist war, and was transformed into a party of millions, which, having overthrown capitalism and transformed the prison of the nationalities that was tsarist Russia into a Country of Soviets, is carrying out the building of socialism in its immense spaces. In this matchless, glorious, and heroic struggle Stalin arose and took shape. Tsarist prison and exile, through which he endured, the richest experience of more than three decades of revolutionary struggle, and the incomparable leadership of Lenin forged this rock-hardened bolshevik, who moved forward after Lenin's death as the leader of the party.

During the past decade of the revolutionary struggle, under the leadership and alongside Lenin, Stalin brick by brick is mustering and strengthening our party, demonstrating himself as the brilliant, professional revolutionary and organizer.

To lead such a party as ours demands much. Thus much is given to comrade Stalin. Stalin unites in himself the quality of the practical organizer and most prominent theoretician of our party. Stalin demonstrates exclusively the clear understanding of leninism; in the struggle with opportunism one sets up and advances forward the development of a series of theoretical problems of imperialism and proletarian dictatorship.

Stalin stands at the head of the leninist Central Committee. Therefore he is the true object of rabid persecution from the world bourgeoisie and social democrats. All the opposition within the party direct always their arrows at comrade Stalin, as the most adamant bolshevik with the most authority, as the most uncompromising defender of leninism from all kinds of misinterpretations.

The enemies of the party know that, while striking at Stalin, they are striking against the bolshevik party, which is leading the entire socialist construction, uniting under its leninist banner all the new millions of workers and laboring people. All the hopes of enemies are futile: The authority of the communist party, authority of the Communist International, and the authority of comrade Stalin steadfastly grow, and the hearts of millions of the oppressed and unfortunate in all the ends of the earth's globe beat in unison with the communist party.

For the past years in the most difficult and complex conditions of reconstruction, while giving a decisive rebuff to the wavering and relentless elements, the Central Committee of our party, at the head of which after Lenin's death stood and stands comrade Stalin, strongly and necessarily led the country on the path toward socialism. The historic change, produced by the Fifteenth Congress, is already giving real results on the experiment of socialist construction, on the experiment of construction in which millions are participating. On this witness the rapid rates of industrialization, the construction of large industrial firms great in size and scale, the construction of a metallurgical base for our socialist economy, grandiose socialist alterations of small and the smallest peasant farms, growth of creative self-criticism of workers, unprecedented rise of activity and initiative of the most extensive masses of laborers. Socialism enters the flesh and blood of millions and therefore its victory is strengthened with each day. But intense socialist construction, which is being conducted with such success in our country, overcoming tremendous difficulties standing on the path toward socialism, and the successful assault of revolutionaries on an international scale presuppose, as the most important condition, firm, bolshevik, leninist leadership, presupposes the most relentless struggle with opportunism, under whatever flag—right or left—that it appears. In the person of Stalin, the party and the entire international working class have the firm leninist, irreconcilable and rock-hard bolshevik.

The example and work of comrade Stalin closes still greater the ranks of our party, the ranks of the international revolution on the eve of the new, decisive battles which the international proletariat is entering.

Long live the dependable, unified leninist party!

Long live its leader comrade Stalin!

Pravda, 21 December 1929, 1.

STALIN, LIQUIDATION OF THE KULAK AS A CLASS

27 December 1929

Stalin used a speech at a conference of Marxist agronomists to call for the elimination of the kulaks as a class. He explained that the time was right for this change in policy because the collective and state farms were able to produce the appropriate marketable amount of grain, thus offsetting that share attributed to the kulaks during the New Economic Policy. This change in policy was an indication of NEP nearing its end and of the unleashing of the offensive in the countryside. Stalin also castigated professed Marxists for writing about non-Marxist economic theories such as the theory of equilibrium, and admonished them for failing to popularize the Marxist theory of reproduction and to analyze the transition of the economy to socialism under the current stage of development.

JOSEPH STALIN

CONCERNING QUESTIONS OF AGRARIAN POLICY IN THE USSR

Speech Delivered at a Conference of Marxist Students of Agrarian Questions

Comrades, the main fact of our social and economic life at the present time, a fact which is attracting universal attention, is the tremendous growth of the collective farm movement.

The characteristic feature of the present collective farm movement is that not only are the collective farms being joined by individual groups of poor peasants, as has been the case hitherto, but that they are being joined by the mass of the middle peasants as well. This means that the collective farm movement has been transformed from a movement of individual groups and sections of the laboring peasants into a movement of millions and millions of the main mass of the peasantry. This, by the way, explains the tremendously important fact that the collective farm movement, which has assumed the character of a mighty and growing *antikulak* avalanche, is sweeping the resistance of the kulak from its path, is shattering the kulak class and paving the way for extensive socialist construction in the countryside.

But while we have reason to be proud of the *practical* successes achieved in socialist construction, the same cannot be said with regard to our *theoretical* work in the economic field in general, and in that of agriculture in particular. More than that, it must be admitted that theoretical thought is not keeping pace with our practical successes, that there is a certain gap between our practical successes and the development of theoretical thought. Yet it is essential that theoretical work should not only keep pace with practical work but should keep ahead of it and equip our practical workers in their fight for the victory of socialism.

I shall not dwell at length here on the importance of theory. You are quite well aware of its importance. You know that theory, if it is genuine theory, gives practical workers the power of orientation, clarity of perspective, confidence in their work, faith in the victory of our cause. All this is, and necessarily must be, immensely important in our work of socialist construction. The unfortunate thing is that precisely in this sphere, in the sphere of the theoretical treatment of questions of our economy, we are beginning to lag behind.

How else can we explain the fact that in our country, in our social and political life, various bourgeois and petty bourgeois theories on questions of our economy are still current? How can we explain that these theories and would-be theories are not yet meeting with proper rebuff? How can we explain the fact that a number of fundamental theses of Marxist-Leninist political economy, which are the most effective antidote to bourgeois and petty bourgeois theories, are beginning to be forgotten, are not popularized in our press, are for some reason not placed in the foreground? Is it difficult to understand that unless a relentless fight against bourgeois theories is waged on the basis of Marxist-Leninist theory, it will be impossible to achieve complete victory over our class enemies?

New practical experience is giving rise to a new approach to the problems of the economy of the transition period. Questions of NEP, of classes, of the rate of construction, of the bond with the peasantry, of the Party's policy, are now presented in a new way. If we are not to lag behind practice we must immediately begin to work on all these problems in the light of the new situation. Unless we do this it will be impossible to overcome the bourgeois theories which are stuffing the heads of our practical workers with rubbish. Unless we do this it will be impossible to eradicate these theories which are acquiring the tenacity of prejudices. For only by combating bourgeois prejudices in the field of theory is it possible to consolidate the position of Marxism-Leninism.

Permit me now to characterize at least a few of these bourgeois prejudices which are called theories, and to demonstrate their unsoundness in the light of certain key problems of our work of construction.

I
THE THEORY OF "EQUILIBRIUM"

You know, of course, that the so-called theory of "equilibrium" between the sectors of our national economy is still current among Communists. This theory, of course, has nothing in common with Marxism. Nevertheless, it is a theory that is being spread by a number of people in the camp of the Right deviators.

This theory assumes that we have, in the first place, a socialist sector—which is one compartment, as it were—and that in addition we have a nonsocialist or, if you like, capitalist sector—which is another compartment. These two "compartments" are on different rails and glide peacefully forward, without touching each other. Geometry teaches that parallel lines do not meet. But the autnors of this remarkable theory believe that these parallel lines will meet eventually, and that when they do, we shall have socialism. This theory overlooks the fact that behind these so-called "compartments" there are classes, and that the movement of these compartments takes place by way of a fierce class struggle, a life and death struggle, a struggle on the principle of "who will beat whom?"

It is not difficult to realize that this theory has nothing in common with Leninism. It is not difficult to realize that, objectively, the purpose of this theory is to defend the position of individual peasant farming, to arm the kulak elements with a "new" theoretical weapon in their struggle against the collective farms, and to discredit the collective farms.

Nevertheless, this theory is still current in our press. And it cannot be said that it has met with a serious rebuff, let alone a crushing rebuff, from our theoreticians. How can this incongruity be explained except by the backwardness of our theoretical thought?

And yet, all that is needed is to take from the treasury of Marxism the theory of reproduction and set it up against the theory of equilibrium of the sectors for the latter theory to be wiped out without leaving a trace. Indeed, the Marxist theory of reproduction teaches that modern society cannot develop without accumulating from year to year, and accumulation is impossible unless there is expanded reproduction from year to year. This is clear and comprehensible. Our large-scale, centralized, socialist industry is developing according to the Marxist theory of expanded reproduction; for it is growing in volume from year to year, it has its accumulations and is advancing with giant strides.

But our large-scale industry does not constitute the whole of the national economy. On the contrary, small-peasant economy still predominates in it. Can we say that our small-peasant economy is developing according to the principle of expanded reproduction? No, we cannot. Not only is there no annual expanded reproduction in the bulk of our small-peasant economy, but, on the contrary, it is seldom able to achieve even simple reproduction. Can we advance our socialized industry at an accelerated rate while we have such an agricultural basis as small-peasant economy, which is incapable of expanded reproduction, and which, in addition, is the predominant force in our national economy? No, we cannot. Can Soviet power and the work of socialist construction rest for any length of time on two *different* foundations: On the most large-scale and concentrated socialist industry, and the most disunited and backward, small-commodity peasant economy? No, they cannot. Sooner or later this would be bound to end in the complete collapse of the whole national economy.

What, then, is the way out? The way out lies in making agriculture large-scale, in making it capable of accumulation, of expanded reproduction, and in thus transforming the agricultural basis of the national economy.

But how is it to be made large-scale?

There are two ways of doing this. There is the *capitalist* way, which is to make agriculture large-scale by implanting capitalism in agriculture—a way which leads to the impoverishment of the peasantry and to the development of capitalist enterprises in agriculture. We reject this way as incompatible with Soviet economy.

There is another way: The *socialist* way, which is to introduce collective and state farms into agriculture, the way which leads to uniting the small-peasant farms into large collective farms, employing machinery and scientific methods of farming, and capable of developing further, for such farms can achieve expanded reproduction.

And so, the question stands as follows: Either one way or the other, either *back*—to capitalism, or *forward*—to socialism. There is not, and cannot be, any third way.

The theory of "equilibrium" is an attempt to indicate a third way. And precisely because it is based on a third (nonexistent) way, it is utopian and antiMarxist.

You see, therefore, that all that was needed was to counterpose Marx' theory of reproduction to this theory of "equilibrium" of the sectors for the latter theory to be wiped out without leaving a trace.

Why, then, do our Marxist students of agrarian questions not do this? In whose interest is it that the ridiculous theory of "equilibrium" should have currency in our press while the Marxist theory of reproduction is kept hidden?

II
THE THEORY OF "SPONTANEITY" IN SOCIALIST CONSTRUCTION

Let us now take the second prejudice in political economy, the second bourgeois type of theory. I have in mind the theory of "spontaneity" in socialist construction—a theory which has nothing in common with Marxism, but which is being zealously advocated by our comrades of the Right camp.

The authors of this theory assert approximately the following. There was a time when capitalism existed in our country, industry developed on a capitalist basis, and the countryside followed the capitalist town spontaneously, automatically, becoming transformed in the image of the capitalist town. Since *that* is what happened under capitalism, why should not the same thing happen under the Soviet economic system as well? Why should not the countryside, small-peasant farming, automatically follow the socialist town, becoming transformed spontaneously in the image of the socialist town? On these grounds the authors of this theory assert that the countryside can follow the socialist town automatically. Hence, the question arises: Is it worth our while bothering about organizing state and collective farms; is it worthwhile breaking lances over this if the countryside may in any case follow the socialist town?

Here you have another theory which, objectively, seeks to supply the capitalist elements in the countryside with a new weapon for their struggle against the collective farms.

The antiMarxist nature of this theory is beyond all doubt.

Is it not strange that our theoreticians have not yet taken the trouble to explode this queer theory which is stuffing the heads of our practical collective-farm workers with rubbish?

There is no doubt that the leading role of the socialist town in relation to the small-peasant, individualist countryside is a great one and of inestimable value. It is indeed upon this that the role of industry in transforming agriculture is based. But is this factor sufficient to cause the small-peasant countryside automatically to follow the town in the work of socialist construction? No, it is not sufficient.

Under capitalism the countryside automatically followed the town because the capitalist economy of the town and the individual small-commodity economy of the peasant are, basically, economies of *the same type*. Of course, small-peasant commodity economy is not yet capitalist economy. But it is, basically, the same type of economy as capitalist economy since it rests on private ownership of the means of production. Lenin was a thousand times right when, in his notes on Bukharin's *Economics of the Transition Period*, he referred to the "commodity-*capitalist* tendency of the peasantry" in contrast to the "*socialist* tendency of the proletariat". It is this that explains why "small production *engenders* capitalism and the bourgeoisie continuously, daily, hourly, spontaneously, and on a mass scale" (*Lenin*).

Is it possible to say that basically small-commodity peasant economy is the same type of economy as socialist production in the towns? Obviously, it is impossible to say so without breaking with Marxism. Otherwise Lenin would not have said that "as long as we live in a small-peasant country, there is a surer economic basis for capitalism in Russia than for communism."

Consequently, in order that the small-peasant countryside should follow the socialist town, it is necessary, apart from everything else, to *introduce* in the countryside large socialist farms in the form of state and collective farms, as bases of socialism, which—headed by the socialist town—will be able *to take the lead* of the main mass of the peasantry.

Consequently, the theory of "spontaneity" in socialist construction is an antiMarxist theory. The socialist town can *lead* the small-peasant countryside, only by *introducing* collective and state farms by transforming the countryside after a new, socialist pattern.

It is strange that the antiMarxist theory of "spontaneity" in socialist construction has hitherto not met with a proper rebuff from our agrarian theoreticians.

III
THE THEORY OF THE "STABILITY" OF SMALL-PEASANT FARMING

Let us now take the third prejudice in political economy, the theory of the "stability" of small-peasant farming. Everybody is familiar with the argument of bourgeois political economy that the well known Marxist thesis about the advantages of large-scale production over small production applies only to industry, and does not apply to agriculture. Social-Democratic theoreticians like David and Hertz, who advocate this theory, have tried to "base themselves" on the fact that the small peasant is enduring and patient, that he is ready to bear any privation if only he can hold on to his little plot of land, and that, as a consequence, small-peasant economy displays stability in the struggle against large-scale economy in agriculture.

It is not difficult to understand such "stability" is worse than any instability. It is not difficult to understand that this antiMarxist theory has only one aim: To eulogize and strengthen the capitalist system which ruins the vast masses of small peasants. And it is precisely because this theory pursues this aim that it has been so easy for Marxists to shatter it.

But that is not the point just now. The point is that our practice, our reality, is providing new arguments against this theory, but our theoreticians, strangely enough, either will not, or cannot, make use of this new weapon against the enemies of the working class. I have in mind our practice in abolishing private ownership of land, our practice in abolishing the land, our practice which liberates the small peasant from his slavish attachment to his little plot of land and thereby helps the change from *small-scale* peasant to *large-scale* collective farming.

Indeed, what is it that has tied, is still tying and will continue to tie the small peasant of Western Europe to his small-commodity farming? Primarily, and mainly, the fact that he owns his little plot of land, the existence of private ownership of land. For years he saved up money in order to buy a little plot of land; he bought it, and of course he does not want to part with it, preferring to endure any privation, preferring to sink into barbarism and abject poverty, if only he can hold on to his little plot of land, the basis of his individual economy.

Can it be said that this factor, in this form, continues to operate in our country, under the Soviet system? No, it cannot be said. It cannot be said because there is no private ownership of land in our country. And precisely because there is no private ownership of land in our country, our peasants do not display that slavish attachment to a plot of land which is seen in the West. And this circumstance cannot but facilitate the change from small-peasant farming to collective farming.

That is one of the reasons why the *large* farms, the collective farms of our countryside, are able in our country, where the land is nationalized, to demonstrate so easily their *superiority* over the *small* peasant farms.

That is the great revolutionary significance of the Soviet agrarian laws which abolished absolute rent, abolished the private ownership of land and carried out the nationalization of the land.

But it follows from this that we now have at our command a new argument against the bourgeois economists who proclaim the stability of small-peasant farming in its struggle against large-scale farming.

Why then is this new argument not sufficiently utilized by our agrarian theoreticians in their struggle against all the various bourgeois theories?

When we nationalized the land our point of departure was, among other things, the theoretical premises laid down in the third volume of *Kapital*, in Marx' well known book *Theories of Surplus-Value*, and in Lenin's works on agrarian questions, which represent an extremely rich treasury of theoretical thought. I am referring to the theory of ground rent in general, and the theory of absolute ground rent in particular. It is now clear that the theoretical principles laid down in these works have been brilliantly confirmed by the practical experience of our work of socialist construction in town and countryside.

The only incomprehensible thing is why the antiscientific theories of "Soviet" economists like Chaianov should be freely current in our press, while Marx', Engels' and Lenin's works of genius dealing with the theory of ground rent and absolute ground rent are not popularized and brought into the foreground, are kept hidden.

You, no doubt, remember Engels' well known pamphlet *The Peasant Question*. You, of course, remember with what circumspection Engels approaches the question of the transition of the small peasants to the path of cooperative farming, to the path of collective farming. Permit me to quote the passage in question from Engels:

"We are decidedly on the side of the small peasant; we shall do everything at all permissible to make his lot more bearable, to facilitate this transition to the cooperative should he decide to do so, and even to make it possible for him to remain *on his little plot of land for a protracted length of time* to think the matter over, should he still be unable to bring himself to this decision." (My italics—*J. Stalin*)

You see with what circumspection Engels approaches the question of the transition of individual peasant farming to collectivist lines. How are we to explain this circumspection displayed by Engels, which at first sight seems exaggerated? What did he proceed from? Obviously, he proceeded from the existence of private ownership of land, from the fact that the peasant has "his little plot of land" which he will find it hard to part with. Such is the peasantry in capitalist countries, where private ownership of land exists. Naturally, great circumspection is needed here.

Can it be said that such a situation exists in our country, in the USSR? No, it cannot. It cannot be said because here we have no private ownership of land chaining the peasant to his individual farm. It cannot be said because in our country the land is nationalized, and this facilitates the transition of the individual peasant to collectivist lines.

That is one of the reasons for the comparative ease and rapidity with which the collective-farm movement has of late been developing in our country.

It is to be regretted that our agrarian theoreticians have not yet attempted to bring out with the proper clarity this difference between the situation of the peasantry in our country and in the West. And yet this would be of the utmost value not only for us, working in the Soviet Union, but for Communists in all countries. For it is not a matter of indifference to the proletarian revolution in the capitalist countries whether, from the first day of the seizure of power by the proletariat, socialism will have to be built there on the basis of the nationalization of the land or without this basis.

In my recent article ("A Year of Great Change"), I advanced certain arguments to prove the superiority of large-scale farming over small farming; in this I had in mind large state farms. It is self-evident that all these arguments fully and entirely apply also to collective farms, as large economic units. I am speaking not only of developed collective farms, which have machines and tractors at their disposal, but also of collective farms in their primary stage, which represent, as it were, the manufacture period of collective-farm development and are based on peasant farm implements. I am referring to the collective farms in their primary state which are not being formed in the areas of complete collectivization, and which are based upon the simple pooling of the peasants' implements of production.

Take, for instance, the collective farms of the Khoper area in the former Don region. Outwardly, from the point of view of technical equipment, these collective farms scarcely differ from small-peasant farms (few machines, few tractors). And yet the simple pooling of the peasants' implements of production within the collective farms has produced results of which our practical workers have never dreamt. What are these results? The fact that the transition to collective farming has brought about an increase of the crop area by 30, 40 and 50 percent. How are these "dizzying" results to be explained? By the fact that the peasants, who were powerless under the conditions of individual labor, have been transformed into a mighty force once they have pooled their implements and have united in collective farms. By the fact that it has become possible for the peasants to till neglected land and virgin soil, which is difficult to cultivate by individual labor. By the fact that the peasants have been enabled to avail themselves of virgin soil. By the fact that wasteland, isolated plots, field boundaries, etc., etc., could now be cultivated.

The question of cultivating neglected land and virgin soil is of tremendous importance for our agriculture. You know that the pivot of the revolutionary movement in Russia in the old days was the agrarian question. You know that one of the aims of the agrarian movement was to do away with the shortage of land. At that time there were many who thought that this shortage of land was absolute, i.e., that there was in Russia no more free land suitable for cultivation. And what has actually proved to be the situation? Now it is quite clear that scores of millions of hectares of free land were and still are available in the USSR. But the peasants were quite unable to till this land with their wretched implements. And precisely because they were unable to till neglected land and virgin soil, they longed for "soft soil", for the soil which belonged to the landlords, for soil which could be tilled with the aid of peasant implements by individual labor. That was at the bottom of the "land shortage". It is not surprising, therefore, that our Grain Trust, which is equipped with tractors, is now able to place under cultivation some twenty million hectares of free land, land unoccupied by peasants and unfit for cultivation by individual labor with the aid of small-peasant implements.

The significance of the collective-farm movement in all its phases—both in its primary and in its more developed phase when it is equipped with tractors—lies, for one thing, in the fact that it is now possible for the peasants to place under cultivation neglected land and virgin soil. That is the secret of the tremendous expansion of the crop area attending the transition of the peasants to collective labor. That is one of the reasons for the superiority of the collective farms over individual peasant farms.

It goes without saying that the superiority of the collective farms over the individual peasant farms will become even more incontestable when our machine and tractor stations and tractor columns come to the aid of the newly-formed collective farms in the areas of complete collectivization, and when the collective farms will be in a position to own tractors and harvester columns.

IV
TOWN AND COUNTRY

In regard to the so-called "scissors", there is a prejudice, fostered by bourgeois economists, against which a merciless war must be declared, as against all the other bourgeois theories that, unfortunately, are circulated in the Soviet press. I have in mind the theory which alleges that the October Revolution brought the peasantry fewer benefits than the February Revolution, that, in fact, the October Revolution brought no benefits to the peasantry.

At one time this prejudice was boosted in our press by a "Soviet" economist. This "Soviet" economist, it is true, later renounced his theory. (*A voice*: "Who was it?") It was Groman. But this theory was seized upon by the Trotsky-Zinoviev opposition and used against the Party. Moreover, there are no grounds for claiming that it is not current even now in "Soviet" public circles.

This is a very important question, comrades. It touches upon the problem of the relations between town and country. It touches upon the problem of eliminating the antithesis between town and country. It touches upon the very urgent question of the "scissors". I think, therefore, that it is worthwhile examining this strange theory.

Is it true that the October Revolution brought no benefits to the peasants? Let us turn to the facts.

I have before me the table drawn up by Comrade Nemchinov, the well known statistician, which was published in my article "On the Grain Front". From this table it is seen that in prerevolutionary times the landlords "produced" not less than 600,000,000 puds of grain. Hence, the *landlords* were then the holders of 600,000,000 puds of grain.

The *kulaks*, as shown in this table, at that time "produced" 1,900,000,000 puds of grain. That represents the very great power which the kulaks wielded at that time.

The *poor* and *middle* peasants, as shown in the same table, produced 2,500,000,000 puds of grain.

That was the situation in the old countryside, prior to the October Revolution.

What changes have taken place in the countryside since October? I quote the figures from the same table. Take, for instance, the year 1927. How much did the *landlords* produce that year? Obviously, they produced nothing and could not produce anything because they had been abolished by the October Revolution. You will realize that that must have been a great relief to the peasantry; for the peasants were liberated from the yoke of the landlords. That, of course, was a great gain for the peasantry, obtained as a result of the October Revolution.

How much did the *kulaks* produce in 1927? Six hundred million puds of grain instead of 1,900,000,000. Thus, during the period following the October Revolution the kulaks had lost more than two-thirds of their power. You will realize that this was bound to ease the situation of the poor and middle peasants.

And how much did the poor and middle peasants produce in 1927? Four thousand million puds, instead of 2,500,000,000 puds. Thus, after the October Revolution the poor and middle peasants began to produce 1,500,000,000 puds more grain than in prerevolutionary times.

There you have facts which show that the October Revolution brought colossal gains to the poor and middle peasants.

That is what the October Revolution brought to the poor and middle peasants.

How, after this, can it be asserted that the October Revolution brought no benefits to the peasants?

But that is not all, comrades. The October Revolution abolished private ownership of land, did away with the purchase and sale of land, carried out the nationalization of the land. What does this mean? It means that now the peasant has no need to buy land in order to produce grain. Formerly he was saving up for years in order to acquire land; he got into debt, went into bondage, if only he could buy a piece of land. The expense which the purchase of land involved naturally increased the cost of production of grain. Now, the peasant does not have to do that. He can produce grain now without buying land. Consequently, the hundreds of millions of rubles that formerly were spent by the peasants for the purchase of land now remain in their pockets. Does this ease the situation of the peasants or not? Obviously, it does.

Further. Until recently, the peasant was compelled to dig the soil with old-fashioned implements by individual labor. Everyone knows that individual labor, equipped with old-fashioned, now unsuitable, instruments of production, does not bring the gains required to enable one to lead a tolerable existence, systematically improve one's material position, develop one's culture and emerge on to the high road of socialist construction. Today, after the accelerated development of the collective-farm movement, the peasants are able to combine their labor with that of their neighbors, to unite in collective farms, to plough virgin soil, to utilize neglected land, to obtain machines and tractors and thereby double or even treble the productivity of labor. And what does this mean? It means that today the peasant, by joining the collective farm, is able to produce much more than formerly with the same expenditure of labor. It means, therefore, that grain will be produced much more cheaply than was the case until quite recently. It means, finally, that, with stable prices, the peasant can obtain much more for his grain than he has obtained up to now.

How, after all this, can it be asserted that the October Revolution brought no gains to the peasantry?

Is it not clear that those who utter such fictions obviously slander the Party and Soviet power?

But what follows from all this?

It follows that the question of the "scissors", the question of doing away with the "scissors", must now be approached in a new way. It follows that if the collective-farm movement grows at the present rate, the "scissors" will be abolished in the near future. It follows that the question of the relations between town and country is now put on a new basis, that the antithesis between town and country will disappear at an accelerated pace.

This circumstance, comrades, is of very great importance for our whole work of construction. It transforms the mentality of the peasant and turns him towards the town. It creates the basis for eliminating the antithesis between town and country. It creates the basis for the slogan of the Party—"face to the countryside"—to be supplemented by the slogan of the peasant collective farmers: "face to the town".

Nor is there anything surprising in this, for the peasant is now receiving from the town machines, tractors, agronomists, organizers and, finally, direct assistance in fighting and overcoming the kulaks. The old type of peasant, with his savage distrust of the town, which he regarded as a plunderer, is passing into the background. His place is being taken by the new peasant, by the collective-farm peasant, who looks to the town with the hope of receiving real assistance in *production*. The place of the old type of peasant who was afraid of sinking to the level of the poor peasants and only stealthily (for he could be deprived of the franchise!) rose to the position of a kulak, is being taken by the new peasant, with a new prospect before him—that of joining a collective farm and emerging from poverty and ignorance on to the high road of economic and cultural progress.

That is the turn things are taking, comrades.

It is all the more regrettable, comrades, that our agrarian theoreticians have not taken all measures to explode and eradicate all bourgeois theories which seek to discredit the gains of the October Revolution and the growing collective-farm movement.

V
THE NATURE OF COLLECTIVE FARMS

The collective farm, as a *type* of economy, is one of the forms of socialist economy. There can be no doubt whatever about that.

One of the speakers here tried to discredit the collective farms. He asserted that the collective farms, as economic organizations, have nothing in common with the socialist form of economy. I must say, comrades, that such a characterization of the collective farms is absolutely wrong. There can be no doubt that it has nothing in common with the true state of affairs.

What determines the type of an economy? Obviously, the relations between people in the process of production. How else can the type of an economy be determined? But is there in the collective farms a class of people who own the means of production and a class of people who are deprived of these means of production? Is there an exploiting class and an exploited class in the collective farms? Does not the collective farm represent the socialization of the principal instruments of production on land belonging to the state? What grounds are there for asserting that the collective farms, as a type of economy, do not represent one of the forms of socialist economy?

Of course, there are contradictions in the collective farms. Of course, there are individualistic and even kulak survivals in the collective farms, which have not yet disappeared, but which are bound to disappear in the course of time as the collective farms become stronger, as they are provided with more machines. But can it be denied that the collective farms as a whole, with all their contradictions and shortcomings, the collective farms as an *economic* fact, represent, in the main, a new path of development of the countryside, the path of *socialist* development of the countryside in *contradistinction* to the kulak, *capitalist* path of development? Can it be denied that the collective farms (I am speaking of real, not sham collective farms) represent, under our conditions, a base and center of socialist construction in the countryside—a base and center which have grown up in desperate clashes with the capitalist elements?

Is it not clear that the attempts of some comrades to discredit the collective farms and declare them a bourgeois form of economy are devoid of all foundation?

In 1923 we did not yet have a mass collective-farm movement. Lenin, in this pamphlet *On Cooperatives*, had in mind all forms of cooperatives, both its lower forms (supply and marketing cooperatives) and its higher forms (collective farms). What did he say at that time about cooperatives, about cooperative enterprises? Here is a quotation from Lenin's pamphlet *On Cooperatives*:

"Under our present system, cooperative enterprises differ from private capitalist enterprises because they are collective enterprises, but they *do not differ* from socialist enterprises if the land on which they are situated and the means of production belong to the state, i.e., the working class" (Volume XXVII, p. 396). (My italics—*J. Stalin*)

Hence, Lenin takes the cooperative enterprises not by themselves, but in connection with our present system, in connection with the fact that they function on land belonging to the state, in a country where the means of production belong to the state; and, regarding them in this light, Lenin declares that cooperative enterprises do not differ from socialist enterprises.

That is what Lenin says about cooperative enterprises in general.

It is not clear that there is all the more ground for saying the same about the collective farms in our period?

This, by the way, explains why Lenin regarded the "mere growth of cooperatives" under our conditions as "identical with the growth of socialism."

As you see, the speaker I referred to above, in trying to discredit the collective farms, committed a grave mistake against Leninism.

This mistake led him to another mistake—about the class struggle in the collective farms. The speaker portrayed the class struggle in the collective farms in such vivid colors that one might think that the class struggle in the collective farms *does not differ* from the class struggle in the absence of collective farms. Indeed, one might think that in the collective farms it becomes even fiercer. Incidentally, the speaker mentioned is not the only one who has erred in this matter. Idle talk about the class struggle, squealing and shrieking about the class struggle in the collective farms, is now characteristic of all our noisy "Lefts". The most comical thing about this squealing is that the squealers "see" the class struggle where it does not exist, or hardly exists, but fail to see it where it does exist and is glaringly manifest.

Are these elements of the class struggle in the collective farms? Yes, there are. There are bound to be elements of the class struggle in the collective farms as long as there still remain survivals of individualistic, or even kulak, mentality, as long as there still exists a certain degree of material inequality. Can it be said that the class struggle in the collective farms is equivalent to the class struggle in the absence of collective farms? No, it cannot. The mistake our "Left" phrasemongers make lies precisely in not seeing the difference.

What does the class struggle imply *in the absence of* collective farms, *prior to* the establishment of collective farms? It implies a fight against the kulak who *owns* the instruments and means of production and who keeps the poor peasants *in bondage* with the aid of those instruments and means of production. It is a life and death struggle.

But what does the class struggle imply with the collective farms *in existence*? It implies, firstly, that the kulak has been defeated and deprived of the instruments and means of production. It implies, secondly, that the poor and middle peasants are united in collective farms on the basis of the socialization of the principal instruments and means of production. It implies, finally, that it is a struggle between members of collective farms, some of whom have not yet rid themselves of individualistic and kulak survivals and are striving to turn the inequality that exists to some extent in the collective farms to their own advantage, while the others want to eliminate these survivals and this inequality. Is it not clear that only the blind can fail to see the difference between the class struggle in the absence of collective farms?

It would be a mistake to believe that once collective farms exist we have all that is necessary for building socialism. It would be all the more a mistake to believe that the members of the collective farms have already become Socialists. No, a great deal of work has still to be done to remold the peasant collective farmer, to set right his individualistic mentality and to transform him into a real working member of a socialist society. And the more rapidly the collective farms are provided with machines, the more rapidly they are supplied with tractors, the more rapidly will this be achieved. But this does not in the least belittle the very great importance of the collective farms as a lever for the socialist transformation of the countryside. The great importance of the collective farms lies precisely in that they represent the principal base for the employment of machinery and tractors in agriculture, that they constitute the principal base for remolding the peasant, for changing his mentality in the spirit of socialism. Lenin was right when he said:

"The remaking of the small tiller, the remolding of his whole mentality and habits, is a work of generations. As regards the small tiller, this problem can be solved, his whole mentality can be put on healthy lines, so to speak, only by the material base, by technical means, by introducing tractors and machines in agriculture on a mass scale, by electrification on a mass scale" (Volume XXVI, p. 239).

Who can deny that the collective farms are indeed that form of socialist economy which alone can draw the vast masses of the small individual peasants into large-scale farming, with its machines and tractors as the levers of economic progress, the levers of the socialist development of agriculture?

Our "Left" phrasemongers have forgotten all that.

And our speaker has forgotten about it, too.

VI
THE CLASS CHANGES AND THE TURN IN THE PARTY'S POLICY

Finally, the question of the class changes in our country and the offensive of socialism against the capitalist elements in the countryside.

The characteristic feature in the work of our Party during the past year is that we, as a Party, as Soviet power:

a) have developed an offensive along the whole front against the capitalist elements in the countryside;

b) that this offensive, as you know, has yielded and continues to yield very appreciable, *positive* results.

What does this mean? It means that we have passed from the policy of *restricting* the exploiting tendencies of the kulaks to the policy of *eliminating* the kulaks as a class. It means that we have carried out, and are continuing to carry out, one of the decisive turns in our whole policy.

Until recently the Party adhered to the policy of restricting the exploiting tendencies of the kulaks. As you know, this policy was proclaimed as far back as the Eighth Party Congress. It was again announced at the time of the introduction of the NEP and at the Eleventh Congress of our Party. We all remember Lenin's well known letter about Preobrazhensky's theses (1922), in which Lenin once again returned to the need for pursuing this policy. Finally, this policy was confirmed by the Fifteenth Congress of our Party. And it was this policy that we are pursuing until recently.

Was this policy correct? Yes, it was absolutely correct at the time. Could we have undertaken such an offensive against the kulaks some five years or three years ago? Could we then have counted on success in such an offensive? No, we could not. That would have been the most dangerous adventurism. It would have been a very dangerous playing at an offensive. For we should certainly have failed, and our failure would have strengthened the position of the kulaks. Why? Because we did not yet have in the countryside strong points in the form of a wide network of state and collective farms which could be the basis for a determined offensive against the kulaks. Because at that time we were not yet able to *replace* the capitalist production of the kulaks by the socialist production of the collective and state farms.

In 1926-1927, the Zinoviev-Trotsky opposition did its utmost to impose upon the Party the policy of an immediate offensive against the kulaks. The Party did not embark on that dangerous adventure, for it knew that serious people cannot afford to play at an offensive. An offensive against the kulaks is a serious matter. It should not be confused with declamations against the kulaks. Nor should it be confused with a policy of pinpricks against the kulaks, which the Zinoviev-Trotsky opposition did its utmost to impose upon the Party. To launch an offensive against the kulaks means that we must smash the kulaks, eliminate them as a class. Unless we set ourselves these aims, an offensive would be mere declamation, pinpricks, phrasemongering, anything but a real Bolshevik offensive. To launch an offensive against the kulaks means that we must prepare for it and then strike at the kulaks, strike so hard as to prevent them from rising to their feet again. That is what we Bolsheviks call a real offensive. Could we have undertaken such an offensive some five years or three years ago with any prospect of success? No, we could not.

Indeed, in 1927 the kulaks produced over 600,000,000 puds of grain, about 130,000,000 of which they marketed outside the rural districts. That was a rather serious power, which had to be reckoned with. How much did our collective and state farms produce at that time? About 80,000,000 puds, of which about 35,000,000 puds were sent to the market (marketable grain). Judge for yourselves, could we at that time have *replaced* the kulak output and kulak marketable grain by the output and marketable grain of our collective and state farms? Obviously, we could not.

What would it have meant to launch a determined offensive against the kulaks under such conditions? It would have meant certain failure, strengthening the position of the kulaks and being left without grain. That is why we could not and should not have undertaken a determined offensive against the kulaks at that time, in spite of the adventurist declamations of the Zinoviev-Trotsky opposition.

But today? What is the position now? Today, we have an adequate material base for us to strike at the kulaks, to break their resistance, to eliminate them as a class, and to *replace* their output by the output of the collective and state farms. You know that in 1929 the grain produced on the collective and state farms has amounted to not less than 400,000,000 puds (200,000,000 puds less than the gross output of the kulak farms in 1927). You also know that in 1929 the collective and state farms have supplied more than 130,000,000 puds of marketable grain (i.e., more than the kulaks in 1927). Lastly, you know that in 1930 the gross output of the collective and state farms will amount to not less than 900,000,000 puds of grain (i.e., more than the gross output of the kulaks in 1927), and their output of marketable grain will be not less than 400,000,000 puds (i.e., incomparably more than the kulaks supplied in 1927).

That is how matters stand with us now, comrades.

There you have the change that has taken place in the economy of our country.

Now, as you see, we have the material base which enables us to *replace* the kulak output by the output of the collective and state farms. It is for this very reason that our determine offensive against the kulaks is now meeting with undeniable success.

That is how an offensive against the kulaks must be carried on, if we mean a genuine and determined offensive and not mere futile declamations against the kulaks.

That is why we have recently passed from the policy of *restricting* the exploiting tendencies of the kulaks to the policy of *eliminating the kulaks as a class.*

Well, and what about the policy of dekulakization? Can we permit dekulakization in the areas of complete collectivization? This question is asked in various quarters. A ridiculous question! We could not permit delulakization as long as we were pursuing the policy of restricting the exploiting tendencies of the kulaks, as long as we were unable to go over to a determined offensive against the kulaks, as long as we were unable to replace the kulak output by the output of the collective and state farms. At that time the policy of not permitting dekulakization was necessary and correct. But now? Now things are different. Now we are able to carry on a determined offensive against the kulaks, break their resistance, eliminate them as a class and replace their output by the output of the collective and state farms. Now, dekulakization is being carried out by the masses of poor and middle peasants themselves, who are putting complete collectivization into practice. Now, dekulakization in the areas of complete collectivization is no longer just an administrative measure. Now, it is an integral part of the formation and development of the collective farms. Consequently, it is now ridiculous and foolish to discourse at length on dekulakization. When the head is off, one does not mourn for the hair.

There is another question which seems no less ridiculous: Whether the kulaks should be permitted to join the collective farms. Of course not, for they are sworn enemies of the collective-farm movement.

VII
CONCLUSIONS

The above, comrades, are six key questions which the theoretical work of our Marxist students of agrarian questions cannot ignore.

The importance of these questions lies, above all, in the fact that a Marxist analysis of them makes it possible to eradicate all the various bourgeois theories which sometimes—to our shame—are circulated by our own comrades, by Communists, and which stuff the heads of our practical workers with rubbish and these theories should have been eradicated and discarded long ago. For only in a relentless fight against these and similar theories can theoretical thought among Marxist students of agrarian questions develop and grow strong.

The importance of these questions lies, lastly, in the fact that they give a new aspect to the old problems of the economy of the transition period.

Questions of NEP, of classes, of the collective farms, of the economy of the transition period, are now presented in a new way.

The mistake of those who interpret NEP as a retreat, and only as a retreat, must be exposed. As a matter of fact, even when the New Economic Policy was being introduced, Lenin said that it was not only a retreat, but also the preparation for a new, determined offensive against the capitalist elements in town and country.

The mistake of those who think that NEP is necessary only as a link between town and country must be exposed. It is not just any kind of link between town and country that we need. What we need is a link that will ensure the victory of socialism. And if we adhere to NEP it is because it serves the cause of socialism. When it ceases to serve the cause of socialism we shall get rid of it. Lenin said that NEP had been introduced in earnest and for a long time. But he never said it had been introduced for all time.

We must also raise the question of popularizing the Marxist theory of reproduction. We must examine the question of the structure of the balance sheet of our national economy. What the Central Statistical Administration published in 1926 as the balance sheet of the national economy is not a balance sheet, but a juggling with figures. Nor is the manner in which Bazarov and Groman treat the problem of the balance sheet of the national economy suitable. The structure of the balance sheet of the national economy of the USSR must be worked out by the revolutionary Marxists if they desire at all to devote themselves to the questions of the economy of the transition period.

It would be a good thing if our Marxist economists were to appoint a special group to examine the problems of the economy of the transition period in the new way in which they are presented at the present stage of development.

Stalin, *Works*, XII, 147-170.

2 THE YEAR 1930

PARTY CENTRAL COMMITTEE RESOLUTION ON INCREASING RATE OF COLLECTIVIZATION

5 January 1930

Based on the work of a special Politburo commission that predicted an exceedingly rapid increase in collectivization, the Party Central Committee resolved to almost double the funding for collectivization and increase considerably the production of tractors and agricultural machinery. It also resolved to move toward the liquidation of kulaks as a class. The special Politburo commission, formed on 5 December 1929 in response to the November plenum decision to proceed with general collectivization, submitted a draft resolution to the Central Committee after repeated criticism and revisions by Stalin, who wanted to accelerate collectivization and exclude kulaks from kolkhozes. The resolution below stopped short of providing specific guidance to Party and Government officials concerning the formation and organization of kolkhozes, and how to manage the kulaks in the process. As a result, tensions were raised in the countryside through the confiscation of kulaks' property and their deportation to remote areas. Moreover, peasants were forced to form kolkhozes despite the resolution's warning against such by decree from above, i.e., from the central bureaucracy.

RESOLUTION OF THE TSK VKP(B) ON THE RATE OF COLLECTIVIZATION AND STATE ASSISTANCE TO KOLKHOZ CONSTRUCTION

1. In recent months the collectivization movement has taken a new stride forward, encompassing not only isolated groups of private farms but also whole raions, okrugs, and even oblasts and krais. At the basis of the movement is the collectivization of the means of production of the poor and middle peasant farms.

All of the contemplated planned rates of development of the collectivization movement have been exceeded. In the spring of 1930 the sown area cultivated on a socialized basis is already considerably in excess of 30 million hectares; thus the five year plan for collectivization, which proceeded on the assumption that 22-24 million hectares would be in collectives by the end of the five year period, will already be substantially overfulfilled this year.

Thus we have the material basis for *replacing* large-scale kulak production by *large-scale* production in the kolkhozes, for a mighty advance in creating a socialist agriculture, not to mention the sovkhozes whose growth is substantially exceeding all planning assumptions.

This circumstance, which is of decisive significance for the whole economy of the USSR, has given the party ample grounds for passing in its practical work from a policy of limiting the exploitive tendencies of the kulaks to a policy of liquidating the kulaks as a class.

2. On the basis of all of this it can undoubtedly be established that, by the end of the five year period, instead of collectivizing 20 percent of the sown area as provided in the five year plan, we can resolve the task of collectivizing the overwhelming majority of peasant farms; the collectivization of such very important grain regions as the Lower Volga, Middle Volga, and North Caucasus may be basically completed by the autumn of 1930 or, at any rate, the spring of 1931, and the collectivization of other grain regions may be basically completed by the autumn of 1931 or, at any rate, the spring of 1932.

3. Because of the increasing rate of collectivization, it is necessary to intensify further the construction of factories producing tractors, combines, and auxiliary farm machinery, so that the deadlines established by the VSNKh for completing the building of new factories will in no circumstances be exceeded. At the same time the TsK orders the VSNKh to report to the TsK not later than 15 March of this year on measures taken to ensure an increase next year in the overall production of complex agricultural machinery in existing plants and, especially, a considerable increase in the production of complex tractor- and horse-drawn machinery instead of simple models.

4. Inasmuch as the problem of the complete replacement of horse-drawn equipment by power-driven models cannot be solved in a short time but requires a number of years, the TsK VKP(b) demands that tendencies to underestimate the role of the horse at this stage in the kolkhoz movement, which lead to the squandering and selling-off of horses, be decisively rejected. The TsK VKP(b) emphasizes the exceptional importance under present conditions, of establishing in the kolkhozes, as a transitional measure, pools of *horse-drawn farm machinery* and *combined horse- and tractor-drawn machinery*, the latter being a mixture of tractor- and horse-powered machinery.

5. In connection with the increasing tempo of the movement toward collectivization, the TsK orders Narkomzem of the USSR to regroup the forces and equipment that are dealing with land tenure [such as surveyors] so as to satisfy fully the needs of the regions of complete collectivization with respect to land tenure, setting aside work on individual land tenure. This does not apply to certain national regions and separate zones that specialize in consumer crops in which the collectivization movement has not yet been broadly developed.

6. In accordance with the above, the TsK considers it absolutely necessary that the total credits made available to the kolkhoz sector in 1929/30 be increased from 270 to 500 million rubles, the credits supplied to other sectors being reduced in proportion.

7. In accordance with the changed conditions in the regions of complete collectivization, the machine tractor stations, coordinated by the All-Union tractor center, must reorganize their work on the following basis:

a) agreements are to be made primarily, and even exclusively, with collectives;

b) peasants are given three years within which to pay for the stations.

At the same time, in regions where sovkhozes are extensive (for example, the Middle Volga and some raions of the North Caucasus), a combined economy in which the sovkhozes assist the kolkhozes, on a contractual basis and for pay, by tractor-plowing their land and harvesting their crops with machinery, should be tested in practice.

8. In view of the particular significance of cadres, the TsK orders the Narkomzem of the USSR, Kolkhoztsentr, and the oblast party committees to accelerate their training of kolkhoz cadres and make them available to the kolkhozes more rapidly, for this purpose setting up a broad network of accelerated courses. Peasants who have distinguished themselves in practical work in the kolkhoz movement and the members of workers' brigades who have proven to be good organizers of the kolkhoz movement must be attracted to these accelerated courses.

9. Inasmuch as the experience of complete collectivization at the present stage of kolkhoz development shows that the artel is the most widespread form of kolkhoz, in which the *basic* instruments of production (livestock and dead stock, farm buildings, commercial herds) are collectivized, instead of the TOZ, in which the labor is socialized while the instruments of production remain in private hands, the Central Committee of the VKP(b) charges the Narkomzem of the USSR, working generally with the kolkhoz organizations, to develop the shortest possible time a model Charter of the agricultural kolkhoz artel as a transitional form of kolkhoz on the way to the commune—bearing in mind the inadmissibility of allowing kulaks to join kolkhozes.

10. The party organizations must head and shape the kolkhoz movement, which is developing spontaneously from below, so as to ensure the organization of *genuinely*

collective production in the kolkhozes, and on this basis not only fully to fulfil the contemplated plan for expanding the sown area and increasing the yields, but also—in accordance with the decision of the November plenum of the TsK—to convert the present sowing campaign into the starting point of a new advance in the kolkhoz movement.

11. The TsK VKP(b) emphasizes the necessity of a resolute struggle against any attempts to hinder the development of the kolkhoz movement because of the insufficiency of tractors and complex machinery. At the same time the TsK with all seriousness warns party organizations against guiding the kolkhoz movement "by decree" from above; this could give rise to the danger of replacing genuine socialist competition in the organization of kolkhozes by mere playing at collectivization.

McNeal/Gregor, Vol. 3, 40-43.
KPSS v rezoliutsiiakh, Vol. 4, 383-386.

DECREE ON HARSH MEASURES AGAINST KULAKS

1 February 1930

The Politburo formed a commission on 15 January, with V. Molotov as chairman, to establish measures to apply against the kulaks. It received a draft resolution from the commission, approved the final resolution on 30 January, and sent the resolution to all local party organizations. The resolution was not published; the decree below by the Central Executive Committee and the Council of People's Commissars indicates the harsh measures reflected in the Politburo resolution. The resolution abolished the right to rent land and hire labor, and authorized local governments to confiscate property of kulaks and to exile them from the local areas.

ON MEASURES TO STRENGTHEN SOCIALIST RECONSTRUCTION OF AGRICULTURE IN REGIONS OF COMPLETE COLLECTIVIZATION AND ON THE STRUGGLE WITH THE KULAKS

With the aim of securing the most advantageous conditions for the socialist reconstruction of agriculture, the Central Executive Committee and Council of People's Commissars of the USSR decree:

1. To abolish in the regions of complete collectivization the operation of the law to authorize the renting of land and the use of hired labor on individual peasant farms (sections VII and VIII of the general principles of land tenure).

Exceptions from this law as concern middle-peasant farms are regulated by raion executive committees under the management and control of okrug executive committees.

2. To grant krai (oblast) executive committees and governments of autonomous republics the right to use in these regions all the necessary measures in the struggle with the kulaks up to and including the complete confiscation of their property and their exile from the boundaries of the individual raions and krais (oblasts).

The confiscated property of kulak farms, except for that part which becomes part of liquidation of obligations (debts) added on to the kulaks by state and cooperative organs, must be transferred to the indivisible fund of the kolkozes in lieu of payment of the entry fees by the poor peasants and day laborers who join the kolkhoz.

3. To propose to the governments of union republics, in the development of the present decree, to issue the necessary instructions to krai (oblast) executive committees and governments of autonomous republics.

Sobranie Zakonov i Rasporiazhenii, No. 9 (24 February 1930), Article 105, 187-188.

STALIN ENCOURAGES FURTHER EXTENSION OF COLLECTIVIZATION

9 February 1930

Following a speech at the Sverdlov Academy in Moscow about agrarian issues, Stalin received and answered questions submitted by students. He encouraged the further extension of collectivization and the policy of eliminating kulaks as a class. He insisted on mass collectivization as the best approach to eliminating kulaks as a class. He stopped short of saying that the New Economic Policy was at an end.

JOSEPH STALIN
REPLY TO THE SVERDLOV COMRADES

I

THE SVERDLOV STUDENTS' QUESTIONS

1. In the theses on the tactics of the RCP(B), adopted by the Third Congress of the Comintern, Lenin spoke of the existence of two main classes in Soviet Russia.

We now speak of eliminating the kulaks and the new bourgeoisie as a class.

Does this mean that in the NEP period a third class has taken shape in our country?

2. In your address to the conference of Marxist students of agrarian questions, you said: "If we adhere to NEP it is because it serves the cause of socialism. When it ceases to serve the cause of socialism we shall get rid of it." How is this "getting rid of" to be understood, and what form will it take?

3. What amendments will the Party, as decisive successes in collectivization and in eliminating the kulaks as a class are achieved, have to make in the slogan which now determines the relations between the proletariat and the various strata of the peasantry: "To come to an agreement with the middle peasant, while never for a moment renouncing the fight against the kulak, and firmly relying solely on the poor peasant" (*Lenin*)?

4. By what methods should the elimination of the kulaks as a class be brought about?

5. Will not the simultaneous application of two slogans: One for the areas of complete collectivization—elimination of the kulaks as a class, and the other for the areas of incomplete collectivization—restriction and ousting of the kulaks, lead in the latter areas to the self-elimination of the kulaks (dissipation of their property, means of production)?

6. What influence may the elimination of the kulaks as a class and the sharpening of the class struggle in our country, and the economic crisis and the rise of the tide of revolution in the capitalist countries, have on the duration of the "respite"?

7. What is your opinion of the possibility of the present revolutionary upsurge in the capitalist countries passing into a direct revolutionary situation?

8. How should the new advances among the working class, characterized by the decision of entire factory shops to join the Party, be assessed from the standpoint of the further relations between the Party and the working class?

9. In connection with the tremendous scope of the collective-farm movement, the extension of the Party organization in the countryside becomes a practical question. What should be our policy in relation to the limits of such extension, and in relation to admission of the various groups of collective farmers into the Party?

10. What is your attitude towards the disputes that are taking place among the economists on cardinal problems of political economy?

II

COMRADE STALIN'S REPLY

First question. Lenin spoke of two *main* classes. But he knew, of course, that there was a third, the capitalist class (the kulaks, the urban capitalist bourgeoisie). The kulaks and the urban bourgeoisie did not, of course, "take shape" as a class only after the introduction of NEP. They existed also before NEP, but as a *secondary* class. NEP, in its first stages, to some extent facilitated the growth of this class. But it assisted the growth of the socialist sector to an even greater extent. With the launching by the Party of an offensive along the whole front, matters have taken a sharp turn towards the undermining and abolition of the class of rural, and partly of urban, capitalists.

For the sake of accuracy, it should be noted that the Party has not given instructions to extend the slogan of eliminating the kulaks as a class to the new, urban bourgeoisie. It is necessary to distinguish between the Nepmen, who were in the main deprived of their *production* base long ago, and therefore play no substantial part in our economic life, and the kulaks, who until very recently possessed enormous economic weight in the countryside, and whom we are *only now* depriving of their *production* base.

It seems to me that some of our organizations forget this difference and commit the error of trying to "supplement" the slogan of eliminating the kulaks as a class with the slogan of eliminating the urban bourgeoisie.

Second question. The sentence in my speech at the conference of Marxist students of agrarian questions should be understood as meaning that we shall "get rid of NEP" when we are no longer under the necessity of permitting a certain freedom for private trade, when permitting it would yield only adverse results, and when we are in a position to establish economic relations between town and country through our own trading organizations, without private trade with its private turnover and tolerance of a certain revival of capitalism.

Third question. It is clear that as the collectives come to embrace the majority of the areas of the USSR, the kulaks will be eliminated—hence this part of Il'ich's formula will lapse. As regards the middle and poor peasants in the collective farms, they will, as the latter become equipped with machines and tractors, merge into a single category of working members of the collectivized countryside. Correspondingly, the concepts "middle peasant" and "poor peasant" should in the future disappear from our slogans.

Fourth question. The principal method of bringing about the elimination of the kulaks as a class is that of mass collectivization. All other measures must be adapted to this principal method. Everything that runs counter to this method or detracts from its effectiveness must be rejected.

Fifth question. The slogans, "elimination of the kulaks as a class" and "restriction of the kulaks" must not be conceived as two *independent* and *equal* slogans. From the moment we passed to the policy of eliminating the kulaks as a class, this slogan became the *chief* slogan; and in the areas of incomplete collectivization the slogan of restricting the kulaks changed from an independent slogan into a *subsidiary* slogan, an *auxiliary* of the chief slogan, into a slogan which facilitates the creation in these areas of the conditions for a transition to the chief slogan. As you see, in the new conditions of today, the status of the slogan "restriction of the kulaks" is radically different from what it was a year ago and earlier.

It is to be noted that, unfortunately, some of our press organs do not appreciate this specific feature.

It is possible and probable that in the areas of incomplete collectivization a section of the kulaks, in anticipation of dekulakization, will resort to "self-elimination" and "dissipate their property and means of production". Measures, of course, must be taken to prevent this. But it does not at all follow that we should permit dekulakization, not as part of the collectivization, but as something independent, undertaken before and without collectivization. To permit that would be to replace the policy of *socializing* confiscated kulak property in the collective farms by a policy of *sharing out* this property for the personal enrichment of individual peasants. Such replacement would be a step backward, not forward. There is only one way of preventing "dissipation" of kulak property, and that is to work harder for collectivization in the areas where it is incomplete.

Sixth question. The means and conditions you enumerate *may* considerably shorten the duration of the "respite". But they are certainly *bound* to strengthen and multiply our means of defense. Very much will depend on the international situation, on the growth of the contradictions within the camp of international capitalism, on the further development of the international economic crisis. But that is another question.

Seventh question. No hard and fast line can be drawn between a "revolutionary upsurge" and a "direct revolutionary situation". One cannot say: "Up to this point we have a revolutionary upsurge; beyond it, we have a leap to a direct revolutionary situation." Only scholastics can put the question in that way. The first usually passes "imperceptibly" into the second. The task is to prepare the proletariat *at once* for decisive revolutionary battles, *without waiting* for the "onset" of what is called a direct revolutionary situation.

Eighth question. The desire of entire factory shops and even of whole factories to join the Party is a sign of the tremendous revolutionary upsurge of the vast masses of the working class, a sign of the correctness of the Party's policy, a sign of publicly expressed approval of this policy by the broad masses of the working class. But it does not at all follow from this that we must admit into the Party all who desire to join it. In the shops and factories there are all sorts of people, even saboteurs. The Party must therefore continue to apply its tried and tested method of *individual* approach to each applicant for membership, and of *individual* admission to the Party. We need not only quantity, but quality.

Ninth question. It goes without saying that numerically the Party in the collective farms will grow at a more or less rapid rate. It is desirable that all the elements of the collective-farm movement who have been most steeled in fighting against the kulaks, especially farm laborers and poor peasants, should find application for their energies in the ranks of the Party. Naturally, individual approach and individual admission into the Party must be applied here with especial persistence.

Tenth question. It seems to me that in the disputes among the economists there is much that is scholastic and farfetched. Setting aside the external aspect of the disputes, the main errors of the contending sides are the following:

a) neither side has proved capable of properly applying the method of fighting on two fronts: Both against "Rubinism" and against "mechanism",

b) both sides have been diverted from the basic questions of Soviet economy and world imperialism into the realm of talmudic abstractions, thus wasting two years of effort on abstract themes—to the satisfaction and advantage, of course, of our enemies.

Stalin, *Works*, XII, 190-196.

COLLECTIVIZATION AND LIQUIDATION OF THE KULAK IN THE COUNTRYSIDE

12-19 February 1930

As the regions received instructions to collectivize and liquidate the kulak as a class, officials quickly drafted memoranda and letters for their subordinates. The two top secret documents below, from the Okrug troika in the Western Oblast near Smolensk, illustrate how local party, government, and security officials interpreted and executed the instructions. The troika, a committee consisting of the first party secretary, chairman of the executive committee, and head of the local OGPU, sought to regularize and standardize collectivization and dekulakization as much as possible to prevent anarchy and to maintain the momentum of the collectivization drive. Despite precise instructions, local authorities interpreted the kulak category broadly. Abuse, vendettas, and opportunities for sordid gain were prevalent. The first document, a letter from the troika, gave specific instructions on how to identify kulaks, confiscate their property, and resettle or deport them to remote areas. The second document, the minutes of a troika meeting, indicates the difficulty and complexity of dekulakization. Both documents show the urgency of dekulakization, the involvement of day laborers, and poor and middle peasants in the process, and, at the same time, words of caution about dekulakization at the expense of collectivization.

ON THE LIQUIDATION OF THE KULAK AS A CLASS TOP SECRET LETTER

12 February 1930

Comrades!

"The introduction of measures to liquidate kulak farms in the regions of complete collectivization—says the TsK decision—must be found in the organic link with the actual mass kolkhoz movement of the poor and middle peasants and is the indissoluble component of the process of complete collectivization."

The Western Oblast Committee warns local organizations against the substitution, which has taken place in a series of regions, of the work for mass collectivization by naked dekulakization. Only in combination with the most extensive organization of day laborers and poor peasants and united masses of poor and middle peasants, can the administrative measures introduced for dekulakization bring a successful resolution of the Party's tasks in connection with socialist reconstruction of the countryside and liquidation of the kulaks.

The Okrug Committee considers it necessary that the process of liquidating kulak farms begun in the regions of complete collectivization would be introduced in the most organized way, that it is especially necessary in the Velikolutsk okrug, as the boundary. So, by these measures we must decisively crush the kulaks' attempts at counterrevolutionary opposition to the kolkhoz movement, tear out the kulaks' means of exploitation, and take from him all possibility of organization against the Party and Soviet power.

For introducing measures to liquidate the kulaks, the Okrug proposes:

1. For the raion committee troika to give immediate instructions, through raion executive committees and village soviets, to register the entire property of the kulaks, with the aim of ending the squandering of these farms. For compiling the list, village soviets must enlist the help of the active of poor peasants and day laborers. Village soviets must immediately warn the kulak farms that the confiscation of the entire property will be applied to those who squander and flee the farms.

2. To introduce in two weeks' time in the entire region the registration and revelation of kulak farms and divide all of them into three groups:

a) First category is the counterrevolutionary active, being arrested at the present time by the OGPU. In connection with this category, the troikas can add to the list, on the basis of the decision of meetings of day laborers and poor and middle peasants, to transfer property and materials to OGPU organs.

b) The second category is the individual elements of the kulak active, especially those of the richest kulaks and semilandowners who will be exiled to the distant areas of the Soviet Union.

The second group and families of the first group will be exiled beyond the boundaries of the okrug in accordance with the order of the okrug troikas. The property of the first group is confiscated and transferred to the kolkhozes. Where there are not any kolkhozes, measures are to be taken to organize kolkhozes from the confiscated property or transferred to the nearest kolkhoz. The property of the second group is confiscated upon their exile, in accordance with the order of the okrug troika; during the creation of kolkhozes, the second group is resettled on those bases as the first group on plots or in temporary locations outside of the boundaries of the kolkhozes;

c) Third category, kulaks remaining within the boundary of the kolkhozes who are subject to exile from the boundaries of the kolkhozes and regions of complete collectivization and to resettlement on plots, beyond the boundaries of the kolkhozes, allotted to them by the Raion Executive Committees, after approval by the okrug troika.

Raion Troikas are obliged in two weeks' time to present to the okrug troika information about the number of kulak farms of the third category. The okrug troika, after receiving the above data from the regions, gives the localities the precise allotment for the settlement by raion of the kulak farms in category III.

3. With the aim of the best understanding of the raions during the compilation of figures for exiling from the boundaries the kulak farms of category II, the okrug troika gives per your raion the following approximate figures....

The okrug troika points out that in the approximate figures by raion, the families of arrested kulak elements in the first category are included in the number of kulak elements of category II.

4. To the kulak farms of the first and second group upon confiscating their property must be left only the most necessary household articles, certain number of elementary means of production, and necessary provisions prior to the new harvest, approximately in the amount of 4 kg. of grain per mouth per month, 8 kg. of potatoes per month, vegetables, etc. To the families with children are to be left the cattle prior to the exile, saws, axes, shovels, hoe, one set of harness. The monetary means of the exiled kulaks are confiscated, allowing them to keep in their hands a minimal sum of up to 500 rubles, needed by the family for the trip to and settling themselves in the new location.

5. In connection with the kulak farms of the third group who are exiled from the boundaries of kolkhozes and regions of complete collectivization to plots allotted by the raion executive committees, the okrug troika proposes: a) For the means of production to leave that necessary to farm on the newly allotted plots; b) for the raion troikas and fractions of the Okrug Executive Committee to develop quickly the question about the capability of using exiled kulaks as labor in special labor brigades in forestry, road, land improvement, and other work; c) in settlements where kulaks are exiled, administration will be carried out by special troikas or plenipotentaries appointed by raion executive committees and approved by troikas of the Okrug executive committees.

6. To all kulak farms located outside kolkhozes, advice is to be given immediately on definite production tasks for farming and delivery to state and cooperative organs and measures to be taken that would obligate kulak farms, which are not exiled, to the full area under crops, under the threat of confiscation of all property and criminal responsibility.

7. The division of plots for settling kulak farms of the third category is carried out by the raion troikas, in the 16 raions: Velikolutsk, Nasvinsk, Rykovsk, Tsevel', Lovetsk,

Kholmsk, Bologovsk, Sovetsk, Leninsk, Oktiabr'sk, Novo-Sokol'nitsk, Nevelsk, Ust'-Dolyssk, Penovsk, Porech'e.

Raion troikas must immediately seek out low grade land, deforested swampy plots, etc. that require improvement, and inform the Okrug troika concerning all such plots the size of the plots, nature of the soil, location, etc.

The allotment to kulak farms of category I being resettled to the above sixteen regions will be supplemented with the registration also of regions for completing parts of 43 divisions.

8. It is absolutely forbidden to extend measures for exile, resettlement, and confiscation to poor and middle peasant farms. It is necessary to prevent this because certain workers, proceeding from the explanation that they are semikulaks of kulak ideology among the poor and middle peasants, who arrest individual poor and middle peasants. On the question of liquidating the kulak as a class, the precise class line must be carried out. We are liquidating, arresting, and confiscating the property of our class enemy. But it is necessary to mobilize the poor and middle peasant masses against the enemy, so our task is the necessity of adding to the poor and middle peasant his separation from the kulak and the understanding of the task to liquidate the kulaks.

It is forbidden to extend the above measures to families of both Red Army soldiers and officers, even though they would be kulaks. In all cases in identifying kulak farms which contain Red Army soldiers and officers, it is necessary immediately to inform the Okrug troika.

9. It is necessary for all party organizations together with trade union organizations to adopt measures for purging industrial enterprises of kulak elements. While not permitting any such general purges, take further measures to disallow such elements into production. The kulak is now fleeing the countryside to the town, he is trying to bury himself into production, in other work, so that is why it is now necessary for all party and trade union organizations to adopt all measures to disallow kulak elements into enterprises and plants, especially into trade unions of construction workers, woodworkers, etc.

In relation to kulak families the members of whom have worked for a continuous period of time in factories and plants, must be given the most cautious approach and must be decided each time by the Okrug troika, in agreement with the corresponding plant organizations.

10. In relation to the procedure for confiscating and using confiscated property, to be guided by the following:

a) Confiscation of kulaks' property is carried out by special authorities of Raion Executive Committees with the compulsory participation of the village soviet, representatives of kolkhozes, groups of day laborers and poor peasants, and day laborers; b) during confiscation a precise list and evaluation is made of the property being confiscated, placing the responsibility on the village soviet the complete revelation of the confiscated property; c) the kulaks' means of production and property being confiscated are transferred by the Raion Executive Committees to the kolkhozes in lieu of entry fees for day laborers and poor peasants, including the confiscated in the indivisible fund of the kolkhozes with the full liquidation from the property being confiscated that are added to the debts of the liquidated kulak farms by the state and cooperative organs; d) kolkhozes, which receive land and confiscated property, must guarantee the full sowing of the transferred land and delivery of all produce to the state; e) the confiscated dwellings of the kulaks are used for the social needs of village soviets and kolkhozes, or for the communal life of those who join the kolkhoz and day laborers who do not have their own dwellings; f) kulaks' savings bank books and state bonds of all three categories are seized and entered on a list with payment of receipts and their sending for deposit to the corresponding organs of the People's Commissariat for Finance. All such payment to the exiled kulak farms from the fees to the savings banks, also the payment of loans on security bonds in the regions of complete collectivization are absolutely forbidden; g) shares and investments of kulaks of all three categories in cooperative associations are transferred to the collectivization fund of poor peasants and day laborers, and landowners are excluded from all forms of cooperatives.

11. According to information at the Oblast Committee, it is totally disallowed to confiscate and exile kulaks in individual raions, for example Idrutsk, Velikolutsk, Kun'insk, without any kind of plan and preparation. It is necessary for the Raion Committees from the beginning to carry through all the necessary measures for preparation, in the time frame indicated by the present letter, after the approval of the necessary measures by the Okrug troika and proceed with the exiling and settlement. During the exiling and confiscation of the kulaks' property, their dwellings must be immediately transferred to the kolkhozes, and kulak families are resettled in other areas outside of the kolkhozes. However, work among the masses of day laborers and poor and middle peasants must now immediately be expanded, and what must be carried out are the listing of property, seeking of plots, accounting and revelation of kulak farms, and other measures indicated in the present letter.

12. Party organizations must immediately, widely expand work among the masses of day laborers and poor and middle peasants to discuss exiling, settlement, and confiscation of property. Such work, on the one hand, will advance the deepest class demarcation from the kulak in the countrysi e and mobilize the masses of day laborers and poor and middle peasants in the struggle with the kulak, under the leadership of the Party, and, on the other hand, this work gives concrete material to the raion troikas to register and divide the kulaks into groups, in addition to the first and second categories.

The okrug troika once again stresses with special urgency that the liquidation of the kulaks must proceed during the most extensive mobilization of the masses of day laborers, and poor and middle peasants. It is necessary to get each day laborer, each poor peasant, and each middle peasant to understand the measures being advanced by the party and Soviet power.

There are not to be any vacillations, any indulgences to right deviation moods or the spirit of compromise.

The expansion of kolkhoz construction and the liquidation of the kulaks, these are the tasks which must be decided by the party in the very shortest period of time.

On all questions about which you are not entirely clear, immediately inquire at the Okrug with Comrades Loktev, D. Ivanov, or Dabolin.

Smolensk Archives, U.S. National Archives II, WKP53, 6-8.

TOP SECRET MINUTES OF SESSION OF OKRUG TROIKA

19 February 1930

Attending: Members of the troika: Comrades Loktev, Ivanov, Dabolin.
Representing the Western Oblast: Comrades Shelekhov, Kirovsky, Pedankin, M. Ivanov.
Invited: Comrade Filippov.
1. On the progress of liquidation of the kulak as a class in the Okrug.

Comrade Dabolin.

Noting the expanding work on the liquidation of the kulak as a class in the okrug, the troika verifies that there are violations and distortions of the Okrug troika's directives in a series of raions. In the Indritsk raion there took place the arrest of the village intelligentsia;

in the Dokniansk region an inventory was conducted of kulak farms which have two sons of Red Army commanders; in the Toropetsk raion there took place the accusation by poor peasants that the kulaks incorrectly arrested were fine kulaks, and the resolution of day laborers and poor peasants against the seed fund; in the Usmynsk raion there took place the disgraceful fact that 1 poor peasant and 2 middle peasants were arrested by the plenipotentaries of the Raion troika meeting for dekulakization, and the same Raion troika plenipotentaries arrested 2 kulaks and 3 middle peasants; there are cases noted of spreading provocative rumors of uprisings in the Kuninsk raion.

The Okrug troika orders the raion troikas:

1. To take measures to prevent and immediately correct admitted distortions, bringing the guilty to account.

2. To order the Okrug procuracy to investigate the inventory list of the kulak farm in the Dokniansk raion which has 2 sons of Red Army commanders.

3. All Raion committees are to take measures to strengthen military training and organization in the military relationship of communists.

4. The issue on the passage through the okrug of a special kulak train to be examined tomorrow, 19 February, at 9:00 am.

2. On the appearance of banditry in the Velizh raion.

To order the Okrug OGPU to take all measures to expose and liquidate the band.

To instruct Comrade Filippov to write a letter to all Raion committees on the possibility of increased banditry in the okrug and on the measures to combat banditry.

3. On National Minority Kolkhozes.

Order Comrades Filippov and Belousov to work the issue.

4. Results of the work of the commission on relieving the repair of labor residences in the okrug.

To hear the report at the troika session on 20 February.

5. On workers for the OGPU.

To instruct the Allocations Department in three days' time to come to agreement with the collective of the VKP(b) of the Plant to select three workers for work in the Okrug OGPU.

Smolensk Archives, U.S. National Archives II, WKP53, 9.

STALIN, "DIZZY WITH SUCCESS"
2 March 1930

By late February, escalating series of peasant violence and state repression associated with the collectivization drive and dekulakization compelled the Politburo to stop the drive and modify its policy, particularly on the issue of private property, animals, and agricultural tools. The Politburo commissioned Stalin to draft the modified policy that would permit peasants to retain private garden plots, small-scale tools, and a few animals. Without consulting the Politburo, Stalin announced that collectivization was successful, but there were excesses committed by overzealous party and government officials, who, overconfident or dizzy from previous successes in overcoming obstacles, violated the voluntary principle of forming collective farms and organized collectives by decree. By circumventing the Politburo and blaming overzealous officials, he appeased the peasants and freed himself from blame. He emphasized the restoration of the voluntary principle of and slower rate in collectivization, and condemned the socialization of animals and tools. Following the publication of Stalin's speech, violence and repression ended in the countryside, and peasants left collective farms en masse. Stalin became a hero to peasants and most likely saved his political power.

JOSEPH STALIN

DIZZY WITH SUCCESS

Concerning Questions of the Collective Farm Movement

The Soviet government's successes in the sphere of the collective-farm movement are now being spoken of by everyone. Even our enemies are forced to admit that the successes are substantial. And they really are very great.

It is a fact that by 20 February of this year 50 percent of the peasant farms throughout the USSR had been collectivized. That means that by 20 February 1930, we had *overfulfilled* the five year plan of collectivization by more than 100 percent.

It is a fact that on 28 February of this year the collective farms had *already succeeded* in stocking upwards of 36,000,000 centners, i.e., about 220,000,000 puds, of seed for the spring sowing, which is more than 90 percent of the plan. It must be admitted that the accumulation of 220,000,000 puds of seed by the collective farms alone—after the successful fulfillment of the grain-procurement plan—is a tremendous achievement.

What does all this show?

That a *radical turn of the countryside towards socialism may be considered as already achieved.*

There is no need to prove that these successes are of supreme importance for the fate of our country, for the whole working class, which is the directing force of our country, and, lastly, for the Party itself. To say nothing of the direct practical results, these successes are of immense value for the internal life of the Party itself, for the education of our Party. They imbue our Party with a spirit of cheerfulness and confidence in its strength. They arm the working class with confidence in the victory of our cause. They bring forward additional millions of reserves for our Party.

Hence the Party's task is: To *consolidate* the successes achieved and to *utilize* them systematically for our further advancement.

But successes have their seamy side, especially when they are attained with comparative "ease"—"unexpectedly", so to speak. Such successes sometimes induce a spirit of vanity and conceit: "We can achieve anything!", "There's nothing we can't do!" People not infrequently become intoxicated by such success; they become dizzy with success, lose all sense of proportion and the capacity to understand realities; they show a tendency to overrate their own strength and to underrate the strength of the enemy; adventurist attempts are made to solve all questions of socialist construction "in a trice": "We can achieve anything!", "There's nothing we can't do!"

Hence the Party's task is: To wage a determined struggle against those sentiments, which are dangerous and harmful to our cause, and to drive them out of the Party.

It cannot be said that these dangerous and harmful sentiments are at all widespread in the ranks of our Party, But they do exist in our Party, and there are no grounds for asserting that they will not become stronger. And if they should be allowed free scope, then there can be no doubt that the collective-farm movement will be considerably weakened and the danger of its breaking down may become a reality.

Hence the task of our press is: Systematically to denounce these and similar antiLeninist sentiments.

A few facts.

1. The successes of our collective-farm policy are due, among other things, to the fact that it rests on the *voluntary character* of the collective-farm movement and on *taking into account the diversity of conditions* in the various regions of the USSR. Collective farms must not be established by force. That would be foolish and reactionary. The collective-farm movement must rest on the active support of the main mass of the peasantry. Examples of the formation of collective farms in the developed areas must not be mechanically transplanted to underdeveloped areas. That would be foolish and reactionary. Such a "policy" would discredit the collectivization idea at one stroke. In determining the speed and methods of collective-farm development, careful consideration must be given to the diversity of conditions in the various regions of the USSR.

Our grain-growing areas are ahead of all others in the collective-farm movement. Why is this?

Firstly, because in these areas we have the largest number of already firmly-established state and collective farms, thanks to which the peasants have had the opportunity to convince themselves of the power and importance of the new technical equipment, of the power and importance of the new, collective organization of farming.

Secondly, because these areas have had two-years' schooling in the fight against the kulaks during the grain-procurement campaigns, and this could not but facilitate the development of the collective-farm movement.

Lastly, because these areas in recent years have been extensively supplied with the best cadres from the industrial centers.

Can it be said that these especially favorable conditions also exist in other areas, the consuming areas, for example, such as our northern regions, or in areas where there are still backward nationalities, such as Turkestan, say?

No, it cannot be said.

Clearly, the principle of taking into account the diversity of conditions in the various regions of the USSR is, together with the voluntary principle, one of the most important prerequisites for a sound collective-farm movement.

But what actually happens sometimes? Can it be said that the voluntary principle and the principle of taking local peculiarities into account are not violated in a number of areas? No, that cannot be said, unfortunately. We know, for example, that in a number of the northern areas of the consuming zone, where conditions for the immediate organization of collective farms are comparatively less favorable than in the grain-growing areas, attempts are not infrequently made to *replace* preparatory work for the organization of collective farms by bureaucratic decreeing of the collective-farm movement, paper resolutions on the growth of collective farms, organization of collective farms on paper—collective farms which have as yet no reality, but whose "existence" is proclaimed in a heap of boastful resolutions.

Or take certain areas of Turkestan, where conditions for the immediate organization of collective farms are even less favorable than in the northern regions of the consuming zone. We know that in a number of areas of Turkestan there have already been attempts to "overtake and outstrip" the advanced areas of the USSR by threatening to use armed force, by threatening that peasants who are not yet ready to join the collective farms will be deprived of water for irrigation and manufactured goods.

What can there be in common between this Sergeant Pribishbeev "policy" and the Party's policy of relying on the voluntary principle and of taking local peculiarities into account in collective-farm development? Clearly, there is not and cannot be anything in common between them.

Who benefits from these distortions, this bureaucratic decreeing of the collective—farm movement, these unworthy threats against the peasants? Nobody, except our enemies!

What may these distortions lead to? To strengthening our enemies and to discrediting the idea of the collective-farm movement.

Is it not clear that the authors of these distortions, who imagine themselves to be "Lefts", are in reality bringing grist to the mill of Right opportunism?

2. One of the greatest merits of our Party's political strategy is that it is able at any given moment to pick out the *main link* in the movement, by grasping which the Party draws the whole chain towards one common goal in order to achieve the solution of the problem. Can it be said that the Party has already picked out the main link of the collective-farm movement in the system of collective-farm development? Yes, this can and should be said.

What is this chief link?

Is it, perhaps, *association for joint cultivation* of the land? No, it is not that. Associations for joint cultivation of the land, in which the means of production are not yet socialized, are already a past stage of the collective-farm movement.

Is it, perhaps, the *agricultural commune*? No, it is not that. Communes are still of isolated occurrence in the collective-farm movement. The conditions are not yet ripe for agricultural communes—in which not only production, but also distribution is socialized—to be the *predominant* form.

The main link of the collective-farm movement, its *predominant* form at the present moment, the link which has to be grasped now, is the *agricultural artel*.

In the *agricultural artel*, the basic means of production, primarily for grain-farming—labor, use of the land, machines and other implements, draught animals and farm buildings—are socialized. In the artel, the household plots (small vegetable gardens, small orchards), the dwelling houses, a part of the dairy cattle, small livestock, poultry, etc., are *not socialized*.

The artel is the *main link of the collective-farm movement* because it is the form best adapted for solving the grain problem. And the grain problem is the *main link in the whole system of agriculture* because, if it is not solved, it will be impossible to solve either the problem of stock-breeding (small and large), or the problem of the industrial and special crops that provide the principal raw materials for industry. That is why the agricultural artel is the main link in the system of the collective-farm movement at the present moment.

That is the point of departure of the "Model Rules" for collective farms, the final text of which is published today.

And that should be the point of departure of our Party and Soviet workers, one of whose duties it is to make a thorough study of these Rules and to carry them out down to the last detail.

Such is the line of the Party at the present moment.

Can it be said that this line of the Party is being carried out without violation or distortion? No, it cannot, unfortunately. We know that in a number of areas of the USSR, where the struggle for the existence of the collective farms is still far from over, and where artels are not yet consolidated, attempts are being made to skip the artel framework and to leap straight away into the agricultural commune. The artel is still not consolidated, but they are already "socializing" dwelling houses, small livestock and poultry; moreover, this "socialization" is degenerating into bureaucratic decreeing on paper, because the conditions which would make such socialization necessary do not yet exist. One might think that the grain problem has already been solved in the collective farms, that it is already a past stage, that the principal task at the present moment is not solution of the grain problem, but solution of the problem of livestock and poultry-breeding. Who, we may ask, benefits from this blockheaded "work" of lumping together different forms of the collective-farm movement? Who benefits from this running too far ahead, which is stupid and harmful to our cause? Irritating the collective-farm peasant by "socializing" dwelling houses, all dairy cattle, all small livestock and poultry, when the grain problem is still unsolved, when the artel form of collective farming is *not yet consolidated*—is it not obvious that such a "policy" can be to the satisfaction and advantage only of our sworn enemies.?

One such overzealous "socializer" even goes so far as to issue an order to an artel containing the following instructions: "Within three days, register all the poultry of every household," establish posts of special "commanders" for registration and supervision; "occupy the key positions in the artel;" "command the socialist battle without quitting your posts" and—of course—get a tight grip on the whole life of the artel.

What is this—a policy of directing the collective farms, or a policy of *disrupting* and *discrediting* them?

I say nothing of those "revolutionaries"—save the mark!—who *begin* the work of organizing artels by removing the bells from churches. Just imagine, removing the church bells—how r-r-revolutionary!

How could there have arisen in our midst such blockheaded exercises in "socialization", such ludicrous attempts to overleap oneself, attempts which aim at bypassing classes and the class struggle, and which in fact bring grist to the mill of our class enemies?

They could have arisen only in the atmosphere of our "easy" and "unexpected" successes on the front of collective-farm development.

They could have arisen only as a result of the blockheaded belief of a section of our Party: "We can achieve anything!", "There's nothing we can't do!"

They could have arisen only because some of our comrades have become dizzy with success and for the moment have lost clearness of mind and sobriety of vision.

To correct the line of our work in the sphere of collective-farm development, *we must put an end to these sentiments.*

That is now one of the immediate tasks of the Party.

The art of leadership is a serious matter. One must not lag behind the movement, because to do so is to lose contact with the masses. But neither must one run too far ahead, because to run too far ahead is to lose the masses and to isolate oneself. He who wants to lead a movement and at the same time keep in touch with the vast masses must wage a fight on two fronts—against those who lag behind and against those who run too far ahead.

Our Party is strong and invincible because, when leading a movement, it is able to preserve and multiply its contacts with the vast masses of the workers and peasants.

Stalin, *Works*, XII, 197-205.

PARTY RESOLUTION. PARTY CENTRAL COMMITTEE FORMALIZES MODIFIED COLLECTIVIZATION POLICY

10 March 1930

The Party Central Committee sent a resolution to local organizations on 10 March 1930 instructing officials how to proceed in collectivization. It decided to make the resolution public, appearing in the press four days later. The resolution condemned compulsory or forcible collectivization and excessive socialization of tools and animals. It prohibited the closing of markets, bazaars, and churches. It warned officials of removal for violation of distortions of the Party line.

RESOLUTION OF THE TSK VKP(B)

14 March 1930

On the Struggle Against Distortions of the
Party Line in the Kolkhoz Movement
(To all the TsKs of National Republics, to all Krai,
Oblast, Okrug and Raion Party Committees)

The information received by the party Central Committee on the course of the kolkhoz movement indicates that along with the real and serious successes of collectivization, there are also instances of distortion of the party line in various regions of the USSR.

First of all, the *voluntary* principle in kolkhoz construction is being violated. In many regions the voluntary principle is replaced by *forced* entry into kolkhozes under the threat of being dispossessed as a kulak, of being deprived of electoral rights, etc. As a result, a part of the middle peasants and even of the poor peasants have sometimes been "dispossessed as kulaks", the figure in some regions being as high as 15 percent, and as many as 15-20 percent being deprived of their electoral rights. There have been instances of exceptionally rough, outrageous, and criminal behavior toward the population on the part of certain lower-level persons who were sometimes the victims of provocation by counterrevolutionary elements who had wormed their way in (pillaging, dividing up property, arrests of middle peasants and even of poor peasants, etc.). In a number of raions, furthermore, preparatory work on collectivization and the patient explanation of the bases of the party's policy to the poor and middle peasants is *replaced* by the bureaucratic decreeing of inflated figures from above and artificial exaggeration of the percentage of collectivization (in some raions the percentage of collectivization "passed" in a few days from 10 to 90 percent).

This is a violation of Lenin's well known instruction that the kolkhozes can be firmly established and vital only if they arise voluntarily. This is a violation of the resolution of the Sixteenth Conference of our party prohibiting the use of forcible measures in forming the kolkhozes. It is a violation of the Charter of the agricultural artel approved by the SNK and TsIK of the USSR which states perfectly straightforwardly that the farm laborers, poor peasants, and middle peasants of such-and-such village "unite *voluntarily* in an agricultural artel".

In addition to these distortions, in some places there have been instances of the *compulsory* socialization of living quarters, sheep, goats, fowl, and milk cows (not used for the sale of dairy products), all of which are forbidden and harmful for the cause. Moreover, there have been attempts to leap in a stupid and bungling way from the artel form of kolkhoz, which is the fundamental link in the kolkhoz movement, to the commune. They forget that in our country the basic agricultural problem is not a "chicken" problem or a "cucumber" problem but the *grain* problem. They forget that at the present moment the basic link in the kolkhoz movement is not the commune but the *agricultural artel*. They forget that this is precisely why the party found it necessary to issue a model Charter not for the agricultural *commune*, but for the agricultural *artel*. These stupid and bungling distortions have in many raions discredited the kolkhoz movement and caused the peasants to desert these communes and artels, which were hastily thrown together and therefore unstable.

Thus the party's determination that at the present moment the fundamental link in the kolkhoz movement is not the commune but the artel is being violated. There is also violation of the well known resolution of the TsIk of 5 January 1930 (See "Pravda") to the effect that the artel form of the kolkhoz movement is its principal form and that, consequently, there can be no frivolous leaping from the artel form to the commune.

Finally, the TsK finds it necessary to point to the completely impermissible distortions of the party line with respect to the struggle against religious prejudices and also in the matter of commercial exchange between the city and the countryside. We mean the *administrative* closing of churches without the consent of the overwhelming majority of the village, which usually leads to an intensification of religious prejudices, and the *abolition* of markets and bazaars in many places, causing a deterioration in the supplying of the cities. There can be no doubt that such practices, carried on under the flag of "leftist" phrases, actually bring water to the mill of the counterrevolutionaries and have nothing to do with our party's policy.

In the view of the TsK, all of these distortions result from the *direct violation* of the party's policy, the *direct violation* of the decrees of the leading organs of our party, which can only prepare the basis for a strengthening of rightist elements in the party.

The TsK considers all these distortions are now the *basic hindrance* to the further growth of the kolkhoz movement and are of *direct assistance* to our class enemies.

The TsK considers the continued *rapid growth* of the kolkhoz movement, and the *liquidation of the kulaks* as a class, are *impossible* without the immediate liquidation of these distortions.

The TsK orders party organizations:

1. To end the practice, observed in many places, of forcible methods of collectivization, at the same time continuing the stubborn struggle to *draw* the peasants into the kolkhozes voluntarily and to *consolidate* the existing kolkhozes.

2. To concentrate the attention of their workers on the economic improvement of the kolkhozes and the organization of field work, ensuring through appropriate economic and party political measures the *consolidation* of the successes already registered in collectivization and the organizational economic ordering of the agricultural artel.

3. To prohibit the transfer of agricultural artels to the status of agricultural communes without the approval of the okrug kolkhoz unions or the okrug executive committees and to end the *forcible* socialization of habitations, sheep, goats, fowl, and noncommercial milk cows.

4. To check the lists of those who have been suppressed as kulaks and deprived of electoral rights and immediately *to right any errors committed* with respect to middle peasants, former red partisans, members of families of village teachers, Red Army men and Red Sailors (both rank and file and those in positions of command).

5. While being guided strictly by the rule that kulaks and other persons deprived of electoral rights are not to be admitted into the kolkhozes, to *permit waivers* to this rule with respect to members of families containing red partisans, Red Army men, and Red Sailors (both rank and file and those in positions of command), and village teachers, if they are loyal to Soviet power and willing to stand guarantee for members of their families.

6. To *forbid* the closing of markets, *restore* bazaars, and *allow* peasants, including kolkhoz members, to sell their products on the market without hindrance.

7. To *put a decisive end* to the practice of closing churches by administrative order covered by the fiction that this expresses the public voluntary desire of the population. To *permit* the closing of churches only when this really expresses the will of the overwhelming majority of the peasants and when the decree of the peasant gathering has been approved by the oblast executive committee. Those guilty of mockery or pranks against the religious feelings of the peasants are to be held accountable in the strictest fashion.

8. To *remove* persons who are unable or unwilling to fight resolutely against distortions of the party line, *replacing* them by others.

McNeal/Gregor, Vol. 3, 47-50.
KPSS v rezoliutsiiakh, Vol. 4, 394-397.

STALIN RALLIES TROOPS FOR COLLECTIVIZATION AND AGAINST KULAKS

3 April 1930

In response to letters from collective farmers, Stalin attempted to restore confidence in the party leadership for collectivization and the war against the kulaks. Using military terminology, he described the retreat in the collectivization drive as a phase in a military campaign eventually to eliminate kulaks as a class. He criticized the previous excesses in the collectivization drive, depicted the decline in collective farms as a minor matter, and rationalized that it was advantageous that hostile elements were leaving the collective farms.

REPLY TO COLLECTIVE-FARM COMRADES

It is evident from the press that Stalin's article, "Dizzy With Success," and the decision adopted by the Central Committee on "The Fight Against Distortions of the Party Line in the Collective Farm Movement" have evoked numerous comments among practical workers in the collective-farm movement. In this connection, I have received lately a number of letters from collective-farm comrades asking for replies to questions raised in them. It was my duty to reply to these letters in private correspondence. But this proved impossible, because more than half the letters contained no indication of the addresses of their writers (they had forgotten to give them). Yet the questions touched upon in the letters are of immense political interest for all our comrades. Moreover, I could not, of course, leave unanswered those comrades who forgot to give their addresses. I am therefore obliged to reply to the letters of the collective-farm comrades publicly, that is, through the press, extracting from them all the questions requiring to be dealt with. I do this all the more readily as I have a direct decision of the Central Committee on this subject.

First question. What is the *root* of the errors in the peasant question?

Reply. A wrong approach to the middle peasant. Resort to coercion in economic relations with the middle peasant. Forgetfulness of the fact that the economic bond with the masses of the middle peasants must be built not on the basis of coercive measures, but on the basis of agreement with the middle peasant, of alliance with him. Forgetfulness of the fact that the basis of the collective-farm movement at the present moment is an alliance of the working class and poor peasantry with the middle peasant against capitalism in general, against the kulaks in particular.

As long as the offensive against the kulak was waged in a united front with the middle peasant, all went well. But when some of our comrades became intoxicated with success and began imperceptibly to slip from the path of an offensive against the kulaks on to the path of a struggle against the middle peasant, when, in pursuit of high collectivization percentages, they began to apply coercion to the middle peasant, depriving him of the suffrage, "dekulakizing" and expropriating him, the offensive began to assume a distorted form and the united front with the middle peasant be undermined, and, naturally, the kulak obtained an opportunity of trying to rise to his feet again.

It has been forgotten that coercion, which is necessary and useful in the fight against our class enemies, is impermissible and disastrous when applied to the middle peasant, who is our ally.

It has been forgotten that cavalry charges, which are necessary and useful for accomplishing tasks of a military character, are unsuitable and disastrous for accomplishing the tasks of collective farm development, which, moreover, is being organized in alliance with the middle peasant.

That is the root of the errors in the peasant question.

Here is what Lenin says about economic relations with the middle peasant:

"Most of all, we must take as our basis the truth that here, by the very nature of the case, nothing can be achieved by methods of coercion. Here the economic task is an entirely different one. Here there is not that top section which can be cut away, while leaving the whole foundation and the whole building intact. That top section, which in the town was represented by the capitalists, does not exist here. *To apply coercion here would ruin the whole matter.... Nothing could be more stupid than the very idea of coercion in the sphere of the economic relations of the middle peasant*" (Volume XXIV, p. 168).

Further:

"*The use of coercion against the middle peasantry would do very great harm.* This stratum is a numerous one, many millions strong. Even in Europe—where it nowhere attains to such strength, where technology and culture, urban life, railways, are immensely developed, has ever proposed the use of coercive measures against the middle peasantry" (Volume XXIV, p. 167).

That is clear, I think.

Second question. What are the chief errors in the collective farm movement?

Reply. There are, at least, three such errors.

1) In building collective farms, Lenin's voluntary principle has been violated. The basic directives of the Party and the Model Rules of the Agricultural Artel about the voluntary character of collective farm development have been violated.

Leninism teaches that the peasants must be brought to adopt collective farming voluntarily, by convincing them of the advantages of socially-conducted, collective farming over individual farming. Leninism teaches that the peasants can be convinced of the advantages of collective farming only if it is *demonstrated* and *proved* to them in actual fact and by experience that collective farming is better than individual farming, that it is more profitable than individual farming and that it offers both poor and middle peasant a way out of poverty and want. Leninism teaches that, without these conditions, collective farms cannot be stable. Leninism teaches that any attempt to impose collective farming by force, any attempt to establish collective farms by compulsion can only have adverse results, can only repel the peasants from the collective-farm movement.

And, indeed, as long as this basic rule was observed, the collective farm movement registered success after success. But some of our comrades, intoxicated with success, began to neglect this rule, began to display excessive haste and, in their pursuit of high collectivization percentages, began to establish collective farms by means of compulsion. It is not surprising that the adverse results of such a "policy" soon showed themselves. The collective farms which had sprung up so rapidly began to melt away just as rapidly, and a section of the peasantry, who only yesterday had had the greatest confidence in the collective farms, began to turn away from them.

That is the first and chief error in the collective farm movement.

Here is what Lenin says concerning the voluntary principle of building collective farms:

"Our task now is to pass to *socially-conducted* cultivation of the land, to *large-scale* farming in common. But there can be no compulsion by the Soviet government; there is no law that makes it compulsory. The agricultural *commune* is founded *voluntarily*, the passing to *socially-conducted cultivation* of the land can only be *voluntary*; there cannot be the slightest compulsion by the workers' and peasants' government in this respect, nor does the law allow it. If any of you has observed such compulsion, you must know that it is an abuse, a violation of the law, which we are doing our utmost to correct, and shall correct" (Volume XXIV, p. 43). (My italics.—*J. Stalin*)

Further:

"Only if we succeed in practice in *showing* the peasants the advantages of common, collective, cooperative, artel cultivation of the soil, only if we succeed in helping the peasant by means of cooperative, artel farming, will the working class, which holds state power in its hands, actually prove to the peasant the correctness of its policy and actually secure the real and durable following of the vast masses of the peasantry. Hence the importance of every kind of measure to promote cooperative, artel agriculture can hardly be overestimated. We have millions of individual farms in our country, scattered and dispersed in the depths of the countryside.... Only when it is *proved in practice, by experience* easily understood by the peasants, that the transition to the cooperative, artel form of agriculture is essential and possible, only then shall we be entitled to say that in this vast peasant country, Russia, an important step towards socialist agriculture has been taken" (Volume XXIV, pp. 579-80).

Lastly, one more passage from the works of Lenin:

"While encouraging cooperative associations of all kinds, and equally agricultural communes of middle peasants, the representatives of the Soviet government must not allow their formation to involve *the slightest compulsion*. Only such associations are valuable as are constituted by the peasants themselves on their free initiative, and the advantages of which have been verified by them in practice. *Excessive haste in this matter is harmful*, because it is only capable of strengthening the middle peasants' prejudice against innovations. Representatives of the Soviet government who take the liberty of resorting even to indirect, to say nothing of direct, compulsion with a view to uniting the peasants in communes must be called to the strictest account and removed from work in the countryside." (Volume XXIV, p. 174).

That is clear, I think.

It scarcely needs proof that the Party will carry out these injunctions of Lenin's with the utmost stringency.

2) In building collective farms, Lenin's principle of taking into account the diversity of conditions in the various regions of the USSR has been violated. It has been forgotten that among them there are advanced regions, average regions and backward regions. It has been forgotten that rates of progress of the collective farm movement and the methods of collective-farm development *cannot be uniform* in these far from uniform regions.

"It would be a mistake," Lenin says, "if we were simply to write stereotyped decrees for all parts of Russia, if the Bolshevik Communists, Soviet officials in the Ukraine and the Don region, began extending them wholesale and without discrimination in other regions"... for "under no circumstances do we bind ourselves to a single stereotyped pattern, or decide once and for all that our experience, the experience of Central Russia, can be transplanted in its entirety to all the border regions" (Volume XXIV, pp. 125-26).

Lenin further says:

"To stereotype Central Russia, the Ukraine and Siberia, to make them conform to a particular stereotyped pattern, would be the greatest folly" (Volume XXVI, p. 243).

Lastly, Lenin makes it obligatory for the Caucasian Communists

"to understand *the specific character of their position, of the position of their republics, as distinct from the position and conditions of the RSFSR; to understand the necessity of not copying our tactics, but of thoughtfully modifying them in accordance with the difference in the concrete conditions*" (Volume XXVI, p. 191).

That is clear, I think.

On the basis of these injunctions of Lenin, the Central Committee of our Party, in its decision on "The Rate of Collectivization" (See *Pravda*, 6 January 1930), divided the regions of the USSR, as regards the rate of collectivization, into three groups, of which the North Caucasus, Middle Volga and Lower Volga may in the main complete collectivization by the spring of 1931, other grain-growing regions (Ukraine, Central Black Earth region, Siberia, Urals, Kazakhstan, etc.,) by the spring of 1932, while the remaining regions may extend collectivization to the end of the five year plan period, that is, until 1933.

But what actually happened? It turned out that some of our comrades, intoxicated by the first successes of the collective farm movement, cheerfully forgot both Lenin's injunctions and the Central Committee's decisions. The Moscow Region, in its feverish pursuit of inflated collectivization figures, began to orientate its officials towards completing collectivization in the spring of 1930, although it had no less than three years at its disposal (to the end of 1932). The Central Black Earth region, not desiring to "lag behind the others," began to orientate its officials towards completing collectivization by the first half of 1930, although it had no less than two years at its disposal (to the end of 1931). And the Transcaucasians and Turkestanians, in their eagerness to "overtake and outstrip" the advanced regions, began to orientate themselves on completing collectivization "at the earliest", although they had fully four years at their disposal (to the end of 1933).

Naturally, with such a quick-fire "tempo" of collectivization, the areas less prepared for the collective farm movement, in their eagerness to "outstrip" the better prepared areas, found themselves obliged to resort to strong administrative pressure, endeavoring to compensate the missing factors needed for a rapid rate of progress of the collective farm movement by their own administrative ardor. The consequences are known. Everyone knows of the muddle which resulted in these areas, and which had to be straightened out by the interference of the Central Committee.

That is the second error in the collective farm movement.

3) In building collective farms, Lenin's principle that it is impermissible to skip over an uncompleted form of movement was violated. Also violated was Lenin's principle of not running ahead of the development of the masses, of not decreeing the movement of the masses, of not becoming divorced from the masses, but of moving together with the masses and impelling them forward, bringing them to our slogans and helping them to convince themselves of the correctness of our slogans through their own experience.

"When the Petrograd proletariat and the soldiers of the Petrograd garrison took power," says Lenin, "they fully realized that our constructive work in the countryside would encounter great difficulties; that there it was necessary to proceed more gradually; that to *attempt to introduce collective cultivation of the land by decrees*, by legislation, would be the *height of folly*; that an insignificant number of enlightened peasants might agree to this, but that the vast majority of the peasants had no such object in view. We, therefore, confined ourselves to what was absolutely essential in the interests of the development of the revolution; in no case *to run ahead of the development of the masses*, but to wait until, as a result of their own experience and their own struggle, a progressive movement grew up" (Volume XXII, p. 252). (My italics—*J. Stalin*)

Proceeding from these injunctions of Lenin, the Central Committee, in its decision on "The Rate of Collectivization" (see *Pravda*, 6 January 1930), laid down that:

a) the chief form of the collective-farm movement at the present moment is the agricultural artel,

b) in view of this, it is necessary to draw up model rules for the agricultural artel, as the chief form of the collective farm movement,

c) "decreeing" the collective-farm movement from above and "playing at collectivization" must not be allowed in our practical work.

That means that at the present time we must steer our course not towards the commune, but towards the agricultural artel, as the chief form of collective farm development; that we must not allow skipping over the agricultural artel to the commune; that "decreeing" of collective farms and "playing at collective farms" must not be substituted for the mass movement of the peasants in favor of collective farms.

That is clear, I think.

But what actually happened? It turned out that some of our comrades, intoxicated by the first successes of the collective farm movement, cheerfully forgot both Lenin's injunctions and the CC's decision. Instead of organizing a mass movement in favor of the agricultural artel, these comrades began to "transfer" the individual peasants straight to the rules of the commune. Instead of consolidating the artel form of the movement, they began compulsorily "socializing" small livestock, poultry, noncommercial dairy cattle and dwelling houses.

The results of this haste, which is impermissible for a Leninist, are now known to all. As a rule, of course, they failed to create stable communes. But, on the other hand, they lost control of a number of agricultural artels. True, "good" resolutions remained. But what is the use of them?

That is the third error in the collective farm movement.

Third question. How could these errors have arisen, and how must the Party correct them?

Reply. They arose because of our rapid successes in the collective farm movement. Success sometimes turns people's heads. It not infrequently gives rise to extreme vanity and conceit.

That may very easily happen to representatives of a party which is in power, especially in the case of a party like ours, whose strength and prestige are almost immeasurable. Here, instances of communist vainglory, which Lenin combated so vehemently, are quite possible. Here, belief in the omnipotence of decrees, resolutions and orders is quite possible. Here, there is a real danger of the Party's revolutionary measures being converted into empty bureaucratic decreeing by individual representatives of the Party in one corner or another of our boundless country. I have in mind not only local officials, but also individual regional officials, and even individual members of the Central Committee.

"Communist vainglory," says Lenin, "means that a man, who is a member of the Communist Party, and has not yet been purged from it, imagines that he can solve all his problems by issuing communist decrees" (Volume XXVII, pp. 50-51).

That is the soil from which sprang the errors in the collective farm movement, the distortions of the Party line in collective-farm development.

Wherein lies the danger of these errors and distortions, if they are persisted in, if they are not eliminated rapidly and completely?

The danger here lies in the fact that these errors lead us straight to the discrediting of the collective farm movement, to dissension in our relations with the middle peasants, to the disorganization of the poor peasants, to confusion in our ranks, to the weakening of all our work of socialist construction, to the revival of the kulaks.

In short, these errors have a tendency to push us from the path of strengthening the alliance with the main mass of the peasantry, of strengthening the proletarian dictatorship, on to the path of a rupture with these masses, on to the path of undermining the proletarian dictatorship.

This danger was already in evidence in the latter half of February, at the time when a section of our comrades, dazzled by the earlier successes, went off at a gallop from the Leninist path. The Central Committee of the Party was alive to this danger and intervened without delay, instructing Stalin to issue a warning to the overpresumptuous comrades in a special article on the collective-farm movement. "Dizzy With Success," was the result of Stalin's personal initiative. That, of course, is nonsense. It is not in order that personal initiative in a matter like this may be taken by anyone, whoever he might be, that we have a Central Committee. It was a reconnaisance-in-depth by the CC. And when the depth and extent of the errors were ascertained, the CC lost no time in striking at these errors with all the strength of its authority, by publishing its well known resolution of 15 March 1930:

It is with difficulty that people who in their frantic course are dashing headlong towards the abyss can be halted and turned back to the right path. But our CC is called the Central Committee of the Leninist party precisely because it is able to overcome difficulties even greater than these. And, in the main, it has already overcome these difficulties.

It is difficult in cases like this for whole detachments of the Party to stop in their course, to turn back time to the right path and to reform their ranks on the march. But our Party is called Lenin's party precisely because it is sufficiently flexible to overcome such difficulties. And, in the main, it has already overcome these difficulties.

The chief thing here is to have the courage to acknowledge one's errors and the moral strength to eliminate them as quickly as possible. Fear of acknowledging one's errors after being intoxicated by recent successes, fear of self-criticism, reluctance to correct one's errors rapidly and resolutely—that is the chief difficulty. One has only to overcome this difficulty, one has only to cast aside inflated numerical targets and bureaucratic maximalism, one has only to transfer one's attention to the tasks of building the collective farms organizationally and economically, and not a trace of the errors will remain. There is no reason to doubt that, in the main, the Party has already overcome this dangerous difficulty.

"All revolutionary parties which have hitherto perished," Lenin says, "did so because they *grew conceited*, failed to see where their strength lay, *and feared to speak of their weaknesses*. But we shall not perish, for we do not fear to speak of our weaknesses and shall learn to overcome them." (Volume XXVII, pp. 260-61). (My italics—J. *Stalin*)

These words of Lenin must not be forgotten.

Fourth question. Is not the fight against distortions of the Party line a step backward, a retreat?

Reply. Of course not! This can be said to be a retreat only by people who consider persistence in errors and distortions an advance, and the fight against errors, a retreat. Advancing by piling up errors and distortions!—a fine "advance", there's no gainsaying....

We have put forward the agricultural artel as the principal form of the collective farm movement at the present moment, and have provided appropriate model rules to serve as a guide in the work of the collective farm development. Are we retreating from that? Of course not!

We have put forward consolidation of the production bond of the working class and the poor peasants with the middle peasants as the basis of the collective-farm movement at the present moment. Are we retreating from that? Of course not!

We have put forward the slogan of eliminating the kulaks as a class as the chief slogan of our practical work in the countryside at the present moment. Are we retreating from that? Of course not!

Already in January 1930 we adopted a definite rate of collectivization of the USSR into a number of groups, and fixing its own special rate for each group. Are we retreating from that? Of course not!

How, then, can it be said that the Party is "retreating"?

We want people who have committed errors and distortions to retreat from their errors. We want blockheads to retreat from their blockheadedness to the position of Leninism. We want this, because only then will it be possible to continue the *real* offensive against our class enemies. Does this mean that we are taking a step backward? Of course not! It only means that we want to carry out a *proper* offensive, and not blockheaded playing at an offensive.

Is it not obvious that only cranks and "Left" distorters can consider this stand of the Party as a retreat?

People who talk about a retreat fail to understand at least two things.

a) They do not know the laws of an offensive. They do not understand than an offensive *without consolidating* captured positions is an offensive that is doomed to failure.

When may an offensive—in the military sphere, say—be successful? When you do not confine yourself to advancing headlong, but endeavor at the same time to *consolidate* the positions captured, *regroup* your forces in conformity with changing conditions, *move up* the rear services, and *bring up* the reserves. Why is all this necessary? In order to guarantee yourself against surprises, to liquidate any breakthroughs, against which no offensive is guaranteed, and thus pave the way for the complete rout of the enemy. The mistake made by the Polish army in 1920, if we consider only the military side of the matter, was that it ignored this rule. That, incidentally, explains why, after having dashed headlong to Kiev, it was then forced to make just as headlong a retreat to Warsaw. The mistake made by the Soviet army in 1920, if again we consider only the military side of the matter, was that it duplicated the mistake of the Poles in its advance on Warsaw.

The same must be said about the laws of an offensive on the front of the class struggle. It is impossible to conduct a successful offensive with the object of annihilating the class enemies, *without consolidating* captured positions, *without regrouping* forces, without providing *reserves* for the front, without moving up *rear services*, and so on.

The whole point is that the blockheads do not understand the laws of an offensive. The whole point is that the Party does understand them and puts them into effect.

b) They do not understand the class nature of the offensive. They shout about an offensive. But an offensive against *which* class, and in alliance with *which* class? We are conducting an offensive against the capitalist elements in the countryside in alliance with the middle peasant, because only such an offensive can bring us victory. But what is to be done if, owing to the misguided ardor of individual sections of the Party, the offensive begins to slide from the proper path and its sharp edge is turned against our ally, the middle peasant? Is it just *any kind* of an offensive that we need, and not an offensive against a definite class, and in alliance with a definite class? Don Quixote also imagined he was conducting an offensive against his enemies when he attacked a windmill. But we know that he got his head broken in this offensive, if one can call it that.

Apparently, our "Left" distorters are envious of the laurels of Don Quixote.

Fifth question. Which is our chief danger, the Right or the "Left"?

Reply. Our chief danger at the present time is the Right danger. The Right danger has been, and still is, the chief danger.

Does not this thesis contradict that in the Central Committee's decision of 15 March 1930, to the effect that the errors and distortions of the "Left" distorters are now the chief hindrance to the collective-farm movement? No, it does not. The fact of the matter is that the errors of the "Left" distorters in regard to the collective farm movement are such as create a favorable situation for the strengthening and consolidation of the Right deviation in the Party. Why? Because these errors present the Party's line in a false light—consequently, they make it easier to discredit the Party, and therefore they facilitate the struggle of the Right elements against the Party's leadership. Discrediting the Party leadership is just that elementary ground on which alone the struggle of the Right deviators against the Party can be waged. This ground is provided for the Right deviators by the "Left" distorters, by their errors and distortions. Therefore, if we are to fight successfully against Right opportunism, we must overcome the errors of the "Left" opportunists. Objectively, the "Left" distorters are allies of the Right deviators.

Such is the peculiar connection between "Left" opportunism and Right deviationism.

It is this connection that explains the fact that some of the "Lefts" so often suggest a bloc with the Rights. This, too, explains the peculiar phenomenon that a section of the "Lefts", who only yesterday were "executing" a dashing offensive and trying to collectivize the USSR in a matter of two or three weeks, are today lapsing into passivity, losing heart and effectively surrendering the field to the Right deviators, thus pursuing a line of real retreat (without quotation marks!) in face of the kulaks.

The specific feature of the present moment is that a fight against the errors of the "Left" distorters is a precondition for a successful fight against Right opportunism and a distinctive form of this fight.

Sixth question. How is the exodus of a section of the peasants from the collective farms to be assessed?

Reply. The exodus of a section of the peasants signifies that of late a certain number of unsound collective farms were formed which are now being cleansed of their unstable elements. That means that sham collective farms will disappear, while the sound ones will remain and grow stronger. I consider this a perfectly normal thing. Some comrades are driven to despair by it, give way to panic, and convulsively clutch at inflated collectivization percentages. Others gloat over it and prophesy the "collapse" of the collective-farm movement. Both are cruelly mistaken. Both are far removed from a Marxist understanding of the nature of the collective farm movement.

Primarily, it is so-called dead souls that are withdrawing from the collective farms. It is not even a withdrawal but rather the revelation of a vacuum. Do we need dead souls? Of course not. I think that the North Caucasians and the Ukrainians are acting quite rightly in dissolving collective farms with dead souls and in organizing really live and really stable collective farms. The collective-farm movement will only benefit from this.

Secondly, it is alien elements, which are definitely hostile to our cause, that are withdrawing. It is obvious that the sooner such elements are ejected, the better it will be for the collective-farm movement.

Lastly, it is vacillating elements, which cannot be called either alien elements or dead souls, that are withdrawing. These are peasants whom *today* we have not yet succeeded in convincing of the rightness of our cause, but whom we shall certainly convince *tomorrow*. The withdrawal of such peasants is a serious, although temporary, loss to the collective farm movement. Consequently, one of the most urgent tasks of the collective farm movement now is to fight for the vacillating elements in the collective farms.

It follows that the exodus of a section of the peasants from the collective farms is not entirely a bad thing. It follows that, inasmuch as this exodus relieves the collective farms of dead souls and definitely alien elements, it is the sign of a beneficent process making the collective farms healthier and stronger.

A month ago it was estimated that collectivization in the grain-growing regions amounted to over 60 percent. It is now clear that, as regards genuine and more or less stable collective farms, that figure was definitely exaggerated. If, after the exodus of a section of the peasants, the collective farm movement is consolidated at 40 percent collectivization in the grain-growing regions—and that is certainly feasible—it will be a very great achievement for the collective-farm movement at the present moment. I take an average figure for the grain-growing regions, although I am well aware that we have individual areas of complete collectivization where the figure is 80-90 percent. Forty percent collectivization in the grain-growing regions means that by the spring of 1930 we shall have succeeded in fulfilling the original five year plan of collectivization *twice over*.

Who will venture to deny the *decisive* character of this *historic* achievement in the socialist development of the USSR?

Seventh question. Are the vacillating peasants acting rightly in withdrawing from the collective farms?

Reply. No, they are acting wrongly. In withdrawing from the collective farms they are going against their own interests, for only the collective farms offer the peasants a way out of poverty and ignorance. In withdrawing from the collective farms, they make their position worse, because they deprive themselves of those privileges and advantages which the Soviet government accords the collective farms. Errors and distortions in the collective farms are no reason for withdrawing from them. Errors must be corrected by joint effort, while remaining in the collective farms. They can be corrected the more easily as the Soviet government will fight them with might and main.

Lenin says:

"The small-farming system under commodity production *cannot* save mankind from the poverty and oppression of the masses" (Volume XX, p. 122).

Lenin says:

"There is no escape from poverty for the small farm" (Volume XXIV, p. 540),

Lenin says:

"If we continue as of old on our small farms, even as free citizens on free land, we shall still be faced with inevitable ruin" (Volume XX, p. 417).

Lenin says:

"Only with the help of common, artel, cooperative labor can we escape from the impasse into which the imperialist war has landed us" (Volume XXIV, p. 537).

Lenin says:

We must pass to common cultivation in large model farms," or "otherwise there will be no escaping from the dislocation, from the truly desperate situation in which Russia finds itself" (Volume XX, p. 418).

What does all that signify?

It signifies that collective farms are only the *sole* means that offer the peasants a way out of poverty and ignorance.

Clearly, peasants who withdraw from the collective farms are acting wrongly.

Lenin says:

"You all know, of course, from all the activity of the Soviet government what *immense importance* we attach to communes, artels and all organizations generally which aim at the transformation, at gradually assisting this transformation, of small, individual peasant farming into socially-conducted, cooperative or artel farming" (Volume XXIV, p. 579).

Lenin says:

"The Soviet government gave direct *preference* to communes and cooperatives by putting them in the *forefront*? (Volume XXIII, p. 399). (My italics—*J. Stalin*)

What does that mean?

It means that the Soviet government will accord privileges and preferences to the collective farms as compared with the individual farms. It means that it will accord privileges to the collective farms as regards provision of land, as regards supply of machines, tractors, seed grain, etc., as regards tax relief, and as regards provision of credits.

Why does the Soviet government accord privileges and preferences to the collective farms?

Because the collective farms are the only means by which the peasants can rid themselves of poverty.

Because preferential assistance to the collective farms is the most effective form of assistance to the poor and middle peasants.

A few days ago the Soviet government decided to *exempt* from taxation *for two years* all socially-owned draught animals in the collective farms (horses, oxen, etc.), and all cows, pigs, sheep and poultry, both those collectively owned by the collective farms and those individually owned by the collective farmers.

The Soviet government has decided, in addition, to *postpone* to the end of the year repayment of arrears on credits granted to collective farmers and to *cancel* all fines and court penalties levied prior to 1 April on peasants who have joined collective farms.

It has decided, lastly, to carry out without fail the granting of credits to collective farms in the present year to the amount of 500,000,000 rubles.

Those privileges will aid the peasant collective farmers. They will aid those peasant collective farmers who have stood firm against the exodus, who have become steeled in the fight against the enemies of the collective farms, who have defended the collective farms and have held aloft the great banner of the collective farm movement. They will aid the poor- and middle-peasant collective farmers, who now constitute the main core of our collective farms, who will strengthen and give shape to our collective farms, and who will win millions upon millions of peasants for socialism. They will aid those peasant collective farmers who now constitute the principal cadres of the collective farms, and who fully deserve to be called heroes of the collective-farm movement.

These privileges the peasants who have left the collective farms *will not receive*.

Is it not clear that peasants who withdraw from the collective farms are making a mistake?

Is it not clear that only by returning to the collective farms can they ensure receiving these privileges?

Eighth question. What is to be done with the communes? Should they not be dissolved?

Reply. No, they should not be dissolved and there is no reason for doing so. I am referring to real communes, not those existing on paper. In the grain-growing regions of the USSR there are a number of splendid communes which deserve to be encouraged and supported. I have in mind the old communes which have withstood years of ordeal, which have become steeled in the struggle and have fully justified their existence. They should not be dissolved, but should be converted into artels.

The formation and management of communes is a complicated and difficult matter. Large and stable communes can exist and develop only if they have experienced cadres and tried and tested leaders. A hasty replacement of the rules of the artel by the rules of the commune can only repel the peasants from the collective farm movement. Hence this matter must be approached with the utmost care and without any sort of haste. The artel is a simpler affair and more easily understood by the broad masses of the peasants. That is why at the present time the artel is the most widespread form of the collective farm movement. Only as the agricultural artels become stronger and more firmly established can the basis be created for a mass movement of the peasants towards communes. But that will not be soon. Hence the commune, which constitutes a higher form, can become the chief link in the collective farm movement only in the future.

Ninth question. What is to be done with the kulaks?

Reply. So far we have spoken of the middle peasant. The middle peasant is an ally of the working class, and our policy towards him must be a friendly one. As for the kulak, that is another matter. The kulak is an enemy of the Soviet regime. There is not and cannot be peace between him and us. Our policy towards the kulaks is to eliminate them as a class. That does not mean, of course, that we can eliminate them at one stroke. But it does mean that we shall work to surround them and to eliminate them.

Here is what Lenin says about the kulaks:

"The kulaks are the most bestial, brutal and savage exploiters, who in the history of other countries have time and again restored the power of the landlords, tsars, priests and capitalists. The kulaks are more numerous than the landlords and capitalists. Nevertheless, the kulaks are a minority of the people.... These bloodsuckers have grown rich on the want suffered by the people during the war; they have raked in thousands and hundreds of thousands of rubles by raising the prices of grain and other products. These spiders have grown fat at the expense of the peasants who have been ruined by the war, and at the expense of the hungry workers. These leeches have sucked the blood of the toilers and have grown the richer, the more the workers in the cities and factories have suffered hunger. These vampires have been gathering and are gathering the landed estates into their hands; they keep on enslaving the poor peasants" (Volume XXIII, pp. 206-07).

We tolerated these bloodsuckers, spiders and vampires, while pursuing a policy of restricting their exploiting tendencies. We tolerated them, because we had nothing with which to replace kulak farming, kulak production. Now we are in a position to replace, and more than replace, their farming by our collective farms and state farms. There is no reason to tolerate these spiders and bloodsuckers any longer. To tolerate any longer these spiders and bloodsuckers, who set fire to collective farms, murder collective-farm leaders and try to disrupt crop-sowing, would be going against the interests of the workers and peasants.

Hence the policy of eliminating the kulaks as a class must be pursued with all the persistence and consistency of which Bolsheviks are capable.

Tenth question. What is the immediate practical task of the collective farms?

Reply. The immediate practical task of the collective farms lies in the fight for crop-sowing, for the maximum enlargement of crop areas, for proper organization of crop-sowing.

All other tasks of the collective farms must now be adapted to the task of sowing the crops.

All other work in the collective farms must be subordinated to the work of organizing the sowing of the crops.

That means that the stamina of the collective farms and of their nonParty active, the ability of the leaders and Bolshevik core of the collective farms will be tested not by resounding resolutions of high-flown greetings, but by practical performance in properly organizing the crop-sowing.

But to fulfil this practical task with honor, the attention of collective farm officials must be turned to the *economic* questions of collective farm development, to the questions of the *internal* development of the collective farms.

Until recently, the attention of collective farm officials was focused on the chase for high collectivization figures; moreover, people refused to see the difference between real collectivization and collectivization on paper. This infatuation for figures must now be discarded. The attention of the officials must now be concentrated on *consolidating* the collective farms, on giving them organizational *shape*, on *organizing* their practical work.

Until recently, the attention of collective-farm officials was concentrated on organizing large collective farm units, so-called "giants", which not infrequently degenerated into cumbrous bureaucratic headquarters, devoid of economic roots in the villages. Consequently, real work was swamped by window-dressing. This infatuation for display must now be discarded. The attention of officials must now be concentrated on the organizational and economic work of the collective farms in the villages. When this work achieves proper success, "giants" will make their appearance of themselves.

Until recently, little attention was paid to drawing middle peasants into the work of managing the collective farms. Yet there are some remarkably fine farmers among the middle peasants, who could become excellent collective-farm executives. This defect in our work must now be eliminated. The task now is to draw the finest elements among the middle peasants into the work of managing the collective farms and to give them the opportunity to develop their abilities in this sphere.

Until recently, insufficient attention was paid to work among peasant women. The past period has shown that work among peasant women is the weakest part of our work. This defect must now be eliminated resolutely, once and for all.

Until recently, the Communists in a number of areas assumed that they could solve all the problems of collective farm development, by their own efforts. Because of this assumption, they did not pay sufficient attention to drawing nonParty people into responsible work in the collective farms, to promoting nonParty people to managerial work in the collective farms, to organizing a large active of nonParty people in the collective farms. The history of our Party has proved, and the past period in collective-farm development has once more demonstrated it, that this line is radically wrong. If Communists were to shut themselves up in their shells and wall themselves off from nonParty people, they would ruin the entire work. If the Communists have succeeded in covering themselves with glory in the battles for socialism, while the enemies of communism have been beaten, it is due, among other things, to the fact that the Communists knew how to enlist the cooperation of the finest elements among the nonParty people, that they knew how to draw forces from the broad nonParty strata, how to surround their Party with broad active of nonParty people. This defect in our work among the nonParty people must now be eliminated resolutely, once and for all.

Correcting these defects in our work, eliminating them completely, means precisely putting the *economic* work of the collective farms on sound lines.

And so:

1) Proper organization of the crop-sowing—that is the task.

2) Concentration of attention on the economic questions of the collective farm movement—that is the means necessary for accomplishing this task.

Stalin, *Works*, XII, 207-234.

★

LAW ON STATE CONCENTRATION CAMPS
7 April 1930

The Soviet drive toward industrialization and collectivization, especially the efforts to deport kulaks to remote areas, led to the expansion of corrective labor camps, otherwise known as concentration camps. The labor camps, placed under the jurisdiction of the Unified State Political Administration, served as a means of punishing kulaks, political opponents, and criminals, while at the same time using them as cheap labor in construction projects in locations hostile to workers and peasants. This document is a decree from the Council of People's Commissars that describes the types of prisoners in the camps, rules and regulations, and incentives for hard work and excellent behavior.

LAW ON CORRECTIVE LABOR CAMPS
(Decree of the USSR SNK)

1. Corrective labor camps have the purpose of protecting society from especially socially dangerous violators of the law by isolating them, uniting them with socially useful labor, and adapting these violators to the conditions of labor communal life.

2. Sent to the corrective labor camps can only be people convicted by a court and deprived of freedom for a period of not less than three years, or people convicted by a special resolution of the OGPU.

3. The camps are under the jurisdiction of the Unified State Political Administration, which exercises general management over their activity.

4. Each corrective labor camp can be administered by a camp chief. The functions of the camp chief shall be:

a) To exercise general guidance, direction, and supervision over camp activities;

b) To carry out all appropriate measures for the isolation of persons sent to the camp, in accordance with the rules prescribed by the present law;

c) To see to it that, appropriately to their purposes, the camps utilize the property and privileges granted to them, and also that the prisoners' labor force is used in a most rational manner in the economic enterprises operated by the camps on a self-supporting basis;

d) To issue, on the basis of the present law, regulations concerning the performance of work by the individual units of the camp, and orders relating to internal management;

e) To impose upon camp [staff] employees disciplinary penalties within the limits prescribed for chiefs of the oblast offices of the OGPU;

f) To direct and guide the activities of productive and other economic enterprises of the corrective labor camp;

g) To manage the property and the finances of the camp and its enterprises within the limits of the production and financial plans approved by the OGPU, to draft production and financial plans promptly and to fulfill them exactly;

h) To enter into all types of contracts and transactions, to issue power of attorney for the transaction of affairs within the limits of authority granted to him by the OGPU;

i) To maintain the application of certain measures designed to increase the cultural level and qualifications of prisoners and to adapt them to the conditions of a productive communal life by training them for socially useful work.

5. In addition to the administrative and production-exploitation units there shall be organized in each camp:

a) A Rating Board;

b) A Cultural and Educational Unit;

c) A Sanitation Unit.

6. It shall be the duty of the Rating Board:

a) To prepare material for the rating of prisoners and, on the basis of this material, to submit the data to the camp chief for consideration of a release prior to the expiration of the prisoner's term or the transfer from one type of regimen to another;

b) To register prisoners in the camp [and] to prepare data with reference to the possible utilization of their labor;

c) To make an accounting of the prisoner manpower with an individual approach to each prisoner, by means of ascertaining his health, inclination to work, qualifications, and conscientiousness in his work;

d) To work out and carry out, upon proper approval, the awarding of bonuses to prisoners for their work.

7. It shall be the duty of the Cultural and Education Unit:

a) To organize schools for the elimination of illiteracy, schools for the literate, and courses of a higher type, and to direct their work;

b) To exercise direction over the content and training methods, and political guidance in schools for industrial training and in technical courses of instruction;

c) To determine the repertoire, to supervise, to instruct, and to control theatrical work in the camps;

d) To direct the organization of libraries in the camp, to supervise the loaning of books to prisoners, and the timely procurement of appropriate additions to the library;

e) To direct the work of clubs, Red Corners, museums, and the like;

f) To conduct the publishing activities of the camp;

g) To supervise physical culture work;

h) To conduct criminological studies of prisoners.

8. It shall be the duty of the Sanitation Unit:

a) To do the prophylactic work in the fight against disease in the camp and to organize medical and sanitation services;

b) To organize, manage, and direct all medical institutions of the camp;

c) To carry out sanitation propaganda work in the camp;

d) To see to it that proper sanitary and medical services are provided for the hired employees and their families.

9. The organizational structure and table of organization for the staff members of each camp shall be approved by the OGPU.

10. Persons sent to camps to serve their term of confinement shall be admitted only by order of the OGPU and only upon presentation of a certified copy of the court sentence, or of the decision of a Collegium or of the Special Conference of the OGPU.

11. Children up to the age of two years may be admitted into the camps together with women prisoners. They shall be placed with their mothers.

Comment: Children over two years of age may be left with their parents until they are transferred to persons designated by the parents, or until they are placed in an orphanage.

12. All prisoners arriving at camps shall be registered and shall undergo a medical examination. Simultaneously, an inspection shall be made of the articles in the possession of the prisoners and those articles which, according to the regulations, may be used by the prisoners, shall remain at their disposal; all other articles shall be surrendered for safekeeping. The list of articles which may be left in the custody of the prisoners shall be established by the OGPU. An inventory of the articles surrendered for safekeeping shall be made and a copy of such inventory given to the prisoner.

Comment: The money taken from a prisoner shall be placed in a personal account for him, and he shall have the right to spend it against the vouchers issued to him for the purchase of food items and other articles from the stores and other organizations of the camp.

13. After registration and examination, all prisoners newly arrived at the camp shall be quarantined for an established period of time, and all personal belongings—clothing, underwear, and other articles that may serve as a source of contagion—shall be disinfected.

14. To secure conditions for the most consecutive and expedient meeting of the purposes of the corrective labor camps, prisoners shall be classified along three categories, depending on their social position and nature of the crime committed.

15. The first category shall be prisoners from among laborers (workers, peasants, and employees), who made use of voting rights before sentencing, are convicted for the first time for a period of not more than five years and not for counterrevolutionary crimes. The second category shall be those prisoners who are convicted for a period of more than five years.

The third category shall be all nonlabor elements and persons convicted of counterrevolutionary crimes.

16. Prisoners in the camps shall conform to three types of regimens: Basic, alleviated, and privileged.

Prisoners subject to the basic regimen shall be used for general labor, live within the boundaries of the camp in special housing, have no right leave these quarters at will, and are directed to work in accordance with a general list.

Prisoners subject to the alleviated regimen shall be used for permanent work in institutions, enterprises, and mines, live in quarters attached to enterprises, have the right to leave their quarters, are directed to work in accordance with labor cards, and can be given bonuses.

In addition to the conditions established for the basic regimen, prisoners subject to the privileged regimen have the right to leave the boundaries of the camp and occupy administrative and economic positions in camp management and production work.

Comment: Nonlabor elements and persons convicted of counterrevolutionary crimes cannot occupy administrative and economic positions.

17. All prisoners entering the camp conform to the basic regimen for the following periods of time: For prisoners of the first category it is not less than half of the year, for prisoners of the second category it is not less than a year, and for prisoners of the third category it is not less than two years.

Comment: Depending on the nature of the work, the conditions for the basic regimen can be changed by the camp chief, but only at the absolute condition so that the regimen would not approximate the conditions of the alleviated or privileged regimens.

18. In accordance with the results of a medical examination, with the status of this or that category (articles 14 and 15), with the conditions of the regimens applied to the prisoner and with his specialty, prisoners shall be divided into the following work assignments: 1) For general work; 2) for work in institutions, enterprises, mines, forestry, etc., and 3) for work in administrative and economic management of the camps.

19. General work is carried out exclusively under surveillance, without the right of free movement not called for by work conditions.

20. Work in institutions, enterprises, and mines is carried out in accordance with the prisoners' specialty and qualifications.

21. All prisoners, regardless of category and regimen, are entitled to food rations in accordance with the nature of the work being fulfilled.

Food rations are divided into four categories: 1) Basic, 2) labor, 3) increased, and 4) punitive.

Comment 1: Ration norms shall be determined by the OGPU, but in all cases not lower than the necessary calories.

Comment 2: The diet of the permanently ill shall be made along special norms. Norms for ambulatory patients are also increased per doctor's conclusions.

22. Prisoners, as necessary, shall be given clothes, shoes, underwear, and bedding.

23. Prisoners who apply themselves diligently to their labor and show excellent indication of corrective behavior may be entitled to the following incentives:

a) Favorable declaration entered in the personal record of the individual camp or management of camps;

b) granting of bonus;

c) improvement in living conditions (granting of personal meetings, freedom for walks, right to receive and send correspondence outside of norms and procedures, etc.).

24. Only prisoners of the alleviated and privileged regimen can receive bonuses. Norms and procedures shall be established by the OGPU.

25. Awards can consist of: 1) Monetary bonuses, 2) increased food rations, 3) quicker transfer to alleviated or privileged regimen, and 4) presentation to Rating Board for reduced time served with or without settlement.

26. For breaking tools intentionally or through negligence, prisoners shall be subject to disciplinary punishment or deduction in bonus payments. For systematically breaking tools and materials with the aim of bringing harm to the enterprise, criminal proceedings shall be brought against prisoners.

27. The working day of prisoners as a general rule shall not be more than eight hours. Deviations from this shall depend on the seasonal nature of the work or in special cases with permission of the USSR People's Commissariat for Labor.

28. Salary norms and the protection of labor of prisoners shall be established by the OGPU in agreement with the USSR People's Commissariat for Labor.

29. In case of sickness, prisoners shall receive medical aid from the medical staff of the camps. Prisoners requiring hospitalization shall be placed in camp infirmaries, and in extreme cases, when there is no camp infirmary, in general hospitals.

30. Depending on the category and type of applicable regimen, prisoners shall live in special premises, dormitories, near enterprises, or at mining sites, and outside the camps.

31. Prisoners who have a bad influence on others or who are suspected of making preparations to escape may be transferred to solitary quarters or to special general cells under special surveillance.

32. Persons who persistently violate the established regimen and order, as well as malingerers, may be sent to penal isolators and to special (punitive) work assignments.

33. Prisoners of corrective labor camps are permitted to receive visitors on the basis of a special instruction issued by the OGPU.

34. Prisoners may carry on correspondence under the following rules:

a) All correspondence shall be examined by the administration;

b) Correspondence from and to prisoners may be confiscated; the prisoner shall be advised of the confiscation.

35. Prisoners shall have the right to receive gifts, postal parcels, and money orders.

The procedure governing the receipt of parcels and money orders shall be established by the OGPU.

Comment: The money received by a prisoner shall be credited to his personal account and not given to him personally.

36. The transfer of prisoners from one camp to another shall be made by the OGPU and from one subdivision of the camp to another, by the camp chief.

When transferred from one subdivision to another, the prisoners shall remain in the same category and under the same regimen as just before the transfer.

37. The period of confinement shall be counted from the date indicated in the sentence or the resolution of the OGPU.

38. In case of receipt of a lawful order for release, the prisoner must be freed immediately.

39. Upon expiration of the designated period of confinement, a prisoner shall be freed immediately by an order to the camp administration, without a special inquiry and without awaiting a resolution from a court or the OGPU.

A prisoner shall be subject to immediate release in case of a general or personal amnesty.

40. A special fund shall be established for the rendering of material aid to persons released from the camps.

This fund shall consist of: 1) partial withholdings from the bonus award due to the prisoners; 2) deductions from the wages of the prisoners; and 3) other receipts.

41. The sanitation unit of the camp shall prepare a proper certificate concerning the death of a prisoner and the causes thereof.

42. Prisoners in camps, who enjoyed their voting rights before sentencing and who are found to be corrected, can receive conditional early release with settlement in the region of the given camp for the unserved period of sentencing or without settlement.

43. During the transfer of the prisoner to the settlement before the end or during the expiration of the end of imprisonment, the place of settlement is determined on the basis of the instruction of the sentence. If the place of the settlement is not indicated in the sentence, then this is determined by the camp chief.

44. For violating the regimen and internal regulations established in the camp, prisoners are subject to the follow disciplinary punishment imposed by the camp chief in accordance with the nature of the misdemeanor:

a) Simple or severe reprimand;

b) limitation or deprivation of right to receive gifts (parcels) for up to one month;

c) limitation or deprivation of right of correspondence for up to three months;

d) limitation of right to money deposited in one's personal account for the same period;

e) isolation in a separate accommodation for up to thirty full days;

f) change in regimen;

g) assignment to punitive work for up to six months;

h) transfer to punitive assignment for up to one year.

The conditions and procedures for applying the enumerated disciplinary measures shall be determined by special instruction of the Unified State Political Administration.

45. Cultural and education work in the camps must correspond to the class nature of the entire corrective labor system with the preferential servicing of prisoners whose origins are from the working class and peasantry.

46. All illiterate prisoners up to the age of 50 years shall be obligated to spend their free time in the cultural and educational institutions of the camp. Club, theater, scientific and lecture, and other work are organized on the basis of the initiative of the prisoners.

47. Persons belonging to the administrative staff and to the guards of the camp, who are granted the right to bear arms, shall have the right to resort to the use of arms in the following instances:

a) To defend a post or person under guard;

b) For self-defense;

c) Against escaping prisoners;

d) In case of a disorderly outbreak or of violence on the part of prisoners against the administration of the camp.

48. The aforementioned persons shall be held criminally liable for the improper use of arms.

49. An appropriate official shall prepare a record describing the circumstances of each case of use of arms, which record shall be forwarded to the OGPU.

50. Absence of a prisoner without proper permission from the area to which he was sent or from the place of work to which the prisoner has been assigned, or his failure to be present at the place of his permanent lodging after the expiration of six hours following the evening roll call shall be regarded as an escape.

51. In each case of escape the camp chief shall conduct an investigation and shall submit a report thereupon to the OGPU.

52. The Public Prosecutor of the constituent republic in whose territory a given corrective labor camp is located, shall be charged with supervision over the observance of the present law and of the proper rules for the maintenance of prisoners; in this connection, such republic prosecutors shall act under a special delegation of authority by the Public Prosecutor of the Supreme Court of the USSR.

53. The prosecutors who supervise the corrective labor camps shall have the right:

a) To visit the camps at any time of the day or night;

b) To interrogate prisoners directly and to receive their complaints;

c) To see that all rules concerning the labor of prisoners, the cultural and educational work, and other rules established by the present law are carried out;

d) To make recommendations to the administration concerning the immediate elimination of any discovered irregularities;

e) To stop the execution of decisions of the administration which violate the present law;

f) To stop the execution of incorrect decisions concerning the release of prisoners prior to the expiration of the term of sentence.

54. Complaints of the administration of the camps with reference to any of the above-mentioned intercessions on the part of the supervisory prosecutors must be directed to the OGPU, without staying the execution of the prosecutor's decision.

Goliakov, 320-323.
Statute on the Corrective Labor Camps, Monograph.

MAIAKOVSKY'S SUICIDE LETTER

12 April 1930

Vladimir Maiakovsky, the poet of the proletarian revolution and avant-garde literary figure, shot himself in his Moscow office on 14 April 1930 at 10:15 in the morning. His latest love interest, the actress Veronika Polonskaia, was the last to see him alive in the morning prior to his suicide. He left a suicide letter, dated 12 April. There was little indication that he contemplated suicided before 14 April. Much was written about the suicide, ranging from the unsuccessful relationship with Lilia Brik to suffering from depression. Maiakovsky's death brought to a close an era of avant-garde art and literature ushered in by the Bolshevik Revolution.

To Everyone

Do not blame anyone for my death and please do not gossip. This deceased hated gossip terribly.

Mama, sisters, and comrades, forgive me—this is not the way (I do not recommend it to others), but I have no other choice.

Lilia—love me.

Comrade government, my family are Lilia Brik, mama, my sisters, and Veronika Vitol'dovna Polonskaia.

If you arrange for them a decent living—thanks.

The verses which I have started give to the Briks, they will figure them out.

As they say—

"the incident is closed",

the love boat
wrecked by daily life.
I am all even with life
and nothing would be gained by a list
mutual hurts,
troubles
and insults.
Good luck,
Vladimir Maiakovsky.
12/IV—1930.

Comrades of VAPP, do not consider me a coward.
Seriously, it could not be helped.
Greetings.
Tell Ermilov that it is too bad—I took down that slogan, should have fought it out.
V.M.
In my desk there are 2,000 rubles—pay my taxes.
The balance get it from Gosizdat.
V.M.

Maiakovsky, 168.

REAFFIRMATION OF 1926 TREATY OF BERLIN
JOINT SOVIET-GERMAN STATEMENT
13 June 1930

There was growing concern in the German Government that the Soviet Union was supporting the Communist Party in Germany and consequently influencing domestic affairs. German and Soviet officials met in January 1929 and agreed to establish a conciliation commission to discuss and resolve any disputes or disagreements concerning the bilateral relations between the two countries. Specific procedures for convening and conducting the commission were also established. Subsequent discussions led to the reaffirmation of the 1926 Treaty of Berlin and the so-called spirit of Rapallo through the statement described in the document below. Both governments agreed to refrain from any attempts at active influence in the domestic affairs of each country.

JOINT SOVIET-GERMAN STATEMENT ON RELATIONS BETWEEN THE TWO COUNTRIES

In the relations between Germany and the USSR, a number of questions have arisen in the course of time which, in the interests of the further development of mutual friendly relations, require to be settled. All these questions taken together have been the object of the general diplomatic conversations which have taken place between the two governments during the past few weeks in Berlin and Moscow, and which are being brought to a definite conclusion at the present time.

Part of the separate claims of each side have already been satisfactorily cleared up in the conversations that have taken place. The remainder must be subject to review by the adjustment commission provided for this purpose by the treaty of 25 April [January] 1929, which must meet annually in the middle of the year, and which this year will meet on 16 June in Moscow for its current session.

In considering the separate questions that have arisen, both governments alike are actuated by a desire to surmount the difficulties that have arisen, in the spirit of the Rapallo Treaty and of other treaties that are in force between them, and by the desire to pursue the policy which they have followed for many years on the basis of these treaties, in the future development of international relations as well.

In the course of a frank exchange of opinion they have again come to the conclusion that the fundamental difference in their systems of government should not be an obstacle to the further fruitful development of amicable relations. In this connection both governments agree that they must refrain from any attempts at active influence in the internal affairs of the other country.

Both governments have decided to support their mutual relations on this basis, and so to approach the questions which may in the future arise between them, whether touching on the direct relations between the two countries or any other matters relating to their interests.

They are convinced that in this way they will serve both the interests of their own countries, and the interests of international peace.

Degras, II, 440.

STALIN'S OPTIMISTIC REPORT TO SIXTEENTH PARTY CONGRESS

27 June 1930

The Sixteenth Party Congress met from 26 June to 13 July 1930. Stalin presented an extensive report from the Central Committee in which he sharply contrasted the growth of the Soviet economic system with the economic crises of capitalist countries affected by the Great Depression. He listed the numerous successes in industrialization, showing the overfulfillment of the Five Year Plan. He predicted industrial output in 1930 at 110 percent of the prewar level. He pointed out that there were still problems with certain branches of industry such as chemicals and transportation. In agriculture, he expressed success despite mistakes made by overzealous officials in the formation of collective farms. The Five Year Plan for collective–farm grain output would be achieved in 1930 by more than 30 percent, thus fulfilling the plan in two years. Stalin described the Fourteenth and Fifteenth Congresses, respectively, as the congress of industrialization and collectivization, and declared the Sixteenth Congress as the sweeping offensive of socialism along the whole front, elimination of the kulaks as a class, and the realization of complete collectivization.

POLITICAL REPORT OF THE CENTRAL COMMITTEE TO THE SIXTEENTH CONGRESS OF THE CPSU(B)

I

THE GROWING CRISIS OF WORLD CAPITALISM AND THE EXTERNAL SITUATION OF THE USSR

Comrades, since the Fifteenth Congress two and a half years have passed. Not a very long period one would think. Nevertheless, during this period most important changes have taken place in the life of peoples and states. If one were to characterize the past period in two words, it could be called a *turning point* period. It marked a turning point not only for us, for the USSR, but also for the capitalist countries all over the world. Between these two turning points, however, there is a fundamental difference. Whereas for the USSR this turning point meant a turn in the direction of a new and bigger economic *upswing*, for the capitalist countries it meant a turn towards economic *decline*. Here, in the USSR, there is a *growing upswing* of socialist development both in industry and in agriculture. There, among the capitalists, there is *growing* economic *crisis* both in industry and in agriculture.

Such is the picture of the present situation in a few words.

Recall the state of affairs in the capitalist countries two and a half years ago. Growth of industrial production and trade in nearly all the capitalist countries. Growth of production of raw materials and food in nearly all the agrarian countries. A halo around the United States as the land of the most full-blooded capitalism. Triumphant hymns of "prosperity". Grovelling to the dollar. Panegyrics in honor of the new technology, in honor of capitalist rationalization. Proclamation of an era of the "recovery" of capitalism and of the unshakable firmness of capitalist stabilization. "Universal" noise and clamor about the "inevitable doom" of the Land of Soviets, about the "inevitable collapse" of the USSR.

That was the state of affairs yesterday.

And what is the picture today?

Today there is an economic crisis in nearly all the industrial countries of capitalism.

Today there is an economic crisis in nearly all the industrial countries of capitalism. Today there is an agricultural crisis in all the agrarian countries. Instead of "prosperity" there is mass poverty and a colossal growth of unemployment. Instead of an upswing in agriculture there is the ruin of the vast masses of the peasants. The illusions about the omnipotence of capitalism in general, and about the omnipotence of North American capitalism in particular, are collapsing. The triumphant hymns in honor of the dollar and of capitalist rationalization are becoming fainter and fainter. Pessimistic wailing about the "mistakes" of capitalism is growing louder and louder. And the "universal" clamor about the "inevitable doom" of the USSR is giving way to "universal" venomous hissing about the necessity of punishing "that country" that dares to develop its economy when crisis is reigning all around.

Such is the picture today.

Things have turned out exactly as the Bolsheviks said they would two or three years ago.

The Bolsheviks said that in view of the restricted limits of the standard of living of the vast masses of the workers and peasants, the further development of technology in the capitalist countries, the growth of productive forces and of capitalist rationalization, must inevitably lead to a severe economic crisis. The bourgeois press jeered at the "queer prophesies" of the Bolsheviks. The Right deviators dissociated themselves from the Bolshevik forecast and for the Marxist analysis substituted liberal chatter about "organized capitalism". But how did things actually turn out? They turned out exactly as the Bolsheviks said they would.

Such are the facts.

Let us now examine the data on the economic crisis in the capitalist countries.

1. THE WORLD ECONOMIC CRISIS

a) In studying the crisis, the following facts, above all, strike the eye:

1. The present economic crisis is a crisis of *overproduction*. This means that more goods have been produced than the market can absorb. It means that more textiles, fuel, manufactured goods and food have been produced than can be purchased for cash by the bulk of the consumers, i.e., the masses of people, whose incomes remain on a low level. Since, however, under capitalism, the purchasing power of the masses of the people remains at a minimum level, the capitalists keep their "superfluous" goods, textiles, grain, etc., in their warehouses or even destroy them in order to bolster up prices; they cut down production and discharge

their workers, and the masses of the people are compelled to suffer hardship because too many goods have been produced.

2. The present crisis is the first postwar *world* economic crisis. It is a world crisis not only in the sense that it embraces all, or nearly all, the *industrial* countries in the world; even France, which is systematically injecting into her organism the billions of marks received as reparations payments from Germany, has been unable to avoid a certain depression, which, as all the data indicate, is bound to develop into a crisis. It is a world crisis also in the sense that the *industrial* crisis has coincided with an *agricultural* crisis that affects the production of all forms of raw materials and food in the chief *agrarian* countries of the world.

3. The present world crisis is developing *unevenly*, notwithstanding its *universal* character; it affects different countries at different times and in different degrees. The industrial crisis began first of all in Poland, Rumania and the Balkans. It developed there throughout the whole of last year. Obvious symptoms of an incipient agricultural crisis were already visible at the end of 1928 in Canada, the United States, the Argentine, Brazil and Australia. During the whole of this period United States industry showed an upward trend. By the middle of 1929 industrial production in the United States had reached an almost record level. A break began only in the latter half of 1929, and then a crisis in industrial production swiftly developed, which threw the United States back to the level of 1927. This was followed by an industrial crisis in Canada and Japan. Then came bankruptcies and crisis in China and in the colonial countries, where the crisis was aggravated by the drop in the price of silver, and where the crisis of overproduction was combined with the ruination of the peasant farms, which were reduced to utter exhaustion by feudal exploitation and unbearable taxation. As regards Western Europe, there the crisis began to gain force only at the beginning of this year, but not everywhere to the same degree, and even in that period France still showed an increase in industrial production.

I do not think there is any need to dwell particularly on the statistics that demonstrate the existence of the crisis. Nobody now disputes the existence of the crisis. I shall therefore confine myself to quoting one small but characteristic table recently published by the German Institute of Economic Research. This table depicts the development of the mining industry and the chief branches of large-scale manufacturing industry in the United States, Britain, Germany, France, Poland and the USSR since 1927; the 1928 level of production is taken as 100.

Here is the table:

Year	USSR	USA	Britain	Germany	France	Poland
1927	82.4	95.5	105.5	100.1	86.6	88.5
1928	100	100	100	100	100	100
1929	123.5	106.3	107.9	101.8	109.4	99.8
1930 (first quarter)	171.4	95.5	107.4	93.4	113.1	84.6

What does this table show?

It shows, first of all, that the United States, Germany and Poland are experiencing *a sharply expressed crisis* in large-scale industrial production; in the first quarter of 1930, in the *United States*, after the *boom* in the first half of 1929, the level of production dropped 10.8 percent compared with 1929 and sank to the level of 1927; in *Germany*, after three years of *stagnation*, the level of production dropped 8.4 percent compared with last year and sank to 6.7 percent below the level of 1927; in *Poland*, after last year's *crisis*, the level of production dropped 15.2 percent compared with last year and sank to 3.9 percent below the level of 1927.

Secondly, the table shows that *Britain* has been marking time for three years, round about the 1927 level, and is experiencing severe economic *stagnation*; in the first quarter of 1930 she even suffered a drop in production of 0.5 percent compared with the previous year, thus entering the first phase of a *crisis*.

Thirdly, the table shows that of the big capitalist countries only in France is there a certain *growth* of large-scale industry; but whereas the increase in 1928 amounted to 13.4 percent and that in 1929 to 9.4 percent, the increase in the first quarter of 1930 is only 3.7 percent above that in 1929, thus presenting from year to a year a picture of a *descending* curve of growth.

Lastly, the table shows that of all the countries in the world, the USSR is the only one in which a powerful upswing of large-scale industry has taken place; the level of production in the first quarter of 1930 was more than twice as high as that in 1927, and the increase rose from 17.6 percent in 1928 to 23.5 percent in 1929 and to 32 percent in the first quarter of 1930, thus presenting from year to year a picture of an *ascending* curve of growth.

It may be said that although such was the state of affairs up to the end of the first quarter of this year, it is not precluded that a turn for the better may have taken place in the second quarter of this year. The returns for the second quarter, however, emphatically refute such an assumption. They show, on the contrary, that the situation has become still worse in the second quarter. These returns show: A further *drop in share prices* on the New York Stock Exchange and a new *wave of bankruptcies* in the United States; a further decline in production, a *reduction of wages* of the workers, and *growth of unemployment* in the United States, Germany, Britain, Italy, Japan, South America, Poland, Czechoslovakia, etc.; the entry of a number of branches of industry in France into a state of *stagnation*, which, in the present international economic situation, is a symptom of incipient crisis. The number of unemployed in the United States is now over 6,000,000, in Germany about 5,000,000, in Britain over 2,000,000, in Italy, South America and Japan a million each, in Poland, Czechoslovakia and Austria half a million each. This is apart from the further intensification of the agricultural crisis, which is ruining millions of farmers and laboring peasants. The crisis of overproduction in agriculture has reached such a pitch that in Brazil, in order to keep up prices and the profits of the bourgeoisie, 2,000,000 bags of coffee have been thrown into the sea; in America maize has begun to be used for fuel instead of coal; in Germany, millions of puds of rye are being converted into pig food; and as regards cotton and wheat, every measure is being taken to reduce the crop area by 10-15 percent.

Such is the general picture of the developing world economic crisis.

b) Now, when the destructive effects of the world economic crisis are spreading, sending to the bottom whole strata of medium and small capitalists, ruining entire groups of the labor aristocracy and farmers, and dooming vast masses of workers to starvation, everybody is asking: What is the cause of the crisis, what is at the bottom of it, how can it be combated, how can it be abolished? The most diverse "theories" about crises are being invented. Whole schemes are being proposed for "mitigating", "preventing", and "eliminating" crises. The bourgeois oppositions are blaming the bourgeois governments because "they failed to take all measures" to prevent the crisis. The "Democrats" blame the "Republicans" and the "Republicans" blame the "Democrats", and all of them together blame the Hoover group with its "Federal Reserve System", which failed to "curb" the crisis. There are even wiseacres who ascribe the world economic crisis to the "machinations of the Bolsheviks". I have in mind the well known "industrialist" Rechberg who, properly speaking, little resembles an industrialist, but reminds one more than anything of an "industrialist" among literary men and a "literary man" among industrialists. (*Laughter*)

It goes without saying that none of these "theories" and schemes has anything in common with science. It must be admitted that the bourgeois economists have proved to be utter bankrupt in face of the crisis. More than that, they have been found to be devoid even of that little sense of reality which their predecessors could not always be said to lack. These gentlemen forget that crises cannot be regarded as something fortuitous under the capitalist system of economy. These gentlemen forget that economic crises are the inevitable result of capitalism. These gentlemen forget that crises were born with the birth of the rule of capitalism. There have been periodical crises during more than a hundred years, recurring every 12, 10, 8 or less years. During this period bourgeois governments of all ranks and colors, bourgeois leaders of all levels and abilities, all without exception tried their strength at the task of "preventing" and "abolishing" crises. But they all suffered defeat. They suffered defeat because economic crises cannot be prevented or abolished within the framework of capitalism. Is it surprising that the present-day bourgeois leaders are also suffering defeat? Is it surprising that far from mitigating the crisis, far from easing the situation of the vast masses of the working people, the measures taken by the bourgeois governments actually lead to new outbreaks of bankruptcy, to new waves of unemployment, to the swallowing up of the less powerful capitalist combines by the more powerful capitalist combines?

The basis, the cause, of economic crises of overproduction lies in the capitalist system of economy itself. The basis of the crisis lies in the contradiction between the social character of production and the capitalist form of appropriation of the results of production. An expression of this fundamental contradiction of capitalism is the contradiction between colossal *growth* of capitalism's potentialities of production, calculated to yield the *maximum* of capitalist profit, and the relative *reduction* of the effective demand of the vast masses of the working people, whose standard of living the capitalists always try to keep at the *minimum* level. To be successful in competition and to squeeze out the utmost profit, the capitalists are compelled to develop their technical equipment, to introduce rationalization, to intensify the exploitation of the workers and to increase the production potentialities of their enterprises to the utmost limits. So as not to lag behind one another, all the capitalists are compelled, in one way or another, to take this path of furiously developing production potentialities. The home market and the foreign market, however, the purchasing power of the vast masses of workers and peasants who, in the last analysis, constitute the bulk of the purchasers, remain on a low level. Hence overproduction crises. Hence the well known results, recurring more or less periodically, as a consequence of which goods remain unsold, production is reduced, unemployment grows and wages are cut, and all this still further intensifies the contradiction between the level of production and the level of effective demand. Overproduction crises are a manifestation of this contradiction in turbulent and destructive forms.

If capitalism could adapt production not to the obtaining of the utmost profit, but to the systematic improvement of the material conditions of the masses of the people, and if it could turn profits not to the satisfaction of the whims of the parasitic classes, not to perfecting the methods of exploitation, not to the export of capital, but to the systematic improvement of the material conditions of the workers and peasants, then there would be no crises. But then capitalism would not be capitalism. To abolish crises it is necessary to abolish capitalism.

Such is the basis of economic crises of overproduction in general.

We cannot, however, confine ourselves to this in characterizing the *present* crisis. The present crisis cannot be regarded as a mere recurrence of the old crises. It is occurring and developing under certain new conditions, which must be brought out if we are to obtain a complete picture of the crisis. It is complicated and deepened by a number of special circumstances which must be understood if we are to obtain a clear idea of the present economic crisis.

What are these special circumstances?

These special circumstances can be reduced to the following characteristic facts:

1. The crisis has most severely affected the principal country of capitalism, its citadel, the United States, in which is concentrated not less than half the total production and consumption of all the countries in the world. Obviously, this circumstance cannot but lead to a colossal expansion of the sphere of influence of the crisis, to the intensification of the crisis and to the accumulation of extra difficulties for world capitalism.

2. In the course of development of the economic crisis, the industrial crisis in the chief capitalist countries did not merely coincide but became *interwoven* with the agricultural crisis in the agrarian countries, thus aggravating the difficulties and predetermining the inevitability of a general decline in economic activity. Needless to say, the industrial crisis will intensify the agricultural crisis, and the agricultural crisis will prolong the industrial crisis, which cannot but lead to the intensification of the economic crisis as a whole.

3. Present day capitalism, unlike the old capitalism, is *monopoly* capitalism, and this predetermines the inevitability of the capitalist combines fighting to keep up the high monopolist prices of goods, in spite of overproduction. Naturally, this circumstance, which makes the crisis particularly painful and ruinous for the masses of the people who constitute the main consumers of goods, cannot but lead to prolonging the crisis, cannot but be an obstacle to resolving it.

4. The present economic crisis is developing on the basis of the *general crises* of capitalism, which came into being already in the period of the imperialist war, and is sapping the foundations of capitalism and has facilitated the advent of the economic crisis.

What does that mean?

It means, first of all, that the imperialist war and its aftermath intensified the decay of capitalism and upset its equilibrium, that we are now living in an epoch of wars and revolutions, that capitalism has already ceased to be the *sole* and *all-embracing* system of world economy, that side by side with the *capitalist* system of economy there is the *socialist* system, which is growing, thriving, stands opposed to the capitalist system and by its very existence demonstrates the decaying state of capitalism, shakes its foundation.

It means, further, that the imperialist war and the victory of the revolution in the USSR have shaken the foundations of imperialism i*n the colonial and dependent* countries, that the prestige of imperialism has already been undermined in those countries, that it is no longer able to lord it in those countries in the old way.

It means, further, that during the war and after it, a young native capitalism appeared and grew up in the colonial and dependent countries, which is successfully competing in the markets with the old capitalist countries, intensifying and complicating the struggle for markets.

It means, lastly, that the war left the majority of capitalist countries a burdensome heritage in the shape of *enterprises chronically working under capacity* and of *an army unemployed numbering millions*, which has been transformed from a reserve into a *permanent army of unemployed*; this created for capitalism a mass of difficulties even before the present economic crisis.

Such are the circumstances which intensify and aggravate the world economic crisis.

It must be admitted that the present economic crisis is the gravest and most profound world economic crisis that has ever occurred.

2. THE INTENSIFICATION OF THE CONTRADICTIONS OF CAPITALISM

A most important result of the world economic crisis is that it is laying bare and intensifying the contradictions inherent in world capitalism.

a) It is laying bare and intensifying the *contradictions between the major imperialist countries*, the struggle for markets, the struggle for raw materials, the struggle for the export of capital. None of the capitalist states is now satisfied with the old distribution of spheres of influence and colonies. They see that the relation of forces has changed and that it is necessary in accordance with it to redivide markets, sources of raw materials, spheres of influence, and so forth. The chief contradiction here is that between the United States and Britain. Both in the sphere of the export of manufactured goods and in the sphere of the export of capital, the struggle is raging chiefly between the United States and Britain. It is enough to read any journal dealing with economics, any document concerning exports of goods and capital, to be convinced of this. The principal arena of the struggle is South America, China, the colonies and dominions of the old imperialist states. Superiority of forces in this struggle—and a definite superiority—is on the side of the United States.

After the chief contradictions come contradictions which, while not the chief ones, are, however, fairly important; between America and Japan, between Germany and France, between France and Italy, between Britain and France, and so forth.

There can be no doubt whatever that owing to the developing crisis, the struggle for markets, for raw materials and for the export of capital will grow more intense month by month and day by day.

Means of struggle: Tariff policy, cheap goods, cheap credits, regrouping of forces and new military-political alliances, growth of armaments and preparation for new imperialist wars, and finally—war.

I have spoken about the crisis embracing all branches of production. There is one branch, however, that has not been affected by the crisis. That branch is the armament industry. It is growing continuously, notwithstanding the crisis. The bourgeois states are furiously arming and rearming. What for? Not for friendly chats, of course, but for war. And the imperialists need war, for it is the only means by which to redivide the world, to redivide markets, sources of raw materials and spheres for the investment of capital.

It is quite understandable that in this situation so-called pacifism is living its last days, that the League of Nations is rotting alive, that "disarmament schemes" come to nothing, while conferences for the reduction of naval armaments become transformed into conferences for renewing and enlarging navies.

This means that the danger of war will grow at an accelerated pace.

Let the Social-Democrats chatter about pacifism, peace, the peaceful development of capitalism, and so forth. The experience of Social-Democrats being in power in Germany and Britain shows that for them pacifism is only a screen needed to conceal the preparation for new wars.

b) It is laying bare and will intensify the *contradictions between the victor countries and the vanquished countries*. Among the latter I have in mind chiefly Germany. Undoubtedly, in view of the crisis and the aggravation of the problem of markets, increased pressure will be brought to bear upon Germany, which is not only a debtor, but also a very big exporting country. The peculiar relations that have developed between the victor countries and Germany could be depicted in the form of a pyramid at the apex of which America, France, Britain and the others are seated in lordly fashion, holding in their hands the Young Plan with the inscription: "Pay up!"; while underneath lies Germany, flattened out, exhausting herself and compelled to exert all her efforts to obey the order to pay thousands of millions in indemnities. You wish to know what this is? It is "the spirit of Locarno". To think that such a situation will have no effect upon world capitalism means not to understand anything in life. To think that the German bourgeoisie will be able to pay 20,000 millions marks within the next ten years and that the German proletariat, which is living under the double yoke of "its own" and the "foreign" bourgeoisie, will allow the German bourgeoisie to squeeze these 20,000 million marks out of it without serious battles and convulsions, means to go out of one's mind. Let the German and French politicians pretend that they believe in this miracle. We Bolsheviks do not believe in miracles.

c) It is laying bare and intensifying the *contradictions between the imperialist states and the colonial and dependent countries*. The growing economic crisis cannot but increase the pressure of the imperialists upon the colonies and dependent countries, which are the chief markets for goods and sources of raw materials. Indeed, this pressure is increasing to the utmost degree. It is a fact that the European bourgeoisie is now in a state of war with "its" colonies in India, Indochina, Indonesia and North Africa. It is a fact that "independent" China is already virtually partitioned into spheres of influence, while the cliques of counterrevolutionary Kuomintang generals, warring among themselves and ruining the Chinese people, are obeying the will of their masters in the imperialist camp.

The mendacious story that officials of the Russian embassies in China are to blame for the disturbance of "peace and order" in China must now be regarded as having been utterly exposed. There have been no Russian embassies for a long time in either South or Central China. On the other hand, there are German, British and Japanese military advisers with the warring Chinese generals. There have been no Russian embassies there for a long time. On the other hand, there are British, American, German, Czechoslovak and all sorts of other guns, rifles, aircraft, tanks and poison gases. Well? Instead of "peace and order" a most unrestrained and most devastating war of the generals, financed and instructed by the "civilized" states of Europe and America, is now raging in South and Central China. We get a rather piquant picture of the "civilizing" activities of the capitalist states. What we do not understand is merely: What have the Russian Bolsheviks to do with it?

It would be ridiculous to think that these outrages will be without consequences for the imperialists. The Chinese workers and peasants have already retaliated to them by forming Soviets and a Red Army. It is said that a Soviet government has already been set up there. I think that if this is true, there is nothing surprising about it. There can be no doubt that only Soviets can save China from utter collapse and pauperization.

As regards India, Indochina, Indonesia, Africa, etc., the growth of the revolutionary movement in those countries, which at times assumes the form of a national war for liberation, leaves no room for doubt. Messieurs the bourgeoisie count on flooding those countries with blood and on relying on police bayonets, calling people like Gandhi to their assistance. There can be no doubt that police bayonets make a poor prop. Tsarism, in its day, also tried to rely on police bayonets, but everybody knows what kind of prop they turned out to be. As regards assistants of the Gandhi type, tsarism had a whole herd of them in the shape of liberal compromisers of every kind, but nothing came of this except discomfiture.

d) It is laying bare and intensifying the *contradictions between the bourgeoisie and the proletariat* in the capitalist countries. The crisis has already increased the pressure exerted by the capitalists on the working class. The crisis has already given rise to another wave of capitalist rationalization, to a further deterioration of the conditions of the working class, to increased unemployment, to an enlargement of the permanent army of the unemployed, to a reduction of wages. It is not surprising that these circumstances are revolutionizing the situation, intensifying the class struggle and pushing the workers towards new class battles.

As a result of this, Social-Democratic illusions among the masses of workers are being shattered and dispelled. After the experience of Social-Democrats being in power, when they broke strikes, organized lockouts and shot down workers, the false promises of "industrial democracy", "peace in industry", and "peaceful methods" of struggle sound like cruel mockery to the workers. Will many workers be found today capable of believing the false doctrines of the social-fascists? The well known workers' demonstrations of 1 August 1929 (against the war danger) and of 6 March 1930 (against unemployment) show that the best members of the working class have already turned away from the social-fascists. The economic crisis will strike a fresh blow at Social-Democratic illusions among the workers. Not many workers will be found now, after the bankruptcies and ruination caused by the crisis, who believe that it is possible for "every worker" to become rich by holding shares in "democratized" joint-stock companies. Needless to say, the crisis will strike a crushing blow at all these and similar illusions.

The desertion of the masses of the workers from the Social-Democrats, however, signifies a turn on their part towards communism. That is what is actually taking place. The growth of the trade-union movement that is associated with the Communist Party, the electoral successes of the Communist Parties, the wave of strikes which the Communists are taking a leading part, the development of economic strikes into political protests organized by the Communists, the mass demonstrations of workers who sympathize with communism, which are meeting a lively response in the working class—all this shows that the masses of the workers regard the Communist Party as the only party capable of fighting capitalism, the only party worthy of the workers' confidence, the only party under whose leadership it is possible to enter, and worthwhile entering, the struggle for emancipation from capitalism. This means that the masses are turning to communism. It is the guarantee that our fraternal Communist Parties will become big mass parties of the working class. All that is necessary is that the Communists should be capable of appraising the situation and making proper use of it. By developing an uncompromising struggle against Social-Democracy, which is capital's agency in the working class, and by reducing to dust all and sundry deviations from Leninism, which bring grist to the mill of Social-Democracy, the Communist Parties have shown that they are on the right road. They must definitely fortify themselves on this road; for only if they do that can they count on winning over the majority of the working class and successfully prepare the proletariat for the coming class battles. Only if they do that can we count on a further increase in the influence and prestige of the Communist International.

Such is the state of the principal contradictions of world capitalism, which have become intensified to the utmost by the world economic crisis.

What do all these facts show?

That the stabilization of capitalism is coming to an end.

That the upsurge of the mass revolutionary movement will increase with fresh vigor.

That in a number of countries the world economic crisis will grow into a political crisis.

This means, firstly, that the bourgeoisie will seek a way out of the situation through further fascization in the sphere of domestic policy, and will utilize all the reactionary forces, including Social-Democracy, for this purpose.

It means, secondly, that in the sphere of foreign policy the bourgeoisie will seek a way out through a new imperialist war.

It means, lastly, that the proletariat, in fighting capitalist exploitation and the war danger, will seek a way out through revolution.

3. THE RELATIONS BETWEEN THE USSR AND THE CAPITALIST STATES

a) I have spoken above about the contradictions of world capitalism. In addition to these, however, there is one other contradiction. I am referring to the contradiction between the capitalist world and the USSR. True, this contradiction must not be regarded as being of the same order as the contradiction *within capitalism*. It is a contradiction between capitalism as a whole and the country that is building socialism. This, however, does not prevent it from corroding and shaking the very foundations of capitalism. More than that, it lays bare all the contradictions of capitalism to the roots and gathers them into a single knot, transforming them into an issue of the life and death of the capitalist order itself. That is why, every time the contradictions of capitalism become acute, the bourgeoisie turns its gaze towards the USSR, wondering whether it would not be possible to solve this or that contradiction of capitalism, or all the contradictions together, at the expense of the USSR, of that Land of Soviets, that citadel of revolution which, but its very existence, is revolutionizing the working class and the colonies, which is hindering the organization of a new war, hindering a new redivision of the world, hindering the capitalists from lording it in its extensive home market which they need so much, especially now, in view of the economic crisis.

Hence the tendency towards adventurist attacks on the USSR and towards intervention, a tendency which will certainly grow owing to the development of the economic crisis.

The most striking expression of this tendency at the present time is present-day bourgeois France, the birthplace of the philanthropic "Pan-Europe" scheme, the "cradle" of the Kellogg

Pact, the most aggressive and militarist of all the aggressive and militarist countries in the world.

But intervention is a two-edged sword. The bourgeoisie knows this perfectly well. It will be all right, it thinks, if intervention goes off smoothly and ends in the defeat of the USSR. But what if it ends in the defeat of the capitalists? There was intervention once and it ended in failure. If the first intervention, when the Bolsheviks were weak, ended in failure, what guarantee is there that the second will not end in failure too? Everybody sees that the Bolsheviks are far stronger now, both economically and politically, and as regards preparedness for the country's defense. And what about the workers in the capitalist countries, who will not permit intervention in the USSR, who will fight intervention and, if anything happens, may attack the capitalists in the rear? Would it not be better to proceed along the line of increasing trade connections with the USSR, to which the Bolsheviks do not object?

Hence the tendency towards continuing peaceful relations with the USSR.

Thus, we have two sets of factors, and two different tendencies operating in opposite directions:

1. The policy of disrupting economic connections between the USSR and the capitalist countries; provocative attacks upon the USSR; open and secret activities in preparation for intervention against the USSR. These are the factors that menace the USSR's international position. It is the operation of these factors that explains such facts as the rupture of relations with the USSR by the British Conservative Cabinet; the seizure of the Chinese Eastern Railway by the Chinese militarists; the financial blockade of the USSR; the clerical "crusade", headed by the Pope, against the USSR; the organization by agents of foreign states of wrecking activities on the part of our specialists; the organization of explosions and incendiarism, such as were carried out by certain employees of the "Lena Gold-Fields"; attempts on the lives of representatives of the USSR (Poland); finding fault with our exports (United States, Poland), and so forth.

2. Sympathy towards and support of the USSR on the part of the workers in capitalist countries; growth of the economic and political might of the USSR; increase in the USSR's defense capacity; the peace policy undeviatingly pursued by the Soviet government. These are the factors that strengthen the USSR's international position. It is the operation of these factors that explains such facts as the successful settlement of the dispute over the Chinese Eastern Railway, the restoration of relations with Britain, the growth of economic connections with capitalist countries, and so forth.

It is the conflict between these factors that determines the USSR's external situation.

b) It is said that the stumbling block to the improvement of economic relations between the USSR and the bourgeois states is the question of the debts. I think that this is not an argument in favor of paying the debts, but a pretext advanced by the aggressive elements for interventionist propaganda. Our policy in this field is clear and well-grounded. On condition that we are granted credits, we are willing to pay a small part of the prewar debts, regarding them as additional interest on the credits. Without this condition we cannot and must not pay. Is more demanded of us? On what grounds? Is it not well known that these debts were contracted by the tsarist government, which was overthrown by the Revolution, and for whose obligations the Soviet Government can take no responsibility? There is talk about international law, about international obligations. But on the grounds of what international obligations did Messieurs the "Allies" sever Bessarabia from the USSR and hand it over to enslavement under the Rumanian boyars? On the grounds of what international obligations did the capitalists and governments of France, Britain, America and Japan attack the USSR, invade it, and for three whole years plunder it and ruin its inhabitants? If this is what is called international law and international obligations, then what will you call robbery? (*Laughter. Applause.*) Is it not obvious that by committing these predatory acts Messieurs the "Allies" have deprived themselves of the right to appeal to international law, to international obligations?

It is said, further, that the establishment of "normal" relations is hindered by the propaganda conducted by the Russian Bolsheviks. With the object of preventing the pernicious effects of propaganda, Messieurs the bourgeoisie every now and again fence themselves off with "cordons" and "barbed-wire fences" and graciously bestow the honor of guarding these "fences" upon Poland, Rumania, Finland and others. It is said that Germany is burning with envy because she is not being permitted to guard the "cordons" and "barbed-wire fences". Does it need to be proved that the chatter about propaganda is not argument against establishing "normal relations", but a pretext for interventionist propaganda? How can people who do not want to appear ridiculous "fence themselves off" from the ideas of Bolshevism if in their own country there exists favorable soil for these ideas? Tsarism in its time also "fenced itself off" from Bolshevism, but, as is well known, the "fence" proved to be useless. It proved to be useless because Bolshevism everywhere does not penetrate from outside, but grows within the country. There are no countries, one would think, more "fenced-off" from the Russian Bolsheviks than China, India and Indochina. But what do we find? Bolshevism is growing in those countries, and will continue to grow, in spite of all "cordons", because, evidently, there are conditions there that are favorable for Bolshevism. What has the propaganda of the Russian Bolsheviks to do with it?

If Messieurs the capitalists could somehow "fence themselves off" from the economic crisis, from mass poverty, from unemployment, from low wages and from the exploitation of labor, it would be another matter; then there would be no Bolshevik movement in their countries. But the whole point is that every rascal tries to justify his weakness or impotence by pleading Russian Bolshevik propaganda.

It is said, further, that another stumbling block is our Soviet system, collectivization, the fight against the kulaks, antireligious propaganda, the fight against wreckers and counter-revolutionaries among "men of science", the banishment of the Besedovskys, Solomons, Dmitrievskys, and other lackeys of capital. But this is becoming quite amusing. It appears that they don't like the Soviet system. But we don't like the capitalist system. (*Laughter. Applause.*) We don't like the fact that in their countries tens of millions of unemployed are compelled to suffer poverty and starvation, while a small group of capitalists own wealth amounting to billions. Since, however, we have agreed not to intervene in the internal affairs of other countries, is it not obvious that it is not worthwhile reverting to this question? Collectivization, the fight against the kulaks, the fight against wreckers, antireligious propaganda, and so forth, are the inalienable right of the workers and peasants of the USSR, sealed by our Constitution. We must and shall implement the Constitution of the USSR, with complete consistency. Naturally, therefore, whoever refuses to reckon with our Constitution can pass on, can go wherever he pleases. As for the Besedovskys, Solomons, Dmitrievskys and so forth, we shall continue to throw out such people like defective goods that are useless and harmful for the Revolution. Let them be made heroes of by those who have a special predilection for offal. (*Laughter.*) The millstones of our Revolution grind exceedingly well. They take all that is useful and give it to the Soviets and cast aside the offal. It is said that in France, among the Parisian bourgeois, there is a big demand for these defective goods. Well, let them import them to their heart's content. True, this will overburden somewhat the import side of France's balance of trade, against which Messieurs the bourgeoisie always protest, but that is their business. Let us not intervene in the internal affairs of France. (*Laughter. Applause.*)

That is how the matter stands with the "obstacles" that hinder the establishment of "normal" relations between the USSR and other countries.

It turns out that these "obstacles" are fictitious "obstacles" raised as a pretext of antiSoviet propaganda.

Our policy is a policy of peace and of increasing trade connections with all countries. A result of this policy is an improvement in our relations with a number of countries and the conclusion of a number of agreements for trade, technical assistance, and so forth. Another result is the USSR's adherence to the Kellogg Pact, the signing of the well known protocol along the lines of the Kellogg Pact with Poland, Rumania, Lithuania, and other countries, the signing of the protocol on the prolongation of the treaty of friendship and neutrality with Turkey. And lastly, a result of this policy is the fact that we have succeeded in maintaining peace, in not allowing our enemies to draw us into conflicts, in spite of a number of provocative acts and adventurist attacks on the part of the warmongers. We shall continue to pursue this policy of peace with all our might and with all the means at our disposal. We do not want a single foot of foreign territory; but of our territory we shall not surrender a single inch to anyone. (*Applause.*)

Such is our foreign policy.

The task is to continue this policy with all the perseverance characteristic of Bolsheviks.

II
THE INCREASING ADVANCE OF SOCIALIST CONSTRUCTION AND THE INTERNAL SITUATION IN THE USSR

Let us pass to the internal situation in the USSR.

In contrast to the capitalist countries, where an economic *crisis* and *growing unemployment* reign, the internal situation in our country presents a picture of *increasing advance* of the national economy and of *progressive diminution* of unemployment. Large-scale industry has grown up, and the rate of its development has increased. Heavy industry has become firmly established. The socialist sector of industry has made great headway. A new force has arisen in agriculture—the state and collective farms. Whereas a year or two ago we had a crisis in grain production, and in our grain-procurement operations we depended mainly on individual farming, now the center of gravity has shifted to the collective and state farms, and the grain crisis can be regarded as having been, in the main, solved. The main mass of the peasantry has definitely turned towards the collective farms. The resistance of the kulaks has been broken. The internal situation in the USSR has been still further consolidated.

Such is the general picture of the internal situation in the USSR at the present time.

Let us examine the concrete facts.

1. THE GROWTH OF THE NATIONAL ECONOMY AS A WHOLE

a) In 1926/27, i.e., at the time of the Fifteenth Congress of the Party, the gross output of *agriculture as a whole*, including forestry, fishing, etc., amounted in prewar rubles to 12,370,000,000 rubles, i.e., 106.6 percent of the prewar level. In the following year, however, i.e., in 1927/28, it was 107.2 percent, in 1928/29 it was 109.1 percent, and this year, 1929/30, judging by the course development of agriculture, it will be not less than 113-114 percent of the prewar level.

Thus we have a steady, although relatively slow, increase in agricultural production as a whole.

In 1926/27, i.e., at the time of the Fifteenth Congress of the Party, the gross output of *industry as a whole*, both small and large scale, including flour milling, amounted in prewar rubles to 8,641,000,000 rubles, i.e., 102.5 percent of the prewar level. In the following year, however, i.e., 1927/28, it was 122 percent, in 1928/29 it was 142.5 percent, and this year, 1929/30, judging by the course of industrial development, it will be not less than 180 percent of the prewar level.

Thus we have an unprecedented rapid growth of industry as a whole.

b) In 1926/27, i.e., at the time of the Fifteenth Congress of the Party, *freight turnover* on our entire *railway system* amounted to 81,700,000,000 ton-kilometers, i.e., 127 percent of the prewar level. In the following year, however, i.e., 1927/28, it was 134.2 percent, in

1928/29 it was 162.4 percent, and this year, 1929/30, it, by all accounts, will be not less than 193 percent of the prewar level. As regards new railway construction, in the period under review, i.e., counting from 1927/28, the railway system has grown from 76,000 kilometers to 80,000 kilometers, which is 136.7 percent of the prewar level.

c) If we take the *trade turnover* (*wholesale and retail*) in the country in 1926/27 as 100 (31,000,000,000 rubles), then the volume of trade in 1927/28 shows an increase to 124.6 percent, that in 1928/29 to 160.4 percent, and this year, 1929/30, the volume of trade will, by all accounts, reach 202 percent, i.e., double that of 1926/27.

d) If we take the *combined balances* of all our *credit institutions* on 1 October 1927 as 100 (9,173,000,000 rubles), then on 1 October 1928, there was an increase to 141 percent, and on 1 October 1929, an increase to 201.1 percent, i.e., an amount double that of 1927.

e) If the *combined state budget* for 1926/27 is taken as 100 (6,371,000,000 rubles) that for 1927/28 shows an increase to 125.5 percent, that for 1928/29 an increase to 146.7 percent, and that for 1929/30 to 204.4 percent, i.e., double the budget for 1926/27 (12,605,000,000 rubles).

f) In 1926/27, our *foreign trade turnover* (exports and imports) was 47.9 percent of the prewar level. In 1927/28, however, our foreign trade turnover rose to 56.8 percent, in 1928/29 to 67.9 percent, and in 1929/30 it, by all accounts, will be not less than 80 percent of the prewar level.

g) As a result, we have the following picture of the growth of the total *national income* during the period under review (in 1926/27 prices): In 1926/27, the national income, according to the data of the State Planning Commission, amounted to 23,127,000,000 rubles; in 1927/28 it amounted to 25,396,000,000 rubles—an increase of 9.8 percent; in 1928/29 it amounted to 28,596,000,000 rubles—an increase of 12.6 percent; in 1929/30 the national income ought, by all accounts, to amount to not less than 34,000,000,000 rubles, thus showing an increase for the year of 20 percent. The average annual increase during the three years under review is, therefore, over 15 percent.

Bearing in mind that the average annual increase in the national income in countries like the United States, Britain and Germany amounts to more than 3-8 percent. It must be admitted that the rate of increase of the national income of the USSR is truly a *record* one.

2. SUCCESSES IN INDUSTRIALIZATION

Our national economy is growing not spontaneously, but in a definite direction, namely, in the direction of industrialization; its keynote is: Industrialization, growth of the relative importance of industry in the general system of the national economy, transformation of our country from an agrarian into an industrial country.

a) The dynamics of the relation between industry as a whole and agriculture as a whole from the point of view of the relative importance of industry in the *gross* output of the entire national economy during the period under review takes the following form: In prewar times, industry's share of the gross output of the national economy was 42.1 percent and that of agriculture 57.9 percent; in 1927/28 industry's share was 45.2 percent and that of agriculture 54.8 percent; in 1928/29 industry's share was 48.7 percent and that of agriculture 51.3 percent; in 1929/30 industry's share ought to, by all accounts, be not less than 53 percent and that of agriculture not more than 47 percent.

This means that the relative importance of industry is already beginning to surpass the relative importance of agriculture in the general system of national economy, and that we are on the eve of the transformation of our country from an *agrarian* into an *industrial* country. (*Applause.*)

b) There is a still more marked preponderance in favor of industry when regarded from the viewpoint of its relative importance in the commodity output of the national economy. In 1926/27, industry's share of the total commodity output of the national economy was 68.8

percent and that of agriculture 31.2 percent. In 1927/28, however, industry's share was 71.2 percent and that of agriculture 28.8 percent; in 1928/29 industry's share was 72.4 percent and that of agriculture 27.6 percent, and in 1929/30, industry's share will, by all accounts, be 76 percent and that of agriculture 24 percent.

This particularly unfavorable position of agriculture is due, among other things, to its character as small-peasant and small-commodity agriculture. Naturally, this situation should change to a certain extent as large-scale agriculture develops through the state and collective farms and produces more for the market.

c) The development of industry in general, however, does not give a complete picture of the rate of industrialization. To obtain a complete picture we must also ascertain the dynamics of the relation between heavy and light industry. Hence, the most striking index of the growth of industrialization must be considered to be the progressive growth of the relative importance of the output of *instruments and means of production* (heavy industry) in the total industrial output. In 1927/28, the share of output of instruments and means of production in the total output of *all* industry amounted to 27.2 percent while that of the output of consumer goods was 72.8 percent. In 1928/29, however, the share of the output of instruments and means of production amounted to 28.7 percent as against 71.3 percent, and in 1929/30, the share of the output of instruments and means of production, will, by all accounts, already amount to 32.7 percent as against 67.3 percent.

If, however, we take not all industry, but *only* that part which is planned by the Supreme Council of the National Economy, and which embraces all the main branches of industry, the relation between the output of instruments and means of production and the output of consumer goods will present a still more favorable picture, namely: In 1927/28, the share of the output of instruments and means of production amounted to 42.7 percent as against 57.3 percent; in 1928/29—44.6 percent as against 55.4 percent, and in 1929/30, it will, by all accounts, amount to not less than 48 percent as against 52 percent for the output of consumer goods.

The keynote of the development of our national economy is industrialization, the strengthening and development of our own heavy industry.

This means that we have already established and are further developing our heavy industry, the basis of our economic independence.

3. THE KEY POSITION OF SOCIALIST INDUSTRY AND ITS RATE OF GROWTH

The keynote of the development of our national economy is industrialization. But we do not need just any kind of industrialization. We need the kind of industrialization that will ensure the growing preponderance of the *socialist forms of industry* over the *small-*commodity and, still more, over the *capitalist* forms of industry. The characteristic feature of our industrialization is that it is *socialist* industrialization, an industrialization which guarantees the victory of the *socialized* sector of industry over the *private* sector, over the small-commodity and capitalist sector.

Here are some data on the growth of capital investments and of gross output according to sectors:

a) Taking the growth of *capital investments* in industry according to sectors, we get the following picture. *Socialized sector*: In 1926/27—1,270,000,000 rubles; in 1927/28—1,614,000,000 rubles; in 1928/29—2,046,000,000 rubles; in 1929/30—4,275,000,000 rubles. *Private and capitalist sector*: In 1926/27—63,000,000 rubles; in 1927/28—64,000,000 rubles; in 1928/29—56,000,000 rubles; 1929/30—51,000,000 rubles.

This means, firstly, that during this period capital investments in the socialized sector of industry have more than *trebled* (335 percent).

It means, secondly, that during this period capital investments in the private and capitalist sector have been *reduced* by *one-fifth* (81 percent).

The private and capitalist sector is living on its old capital and is moving towards its doom.

b) Taking the growth of *gross output* of industry according to sectors we get the following picture. *Socialized sector*: In 1926/27—11,999,000,000 rubles; in 1927/28—15,389,000,000 rubles; in 1928/29—18,903,000,000 rubles; 1929/30—24,740,000,000 rubles. *Private and capitalist sector*: In 1926/27-4,043,000,000 rubles; in 1927/28—3,704,000,000 rubles; 1928/29—3,389,000,000 rubles; in 1929/30—3,310,000,000 rubles.

This means, firstly, that during the three years, the gross output of the socialized sector of industry more than *doubled* (206.2 percent).

It means, secondly, that in the same period the gross industrial output of the private and capitalist sector was *reduced* by nearly *one-fifth* (81.9 percent).

If, however, we take the output not of all industry, but only of *large-scale* (statistically registered) industry and examine it according to sectors, we get the following picture of the relation between the socialized and private sectors. Relative importance of the socialized sector in the output of the country's large-scale industry: 1926/27—97.7 percent; 1927/28—98,6 percent; 1928/29—99.1 percent; 1929/30—99.3 percent. Relative importance of the private sector in the output of the country's large-scale industry: 1926/27—2.3 percent; 1927/28—1.4 percent; 1928/29—0.9 percent; 1929/30—0.7 percent.

As you see, the capitalist elements in large-scale industry have already gone to the bottom.

Clearly, the question "who will beat whom", the question whether socialism will defeat the capitalist elements in industry, or whether the latter will defeat socialism, has already been settled in favor of the socialist forms of industry. Settled finally and irrevocably. (*Applause.*)

c) Particularly interesting are the data on the *rate of development* during the period under review of *state* industry that is planned by the Supreme Council of the National Economy. If the 1926/27 gross output of socialist industry planned by the Supreme Council of the National Economy is taken as 100, the 1927/28 gross output of that industry shows a rise to 127.4 percent, that of 1928/29 to 158.6 percent and that of 1929/30 will show a rise to 209.8 percent.

This means that socialist industry planned by the Supreme Council of the National Economy, comprising all the main branches of industry and the whole of heavy industry, has *more than doubled* during the three years.

It cannot but be admitted that no other country in the world can show such a terrific rate of development of its large-scale industry.

This circumstance gives us grounds for speaking of the five year plan in four years.

d) Some comrades are sceptical about the slogan "the five year plan in four years". Only very recently one section of comrades regarded our five year plan, which was endorsed by the Fifth Congress of Soviets, as fantastic; not to mention the bourgeois writers whose eyes pop out of their heads at the very words "five year plan". But what is the actual situation if we consider the fulfillment of the five year plan during the first two years? What does checking the fulfillment of the optimal variant of the five year plan tell us? It tells us not only that we can carry out the five year plan in four years, it also tells us that in a number of branches of industry we can carry it out in three and even in two-and-a-half years. This may sound incredible to the sceptics in the opportunist camp, but it is a fact which it would be foolish and ridiculous to deny.

Judge for yourselves.

According to the five year plan, the output of the oil industry in 1932/33 was to amount to 977,000,000 rubles. Actually, its output already in 1929/30 amounts to 809,000,000 rubles, i.e., 83 percent of the amount fixed in the five year plan for 1932/33. Thus, we are fulfilling the five year plan for the oil industry in a matter of two-and-a-half years.

The output of the peat industry in 1932/33, according to the five year plan, was to amount to 122,000,000 rubles. Actually, in 1929/30 already its output amounts to over 115,000,000 rubles, i.e., 96 percent of the output fixed in the five year plan for 1932/33. Thus, we are fulfilling the five year plan for the peat industry in two-and-a-half years, if not sooner.

According to the five year plan, the output of the *general machine-building industry* in 1932/33 was to amount to 2,058,000,000 rubles. Actually, in 1929/30 already its output amounts to 1,458,000,000 rubles, i.e., 70 percent of the output fixed in the five year plan for 1932/33. Thus, we are fulfilling the five year plan for the general machine-building industry in two-and-a-half to three years.

According to the five year plan, the output of the agricultural machine-building industry in 1932/33 was to amount to 610,000,000 rubles. Actually, in 1929/30 already its output amounts to 400,000,000 rubles, i.e., over 60 percent of the amount fixed in the five year plan for 193233. Thus, we are fulfilling the five year plan for the agricultural machine-building industry in three years, if not sooner.

According to the five year plan, the output of the *electrotechnical industry* in 1932/33 was to amount to 896,000,000 rubles. Actually, in 1929/30 already it amounts to 503,000,000 rubles, i.e., over 56 percent of the amount fixed in the five year plan for 1932/33. Thus, we are fulfilling the five year plan for the electrotechnical industry in three years.

Such are the unprecedented rates of development of our socialist industries.

We are going forward at an accelerated pace, technically and economically overtaking the advanced capitalist countries.

c) This does not mean, of course, that we have already overtaken them as regards size of output, that our industry has already reached the *level* of the development of industry in the advanced capitalist countries. No, this is far from being the case. The *rate* of industrial development must not be confused with the *level* of industrial development. Many people in our country confuse the two and believe that since we have achieved an unprecedented rate of industrial development we have thereby reached the level of industrial development of the advanced capitalist countries. But that is radically wrong.

Take, for example, the production of electricity, in regard to which our rate of development is very high. From 1924 to 1929 we achieved an increase in the output of electricity to nearly 600 percent of the 1924 figure, whereas in the same period the output of electricity in the United States increased only to 181 percent, in Canada to 218 percent, in Germany to 241 percent and in Italy to 222 percent. As you see, our rate is truly unprecedented and exceeds that of all other states. But if we take the level of development of electricity production in those countries, in 1929, for example, and compare it with the level of development in the USSR, we shall get a picture that is far from comforting for the USSR. Notwithstanding the unprecedented rate of development of electricity production in the USSR, in 1929 output amounted to only 6,465,000,000 kilowatt-hours, whereas that of the United States amounted to 126,000,000,000 kilowatt-hours, Canada 17,628,000,000 kilowatt-hours, Germany 33,000,000,000 kilowatt-hours, and Italy 10,850,000,000 kilowatt-hours.

The difference, as you see, is colossal.

It follows, then, that as regards level of development we are behind all these states.

Or take, for example, our output of pig-iron. If our output of pig-iron for 1926/27 is taken as 100 (2,900,000 tons), the output for the three years from 1927/28 to 1929/30 shows an increase to almost *double*, to 190 percent (5,500,000 tons). The rate of development, as you see, is fairly high. But if we look at it from the point of view of the level of development of pig-iron production in our country and compare the size of the output in the USSR with that in the advanced capitalist countries, the result is not very comforting. To begin with, we are reaching and shall exceed the prewar level of pig-iron production only this year, 1929/30. This alone drives us to the inexorable conclusion that unless we still further accelerate the development of our metallurgical industry we run the risk of jeopardizing our entire industrial production. As regards the level of development of the pig-iron industry in our country and in the West, we have the following picture: The output of pig-iron in 1929 in the United States amounted to 42,300,00 tons; in Germany—13,400,000 tons; in France—10,450,000 tons; in Great Britain—7,700,000 tons; but in the USSR the output of pig-iron at the end of 1929/30 will amount to only 5,500,000 tons.

No small difference, as you see.

It follows, therefore, that as regards level of development of pig-iron production we are behind all these countries.

What does all this show?

It shows that:

1) the rate of development of industry *must not be confused* with its level of development;

2) we are damnably *behind* the advanced capitalist countries as regards level of development of industry;

3) only the *further acceleration* of the development of our industry will enable us to overtake and outstrip the advanced capitalist countries technically and economically;

4) people who talk about the necessity of *reducing* the rate of development of our industry are enemies of socialism, agents of our class enemies. (*Applause.*)

4. AGRICULTURE AND THE GRAIN PROBLEM

Above I spoke about the state of agriculture as a whole, including forestry, fishing, etc., without dividing agriculture into its main branches. If we separate agriculture as a whole into its main branches, such as, for example, grain production, livestock farming and the production of industrial crops, the situation, according to the data of the State Planning Commission and the People's Commissariat for Agriculture of the USSR is seen to be as follows:

a) If the *grain crop* area in 1913 is taken as 100, we get the following picture of the change of the grain crop area from year to year: 1926/27—96.9 percent; 1927/28—94.7 percent; 1928/29—98.2 percent; and this year, 1929/30, the crop area will, by all accounts, be 105.1 percent of the prewar level.

Noticeable is the drop in the grain crop area in 1927/28. This drop is to be explained not by a retrogression of grain farming such as the ignoramuses in the Right opportunist camp have been chattering about, but by the failure of the winter crop on an area of 7,700,000 hectares (20 percent of the winter crop area in the USSR).

If, further, the gross output of grain in 1913 is taken as 100, we get the following picture: 1927—91.9 percent; 1928—90.8 percent; 1929—94.4 percent, and in 1930 we shall, by all accounts, reach 110 percent of the prewar standard.

Noticeable here, too, is the drop in the gross output of grain in 1928 due to the failure of the winter crop in the Ukraine and North Caucasus.

As regards the *marketable* part of the gross output of grain (grain sold outside the rural districts), we have a still more instructive picture. If the marketable part of the grain output of 1913 is taken as 100, then the marketable output in 1927 is found to be 37 percent; in 1928—36.8 percent, in 1929—58 percent, and this year, 1930, it will, by all accounts, amount to not less than 73 percent of the prewar level.

It follows, further, that, as regards the *marketable* part of the grain output, we are still far from having reached the prewar standard and shall remain below it this year too by about 25 percent.

That is the basis of our grain difficulties, which became particularly acute in 1928.

That, too, is the basis of the grain problem.

b) The picture is approximately the same, but with more alarming figures, in the sphere of *livestock farming*.

If the number of head of livestock of all kinds in 1916 is taken as 100, we get the following picture for the respective years. In 1927 the number of horses amounted to 88.9 percent of the prewar level; large horned cattle—114.3 percent; sheep and goats—119.3 percent; pigs—111.3 percent. In 1928, horses—94.6 percent; large horned cattle—118.5 percent; sheep and goats—126 percent; pigs—126.1 percent. In 1929, horses—96.9 percent; large horned cattle—115.6 percent; sheep and goats—127.8 percent; pigs—103 percent. In 1930, horses—88.6 percent; large horned cattle—89.1 percent; sheep and goats—87.1 percent; pigs—60.1 percent of the 1916 standard.

As you see, if we take the figures for the last year into consideration, we have obvious signs of the beginning of a decline in livestock farming.

The picture is still less comforting from the standpoint of the *marketable output* of livestock farming, particularly as regards meat and pork fat. If we take the gross output of meat and pork fat for each year as 100, the marketable output of these two items will be: In 1926—33.4 percent; in 1927—32.9 percent; in 1928—30.4 percent; in 1930—29.2 percent.

Thus we have obvious signs of the instability and economic unreliability of small livestock farming which produces little for the market.

It follows that instead of exceeding the 1916 standard in livestock farming we have in the past year obvious signs of a drop below this standard.

Thus, after the grain problem, which we are already solving in the main successfully, we are faced with the meat problem, the acuteness of which is already making itself felt, and which is still awaiting a solution.

c) A different picture is revealed by the development of *industrial* crops, which provide the raw materials for our light industry. If the industrial *crop area* in 1913 is taken as 100, we have the following: *Cotton*, in 1927—107.1 percent; in 1928—131.4 percent; in 1929—151.4 percent; in 1930—217 percent of the prewar level. *Flax*, in 1927—86.6 percent; in 1928—95.7 percent; in 1929—112.9 percent; in 1930—125 percent of the prewar level. *Sugar-beet*, in 1927—106.6 percent; in 1928—124.2 percent; in 1929—125.8 percent; in 1930—169 percent of the prewar level. *Oil crops*, in 1927—179.4 percent; in 1928—230.9 percent; in 1929—219.7 percent; in 1930—no less than 260 percent of the prewar level.

The same, in the main, favorable picture is presented by the *gross output* of industrial crops. If the gross output in 1913 is taken as 100, we get the following: *Cotton*, in 1928—110.5 percent; 1929—119 percent; in 1930 we shall have, by all accounts, 182.8 percent of the prewar level. *Flax*, in 1928—71.6 percent; in 1929—81.5 percent; in 1930 we shall have, by all accounts, 101.3 percent of the prewar level. *Sugar-beets*, in 1928—93 percent; 1929—58 percent; in 1930 we shall have, by all accounts, 139.4 percent of the prewar level. *Oil crops*, in 1928—161.9 percent; in 1929—149.8 percent; in 1930 we shall have, by all accounts, 220 percent of the prewar level.

As regards industrial crops, we thus have a more favorable picture, if we leave out of account the 1929 beet crop, which was damaged by moths.

Incidentally, here too, in the sphere of industrial crops, serious fluctuations and signs of instability are possible and probable in the future in view of the predominance of small farming, similar to the fluctuations and signs of instability that are demonstrated by the figures for flax and oil crops, which come least under the influence of the collective and state farms.

We are thus faced with the following problems in agriculture:

1) the problem of strengthening the position of industrial crops by supplying the districts concerned with sufficient quantities of cheap grain produce;

2) the problem of raising the level of livestock farming and of solving the meat question by supplying the districts concerned with sufficient quantities of cheap grain produce and fodder;

3) the problem of finally solving the question of grain farming as the chief question in agriculture at the present moment.

It follows that the grain problem is the main link in the system of agriculture and the key to the solution of all the other problems in agriculture.

It follows that the solution of the grain problem is the first in order of a number of problems in agriculture.

But solving the grain problem, and so putting agriculture on the road to really big progress, means completely doing away with the backwardness of agriculture; it means equipping it with tractors and agricultural machines, raising the productivity of labor, and increasing the output for the market. Unless these conditions are fulfilled, it is impossible even to dream of solving the grain problem.

Is it possible to fulfil all these conditions on the basis of small, individual peasant farming? No, it is impossible. It is impossible because small-peasant farming is unable to accept and master new technical equipment, it is unable to raise productivity of labor to a sufficient degree, it is unable to increase the marketable output of agriculture to a sufficient degree. There is only one way to do this, namely, by developing *large-scale* agriculture, by establishing large farms with modern technical equipment.

The Soviet country cannot, however, take the line of organizing large *capitalist* farms. It can and must take only the line of organizing large farms of a *socialist* type, equipped with modern machines. Our *state* and *collective farms* are precisely farms of this type.

Hence the task of establishing state farms and uniting the small, individual peasant farms into large collective farms, as being the *only* way to solve the problem of agriculture in general, and the grain problem in particular.

That is the line the Party took in its everyday practical work after the Fifteenth Congress, especially after the serious grain difficulties that arose in the beginning of 1928.

It should be noted that our Party raised this fundamental problem already at the Fifteenth Congress, when we were not yet experiencing serious grain difficulties. In the resolution of the Fifteenth Congress on "Work in the Countryside" it is plainly said:

"In the present period, the task of uniting and transforming the small, individual peasant farms into large collective farms must be made the Party's *principal task* in the countryside."

Perhaps it will not be superfluous also to quote the relevant passage from the Central Committee's report to the Fifteenth Congress in which the problem of doing away with the backwardness of agriculture on the basis of collectivization was just as sharply and definitely raised. Here is what was stated there:

"What is the way out? The way out is to turn the small and scattered peasant farms into large united farms based on cultivization of the land in common, to go over to collective cultivation of the land on the basis of a new and higher technique.

"The way out is to unite the small and dwarf peasant farms gradually but surely, *not by pressure, but by example and persuasion*, into large farms based on common, cooperative, collective cultivation of the land with the use of agricultural machines and tractors and scientific methods of intensive agriculture.

"There is no other way out"

5. THE TURN OF THE PEASANTRY TOWARDS SOCIALISM AND THE RATE OF DEVELOPMENT OF STATE AND COLLECTIVE FARMS

The turn of the peasantry towards collectivization did not begin all at once. Moreover, it could not begin all at once. True, the Party proclaimed the slogan of collectivization already at the Fifteenth Congress; but the proclamation of a slogan is not enough to cause the peasantry to turn en masse towards socialism. At least one more circumstance is needed for this, namely, that the masses of the peasantry themselves should be convinced that the slogan proclaimed is a correct one and that they should accept it as their own. Therefore, this turn was prepared gradually.

It was prepared by the whole course of our development, by the whole course of development of our industry, and above all the development of the industry that supplies machines and tractors for agriculture. It was prepared by the policy of resolutely fighting the kulaks and by the course of our grain procurements in the new forms that they assumed in 1928 and 1929, which placed kulak farming under the control of the poor- and middle-peasant masses. It was prepared by the development of the agricultural cooperatives, which train the individualist peasant in collective methods. It was prepared by the network of collective farms, in which the peasantry verified the advantages of collective forms of farming over individual farming. Lastly, it was prepared by the network of state farms, spread over the whole of the USSR and equipped with modern machines, which enabled the peasants to convince themselves of the potency and superiority of modern machines.

It would be a mistake to regard our state farms only as sources of grain supplies. Actually, the state farms, with their modern machines, with the assistance they render the peasants in their vicinity, and the unprecedented scope of their farming were the leading force that facilitated the turn of the peasant masses and brought them on to the path of collectivization.

There you have the basis on which arose that mass collective-farm movement of millions of poor and middle peasants which began in the latter half of 1929, and which ushered in a period of great change in the life of our country.

What measures did the Central Committee take so as to meet this movement fully equipped and to lead it?

The measures taken by the Central Committee were along three lines: The line of organizing and financing state farms; the line of organizing and financing collective farms; and lastly, the line of organizing the manufacture of tractors and agricultural machinery and of supplying the countryside with them through machine and tractor stations, through tractor columns, and so forth.

a) As early as 1928, the Political Bureau of the Central Committee adopted a decision to organize *new state farms* in the course of three or four years, calculating that by the end of this period these state farms could provide not less than 100,000,000 puds of marketable grain. Later, this decision was endorsed by a plenum of the Central Committee. The Grain Trust was organized and entrusted with the task of carrying out this decision. Parallel with this, a decision was adopted to strengthen the *old state farms* and to enlarge their crop area. The State Farm Center was organized and entrusted with the task of carrying out this decision.

I cannot help mentioning that these decisions met with a hostile reception from the opportunist section of our Party. There was talk about the money invested in the state farms being money "thrown away". There was also criticism from men of "science", supported by the opportunist elements in the Party, to the effect that it was impossible and senseless to organize large state farms. The Central Committee, however, continued to pursue its line and pursued it to the end in spite of everything.

In 1927/28, the sum of 65,700,000 rubles (not counting short-term credits for working capital) was assigned for financing the state farms. In 1928/29, the sum of 185,800,000 rubles was assigned. Lastly, this year 856,200,000 rubles have been assigned. During the period under review, 18,000 tractors with a total of 350,000 horsepower were placed at the disposal of the state farms.

What are the results of these measures?

In 1928/29, the *crop area* of the *Grain Trust* amounted to 150,000 hectares, in 1929/30 to 1,060,000 hectares, in 1930/31 it will amount to 4,500,000 hectares, in 1931/32 to 9,000,000 hectares, and in 1932/33, i.e., towards the end of the five year plan period, to 14,000,000 hectares. In 1928/29 the crop area of the *State Farm Center* amounted to 430,000 hectares, in 1929/30 to 860,000 hectares, in 1930/31 it will amount to 1,800,000 hectares, in 1931/32 2,000,000 hectares, and in 1932/33 to 2,500,000 hectares. In 1928/29, the crop area of the *Association of Ukrainian State Farms* amounted to 170,000 hectares, in 1929/30 to 280,000 hectares, in 1930/31 it will amount to 500,000 hectares and in 1932/33 to

720,000 hectares. In 1928/29, the crop area of the *Sugar Union* (grain crop) amounted to 780,000 hectares, in 1929/30 to 820,000 hectares, in 1930/31 it will amount to 860,000 hectares, in 1931/32 to 980,000 hectares, and in 1932/33 to 990,000 hectares.

This means, firstly, that at the end of the five year plan period the grain crop of the Grain Trust alone will be *as large* as that of the whole of the Argentine today. (*Applause.*)

This means, secondly, that at the end of the five year plan period, the grain crop area of all the state farms together will be 1,000,000 hectares *larger* than that of the whole of Canada today. (*Applause.*)

As regards the *gross* and *marketable* grain output of the state farms, we have the following picture of the change year by year: In 1927/28, the gross output of all the state farms amounted to 9,500,000 centners, of which marketable grain amounted to 6,400,000 centners; in 1928/29—12,800,000 centners, of which marketable grain amounted to 7,900,000 centners; in 1929/30, we shall have, according to all accounts, 28,200,000 centners, of which marketable grain will amount to 18,000,000 centners (108,000,000 puds); in 1930/31 we shall have 71,700,000 centners, of which marketable grain will amount to 61,000,000 centners (370,000,000 puds), and so on and so forth.

Such are the existing and anticipated results of our Party's state-farm policy.

According to the decision of the Political Bureau of the Central Committee of April 1928 on the organization of new state farms, we ought to receive from the new state farms not less than 100,000,000 puds of marketable grain in 1931/32. Actually, it turns out that in 1931/32 we shall already have from the new state farms alone more than 200,000,000 puds. That means the program will have been fulfilled twice over.

It follows that the people who ridiculed the decision of the Political Bureau of the Central Committee fiercely ridiculed themselves.

According to the five year plan endorsed by the Congress of Soviets, by the end of the five year plan period the state farms controlled by all organizations were to have a total crop area of 5,000,000 hectares. Actually, this year the crop area of the state farms already amounts to 3,800,000 hectares, and next year, i.e., in the third year of the five year period, their crop area will amount to 8,000,000 hectares.

This means that we shall fulfil and overfulfil the five year program of state-farm development in three years.

According to the five year plan, by the end of the five year period the gross grain output of the state farms was to amount to 54,300,000 centners. Actually, this year the gross grain output of the state farms already amounts to 28,200,000 centners, and next year it will amount to 71,700,000 centners.

This means that as regards gross grain output we shall fulfil and overfulfil the five year plan in three years.

The five year plan in three years!

Let the bourgeois scribes and their opportunist echoers chatter now about it being impossible to fulfil and overfulfil the five year plan of state-farm development in three years.

b) As regards *collective-farm* development, we have an even more favorable picture.

As early as July 1928, a plenum of the Central Committee adopted the following decision on collective-farm development:

"Undeviatingly to carry out the task set by the Fifteenth Congress 'to unite and transform the small, individual peasant farms into large collective farms,' as *voluntary associations* organized on the basis of modern technology and representing a higher form of grain farming both as regards the socialist transformation of agriculture and as regards ensuring a radical increase in its productivity and marketable output." (see resolution of the July plenum of the Central Committee on "Grain-Procurement Policy in Connection With the General Economic Situation," 1928).

Later, this decision was endorsed in the resolutions of the Sixteenth Conference of the Party and in the special resolution of the November plenum of the Central Committee, 1929, on the collective-farm movement. In the latter half of 1929, when the radical turn of the peasants towards the collective farms had become evident and when the mass of the middle peasants were joining the collective farms, the Political Bureau of the Central Committee adopted the special decision of 5 January 1930 on "The Rate of Collectivization and State Measures to Assist Collective-Farm Development".

In this resolution, the Central Committee:

1) placed on record the existence of a *mass turn of the peasantry* towards the collective farms and the possibility of overfilling the five year plan of collective-farm development in the spring of 1930;

2) placed on record the existence of the material and other conditions necessary *for replacing kulak production by collective-farm production* and, in view of this, proclaimed the necessity of passing from the policy of restricting the kulaks to the policy of eliminating the kulaks as a class;

3) laid down the prospect that already in the spring of 1930 the crop area cultivated on a socialized basis *would considerably exceed 30,000,000 hectares*;

4) divided the USSR into three groups of districts and fixed *for each of them approximate dates* for the completion, in the main, of collectivization;

5) *revised the land settlement method* in favor of the collective farms and the forms of financing agriculture, assigning for the collective farms in 1929/30 credits amounting to not less than 500,000,000 rubles;

6) refined the *artel form* of the collective-farm movement as the *main link in the collective-farm system* at the present time;

7) rebuffed the opportunist elements in the Party who were trying to retard the collective-farm movement on the plea of a shortage of machines and tractors;

8) lastly, warned Party workers against possible excesses in the collective-farm movement, and against the danger of decreeing collective-farm development from above, a danger that would involve the threat of playing at collectivization taking the place of a genuine and mass collective-farm movement.

It must be observed that this decision of the Central Committee met with a more than unfriendly reception from the opportunist elements of our Party. There was talk and whispering about the Central Committee indulging in fantasies, about it "squandering" the people's money on "nonexistent" collective farms. The Right-wing elements rubbed their hands in gleeful anticipation of "certain" failure. The Central Committee, however, steadfastly pursued its line and pursued it to the end in spite of everything, in spite of the philistine sniggering of the Rights, and in spite of the excesses and dizziness of the "Lefts".

In 1927/28, the sum of 76,000,000 rubles was assigned for financing the collective farms, in 1928/29—170,000,000 rubles, and, lastly, this year 473,000,000 rubles have been assigned. In addition, 65,000,000 rubles have been assigned for the collectivization fund. Privileges have been accorded the collective farms which have increased their financial resources by 200,000,000 rubles. The collective farms have been supplied with confiscated kulak farm property to the value of over 400,000,000 rubles. There has been supplied for use on collective-farm fields not less than 30,000 tractors of a total of 400,000 horsepower, not counting the 7,000 tractors of the Tractor Center which serve the collective farms and the assistance in the way of tractors rendered the collective farms by the state farms. This year the collective farms have been granted seed loans and seed assistance amounting to 10,000,000 centners of grain (61,000,000 puds). Lastly, direct organizational assistance has been rendered the collective farms in the setting up of machine and horse stations to a number exceeding 7,000, in which the total number of horses available for use is not less than 1,300,000.

What are the results of these measures?

The crop area of the collective farms in 1927 amounted to 800,000 hectares, in 1928—1,400,000 hectares, in 1929—4,300,000 hectares, in 1930—not less than 36,000,000 hectares, counting both spring and winter crops.

This means, firstly, that in three years the crop area of the collective farms has grown more than forty-fold. (*Applause.*)

As regards *gross* grain output and the part available for the *market*, we have the following picture. In 1927 we had from the collective farms 4,900,000 centners, of which marketable grain amounted to 2,000,000 centners; in 1928—8,400,000 centners, of which 3,600,000 centners was marketable grain; in 1929—29,100,000 centners, of which 12,700,000 centners was marketable grain; in 1930 we shall have, according to all accounts, 256,000,000 centners (1,550,000,000 puds), of which marketable grain will amount to not less than 82,000,000 centners (over 500,000,000 puds).

It must be admitted that not a single branch of our industry, which, in general, is developing at quite a rapid rate, has shown such an unprecedented rate of progress as our collective-farm development.

What do these figures show?

They show, first of all, that during three years the gross grain output of the collective farms has increased more than fifty-fold, and its marketable part more than forty-fold.

They show, secondly, that the possibility exists of our receiving from the collective farms this year *more than half* of the total marketable grain output of the country.

They show, thirdly, that henceforth, the fate of our agriculture and of its main problems will be determined not by the individual peasant farms, but by the collective and state farms.

They show, fourthly, that the process of eliminating the kulaks as a class in our country is going full steam ahead.

They show, lastly, that such economic changes have already taken place in the country as give us full grounds for asserting that we have succeeded in turning the countryside to the new path, to the path of collectivization, thereby ensuring the successful building of socialism not only in the towns, but also in the countryside.

In its decision of 5 January 1930, the Political Bureau of the Central Committee laid down for the spring of 1930 a program of 30,000,000 hectares of collective-farm crop area cultivated on a socialized basis.

Actually, we already have 36,000,000 hectares. Thus, the Central Committee's program has been overfulfilled.

It follows that the people who ridiculed the Central Committee's decision fiercely ridiculed themselves. Nor have the opportunist chatterboxes in our Party derived any benefit either from the petty-bourgeois elemental forces or from the excesses in the collective-farm movement.

According to the five year plan, by the end of the five year period we were to have a collective-farm crop area of 20,600,000 hectares. Actually, we have already this year a collective-farm crop area of 36,000,000 hectares.

This means that already in two years we shall have overfulfilled the five year plan of collective-farm development by over fifty percent. (*Applause.*)

According to the five year plan, by the end of the five year period we were to have a gross grain output from the collective farms amounting to 190,500,000 centners. Actually, already this year we shall have a gross grain output from the collective farms amounting to 256,000,000 centners.

This means that already in two years we shall have overfulfilled the five year program of collective-farm grain output by over 30 percent.

The five year plan in two years!

Let the opportunist gossips chatter now about it being impossible to fulfil and overfulfil the five year plan of collective-farm development in two years.

6. THE IMPROVEMENT IN THE MATERIAL AND CULTURAL CONDITIONS OF THE WORKERS AND PEASANTS

It follows, therefore, that the progressive growth of the socialist sector in the sphere of industry and in the sphere of agriculture is a fact about which there cannot be the slightest doubt.

What can this signify from the point of view of the material conditions of the working people?

Why? How?

Because, firstly, the growth of the socialist sector signifies, above all, a diminution of the exploiting elements in town and country, a decline in their relative importance in the national economy. And this means that the workers' and peasants' share of the national income must inevitably increase owing to the reduction of the share of the exploiting classes.

Because, secondly, with the growth of the socialized (socialist) sector, the share of the national income that has hitherto gone to feed the exploiting classes and their hangers-on, is bound henceforth to remain in production, to be used for the expansion of production, for building new factories and mills, for improving the conditions of life of the working people. And this means that the working class is bound to grow in numbers and strength, and unemployment to diminish and disappear.

Because, lastly, the growth of the socialized sector, inasmuch as it leads to an improvement in the material conditions of the working class, signifies a progressive increase in the capacity of the home market, an increase in the demand for manufactured goods on the part of the workers and peasants. And this means that the growth of the home market will outstrip the growth of industry and push it forward towards continuous expansion.

All these and similar circumstances are leading to a steady improvement in the material and cultural conditions of the workers and peasants.

a) Let us begin with the *numerical growth* of the working class and the *diminution of unemployment.*

In 1926/27, the number of wage-workers (not including unemployed) was 10,900,000. In 1927/28, however, we had 11,456,000, in 1928/29—11,997,000 and in 1929/30, we shall, by all accounts, have not less than 13,129,000. Of these, manual workers (including agricultural laborers and seasonal workers) numbered in 1926/27—7,069,000, in 1927/28—7,404,000, in 1928/29—7,758,00, in 1929/30—8,533,000. Of these, workers employed in large-scale industry (not including office employees) numbered in 1926/27—2,439,000, in 1927/28—2,632,000, in 1928/29—2,858,000, in 1929/30—3,029,000.

Thus, we have a picture of the progressive numerical growth of the working class; and whereas the number of wage-workers has increased 19.5 percent during the three years and the number of manual workers 20.7 percent, the number of industrial workers has increased 24.2 percent.

Let us pass to the question of *unemployment.* It must be said that in this sphere considerable confusion reigns both at the People's Commissariat for Labor and at the All-Union Central Council of Trade Unions.

On the one hand, according to the data of these institutions we have about a million unemployed, of whom, those to any degree skilled constitute only 14.3 percent, while about 73 percent are those engaged in so-called intellectual labor and unskilled workers; the vast majority of the latter are women and young persons not connected with industrial production.

On the other hand, according to the same data, we are suffering from a frightful shortage of skilled labor, the labor exchanges are unable to meet about 80 percent of the demands for labor by our factories and thus we are obliged hurriedly, literally as we go along, to train absolutely unskilled people and make skilled workers out of them in order to satisfy at least the minimum requirements of our factories.

Just try to find our way out of this confusion. It is clear, at all events, that these unemployed do not constitute a *reserve* and still less a *permanent* army of unemployed workers of our industry. Well? Even according to the data of the People's Commissariat for Labor it appears that in the recent period the number of unemployed has *diminished* compared with last year by over 700,000. This means that by 1 May, this year, the number of unemployed had dropped by over 42 percent.

There you have another result of the growth of the socialist sector of our national economy.

b) We get a still more striking result when we examine the matter from the point of view of the distribution of the national income according to classes. The question of the distribution of the national income according to classes is a fundamental one from the point of view of the material and cultural conditions of the workers and peasants. It is not for nothing that the bourgeois economists of Germany, Britain and the United States try to confuse this question for the benefit of the bourgeoisie by publishing, every now and again, their "absolutely objective" investigations on this subject.

According to data of the German Statistical Board, in 1929 the share of wages in Germany's national income was 70 percent, and the share of the bourgeoisie was 30 percent. According to data of the Federal Trade Commission and the National Bureau of Economic Research, the workers' share of the national income of the United States in 1923 amounted to over 54 percent and the capitalists' share to over 45 percent. Lastly, according to data of the economists Bowley and Stamp, the share of the working class in Britain's national income in 1924 amounted to a little over 50 percent.

Naturally, the results of these investigations cannot be taken on trust. This is because, apart from faults of a purely economic order, these investigations have also another kind of fault, the object of which is partly to conceal the incomes of the capitalists and to minimize them, and partly to inflate and exaggerate the incomes of the working class by including in it officials who receive huge salaries. And this is apart from the fact that these investigations often do not take into account the incomes of farmers and of rural capitalists in general.

Comrade Varga has subjected these statistics to a critical analysis. Here is the result that he obtained. It appears that the share of the workers and of the working people generally in town and country, who do not exploit the labor of others, was in Germany 55 percent of the national income, in the United States—54 percent, in Britain—45 percent; whereas the capitalists' share in Germany was 45 percent, in the United States—46 percent, and in Britain—55 percent.

That is how the matter stands in the biggest capitalist countries.

How does it stand in the USSR?

Here are the data of the State Planning Commission. It appears that:

a) The share of the *workers and working peasants, who do not exploit the labor of others*, constituted in our country, in 1927/28, 75.2 percent of the total national income (including the share of urban and rural wage-workers—33.3 percent); in 1928/29 it was 76.5 percent (including the share of urban and rural wage-workers—33.2 percent); in 1929/30 it was 77.1 percent (including the share of urban and rural wage-workers—33.5 percent).

b) The share of the *kulaks and urban capitalists* was in 1927/28 8.1 percent; in 1928/29—6.5 percent; in 1929/30—1.8 percent.

c) The share of *handicraftsmen*, the majority of whom are working people, was in 1927/28—6.5 percent; in 1928/29—5.4 percent; in 1929/30—4.4 percent.

d) The share of the *state sector*, the income of which is the income of the working class and of the working people generally, was in 1927/28—8.4 percent; in 1928/29—10 percent; in 1929/30—15.2 percent.

e) Lastly, the share of the so-called *miscellaneous* (meaning pensions) was in 1927/28—1.8 percent; in 1928/29—1.6 percent; in 1929/30—1.5 percent.

Thus, it follows that, whereas *in the advanced capitalist countries the share of the exploiting classes in the national income is* about *50* percent and even more, here, *in the USSR, the share of the exploiting classes in the national income is not more than* 2 percent.

This, properly speaking, explains the striking fact that in the United States in 1922, according to the American bourgeois writer *Denny* "one percent of estate holders owned 59 percent of the total wealth", and in Britain, in 1920-21, according to the same *Denny*, "less than two percent of the owners held 64 percent of the total wealth" (see *Denny*'s book *America Conquers Britain*).

Can such things happen in our country, in the USSR, in the Land of Soviets? Obviously, they cannot. There have long been no "owners" of this kind in the USSR, nor can there be any.

But if in the USSR, in 1929/30, only about two percent of the national income falls to the share of the exploiting classes, what happens to the rest, the bulk of the national income?

Obviously, it remains in the hands of the workers and working peasants.

There you have the source of the strength and prestige of the Soviet regime among the vast masses of the working class and peasantry.

There you have the basis of the systematic improvement in the material welfare of the workers and peasants in the USSR.

f) In the light of these decisive facts, one can quite understand the systematic increase in the real wages of the workers, the increase in the workers' social insurance budget, the increased assistance to poor- and middle-peasant farms, the increased assignments for workers' housing, for the improvement of the workers' living conditions and for mother and child care, and, as a consequence, the progressive growth of the population of the USSR and the decline in mortality, particularly in infant mortality.

It is known, for example, that the *real wages* of the workers, including social insurance and allocations from profits to the fund for improvement of the workers' living conditions, have risen to 167 percent of the prewar level. During the past three years, the workers' social insurance budget alone has grown from 980,000,000 rubles in 1927/28 to 1,400,000,000 rubles in 1929/30. The amount spent on mother and child care during the past three years (1927/28—1929/30) was 494,000,000 rubles. The amount spent on preschool education (kindergartens, playgrounds, etc.) during the same period was 204,000,000 rubles. The amount spent on workers' housing was 1,880,000,000 rubles.

This does not mean, of course, that everything necessary for an important increase in real wages has already been done, that real wages could not have been raised to a higher level. If this has not been done, it is because of the bureaucracy in our supply organizations in general, and primarily and particularly because of the bureaucracy in the consumers' cooperatives. According to the data of the State Planning Commission, in 1929/30 the socialized sector of internal trade embraced over 99 percent of wholesale trade and over 89 percent of retail trade. This means that the cooperatives are systematically ousting the private sector and are becoming the monopolists in the sphere of trade. That, of course, is good. What is bad, however, is that in a number of cases this monopoly operates to the detriment of the consumers. It appears, that in spite of the almost monopolist position they occupy in trade, the cooperatives prefer to supply the workers with more "paying" goods, which yield bigger profits (haberdashery, etc.), and avoid supplying them with less "paying", although more essential, goods for the workers (agricultural produce). As a result, the workers are obliged to satisfy about 25 percent of their requirements for agricultural produce in the private market, paying higher prices. That is apart from the fact that the cooperative apparatus is concerned most of all with its balance and is therefore reluctant to reduce retail prices in spite of the categorical instructions of the leading centers. It follows, therefore, that in this case the cooperatives function not as a socialist sector, but as a peculiar sector that is infected with a sort of Nepman spirit. The question is, does anyone need cooperatives of this sort, and what benefit do the workers derive from their monopoly if they do not carry out the function of seriously raising the workers' real wages?

If, in spite of this, real wages in our country are steadily rising from year to year, it means that our social system, our system of distribution of the national income, and our entire wages policy, are such that they are able to neutralize and make up for all defects arising from the cooperatives.

If to this circumstance we add a number of other factors, such as the increase in the role of public catering, lower rents for workers, the vast number of stipends paid to workers and workers' children, cultural services, and so forth, we may boldly say that the percentage increase of workers' wages is much greater than is indicated in the statistics of some of our institutions.

All this taken together, plus the introduction of the seven-hour day for over 830,000 industrial workers (33.5 percent), plus the introduction of the five-day work week for over a million and a half industrial workers (33.4 percent) plus the extensive network of rest homes, sanatoria and health resorts for workers, to which more than 1,700,000 workers have gone during the past three years—all this creates conditions of work and life for the working class that enable us to rear a new generation of workers who are healthy and vigorous, who are capable of raising the might of the Soviet country to the proper level and of protecting it with their lives from attacks by its enemies. (*Applause.*)

As regards assistance to the peasants, both individual and collective-farm peasants, and bearing in mind also assistance to poor peasants, this in the past three years (1927/28—1929/30) has amounted to a sum of not less than 4,000,000,000 rubles, provided in the shape of credits and assignments from the state budget. As is known, assistance in the shape of seeds alone has been granted the peasants during the past three years to the amount of not less than 154,000,000 puds.

It is not surprising that the workers and peasants in our country are living fairly well on the whole, that general mortality has dropped 36 percent, and infant mortality 42.5 percent, below the prewar level, while the *annual increase* in population in our country is about three million. (*Applause.*)

As regards the cultural conditions of the workers and peasants, in this sphere too we have some achievements, which, however, cannot under any circumstances satisfy us, as they are still small. Leaving out of account workers' clubs of all kinds, village reading rooms, libraries and abolition of illiteracy classes, which this year are being attended by 10,500,000 persons, the situation as regards cultural and educational matters is as follows. This year elementary schools are being attended by 11,638,000 pupils; secondary schools—1,945,000; industrial and technical, transport and agricultural schools and classes for training workers of ordinary skill—333,100; secondary technical and equivalent trade schools—238,700; colleges, general and technical—190,400. All this has enabled us to raise literacy in the USSR to 62.6 percent of the population, compared with 33 percent in prewar times.

The chief thing now is to pass to universal, compulsory elementary education. I say the "chief" thing, because this would be a decisive step in the cultural revolution. And it is high time we took this step, for we now possess all that is needed to organize compulsory, universal elementary education in all areas of the USSR.

Until now we have been obliged to "exercise economy in all things, even in schools" in order to "save, to restore heavy industry" (*Lenin*). During the recent period, however, we have already restored heavy industry and are developing it further. Hence, the time has arrived when we must set about fully achieving universal, compulsory elementary education.

I think that the congress will do the right thing if it adopts a definite and absolutely categorical decision on this matter. (*Applause.*)

7. DIFFICULTIES OF GROWTH, THE CLASS STRUGGLE AND THE OFFENSIVE OF SOCIALISM ALONG THE WHOLE FRONT

I have spoken about our achievements in developing our national economy. I have spoken about our achievements in industry, in agriculture, in reconstructing the whole of our national economy on the basis of socialism. Lastly, I have spoken about our achievements in improving the material conditions of the workers and peasants.

It would be a mistake, however, to think that we achieved all this "easily and quietly", automatically, so to speak, without exceptional effort and exertion of willpower, without struggle and turmoil. Such achievements do not come about automatically. In fact, we achieved all this in a resolute struggle against difficulties, in a serious and prolonged struggle to surmount difficulties.

Everybody among us talks about difficulties, but not everybody realizes the character of these difficulties. And yet the problem of difficulties is of serious importance for us.

What are the characteristic features of our difficulties, what hostile forces are hidden behind them, and how are we surmounting them?

a) When characterizing our difficulties we must bear in mind at least the following circumstances.

First of all, we must take into account the circumstance that our present difficulties are difficulties of the *reconstruction* period. What does this mean? It means that they differ fundamentally from the difficulties of the *restoration* period of our economy. Whereas in the restoration period it was a matter of keeping the old factories running and assisting agriculture on its old basis, today it is a matter of fundamentally rebuilding, reconstructing both industry and agriculture, altering their technical basis and providing them with modern technical equipment. It means that we are faced with the task of reconstructing the entire technical basis of our national economy. And this calls for now, more substantial investments in the national economy, for new and more experienced cadres, capable of mastering the new technology and of developing it further.

Secondly, we must bear in mind the circumstance that in our country the reconstruction of the national economy is not limited to rebuilding its technical basis, but that, on the contrary, parallel with this, it calls for the reconstruction of social-economic relationships. Here I have in mind, mainly, agriculture. In industry, which is already united and socialized, technical reconstruction already has, in the main, a ready-made social-economic basis. Here, the task of reconstruction is to accelerate the process of ousting the capitalist elements from industry. The matter is not so simple in agriculture. The reconstruction of the technical basis of agriculture pursues, of course, the same aims. The specific feature of agriculture in our country, however, is that small-peasant farming still predominates in it, that small farming is unable to master the new technology and that, in view of this, the reconstruction of the technical basis of agriculture is *impossible* without simultaneously reconstructing the old social-economic order, without uniting the small individual farms into large, collective farms, without tearing out the roots of capitalism in agriculture.

Naturally, these circumstances cannot but complicate our difficulties, cannot but complicate our work in surmounting these difficulties.

Thirdly, we must bear in mind the circumstance that our work for the socialist reconstruction of the national economy, since it breaks up the economic connections of capitalism and turns all the forces of the old world upside down, cannot but rouse the desperate resistance of these forces. Such is the case, as you know. The malicious wrecking activities of the top stratum of the *bourgeois intelligentsia* in all branches of our industry, the brutal struggle of the *kulaks* against collective forms of farming in the countryside, the sabotage of the Soviet government's measures by *bureaucratic elements* in the state apparatus, who are agents of our class enemy—such, so far, are the chief forms of the resistance of the moribund classes in our country. Obviously, these circumstances cannot facilitate our work of reconstructing the national economy.

Fourthly, we must bear in mind the circumstance that the resistance of the moribund classes in our country is not taking place in isolation from the outside world, but is receiving the support of the capitalist encirclement. Capitalist encirclement must not be regarded simply as a geographical concept. Capitalist encirclement means that the USSR is surrounded by hostile class forces, which are ready to support our class enemies within the USSR morally, materially, by means of a financial blockade and, if the opportunity offers, by military intervention. It has been proved that the wrecking activities of our specialists, the antiSoviet activities of the kulaks, and the incendiarism and explosions at our factories and installations are subsidized and inspired from abroad. The imperialist world is not interested in the USSR standing up firmly and becoming able to overtake and outstrip the advanced capitalist countries. Hence, the assistance it renders the forces of the old world in the USSR. Naturally, this circumstance, too, cannot serve to facilitate our work of reconstruction.

The characterization of our difficulties will not be complete, however, if we fail to bear in mind one other circumstance. I am referring to the special character of our difficulties. I am referring to the fact that our difficulties are not difficulties of *decline*, or of *stagnation*, but difficulties of *growth*, difficulties of *ascent*, difficulties of *progress*. This means that our difficulties differ fundamentally from those encountered by the capitalist countries. When people in the United States talk about difficulties, they have in mind, difficulties due to *decline*, for America is now going through a crisis, i.e., economic decline. When people in Britain talk about difficulties they have in mind difficulties due to *stagnation*, for Britain, for a number of years already, has been experiencing stagnation, i.e., cessation of progress. When we speak about difficulties, however, we have in mind not decline and not stagnation in development, but *growth* of our forces, *upswing* of our forces, the *progress* of our economy. How many points shall we *move further forward* by a given date? What percent *more* goods shall we produce? How many million *more* hectares shall we sow? How many months *earlier* shall we erect a factory, a mill, a railway?—such are the questions that we have in mind when we speak of difficulties. Consequently, our difficulties, unlike those encountered by, say, America or Britain, are difficulties of *growth*, difficulties of *progress*.

What does this signify? It signifies that our difficulties are such as *contain within themselves the possibilities of surmounting them*. It signifies that the distinguishing feature of our difficulties is that *they themselves give us the basis for surmounting them*.

What follows from this?

It follows from this, first of all, that our difficulties are not difficulties due to minor and accidental "derangements", but difficulties arising from the class struggle.

It follows from this, secondly, that behind our difficulties are hidden our class enemies, that these difficulties are complicated by the desperate resistance of the moribund classes in our country, by the support that these classes receive from abroad, by the existence of bureaucratic elements in our own institutions, by the existence of unsureness and conservatism among certain sections of our Party.

It follows from this, thirdly, that to surmount the difficulties it is necessary, first of all, to repulse the attacks of the capitalist elements, to crush their resistance and thereby clear the way for rapid progress.

It follows from this, lastly, that the very character of our difficulties, being difficulties of *growth*, creates the *possibilities* that we need for crushing our class enemies.

There is only one means, however, of taking advantage of these *possibilities* and of converting them into *reality*, of crushing the resistance of our class enemies and surmounting the difficulties, and that is to organize an *offensive* against the capitalist elements *along the whole front* and to isolate the opportunist elements in our own ranks, who are hindering the offensive, who are rushing in panic from one side to another and sowing doubt in the Party about the possibility of victory. (*Applause.*)

There are no other means.

Only people who have lost their heads can seek a way out in Bukharin's childish formula about the capitalist elements peacefully growing into socialism. In our country development has not proceeded and is not proceeding according to Bukharin's formula. Development has proceeded, and is proceeding, according to Lenin's formula "who will beat whom". Either we vanquish and crush them, the exploiters, or they will vanquish and crush us, the workers and peasants of the USSR—that is how the question stands, comrades.

Thus, *the organization of the offensive of socialism along the whole front*—that is the task that arose before us in developing our work of reconstructing the *entire* national economy.

That is precisely how the Party interpreted its mission in organizing the offensive against the capitalist elements in our country.

b) But is an offensive, and an offensive along the whole front at that, permissible at all under the conditions of NEP?

Some think that an offensive is incompatible with NEP, that NEP is essentially a retreat, that, since the retreat has ended, NEP must be abolished. That is nonsense, of course. It is nonsense that emanates either from the Trotskyists, who have never understood anything about Leninism and who think of "abolishing" NEP "in a trice", or from the Right opportunists, who have also never understood anything about Leninism and think that by chattering about "the threat to abolish NEP" they can manage to secure the abandonment of the offensive. If NEP was nothing but a retreat, Lenin would not have said at the Eleventh Congress of the Party, when we were implementing NEP with the utmost consistency, that "the retreat has ended." When Lenin said that the retreat had ended, did he not also say that we were thinking of carrying out NEP "in earnest and for a long time"? It is sufficient to put this question to understand the utter absurdity of the talk about NEP being incompatible with an offensive. In point of fact, NEP does not merely presuppose a *retreat* and permission for the revival of private trade, permission for the revival of capitalism while ensuring the regulating role of the state (the initial stage of NEP). In point of fact, NEP also presupposes, at a certain stage of development, the *offensive* of socialism against the capitalist elements, the *restriction* of the field of activity of private trade, the relative and absolute *dimunition* of capitalism, the increasing *preponderance* of the socialized sector over the nonsocialized sector, the victory of socialism over capitalism (the present stage of NEP). NEP was introduced to ensure the victory of socialism over the capitalist elements. In passing to the offensive along the whole front, we do not yet abolish NEP, for private trade and the capitalist elements still remain, "free" trade still remains—but we are certainly abolishing the initial stage of NEP, while developing its next stage, the present stage, which is the last stage of NEP.

Here is what Lenin said in 1922, a year after NEP was introduced:

"We are now retreating, going back as it were; but we are doing this in order, by retreating first, afterwards to take a run and make a more powerful leap forward. It was on this condition alone that we retreated in pursuing our New Economic Policy. We do not yet know where and how we must now regroup, adapt and reorganize our forces in order to start a most persistent advance after our retreat. In order to carry out all these operations in proper order we must, as the proverb says, measure not ten times, but a hundred times before we decide" (Volume XXVII, pp. 361-62).

Clear, one would think.

But the question is: Has the time already arrived to pass to the offensive, is the moment ripe for an offensive?

Lenin said in another passage in the same year, 1922, that it was necessary to:

"Link up with the peasant masses, with the rank-and-file toiling peasants, and begin to move forward immeasurably, infinitely, more slowly than we imagined, but in such a way that the entire mass will actually move forward with us"... that if we do that we shall in time get such an acceleration of progress as we cannot dream of now" (Volume XXVII, pp. 231-32).

And so the same question arises: Has the time already arrived for such an acceleration of progress, for speeding up the rate of our development? Did we choose the right moment in passing to the decisive offensive along the whole front in the latter half of 1929?

To this question the Party has already given a clear and definite answer.

Yes, that moment had already arrived.

Yes, the Party chose the right moment to pass to the offensive along the whole front.

This is proved by the growing activity of the working class and by the unprecedented growth of the Party's prestige among the vast masses of the working people.

It is proved by the growing activity of the masses of the poor and middle peasants, and by the radical turn of these masses towards collective-farm development.

It is proved by our achievements both in the development of industry and in the development of state and collective farms.

It is proved by the fact that we are now in a position not only to replace kulak production by collective- and state-farm production, but to exceed the former several times over.

It is proved by the fact that we have already succeeded, in the main, in solving the grain problem and in accumulating definite grain reserves, by shifting the center of the production of marketable grain from the sphere of individual production to that of collective- and state-farm production.

There you have the proof that the Party chose the right moment to pass to the offensive along the whole front and to proclaim the slogan of eliminating the kulaks as a class.

What would have happened had we heeded the Right opportunists of Bukharin's group, had we refrained from launching the offensive, had we slowed down the rate of development of industry, had we retarded the development of collective and state farms and had we based ourselves on individual farming?

We should certainly have wrecked our industry, we should have ruined the socialist reconstruction of agriculture, we should have been left without bread and have cleared the way for the predominance of the kulaks. We should have been as badly off as before.

What would have happened had we heeded the "Left" opportunists of the Trotsky-Zinoviev group and launched the offensive in 1926/27, when we had no possibility of replacing kulak production by collective- and state-farm production?

We should certainly have met with failure in this matter, we should have demonstrated our weakness, we should have strengthened the position of the kulaks and of the capitalist elements generally, we should have pushed the middle peasants into the embrace of the kulaks, we should have disrupted our socialist development and have been left without bread. We should have been as badly off as before.

The results would have been the same.

It is not for nothing that our workers say: "When you go to the 'left' you arrive at the right." (*Applause.*)

Some comrades think that the chief thing in the offensive of socialism is measures of repression, that if there is no increase of measures of repression there is no offensive.

Is that true? Of course, it is not true.

Measures of repression in the sphere of socialist construction are a necessary element of the offensive, but they are an auxiliary, not the chief element. The chief thing in the offensive of socialism under our present conditions is to speed up the rate of development of our industry, to speed up the rate of state- and collective-farm development, to speed up the rate of the economic ousting of the capitalist elements in town and country, to mobilize the masses around socialist construction, to mobilize the masses against capitalism. You may arrest and deport tens and hundreds of thousands of kulaks, but if you do not at the same time do all that is necessary to speed up the development of the new forms of farming, to replace the old, capitalist forms of farming by the new forms, to undermine and abolish the production sources of the economic existence and development of the capitalist elements in the countryside—the kulaks will, nevertheless, revive and grow.

Others think that the offensive of socialism means advancing headlong, without proper preparation, without regrouping forces in the course of the offensive, without consolidating captured positions, without utilizing reserves to develop successes, and that if signs have appeared of, say, an exodus of a section of the peasants from the collective farms it means that there is already the "ebb of the revolution", the decline of the movement, the cessation of the offensive.

Is that true? Of course, it is not true.

Firstly, no offensive, even the most successful, can proceed without some breaches or incursions on individual sectors of the front. To argue, on these grounds, that the offensive has stopped, or has failed, means not to understand the essence of an offensive.

Secondly, there has never been, nor can there be, a *successful* offensive without regrouping forces in the course of the offensive itself, without consolidating captured positions, without utilizing reserves for developing success and for carrying the offensive through to the end. Where there is a headlong advance, i.e., without observing these conditions, the offensive must inevitably peter out and fail. A headlong advance means death to the offensive. This is proved by the wealth of experience of our Civil War.

Thirdly, how can an analogy be drawn between the "ebb of the revolution", which usually takes place on the basis of a *decline* of the movement, and the withdrawal of a section of the peasantry from the collective farms, which took place against a background of the continuing *upswing* of the movement, against a background of the continuing *upswing* of the whole of our socialist development, both industrial and collective-farm, against a background of the continuing *upswing* of our revolution? What can there be in common between these two totally different phenomena?

c) What is the essence of the Bolshevik offensive under our present conditions?

The essence of the Bolshevik offensive lies, first and foremost, in mobilizing the class vigilance and revolutionary activity of the masses against the capitalist elements in our country; in mobilizing the creative initiative and independent activity of the masses against bureaucracy in our institutions and organizations, which keeps concealed the colossal reserves latent in the depths of our system and prevents them from being used; in organizing competition and labor enthusiasm among the masses for raising the productivity of labor, for developing socialist construction.

The essence of the Bolshevik offensive lies, secondly, in organizing the reconstruction of the entire practical work of the trade-union, cooperative, Soviet and all other mass organizations to fit the requirements of the reconstruction period; in creating in them a core of the most active and revolutionary functionaries, pushing aside and isolating the opportunist, trade-unionist, bureaucratic elements; in expelling from them the alien and degenerate elements and promoting new cadres from the rank and file.

The essence of the Bolshevik offensive lies, further, in mobilizing the maximum funds for financing our industry, for financing our state and collective farms, in appointing the best people in our Party for developing all this work.

The essence of the Bolshevik offensive lies, lastly, in mobilizing the Party itself for organizing the whole offensive; in strengthening and giving a sharp edge to the Party organizations, expelling elements of bureaucracy and degeneration from them; in isolating and thrusting aside those that express Right or "Left" deviations from the Leninist line and bringing to the fore genuine, staunch Leninists.

Such are the principles of the Bolshevik offensive at the present time.

How has the Party carried out this plan of the offensive?

You know that the Party has carried out this plan with the utmost consistency.

Matters started by the Party developing wide *self-criticism*, concentrating the attention of the masses upon shortcomings in our work of construction, upon shortcomings in our organizations and institutions. The need for intensifying self-criticism was proclaimed already at the Fifteenth Congress. The Shakhty affair and the wrecking activities in various branches of industry, which revealed the absence of revolutionary vigilance in some of the Party organizations, on the one hand, and the struggle against the kulaks and the defects revealed in our rural organizations, on the other hand, gave a further impetus to self-criticism. In its appeal of 2 June 1928, the Central Committee gave final shape to the campaign for self-criticism, calling upon all the forces of the Party and the working class to develop self-criticism "from top to bottom and from the bottom up", "irrespective of persons". Dissociating itself from the Trotskyist "criticism" emanating from the other side of the barricade and aiming at discrediting and weakening the Soviet regime, the Party proclaimed the task of self-criticism to be the ruthless exposure of shortcomings in our work for the purpose of *improving* our work of construction and *strengthening* the Soviet regime. As is known, the Party's appeal met with a most lively response among the masses of the working class and peasantry.

Further, the Party organized a wide campaign for the struggle against *bureaucracy* and issued the slogan of *purging* the Party, trade-union, cooperative and Soviet organizations of alien and bureaucratized elements. A sequel to this campaign was the well known decision of the Central Committee and Central Control Commission of 16 March 1930, concerning the promotion of workers to posts in the state apparatus and the organization of mass workers' control of the Soviet apparatus (patronage by factories). As is known, this campaign evoked tremendous enthusiasm and activity among the masses of the workers. The result of this campaign has been an immense increase in the Party's prestige among the masses of the working people, an increase in the confidence of the working class in the Party, the influx into the Party of further hundreds of thousands of workers, and the resolutions passed by workers expressing the desire to join the Party in whole shops and factories. Lastly, a result of this campaign has been that our organizations have got rid of a number of conservative and bureaucratic elements, and the All-Union Central Council of Trade Unions has got rid of the old, opportunist leadership.

Further, the Party organized wide socialist *competition* and mass *labor enthusiasm* in the factories and mills. The appeal of the Sixteenth Party Conference concerning competition started the ball rolling. The shock brigades are pushing it on further. The Leninist Young Communist League and the working-class youth which it guides are crowning the cause of competition and shock-brigade work with decisive successes. It must be admitted that our revolutionary youth have played an exceptional role in this matter. There can be no doubt now that one of the most important, if not the most important, factor in our work of construction at the present time is socialist competition among factories and mills, the interchange of challenges of hundreds of thousands of workers on the results achieved in competition, the wide development of *shock-brigade work.*

Only the blind fail to see that a tremendous change has taken place in the mentality of the masses and in their attitude to work, a change which has radically altered the appearance of our mills and factories. Not so long ago voices were still heard among us saying that competition and shock-brigade work were "artificial inventions", and "unsound". Today, these "sages" do not even provoke ridicule, they are regarded simply as "sages" who have outlived their time. The cause of competition and shock-brigade work is now a cause that has been won and consolidated. It is a fact that over two million of our workers are engaged in competition, and that not less than a million workers belong to shock brigades.

The most remarkable feature of competition is the radical revolution it brings about to people's views of labor, for it transforms labor from a degrading and heavy burden, as it was considered before, into a matter of *honor*, a matter of *glory*, a matter of *valor* and *heroism.* There is not, nor can there be, anything of the sort in capitalist countries. There, among the capitalists, the most desirable thing, deserving of public approval, is to be a bondholder, to live on interest, not to have to work, which is regarded as a contemptible occupation. Here, in the USSR, on the contrary, what is becoming the most desirable thing, deserving of public approval, is the possibility of being a hero of labor, the possibility of being a hero in shock-brigade work, surrounded with an aureole of esteem among millions of working people.

A no less remarkable feature of competition is the fact that it is beginning to spread also in the countryside, having already spread to our state and collective farms. Everybody is aware of the numerous cases of genuine labor enthusiasm being displayed by the vast masses of state-farm workers and collective farmers.

Who could have dreamed of such successes in competition and shock-brigade work a couple of years ago?

Further, the Party mobilized the country's financial resources for the purpose of developing state and collective farms, supplied the state farms with the best organizers, sent 25,000 front-rank workers to assist the collective farms, promoted the best people among the collective-farm peasants to leading posts in the collective farms and organized a network of training classes for collective farmers, thereby laying the foundation for the training of staunch and tried cadres for the collective-farm movement.

Lastly, the Party reformed its own ranks in battle order, reequipped the press, organized the struggle on two fronts, routed the remnants of Trotskyism, utterly defeated the Right deviators, isolated the conciliators, and thereby ensured the unity of its ranks on the basis of the Leninist line, which is essential for a successful offensive, and properly led this offensive, pulling up and putting in their place both the gradualists of the camp of the Rights and the "Left" distorters in regard to the collective-farm movement.

Such are the principal measures that the Party carried out in conducting the offensive along the whole front.

Everybody knows that this offensive has been crowned with success in all spheres of our work.

That is why we have succeeded in surmounting a whole number of difficulties of the period of reconstruction of our national economy.

That is why we are succeeding in surmounting the greatest difficulty in our development, the difficulty of turning the main mass of the peasantry towards socialism.

Foreigners sometimes ask about the internal situation in the USSR. But can there be any doubt that the internal situation USSR is firm and unshakable? Look at the capitalist countries, at the growing crisis and unemployment in those countries, at the strikes and lockouts, at the antigovernment demonstrations—what comparison can there be between the internal situation in those countries and the internal situation in the USSR?

It must be admitted that the Soviet regime is now the most stable of all the regimes in the world. (*Applause.*)

8. THE CAPITALIST OR THE SOCIALIST SYSTEM OF ECONOMY

Thus, we have the picture of the internal situation in the USSR.

We also have the picture of the internal situation in the chief capitalist countries.

The question involuntarily arises: What is the result if we place the two pictures side by side and compare them?

This question is all the more interesting for the reason that the bourgeois leaders in all countries and the bourgeois press of all degrees and ranks, from the arrant capitalist to the Menshevik-Trotskyist, are all shouting with one accord about the "prosperity" of the capitalist countries, about the "doom" of the USSR, about the "financial and economic bankruptcy" of the USSR, and so forth.

And so, what is the result of the analysis of the situation in our country, the USSR, and over there, in the capitalist countries?

Let us note the main, generally known facts.

Over there, in the capitalist countries, there is economic *crisis* and a *decline* in production, both in industry and in agriculture.

Here, in the USSR, there is an economic *upswing* and *rising* production in all spheres of the national economy.

Over there, in the capitalist countries, there is *deterioration* of the material conditions of the working people, *reduction* of wages and *increasing* unemployment.

Here, in the USSR, there is *improvement* in the material conditions of the working people, *rising* wages and *diminishing* unemployment.

Over there, in the capitalist countries, there are *increasing* strikes and demonstrations, which lead to the *loss* of millions of workdays.

Here, in the USSR, there are no strikes, but *rising* labor enthusiasm among the workers and peasants, by which our social system *gains* millions of additional workdays.

Over there, in the capitalist countries, there is *increasing* tension in the internal situation and *growth* of the revolutionary working-class movement against the capitalist regime.

Here, in the USSR, there is *consolidation* of the internal situation and the vast masses of the working class are *united* around the Soviet regime.

Over there, in the capitalist countries, there is *growing acuteness* of the national question and *growth* of the national-liberation movement in India, Indochina, Indonesia, in the Philippines, etc., developing into national war.

Here, in the USSR, the foundations of national fraternity have been *strengthened*, *peace* among the nations is ensured and the vast masses of the peoples in the USSR are *united* around the Soviet regime.

Over there, in the capitalist countries, there is *confusion* and the prospect of further *deterioration* of the situation.

Here, in the USSR, there is *confidence in our strength* and the prospect of further *improvement* in the situation.

They chatter about the "doom" of the USSR, about the "prosperity" of the capitalist countries, and so forth. Would it not be more correct to speak about the inevitable doom of those who have so "unexpectedly" fallen into the maelstrom of economic crisis and to this day are unable to extricate themselves from the slough of despond?

What are the causes of such a grave *collapse* over there, in the capitalist countries, and of the important *successes* here, in the USSR?

It is said that the state of the national economy depends in large measure upon the abundance or dearth of capital. That, of course, is true! But can the crisis in the capitalist countries and the upswing in the USSR be explained by abundance of capital here and a dearth of capital over there? No, of course not. Everybody knows that there is much less capital in the USSR than there is in the capitalist countries. If matters were *decided* in the present instance by the state of accumulations, there would be a crisis here and a boom in the capitalist countries.

It is said that the state of economy depends in a large measure on the technical and organizing experience of the economic cadres. That, of course, is true. But can the crisis in the capitalist countries and the upswing in the USSR be explained by the dearth of technical cadres over there and to an abundance of them here? No, of course not! Everybody knows that there are far more technically experienced cadres in the capitalist countries than there are here, in the USSR. We have never concealed, and do not intend to conceal, that in the sphere of technology we are the pupils of the Germans, the British, the French, the Italians, and, first and foremost, of the Americans. No, matters are not decided by the abundance or dearth of technically experienced cadres, although the problem of cadres is of great importance for the development of the national economy.

Perhaps the answer to the riddle is that the cultural level is higher in our country than in the capitalist countries? Again, no. Everybody knows that the general level of the masses is lower in our country than in the United States, Britain or Germany. No, it is not a matter of the cultural level of the masses, although this is of enormous importance for the development of the national economy.

Perhaps the cause lies in the personal qualities of the leaders of the capitalist countries? Again, no. Crises were born together with the advent of the rule of capitalism. For over a hundred years already there have been periodic economic crises of capitalism, recurring every 12, 10, 8 or fewer years. All the capitalist parties, all the more or less prominent capitalist leaders, from the greatest "geniuses" to the greatest mediocrities have tried their hand at "preventing" or "abolishing" crises. But they have all suffered defeat. Is it surprising that Hoover and his group have also suffered defeat? No, it is not a matter of capitalist leaders or parties, although both the capitalist leaders and parties are of no little importance in this matter.

What is the cause, then?

What is the cause of the fact that the USSR, despite its cultural backwardness, despite the dearth of capital, despite the dearth of technically experienced economic cadres, is in a state of increasing economic *upswing* and has achieved decisive *successes* on the front of economic construction, whereas the advanced capitalist countries, despite their abundance of capital, their abundance of technical cadres and their higher cultural level, are in a state of growing economic *crisis* and in the sphere of economic development are suffering *defeat after defeat*?

The cause lies in the *difference* in the economic systems here and in the capitalist countries.

The cause lies in the *bankruptcy* of the capitalist system of economy.

The cause lies in the *advantages* of the Soviet system of economy over the capitalist economy.

What is the Soviet system of economy?

The Soviet system of economy means that:

1) the power of the class of capitalists and landlords has been overthrown and replaced by the power of the working class and laboring peasantry;

2) the instruments and means of production, the land, factories, mills, etc., have been taken from the capitalists and transferred to the ownership of the working class and the laboring masses of the peasantry;

3) the development of production is subordinated not to the principle of competition and of ensuring capitalist profit, but to the principle of planned guidance and of systematically raising the material and cultural level of the working people;

4) the distribution of the national income takes place not with a view to enriching the exploiting classes and their numerous parasitical hangers-on, but with a view to ensuring the systematic improvement of the material conditions of the workers and peasants and the expansion of socialist production in town and country;

5) the systematic improvement in the material conditions of the working people and the continuous increase in their requirements (purchasing power), being a constantly increasing source of the expansion of production, guarantees the working people against crises of overproduction, growth of unemployment and poverty;

6) the working class and the laboring peasantry are the masters of the country, working not for the benefit of capitalists, but for their own benefit, the benefit of the working people.

What is the capitalist system of economy?

The capitalist system of economy means that:

1) power in the country is in the hands of the capitalists;

2) the instruments and means of production are concentrated in the hands of the exploiters;

3) production is subordinated not to the principle of improving the material conditions of the masses of the working people, but to the principle of ensuring high capitalist profit;

4) the distribution of the national income takes place not with a view to improving the material conditions of the working people, but with a view to ensuring the maximum profits for the exploiters;

5) capitalist rationalization and the rapid *growth* of production, the object of which is to ensure high profits for the capitalists, encounters an obstacle in the shape of the poverty-stricken conditions and the *decline* in the material security of the vast masses of the working people, who are not always able to satisfy their needs even within the limits of the extreme minimum, which inevitably creates the basis for unavoidable crises of overproduction, growth of unemployment, mass poverty;

6) the working class and the laboring peasantry are exploited, they work not for their own benefit, but for the benefit of an alien class, the exploiting class.

Such are the advantages of the *Soviet* system of economy over the *capitalist* system.

Such are the advantages of the *socialist* organization of economy over the *capitalist* organization.

That is why here, in the USSR, we have an increasing economic upswing, whereas in the capitalist countries there is growing economic crisis.

That is why here, in the USSR, the increase of mass consumption (purchasing power) continuously outstrips the growth of production and pushes it forward, whereas over there, in the capitalist countries, on the contrary, the increase of mass consumption (purchasing power) never keeps pace with the growth of production and continuously lags behind it, thus dooming industry to crises from time to time.

That is why over there, in the capitalist countries, it is considered quite a normal thing during crises to destroy "superfluous" goods and to burn "superfluous" agricultural produce in order to bolster up prices and ensure high profits, whereas here, in the USSR, anybody guilty of such crimes would be sent to a lunatic asylum. (*Applause.*)

That is why over there, in the capitalist countries, the workers go on strike and demonstrate, organizing a revolutionary struggle against the existing capitalist regime, whereas here, in the USSR, we have the picture of great labor emulation among millions of workers and peasants who are ready to defend the Soviet regime with their lives.

That is the cause of the stability and security of the internal situation in the USSR and of the instability and insecurity of the internal situation in the capitalist countries.

It must be admitted that a system of economy that does not know what to do with its "superfluous" goods and is obliged to burn them at a time when want and unemployment, hunger and ruin reign among the masses—such a system of economy pronounces its own death sentence.

The recent years have been a period of practical test, an examination period of the two opposite systems of economy, the Soviet and capitalist. During these years we have heard more than enough prophesies of the "doom", of the "downfall" of the Soviet system. There has been even more talk and singing about the "prosperity" of capitalism. And what has happened? These years have proved once again that the capitalist system of economy is a *bankrupt* system, and that the Soviet system of economy possesses *advantages* of which not a single bourgeois state, even the most "democratic", most "popular", etc. dares to dream.

In his speech at the conference of the RCP(B) in May 1921, Lenin said:

"At the present time we are exercising our main influence on the international revolution by our economic policy. All eyes are turned on the Soviet Russian Republic, the eyes of all toilers in all countries of the world without exception and without exaggeration. This we have achieved. The capitalists cannot hush up, conceal, anything, that is why they most of all seize upon our economic mistakes and our weakness. That is the field to which the struggle has been transferred on a worldwide scale. If we solve this problem, we shall have won on an international scale surely and finally" (Volume XXVI, pp. 410-11).

It must be admitted that our Party is successfully carrying out the task set by Lenin.

9. THE NEXT TASKS

a) General

1) First of all there is the problem of the *proper distribution of industry throughout the USSR*. However much we may develop our national economy, we cannot avoid the question of how properly to distribute industry, which is the leading branch of the national economy. The situation at present is that our industry, like the whole of our national economy, rests, in the main, on the coal and metallurgical base in the Ukraine. Naturally, without such a base, the industrialization of the country is inconceivable. Well, the Ukraine fuel and metallurgical base serves us as such a base.

But can this one base satisfy in future the south, the central part of the USSR, the north, the northeast, the Far East and Turkestan? All the facts go to show that it cannot. The new feature of the development of our national economy is, among other things, that this base has already become inadequate for us. The new feature is that, while continuing to develop this base to the utmost, we must begin immediately to create a second coal and metallurgical base. This base must be the Urals-Kuznetsk Combine, the combination of Kuznetsk coking coal with the ore of the Urals. (*Applause.*) The construction of the automobile works in Nizhni-Novgorod, the tractor works in Cheliabinsk, the machine-building works in Sverdlovsk, the harvester-combine works in Saratov and Novosibirsk; the existence of the growing nonferrous metal industry in Siberia and Kazakhstan, which calls for the creation of a network of repair shops and a number of major metallurgical factories in the east, and, lastly, the decision to erect textile mills in Novosibirsk and Turkestan—all this imperatively demands that we should proceed immediately to create a second coal and metallurgical base in the Urals.

You know that the Central Committee of our Party expressed itself precisely in this spirit in its resolution on the Urals Metal Trust.

2) Further, there is the problem of *the proper distribution of the basic branches of agriculture throughout the USSR*, the problem of *our regions specializing in particular agricultural crops and branches of agriculture*. Naturally, with small-peasant farming real specialization is impossible. It is impossible because small farming being unstable and lacking the necessary reserves, each farm is obliged to grow all kinds of crops so that in the event of one crop failing it can keep going with the others. Naturally, too, it is impossible to organize specialization unless the state possesses certain reserves of grain. Now that we have passed over to large-scale farming and ensured that the state possesses reserves of grain, we can and must set ourselves the task of properly organizing specialization according to crops and branches of agriculture. The starting point for this is the complete solution of the grain problem. I say "starting point", because unless the grain problem is solved, unless a large network of granaries is set up in the livestock, cotton, sugar-beet, flax and tobacco districts, it will be impossible to promote livestock farming and industrial crop cultivation, it will be impossible to organize the specialization of our regions according to crops and branches of agriculture.

The task is to take advantage of the possibilities that have opened up and to push this matter forward.

3) Next comes the problem of *cadres* both for industry and for agriculture. Everybody is aware of the lack of technical experience of our economic cadres, of our specialists, technicians and business executives. The matter is complicated by the fact that a section of the specialists, having connections with former owners and prompted from abroad, was found to be at the head of the wrecking activities. The matter is still more complicated by the fact that a number of our communist business executives failed to display revolutionary vigilance and in many cases proved to be under the ideological influence of the wrecker elements. Yet, we are faced with the colossal task of reconstructing the whole of our national economy, for which a large number of new cadres capable of mastering the new technology is needed. In view of this, the problem of cadres has become a truly vital problem for us.

This problem is being solved by measures along the following lines:

1) resolute struggle against wreckers;

2) maximum care and consideration for the vast majority of specialists and technicians who have dissociated themselves from the wreckers (I have in mind not windbags and poseurs of the Ustrialov type, but the genuine scientific workers who are working honestly, hand in hand with the working class);

3) the organization of technical aid from abroad;

4) sending our business executives abroad to study and generally to acquire technical experience;

5) transferring technical colleges to the respective economic organizations with a view to training quickly a sufficient number of technicians and specialists from people of working-class and peasant origin.

The task is to develop work for the realization of these measures.

4) The problem of *combatting bureaucracy.* The danger of bureaucracy lies, first of all, in that it keeps concealed the colossal reserves latent in the depths of our system and prevents them from being utilized, in that it strives to nullify the creative initiative of the masses, ties it hand and foot with red tape and reduces every new undertaking by the Party to petty and useless trivialities. The danger of bureaucracy lies, secondly, in that it does not tolerate the checking of fulfillment and strives to convert the basic directives of the leading organizations into mere sheets of paper divorced from life. It is not only, and not so much, the old bureaucratic stranded in our institutions who constitute this danger; it is also, and particularly, the new bureaucrats, the Soviet bureaucrats; and the "Communist" bureaucrats are by no means the least among them. I have in mind those "Communists" who try to substitute bureaucratic orders and "decrees", in the potency of which they believe as in a fetish, for the creative initiative and independent activity of the vast masses of the working class and peasantry.

The task is to smash bureaucracy in our institutions and organizations, to rid of bureaucratic "habits" and "customs" and to clear the way for utilizing the reserves of our social system, for developing the creative initiative and independent activity of the masses.

That is not an easy task. It cannot be carried out "in a trice". But it must be carried out at all costs if we really want to transform our country on the basis of socialism.

In the struggle against bureaucracy, the Party is working along four lines: That of developing *self-criticism*, that of organizing the *checking of fulfillment*, that of *purging* the apparatus and, lastly, that of *promoting* from below to posts in the apparatus devoted workers from those of working-class origin.

The task is to exert every effort to carry out all these measures.

5) The problem of increasing the productivity of labor. If there is not a systematic increase in the productivity of labor both in industry and agriculture we shall not be able to carry out the tasks of reconstruction, we shall not only fail to overtake and outstrip the advanced capitalist countries, but we shall not even be able to maintain our independent existence. Hence, the problem of increasing the productivity of labor is of prime importance for us.

The Party's measures for solving this problem are along three lines: That of systematically *improving the material conditions* of the working people, that of implanting *comradely labor discipline* in industrial and agricultural enterprises, and, lastly, that of organizing *socialist competition* and *shock-brigade* work. All this is based on improved technology and the rational organization of labor.

The task is to further develop the mass campaign for carrying out these measures.

6) The problem of *supplies*. This includes the questions of *adequate supplies* of necessary produce for the working people in town and country, of adapting the *cooperative apparatus* to the needs of the workers and peasants, of systematically raising the *real wages* of the workers, of *reducing prices* of manufactured goods and agricultural produce. I have already spoken about the shortcomings of the consumers' cooperatives. These shortcomings must be eliminated and we must see to it that the *policy of reducing prices* is carried out. As regards the inadequate supply of goods (the "goods shortage"), we are now in a position to enlarge the raw materials base of light industry and increase the output of urban consumer goods. The bread supply can be regarded as already assured. The situation is more difficult as regards the supply of meat, dairy produce and vegetables. Unfortunately, this difficulty cannot be removed within a few months. To overcome it will require at least a year. In a year's time, thanks primarily to the organization of state and collective farms for this purpose, we shall be in a position to ensure full supplies of meat, dairy produce and vegetables. And what does controlling the supply of these products mean when we already have grain reserves, textiles,

increased housing construction for workers and cheap municipal services? It means controlling all the principal factors that determine the workers' budget and his real wages. It means guaranteeing the rapid rise of workers' real wages surely and finally.

The task is to develop the work of all our organizations in this direction.

7) The problem of *credits* and *currency*. The rational organization of credit and correct maneuvering with our financial reserves are of great importance for the development of the national economy. The Party's measures for solving this problem are along two lines: That of concentrating all short-term credit operations in the State Bank, and that of organizing noncash settlement of accounts in the socialized sector. This, firstly, transforms the State Bank into a nationwide apparatus for keeping account of the production and distribution of goods; and, secondly, it withdraws a large amount of currency from circulation. There cannot be the slightest doubt that these measures will introduce (are already introducing) order in the entire credit system and strengthening our chervonets.

8) The problem of *reserves*. It has already been stated several times, and there is no need to repeat it, that a state in general, and our state in particular, cannot do without reserves. We have some reserves of grain, goods and foreign currency. During this period our comrades have been able to feel the beneficial effects of these reserves. But "some" reserves is not enough. We need bigger reserves in every direction.

Hence, the task is to accumulate reserves.

b) Industry

1) The chief problem is to force the development of the *iron and steel industry*. You must bear in mind that we have reached and are exceeding the prewar level of pig-iron output only this year, in 1929/30. This is a serious threat to the whole of our national economy. To remove this threat we must force the development of the iron and steel industry. By the end of the five year period we must reach an output not of 10,000,000 tons as is laid down in the five year plan, but of 15-17 million tons. We must achieve this aim at all costs if we want really to develop the work of industrializing our country.

Bolsheviks must show that they are able to cope with this task.

That does not mean, of course, that we must abandon *light* industry. No, it does not mean that. Until now we have been economizing in all things, including light industry, in order to restore heavy industry. But we have already restored heavy industry. Now it only needs to be developed further. Now we can turn to light industry and push it forward at an accelerated pace. One of the new features in the development of our industry is that we are now in a position to develop both heavy and light industry at an accelerated pace. The overfulfilment of the cotton, flax and sugar-beet crop plans this year, and the solution of the problem of kendyr and artificial silk, all this shows that we are in a position really to push forward light industry.

2) The problem of *rationalization, reducing production costs* and *improving the quality* of production. We can no longer tolerate defects in the sphere of rationalization, nonfulfilment of the plan to reduce production costs and the outrageous quality of the goods turned out by a number of our enterprises. These gaps and defects are harmfully affecting the whole of our national economy and hindering it from making further progress. It is time, high time, that this disgraceful stain was removed.

Bolsheviks must show that they are able to cope with this task.

3) The problem of *one-man management*. Infringements in the sphere of introducing one-man management in the factories are also becoming intolerable. Time and again the workers complain: "There is nobody in control in the factory," "confusion reigns at work." We can no longer allow our factories to be converted from organisms of production into parliaments. Our Party and trade-union organizations must at last understand that unless we ensure one-man management and establish strict responsibility for the way the work proceeds we shall not be able to cope with the task of reconstructing industry.

c) Agriculture

1) The problem of *livestock farming* and *industrial crops*. Now that we have, in the main, solved the grain problem, we can set about solving simultaneously both the livestock farming problem, which is a vital one at the present time, and the industrial crops problem. In solving these problems we must proceed along the same lines as we did in solving the grain problem. That is to say, by organizing state and collective farms, which are the strong points for our policy, we must gradually transform the technical and economic basis of present-day small-peasant livestock farming and industrial crops growing. The Livestock Trust, the Sheep Trust, the Pig Trust and the Dairy Trust, plus livestock collective farms, and the existing state and collective farms which grow industrial crops—such are our points of departure for solving the problems that face us.

2) The problem of *further promoting the development of state and collective farms*. It is scarcely necessary to dwell at length on the point that for us this is the *primary* problem of the whole of our development in the countryside. Now, even the blind can see that the peasants have made a tremendous, a radical turn from the old to the new, from kulak bondage to free collective-farm life. There is no going back to the old. The kulaks are doomed and will be eliminated. Only one path remains, the collective-farm path. And the collective-farm path is no longer for us an unknown and unexplored path. It has been explored and tried in a thousand ways by the peasant masses themselves. It has been explored and appraised as a new path that leads the peasants to emancipation from kulak bondage, from want and ignorance. That is the basis of our achievements.

How will the new movement in the countryside develop further? In the forefront will be the state farms as the backbone of the reorganization of the old way of life in the countryside. They will be followed by the numerous collective farms, as the strong points of the new movement in the countryside. The combined work of these two systems will create the conditions for the complete collectivization of all the regions in the USSR.

One of the most remarkable achievements of the collective-farm movement is that it has already brought to the forefront thousands of *organizers* and tens of thousands of *agitators* in favor of collective farms from among *the peasants themselves*. Not we alone, the skilled Bolsheviks, but the collective-farm peasants themselves, tens of thousands of peasant organizers of collective farms and agitators in favor of them will now carry forward the banner of collectivization. And the peasant agitators are splendid agitators for the collective-farm movement, for they will find arguments in favor of collective farms, intelligible and acceptable to the rest of the peasant masses, of which we skilled Bolsheviks cannot even dream.

Here and there voices are heard saying that we must abandon the policy of complete collectivization. We have information that there are advocates of this "idea" even in our Party. That can be said, however, only by people who, voluntarily or involuntarily, have joined forces with the enemies of communism. The method of complete collectivization is that essential method without which it will be impossible to carry out the five year plan for the collectivization of all the regions of the USSR. How can it be abandoned without betraying communism, without betraying the interests of the working class and peasantry?

This does not mean, of course, that everything will go "smoothly" and "normally" for us in the collective-farm movement. There will still be vacillation within the collective farms. There will still be flows and ebbs. But this cannot and must not daunt the builders of the collective-farm movement. Still less can it serve as a serious obstacle to the powerful development of the collective-farm movement. A sound movement, such as our collective-farm movement undoubtedly is, will achieve its goal in spite of everything, in spite of individual obstacles and difficulties.

The task is to train the forces and to arrange for the further development of the collective-farm movement.

3) The problem of *bringing the apparatus as close as possible to the districts* and *villages*. There can be no doubt that we would have been unable to cope with the enormous task of reconstructing agriculture and of developing the collective-farm movement had we not carried out *redelimitation of administrative areas*. The enlargement of the volosts and their transformation into districts, the abolition of gubernias and their transformation into smaller units (okrugs), and lastly, the formation of regions as direct strong points of the Central Committee—such are the general features of this redelimitation. Its object is to bring the Party and Soviet and the economic and cooperative apparatus closer to the districts and villages in order to make possible the timely solution of the vexed questions of agriculture, of its upswing, of its reconstruction. In this sense, I repeat, the redelimitation of administrative areas has been of immense benefit to the whole of our development.

But has everything been done to bring the apparatus really and effectively closer to the districts and villages? No, not everything. The center of gravity of collective-farm development has now shifted to the district organizations. They are the centers on which converge all the threads of collective-farm development and of all other economic work in the countryside, as regards both cooperatives and Soviets, credits and procurements. Are the district organizations adequately supplied with the workers they need, and must have, to cope with all the diverse tasks? There can be no doubt that they are extremely inadequately staffed. What is the way out? What must be done to correct this defect and to supply the district organizations with a sufficient number of the workers required for all branches of our work? At least two things must be done:

1) abolish the okrugs (*applause*), which are becoming an unnecessary barrier between the region and the districts, and use the released okrug personnel to strengthen the district organizations;

2) link the district organizations directly with the region (Territorial Committee, national Central Committee).

That will complete the redelimitation of administrative areas, complete the process of bringing the apparatus closer to the districts and villages.

There was applause here at the prospect of abolishing the okrugs. Of course, the okrugs must be abolished. It would be a mistake, however, to think that this gives us the right to decry the okrugs, as some comrades do in the columns of *Pravda*. It must not be forgotten that the okrugs have shouldered the burden of tremendous work, and in their time played a great historical role. (*Applause*.)

I also think that it would be a mistake to display too much haste in abolishing the okrugs. The Central Committee has adopted a decision to abolish the okrugs. It is not at all of the opinion, however, that this must be done immediately. Obviously, the necessary preparatory work must be carried out before the okrugs are abolished.

d) Transport

Lastly, the *transport* problem. There is no need to dwell at length on the enormous importance of transport for the whole of the national economy. And not only for the national economy. As you know, transport is of the utmost importance also for the defense of the country. In spite of the enormous importance of transport, however, the transport system, the reconstruction of this system, still lags behind the general rate of development. Does it need to be proved that in such a situation we run the risk of transport becoming a "bottleneck" in the national economy, capable of retarding our progress? Is it not time to put an end to this situation?

Matters are particularly bad as regards river transport. It is a fact that the Volga steamship service has barely reached 60 percent, and the Dnieper steamship service 40 percent, of the prewar level. Sixty and forty percent of the prewar level—this is all that river transport can enter in its record of "achievements". A big "achievement" to be sure! Is it not time to put an end to this disgrace? (*Voices*: "It is.")

The task is to tackle the transport problem, at last, in the Bolshevik manner and to get ahead with it.

Such are the Party's next tasks.

What is needed to carry out these tasks?

Primarily and chiefly, what is needed is to *continue* the sweeping offensive against the capitalist elements along the whole front and *to carry it through to the end.*

That is the center and basis of our policy at the present time. (*Applause.*)

III
THE PARTY

I pass to the question of the Party.

I have spoken about the advantages of the Soviet system of economy over the capitalist system. I have spoken about the colossal possibilities that our social system affords us in fighting for the complete victory of socialism. I said that without these possibilities, without utilizing them, we could not have achieved the successes gained by us in the past period.

But the question arises: Has the Party been able to make proper use of the possibilities afforded us by the Soviet system; has it not kept these possibilities concealed, thereby preventing the working class from fully developing its revolutionary might; has it been able to squeeze out of these possibilities all that could be squeezed out of them for the purpose of promoting socialist construction along the whole front?

The Soviet system provides colossal *possibilities* for the complete victory of socialism. But *possibility* is not *actuality*. To transform possibility into actuality a number of conditions are needed, among which the Party's line and the correct carrying out of this line play by no means the least role.

Some examples.

The Right opportunists assert that NEP guarantees us the victory of socialism; therefore, there is no need to worry about the rate of industrialization, about developing state and collective farms, and so forth, because the arrival of victory is assured in any case, automatically, so to speak. That, of course, is wrong and absurd. To speak like that means denying the Party's role in the building of socialism, denying the Party's responsibility for the work of building socialism. Lenin by no means said that NEP guarantees us the victory of socialism. Lenin merely said that "economically and politically, NEP fully ensures us the *possibility* of laying the foundation of a socialist economy." But possibility is not yet *actuality*. To convert possibility into actuality we must first of all cast aside the opportunist theory of things going of their own accord, we must rebuild (reconstruct) our national economy and conduct a determined offensive against the capitalist elements in town and country.

The Right opportunists assert, further, that there are no grounds inherent in our social system for a split between the working class and the peasantry—consequently we need not worry about establishing a correct policy in regard to the social groups in the countryside, because the kulaks will grow into socialism in any case, and the alliance of the workers and peasants will be guaranteed automatically, so to speak. That, too, is wrong and absurd. Such a thing can be said only by people who fail to understand that the policy of the Party, and especially because it is a party that is in power, is the chief factor that determines the fate of the alliance of the workers and peasants. Lenin by no means considered that the danger of a split between the working class and the peasantry was out of the question. Lenin said that "the grounds for such a split *are not necessarily inherent* in our social system," but "*if* serious class disagreements *arise* between these classes, a split *will be inevitable*."

In view of this, Lenin considered that:

"The chief task of our Central Committee and Central Control Commission, as well as of our Party as a whole, is to watch very closely for the circumstances that may cause a split and to *forestall* them; for, in the last resort, the fate of our Republic will depend on whether the masses of the peasants march with the working class and keep true to the alliance with it, or whether they permit the 'Nepmen', i.e., the new bourgeoisie, to drive a wedge between them and the workers, to split them off from the workers."

Consequently, a split between the working class and the peasantry is not precluded, but it is not at all inevitable, for inherent in our social system is the *possibility* of preventing such a split and of strengthening the alliance of the working class and peasantry. What is needed to convert this possibility into actuality? To convert the possibility of *preventing* a split into actuality we must first of all bury the opportunist theory of things going of their own accord, tear out the roots of capitalism by organizing collective and state farms, and pass from the policy of restricting the exploiting tendencies of the kulaks to the policy of eliminating the kulaks as a class.

It follows, therefore, that a strict distinction must be drawn between the *possibilities* inherent in our social system and the *utilization* of these possibilities, the conversion of these possibilities into *actuality*.

It follows that cases are quite conceivable when the possibilities of victory exist, but the Party does not see them, or is incapable of utilizing them properly, with the result that instead of victory there may come defeat.

And so the same question arises: Has the Party been able to make proper use of the *possibilities* and *advantages* afforded us by the Soviet system? Has it done everything to *convert these possibilities into actuality* and thus guarantee the maximum success for our work of construction?

In other words: Has the Party and its Central Committee correctly guided the building of socialism in the past period?

What is needed for correct leadership by the Party under our present conditions?

For correct leadership by the Party it is necessary, apart from everything else, that the Party should have a correct line; that the masses should understand that the Party's line is correct and should actively support it; that the Party should not confuse itself to drawing up a general line, but should day by day guide the carrying out of this line; that the Party should wage a determined struggle against deviations from the general line and against conciliation towards such deviations; that in the struggle against deviations the Party should forge the unity of its ranks and iron discipline.

What has the Party and its Central Committee done to fulfil these conditions?

1. QUESTIONS OF THE GUIDANCE OF SOCIALIST CONSTRUCTION

a) The Party's principal line at the present moment is *transition* from the offensive of socialism on *separate sectors* of the economic front to an offensive *along the whole front* both in industry and in agriculture.

The Fourteenth Congress was mainly the congress of *industrialization*.

The Fifteenth Congress was mainly the congress of *collectivization*.

This was the preparation for the *general* offensive.

As distinct from the past stages, the period before the Sixteenth Congress was a period of the *general* offensive of socialism *along the whole front*, a period of intensified socialist construction both in industry and in agriculture.

The Sixteenth Congress of the Party is the congress of the *sweeping offensive* of socialism *along the whole front*, of the elimination of the kulaks as a class, and of the realization of complete collectivization.

There you have in a few words the essence of our Party's general line.

Is this line correct?

Yes, it is correct. The facts show that our Party's general line is the only correct line. (*Applause*.)

This is proved by our successes and achievements on the front of socialist construction. It was not and cannot be the case that the decisive victory won by the Party on the front of socialist construction in town and country during the past period was the result of an incorrect policy. Only a correct general line could give us such a victory.

It is proved by the frenzied howl against our Party's policy raised lately by our class enemies, the capitalists and their press, the Pope and bishops of all kinds, the Social-Democrats and the "Russian" Mensheviks of the Abramovich and Dan type. The capitalists and their lackeys are abusing our Party—that is a sign that our Party's general line is correct. (*Applause.*)

It is proved by the fate of Trotskyism, with which everybody is now familiar. The gentlemen in the Trotsky camp chattered about the "degeneration" of the Soviet regime, about "Thermidor", about the "inevitable victory" of Trotskyism, and so forth. But, actually, what happened? What happened was the collapse, the end of Trotskyism. One section of the Trotskyists, as is known, broke away from Trotskyism and in numerous declarations of its representatives admitted that the Party was right, and acknowledged the counterrevolutionary character of Trotskyism. Another section of the Trotskyists really degenerated into typical petty-bourgeois counterrevolutionaries, and actually became an information bureau of the capitalist press on matters concerning the CPSU(B). But the Soviet regime, which was to have "degenerated" (or "had already degenerated"), continues to thrive and to build socialism, successfully breaking the backbone of the capitalist elements in our country and their petty-bourgeois yes-men.

It is proved by the fate of the Right deviators, with which everybody is now familiar. They chattered and howled about the Party line being "fatal", about the "probable catastrophe" in the USSR, about the necessity of "saving" the country from the Party and its leadership, and so forth. But what actually happened? What actually happened was that the Party achieved gigantic successes on all the fronts of socialist construction, whereas the group of Right deviators, who wanted to "save" the country but who later admitted that they were wrong, are now left high and dry.

It is proved by the growing revolutionary activity of the working class and peasantry, by the active support for the Party's policy by the vast masses of the working people, and lastly, by that unprecedented labor enthusiasm of the workers and peasant collective farmers, the immensity of which astonishes both the friends and the enemies of our country. That is apart from such signs of the growth of confidence in the Party as the applications from workers to join the Party in whole shops and factories, the growth of the Party membership between the Fifteenth and Sixteenth Congresses by over 600,000, and the 200,000 new members who joined the Party in the first quarter of this year alone. What does all this show if not that the vast masses of the working people realize that our Party's policy is correct and are ready to support it?

It must be admitted that these facts would not have existed if our Party's general line had not been the only correct one.

b) But the Party cannot confine itself to drawing up a general line. It must also, from day to day, keep check on how the general line is being carried out in practice. It must guide the carrying out of the general line, improving and perfecting the adopted plans of economic development in the course of the work, and correcting and preventing mistakes.

How has the Central Committee of our Party performed this work?

The Central Committee's work in this sphere has proceeded mainly along the line of amending and giving precision to the five year plan by accelerating tempo and shortening time schedules, along the line of checking the economic organizations' fulfillment of the assignments laid down.

Here are a few of the principal decisions adopted by the Central Committee amending the five year plan in the direction of speeding up the rate of development and shortening time schedules of fulfillment.

In the iron and steel industry: The five year plan provides for the output of pig-iron to be brought up to 10,000,000 tons in the last year of the five year period; the Central

Committee's decision, however, found that this level is not sufficient, and laid it down that in the last year of the five year period the output of pig-iron must be brought up to 17,000,000 tons.

Tractor construction: The five year plan provides for the output of tractors to be brought up to 55,000 in the last year of the five year period; the Central Committee's decision, however, found that this target is not sufficient, and laid it down that the output of tractors in the last year of the five year period must be brought up to 170,000.

The same must be said about *automobile construction*, where, instead of an output of 100,000 cars (lorries and passenger cars) in the last year of the five year period as provided for in the five year plan, it was decided to bring it up to 200,000.

The same applies to *nonferrous metallurgy*, where the five year plan estimates were raised by more than 100 percent; and to *agricultural machine-building*, where the five year plan estimates were also raised by over 100 percent.

That is apart from *harvester-combine* building, for which no provision at all was made in the five year plan, and the output of which must be brought up to at least 40,000 in the last year of the five year period.

State-farm development: The five year plan provides for the expansion of the crop area to be brought up to 5,000,000 hectares by the end of the five year period; the Central Committee's decision, however, found that this level was not sufficient and laid it down that by the end of the five year period the state-farm crop area must be brought up to 18,000,000 hectares.

Collective-farm development: The five year plan provides for the expansion of the crop area to be brought up to 20,000,000 hectares by the end of the five year period; the Central Committee's decision, however, found that this level was obviously not sufficient (it has already been exceeded this year) and laid it down that by the end of the five year period the collectivization of the USSR should, in the main, be completed, and by that time the collective-farm crop area should cover nine-tenths of the crop area of the USSR now cultivated by individual farms. (*Applause.*)

And so on and so forth.

Such, in general, is the picture of the way the Central Committee is guiding the carrying out of the Party's general line, the planning of socialist construction.

It may be said that in altering the estimates of the five year plan so radically the Central Committee is violating the principle of planning and is discrediting the planning organizations. But only hopeless bureaucrats can talk like that. For us Bolsheviks, the five year plan is not something fixed once and for all. For us the five year plan, like every other, is merely a plan adopted as a first approximation, which has to be made more precise, altered and perfected in conformity with the experience gained in the localities, with the experience gained in carrying out the plan. No five year plan can take into account all the possibilities latent in the depths of our system and which reveal themselves only in the course of the work, in the course of carrying out the plan in the factory and mill, in the collective and state farms, in the district, and so forth. Only bureaucrats can think that the work of planning *ends* with the drafting of a plan. The drafting of a plan is only the *beginning of planning*. Real guidance in planning develops only after the plan has been drafted, after it has been tested in the localities, in the course of carrying it out, correcting it and making it more precise.

That is why the Central Committee and the Central Control Commission, jointly with the planning bodies of the Republic, deemed it necessary to correct and improve the five year plan on the basis of experience, in the direction of speeding up the rate of development and shortening time schedules of fulfillment.

Here is what Lenin said about the principle of planning and guidance in planning at the Eighth Congress of Soviets, when the ten year plan of the GOELRO was being discussed:

"Our Party program cannot remain a Party program. It must become the program of our economic work of construction, otherwise it is useless even as a Party program. It must be supplemented by a second Party program, by a plan for the restoration of our entire national economy and for raising it to the level of modern technology.... We must come to the point of adopting a certain plan; of course, this will be a plan adopted only as a first approximation. This Party program will not be as unalterable as our actual Party program, which can be altered only at Party congresses. No, this program will be improved, worked out, perfected and altered every day, in every workshop, in every volost.... Watching the experience of science and practice, the people of the localities must undeviatingly strive to get the plan carried out earlier than had been provided for, in order that the masses may see that the long period that separates us from the complete restoration of industry can be shortened by experience. This depends upon us. Let us in every workshop, in every railway depot, in every sphere, improve our economy, and then we shall reduce the period. And we are already reducing it" (Volume XXVI, pp. 45,46,43).

As you see, the Central Committee has followed the path indicated by Lenin, altering and improving the five year plan, shortening time schedules and speeding up the rate of development.

On what possibilities did the Central Committee rely when speeding up the rate of development and shortening the time schedules for carrying out the five year plan? On the reserves latent in the depths of our system and revealed only in the course of the work, on the possibilities afforded us by the reconstruction period. The Central Committee is of the opinion that the reconstruction of the technical basis of industry and agriculture *under the socialist organization of production* creates such possibilities of accelerating tempo as no capitalist country can dream of.

These circumstances alone can explain the fact that during the past three years our socialist industry has more than doubled its output and that the output of this industry in 1930/31 should be 47 percent above that of the current year, while the volume of *this increase alone* will be equal to the volume of output of the *entire* prewar large-scale industry.

These circumstances alone can explain the fact that the five year plan of state-farm development is being overfulfilled in three years, while that of collective-farm development has already been overfulfilled in two years.

There is a theory according to which high rates of development are possible only in the restoration period and that with the transition to the reconstruction period the rate of development must diminish sharply year by year. This theory is called the theory of the "descending curve". It is a theory for justifying our backwardness. It has nothing in common with Marxism, with Leninism. It is a bourgeois theory, designed to perpetuate the backwardness of our country. Of the people who have had, or have, connection with our Party, only the Trotskyists and Right deviators uphold and preach this theory.

There exists an opinion that the Trotskyists are superindustrialists. But this opinion is only partly correct. It is correct only insofar as it applies to the end of the *restoration* period, when the Trotskyists did, indeed, develop superindustrialist fantasies. As regards the *reconstruction* period, however, the *Trotskyists, on the question of tempo, are the most extreme minimalists and the most wretched capitulators.* (*Laughter. Applause.*)

In their platforms and declarations the Trotskyists gave no figures concerning tempo, they confined themselves to general chatter about tempo. But there is one document in which the Trotskyists did depict in figures their understanding of the rate of development of state industry. I am referring to the memorandum of the "Special Conference on the Restoration of Fixed Capital of State Industry" (OSVOK) drawn up on the principles of Trotskyism. It will be interesting briefly to analyze this document, which dates back to 1925/26. It will be interesting to do so, because it fully reflects the Trotskyist scheme of the descending curve.

According to this document, it was proposed to *invest* in state industry 1,543,000,000 rubles in 1926/27; 1,490,000,000 rubles in 1927/28, 1,300,000,000 rubles in 1928/29, 1,060,000,000 rubles in 1929/30 (at 1926/27 prices).

Such is the picture of the *descending* Trotskyist curve.

But how much did we actually invest? Actually we invested in state industry 1,065,000,000 rubles in 1926/27; 1,490,000,000 rubles in 1927/28; 1,819,000,000 rubles in 1928/29; 4,775,000,000 rubles in 1929/30 (at 1927/28 prices).

Such is the picture of the *ascending* Bolshevik curve.

According to this document, the *output* of state industry was to increase by 31.6 percent in 1926/27; by 22.9 percent in 1927/28; by 15.5 percent in 1928/29; by 15 percent in 1929/30.

Such is the picture of the *descending* Trotskyist curve.

But what actually happened? Actually, the increase in the output of state industry was 19.7 percent in 1926/27; 26.3 percent in 1927/28; 24.3 percent in 1928/29; 32 percent in 1929/30, and in 1930/31 the increase will amount to 47 percent.

Such is the picture of the *ascending* Bolshevik curve.

As you know, Trotsky specially advocates this defeatist theory of the descending curve in his pamphlet *Towards Socialism or Capitalism*? He plainly says there that since "before the war, the expansion of industry consisted, in the main, in the construction of new factories," whereas "in our times expansion, to a much larger degree, consists in utilizing the old factories and in keeping the old equipment running," therefore, it "naturally follows that *with the completion of the restoration process* the coefficient of growth must *considerably diminish*," and so he proposes that "during the next few years the coefficient of industrial growth be raised not only to twice, but to three times the prewar 6 percent, and perhaps even higher."

Thus, three times six percent annual increase of industry. How much does that amount to? Only to an increase of 18 percent per annum. Hence, 18 percent annual increase in the output of state industry is, in the opinion of the Trotskyists, the highest limit that can be reached in planning to accelerate development in the *reconstruction period*, to be striven for as the ideal. Compare this pettiflogging sagacity of the Trotskyists with the actual increase in output that we have had during the last three years (1927/28—26.3 percent, 1928/29—24.3 percent; 1929/30—32 percent); compare this defeatist philosophy of the Trotskyists with the estimates in the control figures of the State Planning Commission for 1930/31 of a 47 percent increase, which exceeds the *highest* rate of increase of output in the *restoration* period, and you will realize how utterly reactionary is the Trotskyist theory of the "descending curve", the utter lack of faith of the Trotskyists in the possibilities of the *reconstruction* period.

That is why the Trotskyists are now singing about the "excessive" Bolshevik rates of industrial and collective-farm development.

That is why *the Trotskyists cannot now be distinguished from our Right deviators.*

Naturally, if we had not shattered the Trotskyist-Right-deviation theory of the "descending curve", we should not have been able either to develop real planning or to accelerate tempo and shorten time schedules of development. In order to guide the carrying out of the Party's general line, to correct and improve the five year plan of development, to accelerate tempo and to prevent mistakes in the work of construction, it was necessary first of all to shatter and liquidate the reactionary theory of the "descending curve".

That is what the Central Committee did, as I have already said.

2. QUESTIONS OF THE GUIDANCE OF INNER-PARTY AFFAIRS

It may be thought that the work of guiding socialist construction, the work of carrying out the Party's general line, has proceeded in our Party calmly and smoothly, without struggle or tense effort of will. But that is not so, comrades. Actually, this work has proceeded amid a struggle against inner-Party difficulties, amid a struggle against all sorts of deviations from Leninism both as regards general policy and as regards the national question. Our Party does not live and operate in a vacuum. It lives and operates in the thick of life and is subjected to the influence of the surrounding environment, as you know, consists of different classes and social groups. We have launched a sweeping offensive against the capitalist elements, we have pushed our socialist industry far forward, we have widely developed the formation of state and collective farms. Events like these, however, cannot but affect the exploiting classes. These events are usually accompanied by the ruin of the moribund classes, by the ruin of the kulaks in the countryside, by the restriction of the field of activity of the petty-bourgeois strata in the towns. Naturally, all this cannot but intensify the class struggle, the resistance of these classes to the Soviet government's policy. It would be ridiculous to think that the resistance of these classes will not find reflection in some way or other in the ranks of our Party. And it does indeed find reflection in the Party. All the various deviations from the Leninist line in the ranks of our Party are a reflection of the resistance of the moribund classes.

Is it possible to wage a successful struggle against class enemies without at the same time combating deviations in our Party, without overcoming these deviations? No, it is not. That is because it is impossible to develop a real struggle against class enemies while having their agents in our rear, while leaving in our rear people who have no faith in our cause, and who strive in every way to hinder our progress.

Hence an uncompromising struggle against deviations from the Leninist line is an immediate task of the Party.

Why is the Right deviation the chief danger in the Party at the present time? Because it reflects the kulak danger; and at the present moment, the moment of the sweeping offensive and the tearing out of the roots of capitalism, the kulak danger is the chief danger in the country.

What did the Central Committee have to do to overcome the Right deviation, to deliver the finishing stroke to the "Left" deviation and clear the way for rallying the Party to the utmost around the Leninist line?

a) It had, first of all, to put an end to the remnants of Trotskyism in the Party, to the survivals of the Trotskyist theory. We had long ago routed the Trotskyist group as an opposition, and had expelled it. The Trotskyist group is now an antiproletarian and an antiSoviet counter-revolutionary group, which is zealously informing the bourgeoisie about the affairs of our Party. But the remnants of the Trotskyist theory, the survivals of Trotskyism, have not yet been completely swept out of the Party. Hence, the first thing to be done was to put an end to these survivals.

What is the essence of Trotskyism?

The essence of Trotskyism is, first of all, denial of the possibility of completely building socialism in the USSR by the efforts of the working class and peasantry of our country. What does this mean? It means that if a victorious world revolution does not come to our aid in the near future, we shall have to surrender to the bourgeoisie and clear the way for a bourgeois-democratic republic. Consequently, we have here the bourgeois denial of the possibility of completely building socialism in our country, disguised by "revolutionary" phrases about the victory of the world revolution.

Is it possible, while holding such views, to rouse the labor enthusiasm of the vast masses of the working class, to rouse them for socialist competition, for mass shock-brigade work, for a sweeping offensive against the capitalist elements? Obviously not. It would be foolish to think that our working class, which has made three revolutions, will display labor enthusiasm and engage in mass shock-brigade work in order to manure the soil for capitalism. Our working class is displaying labor enthusiasm not for the sake of capitalism, but in order to bury capitalism once and for all and to build socialism in the USSR. Take from it its confidence in the possibility of building socialism, and you will completely destroy the basis for competition, for labor enthusiasm, for shock-brigade work.

Hence the conclusion: In order to rouse labor enthusiasm and competition among the working class and to organize a sweeping offensive, it was necessary, first of all, to bury the bourgeois theory of Trotskyism that it is impossible to build socialism in our country.

The essence of Trotskyism is, secondly, denial of the possibility of drawing the main mass of the peasantry into the work of socialist construction in the countryside. What does this mean? It means that the working class is incapable of leading the peasantry in the work of transferring the individual peasant farms to collectivist lines, that if the victory of the world revolution does not come to the aid of the working class in the near future, the peasantry will restore the old bourgeois order. Consequently, we have here the bourgeois denial of the capacity or possibility of the proletarian dictatorship to lead the peasantry to socialism, disguised by a mass of "revolutionary" phrases about the victory of the world revolution.

Is it possible, while holding such views, to rouse the peasant masses for the collective-farm movement, to organize a mass collective-farm movement, to organize the elimination of the kulaks as a class? Obviously not.

Hence the conclusion: In order to organize a mass collective-farm movement of the peasantry and to eliminate the kulaks, it was necessary, first of all, to bury the bourgeois theory of Trotskyism that it is impossible to bring the laboring masses of the peasantry to socialism.

The essence of Trotskyism is, lastly, denial of the necessity for iron discipline in the Party, recognition of the need to form a Trotskyist party. According to Trotskyism, the CPSU(B) must be not a single, united militant party, but a collection of groups and factions, each with its own center, its own discipline, its own press, and so forth. What does this mean? It means proclaiming freedom for political factions in the Party. It means that freedom for political groupings in the Party must be followed by freedom for political parties in the country, i.e., bourgeois democracy. Consequently, we have here recognition of freedom for factional groupings in the Party right up to permitting political parties in the land of the dictatorship of the proletariat, disguised by phrases about "inner-party democracy", about "improving the regime" in the Party. That freedom for factional squabbling of groups of intellectuals is not inner-party democracy, that the widely-developed self-criticism conducted by the Party and the colossal activity of the mass of the Party membership is real and genuine inner-party democracy—Trotskyism cannot understand.

Is it possible, while holding such views about the Party, to ensure iron discipline in the Party, to ensure the iron unity of the Party that is essential for waging a successful struggle against class enemies? Obviously not.

Hence the conclusion: In order to guarantee the iron unity of the Party and proletarian discipline in it, it was necessary, first of all, to bury the Trotskyist theory of organization.

Capitulation in practice as the *content*, "Left" phrases and "revolutionary" adventurist postures, as the *form* disguising and advertising the defeatist content—such is the essence of Trotskyism.

This duality of Trotskyism reflects the duality of the position of the urban petty bourgeoisie, which is being ruined, cannot tolerate the "regime" of the dictatorship of the proletariat and is striving either to jump into socialism "at one go" in order to avoid being ruined (hence *adventurism* and *hysterics* in policy), or, if this is impossible, to make every conceivable concession to capitalism (hence *capitulation* in policy).

The duality of Trotskyism explains why it usually crowns its supposedly "furious" attacks on the Right deviators by a *bloc* with them, as undisguised capitulators.

And what are the "Left" excesses that have occurred in the Party in connection with the collective-farm movement? They represent a certain attempt, true an unconscious one, to revive among us the traditions of Trotskyism in practice, to revive the Trotskyist attitude towards the middle peasantry. They are the result of that mistake in policy which Lenin called "overadministration". This means that some of our comrades, infatuated by the successes of the collective-farm movement, began to approach the problem of collective-farm movement not as builders, but mainly as administrators and, as a result, committed a number of very gross mistakes.

There are people in our Party who think that the "Left" distorters should not have been pulled up. They think that our officials should not have been taken to task and their infatuation should not have been counteracted even though it led to mistakes. That is nonsense, comrades. Only people who are determined to swim with the stream, can talk like that. These are the very same people who can never understand the Leninist policy of going against the stream when the situation demands it, when the interests of the Party demand it. They are khvostists, not Leninists. The reason why the Party succeeded in turning whole detachments of our comrades on to the right road, the reason why the Party succeeded in rectifying mistakes and achieving successes is just because it resolutely went against the stream in order to carry out the Party's general line. That is Leninism in practice, Leninism in leadership.

That is why I think that if we had not overcome the "Left" excesses we could not have achieved the successes in the collective-farm movement that we have now achieved.

That is how matters stand as regards the struggle against the survivals of Trotskyism and against the recurrence of them in practice.

Matters are somewhat different as regards Right opportunism, which was, or is, headed by Bukharin, Rykov and Tomsky.

It cannot be said that the Right deviators do not admit the possibility of completely building socialism in the USSR. No, they do admit it, and that is what distinguishes them from the Trotskyists. But the misfortune of the Right deviators is that, while formally admitting that it is possible to build socialism in one country, they refuse to recognize the ways and means of struggle without which it is impossible to build socialism. They refuse to admit that the utmost development of industry is the key to the transformation of the entire national economy on the basis of socialism. They refuse to admit the uncompromising class struggle against the capitalist elements and the sweeping offensive of socialism against capitalism. They fail to understand that all these ways and means constitute the system of measures without which it is impossible to retain the dictatorship of the proletariat and to build socialism in our country. They think that socialism can be built on the quiet, automatically, without class struggles, without an offensive against the capitalist elements. They think that the capitalist elements will either die out imperceptibly or grow into socialism. As, however, such miracles do not happen in history, it follows that *the Right deviators are in fact slipping into the viewpoint of denying the possibility of completely building socialism in our country.*

Nor can it be said that the Right deviators deny that it is possible to draw the main mass of the peasantry into the work of building socialism in the countryside. No, they admit that it is possible, and that is what distinguishes them from the Trotskyists. But while admitting it formally, they will not accept the ways and means without which it is impossible to draw the peasantry into the work of building socialism. They refuse to admit that state and collective farms are the principal means and the "high road" for drawing the main mass of the peasantry into the work of building socialism. They refuse to admit that unless the policy of eliminating the kulaks as a class is carried out it will be impossible to transform the countryside on the basis of socialism. They think that the countryside can be transformed to socialist lines on the quiet, automatically, without class struggle, merely with the aid of supply and marketing cooperatives, for they are convinced that the kulaks themselves will grow into socialism. They think that the chief thing now is not a high rate of industrial development, and not collective and state farms, but to "release" the elemental forces of the market, to "emancipate" the market and to "remove the shackles" from the individual farms, up to and including those of the capitalist elements in the countryside. As, however, the kulaks cannot grow into socialism, and "emancipating" the market means arming the kulaks and disarming the working class, it follows that *the Right deviators are in fact slipping into the viewpoint of denying that it is possible to draw the main mass of the peasantry into the work of building socialism.*

It is this, really, that explains why the Right deviators usually crown their sparring with the Trotskyists by backstairs negotiations with them on the subject of a *bloc* with them.

The chief evil of Right opportunism is that it *breaks* with the Leninist conception of the class struggle and slips into the viewpoint of *petty-bourgeois liberalism.*

There can be no doubt that the victory of the Right deviation in our Party would have meant completely disarming the working class, arming the capitalist elements in the countryside and increasing the chances of the restoration of capitalism in the USSR.

The Right deviators do not take the stand of forming another party, and that is another thing that distinguishes them from the Trotskyists. The leaders of the Right deviators have openly admitted their mistakes and have surrendered to the Party. But it would be foolish to think, on these grounds, that the Right deviation is already buried. The strength of Right opportunism is not measured by this circumstance. The strength of Right opportunism lies in the strength of the petty-bourgeois elemental forces, in the strength of the pressure on the Party exercised by the capitalist elements in general, and by the kulaks in particular. And it is precisely because the Right deviation reflects the resistance of the chief elements of the moribund classes that the Right deviation is the principal danger in the Party at the present time.

That is why the Party considered it necessary to wage a determined and uncompromising struggle against the Right deviation.

There can be no doubt that if we had not waged a determined struggle against the Right deviation, if we had not isolated its leading elements, we would not have succeeded in mobilizing the forces of the Party and of the working class, in mobilizing the forces of the poor- and middle-peasant masses, for the sweeping offensive of socialism, for the organization of state and collective farms, for the restoration of our heavy industry, for the elimination of the kulaks as a class.

That is how matters stand as regards the "Left" and Right deviations in the Party.

The task is to continue the uncompromising struggle *on two fronts*, against the "Lefts", who represent *petty-bourgeois radicalism*, and against the Rights, who represent *petty-bourgeois liberalism.*

b) The picture of the struggle against deviations in the Party will not be complete if we do not touch upon the deviations that exist in the Party on the *national question.* I have in mind, firstly, the deviation towards Great-Russian chauvinism, and secondly, the deviation towards local nationalism. These deviations are not so conspicuous and assertive as the "Left" or the Right deviation. They could be called creeping deviations. But this does not mean that they do not exist. They do exist, and what is most important—they are growing. There can be no doubt whatever about that. There can be no doubt about it, because the general atmosphere of more acute class struggle cannot fail to cause some intensification of national friction, which finds reflection in the Party. Therefore, the features of these deviations should be exposed and dragged into the light of day.

What is the essence of the deviation towards Great-Russian chauvinism under our present conditions?

The essence of the deviation towards Great-Russian chauvinism lies in the striving to ignore national differences in language, culture and way of life; in the striving to prepare for the liquidation of the national republics and regions; in the striving to undermine the principle of national equality and to discredit the Party's policy of nationalizing the administrative apparatus, the press, the schools and other state and public organizations.

In this connection, the deviators of this type proceed from the view that since, with the victory of socialism, the nations must merge into one and their national languages must be transformed into a single common language, the time has come to abolish national differences and to abandon the policy of promoting the development of the national cultures of the formerly oppressed peoples.

In this connection, they refer to Lenin, misquoting him and sometimes deliberately distorting and slandering him.

Lenin said that under socialism the interests of the nationalities will merge into a single whole—does it not follow from this that it is time to put an end to the national republics and regions in the interests of... internationalism? Lenin said in 1913, in his controversy with the Bundists, that the slogan of national culture is a bourgeois slogan—does it not follow from this that it is time to put an end to the national cultures of the peoples of the USSR in the interests of... internationalism?

Lenin said that national oppression and national barriers are destroyed under socialism—does it not follow from this that it is time to put a stop to the policy of taking into account the specific national features of the peoples of the USSR and to go over to the policy of assimilation in the interests of... internationalism?

And so on and so forth.

There can be no doubt that this deviation on the national question, disguised, moreover, by a mask of internationalism and by the name of Lenin, is the most subtle and therefore the most dangerous species of Great-Russian nationalism.

Firstly, Lenin never said that national differences must disappear and that national languages must merge into one common language within the borders of *a single* state *before the victory* of socialism *on a world scale*. On the contrary, Lenin said something that was the very opposite of this, namely, that "national and state *differences* among peoples and countries... will continue to exist *for a very, very long time* even *after* the dictatorship of the proletariat has been established on a *world* scale" (Volume XXV, p. 227). (My italics—*J. Stalin*)

How can anyone refer to Lenin and forget about this fundamental statement of his?

True, Mr. Kautsky, an ex-Marxist and now a renegade and reformist, asserts something that is the very opposite of what Lenin teaches us. Despite Lenin, he asserts that the victory of the proletarian revolution in the Austro-German federal state in the middle of the last century would have led to the formation of *a single, common* German language and to the *Germanization* of the Czechs, because "the mere force of the unshackled intercourse, the mere force of modern culture of which the Germans were the vehicles, without any forcible Germanization, *would have converted into Germans the backward Czech petty bourgeois, peasants and proletarians who had nothing to gain from their decayed nationality*" (see Preface to the German edition of *Revolution and Counterrevolution*).

It goes without saying that such a "conception" is in full accord with Kautsky's social-chauvinism. It was these views of Kautsky's that I combated in 1925 in my speech at the University of the Peoples of the East. But can this antiMarxist chatter of an arrogant German social-chauvinist have any positive significance for us Marxists, who want to remain consistent internationalists?

Who is right, Kautsky or Lenin?

If Kautsky is right, then how are we to explain the fact that relatively backward nationalities like the Belorussians and Ukrainians, who are closer to the Great-Russians than the Czechs are to the Germans, have not become Russified as a result of the victory of the proletarian revolution in the USSR, but, on the contrary, have been regenerated and have developed as independent nations? How are we to explain the fact that nations like the Turkmen, Kirghiz, Uzbeks, Tajiks (not to speak of the Georgians, Armenians, Azerbaijanians, and others), in spite of their backwardness, far from becoming Russified as a result of the victory of socialism in the USSR, have, on the contrary, been regenerated and have developed into independent nations? Is it not evident that our worthy deviators, in their hunt after a sham internationalism, have fallen into the clutches of Kautskyan social-chauvinism? Is it not evident that in advocating a single, common language within the borders of *a single* state, within the borders of the USSR, they are, in essence, striving to restore the *privileges* of the formerly predominant language, namely, the *Great-Russian* language?

What has this to do with internationalism?

Secondly, Lenin never said that the abolition of national oppression and the merging of the interests of nationalities into one whole is tantamount to the abolition of national differences. We have abolished national oppression. We have abolished national privileges and have established national equality of rights. We have abolished state frontiers in the old sense of the term, frontier posts and customs barriers between the nationalities of the USSR. We have established the unity of the economic and political interests of the peoples of the USSR. But does this mean that we have thereby abolished national differences, national languages, culture, manner of life, etc.? Obviously it does not mean this. But if national differences, languages, culture, manner of life, etc., have remained, is it not evident that the demand for the abolition of the national republics and regions in the present historical period is a reactionary demand directed against the interests of the dictatorship of the proletariat? Do our deviators understand that to abolish the national republics and regions at the present time means depriving the vast masses of the peoples of the USSR of the possibility of receiving education in their *native* languages, depriving them of the possibility of having schools, courts, administration, public and other organizations and institutions in their *native* languages, depriving them of the possibility of being drawn into the work of socialist construction?

Thirdly, Lenin never said that the slogan of developing national culture *under the conditions of the dictatorship of the proletariat* is a reactionary slogan. On the contrary, Lenin always stood for *helping* the peoples of the USSR to develop their national cultures. It was under the guidance of none other than Lenin that at the Tenth Congress of the Party, the resolution on the national question was drafted and adopted, in which it is plainly stated that:

"The Party's task is to *help* the laboring masses of the nonGreat-Russian peoples to catch up with Central Russia, which has gone in front, to *help* them; a) to develop and strengthen Soviet statehood among them in forms corresponding to the national conditions and manner of life of these peoples; b) to develop and strengthen among them courts, administrations, economic and government bodies functioning in their native languages and staffed with local people familiar with the manner of life and mentality of the local inhabitants; c) to develop among them press, schools, theaters, clubs, and cultural and educational institutions in general, functioning in the native languages; d) to set up and develop a wide network of general-educational and trade and technical courses and schools, functioning in the native languages."

Is it not obvious that Lenin stood wholly and entirely for the slogan of developing national culture *under the conditions of the dictatorship of the proletariat*?

Is it not obvious that to deny the slogan of national culture under the conditions of the dictatorship of the proletariat means denying the necessity of raising the cultural level of the nonGreat-Russian peoples of the USSR, denying the necessity of compulsory universal education for these peoples, means putting these peoples into spiritual bondage to the reactionary nationalists?

Lenin did indeed qualify the slogan of national culture *under the rule of the bourgeoisie* as a reactionary slogan. But could it be otherwise?

What is national culture under the rule of the national bourgeoisie? It is culture that is *bourgeois* in content and national in form, having the object of doping the masses with the poison of nationalism and of strengthening the rule of the bourgeoisie.

What is national culture under the dictatorship of the proletariat? It is culture that is *socialist* in content and national in form, having the object of educating the masses in the spirit of socialism and internationalism.

How is it possible to confuse these two fundamentally different things without breaking with Marxism?

Is it not obvious that in combating the slogan of national culture under the bourgeois order, Lenin was striking at the bourgeois *content* of national culture and not at its national form?

It would be foolish to suppose that Lenin regarded socialist culture as *nonnational*, as not having a particular national form. The Bundists did at one time actually ascribe this nonsense to Lenin. But it is known from the works of Lenin that he protested sharply against this slander, and emphatically dissociated himself from this nonsense. Have our worthy deviators really followed in the footsteps of the Bundists?

After all that has been said, what is left of the arguments of our deviators?

Nothing, except juggling with the flag of internationalism and slander against Lenin.

Those who are deviating towards Great-Russian chauvinism are profoundly mistaken in believing that the period of building socialism in the USSR is the period of the collapse and abolition of national cultures. The very opposite is the case. In point of fact, the period of the dictatorship of the proletariat and of the building of socialism in the USSR is a period of the *flowering* of national cultures that are *socialist* in content and national inform; for, under the Soviet system, the nations themselves are not the ordinary "modern" nations, but *socialist* nations, just as in content their national cultures are not the ordinary bourgeois cultures, but *socialist* cultures.

They apparently fail to understand that national cultures are bound to develop *with new strength* with the introduction and firm establishment of compulsory universal elementary education in the native languages. They fail to understand that only if the national cultures are developed will it be possible really to draw the backward nationalities into the work of socialist construction.

They fail to understand that it is just this that is the basis of the Leninist policy of *helping* and *promoting* the development of the national cultures of the peoples of the USSR.

It may seem strange that we who stand for the future *merging* of national cultures into one common (both in form and content) culture, with one common language, should at the same time stand for the *flowering* of national cultures at the present moment, in the period of the dictatorship of the proletariat. But there is nothing strange about it. The national cultures must be allowed to develop and unfold, to reveal all their potentialities, in order to create the conditions for merging them into one common culture with one common language in the period of the victory of socialism all over the world. The flowering of cultures that are national in form and socialist in content under the dictatorship of the proletariat in one country *for the purpose* of merging them into one common socialist (both in form and content) culture, with one common language, when the proletariat is victorious all over the world and when socialism becomes the way of life—it is just this that constitutes the dialectics of the Leninist presentation of the question of national culture.

It may be said that such a presentation of the question is "contradictory". But is there not the same "contradictoriness" in our presentation of the question of the state? We stand for the withering away of the state. At the same time we stand for the strengthening of the dictatorship of the proletariat, which is the mightiest and strongest state power that has ever existed. The highest development of state power with the object of preparing the conditions *for* the withering away of state power—such is the Marxist formula. Is this "contradictory"? Yes, it is "contradictory". But this contradiction is bound up with life, and it fully reflects Marx' dialectics.

Or, for example, Lenin's presentation of the question of the right of nations to self-determination, including the right to secession. Lenin sometimes depicted the thesis on national self-determination in the guise of the simple formula: "Disunion for union". Think of it—disunion for union. It even sounds like a paradox. And yet, this "contradictory" formula reflects that living truth of Marx' dialectics which enables the Bolsheviks to capture the most impregnable fortresses in the sphere of the national question.

The same may be said about the formula relating to national culture: The flowering of national cultures (and languages) in the period of the dictatorship of the proletariat in one country with the object of preparing the conditions for their withering away and merging into one common socialist culture (and into one common language) in the period of the victory of socialism all over the world.

Anyone who fails to understand this peculiar feature and "contradiction" of our transition period, anyone who fails to understand these dialectics of the historical processes, is dead as far as Marxism is concerned.

The misfortune of our deviators is that they do not understand, and do not wish to understand, Marx' dialectics.

That is how matters stand as regards the deviation towards Great-Russian chauvinism.

It is not difficult to understand that this deviation reflects the striving of the moribund classes of the formerly dominant Great-Russian nation to recover their lost privileges.

Hence the danger of Great-Russian chauvinism as the chief danger in the Party in the sphere of the national question.

What is the essence of the deviation towards local nationalism?

The essence of the deviation towards local nationalism is the endeavor to isolate and segregate oneself within the shell of one's own nation, the endeavor to slur over class contradictions within one's own nation, the endeavor to protect oneself from Great-Russian chauvinism by withdrawing from the general stream of socialist construction, the endeavor not to see what draws together and unites the laboring masses of the nations of the USSR and to see only what can draw them apart from one another.

The deviation towards local nationalism reflects the discontent of the moribund classes of the formerly oppressed nations with the regime of the dictatorship of the proletariat, their striving to isolate themselves in their national bourgeois state and to establish their class rule there.

The danger of this deviation is that it cultivates bourgeois nationalism, weakens the unity of the working people of the different nations of the USSR and plays into the hands of the interventionists.

Such is the essence of the deviation towards local nationalism.

The Party's task is to wage a determined struggle against this deviation and to ensure the conditions necessary for the education of the laboring masses of the peoples of the USSR in the spirit of internationalism.

That is how matters stand with the deviations in our Party, with the "Left" and Right deviations in the sphere of general policy, and with the deviations in the sphere of the national question.

Such is our inner-Party situation.

Now that the Party has emerged victoriously from the struggle for the general line, now that our Party's Leninist line is triumphant along the whole front, many are inclined to forget the difficulties that were created for us in our work by all kinds of deviators. More than that, to this day some philistine-minded comrades still think that we could have managed without a struggle against the deviators. Needless to say, those comrades are profoundly mistaken. It is enough to look back and recall the handiwork of the Trotskyists and Right deviators, it is enough to recall the history of the struggle against deviations during the past period, to understand the utter vacuity and futility of this party philistinism. There can be no doubt that if we had not curbed the deviators and routed them in open struggle, we could not have achieved the successes of which our Party is now justly proud.

In the struggle against deviations from the Leninist line our Party grew and gained strength. In the struggle against deviations it forged the *Leninist unity* of its ranks. Nobody now denies the indisputable fact that the Party has never been so united around its Central Committee as it is now. Everybody is now obliged to admit that the Party is now more *united* and *solid* than ever before, that the Sixteenth Congress is one of the few congresses of our

Party at which there is no longer a definitely formed and united opposition capable of counterposing its separate line to the Party's general line.

To what is the Party indebted for this decisive achievement?

It is indebted for this achievement to the circumstance that in its struggle against deviations it always pursued a policy *based on principle*, that it never sank to backstairs combinations or diplomatic huckstering.

Lenin said that a policy based on principle is the *sole* correct policy. We emerged victoriously from the struggle against deviations because we honestly and consistently carried out this behest of Lenin's (*Applause.*)

I shall now conclude, comrades.

What is the general conclusion?

During the past period we have achieved a number of decisive successes on all the fronts of socialist construction. We achieved these successes because we were able to hold aloft the great banner of Lenin. If we want to be victorious we must continue to hold aloft the banner of Lenin and keep it pure and unstained. (*Applause.*)

Such is the general conclusion.

With the banner of Lenin we triumphed in the battles for the October Revolution.

With the banner of Lenin we have achieved decisive successes in the struggle for the victory of socialist construction.

With this banner we shall triumph in the proletarian revolution all over the world.

Long live Leninism! (*Loud and prolonged applause. An ovation from the entire hall.*)

Stalin, *Works*, XII, 242-385.

STALIN TRIUMPHS AT SIXTEENTH PARTY CONGRESS
OBSERVATION BY LOUIS FISCHER
22 July 1930

Louis Fischer, a journalist and astute observer of Soviet politics, wrote an article for The Nation following the Sixteenth Party Congress. He witnessed how Stalin had prevailed over his political opponents, his political power and strength, and the change in the mood and character of Party members over the past decade. He also noted Stalin's need for praise and adulation.

LOUIS FISCHER
WHY STALIN WON
22 July 1930

The sixteenth party congress just ended was a complete victory for Stalin. Premier Rykov was unexpectedly retained in the Politburo, and Tomsky and Bukharin, his Right-wing colleagues, were reelected into the Central Committee on Stalin's own wish. They get another trial. They could easily have been eliminated. The congress did Stalin's bidding. What is the secret of Stalin's unquestioned strength? He controls every wheel and secret of the party machine, which is the source of authority and power in the Soviet Union. This is extremely important. For dynamic energy, driving force, and discipline the Russian Communist Party is unique the world over, perhaps even throughout history. But party manipulations are not everything. To explain Stalin's influence by his absolute domination of the party apparatus is to neglect the most decisive psychological and economic factors of the Soviet situation.

Russia today is the strangest combination of brightest white and darkest black. You may spend one evening in a discussion of unprecedented, exciting achievements and the next evening—often among foreigners who suffer the least—listening to distressing tales of hardships. Both are true. Communists, however, are an optimistic, enthusiastic race. They glory in their accomplishments but wave away difficulties. This was the spirit of the delegates who defeated Rykov, Bukharin, and Tomsky and riotously hailed Stalin as their chief.

I encountered some of the delegates. If you mentioned the food shortage they spoke of Dnieperstroi, Kuznetskstroi, Magnitorgorsk, and the other huge power, iron, and steel works which will be larger than any in Europe. If you reminded them that people cannot buy shoes and textiles they told you that in three years Russia will be the world's second-largest producer of cast iron, that the Soviet Union is turning out more and more machines, that its industrial output is double the prewar amount and will soon be doubled again, that collectives and state farms will eliminate the food shortage, that at the end of the Five Year Plan—in 1933—Russia will be manufacturing more tractors than America, that she will then export grain, grow her own cotton, and have enough livestock to satisfy home demands, and, finally, that the Soviet Union is quickly ceasing to be a backward, semiAsiatic country.

Men in this optimistic mood, convinced that they are about to "overtake and outstrip" capitalist nations, and themselves responsible for the construction now in progress, do not want it interrupted, will not listen to Cassandra warnings, and will not applaud meek-minded moderates who caution against excessive haste in industrialization and collectivization. The Right-wingers irritate them; Stalin, on the other hand, makes faith in victory a doctrine. This same faith then becomes another factor in that victory. Stalin fires his followers with additional zeal by preaching selfassurance; he increases the construction tasks assigned, introducing a sporting element into their fulfillment, and mows down the doubters. Seers of evil, prophets of disaster have no place in Bolshevik psychology. This is one of the outstanding subjective weaknesses of the Right cause, and one of Stalin's greatest advantages.

The Right platform stands on three pillars: (1) more freedom to the kulak, or rich peasant, (2) less collectivization, and (3) stimulation of light industries which produce goods for immediate consumption. But all these proposals are impracticable. Why? Public recantations do not change the leopard's spots, and Rykov, Tomsky, and especially Bukharin want the upper layer of the peasantry to work with less official interference. It is Bukharin's old summons to the muzhik to "get rich", which he retracted under pressure in 1925 but which he obviously still upholds. If the kulak could become rich every sredniak, or middle peasant, would follow in his footsteps, for the sredniak, as Trotsky writes, "is the kulak conveyor". (He feeds the kulak ranks belt-fashion.) And that would spell the end of collectivization. Immersed in private-capitalistic instincts, not wholly prepared psychologically for cooperative cultivation, and not yet completely convinced of the benefits of collective farming, the sredniak submitted to collectivization because the door to individual enrichment was closed by the government's suppression of the kulak. The reversal of this policy would throw the sredniak—40 percent or so of the peasantry—into the antiCommunist camp, suspend collectivization, and obstruct the socialization of the village. A large class of prosperous individualistic farmers in Russia would mean a liberal, petty bourgeois Russia with soviets persisting only as an outward form.

The suppression of the kulak class is the corollary of collectivization and vice versa. Collectivization is the cornerstone of Bolshevik agrarian policy. It is inconceivable that the Communists should suspend or weaken collectivization or support any leaders who suggest such a measure. The Right may perform a useful function in drawing attention to uneconomic means of collectivizing and to the need of improving the internal organization of collectives, but it cannot gain a wide party following by condemning collectivization as a system. For without collectivization there can be so socialism and no Bolshevik solution of the peasant problem.

The strength of the Right-wingers lies in the friendly echo their views arouse among the peasant and petty bourgeois masses. But this is the very cause of their downfall within the party, which sees the danger of tolerating prominent Communists who advocate heterodox policies with a broad appeal. For the same reason, on the other hand, the Right cannot be dealt with so summarily as the Trotsky opposition. The Bukharin opposition has roots. Less is achieved by merely cutting off the plant above the ground. The Right-wingers' peasant policy demands the stimulation of light industry. To induce the peasant to part with his increased yield resulting from greater individual freedom, they say, the city must offer him more goods for immediate consumption. The impulse thus given to light industry will also react to the benefit of the urban population.

Now nobody would object to the alleviation of the "goods famine" if it could be attained without damage to heavy industry. The heavy industries must not suffer. They are the solid foundation which bolshevism is laying for Russia's future development. Without them the country is dependent, incapable of defense in war, and doomed to a low standard of living. Moreover, if agricultural overproduction continues throughout the world, and if the Soviet Union were to remain a predominantly agrarian country, nobody would desire her exports, her foreign trade would shrink and her growth would be stunted. Industrialization is the historic function of bolshevism and answers the highest national interests. In the end the nation will be grateful to the Soviet regime for its persistence and courage in carrying out a difficult program despite the terrific costs to all inhabitants of the Union. The heavy industrialization base of the new structure is of course not an end in itself but a means whereby light industry may prosper. Ultimately, more coal, cast iron, steel, turbines, chemicals, spindles, locomotives must mean more shoes, shirts, clothing, and more food too. But is just this "ultimately"—the time element—that is so trying. While the foundation is under construction the people forego many necessities. In two years, in three years at the most, the dividends on the present sacrifice investment will probably be paid. This intervening period is inevitably filled with murmurs, complaints, and sour "anecdotes". The Right wing reflects this displeasure.

A compromise on this issue is not impossible. For whereas surrender on collectivization might be disastrous, a slackening of the pace of heavy industrialization so that textile, leatherwear, clothing, and food industries would receive more money and materials is not precluded. There is at least margin here for maneuvering. Yet I do not think it realistic to expect any very appreciable improvement of light industry in the near future. The state cannot well discontinue the construction of the great metallurgical plants at Magnitogorsk, in the Kuznetsk basin in Siberia, and around Dnieperstroi, nor of the two huge additional tractor factories in Cheliabinsk and Kharkov, nor of the Nizhni Novgorod automobile factory, nor of the numerous other heavy industrial "giants" which have been started in the past year or two. The government, as Kuibyshev, reporting on industry, told the party congress, must also carry out the program of 15,000,000 tons of cast iron by 1932/33 (compared with 5,500,000 tons this year and 4,200,000 tons in 1913), which requires corresponding increases in kindred heavy industries like coal, oil, electricity, transport. This being the case, little surplus strength or funds will be left for light industry.

These and other Soviet economic problems meet at one focal point—foreign trade. Although the means of production are being manufactured in Russia in mounting quantities, the Bolsheviks must turn to foreign countries for much of the equipment of their big steel and electrical power plants and for technical engineering assistance. This costs money. It must be paid for in foreign currency or gold, which Moscow does not possess in abundance.

Further depletion of the solid metal cover of the ruble would induce further inflation with all its initial benefits and all its disastrous aftereffects. Moscow must therefore husband its valuta, force exports even at the expense of prime domestic necessities, and cut imports to the bone so as to include little else than the indispensable needs of heavy industry. This is the root of the people's hardships. For instance, Russia must import cotton from the United States. But it prefers to spend its dollars on drills, compressors, and turbines for the Stalingrad tractor works and similar undertakings. Cotton, consequently, reaches the Soviet Union in reduced volume, the country is textile-hungry, and textile factories, some of them new, close down for want of raw material.

The chief hope for an early improvement on the internal market lies in foreign credits, which would make it unnecessary for Russia to export food, tobacco, and other products its own population needs and at the same time allow the government to import more raw materials—in addition, of course, to machinery. Foreign credits, on good terms, would bring a sigh of relief to Moscow. We may therefore see a more liberal Soviet foreign policy under a very influential new commissar. But observers who interpret the first signs of such a policy as the beginnings of a swerve to the Right internally are quite mistaken. The contrary is true, for the principle holds almost invariably that a Left policy which produces the greatest strain inside may well be complemented by a Right strategy to win the most help abroad.

Special difficulties arise this year owing to the fall of world prices. Russia's exports will expand in volume, but oil, lumber, and cereals will fetch relatively less-an estimated 28 percent less. Considerable grain sales to foreign customers—the Union may export some 2,500,000 tons after the present harvest—should, however, repair this loss. The final solution of the shortages will come, nevertheless, not through outside assistance but from the reorganization of agriculture. Kuibyshev said this to the party congress in almost so many words. Only when the state farms and collectives yield vastly more livestock, poultry, bread, dairy products, cotton, tobacco, sugar, vegetables, flax, fats, and fruit will the problem of internal supply be settled satisfactorily. Here again, therefore, everything hinges on collectivization—and on tractors, fertilizer, agricultural machinery, in other words, on heavy industry. Heavy industrialization and collectivization are Siamese twins. Collectivization implies an antikulak war.

Since light industries cannot be greatly stimulated, since collectivization must not be undermined, since the kulak will be amnestied, the Right platform collapses, the Right-wingers suffer defeat, and Stalin wins. I think the Right wing, though convinced of the justice of its negative criticism, fears the possible results of its positive recommendations. To turn back in 1930 might signify a retreat down a decline which offered no opportunities for digging in at halfway stations. In *The Nation* of 30 April 1930, I suggested that despite the rightward zigzag of March "a large potential of Leftness" remained which would act as a "guaranty against any permanent or far-reaching swing to the Right". This has certainly been borne out by events since that date. And the "potential of Leftness" is far from exhausted. Nothing but a severe economic crisis will force a change of policy under Stalin's leadership.

Psychology and economics are Stalin's favorable winds. He is also the party "boss". But he is, in addition, the Soviet Union's most striking personality. He outranks all other Russian statesmen in courage, willpower, maneuvering talents, political organizing ability, and primitive tenacity. If he lacks the intellectual attainments of a Trotsky or Bukharin his very directness, force, and even crudeness appeal to a party whose membership has changed radically since 1924 and in which the prerevolutionary "highbrow" feels himself slightly out in the cold. Stalin's job, of course, is no bed of roses. But he weathered the mad tempest that raged in the villages during January and February, and even emerged from it strengthened. Now he will do well to look to the mood of the workers. Their real wages must not fall below the present level. Prices should be pegged, and the criminal inefficiency of the cooperatives eradicated.

A good friend might also advise Stalin to put a stop to the orgy of personal glorification of Stalin which has been permitted to sweep the country. This is Stalin's Achilles heel. From being the modest, retiring leader whom few saw or heard—the silent power behind the "throne"—he has in recent months stepped forth into the brightest limelight and seems to enjoy it. He has become the object of thickly smeared praise, fawning adulation, and tasteless obeisance. Bolshevik politicians go out of their way to sing extravagant odes to Stalin's person (Zinoviev is the last to do it). Daily, hundreds of telegrams pour in on him brimming over with Oriental supercompliments: "Thou art the greatest leader... the most devoted disciple of Lenin," and the like. Three cities, innumerable villages, collectives, schools, factories, and institutions have been named after him, and now somebody has started a movement to christen the Turksib the "Stalin Railway". I have gone back over the newspapers from 1919 to 1922: Lenin never permitted such antics and he was more popular than Stalin can ever hope to be. It exposes a weak side of Stalin's character which his enemies, who are numerous, are sure to exploit, for it is as unBolshevik as it is politically unwise. If Stalin is not responsible for this performance he at least tolerates it. He could stop it by pressing a button.

Fischer, *The Nation*, Vol. 131, No. 3397, 13 August 1930, 174-176.

ELIMINATION OF VESTIGES OF PEASANT CONTROL IN THE COUNTRYSIDE
23-30 July 1930

The forced collectivization of farms and dekulakization literally destroyed the old commune and village system. The party and government filled the void by focusing on the village soviet as the new basis of authority. They abolished the okrug administrative unit and transferred personnel and authority to the raions, which in turn took on greater control and responsibility for the countryside. They also created associations of collective farms and cooperatives to manage production and services in the countryside as well as to be the link between the peasant and the state. The first document below is a decree from the Council of People's Commissars and Central Executive Council that abolished the okrug and transferred resources and authority to the raions. Stalin recommended the abolishment of the okrug in his report to the Sixteenth Party Congress. The second document, a resolution of the Party Central Committee, describes the functions and responsibilities of raion associations of kolkhozes and cooperatives.

DECREE. ON THE LIQUIDATION OF THE OKRUGS
23 July 1929

The tremendous successes of the socialist reconstruction of industry, the extensive spreading of the kolkhoz movement in the countryside and liquidation of the kulak as a class on the basis of complete collectivization, the active participation of widespread masses of workers, day laborers, and poor and middle peasants in the socialist reconstruction of the entire national economy require from the entire Soviet bureaucracy, primarily from its lower organs, the precise leadership to carry out the tasks connected with the expanded socialist offensive and alteration of farming, culture, and way of life.

For this what is necessary is the maximum approximation of authoritative organs to the population and strengthening them with all the means at their disposal, extending their rights and responsibilities and establishing their direct link with higher central organs of authority, the central executive committees and councils of people's commissars of union and autonomous republics, and krai (oblast) executive committees.

The approximation of authoritative organs to the population will contribute to the simplification of the bureaucracy, to the decisive struggle with bureaucratism, and to the still greater attraction of the wide masses of workers and peasants to the practical work of the soviets.

As a result of this, the Central Executive Committee and the Council of People's Commissars of the USSR resolve:

1. To abolish the okrug, establishing 1 October 1930 as the deadline for the liquidation of okrug organs.

2. Upon the abolishment of the okrugs, to base the raions and village soviets on the existing boundaries, while not permitting their enlargement.

During the period of liquidating the okrugs, changes in the boundaries of raions and village soviets cannot proceed any further without the permission of the presidium of the USSR Central Executive Committee.

3. In connection with the liquidation of the okrugs, transfer their materials and resources to the raion executive committees, creating from these authoritative organs that are stronger and closer to the population and the leadership over the entire political, economic, social, and cultural life of the raions.

4. To propose to the governments of the union and autonomous republics, as well as to the krai (oblast) executive committees to increase work on the leadership of the lower organs of authority and to establish immediately the direct link with the raion executive committees.

With these aims, to strengthen the instructional and inspection bureaucracy of the central executive committees of the union and autonomous republics, and the krai (oblast) executive committees.

5. To transfer to the raion executive committees the right and to place on them the responsibilities given to the okrug executive committees for effective legislation.

6. To allot for the raion executive committees and city soviets the revenue granted to okrug executive committees for effective legislation.

7. To acknowledge the necessity of transferring to the management of raion executive committees and city soviets the enterprises and social and cultural institutions under the management of okrug executive committees, except for those which, on the basis of special resolutions, must be allotted through the proper channels for krai (oblast) executive committees and central organs of union republics.

8. With the aim of greater strengthening and expansion of the material bases of the lower soviets, to expedite the introduction of budgets in all the village soviets of the USSR.

9. To direct to the raions not less than 90 percent of okrug personnel.

At the same time to adopt decisive measures to strengthen the cadre of village soviets and increase the material situation of employees of the raions and village soviets.

10. During the process of liquidating the okrugs, to preserve in full the rights of the autonomous republics and oblasts. The network of village soviets and raions of national minorities must also be completely preserved.

11. The organization of the raion system on the foundations indicated above must be carried out so that the administrative and managerial expenditures for the 1930/1931 budget year, for both the state and local budgets, do not exceed the sum designated for supporting the okrug and raion bureaucracy in 1929/1930.

12. To instruct the central executive committees of union and autonomous republics, and the krai (oblast) executive committees to assign immediately special commissions to develop all measures connected with bringing to life the liquidation of the okrugs.

13. In connection with liquidating the okrugs and abolishing the okrug budgets, to instruct the USSR People's Commissariat for Finance to give in five days' time instructions about the procedure for establishing local budgets that would provide for the increase in the raion budgets and bringing them to life beginning on 1 October 1930.

14. To instruct the central executive committees of the union republics to present in twenty days' time to the presidium of the USSR Central Executive Committee reports on measures adopted to liquidate the okrugs and strengthen the work of raion executive committees.

15. To instruct the USSR Council of People's Commissars to develop a draft law on the bases for organizing raion organs of authority and in one month's time to present it for examination by the presidium of the USSR Central Executive Committee.

Sobranie Zakonov i Rasporiazhenii, No. 37 (8 August 1930), Article 400, 676-678.

PARTY RESOLUTION. ON THE REORGANIZATION OF THE KOLKHOZ AND COOPERATIVE SYSTEM

30 July 1930

In execution of the decisions of the Sixteenth Party Congress on the reorganization of the kolkhoz and cooperative system, the TsK VKP(b) resolves:

1. To concentrate in a single raion kolkhoz association all the organizational and production management of kolkhoz construction in a raion.

2. To concentrate in a single raion cooperative association all the work for the production and services of individual farms as well as the procurement, sales, and supply foundations in relation to all kolkhozes, cooperative farms, and individual holdings. In the raions where there is an extremely low percentage of collectivized farms, to permit an exception to the raion kolkhoz association by creating kolkhoz autonomous sections attached to the raion cooperative association, for which this question is to be decided in each separate case by oblast organizations and approved by the Union of associations and the Kolkhoz Center.

3. The raion kolkhoz association, while developing the specialization of kolkhozes according to the basic direction of agriculture in the raion, manages and services kolkhozes united around them also along the lines of the given raion's minor branches of agricultural production.

It is precisely the raion cooperative association, side by side with the servicing of the simplest production associations for the basic branch of agriculture in the raion, manages their activity also in relation to all minor branches of agricultural production.

The staff of the raion kolkhoz association and raion cooperative association must be filled accordingly with specialists and must possess the necessary flexibility to provide for the thorough organizational and production services for agricultural production in a given raion.

4. Because of the need to accelerate the development of cattle breeding, to pay special attention to the increased construction of raion cooperative associations and low level production associations for cattle breeding.

5. To reduce the number of special centers of agricultural cooperatives, leaving in the oblasts and krais not more than four special associations in accordance with the basic market

direction of agricultural production in an oblast or krai. To acknowledge the need to create, in addition to the All-Union Grain Center, also all-union centers of cooperatives for cattle breeding, fruit and vegetables, flax, cotton, and sugar beets.

6. Keeping in mind the specific task placed on seed growing cooperatives for expanding the production of pure, high quality seed to the sowed area in the quickest time, to keep in the form of a separate existing organization the all-union seed growing center and, per the decision of the USSR People's Commissar for Agriculture, there will be in those oblasts, where it would be necessary, an oblast association of seed growing cooperatives which rely for their work on seed growing kolkhozes and clusters of companies.

7. To reorganize republic and oblast (krai) kolkhoz associations to manage the activity of raion kolkhoz associations.

8. The general management of the kolkhoz and cooperative system is exercised by the Union of associations organized from: Representatives of special cooperative centers, Kolkhoz Center with the Tractor Center, and the Union Kolkhoz Bank. In republics, oblasts, and krais, there are created cooperative councils for the exchange of experience and the coordination of activities among various cooperative systems.

9. The TsK emphasizes that the reorganization of the kolkhoz and cooperative system can give results only if there would be the actual strengthening of the kolkhoz and cooperative system with the appropriate cadre of both specialists and leading party workers.

Upon the liquidation of the okrugs, the cadre of kolkhoz and special associations of agricultural cooperatives must be transferred to the corresponding raion kolkhoz and cooperative associations. Kolkhoz organs must be strengthened also with new workers at the expense of the liquidated soviet, economic, and other okrug organizations. The reorganization of the kolkhoz and cooperative system must effectively reduce the staff and rationalize the entire work of the kolkhoz and cooperative bureaucracy.

To commit a fraction of the Union of associations, the USSR Narkomzem, and the USSR People's Commissar of the Workers' and Peasants' Inspectorate to reduce managerial expenses along the entire kolkhoz and cooperative system from top to bottom by not less than 50 percent in relation to the bureaucracy at a given moment.

10. Because the network of low level settlements of the cooperative system is extremely weak and shattered, and the local areas are completely liquidated, the TsK commits the fraction of the Union of associations and centers of agricultural cooperatives as well as local party organizations to take timely and energetic measures to reconstruct and strengthen the network of settlement cooperatives. The harvest and autumn sowing campaign must be used to the utmost for carrying out this task.

11. With the aim of regulating the supply to farms of agricultural machinery and equipment, to instruct the USSR Narkomzem to establish the following procedure to supply farms with agricultural machinery:

a) the supply of machines and equipment to sovkhozes and kolkhozes within the limits of plans approved by USSR Narkomzem is carried out by the joint stock company "Sel'khozsnabzhenie" directly and as a rule, as transit goods (agricultural machine building plan - sovkhoz or kolkhoz);

b) the supply of agricultural machinery and equipment to the simplest cooperative production associations and individual poor and middle peasant farms, as well as the supply to kolkhozes of small tools, is carried out by the joint stock company "Sel'khozsnabzhenie" through the raion cooperative associations of agricultural cooperatives in accordance with their plans;

c) movable stock, spare parts, unseasonable agricultural machinery and that machinery which cannot be shipped as transit goods are delivered to interraion warehouses by the joint stock company "Sel'khozsnabzhenie" to supply both sovkhozes and kokhozes, and raion associations of agricultural cooperatives.

12. To introduce the reorganization of the kolkhoz and cooperative system not later than one month's time.

13. In view of the special importance of the tasks placed on the Grain Center and its entire system of grain procurement, the TsK commits party organizations to strengthen the grain cooperative and not to permit the withdrawing of workers from the Grain Center system prior to the conclusion of the grain procurement campaign, except for part of the special production workers who are being transferred to the kolkhoz system.

14. To instruct the TsKK, RKI, USSR Narkomzem, and Gosbank to develop in one month's time the question on the financial and credit system in the raion.

Pravda, 2 August 1930, 3.

LITVINOV BECOMES PEOPLE'S COMMISSAR FOR FOREIGN AFFAIRS. PRESS STATEMENT

25 July 1930

Maxim Litvinov officially succeeded G. Chicherin as People's Commissar for Foreign Affairs after the latter's death following years of ill health. Litvinov was in fact commissar during the last two years of Chicherin's illness. In a press statement, he explained that his appointment did not signify a change in Soviet foreign policy, and that the Soviet Union wanted to maintain a peaceful coexistence with the capitalist countries through trade and security agreements. Foreign policy would protect the Soviet Union during the building of socialism and expand trade. Litvinov's official appointment emphasized the Soviet Union's greater participation in world organizations, such as the League of Nations, and deemphasized reliance on relations with Germany.

PRESS STATEMENT BY LITVINOV ON HIS APPOINTMENT AS COMMISSAR FOR FOREIGN AFFAIRS

The decision of the Central Executive Committee of the USSR on my appointment as People's Commissar cannot in any way signify any change whatever in the foreign policy of the Union; not merely because I have already been working for the past ten years in the Commissariat for Foreign Affairs in close collaboration with my predecessor, Comrade Chicherin, with whom I have actively shared in working out and conducting questions of foreign policy, while in the past two years I have in fact been in charge of the Commissariat, but chiefly because a change in the heads of departments in the Soviet State cannot have the same significance as in capitalist countries. In these, changes in the Government, and in particular among those in charge of foreign policy, are in the majority of cases the result of a struggle among political parties and the class interests they represent, and sometimes of adaptation to a changing international situation or even to external influence. In the country of the proletarian dictatorship, where the workers and peasants exercise full and undivided power, foreign policy is wholly determined by the will of the working and peasant masses, which finds its expression in the decisions of the Soviet Government.

The principles of the October revolution are the foundations of the Union's foreign policy, and the defense of the conquests of the revolution from external action and intervention is one of its principal objects. No less important as an object of Soviet diplomacy is to secure conditions of peace and freedom from external disturbances for our socialist construction.

The greater our plans of development, the more rapid their pace, the greater is our interest in the preservation of peace. Our efforts have been directed to this end up to now, and will continue to be directed thereto in an even greater degree in the future.

We have to build socialism in our own country, surrounded by capitalist countries occupying five-sixths of the earth's surface. We cannot ignore this fact and do not ignore it, and we are therefore trying to discover and put into operation methods for the peaceful coexistence of the two social systems. We have, and shall have in the future, to make the greatest efforts to combat the aggressive tendencies of certain capitalist groups making for the creation of constant disputes and conflicts between the two systems; therefore these efforts will be directed to the consolidation and maintenance of peace among the nations.

However, the important national, political, and economic antagonisms existing within the capitalist world prevent the adoption of a uniform attitude towards the Soviet Union and the elaboration of unified methods of struggle against it. The so-called peace treaties which brought the imperialist war to an end, which imposed tremendous burdens on some countries for the benefit of the others, have aggravated these antagonisms, tracing an ineffaceable barrier between the so-called victors and vanquished. Because of our natural sympathy with countries where the greatest weight of the burdens imposed falls on the workers, and also because the States interested in the perpetuation of the consequences and injustices embodied in these treaties are also at the same time conducting a most aggressive and hostile policy towards our Union, a certain community of interests has been established between the Soviet Union and the States which suffered from the war. On the basis of this community of interests there have developed with some of these States wholly correct, normal, and even in some cases friendly relations, which we are anxious to develop and strengthen in a loyal fashion in the future. We do not, however, seek to take part in the grouping of some States against others; we shall sincerely try at the same time to establish relations with all States that wish to do so.

We do not deny that in carrying out the plans for our expanding economy, we should like to be able to count on the further expansion of our economic intercourse with other States. The more our economy expands, the greater the field for the application of foreign technique, foreign labor, the products of foreign industry, and even of certain raw materials. But even here we encounter inimical tendencies among certain hostile capitalist groups, who are conducting a campaign for the severance of economic relations with our Union. Their efforts appear to be directed chiefly against our exports, but in fact they are against our entire foreign trade, for a reduction in our exports would inevitably mean a corresponding reduction in our imports. The foreign exchange connection between exports and imports is so clear that it is unnecessary to dwell upon it. The States being subjected to this campaign, emanating from interested but insignificant groups of our competitors in the export markets, and which have placed artificial legislative or other obstacles in the way of the import of our raw materials and goods, should not naively believe that these measures will not involve the reduction or cessation of our imports from them. We are, however, convinced that all these antiSoviet campaigns are doomed to failure, for in the long run they must injure not only our interests, but even the interests of those countries which join in such campaigns. At the present time, when the economic crisis is spreading so deep and wide, when the economic crisis is spreading so deep and wide, affecting almost all European and nonEuropean countries, the exclusion from world trade of a country as vast as our Union, which is growing stronger economically and which alone is free from depression, will scarcely be regarded as an appropriate measure in keeping with the interests of a realistic policy. A real and correct understanding of the interests of the capitalist countries themselves must impel them to prolong and extend their economic relations with the Soviet Union.

We ourselves take full account of the necessity for economic relations and trade agreements in the given historical circumstances. We therefore did not in the past decline, and we do not intend to decline to meet representatives of other countries, and examine jointly with them the problems which may affect the interests of our Union. We shall willingly support designs and proposals aimed at removing the possibility of armed conflicts and of securing general peace. We shall, however, take the part of merciless prosecutor whenever we find that under the hypocritical mask of pacifist phrases there are concealed appetites and interests that have nothing to do with peace and with the real interests of the nations. We shall confine ourselves to the role of observer in those cases where the real aims of international gestures are insufficiently clear to us and require greater precision and exposition. We remain resolutely hostile to any international actions which might in any degree favor the oppression of some nations by others or the preparation of new wars.

We shall with particular attention follow the policy of our nearest neighbors, where a strengthening of aggressive and chauvinist movements has recently become discernible, representing a serious threat to peace; now as before we are of the opinion that one of the most important tasks of our diplomacy is to strengthen peaceful good-neighborly relations with these countries in the spirit of the pacific proposals we have repeatedly made and of the Moscow protocol.

In general we shall continue our old and tried foreign policy in the consciousness of its correctness, its accordance with the interests of all peoples, and also in the consciousness of the growing might of the Soviet Union.

Degras, II, 449-451.

PARTY RESOLUTION. INTRODUCTION OF COMPULSORY EDUCATION

25 July 1930

The Party Central Committee and the Sixteenth Party Congress called for the introduction of three years of compulsory primary education. They recognized the need to improve the education level of the Soviet population, especially in the countryside where education was weak, so as to provide the technical personnel to make industrialization a success.

RESOLUTION OF THE TSK VKP(B) ON GENERAL COMPULSORY EDUCATION

The development of socialist construction and the great tasks connected with this for the training of cadre, liquidation of cultural and technical backwardness, and the communist education of the broad masses require the quickest introduction of general compulsory education as the most important precondition for the most further development of the cultural revolution.

The successful carrying out of general compulsory education "will be the greatest victory not only on the cultural, but also on the political and economic fronts" (Stalin).

In spite of the significant growth of children who have acquired an elementary education, compared to the prerevolutionary situation, the TsK acknowledges it as completely unsatisfactory the rate of preparation and introduction of general compulsory education. Noting the weak work for introducing general compulsory education by soviet organs, particularly the people's commissariats for education, their organs in the local areas and the executive committees in the majority of the republics and oblasts, as well as the completely insufficient attention and effect in this work by party, trade union and other organizations, the TsK considers it necessary:

1. Beginning with the year 1930/31 to introduce compulsory education for children of the age of 8, 9 and 10 years, and subsequently to extend general compulsory education to children of age 11, beginning with the year 1931/32.

In this respect the particular local customs and organizational difficulties are to be taken into account in suburban settlements, in various national republics and oblasts, as well as in distant provinces, but only to the extent that the nonfulfillment of the terms must not exceed one and two years, respectively. In each individual case the approval of the government of the respective union republic must be obtained.

Beginning with the year 1930/31 general compulsory education is introduced for children 11 to 15 years of age who have passed through the elementary school. These children will attend courses of one to two years.

Beginning with the year 1930/31 general compulsory education extending over seven years is being introduced in the industrial towns, factory districts and workers' settlements for those children who passed through the elementary school (first stage) in the respective year.

To render special attention to the development of seven-year factory and plant schools.

In particular the school for the youth of collective farms (day and night schools) are to be developed in order to include the main mass of the youth in collective farms at the end of five years.

2. In addition to a considerable increase in the financial means for meeting the cost of general compulsory education as well as the construction, maintenance and equipment of the elementary schools, the economic, trade union, cooperative and social organizations are to be drawn into this work. Further, the initiative of the broad masses is to be mobilized for this purpose (i.e., in the form of socialist competitions, allotting for these purposes the revenues obtained by the collective farms from their market produce, support afforded by the patronage organizations, assistance by gratuitous labor, etc.).

The economic organizations, in accordance with the decisions of the SNK of the USSR and SNK of union republics, must include in their industrial and financial plans the means for the construction of schools and for general compulsory education, under the same heading as the means for the construction of big buildings.

Beginning with the year 1930/31 to increase significantly the funds for construction of schools for general compulsory education with special subsidies in connection with the introduction of general compulsory education specified in the all-union budget. The size of these subsidies are established by the SNK of the USSR corresponding with the general education plan.

Former landowners' houses, confiscated kulak buildings, etc. are to be used for schools. In the expenditure of means on the construction of schools, consideration is to be given in the first place to the requirements of the chief industrial districts, the workers' centers, the districts with complete collectivization, as well as all the culturally backward districts.

3. In order to guarantee the schools the educational staff which is necessary for general compulsory education:

a) The network of pedagogical institutes, seminaries, and special pedagogical courses is to be extended.

b) In view of the new tasks of the teachers, the material position of the elementary school teachers must be considerably raised. The village school teacher shall be granted rations equal to those of the workers.

c) The Marxist-Leninist training and the technical qualifications of the teachers in particular is necessary.

The nucleus of Communist workers among the teachers must be enlarged. The Central Committee of the Komsomol is to be called upon to mobilize at least 20,000 VLKSM members annually for work in the schools and for training in the pedagogical institutions.

4. In order to guarantee the practical results of school education the quality of instruction must be raised. Beginning with 1930/31 material support of the scholars with gratuitous school material, shoes, clothes, food, fares, etc. for the children of the poor peasantry is to be granted. For this purpose the budgets must be enlarged, among other ways, by making use of the means available in the new special funds formed by the social organizations. At the same time the formation of preparatory groups of the children of workers, day laborers and poor peasants before their entrance into the schools shall be taken in hand by means of the cultural campaigns.

5. In order to facilitate the preparation for the introduction of general compulsory education, the TsK calls upon the Party organizations:

a) To consider the introduction of general compulsory education as the most important political campaign during the whole of the next period;

b) To induce the Party members to participate actively and systematically in the work of the auxiliary committees and of the elected school organizations (school councils and parents' councils);

c) The Party committees must receive, at least twice annually, the reports of the fractions of the executive committees and Soviets regarding the progress of the introduction of general compulsory education, and systematically discuss in the nuclei meetings the questions of its practical carrying out under the local conditions (factory-plant region, settlement, village).

6. Carrying out in the shortest time the general compulsory education is connected with a series of tremendous difficulties. The decisive surmounting of these difficulties can be achieved only under conditions when the matter of introducing general compulsory education is transformed into a massive public and political campaign, relying on the initiative and independence of the entire proletarian society and on the wide use of such work methods as cultural campaigns, socialist competitions, patronage of enterprises over schools, public review, mass conferences, etc.

The TsK considers it necessary, in order to mobilize means and teachers for the introduction of general compulsory education, to form auxiliary committees of active workers and functionaries of the collective farms who are working in cultural spheres for the introduction of general compulsory education in the town and village soviets, and executive committees, with the participation of people's education departments, trade union organizations, komsomol, society for the liquidation of illiteracy, society of children's friends.

The TsK calls upon the local and central press to develop a large-scale campaign in connection with the introduction of general compulsory education by means of systematic discussion of all questions of this work.

International Press Correspondence, Vol. 10, No. 36 (7 August 1930), 706.
KPSS v rezoliutsiiakh, Vol. 4, 473-476.

DECREE ON CHANGE FROM ECONOMIC TO CALENDAR YEAR

20 September 1930

Faced with setbacks in industrial production and the inability to meet the accelerated rates established for the economic years 1930/31-1932/33, the Soviet Government found the solution in postponing by one quarter the goals for 1931/32 and decreed that annual plans would henceforth coincide with the calendar year.

DECREE OF USSR TSIK AND SNK ON THE TRANSFER OF THE BEGINNING OF THE ECONOMIC YEAR FROM 1 OCTOBER TO 1 JANUARY

After the difficult years of the civil war, Soviet power, having set about restoring the national economy, established for calculation purposes the economic year from 1 October through 30 September instead of the customary calendar year. This decision was carried out with the goal of taking in the calculation of the economic year the cycle of agricultural production which at the time rested on individual, small-scale agriculture.

At the present time, the tremendous growth of sovkhozes and kolkhozes, which carry on planned farming and the planned introduction of sowing campaigns, enable to a significant degree to determine the results of the subsequent following agricultural year.

The successes already achieved in the organization of socialist agriculture to a tremendous degree strengthened and increased the role of the planning principle in the entire national economy. The role of new construction, growing with each year, both in the development of industry and agricultural production and in communal and living matters and in the cultural development of the country, require that the planning of the economic year will take in the entire construction season, which ends in the month of November-December.

As a result of this, the Central Executive Committee and the Council of People's Commissars of the USSR decree:

1. To establish the economic year from 1 January through 31 December, beginning with 1931.

2. To instruct the Council of People's Commissars of the USSR to approve not later than 5 October 1930 a national economic and financial plan and budget for October-December 1930.

3. The control figures, financial plan, and a single state budget of the USSR for 1931 must be completed with such a calculation that the final economic task would be sent to plants, factories, and other enterprises not later than the end of December 1930.

The control figures, financial plan, and single state budget of the USSR for 1931 must be submitted for approval at the session of the USSR Central Executive Committee not later than the middle of December 1930.

Resheniia, 243.

DECREE ON MEASURES TO MEET LABOR SHORTAGE

9 October 1930

Rapid industrialization compelled the Soviet Government to find ways to meet a growing labor shortage in industry. In the 1920s there was a general surplus of labor and entry into the labor market was the prerogative of the trade unions. The decree below from the People's Commissariat for Labor discontinued unemployment benefits and replaced the trade-union responsibility with the direction and planned placement by the Commissariat's labor exchanges. The Soviet propaganda machine used the lack of unemployment to contrast the

Soviet regime with that of capitalist countries where unemployment was increasing as a result of the Great Depression.

DECREE OF THE PEOPLE'S COMMISSARIAT FOR LABOR OF THE USSR REGARDING THE IMMEDIATE DISPATCH OF ALL UNEMPLOYED TO WORK AND THE CESSATION OF PAYMENT OF UNEMPLOYMENT BENEFITS

The People's Commissariat for Labor decrees as follows:

1. In view of the great shortage of labor in all branches of State industry, insurance bureaus are requested to discontinue payment of unemployment benefits. No provision for the payment of unemployment benefits has been made in the Budget of Social Insurance for the supplementary quarter October-December 1930.

2. Labor exchanges are instructed to take all necessary measures in order that the unemployed be immediately sent to work, and of these the first to be sent are persons entitled to draw unemployment benefits.

3. Unemployed persons are to be drafted not only to work in their own trades, but also to other work, necessitating special qualifications.

At the same time labor exchanges, according to local conditions (the needs of any particular trade) should extend their activities in the training and retraining of the unemployed.

4. No excuse for refusal of work, with the exception of illness, supported by a medical certificate, should be considered. Refusal of work carries with it removal from the registers of the labor exchanges.

Medical certificates should be issued to the unemployed by medical boards and medical control boards. Unemployed in possession of medical certificates will receive benefits under the heading of unemployment benefits, but the benefits will come out of the sums allocated for temporary capacity.

5. The personal responsibility for the due and correct execution of the present decree is placed upon the heads of the labor exchanges (and in districts where these are not in existence on the directors of labor organizations) and upon the chairmen of insurance bureaus.

6. Article 1 of the present decree is to be put into force by telegraph.

Selection of Documents, 425-426.

THE SYRTSOV-LOMINADZE PLOT
DECISION BY MOSCOW PARTY COMMITTEE
12 November 1930

The party suddenly uncovered a plot in October 1930 of the "right-ultraleft bloc," which was secretly formed to undermine the collectivization and industrialization policies of the Sixteenth Party Congress. This fictitious plot, under the leadership of S.I. Syrtsov and V.V. Lominadze, openly agreed with the general party line, but secretly conspired to undermine it. In fact, Syrtsov, who became one of the darlings of the party leadership, Lominadze, and others criticized the administrative and bureaucratic measures used to collectivize and industrialize the country. The Moscow Party Committee submitted its decision to condemn and expel the bloc members (to the Party Central Committee). The Party Central Committee agreed with the decision, removed them from their posts, and expelled them from the party. Criticism of the party line now carried grave consequences.

DECISION OF THE MOSCOW COMMITTEE AGAINST THE SECRET FRACTIONAL ACTIVITY IN THE CPSU

After hearing the report on the fractional activity of Comrades Syrtsov and Lominadze directed against the Party and its CC, the Bureau of the Moscow Committee of the CPSU together with the Presidium of the Moscow Control Commission and the secretaries of the district party committees of Moscow, adopted the following decision:

The Bureau considers it to be evident that Comrade Syrtsov founded a secret faction central to which Comrades Nusinov, Kavraisky, Galperin and others, belonged; that Comrade Lominadze stood at the head of a secret fraction group to which belonged Comrades Shatskin, Reznikov and others, and that these two fractional groups concluded a bloc for the common struggle against the Party and its leadership. These groupings have existed for a long time (before, during and after the Sixteenth Party Congress), masking their activity by declarations of their complete agreement with the general line of the Party and the recognition of the correctness of the Party leadership. The Syrtsov-Lominadze group like all Right opportunist and Trotskyist elements, ignored the peculiarity of the present period of the proletarian revolution as a period of enhanced socialist offensive along the whole front, of gigantic development of socialist economy, which is closely bound up with the accentuation of the class struggle and the inevitable difficulties to overcome which the Party is exerting all its forces and mobilizing the broadest proletarian masses. Comrades Syrtsov, Lominadze and Shatskin, et. al. carefully concealed their real antiParty views, penetrated into leading Party organs and in a provocatory manner made use of their positions in order to organize the fraction struggle against the policy of the Party and its CC. Comrades Syrtsov and Lominadze commenced the fight against the Party at a moment when the class enemies of the proletariat mobilized all their forces for the struggle against the proletarian dictatorship and our Party, when the counterrevolutionary sabotage organizations (Industrial party, party of the toiling peasants, etc.) were discovered and their connection with the imperialist interventionists ascertained, at a moment when the Right opportunists in the Party increased their struggle against the CC and ideologically more and more approach to the counterrevolutionary sabotage organizations. Under these conditions the Syrtsov-Lominadze group has by its secret fraction struggle against the Party and its CC taken up the position of the Right opportunists and of the counterrevolutionary Trotskyists and entered the path of undermining the dictatorship of the proletariat.

Instead of actively supporting the Party in its fight for a rapid rate of industrialization of the country, for the socialist transformation of agriculture, for the liquidation of the kulaks as a class, the Syrtsov-Lominadze group, under the mask of self-criticism, discredits these slogans and its speculating upon the difficulties. In its struggle against the Party it is repeating the Trotskyist and Right opportunist assertions of an "inner-Party regime"; it is repeating all the shameful calumnies of the enemies of the proletariat and its henchmen against the Party leadership of the CPSU. The bloc of the Right opportunist Syrtsov group, which formerly proclaimed the slogan: "Accumulate calmly" and its leader, the "Left" semi-Trotskyist Lominadze, represents only another attempt on the part of the Right opportunist elements (Bukharin, Rykov, Tomsky group) to unite with the Trotskyist and semi-Trotskyist elements for a common struggle against the Party.

The fact that the Right and "Left" Syrtsov-Lominadze group are adhering to the Right opportunist standpoint (the question of the rate of socialist construction, etc.) and conducting the fight against the Party, fully exposes the altered Left position of the semi-Trotskyist and Trotskyist "Left" elements and again confirms the statement that the Right danger is the main danger in the Party.

The Sixteenth Party Congress has called the attention of the whole Party to the new maneuver of the Right and other opportunist elements, which is expressed in their formal recognition of their mistakes and their formal agreement with the general line of the Party without, however, this recognition being confirmed by work and fight for the general line which attitude in reality only represents the transition from the open fight against the Party to a concealed fight or to waiting for a more favorable moment in order to resume the attacks upon the Party. This double game is further confirmed by the fact that the leaders of the Syrtsov-Lominadze fraction bloc, who have been proved guilty of antiParty activity up to the last moment attempted to conceal their fraction activity by designating the statement regarding their antiParty activity as calumnies and malicious talk. The fraction work of the Syrtsov-Lominadze group again confirms the correctness of the warning issued by the Sixteenth Party Congress in regard to the new maneuvers of the Right and "Left" opportunists and in regard to the necessity of waging a ruthless struggle against them.

The Bureau of the Moscow Committee is convinced that the CC and CCC will adopt against Comrades Syrtsov and Lominadze the organizational measures resulting from the decisions of the Sixteenth Party Congress, and if necessary expel them from the ranks of the CPSU. In view of the discovery of the fractional double game of the Syrtsov-Lominadze group, in view of the enhanced activity of all opportunist and in particular of the Right elements (Riutin, Slepkov, Maretsky, et. al.), and in view of the attitude of the former leaders of the Right opposition (Bukharin, Rykov and Tomsky), who have not carried out the decisions of the Sixteenth Party Congress regarding the active struggle for the general line of the Party, further iteration cannot be permitted. The Bureau of the Moscow Committee believes that such an attitude on the part of the members of the CC—Bukharin, Rykov, Tomsky, must become the object of special investigation on the part of the CC and of the CCC. The Moscow Committee of the CPSU calls upon all Bolsheviks of the Moscow Party organizations to rally still more closely around the Leninist CC and to display a still greater vigilance, ideological and organizational ruthlessness in the fight against the Right and "Left" opportunists and hypocrites as well as also against the conciliators. The Moscow Committee of the CPSU expresses the firm conviction that our Party, in spite of antiParty and fractional attacks, in spite of the attempts on the Party of the petty bourgeois elements to disorganize the work of the Party and to undermine the iron unity of its ranks, will, under the leadership of its CC, continue to march firmly and unshakably along the path of successful socialist construction, along the path of carrying out the general line of the Party.

International Press Correspondence, Vol. 10, No. 52 (20 November 1930), 1073-1074.

MAXIM GORKY DECLARES CIVIL WAR AGAINST KULAKS AND OTHER CAPITALIST ENEMIES

15 November 1930

Beginning in the autumn of 1930, party officials renewed the collectivization drive and dekulakization, but, much more cautiously than they did early in 1930. The poor showing of industrial production in the last quarter of the economic year led to the intensification of industrialization. Propaganda became one of many weapons used. Maxim Gorky used his fame and pen to publish an article simultaneously in Pravda and Izvestiia to justify collectivization, dekulakization, and a civil war against domestic and foreign bourgeois and capitalist enemies. His article below was publicized in other media.

"IF THE ENEMY DOES NOT SURRENDER—
DESTROY HIM"

The energy of the advanced ranks of the workers and peasants has been organized by the teachings of Marx and Lenin to lead the masses of toiling people in the Soviet Union to a goal which can be expressed in four simple words: *Create a new world.* In the Soviet Union, even the Pioneers, the children, understand that to create a new world, to set up new conditions of life, it is necessary:

To make it impossible for individuals to amass riches which are always squeezed out of the sweat and blood of the workers and peasants; to abolish the division of people into classes, to abolish every possibility of the exploitation of the creative energy and the labor of the majority by a minority; to expose the poisonous lies of religious and national prejudices, which disunite people, making them hostile and incomprehensible to each other; to cleanse the lives of the workers from the savage and filthy habits of life which have been forced on them by centuries of slavery; to destroy everything, which, by hindering the growth of the consciousness of their community of interests among the working people, allows the capitalists to organize wholesale slaughter to drive millions of workers to fight against each other, to wars which have always one single purpose; to strengthen the predatory rights of the capitalists, to increase their senseless passion for profits and for power over the workers.

In the long run, this means to set up conditions for all to reach the heights which have been attained with a useless expenditure of energy only by exceptional, so-called "great men".

Is this fantastical dreaming, romancing? No, it is reality. It is the enemies of the workers and peasants, who describe this mass movement for the building of a new world as fantastic romancing, people who, as a "Russian woman" recently wrote to me, form a "thin stratum of educated and European thinkers", and who, as she writes, are convinced that "intelligence belongs to the few, cannot be formed among the masses." Culture is the creation of a few highly gifted people.

In these words, the "Russian woman" crudely but correctly expressed the whole philosophy and poverty of bourgeois ideology, expressed everything that bourgeois philosophy can bring forward in opposition to the spiritual renaissance of the proletarian masses. The spiritual renaissance of the proletariat throughout the world is an indisputable fact. The working class of the Soviet Union, marching ahead of the proletarians of all countries, well confirms this new reality. It has set itself a grandiose task, and is successfully carrying it out by concentrated energy. The difficulties of fulfillment are enormous, but where there's a will there's a way. Ten years ago, the working class, almost without arms, bootless, ragged, hungry, drove out of their country the well armed white armies of the European capitalists, drove out the troops of the interventionists.

For thirteen years, working for the construction of their own government with a small number of honest and loyal specialists, intermingled with a mass of the vilest traitors, who compromise not only their comrades but science itself, working in an atmosphere of the hate of the world bourgeoisie, and the sneers of the "advanced bourgeois technicians" who maliciously point to all the small mistakes, shortcomings, defects, working under conditions the difficulties of which they themselves have no clear idea,—in these hellish conditions the working class has developed an absolutely stupendous concentration of genuine revolutionary and miraculous energy.

Only the heroic courage of the workers and of the Party which expresses the mind of the revolutionary masses could have made such advances under these unfavorable conditions, such as, for example, increasing industry by 25 percent in 1929/30 instead of the 22 percent stipulated in the plan, cultivating 36 million hectares in the collective farms instead of 20 millions! In addition to all this, while expending their energy on the construction of industry, while guiding the reorganization of the villages, the working class and the peasants are continually producing from among their ranks hundreds of talented administrators, shock brigadiers, worker correspondents, writers, inventors, and new intellectual forces in general.

Within the country, the cunning foe is organizing against us a shortage of food, the kulaks are terrorizing the collectivized peasants by murders, incendiarism, by all kinds of crimes, against us are aligned all who have outlived their historical age, and this gives us the right to consider that we are still in the midst of a civil war. Hence, the natural conclusion to be drawn is if the enemy does not surrender, destroy him.

From abroad, European capital is fighting against the creative work of the Soviet Union. It has also outlived its age and is doomed to destruction. But it still wishes and still has the power to resist the inevitable. It has connections with all those traitors who are carrying on their work of destruction within the Union, and who are shameless enough to assist the predatory intentions of the capitalists.

Poincare, one of the organizers of the European slaughter of 1914-1918, with the nickname "Poincare la guerre", the man who almost lost the war for the capitalists of France, the former socialist Briand, the famous drunkard Lord Birkenhead who recently died, and other faithful lackeys of capital are preparing a robber attack on the Soviet Union, with the blessing of the head of the Christian church.

We are living under conditions of unceasing war against the whole bourgeois world. This compels the working class to make real preparations for self-defense, in defense of their historic role, in defense of all that they have created for themselves or for the enlightenment of the proletariat of all countries during the course of thirteen years of heroic self-sacrificing work on the construction of the new world.

The working class and the peasants must arm themselves, remembering that the power of the Red Army was able victoriously to brave the onslaught of world capitalism without arms, hungry, ragged, bootless, and led by their comrades who were not well acquainted with the stratagems of war. We have now a Red Army, an army of warriors, each of whom understands what he will fight for. And if, absolutely panic stricken in their terror of the inevitable future, the capitalists of Europe nevertheless dare to send against us their workers and peasants, it is necessary to deal them such a blow that it will be the death blow which will cast capitalism into the grave that has been dug for it by history.

International Press Correspondence, Vol. 10, No. 54 (27 November 1930), 113-114.
Pravda, 15 November 1930, 1.

THE INDUSTRIAL PARTY SHOW TRIAL COURT VERDICT

8 December 1930

Between 25 November and 7 December 1930, the Soviet Government staged the spectacular show trial of eight members of a fictional organization, the so-called Industrial Party, who were accused and found guilty of wrecking, economic sabotage, treason, espionage, and undermining socialist construction. The verdict, delivered by the Soviet Supreme Court, claimed that the Industrial Party grew from a coordinating center for wrecking activities into an underground political organization in 1925 with the purpose of preparing the ground for a coup d'etat in 1930 or 1931. Supported primarily by French government officials and financiers, the Industrial Party was making preparations for military intervention by France and its allies. It was estimated that the party consisted of as many as 2,000 members. The trial consisted of rehearsed testimonies of leading engineers, such as Leonid Ramzin. It was an attempt to make the technical intelligentsia more responsive to pressures to support Soviet industrialization. It was also convenient for the Soviets to find a scapegoat for the poor performance of industrialization.

VERDICT OF THE SUPREME COURT OF THE SOVIET UNION
IN THE SPECIAL INVESTIGATION INTO THE CASE OF THE
COUNTERREVOLUTIONARY ORGANIZATION, "THE INDUSTRIAL PARTY"

In the name of the Union of Socialist Soviet Republics the Special Investigation of the Supreme Court of the USSR composed as follows: President comrade A.Zh. Vishinsky, and judges comrades V.P. Antonov-Saratovsky and Vl. L'vov, the secretaries comrades A.F. Iakovlev, G.I. Ivanenko and P.I. Sharutin in the presence of the State Prosecutor, the Public Prosecutor of the RSFSR comrade N.V. Krylenko and the Vice-Public Prosecutor of the RSFSR comrade V.I. Fridberg, and the members of the Moscow District Collegium of Advocates, the defending lawyers comrades I.D. Braude and M.A. Ozep, which sat in public and closed sessions from 25 November to 7 December 1930 to investigate case No. 38 of the counterrevolutionary organization known as "The Association of Engineers Organizations" ("Industrial Party") with the following accused:

1. Leonid Konstantinovich Ramzin, 43 years old, a citizen of the Soviet Union, former Professor of the Moscow Academy for Mechanical Engineering and former Director of the Thermal Technical Institute;

2. Ivan Andreevich Kalinnikov, 56 years old, a citizen of the Soviet Union, former Vice-Chairman of the productive sector of the State Planning Commission and former Professor of the Military Air Academy and other Academies;

3. Viktor Alekseevich Larichev, 43 years old, a citizen of the Soviet Union, former Chairman of the Fuel Section and a former member of the Presidium of the State Planning Commission of the Soviet Union;

4. Nikolai Franzevich Charnovsky, 62 years old, a citizen of the Soviet Union, former Vice-Chairman of the Scientific and Technical Council of the Engineering Industry in the Engineering Department of the Supreme Council of the National Economy of the Soviet Union and former Professor of various Academies;

5. Aleksandr Aleksandrovich Fedotov, 66 years old, a citizen of the Soviet Union, former Chairman of the Collegium of the Scientific Research Institute for the Textile Industry and former Professor of various Technical Academies;

6. Sergei Viktorovich Kuprianov, 59 years old, a citizen of the Soviet Union, former Technical Director of the Textile Organization of the Supreme Council of the National Economy of the Soviet Union;

All charged with offenses under Article 58, Paragraphs 3, 4 and 6 of the Penal Code of the RSFSR; and;

7. Vladimir Ivanovich Ochkin, 39 years old, a citizen of the Soviet Union, former Scientific Secretary of the Thermal Technical Institute, and former Chairman of the Scientific Research Department of the Supreme Council of the National Economy of the Soviet Union;

Charged with offenses under Article 58, Paragraphs 3 and 6 of the Penal Code of the RSFSR; and;

8. Ksenofon Vasileevich Sitnin, 52 years old, a citizen of the Soviet Union, and former Engineer of the All-Russian Textile Syndicate;

Charged with offenses under Article 58, Paragraphs 3 and 4 of the Penal Code of the RSFSR;

has come to the following conclusions:

The final destruction of the armies of the white-guards Generals, which were organized and led by the imperialist States and which tried to overthrow Soviet power and restore the power of the landowners and capitalists, by the Red Army in the year 1920 opened up the path to the peaceful economic constructive work of the toilers of the Soviet Union on a socialist basis. In alliance with the decisive masses of the peasantry, the working class of the Soviet Union liquidated with great efforts during the course of the following years the worst results of the imperialist and the civil wars, overcame numerous difficulties during the reconstruction period which was concluded in these years, and proceeded under new circumstances to a widespread socialist offensive along the whole front.

During the course of the whole reconstruction period, the struggle of the working class for the speediest possible regulation of the economic life of the Soviet Union and for the success of the socialist constructive work, met with violent and unrelenting resistance on the part of those capitalist elements which had remained in our country and on the part of those sections of the bourgeois intelligentsia which had made common cause with them. These elements worked with all methods, sabotage, direct destruction of State property and even the destruction of whole undertakings, to disorganize, hold up and prevent the victorious advance of the proletariat on the way to the economic reconstruction of the proletarian State and the consolidation of its socialist constructive work.

The successes of this constructive work on the one hand and the energetic struggle of the proletariat against all attempts to prevent this work on the other hand, paralyzed these efforts of the capitalist elements and accelerated the process of differentiation in the ranks of the bourgeois intelligentsia, as a result of which antisoviet and antiproletarian feelings became the common property of the leading section of this intelligentsia, which in the past was closely connected with capitalist circles and enjoyed a privileged position under capitalism. The most irreconcilable and venomous organizers of and participants in every form of counterrevolutionary conspiracy directed against the soviet economic system, for the destruction of Soviet industry, of socialist transport, traffic and agriculture, and for the preparation of the overthrow of Soviet power with armed force, came from this environment of the leading section of the specialists who were permeated with a bourgeois-capitalist ideology and were convinced opponents of the October Revolution and the work of socialist construction.

The development from the period of reconstruction into the period of construction, the growing progress of the whole economic system of the Soviet Union and the tremendous successes of the socialist constructive work on the one hand and the increasing crisis in the capitalist countries on the other caused bitter resistance on the part of the capitalist elements and those sections of the technical intelligentsia bound up with them in the Soviet Union and over the whole world. In spite of the ever strengthening and increasing economic, political and military power of the Soviet Union, all the forces of the old world formed a united front for a "crusade" against the proletarian State, the Fatherland of the world proletariat and of all toilers, and proceeded to mobilize all the methods of overt and covert attack.

This was the situation in which the counterrevolutionary organization, "The Association of Engineer Organizations" (Industrial Party) came into being, began its activity and united all those sabotage groups which were at work in the various branches of industry into a uniform organization.

The trial of the so-called Industrial Party revealed the fact that the crystallization of these various groups in the Industrial Party was furthered to a certain extent by the fact that the chief group of its participants consisted of the members of the counterrevolutionary organization known as the "Engineers Central Committee" which was formed in 1925 and which was led by the engineer Palchinsky who was executed in 1930 for sabotage in the gold and platinum industry, the former capitalist and millowner Rabinovich who was sentenced in the Shakhty trial and the engineer Fedorovich. The "Engineers Central Committee" itself developed out of two counterrevolutionary organizations which existed still earlier in the form of the so-called Club of "Mine Managers" and the All-Russia Engineers Association which had as their members the most reactionary and most antisoviet elements of the old engineering circles. This section of the old engineers worked chiefly in the mining industry and in the transport industry and consisted for the most part of former owners and shareholders of capitalist enterprises. The "Industrial Party", which consisted of persons out of the narrow stratum of the bourgeois intelligentsia, had no touch of any kind with the broad masses of the people and no support of any kind from these masses, so that it was condemned to maintain a narrow caste spirit.

The accused (Ramzin, Larichev and the others) were compelled to admit that the Industrial Party was unable to reckon with the sympathy of the masses, even in words, and still further that it was unable to reckon with the sympathy of the broad masses of the peasantry. The fact that the Industrial Party could reckon on no sympathy or support of any kind from the toiling masses explains why its leaders placed their hopes for the realization of their criminal plans not on internal but external forces.

The Special Investigation recorded the fact that in its efforts to recruit members from amongst the ranks of the engineers, technicians, Professors, the lecturers at the various institutions and enterprises, scientific research institutes and academies, the Central Committee of the Industrial Party adopted most varied methods beginning with propaganda and the payment of monies, as a reward for carrying out the instructions of the Industrial Party, and ending with threats of damaging the careers, the economic situation and the social position of those who hesitated or refused to join the Industrial Party. The activity of the Industrial Party was conducted on a strictly conspirative basis, and the connections between the members were only permitted within the framework of the branch organizations, so that the members of different branch organizations did not know each other. The judicial investigation revealed the fact that the Industrial Party was led by a Central Committee which had developed from the main group of the old Engineers Central Committee whose chief leaders were Palchinsky, Rabinovich, Fedorovich, Krennikov and Krasovsky and later Ramzin, Larichev, Kalinnikov, Charnovsky, Fedotov, Osadchy, Shein and others, whereby after the arrest of Palchinsky and Krennikov the leading position in the Industrial Party was taken by Ramzin. In the Engineers Central Committee and later in the Central Committee of the Industrial Party, the leadership of the counterrevolutionary work was also divided amongst the members according to the principle of "branches". Accordingly, Palchinsky directed the counterrevolutionary work in the mining industry, in the gold mining industry, in the platinum industry and in the Biological Committee; Rabinovich directed the work in the mining industry with Palchinsky; Krennikov and Charnovsky directed the work in the ferrous metallurgical industry; Fedotov in the textile industry; Larichev in the fuel supply industry and above all in the oil industry; Krasovsky in the transport industry; Kalinnikov in the "Economic Group"; and Ramzin, apart from the general control of all the work, in the fuel and power supply industries.

In this way the reorganization of the "Engineers Central Committee" into the "Industrial Party" was completed towards the end of 1927. The trial revealed the fact that one of the factors accelerating this development was the desire of the "Engineers Central Committee" to mobilize all the counterrevolutionary elements of the technical intelligentsia in a struggle for power. Other very important factors in this process were the influence of such foreign counterrevolutionary organizations as the Trade and Industrial Committee (Torgprom), the association of former Russian capitalists under the leadership of Denisov, Riabushinsky, Tretiakov, Konovalov, Gusakov, Nobel, Mantachev and others with its seat in Paris, and further, the influence of the most aggressive imperialist circles in France.

The Industrial Party based its criminal sabotage activity on a program whose chief aim was the destruction of Soviet power and the restoration of the power of the capitalists and landowners by the establishment of a military dictatorship. The military dictator was to have been the white-guardist General Lukonisky or the leader of the Central Committee of the Industrial Party Palchinsky. The economic part of the program of the Industrial Party provided for the return of the factories, etc. to their former owner, or where such enterprises had been reconstructed, the compensation of the former owners by the issue to them of shares. In this way the action of the Industrial Party would have more than compensated the former owners by giving them the increased values created by the heroic efforts of the toiling masses of the Soviet Union in the refitted, reconstructed and newly-built enterprises. On the field of agriculture the program of the Industrial Party was the restoration of the large land owning system and the consolidation of the rich peasant enterprises, the return of the land to its former owners, or otherwise the compensation of the former owners from a special fund formed by the transformation of the soviet industrial enterprises into joint-stock companies. The methods used to carry this program into operation were different at different periods of the criminal activity of the Engineers Central Committee and of the Industrial Party. In the initial period of its criminal activity, for instance at the time of the introduction of the New Economic Policy, the Industrial Party (Engineers Central Committee) concentrated its efforts to secure a capitalist degeneration of Soviet power. A number of the accused spoke of this attitude of the Industrial Party (Engineers Central Committee) in their statements in the preliminary examination and during the trial. The accused Larichev, for instance, declared during the proceedings: "The New Economic Policy was to lead to the degeneration of Soviet power." The accused Kalinnikov declared: "When the NEP was introduced in 1921, the engineers began to cooperate gladly with Soviet power for the reconstruction of the economic system, because they were convinced that the reconstruction of industry would inevitably lead to the restoration of the bourgeoisie, because they could not conceive of a reconstruction of industry with any but capitalist methods." The accused Ramzin said the same and declared: "The NEP was regarded by me and the overwhelming majority of the old engineers as the beginning of the degeneration of Soviet power."

It was, however, not long before the Industrial Party was compelled, in view of the successful development of the socialist constructive work in town and country, to recognize that its hopes for the degeneration of Soviet power were baseless. The accused Kalinnikov declared: "In 1926 the reconstruction period of industry and transport was practically at an end... The technical intelligentsia, convinced that the result of the NEP with the conclusion of the reconstruction period must see a transformation to a bourgeois basis for the policy of Soviet power, observed the beginning of the new constructive period on a socialist basis in a very hostile fashion. Their hopes that the NEP would be continued in the new period of construction were not confirmed." This explains the search for new ways and means of the struggle against Soviet power and the gradual development to the preparations for an armed overthrow of Soviet power with the forces of the internal and external counterrevolution. Completely isolated from the masses of the toilers and without any support from these masses, the Industrial Party was soon compelled to realize that its hopes of a coup d'etat with the exclusive means of the counterrevolutionary elements within the Soviet Union were baseless. From this moment on the Industrial Party concentrated on the preparations for a military intervention against the Soviet Union and to this end took up organizational connections with the interventionist organizations both inside and outside the Soviet Union (the Social-Revolutionaries, the Constitutional Democrats, the Rich Peasant Group Kondratiev-Chaianov, the Menshevik group Sukhanov-Groman inside the Soviet Union, and abroad the Torgprom, the Miliukov group and the French interventionists, etc.).

In the first period of the existence of the Engineers Central Committee, the contact between this organization and the representatives of the Trade and Industrial Committee in Paris took the form of individual relations between the individual members of the first named organization and the former owners of the factories. For instance, Palchinsky maintained connections with Meshchersky; Fedotov with Morosov, Konovalov and Riabushinsky; Charnovsky with Denisov and Meshchersky; Rabinovich with Dvorshanchik, Larichev with Bardygin; Strichev with Nobel, Gusakov and Manachov, et. al. But from 1927/28 on these relations became more organized and systematic, whereby the Industrial Party completely subordinated itself to the leaders of the Torgprom and finally became the paid agents of this organization and of the foreign interventionist powers. It was in this period that Ramzin's first meeting took place with Riabushinsky at the instructions of Palchinsky and the Engineers Central Committee.

At this meeting (in the second half of 1927) not only such questions as the turning of the soviet enterprises into joint-stock companies, and the form of their future administration were discussed, but also the negotiations being conducted between the Torgprom and the governing circles of France for the organization of an armed intervention against the Soviet Union to take place in 1928. At this meeting Riabushinsky conveyed through Ramzin the demand of the Torgprom and of French capitalist circles that the Industrial Party should increase its work for the internal preparations for an intervention.

Considerable progress in this direction was made in 1928 when a number of members of the Central Committee of the Industrial Party (Ramzin, Larichev, Fedotov, Sitnin and others) visited the leaders of the white-guardist organization in Paris. As a result of this visit a concrete and detailed plan for the methods of the intervention preparations was worked out, with the tasks of the Torgprom, the aggressive militarist circles in France and the Central Committee of the Industrial Party specialized. The negotiations between Ramzin and Larichev in October 1928 in Paris with the leaders of the Torgprom (Denisov, Riabushinsky, Nobel, Gusakov, Konovalov, Starinkevich and Manachov) were of especial importance in this respect, as also were the discussions between Ramzin and General Lukomsky, Colonel Joinville and Colonel Richard. As revealed during the cross-examination of the accused Ramzin and Larichev, the conferences with the Torgprom paid special attention to those events which had interfered with the activity of the Industrial Party, such as the discovery of the sabotage organization in the Don Basin, the Shakhty Trial, and the discovery of the sabotage organization in the transport industry. The Torgprom (Denisov and Riabushinsky) was greatly interested in these questions because they complicated the sabotage work of the Industrial Party. Denisov exercised pressure in order to secure from that time on more attention for the metallurgical industry in order to bring about acute disproportions and to diminish the usefulness of the capital being invested. Nobel and Gukasov put questions concerning the oil industry and the firmness of the sabotage organization there, concerning the carrying out of sabotage to prevent the installation of new equipment, and to throttle export. They pointed out that they had given the general instructions for the sabotage activity in the oil industry to Strichov (a member of the Industrial Party) during his stay in Paris. With regard to the general situation of the Torgprom and the Industrial Party, Denisov pointed out that the work must be continued at all costs despite the discovery of individual sabotage organizations. Denisov also stressed in particular the fact that although the date of the intervention had been postponed from 1928 to 1930, there was no question of it being abandoned; on the contrary, that intensive preparations were being conducted abroad for the organization of the intervention and in consequence the sabotage activity of the Industrial Party in the Soviet Union was of greatest importance. At this conference the chairman of the Torgprom, Denisov, announced that French governing circles had decided on the organization of an armed intervention against the Soviet Union. Denisov also announced during the discussion of the intervention preparations, that a special military commission had been formed under the chairmanship of General Jeannim, the former French military representative with the Staff of Kolchak and that this commission was already at work.

The Paris conference in October 1928 was of decisive importance because:

1. the main lines of the work of the sabotage organizations, of the Torgprom and of the French interventionists were laid down and agreed upon;

2. the forms of the connections between the Torgprom and these circles were laid down in detail and the tasks for the preparation of the intervention were distributed. At the same time the form in which the sabotage activity of the Industrial Party was to be financed by these circles and the Torgprom were laid down.

The proceedings at the trial revealed the fact that during his stay in Paris in 1927 and 1928, the accused Ramzin was put into touch with agents of the French Service in Moscow, known as Mr. K. and Mr. R. The connection between the Industrial Party in the persons of Ramzin, and then Larichev, Kalinnikov and Ochkin with the agents of the French Service mentioned continued right throughout the following period and up to the time of the arrest of the accused in the present case in the summer of 1930. This connection was used for the transmission of various instructions in connection with the preparations of the Industrial Party for intervention and also for the transmission of espionage material collected by the Industrial Party to be sent abroad.

The Special Investigation of the Supreme Court of the Soviet Union which examined this side of the criminal activity of the accused in closed session and revealed facts concerning Mr. K. and Mr. R., which completely confirmed the statements made by the accused, has decided to place this matter before the Soviet government.

In accordance with the agreement concluded with the Torgprom at the conference in Paris in October 1928, the Industrial Party began from this moment to force its work to bring about an "artificial deterioration of the economic life of the country", whereby it adopted sabotage methods on a wide and systematized scale. The systematic sabotage work was carried out chiefly with the assistance of the following methods:

1. The method of the drawing up of minimal plans, with which was connected the question of the diminution of the tempo of the industrialization and of the growth of the whole economic system. As the accused Fedotov declared before the court, the Industrial Party operated with these methods with the support of the ideas of the right-wing deviation. He declared: "These ideas proved useful and seemed to offer such high hopes of a development of the NEP and the development of ideas of a basically bourgeois character that the support of these ideas was necessary and desirable." This method was connected with the struggle for a minimal Five Year Plan.

2. The method of bringing about disproportions between the individual branches of the economic system, and between individual parts of the same branches of the economy.

3. The method of "freezing up" capital investments by causing them to be made in unnecessary enterprise, or by an irrational utilization of the invested capital, with the aim of diminishing the tempo of the industrialization, lowering the value of industrialization and diminishing the successes of the socialist constructive work.

Ramzin declared before the court: "These three methods were applied as the fundamental methods for the systematic sabotage work."

The facts revealed by the Special Investigation of the Supreme Court concerning the sabotage offered a complete picture of this side of the criminal activity of the Industrial Party which was thus able to damage our socialist economic systems, but was quite unable to destroy our Five Year Plan or prevent our continued advance. The sabotage activity of the Industrial Party was effectively countered by the tremendous labor impulse of the working masses, their great labor enthusiasm and their persistent struggle to carry out the industrial and finance plans and even to exceed them. The shock group movement and the socialist competitive scheme which took on a mass character, the increase of the class watchfulness of the proletariat and the counterplans of the masses in industry and finance guaranteed the success of the work of socialist construction to such an extent that the minimal Five Year Plan set up by the Industrial Party proved to be inadequate and was exceeded in the first two years.

In its development to systematic sabotage the Industrial Party concentrated its criminal activities on the most important branches of industry and transport. It delivered its blows against the metallurgical industry, the fuel supply, the power supply, the chemical and textile industries, and transport with a view to producing losses in production, disproportions and a crisis.

With regard to the fuel supply, the Industrial Party reckoned on producing a crisis by guiding the development of this branch of our economic system in a direction intended to facilitate as far as possible the task of the intervention. With this end in view the Industrial Party did everything possible in order to prevent the exploitation of local fuel resources, in particular the coal and peat resources of the Moscow district, and the coal resources of the Kuznets Basin. The Industrial Party also prepared the conditions under which such districts as the central industrial district, the northwest district and great centers like Moscow and Leningrad would come into a precarious situation. This was to be done by delivering the main blow against the railway communications connecting these districts with the Don Basin and thus cutting off the supply of fuel from the Don Basin. At the same time the Industrial Party carried on a struggle against all forms of rational productive methods in the fuel supply industry, and in particular it tried to prevent the use of special cutting-machines for the production of peat fuel. It also tried to prevent the cheapening and the rational usage of peat fuel.

The Special Investigation of the Supreme Court revealed the fact that the Industrial Party not only conducted its sabotage activity through the practical work of its members who held various official positions in the various branches of the economic system, but also that it misused the activity of scientific institutions such as the Thermal Technical Institute under Ramzin's leadership, and the Peat Fuel Institute under the leadership of V. Kirpichnikov, who was also a member of the Industrial Party. The chief methods of sabotage in the fuel supply industry were the drawing up of plans:

1. containing deliberately low coefficients and tempos far below the real potentialities;
2. containing discrepancies between the carrying out of the preparatory work and the operative plans of production;
3. giving the production of less valuable products preference over the production of more valuable products.

The sabotagers paid particular attention to such important fuel supply districts as the Don Basin, the Kuznets Basin, the Kizel Basin and others and directed their main blow against the supply of these districts with electric current. In order to sabotage the power supply, the Industrial Party worked through its branches and individual members to adopt measures for the slowing down of the building or extension of electric power stations (Tver, Bobrikov, Shter, Suevo and others) and for the supply of these stations with unsuitable equipment.

With regard to the power supply, the Industrial Party directed its sabotage activity to bringing about a critical situation at the most important power generating points, arranging that the crisis should make itself particularly felt in the year 1930, i.e., in the fear fixed for the intervention.

Ramzin summed up the results of this criminal activity of the Industrial Party with regard to the power supply as follows in his statement before the court:

"The current was interrupted in the Don Basin, in the Moscow district, in the Leningrad district, in the Kuznets Basin and in the Kizel Basin, and a critical situation brought about, so that at the beginning of military operations a catastrophe would take place."

It must be pointed out, however, that here also the efforts of the Industrial Party suffered a complete lack of success.

With regard to the supply of metals the Industrial Party worked for the increase of the deficit by the creation of disproportions between the production and consumption of metals. This was done by deliberately holding down the plan proposals and the economic coefficients with regard to the possibilities of production (for instance, 7 million tons instead of 17 million tons); by a wrong utilization of the metals produced in the Soviet Union (in particular with regard to boiler-making); by the creation of disproportions between the metallurgical and the foundry industries (disproportions between the various departments); and by a deliberate slowing down of the development of the engineering industry, etc.

With regard to transport the sabotagers aimed at reducing the rolling material in the wagon parks, and in particular the number of locomotives by disorganizing the fuel supply of the carriage and locomotive building works, etc.

The Special Investigation of the Supreme Court revealed the fact through the examination of the accused Ramzin, the statements of the witness Krasovgky and the material in the protocol, that the sabotage in this respect was conducted in one fundamental direction whose main aim was:

1. to weaken the capacity of the repair works and to reduce the efficiency of the railway service;
2. to put forward false figures for the mobilization plans with criminal motives;
3. to secure a criminal reduction of the credits for the railways in the front line network;
4. to apply the "method of the low coefficient", in other words to place the coefficients or index figures too low with the result that in the building of apparatuses for the railway service, figures would be set which were not in accord with the real demands with regard to quantity and nomenclature, whereby a "freezing up" of capital would be obtained.

The aim of all these criminal acts was to disorganize transport by causing a critical situation at a moment of a military attack on the Soviet Union, particularly on the western frontiers, and further, to cut off communications with the Donets Basin and isolate this district from the center.

With regard to the chemical industry, the sabotage work was chiefly expressed in an attempt to install a series of great enterprises at deliberately unfavorable points and in an attempt to hold back apparatuses needed for the chemical industry.

With the regard to the textile industry, the sabotage work aimed at securing an irrational utilization of the invested capital by means of deliberately miscalculating the height of the stories in the newly-built factories so that they should not be in accordance with the needs, by a deliberate failure to utilize considerable floor space in the factory buildings, by preventing the import of the newest American textile machinery, by wrong management of the cotton supply and a deliberately false utilization of the cotton supply by wrong distribution of the yield, etc., and by a deliberately wrong distribution of the various sorts of textile products.

In this connection the sabotage work is worthy of note which aimed at slowing down the development of the linen and hemp industries in order to damage the defensive capacities of the Soviet Union.

The proceedings of the trial also revealed the fact that parallel with the attempts to bring about an economic crisis for the spring of 1930, the Industrial Party also conducted criminal activity for the preparation of acts of sabotage which would facilitate as far as possible the military action of the intervention against the Soviet Union.

The judicial investigation revealed the fact that the first instructions for the carrying out of sabotage were received by the Industrial Party from the Torgprom and from Mr. K. in 1928. The chief instruction in this connection was to avoid fundamental damage in carrying out the sabotage in order not to worsen the situation of the intervention and the future counterrevolutionary government. Therefore it was planned to cut off the electric supply of those power stations which supplied particular groups of factories with the aim of causing them to close down for shorter or longer periods.

The sabotage activity was to be carried out according to the plan of the Industrial Party not only on the field of the power supply, but also on other fields (war industries, transport).

The plan for the sabotage activity in the war industries was worked out by the Central Committee of the Industrial Party with the direct cooperation of the previously mentioned persons of the French Service in Moscow. The chief attention was paid to those factories which produce war materials and ammunition.

With a view to carrying out the sabotage acts successfully, special sabotage groups were formed in a number of factories and institutions (for instance, the Thermal Technical Institute, "Elektrotok", Moscow electricity works, etc.). The task of these groups was to cause the closing down of the most important factories.

The sabotage in the transport industry was to be carried out according to the plan drawn up by the accused Larichev by congestions, disorganization of transport, and direct destruction of bridges, etc.

The proceedings revealed the fact that the nearer the date fixed for the intervention approached, the year 1930, the more decisively was the Industrial Party urged to take up the question of forming special military groups. This task was put forward by the foreign military interventionists in Paris.

During the meeting of Ramzin with Mr. K. which took place in the rooms of Larichev in the autumn of 1928 according to the results of the judicial investigation, Mr. K. demanded more energy from the Industrial Party because its work for the internal preparation of the intervention was unsatisfactory and the internal crisis expected by the interventionists did not materialize.

The judicial investigation revealed the fact that those members of the Industrial Party who were enabled, thanks to their positions in the service of the Soviet State, to take part in various works in the frontier districts, exploited their position in order to direct and organize this work in the direction of their criminal and treasonable plans.

Exploiting their participation in such work as drainage, the laying down of foundations for industrial enterprises, etc., they attempted to create the most favorable conditions possible for the military operations of the interventionist troops against the Soviet Union. They attempted to prepare traversable ways for the troops of intervention, to lay out landing places for the airplanes of the intervention, areas of operation for the deployment of the interventionist armies, dumps for fuel supply, for the supply of the interventionist troops with oil, etc.

The work of the Central Committee of the Industrial Party to supply the interventionists with espionage material was directly connected with its treasonable sabotage and its interventionist activity. The judicial investigation revealed the fact that the Industrial Party received instructions from the Torgprom as early as 1928 to organize a systematic supply of quarterly reports to the counterrevolutionary centers abroad concerning the situation of the Soviet economic system drawn up from the angles of interest to these circles. The Central Committee of the Industrial Party gave Larichev and Kalinnikov the task of drawing up these reports, and the latter systematically carried out his work. These reports were sent abroad through the medium of Mr. K who received apart from these reports, other reports having a direct bearing on the defense of the Soviet Union.

The trial also showed that the accused Ramzin and Ochkin maintained connections with Messrs. R. and K. and gave these persons both in writing and by word of mouth the information they demanded.

This was the widespread sabotage work being conducted under the direction of the Central Committee of the Industrial Party on all fields for the preparation of the intervention in the year 1930.

Three chief forces were active in these preparations: The capitalist and militarist circles in France, Torgprom and the Industrial Party.

The relative importance of these three factors in the preparations for intervention was not equal. The leading role in these preparations was played by the capitalist and militarist circles of France, as irrefutably established by the trial. The influence of these circles is shown in such questions as the working out of the plans and methods for the carrying out of the intervention and the fixing of the date of the intervention.

The strategic plan of the intervention was to deliver a combined drive at Moscow and Leningrad with the united forces of the foreign expeditionary corps with the assistance of the remnants of the Wrangel army and the Krasnov Cossacks.

According to this plan the southern army was to operate in the Ukraine to the right of the Don and supported on the right bank of the Dnieper and move towards Moscow. The northern group of the intervention army was to operate against Leningrad with the support of an air and naval fleet.

The exploitation of some frontier conflict or the other was a part of the intervention plan in order to give the pretext for the intervention. In the course of the development of the conflict the armies of Poland and Rumania which are allied with France, and the armies of the Baltic States were then to be used. According to the aims of the interventionists the successful carrying out of the military operations was to lead to the dismemberment of the Soviet Union, the wrenching off of important areas and the concession of important financial and economic rights to the foreign participants in the intervention. In other words, the enslavement of the toilers of the Soviet Union. According to the intervention plans imperialist France was to be paid the Tsarist debts and in addition to receive important concessions for the exploitation of the iron ore and other natural resources of the Soviet Union. The judicial investigation showed that these concessions were planned in such a way that they would have been practically a direct confiscation.

Imperialist circles in Great Britain were to receive the oil wells in Caucasia.

Imperialist circles in Poland and Rumania insisted on territorial annexations (the Ukraine to the right of the Don, Kiev, Odessa).

The interventionists were compelled to shift the date of the intervention, which was first fixed in 1928, to 1930 and then to 1931. The reason for these postponements was not only that the capitalist States, participating in the intervention were not prepared for it as a result of their own disagreements, but still moreso the fact that the preliminary conditions for the intervention were not present in the Soviet Union itself.

Despite the widespread sabotage work carried on by various counterrevolutionary organizations, including the Industrial Party, which aimed at causing various serious disturbances in the economic life of the masses with the Soviet government on the basis of economic and food difficulties, these efforts showed no results, and this proved that all the calculations of the interventionists based on dissatisfaction of the working masses with the Soviet power are without foundation.

A further important reason for the postponement of the intervention was, as revealed by the judicial investigation, the fact that the interventionists circles in France were unable to ignore the lessons of the Chinese Eastern Railway conflict which proved the power and defensive capacities of the Soviet Union and the united will of the working masses to defend the frontiers of the Soviet Union and to fight for Soviet power and the building up of socialism.

On the basis of the facts set forth above and with the consideration to Articles 319 and 320 of the Penal Code of the RSFSR the Special Investigation of the Supreme Court of the Soviet Union records the following:

1. Leonid Konstantinovich Ramzin, who joined the counterrevolutionary organization "Association of Engineers Organizations" (RIO) or the "Engineers Central Committee" in the first half of the year 1927, took an active part in the organization of a counterrevolutionary party under the name of the "Industrial Party". After the arrest of the leaders of the party,

Palchinsky and Krennikov, he was the head of the Central Committee of this party whose aim it was to overthrow Soviet power with the assistance of foreign military intervention, and to restore the capitalist regime in the Soviet Union.

With these aims and also with the aim of directly preparing the way for an intervention Ramzin:

a) took up connections in the name of the Industrial Party with the white-guardist center of the former owners in Paris (Torgprom);

b) took up connections with interventionist circles in France and established a permanent connection with them through persons of the French Service in Moscow, Messrs. R. and K.;

c) worked to secure the systematic financing of the Industrial Party by the Torgprom and through the persons mentioned in point b);

d) took part together with the Torgprom and the above mentioned circles in the working out of a concrete plan of intervention against the Soviet Union, and declared his agreement in the name of the Industrial Party to the repayment of the Tsarist debts and to the annexation of considerable Soviet territories;

e) was the organizer and leader of a systematic sabotage work on various fields of the Soviet economic system with the same aims in view;

f) is proved guilty of having organized sabotage acts for which he created the necessary sabotage groups, and of having drawn up a plan of sabotage in the power supply;

g) maintained permanent connections with persons of the French Service in Moscow, Messrs. K. and R., and gave them both by word of mouth and in writing information of an espionage character;

h) proved guilty of having organized and carried out the distribution of monies arriving from abroad to finance the criminal activity of the Industrial Party. In short, he has committed crimes under Article 58, Paragraphs 3, 4, 6 and 11 of the Penal Code of the RSFSR.

2. Ivan Andreevich Kalinnikov:

a) through his participation in the same organizations and as a member of the Central Committee of the Industrial Party guided the sabotage and espionage activities of the Industrial Party directed towards the overthrow of Soviet power by a foreign military intervention, and towards the restoration of the capitalist regime in the Soviet Union. Further, in his capacity as the Vice-Chairman of the Industrial Section of the State Planning Commission, he misused his position to organize sabotage and to attempt to destroy the Five Year Plan;

b) together with the accused Charnovsky he laid a plan for sabotage acts in the metallurgical industry before the Central Committee of the Industrial Committee which accepted this plan;

c) he took up connections with persons of the French Service in Moscow, Messrs. K. and R., and collected and tabulated material of an espionage character and sent the same abroad;

d) he divided the monies which came from abroad amongst the members of the Industrial Party who belonged to the chain organization of the field under his control. In short, he has committed crimes under Article 58, Paragraphs 3, 4, 6 and 11 of the Penal Code of the RSFSR.

3. Viktor Alekseevich Larichev, took part as a member of the counterrevolutionary organization "Engineers Central Committee" since 1926, in the organization of the Industrial Party. As a member of the Central Committee of the Industrial Party he directed sabotage and espionage work with the aims mentioned above. Further,

a) in the name of the Industrial Party he took up direct connections with the Torgprom and with interventionist circles in Paris;

b) he took up connections with the above mentioned persons of the French Service in Moscow, Messrs. K. and R.;

c) he distributed monies received from abroad amongst the members of that branch of the sabotage organization which was under his direction;

d) he exploited his position as Chairman of the Fuel Supply Section of the State Planning Commission in order to organize sabotage work for counterrevolutionary aims in the planning work for the fuel supply, and in particular in the oil industry. Further, he took a direct part in the leadership of the sabotage work in the transport industry;

e) by delivering the necessary material to the above mentioned persons of the French Service in Moscow, he carried out espionage. In short, he has committed crimes under Article 58, Paragraphs 3, 4, 6 and 11 of the Penal Code of the RSFSR.

4. Nikolai Frantsevich Charnovsky, carried out active sabotage and espionage work after his entry into the same counterrevolutionary organization in 1927. He took an active part in the leadership of the counterrevolutionary organization the "Industrial Party" and was a member of its Central Committee. Further,

a) he directed the sabotage work of the Industrial Party in the metallurgical industry;

b) carried out sabotage work in connection with the drawing up of projects in the Scientific-Technical Council of which he was the Chairman. As a result of his sabotage work a number of factory building enterprises, including several engineering factories, were held up, disproportions created in the factory departments, irrational capital investments made and in general the development of the metallurgical industry hampered;

c) together with the accused Kalinnikov he worked out a plan for sabotage acts with regard to the supply of military authorities with equipment;

d) he distributed monies received from abroad amongst the members of that branch of the sabotage organization under his leadership;

e) together with the accused Kalinnikov he drew up reports of an espionage character and sent them abroad. In short, he has committed crimes under Article 58, Paragraphs 3, 4, 6 and 11 of the Penal Code of the RSFSR.

5. Aleksandr Aleksandrovich Fedotov joined the sabotage group in the textile industry in 1925 which he later led. He joined the Industrial Party and became a member of its Central Committee. He took part in the leadership of the espionage and sabotage activities of the Industrial Party. Further,

a) he directed the sabotage work in the sabotage branch in the textile industry. He carried out sabotage in his activity for the drawing up of the Five Year Plan and worked to slow down the development of textile production and hinder the building of new factories. He deliberately created difficulties in order to prevent the supply of the textile industry with raw material and imported machinery of a high quality. He also undermined the development of those branches of the textile industry which would have been most necessary for the Soviet Union in case of an open armed intervention;

b) he distributed monies received from the sources mentioned above. In short, he has committed crimes under Article 58, Paragraphs 3, 4, 6 and 11 of the Penal Code of the RSFSR.

6. Sergei Viktorovich Kuprianov, was a member of the counterrevolutionary Industrial Party and had the same aims,

a) he maintained connections with the representatives of the Torgprom with a view to carrying out the sabotage and intervention preparations of the Industrial Party;

b) he carried out the instructions of the Central Committee of the Industrial Party to draw up plans for sabotage in the textile industry by causing the production of commodities not in accord with the need of the market, by holding up the manufacture of textile machinery, by deliberately failing to supply on time and in the required quantities, etc., the various districts with textile goods;

c) he distributed monies received from abroad amongst the members of the textile section of the sabotage organization;

d) he accepted the instructions of the Central Committee of the Industrial Party to organize military groups of former white-guardist officers;

e) he accepted instructions of the Central Committee of the Industrial Party to obtain secret information concerning the mobilization work in the textile industry. In short, he has committed crimes under Article 58, Paragraphs 3, 6 and 11 of the Penal Code of the RSFSR.

7. Vladimir Ivanovich Ochkin, accepted and carried out as a member of the Industrial Party instructions of the Central Committee of that party through the accused Ramzin, to establish connections with persons of the French Service in Moscow, Messrs. K. and R. Further, he was a member of the sabotage group in the Thermal Technical Institute. In short, he has committed crimes under Article 58, Paragraphs 3, 6 and 11 of the Penal Code of the RSFSR.

8. Ksenofon Vasileevich Sitnin, was a member of the counterrevolutionary Industrial Party and was well acquainted with the aims of this party. He undertook to carry out sabotage, and further, he took up connections with the representatives of the Torgprom, informing the latter of the activities of the Industrial Party and forwarding the instructions of the Torgprom to the Industrial Party. In short, he has committed crimes under Article 58, Paragraphs 3, 4 and 11 of the Penal Code of the RSFSR.

On the basis of Article 326, Paragraph 3 of the Law of Criminal Procedure of the RSFSR the Supreme Court of the Soviet Union in special investigation has sentenced the accused as follows:

1. Sergei Viktorovich Kuprianov on the basis of Article 58, Paragraphs 3, 4, 6 and 11 of the Penal Code of the RSFSR to ten years imprisonment, and to the loss of all civil rights in accordance with Article 31, Points a., b., c., d., and f. of the Penal Code of the RSFSR for a period of five years. Further, the Supreme Court orders the confiscation of all his property.

2. Ksenofon Vasileevich Sitnin on the basis of Article 58, Paragraphs 3, 4 and 11 of the Penal Code of the RSFSR to ten years imprisonment, and to the loss of all civil rights in accordance with Article 31, Points a., b., c., d., and f. of the Penal Code of the RSFSR for a period of five years. Further, the Supreme Court orders the confiscation of all his property.

3. Vladimir Ivanovich Ochkin on the basis of Article 58, Paragraphs 3, 6 and 11 of the Penal Code of the RSFSR to ten years imprisonment and to the loss of all civil rights in accordance with Article 31, Points a., b., c., d., and f. of the Penal Code of the RSFSR for a period of five years. Further, the Supreme Court orders the confiscation of all his property.

4. Ivan Andreevich Kalinnikov on the basis of Article 58, Paragraphs 3, 4, 6 and 11 of the Penal Code of the RSFSR to the extreme measure of social defense, execution. Further, the Supreme Court orders the confiscation of all his property.

5. Nikolai Frantsevich Charnovsky on the basis of Article 58, Paragraphs 3, 4, 6 and 11 of the Penal Code of the RSFSR to the extreme measure of social defense, execution. Further, the Supreme Court orders the confiscation of all his property.

6. Viktor Alekseevich Larichev on the basis of Article 58, Paragraphs 3, 4, 6 and 11 of the Penal Code of the RSFSR to the extreme measure of social defense, execution. Further, the Supreme Court orders the confiscation of all his property.

7. Aleksandr Aleksandrovich Fedotov on the basis of Article 58, Paragraphs 3, 4, 6 and 11 of the Penal Code of the RSFSR to the extreme measure of social defense, execution. Further, the Supreme Court orders the confiscation of all his property.

8. Leonid Konstantinovich Ramzin on the basis of Article 58, Paragraphs 3, 4, 6 and 11 of the Penal Code of the RSFSR to the extreme measure of social defense, execution. Further, the Supreme Court orders the confiscation of all his property.

The time spent by the convicted Kuprianov, Sitnin and Ochkin in prison awaiting trial shall be deducted from their sentences.

The Verdict and Sentences are final and not subject to appeal.

International Press Correspondence, Vol. 10, No. 57 (11 December 1930), 1171-1177.

PARTY RESOLUTION. PARTY CALLS FOR ACCELERATION OF FIVE YEAR PLAN IN 1931
17-21 December 1930

The Joint Plenum of the Party Central Committee and Central Control Commission examined the results of the first two years of the Five Year Plan and called for the acceleration of the plan for 1931 to overfulfill the plan in four years. Although it acknowledged problems in parts of the economy, in spite of the effort to overcome these problems in the last quarter of the economic year, it wanted to push the economy toward higher goals.

RESOLUTION OF JOINT PLENUM OF TSK AND TSKK VKP(B) ON THE NATIONAL ECONOMIC PLAN FOR 1931 (CONTROL FIGURES)

I

The preceding economic year 1929/30—the second year of the five year plan—was a year of new and the greatest achievements of the working class in socialist construction.

The goals of the five year plan have been fulfilled with significant increases in all the basic indicators:

a) Large-scale state industry, having a 25 percent rise in gross output in 1929/30, exceeded the goals of the five year plan for this year by 5 percent, and at the same time the first year of the five year plan gave a 3 percent increase over the rough estimate of the five year plan. As a result of the first two years of the five year plan socialist state industry gave the national economy an output of 30.5 billion rubles instead of the 29.3 billion rubles in the five year plan (in constant prices).

Especially significant were the successes of the branches of industry which produce the means of production: For the first two years of the five year plan heavy industry gave the country an output of 13.8 billion rubles instead of 12.5 billion rubles in the five year plan.

In sum, the volume of annual production of all industrial factories and plants of the Union in 1929/30 more than doubled the prewar annual production.

b) The successes of socialist industry provided a radical breakthrough in the socialist development of agriculture.

The sown area rose from 118 million hectares in 1928/29 to 127.8 hectares in the preceding economic year, exceeding the projections of the five year plan in both grain and especially industrial crops (cotton, sugar beets, etc.).

There was a significant rise in agricultural output. The gross yield of bread grains in 1930 consisted of 87.4 million tons against 71.7 tons in 1929 (growth of 21.8 percent). The gross yield of cotton consists of not less than 13.5 million centners against 8.6 million centners in 1929. The gross yield of sugar beets consists of, respectively, 151.7 million centners against 62.5 centners in the previous year.

Earnest achievements in agriculture, the basic solution of the grain problem were the direct result of greatest successes achieved in the area of sovkhoz and kolkhoz construction, and the liquidation of the kulak as a class being carried out without deviation on the basis of complete collectivization.

The goals of the five year plan in the area of collectivization were surpassed some time ago. In kolkhozes already as of 1 December 1930, if you consider all the regions of the USSR and all branches of agriculture (farming, raising livestock, fishing, hunting), more than 6.15 million peasant farms were united, i.e., 24.1 percent. In the basic grain regions the percent of collectivization rose to 49.3 percent.

The land area of kolkhozes sown in the spring and fall of 1930 consisted of 43.4 million hectares against the 20.6 million hectares projected for the *last year* of the five year plan.

This means that for the *first two years* of the five year plan we were able to have already exceeded two times the *entire five year program.*

Thus, the sown area of the entire socialist sector (including the sovkhozes the sown area of which consisted of more than 4.8 million hectares in the spring and fall of 1930) reached 48.2 million hectares.

The percentages of the socialist sector in the commodity output of grain, harvested in 1930, consisted of about 50 percent of the entire commodity output against 43 percent proposed by the five year plan for its *last year*.

At the same time the preceding year gave a tremendous change in the area of socialist livestock. For working horses the percentages of the socialist sector in 1928 consisted of only 0.8 percent, 1.7 percent in 1929, and already 17.2 percent in 1930; for cows, respectively, 0.4, 0.8, and 6.6 percent. This change in the area of collectivizing livestock, together with the organization of large sovkhozes for raising livestock ("Skotovod", "Svinovod", "Ovtsevod") provide a quick solution of the livestock problem.

c) For some time the projections of the five year plan were exceeded in the area of railroad transportation. The turnover of goods in railroad transportation, having reached 235 million tons in the preceding economic year, exceeded more than one-fourth the projections of the five year plan for the second year of the five year plan.

d) This growth of the national economy provided the further increase in the material and cultural level of laborers' lives. The total number of workers and employees significantly exceeded the projections of the five year plan. Workers' wages for the two years of the five year plan increased by 12 percent. By the end of the second year of the five year plan 45.5 percent of all industrial workers had already been transferred to the seven-hour workweek. For the preceding period 67 percent of all industrial workers were transferred to the continuous work week (nepreryvka).

As a result of all this we have basically liquidated unemployment.

The greatest successes achieved in socialist construction are indisputable. The goals of the five year plan have not only been fulfilled, but even *significantly* overfulfilled, guaranteeing the fulfillment of the entire five year plan in four years. In light of these facts what becomes completely obvious is both the complete failure and ideological bankruptcy of the right and "left" opportunist elements, and the ludicrous cries of the bourgeois press about the failure of the five year plan that have been launched above all to hide the existence of the severe economic crisis in the capitalist countries.

The decisive role in this economic rise of the USSR is played by the correct policy of the party, the tremendous growth of the activity and creative labor enthusiasm of millions of masses of the working class and collective farmers (socialist competition, shock work, counter plans), under the sign of which passed the first two years of the five year plan.

II

The successes of the first two years of the five year plan enable the adoption for the upcoming year 1931 of even higher rates of development in socialist construction.

As a result of this, the joint plenum of the TsK and TsKK VKP(b) resolve:

1. On the national economy as a whole

a) To adopt the approximate national revenue of the USSR for 1931 at 49 billion rubles (in 1926/27 prices) against 49.7 billion rubles proposed for the *last year* (1933) of the five year plan, so that the growth of the national revenue in 1931 would consist of not less than 35 percent (against the growth of national revenues in 1930 by 19 percent and by 11 percent in 1929).

b) As a result of this growth of national revenues, capital investment in the socialist sector of the national economy (industry, transportation, agriculture, etc.) is determined at 17 billion rubles against 10 billion rubles in the preceding year.

c) The fund of industrial commodities for general consumption is determined for 1931 at 14.6 billion rubles against 11.5 billion rubles for 1930 (growth for one year at 3.1 billion rubles against the growth in 1929 to the preceding year at 1 billion), together with the growth of the fund for agricultural goods must increase the retail turnover by 25-30 percent against the preceding year.

2. On industry and electrification

a) The capacity of capital construction in socialist industry and electrification (regional power stations) is determined for 1931 at 7470 million rubles, to include electrification at 850 million rubles and being planned by the VSNKh for industry, 5500 million rubles (of these, 500 million rubles in VSNKh reserves for industry and electrification).

The reduction in construction costs is determined at 12 percent.

b) To establish the growth of the gross output of all state industry (for VSNKh and People's Commissariat for Supply) at 45 percent in comparison to 1930, meaning the fulfillment of the entire five year plan for industrial production in the third year of the five year plan, i.e., in 1931, by 79 percent, and for branches of heavy industry by 98 percent.

c) To bring by the end of 1931 the total capacity of all existing electric power stations to 4.5 million kilowatts, and the production of electricity to 12.7 billion kilowatt hours against 8.8 billion kilowatt hours in 1930.

d) To establish for industry, being planned by VSNKh, the growth of the number of workers by 10 percent, growth in labor productivity by 28 percent, reduction in production costs by 10 percent, with the compulsory improvement in the quality of production. In accordance with industry being planned by the People's Commissariat for Supply, the growth of the number of workers by 16 percent, growth in labor productivity by 35 percent, reduction in costs by 11 percent.

3. On agriculture

a) To provide in 1931 the range of collective farms for the Ukraine (Steppe), Northern Caucasus, Lower Volga, Middle Volga (Transvolga) on the average of not less than 80 percent of peasant farms, meaning that for these regions basically the ending of complete collectivization and the liquidation of the kulak as a class. For the remaining grain regions, Central Black Earth Region, Siberia, Urals, Ukraine (Forest Steppe), Kazakhstan (grain regions) are to secure 50 percent collectivization of peasant farms. For the consuming area in grain farming, 20-25 percent. In the cotton and sugar beet regions to provide the range of collective farms of not less than 50 percent of the total number of farms.

To secure in 1931, on the average in the Union of all branches of agriculture, collectivization of not less than half of the peasant farms.

b) The total size of sown area in all crops to reach in 1931 up to 143 million hectares (spring and winter crops in 1931).

The sown area of sovkhozes is determined at 9.5 million hectares (including Zernotrest at 5 million hectares) and of kolkhozes at not Less than 66 million hectares, of these (the kolkhozes) the spring crops are not less than 50 million hectares.

c) To bring the number of MTS' of Traktorotsentr by the end of the year to 1400 with the total capacity of tractors at 980 thousand horsepower.

d) To bring the herd of "Skotovod" to 2800 thousand head; the herd of "Svinovod" to 1900 thousand head; the herd of "Ovtsevod" to 4.4 million head; the herd of the Milk and Butter Trust to 110 thousand cows.

e) The volume of capital investment in the socialist sector (sovkhozes and kolkhozes) of agriculture is determined at 3.8 billion rubles, to include the state sector at 2055 million rubles and the kolkhozes and MTSs at 1745 million rubles.

4. On transportation and communications

a) To adopt the total rate of turnover of goods of railroads in 1931 measuring 330 million meters against 281 million proposed for the *last* year of the five year plan.

b) To secure reduction of the transportation costs of railroads in 1931 at not less than 9 percent compared to the costs in 1930.

c) To adopt the total of capital investment in railroads at 3185 million rubles.

d) To determine the total of capital investment in civil aviation at 135 million rubles (in addition, 15 million rubles for operating costs).

e) To determine the total of capital investment in national communications in 1931 at 260 million rubles.

5. On People's Commissariat for supply and consumer cooperative

To determine the extent of capital investment:

a) For People's Commissariat for Supply (raw materials depot, elevators, refrigerators, warehouses, etc.) it is 230 million rubles (less industry).

b) For the consumer cooperative (public catering, local gardens, construction of shops, etc.), 365 million rubles (less industry).

6. On labor and culture

a) To establish the total number of workers and employees in 1931 at 16 million people against 14 million people in 1930.

b) To establish the growth of wages in 1931 in comparison with 1930 for industrial workers at 6 percent and for railroad workers at 8 percent. To determine respectively the annual wages for 1931 at 15.3 billion rubles against 12.5 million rubles in 1930.

c) To determine the annual social insurance fund of workers and employees in 1931 at 2138 rubles (against 1.6 billion rubles in 1930), that exceeds the goal for the *last year* of the five year plan (1950 million rubles).

d) To determine the total amount of the fund for improving workers' conditions in 1931 at 285 million rubles against 125 million rubles in 1930.

e) To determine the allocation for the protection of labor in industry and transportation at 155 million rubles.

f) To transfer to the seven hour work day by the end of 1931 all railroad workers and 92 percent of industrial workers being planned by VSNKh, and 52 percent of the industrial workers being planned by the People's Commissariat for Supply.

g) To transfer to the five day work week (nepreryvka) in 1931 all industrial workers being planned by VSNKh, except for textile workers, and 98 percent of the industrial workers being planned by the People's Commissariat for Supply.

h) To determine the investment in housing construction in all branches of the socialist national economy at 1.1 billion rubles against 582.5 million rubles in the previous year.

i) To determine the total fund for financing education, cadre, science, health protection, and social security at 6.5 billion rubles against 5 billion rubles in 1930.

7. On the financial plan

1. To approve the amount of the single financial plan (budget, credit system and actual resources of economic organizations) in the sum of 31.1 billion rubles for revenues and 29.6 billion rubles for expenditures (to include the state budget in the sum of 21.2 billion rubles for revenues and 19.7 billion rubles for expenditures) with the exceeding of revenues over expenditures and the formation of the state reserve at 1.5 billion rubles.

2. Considering that: a) the successes of the planned socialist economy enabled the transfer in the area of finances to the system of the single financial plan, which occupies all the means of the country that go into capital construction, the replenishment of the working resources of the socialist economy, to culture, management and the defense of the USSR; b) the single financial plan which involves and redistributes about two-thirds of all the national revenues in socialist construction; c) the successful fulfillment of the financial plan and budget depends directly on the fulfillment of the quantitative and qualitative indicators in all branches of national economic construction; d) without the firm fulfillment of the financial plan it is impossible to carry out the designated economic plan in all branches of the national economy,—the plenum considers it necessary to improve decisively the work of all financial organs, the introduction of the strictest financial discipline and economic regimen, to fulfil without doubt revenues, establish the expenditures of each organization in direct dependence on its fulfillment of its production and financial plans, strengthening of the chervonets and the decisive struggle with the underestimation of the role and importance of the financial system at the given stage of socialist construction.

III

The possibility of solving the greatest tasks established by the national economic plan in 1931 is based to a significant degree on the earnest successes already achieved in the preceding two years of the five year plan and especially in 1929/30. Despite the unfulfilment of the annual plan of 1930 in individual elements of the plan, the goals of the five year plan in the preceding economic year were significantly exceeded. By the same the preconditions were created for the future acceleration of the rates of socialist construction, the rates of the industrialization of the country and the collectivization of agriculture.

It would, however, be radically incorrect to think that these grandiose tasks could be solved "haphazardly", "spontaneously". On the path of solving these tasks stand the greatest difficulties, the overcoming of which requires the greatest organization and discipline, decisive improvement in the quality of work in all levels of state, economic, and cooperative apparata, the decisive introduction into the economic development of a planning foundation and planning discipline, the future growth of the activity and labor enthusiasm of the most extensive masses of laborers (socialist competition, shock brigade, industrial and financial counter plans).

The upcoming year 1931 is the deciding year in the carrying out of the slogan: "The five year plan in four years". The maximum attention, maximum energy must be concentrated on the absolute fulfillment of the above plan in all of its parts, and especially on its qualitative indicators (reduction in the cost of industrial output, reduction in construction costs, improvement in labor productivity, increase in harvests, increase in the indicators of transportation work, improvement in the quality of output, etc.).

Under the special supervision of the working class and its party must be undertaken the fulfillment of the planned goals for coal, for metal, the solution of the livestock problem and for overcoming one of lowest places in the national economy, railroad and water transportation.

Our country, where the socialist sector occupied absolutely the predominant role in the national economy, entered the period of the expanded socialist offensive, the period of socialism. The upcoming year 1931 will be the year of new achievements, new greatest successes of socialism in its struggle with capitalism. The fulfillment of the plan in the area of collectivization will give the absolute superiority of socialist elements over the individual sector in the countryside, strengthen the alliance of the working class with the laboring masses of peasantry and complete the construction of the foundation of the USSR socialist economy. This will be a victory of worldwide historical importance.

The national economy of our Union is standing on the threshold of completing a grandiose plan for the construction of socialism, the five year plan. The perspective of the decisive victory cannot but call for the new burst of enthusiasm and new labor enthusiasm among workers and peasants. But it also cannot but increase the envy and anger of our class enemies. It is namely because of this that the remnants of capitalism within the Soviet Union are so desperately resisting (resistance of kulaks, wrecking, etc.). It is namely because of this that international capitalism is so feverishly preparing armed intervention against the Soviet Union. Under these conditions of the heightened class struggle what is required is the maximum mobilization of the creative forces of the working class, collective farmers, and laborers for the overcoming of difficulties which are standing on the path of socialist construction, on the path of carrying out the slogan: "Five year plan in four years". It is namely under these conditions that what is required of us is the maximum exertion of resources for the future development of industrialization of the country and socialist construction, for the country's defense capability.

KPSS v rezoliutsiiakh, Vol. 4, 490-497.

3 THE YEAR 1931

USSR CRITICIZES DISARMAMENT CONFERENCE NOTE TO FOREIGN GOVERNMENTS

12 January 1931

The Soviet Union and Germany refused to approve the draft convention of the Preparatory Commission for Disarmament adopted by the commission in December 1930. The Soviet Government emphasized its disapproval of the convention by circulating the note below to several governments, including Great Britain, France, and Japan. In the note, the Soviet Government approved the idea of disarmament and sought to continue its participation in the upcoming Disarmament Conference; however, it rejected the contents of the draft convention, the location of the upcoming conference, and the selection of the president of the conference. It also expressed dissatisfaction at being treated as an unequal participant.

TEXT OF NOTE FROM THE GOVERNMENT OF THE SOVIET UNION

In accordance with a resolution of the majority of the Preparatory Commission, the Council of the League of Nations at its next session will probably occupy itself with determining the place and date of the convocation for the Disarmament Conference, and with the appointment of its President.

The Soviet Government is of opinion that this Conference will be of international importance, as from its results must depend in considerable degree the question of the prolongation and stability of peace, or of a new destructive war.

In this sense, the Soviet Government has repeatedly expressed its views that, under existing conditions, the sole guarantee for the preservation of peace would be disarmament; or, at any rate, the greatest possible reduction of armaments.

It has (also) submitted corresponding drafts of a Convention to the Preparatory Commission for Disarmament, and will again put them forward for the consideration of the Conference itself.

This evidences the particular interest taken by the Soviet Union in the success of the Conference, as well as its readiness to take a most active part in the Conference's work.

The Soviet Government is of the opinion that to bring the labors of the Conference to a successful issue requires the unqualified admission of the principle of complete equality of status to each participant in the Conference, whether a great or small Power.

The Soviet Government, however, is compelled to state that such equality has not been observed towards the Soviet Delegation by the Preparatory Commission on Disarmament, not only by the decisions of the Commission itself, but also to a great extent *by the obviously biased behavior of the Commission's President.* Many instances in proof of this statement may be found in the Protocols drawn up by the Commission. It required, indeed, considerable self-restraint and patience on the part of the Soviet Delegation, as well as consciousness of the extreme importance attached by its Government to the problem of disarmament, to prevent its withdrawing itself from further participation in the Commission, on account of the instances of rudeness and want of tact given by the President of the Commission.

Undoubtedly, this conduct of the Commission's President was occasioned by the fact, amongst others, that he was the representative of one of such States that, for fourteen years past, having declined normal relations with the Soviet Union, are thereby cut off from positive sources of information regarding it, and therefore more subject than other capitalistic countries to prejudiced views towards the USSR.

Arising out of this, consequently, *the Soviet Government considers that participation in the election of a President to the Conference should be granted to each member, without exception, of the Conference*, and, therefore, that the President ought to be elected by the *Conference as a whole*, and not by a group of Powers, nor of organizations, to which do not belong all those taking part in the Conference.

Moreover, the Soviet Government is of the opinion that as President, and consequently leader, of a Conference of such worldwide importance, it is not permissible to elect the representative of a State that took up a distinctly negative position towards disarmament at the Preparatory Commission, neither of one that possesses developed armament industries of international significance, through which it is economically interested in the upkeep and increase of armaments, nor—finally—of a State that does not maintain normal relations with all the others participating in the Conference.

It is superfluous to add *that no one should be chosen as President of the Conference, notorious by his public utterances or by his prejudices for hostile feelings towards one or another of the countries represented.*

It is also necessary for a successful issue to the Conference that to every member taking part in it should be secured the requisite conditions allowing peaceful and undisturbed concentration upon the subjects connected with the work of the Conference. The Soviet Delegation to the Preparatory Commission was to a considerable degree deprived of such conditions, owing to the inimical atmosphere created around it by the Geneva Press, and by local antiSoviet societies, among which must be included the notorious International Organization for the Preparation of Intervention in the USSR, with Monsieur Aubert, the counsel for Conradi, the murderer of the USSR plenipotentiary, Monsieur Vorovsky, at its head. Preconceived ideas and prejudices against the USSR are naturally of stronger growth in countries that, not maintaining diplomatic representatives in the Soviet Union, are thereby deprived of authentic information concerning it, and rely for intelligence only upon the statements of irresponsible journalists.

The Soviet Government, therefore, considers that *as meeting-place for the Disarmament Conference, a country should be chosen that maintains normal relations with all other countries taking part in the Conference.*

Documents on International Affairs, 1931, 68-70.

PARTY RESOLUTION. MAGNITOGORSK AS SYMBOL OF FIVE YEAR PLAN

25 January 1931

Founded in 1929 in the Southern Urals, Magnitogorsk became a symbol of what the Five Year Plan promised to industrialization. It began as a construction project to build a massive iron smelting plant as part of the even more massive Urals-Kuznetsk Combine, which would develop the entire region and integrate the potential resources in the region to produce iron and steel. The project encountered numerous difficulties, thus requiring intervention from Stalin and the party leadership. Thousands of dispossessed kulaks were part of the project's workforce. One week after the plant produced the first pig iron an accident disabled the blast furnace. The plant began full production in 1932 and produced prior to World War II ten percent of the Soviet Union's steel.

ON THE CONSTRUCTION OF THE MAGNITOGORSK METALLURGICAL PLANT

The task of creating the Urals-Kuznetsk Combine as a powerful coal-metallurgical base, which was set forth by the Sixteenth Party Congress, is being executed in the forced-pace construction of the Magnitogorsk and Kuznetsk plants.

The significance which the Magnitogorsk plant has for the economy (a capacity of 2.5 million tons of pig iron, increasing to 4 million tons) is strengthened by its geographical position at the junction of the Urals industrial area, the nonferrous metals of the East and Kazakhstan, and the vast agricultural areas of Siberia, Kazakhstan, and Central Asia.

The construction of the Magnitogorsk plant must become a practical school for the creation of new methods and forms of socialist labor, technology, and the preparation of personnel for further industrialization of the Soviet Union.

The Central Committee of the VKP(b) notes that the construction of the Magnitogorsk plant thus far has not attained the required pace and, in the organization of work, real planning and one-man management have not been introduced in all sections of the project.

The Central Committee of the VKP(b) resolves:

1. To ensure that the Magnitogorsk plant begins operation by the date set by the Central Committee VKP(b) on 25 January of this year.

2. To direct the Supreme Council of the National Economy to provide the Magnitogorsk construction project with all necessary financial support as well as with equipment and materials, owing to the necessity of finishing the construction by the deadline.

3. To direct Vostokostal and the chief of Magnitostroi to strengthen decisively planning discipline at the construction site.

In order to secure the necessary pace of construction, to propose to Vostokostal and the chief of Magnitostroi to pay special attention, in the first quarter of the year, to all necessary preparatory and auxiliary works (earth works, auxiliary enterprises, quarries, water supply, etc.) and parallel with this to begin the construction of auxiliary shops (mechanical, boiler rooms, forge, foundry, silicates). The fulfillment of these tasks will be a fundamental turning point.

To propose that Vostokostal develop, no later than 1 March 1931, a plan for the organization of work on Magnitostroi, based on the maximal mechanization and rationalization of labor. The reorganization of all work on Magnitostroi on the basis of this plan should be made the most important task of the next two months.

To direct the chief of Magnitostroi decisively to improve, as soon as possible, the use of the existing administration and to take measures for implementation of the principle of one-man management and operation on a profitable basis in all departments of the project.

4. To direct Comrade Ivanchenko to establish a system of planning in which unified technical leadership of all projected works conducted in the Soviet Union (on and outside the construction site) will be achieved, and work planned in the Soviet Union and executed abroad will be coordinated. To direct the Supreme Council of the National Economy to submit to the Central Committee proof of fulfillment of the above within twenty days.

To direct Comrades Ivanchenko, Kolesnikov, and Postnikov to examine the plans of transportation within the plant and to submit them for approval to the Supreme Council of the National Economy within two weeks.

5. In coordination with the construction project, planning organizations are to devise in a week's time a monthly timetable for the drafting of plans. This will ensure the timely issuance of plans on the dates established by the construction project. The drafting of plans must be given special priority.

To assign Comrade Kolesnikov personal responsibility for putting into practice point No. 5 of this resolution.

6. Noting that work in the mining industry is behind schedule, Vostokostal and the Main Geological Survey Administration are hereby instructed:

a) To provide more exact information by 15 February on deposits of low-sulphur ore which can be used without being enriched, thus securing the operation of the Magnitogorsk and Kuznetsk plants next year;

b) To open the ore crushers not later than 1 June;

c) To start industrial exploitation of the mine by 15 May, producing enough to enable the blast furnaces of both plants to start by 1 October 1931.

To direct special attention to planning the transportation and water supply, which will be needed to open the mine on time.

7. By 1 March 1931, the Main Geological Survey Administration must submit to Magnitostroi the data regarding the sources of the nonmetallic minerals (limestone, dolomite, chromite, fire clay, moulding and other types of sands, etc.) and also the data on manganese for 1931. To conduct during the four-month period prospecting missions in the Magnitogorsk region to secure these materials for the plant.

8. Taking into account the proximity of the Poltava-Bredinsk coal mines to the Magnitogorsk plant, to propose that the Supreme Council of the National Economy begin the immediate organization of the industrial exploitation of these mines and to speed up the prospecting of the indicated deposits so that the main shafts can be sited in May.

9. In connection with the great need for water which has come to light, especially in the enterprises being organized near the Magnitogorsk plant (synthesis of ammonia, sovkhozes, and kolkhozes) to propose that the Supreme Council of the National Economy begin work on the second dam on the Urals River, so that it will be completed in time to collect water during the spring runoff of 1932.

10. So that Magnitostroi and Kuznetskstroi can in time be equipped with machinery manufactured in the USSR, the Supreme Council of the National Economy is to:

a) Work out a schedule for manufacturing and delivering equipment for top-priority plants, with precise orders for the producers and dates for the delivery of equipment;

b) Pay special attention to expediting the delivery of orders directly to the plants which manufacture the equipment, to achieve the detailed work of Vostokostal and the corresponding associations, so that the contracts with the corresponding suppliers can be formulated in the shortest time;

c) Begin immediately the planned preparation of placing orders for equipment of the next priority, singling out especially heavy equipment or those requiring long periods of time for manufacture and installation;

d) Establish no later than 1 April a schedule with precise deadlines for placing orders, manufacturing, delivery, and installation of equipment for the complete productivity of the Magnitogorsk and Kuznetsk plants;

e) For carrying out this work immediately strengthen Vostokostal with qualified specialists.

While attaching special significance to the contemporary manufacture of equipment and construction for Magnitostroi and Kuznetskstroi at Union plants, the TsK commits the VSNKh to enlist directly the directors of plants and plant organizations in the placing of orders.

At the same time the TsK proposes to plant, party, and trade union organizations to assume special observation of the manufacture of equipment and construction for Magnitostroi and Kuznetskstroi, mobilizing for this shock brigades, production conferences, and the plant press.

11. The People's Commissariat for Labor and Supreme Council of the National Economy are to adopt measures without delay for the selection and staffing of the labor force and technical personnel for the Magnitostroi by the beginning of the second quarter (the

completion of construction and installation operations) in accordance with the requirements of the construction project, which must be submitted to the People's Commissariat for Labor within a month.

12. The Supreme Council of the National Economy is to check the work of the Vostokostal and the Magnitogorsk construction project on securing the qualified manpower and management for the Magnitogorsk and Kuznetsk plans on schedule and to take the necessary measures for providing these plants with personnel, not hesitating to transfer the necessary supply of experienced cadres.

13. To instruct the People's Commissariat for Transport to settle within one month the question of the trunk lines and secondary lines associated with the plant, in order to assure the transportation of ore and coal, both to Magnitogorsk, and from Magnitogorsk to Kuznetsk, taking into account the necessity of a connection to Belokurets and Ufa.

14. Noting the totally unsatisfactory condition of the freight flow capacity of the Kartala-Magnitnaia branch line, Comrade Rukhimovich is personally responsible in adoption of all necessary measures to put the branch line into working order, in order to ensure the uninterrupted shipping of freight, which is indispensable for the construction of the Magnitogorsk plant.

15. The People's Commissariat for Transport and the Supreme Council of the National Economy are to organize preparations for the reception and handling of the imported heavy machinery which will arrive in the near future for the Magnitogorsk construction project. To this end Vostokostal is to present a detailed plan within twenty days to direct the heavy freight indicating the size, weight, and number of units.

16. The Supreme Council of the National Economy and People's Commissariat for Transport are to determine within twenty days the type and quantity of rolling stock and engines on the Kuznetsk-Magnitnaia line to supply transportation of ore and coal.

17. Considering that the problem of transportation between Kuznetsk and Magnitnaia has not yet been thoroughly worked out, the People's Commissariat for Transport and the Supreme Council of the National Economy are to deliver a special report on this question to the Central Committee of the VKP(b) in May 1931.

18. The Central Union of Consumer's Cooperatives is to reorganize all cooperative work at Magnitogorsk within two months and to give Magnitostroi first priority in consumer supplies.

19. To oblige the People's Commissariat for Health to secure promptly the medical staff required for the Magnitogorsk plant, also reinforcing the first-aid and ambulance network in the area.

20. Taking note of the insufficient activity by the Urals party organization in the matter of assisting the Magnitogorsk construction, the Central Committee proposes to the Urals Oblast Committee and to the Magnitogorsk local party organizations that they adopt all necessary practical measures toward the realization of the construction and toward a widespread clarification of the political and economical significance of the Magnitogorsk plant.

21. Trade union organizations of the Urals region must take genuine, serious measures to attract the broad laboring masses into participating in the construction; they must introduce new forms of socialist labor on the construction site and the wide development of the shock-work movement, socialist competition, and social teamwork; they must assure the active participation of the laboring mass in the development and accomplishment of the construction plans, placing the everyday cultural facilities of the workers on the requisite level, decisively bringing to a halt instability, self-seeking, etc.

22. The Central Committee considers that economic organizations connected with the project must fulfil their tasks precisely on time and with the quality of products that is required. They must eliminate the formalist bureaucratic attitude toward orders and assignments from the construction project, and must render the maximum technical assistance to

the project in the installation and utilization of machinery that is being supplied according to the deadlines for the opening of the plant.

McNeal/Gregor, Vol. 3, 98-103.
Pravda, 26 January 1931, 1.

STALIN, FIVE YEAR PLAN IN THREE YEARS

4 February 1931

Stalin used the occasion of a conference convened by the new Chairman of the Supreme Council of the National Economy, S. Ordzhonikidze, to increase the pressure on the fulfillment of the Five Year Plan. The attainment of goals in the plan for 1930 were less than predicted. Stalin called for the fulfillment of the Five Year Plan in three years instead of four years. He explained that there were no fortresses that Bolsheviks could not conquer. Old Russia was defeated by Mongols, Turks, and others because of its backwardness, and the USSR was fifty to 100 years behind the advanced countries.

JOSEPH STALIN
THE TASKS OF BUSINESS EXECUTIVES
Speech Delivered at the First All-Union Conference of Leading Personnel of Socialist Industry

Comrades, the deliberations of your conference are drawing to a close. You are now about to adopt resolutions. I have no doubt that they will be adopted unanimously. In these resolutions—I am somewhat familiar with them—you approve the control figures of industry for 1931 and pledge yourselves to fulfil them.

A Bolshevik's word is his bond. Bolsheviks are in the habit of fulfilling promises made by them. But what does the pledge to fulfil the control figures for 1931 mean? It means ensuring a total increase of industrial output by 45 percent. And that is a very big task. More than that. Such a pledge means that you not only pledge yourselves to fulfil our five year plan in four years—that matter has already been settled, and no more resolutions on it are needed—*it means that you promise to fulfil it in three years in all the basic, decisive branches of industry*.

It is good that the conference gives a promise to fulfil the plan for 1931, to fulfil the five year plan in three years. But we have been taught by "bitter experience". We know that promises are not always kept. In the beginning of 1930, too, a promise was given to fulfil the plan for the year. At that time it was necessary to increase the output of our industries by 31 to 32 percent. But that promise was not kept to the full. Actually, the increase in industrial output during 1930 amounted to 25 percent. We must ask: Will not the same thing occur again this year? The managers and leading personnel of our industries now promise to increase industrial output in 1931 by 45 percent. But what guarantee is there that this promise will be kept?

What is needed in order to fulfil the control figures, to achieve a 45 percent increase in output, to secure the fulfillment of the five year plan not in four, but, as regards the basic and decisive branches of industry, in three years?

Two fundamental conditions are needed for this.

Firstly, real or, as we term it, "objective" possibilities.

Secondly, the willingness and ability to direct our enterprises in such a way as to realize these possibilities.

Did we have the "objective" possibilities last year for completely fulfilling the plan? Yes, we had. Incontestable facts testify to this. These facts show that in March and April of last year industry achieved an increase of 31 percent in output compared with the previous year. Why then, it will be asked, did we fail to fulfil the plan for the whole year? What prevented it? What was lacking? *The ability to make use of the existing possibilities were lacking. The ability to manage the factories, mills and mines properly was lacking.*

We had the first condition: The "objective" possibilities for fulfilling the plan. But we did not have in sufficient degree the second condition: The ability to manage production. And precisely because we lacked the ability to manage the factories, the plan was not fulfilled. Instead of a 31-32 percent increase we had one of only 25 percent.

Of course, a 25 percent *increase* is a big thing. Not a single capitalist country *increased* its production in 1930, or is *increasing* production now. In all capitalist countries without exception a sharp *decline* in production is taking place. Under such circumstances a 25 percent *increase* is a big step forward. But we could have achieved more. We had all the necessary "objective" conditions for this.

And so, what guarantee is there that what happened last year will not be repeated this year, that the plan will be fulfilled, that we shall use the existing possibilities in the way that they should be used, that your promise will not to some extent remain a promise on paper?

In the history of states and countries, in the history of armies, there have been cases when there was every possibility for success and victory, but these possibilities were wasted because the leaders failed to notice them, did not know how to take advantage of them, and the armies suffered defeat.

Have we all the possibilities that are needed to fulfil the control figures for 1931?

Yes, we have such possibilities.

What are these possibilities? What is needed in order that these possibilities should really exist?

First of all, adequate *natural resources* in the country: Iron ore, coal, oil, grain, cotton. Have we these resources? Yes, we have. We have them in larger quantity than any other country. Take the Urals, for example, which provide a combination of resources not to be found in any other country. Ore, coal, oil, grain—what is there not in the Urals? We have everything in our country, except, perhaps, rubber. But within a year or two we shall have our own rubber as well. As far as natural resources are concerned we are fully provided. We have even more than necessary.

What else is needed?

A *government* desirous and capable of utilizing these immense natural resources for the benefit of the people. Have we such a government? We have. True, our work in utilizing natural resources does not always proceed without friction among our leading personnel. For instance, last year the Soviet Government had to conduct a certain amount of struggle over the question of creating a second coal and metallurgical base, without which we cannot develop further. But we have already overcome these obstacles and shall soon have this base.

What else is needed?

That this government should enjoy the *support* of the vast masses of workers and peasants. Does our government enjoy such support? Yes, it does. You will find no other government in the world that enjoys such support from the workers and peasants as does the Soviet Government. There is no need for me to refer to the growth of socialist competition, the spread of shock-brigade work, the campaign and struggle for counterplans. All these facts, which vividly demonstrate the support that the vast masses give the Soviet Government, are well known.

What else is needed to order to fulfil and overfulfil the control figures for 1931?

A *system* that is free from the incurable diseases of capitalism and has great advantages over capitalism. Crises, unemployment, waste, destitution among the masses—such are the incurable diseases of capitalism. Our system does not suffer from these diseases because power is in our hands, in the hands of the working class; because we are conducting a planned economy, systematically accumulating resources and properly distributing them among the different branches of the national economy. We are free from the incurable diseases of capitalism. That is what distinguishes us from capitalism; that is what constitutes our decisive superiority over capitalism.

Notice the way in which the capitalists are trying to escape from the economic crisis. They are reducing the workers' wages as much as possible. They are reducing the prices of raw materials as much as possible. But they do not want to reduce the prices of food and industrial commodities for mass consumption to any important extent. This means that they want to escape from the crisis at the expense of the principal consumers, at the expense of the workers and peasants, at the expense of the working people. The capitalists are cutting the ground from under their own feet. And instead of overcoming the crisis they are aggravating it; new conditions are accumulating which lead to a new, even more severe crisis.

Our superiority lies in the fact that we have no crises of overproduction, we have not and never will have millions unemployed, we have no anarchy in production, for we are conducting a planned economy. But that is not all. We are a land of the most concentrated industry. This means that we can build our industry on the basis of the best technique and thereby secure an unprecedented productivity of labor, an unprecedented rate of accumulation. Our weakness in the past was that this industry was based upon scattered and small peasant farming. That *was* so in the past; it is no longer so now. Soon, perhaps within a year, we shall become the country of the largest-scale agriculture in the world. This year, the state and collective farms—and these are forms of large-scale farming—have already supplied half of all our marketable grain. And that means that our system, the Soviet system, affords us opportunities of rapid progress of which not a single bourgeois country can dream.

What else is needed in order to advance with giant strides?

A *party* sufficiently solid and united to direct the efforts of all the best members of the working class to *one point*, and sufficiently experienced to be unafraid of difficulties and to pursue systematically a correct, revolutionary, Bolshevik policy. Have we such a party? Yes, we have. Is its policy correct? Yes, it is, for it is yielding important successes. This is now admitted not only by the friends by also by the enemies of the working class. See how all the well known "honorable" gentlemen, Fish in America, Churchill in Britain, Poincare in France, fume and rave against our Party. Why do they fume and rave? Because the policy of our Party is correct, because it is yielding success after success.

There, comrades, you have all those objective possibilities which assist us in realizing the control figures for 1931, which help us to fulfill the five year plan in four years, and in the key industries even in three years.

Thus we have the first condition for fulfillment of the plan—the "objective" possibilities.

Have we the second condition, the ability to use these possibilities?

In other words, are our factories, mills and mines properly managed? Is everything in order in this respect?

Unfortunately, not everything is in order here. And, as Bolsheviks, we must say this plainly and frankly.

What does management of production mean? There are people among us who do not always have a Bolshevik approach to the question of the management of our factories. There are many people among us who think that management is synonymous with signing papers and orders. This is sad, but true. At times one cannot help recalling Shchedrin's Pompadours. Do you remember how Madame Pompadour taught the young Pompadour: "Don't bother your head with science, don't go into matters, let others do that, it is not your business—your business is to sign papers." It must be admitted to our shame that even among us

Bolsheviks there are not a few who carry out management by signing papers. But as for going into matters, mastering technique, becoming master of the business—why, that is out of the question.

How is it that we Bolsheviks, who have made three revolutions, who emerged victorious from the bitter civil war, who have solved the tremendous task of building a modern industry, who have swung the peasantry on to the path of socialism—how is it that in the matter of the management of production we bow to a slip of paper?

The reason is that it is easier to sign papers than to manage production. And so, many business executives are taking this line of least resistance. We, too, in the center, are also to blame. About ten years ago a slogan was issued: "Since Communists do not yet properly understand the technique of production, since they have yet to learn the art of management, let the old technicians and engineers—the experts—carry on production, and you, Communists, do not interfere with the technique of business; but, while not interfering, study technique, study the art of management tirelessly, in order later on, together with the experts who are loyal to us, to become true managers of production, true masters of the business." Such was the slogan. But what actually happened? The second part of this formula was cast aside, for it is harder to study than to sign papers; and the first part of the formula was vulgarized: Noninterference was interpreted to mean refraining from studying the technique of production. The result has been nonsense, harmful and dangerous nonsense, which the sooner we discard the better.

Life itself has more than once warned us that all was not well in this field. The Shakhty affair was the first grave warning. The Shakhty affair showed that the Party organizations and the trade unions lacked revolutionary vigilance. It showed that our business executives were disgracefully backward in technical knowledge; that some of the old engineers and technicians, working without supervision, rather easily go over to wrecking activities, especially as they are constantly being besieged by "offers" from our enemies abroad.

The second warning was the "Industrial Party" trial.

Of course, the underlying cause of wrecking activities is the class struggle. Of course, the class enemy furiously resists the socialist offensive. This alone, however, is not an adequate explanation for the luxuriant growth of wrecking activities.

How is it that wrecking activities assumed such wide dimensions? Who is to blame for this? We are to blame. Had we handled the business of managing production differently, had we started much earlier to learn the technique of business, to master technique, had we more frequently and efficiently intervened in the management of production, the wreckers would not have succeeded in doing so much damage.

We must ourselves become experts, masters of the business; we must turn to technical science—such was the lesson life itself was teaching us. But neither the first warning nor even the second brought about the necessary change. It is time, high time that we turned towards technique. It is time to discard the old slogan, the obsolete slogan of noninterference in technique, and ourselves become specialists, experts, complete masters of our economic affairs.

It is frequently asked: Why have we not one-man management? We do not have it and we shall not get it until we have mastered technique. Until there are among us Bolsheviks a sufficient number of people thoroughly familiar with technique, economy and finance, we shall not have real one-man management. You can write as many resolutions as you please, take as many vows as you please, but, unless you master technique, economy and finance of the mill, factory or mine, nothing will come of it, there will be no one-man management.

Hence, the task is for us to master technique ourselves, to become masters of the business ourselves. This is the sole guarantee that our plans will be carried out in full, and that one-man management will be established.

This, of course, is no easy matter; but it can certainly be accomplished. Science, technical experience, knowledge, are all things that can be acquired. We may not have them today, but tomorrow we shall. The main thing is to have the passionate Bolshevik desire to master technique, to master the science of production. Everything can be achieved, everything can be overcome, if there is a passionate desire for it.

It is sometimes asked whether it is not possible to slow down the tempo somewhat, to put a check on the movement. No, comrades, it is not possible! The tempo must not be reduced! On the contrary, we must increase it as much as is within our powers and possibilities. This is dictated to us by our obligations to the workers and peasants of the USSR. This is dictated to us by our obligations to the working class of the whole world.

To slacken the tempo would mean falling behind. And those who fall behind get beaten. But we do not want to be beaten. No, we refuse to be beaten! One feature of the history of old Russia was the continual beatings she suffered because of her backwardness. She was beaten by the Mongol khans. She was beaten by the Turkish beys. She was beaten by the Swedish feudal lords. She was beaten by the Polish and Lithuanian gentry. She was beaten by the British and French capitalists. She was beaten by the Japanese barons. All beat her—because of her backwardness, because of her military backwardness, cultural backwardness, political backwardness, industrial backwardness, agricultural backwardness. They beat her because to do so was profitable and could be done with impunity. You remember the words of the prerevolution ry poet: "You are poor and abundant, mighty and impotent, Mother Russia." Those gentlemen were quite familiar with the verses of the old poet. They beat her, saying: "You are abundant," so you can be beaten and plundered with impunity. Such is the law of the exploiters—to beat the backward and the weak. It is the jungle of the law of capitalism. You are backward, you are weak—therefore you are wrong; hence you can be beaten and enslaved. You are mighty—therefore you are right; hence we must be wary of you.

That is why we must no longer lag behind.

In the past we had no fatherland, nor could we have had one. But now that we have overthrown capitalism and power is in our hands, in the hands of the people, we have a fatherland, and we will uphold its independence. Do you want our socialist fatherland to be beaten and to lose its independence? If you do not want this, you must put an end to its backwardness in the shortest possible time and develop a genuine Bolshevik tempo in building up its socialist economy. There is no other way. That is what Lenin said on the eve of the October Revolution: "Either perish, or overtake and outstrip the advanced capitalist countries."

We are fifty or a hundred years behind the advanced countries. We must make good this distance in ten years. Either we do it, or we shall go under.

That is what our obligations to the workers and peasants of the USSR dictate to us.

But we have yet other, more serious and more important, obligations. They are our obligations to the world proletariat. They coincide with our obligations to the workers and peasants of the USSR. But we place them higher. The working class of the USSR is part of the world working class. We achieved victory not solely through the efforts of the working class of the USSR, but also thanks to the support of the working class of the world. Without this support we would have been torn to pieces long ago. It is said that our country is the shock brigade of the proletariat of all countries. That is well said. But it imposes very serious obligations upon us. Why does the international proletariat support us? How did we merit this support? By the fact that we were the first to hurl ourselves into battle against capitalism, we were the first to begin building socialism. By the fact that we are engaged on a cause which, if successful, will transform the whole world and free the entire working class. But what is needed for success? The elimination of our backwardness, the development of a high Bolshevik tempo of construction. We must march forward in such a way that the working class of the whole world, looking at us, may say: There you have my advanced detachment, my shock brigade, my working-class state power, my fatherland; they are engaged on their cause, *our* cause, and they are working well; let us support them against the capitalists and promote the cause of the world revolution. Must we not justify the hopes of the world's working class, must we not fulfil our obligations to them? Yes, we must if we do not want to utterly disgrace ourselves.

Such are our obligations, internal and international.

As you see, they dictate to us a Bolshevik tempo of development.

I will not say that we have accomplished nothing in regard to management of production during these years. In fact, we have accomplished a good deal. We have doubled our industrial output compared with the prewar level. We have created the largest-scale agricultural production in the world. But we could have accomplished still more if we had tried during this period really to master production, the technique of production, the financial and economic side of it.

In ten years at most we must make good the distance that separates us from the advanced capitalist countries. We have all the "objective" possibilities for this. The only thing lacking is the ability to make proper use of these possibilities. And that depends on us. *Only* on us! It is time we learned to make use of these possibilities. It is time to put an end to the rotten line of noninterference in production. It is time to adopt a new line, one corresponding to the present period—the line of *interfering in everything*. If you are a factory manager—interfere in all the affairs of the factory, look into everything, let nothing escape you, learn and learn again. Bolsheviks must master technique. It is time Bolsheviks themselves became experts. In the period of reconstruction, technique decides everything. And a business executive who does not want to study technique, who does not want to master technique, is a joke and not an executive.

It is said that it is hard to master technique. That is not true! There are no fortresses that Bolsheviks cannot capture. We have solved a number of most difficult problems. We have overthrown capitalism. We have assumed power. We have built up a huge socialist industry. We have transferred the middle peasants on to the path of socialism. We have already accomplished what is most important from the point of view of construction. What remains to be done is not so much: To study technique, to master science. And when we have done that we shall develop a tempo of which we dare not even dream at present.

And we shall do it if we really want to.

Stalin, *Works*, XIII, 31-44.

MENSHEVIK PARTY SHOW TRIAL. COURT VERDICT
10 March 1931

On the heels of the "Industrial Party" show trial of 1930, the Soviet Government staged another show trial between 1 and 9 March 1931, during which fourteen individuals were accused of sabotage and counterrevolutionary activity as members of the Menshevik Social Democratic Party. The accused, primarily prominent officials of the State Planning Commission, State Bank, and the Supreme Council of the National Economy, formed the fictitious conspiratorial "All-Union Bureau" to work with the "Industrial Party," Second International, the Menshevik Party in Berlin, Germany, and foreign governments, particularly France, to subvert and attack the Soviet Union. Soviet officials extracted confessions from the accused through torture and promises of leniency. Many of the accused at one time were Mensheviks critical of the Party's industrialization policies. The document below describes the charges, verdict, and punishment against the members of the fictitious "All-Union Bureau."

VERDICT OF THE SUPREME COURT OF THE SOVIET UNION
IN THE TRIAL OF THE COUNTERREVOLUTIONARY ORGANIZATION
THE "ALL-UNION BUREAU" OF THE CC OF THE RSDLP (MENSHEVIKS)

In the name of the Union of Socialist Soviet Republics, the Special Senate of the Supreme Court of the USSR, consisting of the President, Comrade Shvernik and judges Comrades Maranov and Antonov-Saratovsky, the secretaries Comrades Smolitsky, Dubrovsky and Iakovlev, with the participation of the Public Prosecutor of the RSFSR, Comrade Krylenko, and the deputy Public Prosecutor of the RSFSR, Comrade Roginsky, as well as the defenders Komodov and Braude, members of the Moscow collegium of advocates, investigated in public judicial proceedings from 1 to 9 March 1931, the matter of the counterrevolutionary organization the "All-Union Bureau" of the CC of the Russian Social-Democratic Labor Party (Mensheviks).

The accused were:

1. Groman, Vladimir Gustavovich, 56 years old, son of a private tutor, high school education, not previously convicted, economist by profession, former member of the Presidium of the State Planning Commission, member of the RSDLP since its foundation up to the year 1922, with interruptions, and again, from 1926 to 1930 member of the RSDLP (Mensheviks);

2. Sher, Vasilii Vladimirovich, 47 years old, high school education, not previously convicted, formerly member of the directorial board of the State Bank of the Soviet Union, member of the RSDLP from 1923 to 1930;

3. Sukhanov, Nikolai Nikolaevich, 48 years old, son of a commercial employee, high school education, not previously convicted, publicist by profession, a member of the RSDLP (Mensheviks) from 1907 to 1920 (Martov group) and since 1929 a member of the RSDLP (Mensheviks);

4. Ginsburg, Abraham Moiseevich, 52 years old, son of a merchant, high school education, not previously convicted, economist by profession, member of the RSDLP (Mensheviks) from 1897 to 1921 and then again from 1926 to 1930;

5. Iakubovich, Mikhail Petrovich, 39 years old, of aristocratic origin, not previously convicted, high school education, former Vice-Chairman of the Supply Department of the Trade Commissariat of the Soviet Union, a member of the RSDLP (Mensheviks) from 1908 to 1921 and again from 1927 to 1930;

6. Petunin, Kiril Gavrilovich, 47 years old, son of a village tailor, not previously convicted, accountant by profession, a member of the directorial board of the Tsentrosoiuz since 1922, a member of the RSDLP (Mensheviks) from 1905 to 1918 and again from 1925 to 1930;

7. Fin-Ienotaevsky, Aleksandr Iulevich, 58 years old, son of a commercial employee, high school education, not previously convicted, Professor of Political Economy, a member of the RSDLP (Bolsheviks) from 1903 to 1915, a member of the RSDLP (Mensheviks) from 1928 to 1930;

8. Sokolovsky, Aron Lvovich, 47 years old, of petty-bourgeois origin, not previously convicted, economist by profession, a member of the Central Committee of the United Jewish Socialist Party from 1906 to 1920, a member of the RSDLP (Mensheviks) from 1927 to 1930;

9. Salkind, Lazar Borisovich, 45 years old, son of a commercial employee, not previously convicted, high school education, economist by profession, a member of the RSDLP (Bolsheviks) from 1903 to 1907, a member of the RSDLP (Mensheviks) from 1917 to 1921 and again from 1924 to 1930;

10. Berlatsky, Boris Markovich, 41 years old, of petty-bourgeois extraction, not previously convicted, incomplete high school education, former member of the directorial board of the State Bank, a member of the RSDLP (Mensheviks) from 1904 to 1930 with interruptions;

11. Volkov, Ivan Grigorevich, 47 years old, son of a peasant, former worker, not previously convicted, worked as an economist in the Supreme Council of the National Economy of the Soviet Union, a member of the Social-Revolutionary Party from 1902 to 1905, a member of the RSDLP (Mensheviks) from 1905 to 1918 and again from 1928 to 1930.

These eleven persons were accused of having committed crimes coming under Article 58, Paragraphs 4, 7 and 11 of the Penal Code of the RSFSR.

12. Ikov, Vladimir Konstantinovich, 49 years old, of aristocratic extraction, not previously convicted, incomplete high school education, publicist by profession, a member of the RSDLP (Mensheviks) since 1901;

13. Teitelbaum, Moisei Isaevich, 54 years old, of petty-bourgeois extraction, not previously convicted, incomplete high school and legal training, former President of the Department of the Trade Commissariat of the Soviet Union for the Standardization of Exports, a member of the RSDLP (Bolsheviks) from 1900 to 1907, a member of the RSDLP (Mensheviks) from 1925 to 1930;

have violated Article 58, Paragraphs 4 and 11.

The fourteenth accused:

14. Rubin, Isaak Ilich, 45 years old, Professor of Political Economy, member of the Jewish "Bund" from 1904 to 1920, member of the Jewish "Bund" and of the RSDLP (Mensheviks) from 1929 to 1930;

has committed a crime which comes under Article 58, Paragraphs 4, 10 and 11 of the Penal Code of the RSFSR.

After hearing the statements of the accused, of the witnesses, and the speeches of the Prosecution and the Defense, and after investigating the material relating to the matter, the Supreme Court finds that following has been proved:

In the second half of the year 1930 there was discovered in Moscow a sabotage organization which possessed branches in various parts of the State apparatus. This organization was headed by a group which formed the "All-Union Bureau" of the CC of the RSDLP (Mensheviks), which is affiliated to the Second International. The said bureau was founded and confirmed by the CC at the beginning of 1928. It comprised the following persons, who were specially prominent in the circles of the social democrats (Mensheviks) and who for the greater part occupied responsible positions in the central institutions of the Soviet apparatus: Groman, Sher, Ginsburg, Sokolovsky, Salkind, Iakubovich, Volkov, Petunin, and Fin-Ienotaevsky, and, since the beginning of 1929, also Sukhanov, among whom the following played leading roles: Groman, Sher, Ginsburg and Sukhanov.

In order to conduct the counterrevolutionary and sabotage work the Bureau had a Presidium, a Plenum and also a number of commissions: Program, organization, war and finance commissions. The Party documents were handed over to the secretary of the "All-Union Bureau" Sher as well as to Rubin for safekeeping. The task of duplicating the documents was carried out by Iakubovich. For the purpose of coordinating their own activity with the activity of the Foreign Delegation of the RSDLP, whose seat is in Berlin, the "All-Union Bureau" established regular correspondence through the members of its organization Ikov and Fin-Ienotaevsky, as well as direction by means of journeys abroad of members of the Bureau (Groman, Petunin, Ginsburg and others) as well as through journeys of the members of the Foreign Delegation of the RSDLP (Mensheviks) (Abramovich, Braunshtein and others) to Moscow.

The judicial investigation established that sabotage had been carried out by all members of the "All-Union Bureau" and by members of the special sabotage nuclei which were founded by the social democrats (Mensheviks) in a number of Soviet institutions: In the State Planning Commission, in the Supreme Council of the National Economy, in the State Bank, in the People's Commissariat for Trade and in the Cooperative Association, and in the Tsentrosoiuz.

The judicial investigation establishes: The Russian social democrats (Mensheviks), lacking a point of support among the working masses and the peasantry in the country, following the failure of their attempts even by sabotage activity to call forth discontent among the masses and to incite them against Soviet Power, decided on the necessity of intervention and for increasing sabotage work for the purpose of actively supporting intervention. This attitude towards intervention arose both in the "Union Bureau" and in the Foreign Delegation of the Russian social democracy (Mensheviks), the latter expressly demanding the raising of the question in the "All-Union Bureau".

Already at the end of 1927 leading persons of the Foreign Delegation of the Russian social democrats (Mensheviks), Dan and Abramovich, put the question to the "All-Union Bureau".

In the summer of 1928 Abramovich made an illegal journey to Moscow in order to confer with the "All-Union Bureau". He insisted on the acceptance of intervention as the only way out for Russian social democracy (Mensheviks) in their fight against Soviet Power.

After the "All-Union Bureau" had requested Abramovich to send written directives from abroad regarding this question, these directives were sent to the Bureau through Ikov.

Braunshtein, the authorized representative of the same Foreign Delegation of the Russian social democratic party (Mensheviks), made an illegal journey to Moscow in the year 1929 and again confirmed that the Foreign Bureau had adopted the policy of intervention and that it demanded the greatest activity in this direction from the "All-Union Bureau".

In the Autumn of 1929 the second Plenum of the "All-Union Bureau" discussed the directives of the Foreign Delegation regarding intervention and decided that "intervention is a necessary weapon against the proletarian dictatorship, against Soviet Power."

The judicial investigation has ascertained that the adoption of the policy of intervention, and of sabotage work as a means in preparation thereof, induced the Mensheviks to conclude a firm political bloc with the counterrevolutionary Kulak party of Kondratiev-Chaianov as well as with the "Industrial Party", the interventionist espionage and sabotage organization of the big bourgeoisie of the imperialist countries.

All the above-mentioned counterrevolutionary organizations, at a common consultation of leaders which took place at the beginning of 1929, distributed among themselves the functions in the fight against Soviet Power. The Russian social democrats (Mensheviks), with the approval of their Foreign Delegation, took over the control of general sabotage activity especially in the sphere of national economy, concrete sabotage activity in regard to obtaining grain and raw materials and in the distribution of industrial goods, and also in supplies to the working class and in the sphere of finance and credit. In addition, they undertook with the aid of their Foreign Delegation and the Second International to adopt measures to work upon the international proletariat so that it would offer no resistance to an intervention of the capitalist Powers in the Soviet Union.

The judicial investigation ascertained that the Russian social democrats (Mensheviks) received money for the carrying out of their sabotage work from the counterrevolutionary organization of the bourgeoisie, the "Industrial Party", which money originally came from the "Torgprom" in Paris and the imperialist circles allied with it. In the year 1929/30 they received 200,000 rubles from the treasurer of the central committee of the "Industrial Party", Larichev. The second source of finance of the sabotage activity of the Russian social democrats (Mensheviks) was the German social democracy, a section of the Second International. From this source monies were remitted to the All-Union Bureau through the Foreign Bureau of the Russian social democrats through the mediation of Fin-Ienotaevsky. The "All-Union Bureau" received through this source 280,000 rubles, and in addition, at the commencement of the sabotage activity, 20,000 rubles from Dan, which were paid over to the Bureau through Shurigin and Petunin. In addition, 15,000 rubes were received from the "Industrial Party" through Sher and Salkind. In all they received 515,000 rubles.

At the same time the judicial proceedings ascertained that the Foreign Delegation of the Russian social democrats (Mensheviks) carried on its criminal counterrevolutionary work in preparation for intervention and financing the sabotage activity of the "All-Union Bureau", which served the same purpose, with the knowledge and approval of the Second International, which connived at this work and rendered it financial support through the German social democracy. At the same time the Second International (Weis, Hilferding, Blum), in public hypocritically opposed intervention, whilst in reality it developed its counterrevolutionary activity against the Soviet Union by preparing the minds of the workers for the intended intervention and promoting the predatory designs of the imperialists against the Soviet Union.

Under Article 326, Paragraph 3 of the Law of the Criminal Procedure of the RSFSR, the Supreme Court of the Soviet Union has sentenced the accused as follows:

Teitelbaum, Moisei Isaevich, to five years' social isolation and the loss of civil rights, according to Article 31, Paragraphs a., b., c, d., e. of the Penal Code of the RSFSR, for the period of two years.

Rubin, Isaak Ilich, to five years' social isolation and the loss of civil rights, according to Article 31, Paragraphs a., b., c., d., e. of the Penal Code of the RSFSR, for the period of two years.

Volkov, Ivan Grigorevich, to five years' social isolation and the loss of civil rights, according to Article 31, Paragraphs a., b., c., d., e. of the Penal Code of the RSFSR, for the period of two years.

Sokolovsky, Aron Lvovich, to eight years' social isolation and the loss of civil rights, according to Article 31, Paragraphs a., b., c., d., e. of the Penal Code of the RSFSR, for the period of three years.

Salkind, Lazar Borisovich, according to Article 31, Paragraphs a., b., c., d., e. of the Penal Code of the RSFSR, to eight years' social isolation and the loss of civil rights for the period of three years.

Berlatsky, Boris Markovich, under Article 31, Paragraphs a., b., c., d., e. of the Penal Code of the RSFSR, to eight years' social isolation and the loss of civil rights for the period of three years.

Ikov, Vladimir Konstantinovich, under Article 31, Paragraphs a., b., c., d., e. of the Penal Code of the RSFSR, to eight years' social isolation and the loss of civil rights for the period of three years.

Petunin, Kiril Gavrilovich, according to Article 31, Paragraphs a., b., c., d., e. of the Penal Code of the RSFSR, to ten years' social isolation and the loss of civil rights for the period of five years.

Fin-Ienotaevsky, Aleksandr Iulevich, under Article 31, Paragraphs a., b., c., d., e. of the Penal Code of the RSFSR, to ten years' social isolation and the loss of civil rights for the period of five years.

Iakubovich, Mikhail Petrovich, under Article 31, Paragraphs a., b., c., d., e. of the Penal Code of the RSFSR, to ten years' social isolation and the loss of civil rights for the period of five years.

Ginsburg, Abraham Moiseevich, under Article 31, Paragraphs a., b., c., d., e. of the Penal Code of the RSFSR, to ten years' social isolation and the loss of civil rights for the period of five years.

Sukhanov, Nikolai Nikolaevich, under Article 31, Paragraphs a., b., c., d., e. of the Penal Code of the RSFSR, to ten years' social isolation and the loss of civil rights for the period of five years.

Sher, Vasilii Vladimirovich, under Article 31, Paragraphs a., b., c., d., e. of the Penal Code of the RSFSR, to ten years' social isolation and the loss of civil rights for the period of five years.

Groman, Vladimir Gustavovich, under Article 31, Paragraphs a., b., c., d., e. of the Penal Code of the RSFSR, to ten years' social isolation and the loss of civil rights for the period of five years.

In reckoning the sentences the period spent by the accused in prison while awaiting trial is taken into account.

The verdict and the sentences are legally valid and require no confirmation.

International Press Correspondence, Vol. 11, No. 15 (19 March 1931), 301-302.

LITVINOV ON THE WORLD ECONOMIC CRISIS AND THE EUROPEAN UNION

Geneva, 18 May 1931

Several European states, under the auspices of the League of Nations, created a commission early in 1931 to explore the possibilities for a European Union and to convene a conference on 15 May to discuss these as well as to study the world economic crisis as it affected Europe as a whole. Iceland, Turkey, and the Soviet Union were invited to participate in the study of the world economic crisis. Maxim Litvinov, People's Commissar for Foreign Affairs, attended the conference and delivered a speech, in which he gave the Soviet interpretation of the reasons for the world economic crisis and refuted accusations against the Soviet Union for "dumping" grain exports on the world economy at reduced prices to undercut grain exports of other countries.

COMRADE LITVINOV'S SPEECH IN THE EUROPEAN COMMISSION

First of all I wish to express my thanks to the President of the Commission for the welcome he has extended to the new members. The fact that I am present here will undoubtedly please the Geographers of the world, for my presence is a confirmation of the hypothesis which they have formulated concerning the connection of Russia with Europe, a hypothesis which is also confirmed by the decision of the European Conference-Commission.

The position which I take up here is little out of the ordinary, if only as a result of the fact that the country which I represent is very far from experiencing a crisis. On the contrary, it is experiencing a development unexampled in its economic history.

The World Crisis and the Soviet Union

This, however, does not mean that we are not interested in the world crisis, or that this crisis does not affect the interests of the Soviet Union. At the moment the Soviet Union maintains economic relations with the great majority of the European and nonEuropean States, so that the economic disturbances in these countries cannot be a matter of indifference to us. The price vacillations offer an example of how the crisis affects us. The carrying out of the great plan for the speedy industrialization of the Soviet Union demands, and will continue to demand from year to year, the import of industrial goods from other countries. In order to be able to pay for these imports my government must occupy itself with the export of raw materials practically to the exclusion of other exports. The drop in the price of raw materials during the last few years, plus the fact that the prices of finished goods have remained stable, has had damaging results for the economic life of the Soviet Union. Thus the connection between the world economic crisis and the interests of the Soviet Union can be easily appreciated.

Indirectly the interests of the Soviet Union are damaged in consequence of the various plans which have been forged against the Soviet Union, and in some cases actually put into action by certain States. These States are striving without much success to extricate themselves from the crisis at the expense of the Soviet Union, or to take advantage of the crisis.

And finally, and this is not an unimportant point, the relations set up between the Soviet Union and the other European States must inevitably have an effect on the development of the economic crisis.

I think that I have said enough to show you what interest we have in a study of the problems raised by the world economic crisis in the sessions of this Commission.

The Cause of the Crisis

I do not know whether any of my colleagues in this Commission are in a position to offer us any effective cure for the abolition of the crisis through which the world is at present passing. For my part, I do not believe that there can be any such cure. In any case, please do not expect any such proposal from a representative of the Soviet Union.

The whole world knows that in our opinion the economic crisis of overproduction have their roots in the capitalist system itself; they are closely wound up with the capitalist system, and they are based on the conflict of interests which is peculiar to the capitalist system. In consequence they appear at more or less regular intervals.

No one now denies that the present crisis is the worst that the capitalist system has ever experienced. This time we are faced with an industrial crisis which is indissolubly connected, and not fortuitously, with an agricultural crisis. The mutual influences of these crises lead inevitably to an intensification and protraction of the crisis as a whole.

The intensity of the crisis is aggravated by the policy of those organizations which have a monopolist position and are aiming to maintain high prices on the home markets of their various countries. No one can deny that this policy considerably hinders the disposal of warehoused supplies and places almost insuperable hindrances in the way of the purchasers of such commodities, and thus protracts the economic crisis.

It is generally admitted that the intensity of the present crisis, particularly in the European economic system, is to a large extent caused by the special conditions which have resulted from the world war; that its causes lie in the disorganization of the world economic system during the war; that they were perpetuated in the system of treaties which followed on the conclusion of the war, in the indebtedness of the nations to each other as a result of the war, and in the system of military alliances, etc., which was continued after the war. In my opinion, therefore, this Commission must pay particular attention to these contributory causes which have intensified the crisis, and must see what can be done to exclude these factors in order to prevent any further intensification of the crisis, or at least, what can be done to ameliorate the unfortunate results of these factors.

The factors which I have mentioned must be sought for both in politics and economics. They are deeply rooted in the general policy pursued during the world war and after its conclusion. I will deal with these factors briefly.

In my opinion it is hardly necessary to pay any special attention to the close connection between the increase of the burden of taxation and the crisis itself, as this connection is self-evident. It is clear that the increase of taxation is chiefly due to the obstinate persistence of militarism and the consequent continual increase of armaments. Despite the Locarno Pact, the Kellogg Pact and various other Pacts, on which pacifist circles set such great hopes, there is absolutely no sign that the growth of armaments is coming to a stop or even slowing down. The work of the Preparatory Disarmament Commission offers little hope for an improvement in this connection.

The policy of the formation of new military blocs is changing the face of the world. Great armies prepared at a moment's notice to plunge into bloody conflicts, and the existence of these military blocs of course sharpen the armament competition. Every country is compelled to be on the watch not only against this or that other country, but against already existing groups of States, or groups in process of formation.

Apart from the political differences which exist between the capitalist States, it can be observed that the economic differences are sharpening. This is expressed in the growth of protectionism. This intensified economic struggle, of course, also affects unfavorably the postwar economic system of Europe. In this connection it is interesting to note that the national frontiers have been extended since the war by 20,000 kilometers, or almost 30 percent.

Further, we must not conceal from ourselves the fact that another consequence of the war, namely the special burdens which have been placed on certain States either in the form of reparations or inter-allied debts, contributes considerably to the intensification of the crisis. The result is that large sections of the population observe their purchasing power dwindling, and this results again in making it impossible to dispose of a part of the goods produced. Another factor is the unfavorable distribution of the gold reserves throughout the world. Gold reserves are lying unused in the safes of certain countries, whilst other countries are suffering from gold shortage.

Special attention must also be paid to the danger which results from the reduction of the purchasing power of great masses of the population both in town and country. These factors are in their turn closely connected with the unemployment problem, which is acute everywhere to an unexampled degree; they are closely connected with the systematic reduction of wages, with the increase of the working day for those still in employment, with the reduction of benefits under the various social insurance schemes, and with the simultaneous increase of the burden of taxation which weighs with particular severity on the shoulders of the working masses.

All these factors combine to create an atmosphere of political uncertainty not only in Europe, but in the whole world, to create a fear of some terrible catastrophe. This atmosphere affects the credit policy of the banks and prevents the utilization of capital for the purposes of constructive work, and this in its turn again intensifies the crisis. And in this situation the feeling of uncertainty and lack of confidence which exists in Europe is being artificially aggravated by the various antiSoviet campaigns which aim at proving the necessity of a military attack on the part of the capitalist States against the Soviet Union. The plans for this attack and the conditions under which it is to take place are the subject of open discussion in the press and at public meetings. The originators of these campaigns wish to exploit the world economic crisis for the furtherance of their aims. Those capitalist circles which are particularly in concealing the real causes of the crisis from the masses of the people, show great zeal in putting on a false scent those who are studying the causes of the crisis, and persuading them that the only cause of the present crisis is the existence of the Soviet Union.

The Crisis and Soviet Exports

It will not be difficult for me to show you the absurdity of such a contention. All that is necessary is to point to the moderate share taken by the Soviet Union in world trade. It must also not be forgotten that not only those markets which absorb Soviet exports are suffering from the crisis, but also those markets on which the Soviet Union appears exclusively as a purchaser. Figures taken from the reports of the economic organizations of the League of Nations clearly illustrate my contentions. For instance, the price of coffee sunk from 16.25 cents a pound in September 1929 to 10.3 cents a pound in March 1930. In the same period the price of tin fell from 204.9 pounds sterling per ton to 165 pounds sterling per ton. The price of rubber also fell from 10.5 to 7.5. In the same period the price of rice fell by 49.2 percent, the price of olive oil by 23.8 percent, and the price of silk by 48.1 percent.

Economic crises occurred before the existence of the Soviet Union, and that being the case, I think we may say that the present crisis would have occurred, perhaps even in a still more acute and extensive form, did the Soviet Union not exist, but in its place existed a Tsarist or bourgeois Russia, i.e., a political and economic organism similar to the other countries of the world. Without doubt such a country would also have fallen victim to the crisis and the result would have been that the crisis would have been still more severe than it is at present. The Statesmen who are now doing their best to ameliorate the results of the crisis in the other countries, would then have been compelled to call special international conferences with a view to finding ways and means of meeting the danger which would have resulted from a crisis in Russia.

Permit me to ask whether the fact that one-sixth of the globe, or about one-half the area of Europe is immune from the crisis, the fact that there is one country in the world whose imports of finished goods rise from year to year, whose orders keep the factories of other countries busy and thus reduce unemployment and charter foreign vessels to transport these goods, the fact that this country itself has no unemployment problem and that its citizens are not compelled to seek employment in thousands in other countries as was the case under Tsarism, permit me to ask whether all these circumstances aggravate or ameliorate the world economic crisis.

Is the world economic crisis aggravated or ameliorated by the fact that the Soviet Union purchases from 50 to 75 percent of the total export of certain branches of the engineering industry in Germany, Austria, Great Britain and Poland? There can be no doubt that the orders placed by the Soviet Union abroad, orders which increase from year to year, represent a factor which makes for the amelioration of the crisis. In view of the fact that 53 percent of the total tractor export of the United States in 1930 was purchased by the Soviet Union, and that in the same year the Soviet Union purchased 12 percent of the total export of the textile machinery from Great Britain, 23 percent of the total export of agricultural machinery from Germany, 21 percent of the total German export of lathes and 11 percent of the German export of all other classes of machinery, and that in the first quarter of 1930 the Soviet Union purchased 91.5 percent of the total Polish export of foundry products, then there can be only one answer to the question whether the foreign trade of the Soviet Union contributes in the aggravation or the amelioration of the present world economic crisis.

In view of the certainty that Soviet imports contribute towards ameliorating the world economic crisis, and in particular the European economic crisis, for Soviet orders are placed chiefly in the European countries, it is very difficult to raise objections to the export trade of the Soviet Union, because this export trade is necessary if the import trade is to be financed.

The most recent antiSoviet campaigns made great play with the allegedly unfavorable effect of the export of raw materials by the Soviet Union on the level of prices. There is no doubt, of course, that when large quantities of commodities come on to the market the result is a drop in prices, but the result would be the same if these commodities came from other countries and not from the Soviet Union.

The "Soviet Dumping" Fable

Why is the Soviet Union made the scapegoat for the drop in the prices of these raw materials any more than any other exporting country? How is it that the export of certain countries is regarded as legitimate, whilst the export of the Soviet Union is declared to be an attack against the world economic system? What arguments can be advanced in support of cutting down the export trade of the Soviet Union, especially as any such action would only be in the interests of other countries?

Before I go any further, I would like to remind you that the export trade of the Soviet Union is in most cases not as great as the export trade of Tsarist Russia before the war.

In 1910 the grain export of Tsarist Russia totalled 25 percent of the world export, whilst in 1930 the Soviet share of world grain exports was only 20 percent. The same applies to the export of manganese ore (51 percent of world exports under Tsarism, but only 35 percent under the Soviet regime), to the export of flax (53 percent compared with 42 percent), to butter (78 million tons as compared with 10 million tons), and so on. Why, one might ask, was no attempt made to condemn the export trade of Tsarist Russia? Had there been no Tsarist exports, prices would have been at a much lighter level, and this would have been in the interests of those countries which competed with Tsarist Russia.

As far as the export trade is concerned, the Soviet Union is only just beginning to take the place in world trade which it was compelled to relinquish as a consequence of the world war, the military interventions and the blockade.

Why did the growth of the Canadian grain export trade from 2,350,000 tons in 1913 to 10,900,000 tons in 1928, or the increase of the export of Argentine butter in the same period by 810 percent, produce no protest?

A little while ago an attempt was made to justify the campaign against the Soviet export trade by declaring that the Soviet Union was indulging in dumping. This accusation is absolutely without foundation and it has been refuted on many occasions publicly not only by the official representatives of the Soviet Union, but also by the impartial investigations of economic experts from the capitalist countries. We do not deny that the special conditions of our agricultural system and of our foreign trading system permit us to sell agricultural products at lower prices than other countries can. These favorable conditions are the result of the socialization of the land in the Soviet Union, the absence of such heavy burdens as those borne by the peasant population in the capitalist countries, namely lease rent and mortgage interest which account in those countries for about 70 percent of the total costs of production, and the abolition of private profit, speculation and the middleman's profit.

In conclusion, I must point out that the prices on the world market are determined by supply and demand. We are not in the least interested in a fall of prices on the world markets, because then our income from our export trade would correspondingly sink, and it is from this income that we must meet the costs which accrue to us from the machinery imports which we need for the development of our industry and the carrying out of our Five Year Plan.

We have no desire to take any part in booms or slumps at the cost of the consumers, and for this reason we have declared ourselves prepared to take part in the grain conference which is now taking place in London. In any case, one thing is certain, and that is that low prices are not necessarily a sign of dumping. If, however, by dumping is meant the policy of the monopolist organizations which maintain high prices on the home markets in order to make possible low prices for export purposes, then the culprits will be found in the capitalist countries. The report of the International Labor Office contains very interesting figures concerning the great disparity between the home and export prices prevailing in a number of countries. This phenomenon is closely connected with the policy of the monopolist organizations. I could quote innumerable such instances, taken exclusively from the capitalist press. Here is an example from Czechoslovakia: Last year sugar was sold in Czechoslovakia at 550 Czech crowns per 100 kilos wholesale and at 600 Czech crowns per 100 kilos retail. At the same time, however, Czechoslovakia exported the same sugar at 80 crowns per 100 kilos. In Poland for instance, a product which was sold at 400 zloty in Poland was exported by Poland at only 300 zloty. The same was the case in Germany where sugar was sold on the home market at from 23 to 24 marks per 50 kilos, whilst the German sugar-exporters were selling the same sugar at from 5.8 to 6.7 marks per 50 kilos. These are generally known examples of agricultural dumping.

Only a few weeks ago Mr. Holovetz, who was Minister for Trade in Czechoslovakia for some time, declared that it was pharisaical to charge the Soviet Union with dumping, whilst neither Czechoslovakia nor any other capitalist country was free from this sin. To prove his contention he quoted examples from the sugar and iron trades. I also have occupied myself with this question, not only because we have been charged with dumping, but because the permanent policy of forming monopolies on the home markets in order to obtain artificially high prices there, and to utilize the surplus to further the export trade, represents, as I have already pointed out, one of the factors which complicate and aggravate the world economic crisis. The high prices hinder the consumption of the piled up commodities. They are maintained by those organizations which exploit their monopoly in order to export at dumping prices. The great disparity between the export prices and the home prices of the same commodities has been dealt with in the report of the economic organizations of the League of Nations, but this report made no attempt to give any explanation for this disparity or to draw any conclusions from it.

The fact that despite the fall in grain prices by 48.3 percent on the London market in the period from March 1929 to march 1931, and despite the acute agrarian crisis, the grain prices on the Berlin market increased by 28.5 percent, and on the Paris market by 12.9 percent, shows clearly that this price policy reduces the purchasing power of the masses, which is in any case low, still further, and complicates and aggravates the present crisis.

The French Project

The only effective way to secure a solution of the crisis would be to facilitate the growth of the purchasing power of the masses and in this way to secure the absorption of the stored up commodities by the market.

However, the proposals which have been made in this Commission positively tend to aggravate the special factors which prevent any amelioration of the crisis. These proposals are calculated to support the policy of high prices, although this policy is one of the most serious aggravating factors at the moment. Where can the proposal of the French delegate Monsieur Francois Poncet to extend the present practice of the international organization of industry lead? The enlargement of the steel and copper trusts did not prevent the development of the crisis. On the contrary, the extension of the cartels and the fact that they maintain high prices despite continual overproduction, have resulted in the throttling of sales and the development of the present crisis to a greater extent than former crises.

The proposal of the French delegation leads only to an extension of the policy of political blocs to new fields. The proposal cannot do anything else but maintain the present high prices and ensure that the monopolists continue to pocket their excessive profits. It seems to me that this Commission might have expected exactly contrary proposals with a view to ameliorating the crisis.

In view of the importance of this question and in view of the baseless charges of dumping which have been made against the Soviet Union. I propose that the governments represented at this conference should adopt a joint declaration which could later on be turned into an international convention, aiming at abolishing the disparity between home and export prices and containing an undertaking not to permit prices on the home markets to exceed the export prices for the same commodities.

We deny categorically the existence of Soviet dumping, and we should certainly not refuse to take part in an international discussion and an international action on the lines I have just sketched. Such an action would have a most beneficial influence on the economic situation of the broad masses of the people because it would increase their purchasing power, make possible the absorption of the stored up commodities and thus contribute to a solution of the crisis.

I have done my best to point out the course of action which would lead to an amelioration of the crisis. The first step necessary, however, is that false measures should be abandoned, and I must stress strongly that the right way to a solution of the crisis is not to be found in an attack on the Soviet Union, or in the suggestion that this attack represents the only possible means to free the world of the crisis from which it is suffering.

The Campaigns against the Soviet Union

A campaign against the Soviet Union may seem advantageous to certain interested circles for the moment, perhaps even to certain countries which need not necessarily be European countries or competitors of the Soviet Union in the supply of raw materials to the world market. But in any case, such a campaign can have nothing to do with the interests of Europe as a whole. To deprive Europe of such an important market as the Soviet Union, a market which has great potentialities for development, and to deprive European industries of orders from the Soviet Union which enable them to reduce unemployment, would certainly not be a measure calculated to secure a way out of the present crisis. Unfortunately, wrong ideas have been spread almost everywhere concerning the development of economic relations between the Soviet Union and the other countries. The constructive economic work in the Soviet Union and the carrying out of the Five Year Plan will not result in any reduction of the foreign trade of the Soviet Union. The more our economic system develops, the bigger will be its demands on foreign markets. Our capacity for absorbing foreign goods is immense.

Further, experience has shown that these various antiSoviet campaigns are useless. Experience has shown that the most important industrial contracts we ever concluded (with Germany and Italy) were made at the height of these campaigns, and that further we succeeded in increasing our trade with Great Britain and other industrial countries, and in opening up negotiations with other countries which hitherto have hesitated to enter into commercial relations with us. Is this not proof enough that the interests of the capitalist countries do not demand a conflict with the Soviet Union, but that on the contrary they demand the extension and consolidation of relations with the Soviet Union? Is this not proof enough that these campaigns against the Soviet Union can have no beneficial effect whatever on the economic crisis, and that they are bound by narrow and unreasonable aims?

The Capitalist System and the Soviet System

Although I show you the favorable influence of the foreign trade of the Soviet Union on the course of the present world economic crisis, I have no intention of creating the impression that there is any harmony of interests between the capitalist system and the Soviet system. Differences exist between these two systems and they will continue to exist. These two systems are fighting each other and they will continue to do so; this fact is inherent in their simultaneous existence. The question is only whether this struggle is to take place within the limits of the natural methods peculiar to these two systems, or whether the two systems are to adopt mutually hostile measures which can in any case have no decisive influence on the outcome of the struggle, but which would succeed merely in turning these two systems into armed and hostile camps.

There are some people, particularly people connected with the press—I am not sure that it is worthwhile, taking them seriously—who contend that the Soviet government has adopted a devilish plan to secure the disorganization of the capitalist economic system by selling goods below cost price. It would be difficult to imagine anything more absurd than such a plot, which would have no effect whatever on the final fate of capitalism, but which would result merely in cutting down the income of the Soviet Union from its export trade and as a result, reducing the important trade of the Soviet Union. The net result would be that the work of socialist construction in the Soviet Union would be delayed, and this work is a much more important actor in the struggle between the two systems than anything else.

It is no less absurd on the part of our enemies to forge plans for the struggle against our foreign trade. First of all, such plans would not materially affect the future of our foreign trade, and secondly they would be a boomerang for the capitalist States because as a result of them the existing crisis would be still further aggravated.

On the other hand, of course, it would be naive to pretend that the capitalist States are working conscientiously and impartially to assist the building up of Socialism in the Soviet

Union, or that the Soviet Union attempts in any way to strengthen the capitalist system. The truth of the matter is simply that there must be economic agreements and trade relations between the capitalist countries and the Soviet Union, and that these agreements and business relations are profitable to all parties concerned. There are many such agreements to be met with.

For the moment I will ignore the possibility of a military attack on the Soviet Union, and deal only with the possibility of a period of peaceful relations extending over a generous time. I think that the moment has come for the capitalist governments to realize that the Soviet Union is a fact, and a fact that must be reckoned with. The Soviet Union is not to be removed from the face of the earth by the conjurations or resolutions of certain groups or certain individuals who dream of achieving this desirable consummation by some magic trick.

The States which are now represented here, met together at a world conference which took place four years ago in Geneva and decided to adopt a resolution proclaiming the possibility of a peaceful parallel existence of two systems prevailing at a definite historical moment. How much more reasonable it would be were they now to decide to put this resolution into practice. The Soviet Union is much stronger today than it was at that time. During the last four years it has achieved feats of economic reconstruction which have won the admiration of both friends and foes of the Soviet regime, and fostered the enthusiasm of the masses of the people of the Soviet Union without which these feats could never have been accomplished.

A Commission for the Study of the possibilities of a European Union cannot base its work on a campaign on an appeal for a campaign against a country or against a certain group of countries without coming into contradiction with the principles and the aims which it has set itself.

The Dangers of the Preference System

I began my remarks by declaring that I had not intention of proposing any remedy for the solution of those conflicts in the capitalist system which are the basis of the present world economic crisis. However, I believe that something could be done to remove certain contributory factors which intensify these conflicts and lead to the aggravation and protraction of the present crisis. First of all, everything should be avoided which is calculated to increase the atmosphere of suspicion, an atmosphere which makes it impossible to speak of any peaceful economic cooperation between the peoples.

I do not know whether any effective proposals will be made to this Commission. I only know that much has been said and written on the subject, and that the so-called preference system has been in particular the object of interest. I do not know exactly what is meant by this term preference system. Does it mean perhaps that each European State is to grant preferential customs treatment to the exports of certain other European States? It seems to me, however, that something different is meant, namely the extension of the preferential customs treatment and other privileges to a certain group of States, or simply to certain States. If this be the case, is it not practically the extension of those methods used during and after the war on the political field to the economic field? These methods showed no very favorable results in political life. Would not the result be the intensified division of Europe into economic groups, instead of the unification of Europe, which is the avowed object of this Commission? Such a procedure would not lead to cooperation, but to an intensified struggle, whereby the occasion of the struggle would be rather political than economic motives. It will be recalled that when the question of assistance for those States, referred to under the general term of Danubian States, was raised in Paris, M. Fotitch, the representative of the Yugoslav government, if I remember rightly, declared that such assistance would take on a social rather than an economic character. We observe, therefore, that this question was dealt with only from a political standpoint, and that the economic crisis was not taken into consideration thereby. It seems to me that the creation of new blocs and groups which already exist, and the granting of artificial economic assistance to certain States to the disadvantage of other States would result only in intensifying the economic and political struggle which already exists, in increasing the prevailing confusion, and in arriving at a solution which is directly opposed to the aim which this Commission pursues and for which it was created.

The Economic Nonaggression Pact Proposal

If all governments, and particularly the governments of European countries, could agree to adopt a uniform attitude, then the carrying out of the program of this Commission and the peaceful cooperation of the peoples would be greatly facilitated. Of course, it would be necessary for each European State to grant equal treatment in all other European States, and to exclude ruthlessly all elements no matter what their nature, calculated to produce any differential treatment.

I must point out that with my proposal I have no intention of limiting the sovereignty of States which have historically and economically a special position from the point of view of economic relations. However, one principle must be inviolable; the right of every nation to join groupings or federations of nations so long as this is done voluntarily and so long as it is not a question of temporary combinations directed against other States. I may say that my proposal is a sort of economic nonaggression pact. I have laid down my idea of this pact in a special draft resolution to which I permit myself to draw your attention. I do not know what you will think about it, but at least this draft resolution will prove the willingness of the Soviet Union, which is confident in its own strength and which is thoroughly engaged in the tremendous tasks of the constructive work it is conducting, to maintain firmly as in the past the principle of the peaceful parallel existence of the two economic systems which exist simultaneously at a definite historical moment. The draft resolution will serve as an earnest of the fact that the Soviet Union harbors no aggressive intentions either of a political or economic character against any other State.

International Press Correspondence, Vol. 11, No. 26 (21 May 1931), 475-478.

GLAVLIT—MODIFICATION OF CENSORSHIP STATUTE OF 6 JUNE 1922

6 June 1931

*The Council of People's Commissars of the RSFSR modified the decree issued nine years before that established the Main Administration for Literature and Publishing (*Glavlit*). See Volume 2 of this work for the decree of June 1922. The 1931 decree closely resembled the earlier decree. References to the United State Political Administration were deleted. Glavlit now assumed responsibility for radio broadcasts, public lectures, and exhibitions. The decree remained in force throughout the Soviet period.*

LAW ON THE MAIN ADMINISTRATION FOR AFFAIRS OF LITERATURE AND PUBLISHING OF THE RSFSR (GLAVLIT) AND ITS LOCAL ORGAN

1. The main administration for Affairs of Literature and Publishing (Glavit) is established within the People's Commissariat for Education of the RSFSR to execute all forms of

political, ideological, military, and economic control over printed works, manuscripts, photographs, pictures etc., as well as radio programs, lectures and exhibitions that are intended for publication or distribution.

2. Glavlit, to carry out the tasks with which it is charged, forbids the publishing, publication, or distribution of any works which:

a) contain agitation or propaganda against Soviet power and the dictatorship of the proletariat;

2) divulge state secrets;

c) arouse nationalist or religious fanaticism;

d) bear a pornographic character.

3. Glavit is charged with:

a) the general management and inspection of local organs and Glavlit representatives;

b) the preliminary and subsequent control over literature published, both from the political and ideological, and from the military and economic, points of view, as well as over radio programs, lectures, and exhibitions;

c) the confiscation of works not subject to distribution;

d) issuing permits for opening publishing houses and periodical organs, the closure of publishing houses and banning of editions, prohibiting or licensing the import from abroad or export of literature, pictures, etc., in accordance with existing regulations;

e) publishing rules, regulations and instructions on matters which it handles: These rules, etc., are obligatory for all institutions, organizations, and individuals;

f) examining complaints against decisions of local organs and Glavlit representatives;

g) developing, together with the corresponding organizations, an inventory of information which is, by the nature of their contents, specially reserved state secrets and not subject to publication or disclosure;

h) compiling a list of works banned from publication or distribution;

i) prosecuting persons who violate the requirements of Glavit, its organs and representatives.

4. Preliminary control (see paragraph b of Article 3 above) is executed by Glavit through its representatives at publishing houses, editorial boards of periodicals, printing houses, radio stations, telegraph agencies, customs houses, central post offices and similar institutions.

Representatives are nominated and removed by Glavit and maintained at the expense of the organization in which they serve.

Preliminary control of the production of those state publishing houses forming part of the system of the Association of State Publishing Houses (OGIZ) is carried out by the managers of these publishing houses, who are Glavit representatives and act on the basis of a special instruction approved by the RSFSR People's Commissar for Education. The managers of OGIZ publishing houses nominate responsible political editors for executive control work, and these editors are approved by Glavit.

Glavit is granted the right in necessary cases to establish preliminary control both over the entire production and over individual kinds of literature published by the OGIZ state publishing houses through specially nominated Glavit representatives.

5. Publications of the Communist International, the Central Committee of the VKP(B), krai, oblast and raion committees of the VKP(B), together with "Izvestiia of TsIK and VTsIK", the works of the Communist Academy and the Academy of Sciences are freed from the political and ideological control of Glavit.

With regard to these publications, Glavlit and its local organs are responsible, by way of prior examination of the publications, for the complete protection of state secrets.

6. At the head of Glavlit stands a chief under whom a collegium is created. The membership of this collegium is approved by the RSFSR People's Commissariat for Education in agreement with interested organizations.

7. In krais and oblasts, as well as in industrial centers with a well-developed network of factory and plant newspapers and a significant amount of publishing activity, local Glavlit organs are formed and attached to the relevant public education bodies, and conduct their work according to Glavlit directives and goals.

8. The functions indicated in Articles 1 and 2, and in paragraphs "b", "c", "f", "h", and "i" of Article 3 of this law are placed on the local Glavlit organs.

The functions of the local Glavlit organs in the raion are carried out by an official nominated by the raiispolkom in agreement with the corresponding Glavlit organ.

9. The local Glavlit organs are structured similarly to Glavlit itself, while the managers are nominated and removed by the RSFSR People's Commissariat for Education in accordance with Glavlit's recommendation.

10. In all printed works published in the RSFSR there must be the imprimatur of Glavlit or its local organs (krailit, oblit, railit, gorlit, a representative of Glavlit).

11. The managers of printing houses are obligated to submit to Glavlit organs five copies each of any printed work as soon as it leaves the presses and before it is published.

12. Printed works not authorized by Glavlit and its local organs are removed from distribution at the suggestion of Glavlit and its organs by the machinery of the publishing, book-trade, and distribution organizations (OGIZ—Knigotsentr, Soiuzpechat', etc.).

Fogelevich, 93-94.

STALIN REHABILITATES SPECIALISTS AND CALLS FOR WAGE DIFFERENTIATION

23 June 1931

A consensus was evolving among the party and industrial leadership that changes were needed to solve a growing shortage of technicians and engineers in the industrial sphere. Stalin announced these changes by rehabilitating the "bourgeois" specialists and calling for payment of different wages for different skills, and opportunities for upward mobility. After years of "baiting" the old specialists, particularly during the famous show trials, and the Bolshevik commitment to social equality, Stalin's speech represented a departure from previous policies.

JOSEPH STALIN
NEW CONDITIONS—NEW TASKS IN ECONOMIC CONSTRUCTION

Speech Delivered at a Conference of Business Executives

Comrades, the materials presented to this conference show that as regards the fulfillment of the plan our industry presents a rather motley picture. There are branches of industry that have increased their output during the past five months 40 to 50 percent compared with last year. Other branches have increased their output not more than 20 to 30 percent. Lastly, there are certain branches that show a very small increase, some 6 to 10 percent and sometimes less. Among the latter we must include coal mining and the iron and steel industry. The picture, as you see, is a motley one.

How is this diversity to be explained? Why are certain branches of industry lagging behind? Why is it that certain branches of industry show an increase of only 20 to 25 percent, while coal mining and the iron and steel industry show an even smaller increase and are trailing behind other branches?

The reason is that lately the conditions of development of industry have radically changed; new conditions demanding new methods of management have arisen; but some of our business executives, instead of changing their methods of work, are continuing in the old way. The point, therefore, is that the new conditions of development of industry require new methods of work; but some of our business executives do not understand this and do not see that they must now adopt new methods of management.

That is the reason why certain branches of our industry are lagging behind.

What are these new conditions of development of our industry? How did they arise?

There are at least six such new conditions.

Let us examine them.

I
MANPOWER

First of all, there is the question of the supply of *manpower* for our factories. Formerly, the workers usually came of their own accord to the factories and mills—to some extent, therefore, things proceeded automatically in this sphere. And this happened because there was unemployment, there was differentiation in the countryside, there was poverty and fear of starvation, which drove people from the country to the town. You remember the formula: "The flight of the peasant from the country to the town?" What compelled the peasant to flee from the country to the town? The fear of starvation, unemployment, the fact that the village was like a stepmother to him, and he was ready to flee from his village to the devil himself, if only he could find some sort of work.

Such, or nearly such, was the state of affairs in the recent past.

Can it be said that the same conditions prevail now? No, it cannot. On the contrary, conditions have now radically changed. And because conditions have changed we no longer have an automatic influx of manpower.

What, in point of fact, has changed during this period? Firstly, we have done away with unemployment—consequently, we have abolished the force that exercised pressure upon the "labor market". Secondly, we have radically undermined differentiation in the countryside—consequently, we have overcome the mass poverty there, which drove the peasant from the country to the town. Lastly, we have supplied the countryside with tens of thousands of tractors and agricultural machines, we have smashed the kulak, we have organized collective farms and have given the peasants the opportunity to live and work like human beings. Now the countryside cannot any longer be termed a stepmother to the peasant. And precisely because it can no longer be termed a stepmother, the peasant has begun to settle down in the countryside; we no longer have "the flight of the peasant from the country to the town" nor an automatic influx of manpower.

As you see, we now have an entirely new situation and new conditions in regard to the supply of manpower for our factories.

What follows from that?

It follows, firstly, that we must no longer count on an automatic influx of manpower. This means that we must pass from the "policy" of letting things proceed automatically to the policy of *organized* recruiting of workers for industry. But there is only one way of achieving this—that of contracts of economic organizations with collective farms and collective farmers. As you know, certain economic organizations and collective farms have already adopted this method; and experience has shown that this practice yields important advantages both for the collective farms and for the industrial enterprises.

It follows, secondly, that we must pass immediately to *mechanization* of the heavier processes of labor and develop this to the utmost (timber industry, transport, iron and steel industry, etc.). This, of course, does not mean that we must abandon manual labor. On the contrary, manual labor will continue to play a very important part in production for a long time to come. But it does mean that mechanization of labor processes is for us the *new* and *decisive force*, without which neither our tempo nor the new scale of production can be maintained.

There are still quite a number of our business executives who "do not believe" either in mechanization or in contracts with collective farms. These are the very executives who fail to understand the new situation, who do not want to work in the new way and sigh for the "good old times" when manpower "came of its own accord" to the enterprises. Needless to say, such business executives are as remote from the new tasks in economic construction, which are imposed by the new conditions, as the sky from the earth. Apparently they think that the difficulties in regard to manpower are accidental and that the shortage of manpower will disappear automatically, so to speak. That is a delusion, comrades. The difficulties in regard to manpower cannot disappear of themselves. They can disappear only as the result of our own efforts.

Hence the task is *to recruit manpower in an organized way, by means of contracts with the collective farms, and to mechanize labor.*

That is how matters stand with regard to the first new condition of development of our industry.

Let us pass to the second condition.

II
WAGES

I have just spoken about the organized recruiting of workers for our factories. But recruiting workers is not all that has to be done. In order to ensure manpower for our enterprises we must see to it that the workers remain connected with their factories and make the composition of the labor force in the factories more or less constant. It scarcely needs proof that without a constant labor force who have more or less mastered the technique of production and have become accustomed to the new machinery it will be impossible to make any headway, impossible to fulfil the production plans. Unless this is achieved, we shall have to keep on training new workers and to spend half the time on training them instead of making use of this time for production. But what is actually happening now? Can it be said that the composition of the labor force at our factories is more or less constant? Unfortunately, this cannot be said. On the contrary, we still have a so-called *fluidity* of manpower at our factories. More than that, in a number of factories the fluidity of manpower, far from disappearing, is increasing and becoming more marked. At any rate, you will find few factories where the personnel does not change at least to the extent of 30 to 40 percent of the total in the course of a half year, or even in one quarter.

Formerly, during the period of restoration of our industry, when its technical equipment was not very complex and the scale of production not very large, it was more of less possible to "tolerate" this so-called fluidity of manpower. Now it is another matter. Now the situation is radically different. Now, in the period of intensive reconstruction, when the scale of production has become gigantic and technical equipment has become extremely complex, the fluidity of manpower has become a scourge of production and is disorganizing our factories. To "tolerate" the fluidity of manpower now would mean disintegrating our industry, destroying the possibility of fulfilling production plans and ruining any chance of improving the quality of the output.

What is the cause of the fluidity of manpower?

The cause is the wrong structure of wages, the wrong wage scales, the "Leftist" practice of wage equalization. In a number of factories wage scales are drawn up in such a way as to practically wipe out the difference between skilled and unskilled labor, between heavy and light work. The consequence of wage equalization is that the unskilled worker lacks the incentive to become a skilled worker and is thus deprived of the prospect of advancement; as a result he feels himself a "visitor" in the factory, working only temporarily so as to "earn a little money" and then go off to "try his luck" in some other place. The consequence of wage equalization is that the skilled worker is obliged to go from factory to factory until he finds one where his skill is properly appreciated.

Hence, the "general" drift from factory to factory; hence, the fluidity of manpower.

In order to put an end to this evil we must abolish wage equalization and discard the old wage scales. In order to put an end to this evil we must draw up wage scales that will take into account the difference between skilled and unskilled labor, between heavy and light work. We cannot tolerate a situation where a rolling-mill worker in the iron and steel industry earns no more than a sweeper. We cannot tolerate a situation where a locomotive driver earns only as much as a copying clerk. Marx and Lenin said that the difference between skilled and unskilled labor would exist even under socialism, even after classes had been abolished; that only under communism would this difference disappear and that, consequently, even under socialism "wages" must be paid according to work performed and not according to needs. But the egalitarians among our business executives and trade-union officials do not agree with this and believe that under our Soviet system this difference has already disappeared. Who is right, Marx and Lenin or the egalitarians? It must be supposed that it is Marx and Lenin who are right. But it follows from this that whoever draws up wage scale on the "principle" of wage equalization, without taking into account the difference between skilled and unskilled labor, breaks with Marxism, breaks with Leninism.

In every branch of industry, in every factory, in every shop, there is a leading group of more or less skilled workers who first and foremost must be retained if we really want to ensure a constant labor force in the factories. These leading groups of workers are the principal link in production. By retaining them in the factory, in the shop, we can retain the whole labor force and radically prevent the fluidity of manpower. But how can we retain them in the factories? We can retain them only by promoting them to higher positions, by raising the level of their wages, by introducing a system of wages that will give the worker his due according to qualification.

And what does promoting them to higher positions and raising their wage level mean, what can it lead to as far as unskilled workers are concerned? It means, apart from everything else, opening up prospects for the unskilled worker and giving him an incentive to rise higher, to rise to the category of a skilled worker. You know yourselves that we now need hundreds of thousands and even millions of skilled workers. But in order to build up cadres of skilled workers, we must provide for them a prospect of advancement, of rising to a higher position. And the more boldly we adopt this course the better, for this is the principal means of putting an end to the fluidity of manpower. To economize in this matter would be criminal, it would be going against the interests of our socialist industry.

But that is not all.

In order to retain the workers in the factories we must still further improve the supply of goods and the housing conditions of the workers. It cannot be denied that a good deal has been done during the last few years in the sphere of housing construction and supplies for the workers. But what has been done is altogether inadequate compared with the rapidly growing requirements of the workers. It will not do to plead that there were fewer houses before than there are now and that therefore we can be content with the results achieved. Nor will it do to plead that workers' supplies were far worse before than they are now and therefore we can be satisfied with the present situation. Only those who are rotten to the core can content themselves with references to the past. We must proceed, not from the past, but from the growing requirements of the workers at the present time. We must realize that the conditions of life of the workers have radically changed in our country. The worker today is not what he was previously. The worker today, our Soviet worker, wants to have all his material and cultural needs satisfied: In respect of food, housing conditions, cultural and all sorts of other requirements. He has a right to this, and it is our duty to secure these conditions for him. True, our worker does not suffer from unemployment; he is free from the yoke of capitalism; he is no longer a slave, but the master of his job. But this is not enough. He demands that all his material and cultural requirements be met, and it is our duty to fulfil this demand of his. Do not forget that we ourselves are now making certain demands on the worker—we demand from him labor discipline, intense effort, competition, shock-brigade work. Do not forget that the vast majority of workers have accepted these demands of the Soviet Government with great enthusiasm and are fulfilling them heroically. Do not be surprised, therefore, if, while fulfilling the demands of the Soviet Government, the workers in their turn demand that the Soviet Government should fulfill its obligations in regard to further improving their material and cultural condition.

Hence, the task is to *put an end to the fluidity of manpower, to do away with wage equalization, to organize wages properly and to improve the living conditions of the workers.*

That is how matters stand with regard to the second new condition of development of our industry.

Let us pass to the third condition.

III
THE ORGANIZATION OF WORK

I have said that it is necessary to put an end to the fluidity of manpower, to retain the workers in the factories. But retaining the workers in the factories is not all; the matter does not end there. It is not enough to put an end to the fluidity of manpower. We must provide the workers with such working conditions as will enable them to work efficiently, to increase productivity and to improve the quality of the products. Consequently, we must so organize work in the factories as to bring about an increase in labor productivity from month to month, from quarter to quarter.

Can it be said that the present organization of work in our factories meets the modern requirements of production? Unfortunately, this cannot be said. At all events, we still have a number of factories where work is organized abominably, where instead of order and coordination of work there is disorder and muddle, where instead of responsibility for the work there is absolute irresponsibility, *lack of personal responsibility.*

What is meant by lack of personal responsibility? It is the absence of any responsibility for work that is entrusted to one, the absence of responsibility for machinery and tools. Naturally, when there is no personal responsibility there can be no question of any important increase in the productivity of labor, of any improvement in the quality of production, of the exercise of care in handling machinery and tools. You know what lack of personal responsibility led to on the railways. It is leading to the same result in industry. We have abolished the system under which there was lack of personal responsibility on the railways and have thus improved their work. We must do the same in industry in order to raise its work to a higher level.

Formerly, we could "manage" somehow or other with the bad organization of work that goes naturally with lack of personal responsibility, with no worker being responsible for a particular concrete job. Now it is another matter. Now the situation is completely different. With the present vast scale of production and the existence of giant enterprises, lack of personal responsibility has become a scourge of industry that is jeopardizing all our achievements in the factories in the sphere of production and organization.

What enabled lack of personal responsibility to become the rule in a number of our factories? It entered the factories as the illegitimate companion of the uninterrupted working-week. It would be wrong to assert that the uninterrupted working-week necessarily leads to lack of personal responsibility in production. If work is properly organized, if each person is made responsible for a definite job, if definite groups of workers are assigned to machines, if the shifts are properly organized so that they are equal in quality and skill—given such conditions, the uninterrupted working-week leads to a tremendous increase in labor productivity, to an improvement in quality of work and to eliminating lack of personal responsibility. Such is the case on the railways, for example, where the uninterrupted working-week is now in force, but where there is no longer lack of personal responsibility. Can it be said that the position in regard to the uninterrupted working-week is equally satisfactory in industrial enterprises? Unfortunately, this cannot be said. The fact of the matter is that a number of our factories adopted the uninterrupted working-week too hastily, without preparing suitable conditions for it, without properly organizing shifts more or less equal in quality and skill, without making each worker responsible for a particular concrete job. The result is that the uninterrupted working-week, left to itself, has given rise to lack of personal responsibility. The result is that in a number of factories we have the uninterrupted working-week on paper, in words, and lack of personal responsibility not on paper, but in actual operation. The result is that there is no sense of responsibility for the job, machinery is handled carelessly, large numbers of machine tools break down, and there is no incentive for increasing the productivity of labor. It is not for nothing that the workers say: "We could raise the productivity of labor and improve matters; but who is going to appreciate it when nobody is responsible for anything?"

It follows from this that some of our comrades were a little hasty in introducing the uninterrupted working-week, and in their hurry distorted it and transformed it into a system of lack of personal responsibility.

There are two ways of putting an end to this situation and of doing away with lack of personal responsibility. Either change the method of carrying out the uninterrupted working-week so that it does not result in lack of personal responsibility, as was done on the railways. Or, where the conditions do not favor this, abandon the nominal uninterrupted working-week, temporarily adopted the interrupted six-day week, as was recently done in the Stalingrad Tractor Works, and prepare the conditions so as to return, should the need arise, to a real, not nominal, uninterrupted working-week; to return eventually to the uninterrupted working-week, but not to lack of personal responsibility.

There is no other way.

There can be no doubt that our business executives understand all this very well. But they keep silent. Why? Because, evidently, they fear the truth. But since when have the Bolsheviks begun to fear the truth? Is it not true that in a number of factories the uninterrupted working-week has resulted in lack of personal responsibility and has thus been distorted to an extreme degree? The question is: Who wants such an uninterrupted working-week? Who dares assert that the preservation of this nominal and distorted uninterrupted working-week is more important than the proper organization of work, than increased productivity of labor, than a genuine uninterrupted working-week, than the interests of our socialist industry? Is it not clear that the sooner we bury the nominal uninterrupted working-week the sooner shall we achieve a proper organization of work?

Some comrades think that we can do away with the lack of personal responsibility by means of incantations and high-sounding speeches. At any rate, I know a number of business executives who in their fight against lack of personal responsibility confine themselves to speaking at meetings now and again, hurling curses at the lack of personal responsibility, apparently believing that after such speeches lack of personal responsibility is bound to disappear automatically, so to speak. They are grievously mistaken if they think that lack of personal responsibility can be done away with by speeches and incantations. No, comrades, lack of personal responsibility will never disappear of itself. We alone can and must put an end to it; for it is you and I who are at the helm and it is you and I who are answerable for everything, including lack of personal responsibility. I think that it would be far better if our business managers, instead of making speeches and incantations, spent a month or two at some mine or factory, studied all details and "trifles" relating to the organization of work, actually put an end there to lack of personal responsibility and then applied the experience gained at this enterprise to other enterprises. That would be far better. That would be really fighting against lack of personal responsibility, fighting for the proper, Bolshevik organization of work, for the proper distribution of forces in our enterprises.

Hence, the task is *to put an end to lack of personal responsibility, to improve the organization of work and to secure the proper distribution of forces in our enterprises.*

That is how matters stand with regard to the third new condition of development of our industry.

Let us pass to the fourth condition.

IV
A WORKING-CLASS INDUSTRIAL AND TECHNICAL INTELLIGENTSIA

The situation has also changed in regard to the administrative staff of industry in general, and in regard to the engineering and technical personnel in particular.

Formerly, the situation was that the main source of supply for all our industry was the coal and metallurgical base in the Ukraine. The Ukraine supplied metal to all our industrial regions: Both to the South and to Moscow and Leningrad. It also supplied coal to the principal enterprises in the USSR. I leave out the Urals because the relative importance of the entire Urals was very small compared with the Donets Basin. Accordingly, we had three main centers for training an administrative staff for industry: The South, the Moscow district and the Leningrad district. Naturally, under those conditions we could somehow manage with the very small engineering and technical forces that were all that our country could have at its disposal at that time.

That was the position in the recent past.

But the situation is now quite different. Now it is obvious, I think, that with the present rate of development and gigantic scale of production we are already unable to make do with the Ukrainian coal and metallurgical base alone. As you know, the supply of Ukrainian coal and metal is already inadequate, in spite of the increase in their output. As you know, we have been obliged, as a result of this, to create a new coal and metallurgical base in the East—the Urals-Kuznetsk Basin. As you know, our work to create this base has been not without success. But that is not enough. We must, further, create an iron and steel industry in Siberia itself to satisfy its own growing requirements. And we are already creating it. Besides this, we must create a new base for nonferrous metals in Kazakhstan and Turkestan. Finally, we must develop extensive railway construction. That is dictated by the interests of the USSR as a whole—by the interests of the border republics as well as of the center.

But it follows from this that we can no longer make do with the very small engineering, technical and administrative forces of industry with which we managed formerly. It follows that the old centers for training engineers and technical forces are no longer adequate, that we must create a whole network of new centers—in the Urals, in Siberia and in Central Asia. We must now ensure the supply of three times, five times the number of engineering, technical and administrative forces for industry if we really intend to carry out the program of the socialist industrialization of the USSR.

But we do not need just *any kind* of administrative, engineering and technical forces. We need *such* administrative, engineering and technical forces as are capable of understanding the policy of the working class of our country, capable of assimilating that policy and ready to carry it out conscientiously. And what does this mean? It means that our country has entered a phase of development in which the *working class must create its own industrial and technical intelligentsia*, one that is capable of upholding the interests of the working class in production as the interests of the ruling class.

No ruling class has managed without its own intelligentsia. There are no grounds for believing that the working class of the USSR can manage without its own industrial and technical intelligentsia.

The Soviet Government has taken this circumstance into account and has opened wide the doors of all the higher educational institutions in every branch of the national economy to members of the working class and laboring peasantry. You know that tens of thousands of working class and peasant youths are now studying in higher educational institutions. Whereas formerly, under capitalism, the higher educational institutions were the monopoly of the scions of the rich—today, under the Soviet system, the working class and peasant youth predominate there. There is no doubt that our educational institutions will soon be turning out thousands of new technicians and engineers, new leaders for our industries.

But that is only one aspect of the matter. The other aspect is that the industrial and technical intelligentsia of the working class will be recruited not only from those who have had higher education, but also from practical workers in our factories, from the skilled workers, from the working-class cultural forces in the mills, factories and mines. The initiators of competition, the leaders of shock brigades, those who in practice inspire labor enthusiasm, the organizers of operations in the various sectors of our work of construction—such is the new stratum of the working class that, together with the comrades who have had higher education, must form the core of the intelligentsia of the working class, the core of the administrative staff of our industry. The task is to see that these "rank-and-file" comrades who show initiative are not pushed aside, to promote them boldly to responsible positions, to give them the opportunity to display their organizing abilities and the opportunity to supplement their knowledge, to create suitable conditions for their work, not stinting money for this purpose.

Among these comrades there are not a few nonParty people. But that should not prevent us from boldly promoting them to leading positions. On the contrary, it is particularly these nonParty comrades who must receive our special attention, who must be promoted to responsible positions so that they may see for themselves that the Party appreciates capable and gifted workers.

Some comrades think that only Party members may be placed in leading positions in the mills and factories. That is the reason why they do not infrequently push aside nonParty members at the top instead, although they may be less capable and show no initiative. Needless to say, there is nothing more stupid and reactionary than such a "policy", if one may call it such. It scarcely needs proof that such a "policy" can only discredit the Party and repel nonParty workers from it. Our policy does not by any means lie in converting the Party into an exclusive caste. Our policy is to ensure that there is an atmosphere of "mutual confidence", of "mutual control" (*Lenin*), among Party and nonParty workers. One of the reasons why our Party is strong among the working class is that it pursues this policy.

Hence, the task is *to see to it that the working class of the USSR has its own industrial and technical intelligentsia.*

That is how matters stand with regard to the fourth new condition of development of our industry.

Let us pass to the fifth condition.

V
SIGNS OF A CHANGE OF ATTITUDE AMONG THE OLD INDUSTRIAL AND TECHNICAL INTELLIGENTSIA

The question of our attitude towards the old, bourgeois industrial and technical intelligentsia is also presented in a new light.

About two years ago the situation was that the more highly skilled section of the old technical intelligentsia was infected with the disease of wrecking. More than that, at that time wrecking was a sort of fashionable activity. Some engaged in wrecking, others shielded the wreckers, others again washed their hands of what was going on and remained neutral, while still others vacillated between the Soviet regime and the wreckers. Of course, the majority of the old technical intelligentsia continued to work more or less loyally. But we are not speaking here of the majority, but of the most highly skilled section of the technical intelligentsia.

What gave rise to the wrecking movement? What fostered it? The intensification of the class struggle in the USSR, the Soviet Government's policy of offensive against the capitalist elements in town and country, the resistance of these elements to the policy of the Soviet Government, the complexity of the international situation and the difficulties of collective- and state-farm development. While the activities of the militant section of the wreckers were augmented by the interventionist intrigues of the imperialists in the capitalist countries and by the grain difficulties within our country, the vacillations of the other section of the old technical intelligentsia towards the active wreckers were encouraged by utterances that were in fashion among the Trotskyist-Menshevik windbags to the effect that "nothing will come of the collective and state farms anyway," that "Soviet power is degenerating anyway and is bound to collapse very soon," that "the Bolsheviks by their policy are themselves facilitating intervention," etc.. Besides, if even certain old Bolsheviks among the Right deviators could not resist the "epidemic" and swung away from the Party at that time, it is not surprising that a certain section of the old technical intelligentsia who had never had any inkling of Bolshevism should, with the help of God, also vacillate.

Naturally, under such circumstances, the Soviet Government could pursue only one policy towards the old technical intelligentsia—the policy of *smashing* the active wreckers, *differentiating* the neutrals and *enlisting* those who were loyal.

That was a year or two ago.

Can we say that the situation is exactly the same now? No, we cannot. On the contrary, an entirely new situation has arisen. To begin with, there is the fact that we have routed and are successfully overcoming the capitalist elements in town and country. Of course, this cannot evoke joy among the old intelligentsia. Very probably they still express sympathy for their defeated friends. But sympathizers, still less those who are neutral or vacillating, are not in the habit of voluntarily agreeing to share the fate of their more active friends when the latter have suffered severe and irreparable defeat.

Further, we have overcome the grain difficulties, and not only have we overcome them but we are now exporting a larger quantity of grain than has ever been exported since the existence of Soviet power. Consequently, this "argument" of the vacillators also falls to the ground.

Furthermore, even the blind can now see that as regards the front of collective- and state-farm development we have gained a definite victory and achieved tremendous successes.

Consequently, the chief weapon in the "arsenal" of the old intelligentsia has gone by the board. As for the bourgeois intelligentsia's hopes of intervention, it must be admitted that, for the time being at least, they have proved to be a house built on sand. Indeed, for six years intervention has been promised, but not a single attempt at intervention has been made. The time has come to recognize that our sapient bourgeois intelligentsia has simply been led by the nose. That is apart from the fact that the conduct of the active wreckers at the famous trial in Moscow was bound to discredit, and actually did discredit, the idea of wrecking.

Naturally, these new circumstances could not but influence our old technical intelligentsia. The new situation was bound to give rise, and did actually give rise, to new sentiments among the old technical intelligentsia. This, in fact, explains why there are definite signs of a change of attitude in favor of the Soviet regime on the part of a certain section of the intelligentsia that formerly sympathized with the wreckers. The fact that not only this stratum of the old intelligentsia, but even definite wreckers of yesterday, a considerable number of them, are beginning in many factories and mills to work hand in hand with the working class—this fact shows without a doubt that a change of attitude among the old technical intelligentsia has already begun. This, of course, does not mean that there are no longer any wreckers in the country. No, it does not mean that. Wreckers exist and will continue to exist as long as we have classes and as long as capitalist encirclement exists. But it does mean that, since a large section of the old technical intelligentsia who formerly sympathized, in one way or another, with the wreckers have now made a turn to the side of the Soviet regime, the active wreckers have become few in number, are isolated and will have to go deeply underground for the time being.

But it follows from this that we must change our policy towards the old technical intelligentsia accordingly. Whereas during the height of the wrecking activities our attitude towards the old technical intelligentsia was mainly expressed by the policy of routing them, now, even these intellectuals are turning to the side of the Soviet regime, our attitude towards them must be expressed mainly by the policy of enlisting them and showing solicitude for them. It would be wrong and undialectial to continue our former policy under the new, changed conditions. It would be stupid and unwise to regard practically every expert and engineer of the old school as an undetected criminal and wrecker. We have always regarded and still regard "expert-baiting" as a harmful and disgraceful phenomenon.

Hence, the task is to change our attitude towards the engineers and technicians of the old school, to show them greater attention and solicitude, to enlist their cooperation more boldly.

That is how matters stand with regard to the fifth new condition of development of our industry.

Let us pass to the last condition.

VI
BUSINESS ACCOUNTING

The picture would be incomplete if I did not deal with one more new condition. I refer to the sources of capital accumulation for industry, for the national economy; I refer to the need for increasing the rate of accumulation.

What is the new and special feature of the development of our industry from the point of view of accumulation? It is that the old sources of accumulation are already beginning to be inadequate for the further expansion of industry; that it is necessary, therefore, to seek new sources of accumulation and to reinforce the old sources if we really want to maintain and develop the Bolshevik tempo of industrialization.

We know from the history of the capitalist countries that not a single young state that desired to raise its industry to a higher level was able to dispense with external aid in the form of long-term credits or loans. For this reason the capitalists in the Western countries point-blank refused credits or loans to our country, in the belief that the lack of credits and loans would certainly prevent the industrialization of our country. But the capitalists were mistaken. They failed to take into account the fact that our country, unlike the capitalist countries, possesses certain special sources of accumulation sufficient to restore and further develop our industry. And indeed, not only have we restored our industry, not only have we restored our agriculture and transport, but we have already managed to set going the tremendous work of reconstructing heavy industry, agriculture and transport. Of course, this work has cost us many thousand million rubles. Where did we get these thousands of millions from? From light industry, from agriculture and from budget accumulations. This is how we managed until recently.

But the situation is entirely different now. Whereas previously the old sources of capital accumulation were sufficient for the reconstruction of industry and transport, now they are obviously becoming inadequate. Now it is not a question of reconstructing our old industries. It is a question of creating new, technically well-equipped industries in the Urals, in Siberia, in Kazakhstan. It is a question of creating new, large-scale farming in the grain, livestock and raw material regions of the USSR. It is a question of creating a new network of railroads connecting the East and West of the USSR. Naturally, the old sources of accumulation cannot suffice for this gigantic task.

But that is not all. To it must be added the fact that owing to inefficient management the principles of business accounting are grossly violated in a large number of our factories and business organizations. It is a fact that a number of enterprises and business organizations have long ceased to keep proper accounts, to calculate, to draw up sound balance-sheets of income and expenditure. It is a fact that in a number of enterprises and business organizations such concepts as "regime of economy", "cutting down unproductive expenditure," "rationalization of production" have long gone out of fashion. Evidently they assume that the State Bank "will advance the necessary money anyway." It is a fact that production costs in a number of enterprises have recently begun to increase. They were given the assignment of reducing costs by 10 percent and more, but instead they are increasing them. Yet what does a reduction in the cost of production mean? You know that reducing the cost of production by one percent means an accumulation in industry of 150,000,000 to 200,000,000 rubles. Obviously, to raise the cost of production under such circumstances means to deprive industry and the entire national economy of hundreds of millions of rubles.

From all this it follows that it is no longer possible to rely solely on light industry, on budget accumulation and on revenue from agriculture. Light industry is a bountiful source of accumulation, and there is every prospect of its continuing to expand; but it is not an unlimited source. Agriculture is a no less bountiful source of accumulation, but now, during the period of its reconstruction, agriculture itself requires financial aid from the state. As for budget accumulations, you know yourselves that they cannot and must not be unlimited. What, then, remains? There remains heavy industry. Consequently, we must see to it that heavy industry—and above all its machine-building section—also provide accumulations. Consequently, while reinforcing and expanding the old sources of accumulation, we must see to it that heavy industry—and above all machine-building—also provides accumulations.

That is the way out.

And what is needed for this? We must put an end to inefficiency, mobilize the internal resources of industry, introduce and reinforce business accounting in all our enterprises, systematically reduce production costs and increase internal accumulations in every branch of industry without exception.

That is the way out.

Hence, the task is *to introduce and reinforce business accounting, to increase accumulation within industry.*

VII
NEW METHODS OF WORK, NEW METHODS OF MANAGEMENT

Such, comrades, are the new conditions of development of our industry.

The significance of these new conditions is that they are creating a new situation for industry, one which demands new methods of work and new methods of management.

Hence:

a) It follows, therefore, that we can no longer count, as of old, on an automatic flux of manpower. In order to secure manpower for our industries it must be recruited in an organized manner, and labor must be mechanized. To believe that we can do without mechanization, in view of our tempo of work and scale of production, is like believing that the sea can be emptied with a spoon.

b) It follows, further, that we cannot any longer tolerate the fluidity of manpower in industry. In order to do away with this evil, we must organize wages in a new way and see to it that the composition of the labor force in the factories is more or less constant.

c) It follows, further, that we cannot any longer tolerate lack of personal responsibility in industry. In order to do away with this evil, work must be organized in a new way, and the forces must be so distributed that every group of workers is responsible for its work, for the machinery, and for the quality of the work.

d) It follows, further, that we can no longer manage, as of old, with the very small force of old engineers and technicians that we inherited from bourgeois Russia. In order to increase the present rate and scale of production, we must ensure that the working class has its own industrial and technical intelligentsia.

e) It follows, further, that we can no longer, as of old, lump together all the experts, engineers and technicians of the old school. In order to take into account the changed situation we must change our policy and display the utmost solicitude for those experts, engineers and technicians of the old school who are definitely turning to the side of the working class.

f) It follows, lastly, that we can no longer, as of old, manage with the old sources of accumulation. In order to ensure the further expansion of industry and agriculture we must tap new sources of accumulation; we must put an end to inefficiency, introduce business accounting, reduce production costs and increase accumulation within industry.

Such are the new conditions of development of industry, which demand new methods of work and new methods of management in economic construction.

What is needed in order to ensure management along new lines?

First of all, our business executives must understand the new situation; they must study concretely the new conditions of development of industry and reform their methods of work to meet the requirements of the new situation.

Further, our business executives must direct their enterprises not "in general", not "in the abstract," but concretely, specifically; they must approach every question not from the standpoint of general phrases, but in a strictly business-like manner; they must not confine themselves to formal written instructions or general phrases and slogans, but study the technique of the business and enter into details, into "trifles", for it is out of "trifles" that great things are now being built.

Further, our present unwieldy combines, which sometimes consist of as many as 100 to 200 enterprises, must each be immediately split into several combines. Obviously, the chairman of a combine who has to deal with a hundred or more factories cannot really know those factories, their potentialities and their work. Obviously, if he does not know those factories he is not in a position to direct them. Hence, to enable the chairman of a combine to study the factories thoroughly, and direct them, he must be relieved of some of the factories; the combine must be split up into several smaller ones, and the combine headquarters must be brought into closer contact with the factories.

Further, our combines must substitute one-man management for collective management. The position at present is that there are from ten to fifteen persons on the board of a combine, drawing up documents and carrying on discussions. We cannot go on managing in this way, comrades. We must put a stop to paper "management" and switch to genuine, business-like, Bolshevik work. Let one chairman and several vice-chairmen remain at the head of a combine. That will be quite enough for its management. The other members of the board should be sent to the factories and mills. That will be far more useful, both for the work and for themselves.

Further, the chairmen and vice-chairmen of combines must pay more frequent visits to the factories, stay and work there for longer periods, acquaint themselves more closely with the personnel in the factories and not only teach the local people, but also learn from them. To think that you can now direct by sitting in an office, far away from the factories, is a delusion. In order to direct the factories you must come into more frequent contact with the staffs in those factories, maintain live contact with them.

Finally, a word or two about our production plan for 1931. There are certain near-Party philistines who assert that our production program is unrealistic, that it cannot be fulfilled.

They are somewhat like Shchedrin's "sapient gudgeons" who are always ready to spread "a vacuum of ineptitude" around themselves. Is our production program realistic or not? Most certainly, it is. It is realistic if only because all the conditions necessary for its fulfillment are available. It is realistic if only because its fulfillment now depends solely on ourselves, on our ability and willingness to take advantage of the vast opportunities at our disposal. How else can we explain the fact that a whole number of enterprises and industries have already *overfulfilled* their plans? That means that other enterprises and industries, too, can fulfil and overfulfil their plans.

It would be foolish to think that the production plan is a mere enumeration of figures and assignments. Actually, the production plan is the living and practical activity of millions of people. The reality of our production plan lies in the millions of working people who are creating a new life. The reality of our program lies in living people, you and I, our will to work, our readiness to work in the new way, our determination to fulfil the plan. Have we that determination? Yes, we have. Well then, our production program can must be fulfilled. (*Prolonged applause.*)

Stalin, *Works*, XIII, 53-82.

EXTENSION OF SOVIET-GERMAN AGREEMENT OF 1926. JOINT PROTOCOL

24 June 1931

The diplomatic representatives of the USSR and Germany agreed in June 1931 to prolong the 1926 Treaty of Berlin, to 30 June 1933. They also approved, with modification, the Conciliation Convention of 25 January 1929. Germany did not ratify the agreement until 1933.

PROTOCOL PROLONGING THE AGREEMENT REGARDING NEUTRALITY AND NONAGRESSION OF 24 APRIL 1926 AND THE CONCILIATION CONVENTION OF

25 January 1929

The Government of USSR and the German Government, being desirous of continuing the friendly relations existing between them, as well as their mutual cooperation in the interest of both countries, and at the same time of contributing to the consolidation of world peace, have agreed to prolong the Treaty of 24 April 1926 signed at Berlin and the Convention of Conciliation signed at Moscow on 25 January 1929.

For this purpose, they have appointed as their plenipotentiaries:

For USSR: Nikolai Nikolaevich Krestinsky, Member of the Central Executive Committee of USSR, Deputy People's Commissar for Foreign Affairs;

For Germany: Dr. Herbert von Dirksen, German Ambassador in USSR;

Who.... have agreed on the following provisions:

I. The Treaty concluded on 24 April 1926 between the USSR and Germany, including the Notes of the same date annexed thereto, shall be regarded as prolonged from the date of the expiry of its validity. Each of the Contracting Parties shall be entitled at any time, but not earlier than 30 June 1933, to denounce this Treaty at one year's notice.

In modification of Article IX of the Convention of Conciliation of 25 January 1929, the period of validity of the Convention shall be regarded as prolonged in such a manner that it may in future be denounced only at the same time as the Treaty of 24 April 1926, in accordance with the provisions of Article I of the present Protocol.

III. The present Protocol shall be subject to ratification. The exchange of the instruments of ratification shall take place at Moscow.

IV. The present Protocol is drawn up in duplicate in the Russian and German languages. Both texts are equally authentic.

Soviet Treaty Series, II, 34.

PARTY RESOLUTION. PARTY CENTRAL COMMITTEE CALLS FOR FURTHER INCREASE IN COLLECTIVIZATION
2 August 1931

At the beginning of the autumn harvest of 1931, the Party Central Committee called for the completion of its collectivization goals in 1932. It listed in its resolution of 2 August 1931 the major grain-producing regions and the percentages of peasant farms already collectivized and to be collectivized. It warned Party organizations against inflating percentages in this collectivization drive.

RESOLUTION OF TSK VKP(B) ON RATES FOR FUTURE COLLECTIVIZATION AND TASKS FOR STRENGTHENING COLLECTIVE FARMS

The TsK VKP(b) notes the successful fulfillment and overfulfilment of the rates for collectivization of farms established by the decisions of the TsK and Sixteenth Party Congress.

The TsK VKP(b) resolves:

1) To clarify that the standard for completing basically collectivization of this or that region or oblast is not the compulsory inclusion of the entire 100 percent of poor and middle peasant farms, but the joining in the kolkhozes of not less than 68-70 percent of peasant farms with the inclusion of not less than 75-80 percent of the sown area of peasant farms.

2) To consider basically collectivization finished:

a) in the Northern Caucasus (less certain regions of nationalities), where collectivized have already been 82 percent of peasant farms with the inclusion of 92 percent of the peasant sown areas;

b) in the Lower Volga (less the Kalmyk oblast), where collectivized have already been 82 percent of peasant farms with the inclusion of 92 percent of the peasant sown areas;

c) in the Middle Volga (Left Bank), where collectivized have already been 90 percent of peasant farms with the inclusion of 95 percent of the peasant sown areas;

d) in the Ukraine (Steppe), where collectivized have already been 85 percent of peasant farms with the inclusion of 94 percent of the peasant sown areas;

e) in the Ukraine (Left Bank), where collectivized have already been 69 percent of peasant farms with the inclusion of 80 percent of the peasant sown areas;

f) in the Crimea, where collectivized have already been 83 percent of peasant farms with the inclusion of 93 percent of the peasant sown areas;

g) in the Urals (grain regions), where collectivized have already been 75 percent of peasant farms with the inclusion of 82 percent of the peasant sown areas;

h) in Moldavia, where collectivized have already been 68 percent of peasant farms with the inclusion of 75 percent of the peasant sown areas.

The TsK instructs party organizations of the indicated republics and oblasts to center their work on the organizational and economic strengthening of kolkhozes in their present artel stage of development: Organization of labor, registration, piecework, struggle for the quality of work, organization of highly productive collective farms, creation of cadre.

3) Concerning other grain regions of the USSR (grain regions of the Central Black Earth, Western Siberia, Kazakhstan, Bashkiria, Eastern Siberia, Far East krai), as well as the cotton regions of Central Asia, Kazakhstan, and Transcaucasus, and the sugar beet regions of the Ukraine and Central Black Earth, the TsK orders future rates for the joining of peasant farms in kolkhozes to construct in these regions such that collectivization would be basically completed in 1932.

The TsK orders the party organizations of these oblasts and regions to not permit in any case whatsoever the struggle for joining peasants in kolkhozes to turn into an unhealthy chase for inflated percentages of collectivization.

The TsK orders these organizations to concentrate the attention of workers on strengthening the existing achievements in the area of collectivization and increase the work for the organizational and economic strengthening of kolkhozes.

4) In the remaining regions of the USSR, including the regions of consuming areas, the TsK resolves to work for collectivization so that collectivization would be basically completed in 1932-33.

The TsK especially warns the organizations of these regions and oblasts against chasing after inflated percentages of collectivization.

The TsK orders these organizations to concentrate the attention of workers on the task of improving the organizational and construction work of kolkhozes and strengthening above all the flax and vegetable kolkhozes.

KPSS v rezoliutsiiakh, Vol. 4, 559-560.

PARTY RESOLUTION. PARTY DICTATES POLICY FOR PRIMARY AND SECONDARY SCHOOLS

25 August 1931

Throughout the 1920s, various "progressive" experiments were the vogue in Soviet schools. On 25 August 1931, the Party Central Committee declared that the Soviet school was not meeting the pressing need to provide general education and preparation of students for higher education and technical schools, and condemned the "progressive" experiments and the prevalent theory of the "withering away of the school." It called for the reinstitution of physics, chemistry, history, and other traditional subjects and emphasis on the importance of the teacher and discipline. Dissatisfied with the abilities and training of new engineers who were entering industry, the Party Central Committee began to dictate school policy. Other resolutions and decrees followed in subsequent years. The new policy was considered a return to the "old school."

ON PRIMARY AND SECONDARY SCHOOLS

According to the Program of the Communist Party "the school must transmit not only communist principles generally, but also the ideological, organizational, and educational influence of the proletariat on semiproletarian and nonproletarian strata of the toiling masses in order to educate a generation capable of the final establishment of communism." In implementing this Program the proletarian state has achieved gigantic successes in extending the school network and in reconstructing the schools. The number of pupils enrolled in primary and secondary schools grew from 7,800,000 in 1914 to 20 million in 1931. The social makeup of the schools has altered radically: The children of workers and of the broad masses of toilers in the countryside, who formerly had no possibility of giving their children an education, now form the basic contingent in the school. Education is now given in 70 languages, including those of the most culturally backward peoples of the Soviet Union.

The content of all of the schools' work has become essentially different.

The Soviet school, which set as its task the "preparation of comprehensively developed members of a communist society," gives children an incomparably broader sociopolitical outlook and general development than the prerevolutionary bourgeois school. In recent years there has been a rise in the level of the general education of children in the Soviet schools.

The schools have been especially successful since the historic resolution of the Sixteenth Party Congress on the introduction of universal primary education. During the past year alone the number of pupils in primary and secondary schools has risen from 13.5 to 20 million. Another 1,400,000 students are included in the factory apprenticeship schools and technicums.

Along with the decisive steps to implement the compulsory education of school-age children, the schools have made considerable progress in combining education with productive labor and social work, thus laying the foundations for restructuring the schools on a polytechnical basis.

The increasing number of workshops, while still insufficient and poorly equipped from the technical point of view, combined with the progressive attachment of the schools to factories, sovkhozes, MTSs, and kolkhozes, enables the polytechnical transformation of the schools to proceed at an increasingly accelerated tempo and on an increasingly broad basis.

However, despite all these achievements, the Central Committee hereby notes that the Soviet school is still far from meeting the enormous demands placed on it by the present stage of socialist construction. The Central Committee considers the *fundamental inadequacy* of the schools at the present moment to be their inability to provide general education in sufficient volume and their unsatisfactory solution of the problem of producing fully educated people, with knowledge of the basic sciences (physics, chemistry, and mathematics, one's native language, geography, etc.), for the technical colleges and for higher education generally. Because of this the polytechnical transformation of the schools in many instances takes on a formal character and fails to prepare children as comprehensively developed builders of socialism who combine theory and practice and have a mastery of technical knowledge.

Any attempt to divorce the polytechnical transformation of the schools from the systematic and solid assimilation of the sciences, especially physics, chemistry, and mathematics, which must be taught on the basis of strictly defined and carefully worked out programs and study plans and according to strictly established schedules, is an extremely crude distortion of the idea of the polytechnical transformation of the schools. "One can only become a communist when one's memory has been enriched with the knowledge of all those treasures which mankind has developed" (Lenin, Volume XXV, 388).

For the basis of all further work of the school, the TsK proposes to offer Lenin's guidelines given by him back in 1920. Emphasizing that it was impossible to raise abstractly questions of introducing polytechnical education, that it is necessary to resolve these questions in close connection with the concrete tasks standing before the party, Lenin pointed out that it is necessary:

"1) to avoid early specialization; to develop instructions on this.

2) to extend *general education* subjects in all professional technical schools...

3) to establish by absolute tasks the *immediate* transition to *polytechnical* education or, rather, the immediate execution of a series of *achievable steps toward polytechnical education*...

We need joiners, metal workers, *immediately. Absolutely.*

Everyone must become joiners, metal workers, etc., *but* with some addition of a general education and polytechnical minimum.

The task of schools of the second level (rather, the higher classes of the second level) (12-17): Provide the complete expert in his occupation, completely capable of becoming a master and practically prepared for this as *joiners, carpenters, metal workers*, etc., *with the fact, however*, that this 'craftsman' would have an *extensive general education* (know the minimum bases of this and that science; indicate exactly what);

would be a communist (indicate exactly what he must know);

have a polytechnical range of interests and bases (elements) of a polytechnical education, namely:

(aa) *fundamental* understanding of electricity (determine exactly what),

(bb) about the use of electricity in *machine* industry,

(cc) also in the *chemical* industry,

(dd) also about the plan for the electrification of the RSFSR,

(ee) visit not less that 1-3 times an electric power station, plant, sovkhoz,

(ff) know *some* bases of agronomy, etc.

To develop *in detail the minimum of knowledge*."

On the basis of all of the above, the Central Committee resolves:

1. Basic Tasks of Schools

The union-republic people's commissariat for education are ordered to organize forthwith a scientific marxist critique of the programs, ensuring that they contain a precisely outlined area of systematic knowledge (native language, mathematics, physics, chemistry, geography, history), with instruction on the basis of the revised programs commencing on 1 January 1932.

While revising the programs, the people's commissariats for education must at the same time adopt a number of measures to ensure that instruction according to the new programs will actually be possible (teacher training, the issuance of appropriate instructions, etc.).

While introducing in the Soviet schools various new teaching methods that can advance the education of active participants in socialist construction, it is necessary to struggle resolutely against frivolous and harebrained schemes in teaching methods, against the massive introduction of methods which have not previously been tested in practice, as has been especially vividly manifested recently in the application of the so-called "project method". The attempts, deduced from the antileninist theory of the "dying out of the school", to put the so-called "project method" at the basis of all school work have in fact led to the destruction of the school.

The Central Committee hereby obliges the union-republic people's commissariats for education immediately to organize scientific research work and give it the necessary priority, assigning to it the best party personnel and restructuring it on strict marxist-leninist principles.

Considering that an essential component of communist education is polytechnical instruction, which must give the students the "fundamentals of science", acquaint them "in theory and practice with all the major production branches," and establish a "close tie between studies and productive labor", the union-republic people's commissariats for education are ordered throughout 1931 to expand generally the network of shops and workrooms in schools, combining this work with the attachment of schools to enterprises, sovkhozes, MTSs, and kolkhozes on the basis of contracts.

It is necessary to combine instruction with labor productivity on such a basis that the entire social and labor productivity of the studies are subordinated to the educational and training aims of the school.

Enterprises, sovkhozes, MTSs, and kolkhozes are to render all measures of help to the people's commissariats for education in meeting this task by way of allotting the necessary tools and equipment for school workshops and laboratories, allotting qualified workers and specialists for immediate participation in school work, and help to teachers in studying production, etc.

Union-republic people's commissariats for education are to create in each raion and all towns a network of model schools, providing them with more advantageous material conditions and concentrating in them the best pedagogical resources so that the teachers, workers, collective farmers, and students can learn in practice about the construction of the polytechnical school.

To assist the polytechnical school, the union-republic people's commissariats for education are to organize in the 1931/32 school year a network of small polytechnical museums as well as special polytechnical branches in existing museums of local lore, history and economy. The Supreme Council of the National Economy is to render financial and organizational assistance for carrying out this measure. The people's commissariats for education together with state publishing houses are to create standard polytechnical libraries for students and teachers in the native language. The people's commissariats for education together with film organizations are to develop measures to use film in schools, particularly for the introduction of polytechnical education.

In the period of socialism, when the proletariat completes the final destruction of classes under the conditions of the heightened class struggle, solely important significance is gained by consistent communist education in the soviet school and by the increase in the struggle against all kinds of attempts to inculcate elements of antiproletariat ideology in the children of the soviet school.

In connection with this, the TsK proposes to party organizations to strengthen the management of the school and take on the direct supervision of the teaching of social and political discipline in the seven-year schools, technicums, and institutions of higher learning.

Confirming the necessity of the timely fulfillment of the Central Committee resolution of 25 July 1930, on universal compulsory primary education, the Central Committee, for purposes of the most rapid implementation of the demands of the party program with respect to universal and polytechnical education for all children and adolescents under seventeen years of age, hereby orders the Sovnarkom to develop a plan for a *universal, compulsory, seven-year educational program.*

2. Improving the Methodical Guidance of the School

Noting the unsatisfactory state of the cadres and organizations concerned with giving schools methodical guidance, in the national educational system, the Central Committee orders the Culture and Propaganda Section to work together with the people's commissariats for education and culture and propaganda organs of the national communist parties' central committees to prepare marxist-leninist cadres for methodical work in the national educational system and to assign the party's best theoretical and pedagogical personnel to the leading organs concerned with providing methodical guidance.

Noting the considerable gap between the scientific research institutions concerned with pedagogy and the practical tasks of the schools, the Central Committee orders the union-republic people's commissariats for education to concentrate the work of their respective research institutes principally on studying and disseminating the experience acquired by persons doing practical work in the schools, especially in their polytechnical transformation.

The union-republic people's commissariats for education are to introduce into their educational systems the institution of instructor, starting at the raion level, for purposes of steady practical assistance to the teachers in their everyday work in the schools. The instructors are to be recruited from among experienced teachers who are well acquainted with the schools and their tasks, with not less than two per raion. All Communists in leading work in the educational field are to master the methodological side of school work in the shortest time.

The Society of Marxist Teachers of the Communist Academy is to be assigned the task of elaborating, upon the instructions of the People's Commissariat for Education, the basic issues of methodical assistance to the teachers in their day-to-day work.

The existing periodicals dealing with problems of pedagogy are to be reviewed in order to effect a decisive improvement in their quality and to orient them directly to the school and its needs. Teachers must be taken on to their editorial boards.

3. Cadres

Work among teachers is to be governed by the guideline given by Lenin as far back as 1922: "With us the teacher must enjoy greater esteem than he has ever enjoyed, does enjoy, or ever will enjoy in bourgeois society" (Lenin, Volume XVIII, Part 2, 115).

Considering the increasing demand, due to the introduction of universal education, for pedagogical cadres and for a heightening of their skill, the USSR Gosplan and the union-republic commissariats for education are given two months to develop a plan for training pedagogical cadres which will fully satisfy the needs for primary and secondary school teachers, submitting it to the Sovnarkom for approval.

An organized effort will be made to acquaint teachers with the bases of production in factories, sovkhozes, MTSs, and kolkhozes, so that all teaching cadres will have been covered during the years 1931/32.

In deciding upon contingents for educational institutions training agronomists, the USSR Narkomzem will give consideration to the need of the kolkhoz youth for schools and will also extend the necessary assistance to national educational organs in their effort to attract agronomists occupied in production to work in the kolkhoz youth schools.

All institutions of higher industrial and agricultural education are to be acquainted with the methods used in the polytechnical transformation of the schools and with the techniques used in production and technical training.

The Central Committee of the Komsomol and the union-republic people's commissariats for education are hereby ordered to elaborate special measures for selecting Young Pioneer leaders, assigning them to work, heightening their general and specialized pedagogical skills, viewing them as a valuable reserve for training new pedagogical cadres.

Gosplan, the People's Commissariat for Finance, the central committee of the workers' educational union, and the union-republic people's commissariats for education are given ten days to devise measures to increase the salaries of primary and secondary school teachers. The Central Committee of the educational workers' union and the union-republic people's commissariats for education are given one month to develop a system of differentiated pay scales for teachers, based on regional factors, qualifications, and the quality of their work.

Teachers are to be supplied with food and industrial goods in the following way: In cities and industrial regions, by attaching them to closed workers' distribution centers and cafeterias, with the norm of an industrial worker; teachers in kolkhozes are to be supplied with food from the food stocks of the kolkhoz, according to the norm for the industrial workers of the given raion; village teachers are to be supplied with industrial goods and products, and in villages where no kolkhoz has yet been established teachers are to be supplied with food products from central supply stocks at the norm of the industrial workers of the given raion. All work among teachers must aim, in every way, to stimulate socialist competition and the shock-worker movement, with shock-worker teachers being encouraged in every possible way.

4. The Material Base of the Primary and Secondary Schools

Noting that the material base of the schools—the construction of new buildings and the repair of existing ones, the production of teaching equipment and textbooks—is extremely inadequate and is becoming one of the obstacles to an improvement of the work of the schools, the Central Committee orders the Union Gosplan to develop a five year plan for new school construction. In all new construction work the schools must be completed before the enterprise enters into operation.

To increase the number of school buildings, the Central Committee orders the local party and soviet organizations to return to the schools any unreleased former school buildings and also to use confiscated kulak houses as schools. The initiative and funds of the kolkhozes must be broadly involved in improving the material base of the schools and making better provision for the teachers.

The Supreme Council of the National Economy is ordered to establish an All-Union Association of the Textbook and School Equipment Manufacturing Industry and within two months to have examined the production plan of this association so that by 1932 the greater part of both primary and secondary schools will be provided with the necessary minimum of school equipment; the union-republic people's commissariats for education are given one month to develop the appropriate application and submit it to the Supreme Council of the National Economy, having elaborated standards for textbooks and polytechnical equipment.

The USSR Supreme Council of the National Economy is ordered to transfer to the schools any machine tools, instruments, or waste materials (rejects, breakage, scraps) which cannot be used by enterprises and are suitable for school workshops. The union-republic sovnarkoms as well as the krai and oblast executive committees and the organs of industrial cooperation are immediately to organize the local production of textbooks and school equipment—using locally available resources—for mass distribution in the schools.

5. School Administration and Leadership

While noting the successful restructuring of educational work in past years by the union-republic people's commissariats for education, the Central Committee of the party emphasizes that the quality of school work cannot be improved without a decisive improvement in the quality of school leadership by the organs of the People's Commissariat for Education, without their accelerated transition to operative, concrete, and differentiated guidance, with due regard for the economic and political significance of the various oblasts and raions, national characteristics, etc., establishing, in all elements of the educational network, strict responsibility for work assigned which will exclude any evasion by individuals. The Central Committee demands that all organs of the educational system perform their work and give guidance in a new way, one which meets the increasing demands made upon the schools by the socialist reconstruction of the economy.

The Central Committee orders the union-republic people's commissariats for education to effect a thoroughgoing reconstruction of the practical guidance of the educational organs, making it truly operative and differentiated, concentrating attention on the major industrial regions (metal, coal, oil, etc.), on sovkhozes, the MTSs, areas of total collectivization, and new construction sites. The "balanced" approach to the distribution of personnel and funds must be ended, and they must be concentrated primarily in the leading sectors of socialist construction.

The union-republic people's commissariats for education must ensure the implementation of one-man management in school administration. In this the trade union organizations must extend the necessary assistance to the educational organs.

By organizing practical assistance to teachers, the union-republic people's commissariats for education are to heighten the responsibility of teachers for the quality of their work, singling out and encouraging those who are knowledgeable and devoted to their work.

The work of the organs of children's self-government in the schools is to be directed mainly at heightening the quality of school work and reinforcing conscious school discipline.

The Central Committee considers that, to accomplish successfully the tasks set by the present resolution, the union-republic people's commissariats for education must struggle resolutely against those elements in the educational organs which oppose this about-face in the work of the schools as indicated by the present resolution and, instead of raising the quality of instruction, either indulge in leftist phrase-making or pull back in the direction of the bourgeois school.

The Central Committee stresses the growing significance and role of the school in socialist construction and orders all organizations to struggle systematically and unyieldingly against opportunist and antileninist distortions of the party's school policy. The success of the struggle against the major danger on the path to the construction of a polytechnical school—the right opportunist distortion of the party's policy leading to a rejection of the polytechnical transformation of the schools, to attempts to preserve the old system of verbal teaching, to a rift between theoretical studies and practice, is the precondition for an intensified struggle against left-opportunist distortions, the theory of the "dying out" of the school, and the reduction in the role of the teacher.

The Central Committee directs the attention of all party organizations to the need for a resolute concentration of attention on the mass school, the work of the teacher, and on reinforcing the day-to-day concrete guidance of the schools.

McNeal/Gregor, Vol. 3, 108-115.
KPSS v rezoliutsiiakh, Vol. 4, 569-577.

STALIN DICTATES PARTY HISTORY
LETTER TO JOURNAL "PROLETARSKAIA REVOLIUTSIIA"
6 November 1931

In response to an article which cast doubt on Lenin's infallibility as a real Bolshevik and follower of Marx, Stalin furiously and with venom attacked the author and the editors of the journal which published the article. His attack represented a Russocentric view of the history of the European Marxist movement. As a result, his article dictated to historians the infallibility of Lenin and the existence of both Lenin and Stalin as the party's leaders.

SOME QUESTIONS CONCERNING THE HISTORY OF BOLSHEVISM
Letter to the Editorial Board of the Journal "Proletarskaia Revoliutsiia"

Dear Comrades,

I emphatically protest against the publication in the journal *Proletarskaia Revoliutsiia* (No. 6, 1930) of Slutsky's antiParty and semiTrotskyist article, "The Bolsheviks on German Social-Democracy in the Period of Its Prewar Crisis," as an article for discussion.

Slutsky asserts that Lenin (the Bolsheviks) underestimated the danger of *Centrism* in German Social-Democracy and in prewar Social-Democracy in general; that is, he underestimated the danger of camouflaged opportunism, the danger of conciliation towards opportunism. In other words, according to Slutsky, Lenin (the Bolsheviks) did not wage an irreconcilable struggle against opportunism, for, in essence, underestimation of Centrism is tantamount to refraining from a thoroughgoing struggle against opportunism. It follows, therefore, that in the period before the war Lenin was not yet a real Bolshevik; that it was only in the period of the imperialist war, or even at the close of the war, that Lenin became a real Bolshevik.

Such is the tale Slutsky tells in his article. And you, instead of branding this new-found "historian" as a slanderer and falsifier, enter into discussion with him, provide him with a forum. I cannot refrain from protesting against the publication of Slutsky's article in your journal as an article for discussion, for the question of Lenin's *Bolshevism*, the question whether Lenin *did* or *did not wage* an irreconcilable struggle, based on principle, against Centrism as a certain form of opportunism, the question whether Lenin *was* or *was not* a real Bolshevik, cannot be made into a subject of discussion.

In your statement entitled "From the Editorial Board", sent to the Central Committee on 20 October, you admit that the editorial board made a mistake in publishing Slutsky's article as a discussion article. That is all to the good, of course, despite the fact that the statement of the editorial board is very belated. But in your statement you commit a fresh mistake by declaring that "the editorial board consider it to be politically extremely urgent and necessary that the entire complex of problems pertaining to the relations between the Bolsheviks and the prewar Second International be further analyzed in the pages of *Proletarskaia Revolutsiia*." That means that you intend once again to draw people into a discussion on questions which are axioms of Bolshevism. It means that you are again thinking of converting the subject of Lenin's Bolshevism from an axiom into a problem requiring "further analysis". Why? On what grounds?

Everyone knows that Leninism was born, grew up and become strong in relentless struggle against opportunism of every brand, including Centrism in the West (Kautsky) and Centrism in our country (Trotsky, et. al.). This cannot be denied even by the downright enemies of Bolshevism. It is an axiom. But you are dragging us back by trying to turn an axiom into a problem requiring "further analysis". Why? On what grounds? Perhaps through ignorance of the history of Bolshevism? Perhaps for the sake of rotten liberalism, so that the Slutskys and other disciples of Trotsky may not be able to say that they are being gagged? A rather strange sort of liberalism, this, exercised at the expense of the vital interests of Bolshevism....

What exactly, is there in Slutsky's article that the editorial board regard as worthy of discussion?

1) Slutsky asserts that Lenin (the Bolsheviks) did not pursue a line directed towards a rupture, towards a split with the opportunists in German Social-Democracy, with the opportunists in the Second International of the prewar period. You want to open a discussion on this Trotskyist thesis of Slutsky's. But what is there to discuss? Is it not obvious that Slutsky is simply slandering Lenin, slandering the Bolsheviks? Slander must be branded as such and not made the subject of discussion.

Every Bolshevik, if he really is a Bolshevik, knows that long before the war, approximately since 1903-04, when the Bolshevik group in Russia took shape and when the Lefts in German Social-Democracy first raised their voice, Lenin pursued a line directed towards a rupture, towards a split with the opportunists both here, in the Russian Social-Democratic Party, and over there, in the Second International, particularly in the German Social-Democratic Party.

Every Bolshevik knows that it was for that very reason that even at that time (1903-05) in the ranks of the opportunists of the Second International the Bolsheviks won for themselves honorable fame as being "splitters" and "disrupters". But what could Lenin do, what could the Bolsheviks do, if the Left Social-Democrats in the Second International, and above all in the German Social-Democratic Party, were a weak and powerless group, a group without organizational shape, ideologically ill-equipped and afraid even to pronounce the word "rupture", "split"? It cannot be demanded that Lenin, the Bolsheviks, should have, from inside Russia, done the work of the Lefts for them and brought about a split in the parties of the West.

That is apart from the fact that organizational and ideological weakness was a characteristic feature of the Left Social-Democrats not only in the period prior to the war. As is well known, the Lefts retained this negative feature in the postwar period as well. Everyone knows the appraisal of the German Left Social-Democrats given by Lenin in his famous article , "On Junius' Pamphlet," [Junius was the pen name of Rosa Luxemburg—AGC] published in October 1916—that is, more than two years after the beginning of the war—in which Lenin, criticizing a number of very serious political mistakes committed by the Left Social-Democrats in Germany, speaks of "*the weakness of all German Lefts, who are entangled on all sides in the vile net of Kautskyist hypocrisy, pedantry, 'friendship' for the opportunists*"; in which he says that "*Junius has not yet freed himself completely from the 'environment' of the German, even Left Social-Democrats, who are afraid of a split, are afraid to voice revolutionary slogans in the full*".

Of all the groups in the Second International, the Russian Bolsheviks were at that time the only one which, by its organizational experience and ideological equipment, was capable of undertaking anything serious in the sense of a direct rupture, of a split with its own opportunists in its own Russian Social-Democratic Party. Now, if the Slutskys attempted, not even to prove, but simply to assume that Lenin and the Russian Bolsheviks did not exert all their efforts to organize a split with the opportunists (Plekhanov, Martov, Dan) and to oust the Centrists (Trotsky and other adherents of the August bloc), then one could argue about Lenin's Bolshevism, about the Bolsheviks' Bolshevism. But the whole point is that the Slutskys dare not even hint at such a wild assumption. They dare not, for they are aware that the universally known facts concerning the resolute policy of rupture with the opportunists of all brands pursued by the Russian Bolsheviks (1904-12) cry out against such an assumption. They dare not, for they know that they would be pilloried the very next day.

But the question arises: Could the Russian Bolsheviks bring about a split with their opportunists and Centrist conciliators long before the imperialist war (1904-12) without at the same time pursuing a line directed towards a rupture, towards a split with the opportunists and Centrists of the Second International? Who can doubt that the Russian Bolsheviks regarded their policy towards the opportunists and Centrists as a model for the policy of the Lefts in the West? Who can doubt that the Russian Bolsheviks did all they could to push the Left Social-Democrats in the West, particularly the Lefts in the German Social-Democratic Party, towards a rupture, towards a split with their own opportunists and Centrists? It was not the fault of Lenin and of the Russian Bolsheviks that the Left Social-Democrats in the West proved to be too immature to follow in the footsteps of the Russian Bolsheviks.

2) Slutsky reproaches Lenin and the Bolsheviks for not supporting the German Left Social-Democrats resolutely and wholeheartedly, for supporting them only with important reservations, for allowing factional considerations to hinder them from giving all-out support to the Lefts. You want to discuss this fraudulent and utterly false reproach. But what is there indeed to discuss? Is it not obvious that Slutsky is maneuvering and trying, by means of a false reproach against Lenin and the Bolsheviks, to cover up the real gaps in the position of the Lefts in Germany? Is it not obvious that the Bolsheviks could not support the Lefts in Germany, who time and again waivered between Bolshevism and Menshevism, *without* important reservations, *without* seriously criticizing their mistakes, and that to act otherwise

would have been a *betrayal* of the working class and its revolution? Fraudulent manuevers must be branded as such and not made a subject of discussion.

Yes, the Bolsheviks supported the Left Social-Democrats in Germany only with certain important reservations, criticizing their semiMenshevik mistakes. But for this they ought to be applauded, not reproached.

Are there people who doubt this?

Let us turn to the most generally known facts of history.

a) In 1903, serious differences arose between the Bolsheviks and the Mensheviks in Russia on the question of Party membership. By their formula on Party membership the Bolsheviks wanted to set up an organizational barrier against the influx of nonproletarian elements into the Party. The danger of such an influx was very real at that time in view of the bourgeois-democratic character of the Russian revolution. The Russian Mensheviks advocated the opposite position, which threw the doors of the Party wide open to nonproletarian elements. In view of the importance of the questions of the Russian revolution for the world revolutionary movement, the West-European Social-Democrats in Germany, Parvus and Rosa Luxemburg, then the leaders of the Lefts, also intervened. And what happened? Both declared for the Mensheviks and against the Bolsheviks. They accused the Bolsheviks of having ultracentralist and Blanquist tendencies. Subsequently, these vulgar and philistine epithets were seized upon by the Mensheviks and spread far and wide.

b) In 1905, differences developed between the Bolsheviks and the Mensheviks in Russia on the question of the character of the Russian revolution. The Bolsheviks advocated an alliance between the working class and the peasantry under the hegemony of the proletariat. The Bolsheviks asserted that the objective must be a revolutionary-democratic dictatorship of the proletariat and peasantry for the purpose of passing immediately from the bourgeois-democratic revolution to the socialist revolution, with the support of the rural poor secured. The Mensheviks in Russia rejected the idea of the hegemony of the proletariat in the bourgeois-democratic revolution; instead of the policy of an alliance between the working class and the peasantry, they preferred the policy of an agreement with the liberal bourgeoisie, and they declared that the revolutionary-democratic dictatorship of the proletariat and peasantry was a reactionary Blanquist scheme that ran counter to the development of the bourgeois revolution. What was the attitude of the German Left Social-Democrats, of Parvus and Rosa Luxemburg, to this controversy? They invented a utopian and semiMenshevik scheme of permanent revolution (a distorted representation of the Marxist scheme of revolution), which was permeated through and through with the Menshevik repudiation of the policy of alliance between the working class and peasantry, and they counterposed this scheme to the Bolshevik scheme of the revolutionary-democratic dictatorship of the proletariat and peasantry. Subsequently, this semiMenshevik scheme of permanent revolution was seized upon by Trotsky (in part by Martov) and turned into a weapon of struggle against Leninism.

c) In the period before the war, one of the most urgent questions that came to the fore in the parties of the Second International was the national and colonial question, the question of the oppressed nations and colonies, the question of the liberation of the oppressed nations and colonies, the question of the paths to be followed in the struggle against imperialism, the question of the paths to overthrow imperialism. In the interests of developing the proletarian revolution and encircling imperialism, the Bolsheviks proposed the policy of supporting the liberation movement of the oppressed nations and colonies on the basis of the self-determination of nations, and developed the scheme of a united front between the proletarian revolution in the advanced countries and the revolutionary-liberation movement of the peoples of the colonies and oppressed countries. The opportunists of all countries, the social-chauvinists and social-imperialists of all countries hastened to take up arms against the Bolsheviks on this account. The Bolsheviks were baited like mad dogs. What position did the Left Social-Democrats in the West adopt at that time? They developed a semiMenshevik theory of imperialism, rejected the principle of self-determination of nations in its Marxist sense (including secession and formation of independent states), rejected the thesis that the liberation movement in the colonies and oppressed countries is of great revolutionary importance, rejected the thesis that a united front between the proletarian revolution and the movement for national liberation is possible, and counterposed all this semiMenshevik hodgepodge, which is nothing but an underestimation of the national and colonial question, to the Marxist scheme of the Bolsheviks. It is well known that this semiMenshevik hodgepodge was subsequently seized upon by Trotsky, who used it as a weapon in the struggle against Leninism.

Such are the universally known mistakes committed by the Left Social-Democrats in Germany.

I need not speak of the other mistakes of the German Lefts, mistakes which were severely criticized in various articles by Lenin.

Nor need I speak of the mistakes they committed in appraising the policy of the Bolsheviks in the period of the October Revolution.

What do these mistakes of the German Lefts taken from the history of the prewar period indicate, if not that the Left Social-Democrats, despite their Leftism, had not yet rid themselves of Menshevik lumber?

Of course, the record of the Lefts in Germany does not consist only of serious mistakes. They also have great and important revolutionary deeds to their credit. I have in mind a number of their services and revolutionary actions in relation to questions of internal policy and, in particular, of the electoral struggle, questions of the struggle inside and outside parliament, the general strike, war, the Revolution of 1905 in Russia, etc. That is why the Bolsheviks reckoned with them as Lefts, supported them and urged them forward. But it does not and cannot obliterate the fact that at the same time the Left Social-Democrats in Germany did commit a number of serious political and theoretical mistakes; that they had not yet rid themselves of the Menshevik burden and therefore were in need of severe criticism by the Bolsheviks.

Now judge for yourselves whether Lenin and the Bolsheviks could have supported the Left Social-Democrats in the West *without serious reservations, without severely criticizing* their mistakes, and whether it would not have been a betrayal of the interests of the working class, a betrayal of the interests of the revolution, a betrayal of communism, to act otherwise?

Is it not obvious that in reproaching Lenin and the Bolsheviks for something for which he should have applauded them if he were a Bolshevik, Slutsky fully exposes himself as a semiMenshevik, as a camouflaged Trotskyist?

Slutsky assumes that in their appraisal of the Lefts in the West, Lenin and the Bolsheviks were guided by their own factional considerations and that, consequently, the Russian Bolsheviks sacrificed the great cause of the international revolution to the interests of their faction. It scarcely needs proof that there can be nothing more base and disgusting than such an assumption. There can be nothing more base, for even the basest of Mensheviks are beginning to understand that the Russian revolution is not a private cause of the Russians; that, on the contrary, it is the cause of the working class of the whole world, the cause of the world proletarian revolution. There can be nothing more disgusting, for even the professional slanderers in the Second International are beginning to understand that the consistent and thoroughly revolutionary internationalism of the Bolsheviks is a model of proletarian internationalism for the workers of all countries.

Yes, the Russian Bolsheviks did put in the forefront the fundamental questions of the Russian revolution, such questions as those of the Party, of the attitude of Marxists towards the bourgeois-democratic revolution, of the alliance between the working class and the peasantry, of the hegemony of the proletariat, of the struggle inside and outside parliament, of the general strike, of the growing over of the bourgeois-democratic revolution into a socialist revolution, of the dictatorship of the proletariat, of imperialism, of the self-determination of nations, of the liberation movement of the oppressed nations and colonies, of the policy of support for this movement, etc. They advanced these questions as the touchstone by which they tested the revolutionary stamina of the Left Social-Democrats in the West. Had they the right to do so? Yes, they had. They not only had the right, but it was their duty to do so. It was their duty to do so because all these questions were also fundamental questions of the world revolution, to whose aims the Bolsheviks subordinated their policy and their tactics. It was their duty to do so because only through such questions could they really test the revolutionary character of the various groups in the Second International. The question arises: Where is there here any "factionalism" of the Russian Bolsheviks and what have "factional" considerations to do with this?

As far back as 1902 Lenin wrote in his pamphlet *What Is To Be Done?* That "*history has now confronted us with an immediate task which is the most revolutionary of all the immediate tasks that confront the proletariat of any country*," that "*the fulfillment of this task, the destruction of the most important bulwark, not only of European, but also (it may now be said) of Asiatic reaction, would make the Russian proletariat the vanguard of the international revolutionary proletariat*." Thirty years have elapsed since that pamphlet, *What Is To Be Done?*, appeared. No one will dare deny that the events during this period have brilliantly confirmed Lenin's words. But does it not follow from this that the Russian revolution was (and remains) the nodal point of the world revolution, that the fundamental questions of the Russian revolution were at the same time (and are now) the fundamental questions of the world revolution?

Is it not obvious that only through these fundamental questions was it possible to make a real test of the revolutionary character of the Left Social-Democrats in the West?

Is it not obvious that people who regard these questions as "factional" questions fully expose themselves as base and degenerate elements?

3) Slutsky asserts that so far there has not been found a sufficient number of official documents testifying to Lenin's (the Bolsheviks') determined and relentless struggle against Centrism. He employs this bureaucratic thesis as an irrefutable argument in favor of the proposition that Lenin (the Bolsheviks) underestimated the danger of Centrism in the Second International. And you are ready to discuss this nonsense, this rascally chicanery. But what is there indeed to discuss? Is it not obvious anyway that by this talk about documents Slutsky is trying to cover up the wretchedness and falsity of his so-called conception?

Slutsky considers the Party documents now available to be inadequate. Why? On what grounds? Are not the universally known documents relating to the Second International, as well as those relating to the inner-Party struggle in Russian Social-Democracy, sufficient to demonstrate with full clarity the revolutionary relentlessness of Lenin and the Bolsheviks in their struggle against the opportunists and Centrists? Is Slutsky at all familiar with these documents? What more documents does he need?

Let us assume that, in addition to the documents already known, a mass of other documents were found, containing, say, resolutions of the Bolsheviks once again urging the necessity of wiping out Centrism. Would that mean that the mere existence of written documents is sufficient to demonstrate the real revolutionary character and the real relentlessness of the Bolsheviks' attitude toward Centrism? Who, except hopeless bureaucrats, can rely on written documents alone? Who, except archive rats, does not understand that a party and its leaders must be tested primarily by their *deeds* and not merely by their declarations? History knows not a few Socialists who readily signed all sorts of revolutionary resolutions, just for the sake of satisfying importunate critics. But that does not mean that they *carried out* these resolutions. Furthermore, history knows not a few Socialists who, foaming at the mouth, called upon the workers' parties of *other* countries to perform the most revolutionary actions imaginable. But that does not mean that they did not in their own party, or in their own country, *shrink* from fighting *their own* opportunists, *their own* bourgeoisie. Is not this why Lenin taught us to test revolutionary parties, trends and leaders, not by their declarations and resolutions, but by their *deeds*?

Is it not obvious that if Slutsky really wanted to test the relentlessness of Lenin and the Bolsheviks towards Centrism, he should have taken as the *basis* of his article, not individual documents and two or three personal letters, but a test of the Bolsheviks by their *deeds*, their *history*, their *actions*? Did we not have opportunists and Centrists in the Russian Social-Democratic Party? Did not the Bolsheviks wage a determined and relentless struggle against all these trends? Were not these trends both ideologically and organizationally connected with the opportunists and Centrists in the West? Did not the Bolsheviks smash the opportunists and Centrists as no other Left group did anywhere else in the world? How can anyone say after all this that Lenin and the Bolsheviks underestimated the danger of Centrism? Why did Slutsky ignore these facts, which are of decisive importance in characterizing the Bolsheviks? Why did he not resort to the most reliable method of testing Lenin and the Bolsheviks: By their deeds, by their actions? Why did he prefer the less reliable method of rummaging among casually selected papers?

Because recourse to the more reliable method of testing the Bolsheviks by their deeds would have instantaneously upset Slutsky's whole conception.

Because a test of the Bolsheviks by their deeds would have shown that the Bolsheviks are the *only* revolutionary organization in the world which has completely smashed the opportunists and Centrists and driven them out of the Party.

Because recourse to the real deeds and the real history of the Bolsheviks would have shown that Slutsky's teachers, the Trotskyists, were the *principal* and *basic* group which fostered Centrism in Russia, and for this purpose created a special organization, the August bloc, as a hotbed of Centrism.

Because a test of the Bolsheviks by their deeds would have exposed Slutsky once and for all as a falsifier of the history of our Party, who is trying to cover up the Centrism of prewar Trotskyism by slanderously accusing Lenin and the Bolsheviks of having underestimated the danger of Centrism.

That, comrade editors, is how matters stand with Slutsky and his article.

As you see, the editorial board made a mistake in permitting a discussion with a falsifier of the history of our Party.

What could have impelled the editorial board to take this wrong road?

I think that they were impelled to take that road by rotten liberalism, which has spread to some extent among a section of the Bolsheviks. Some Bolsheviks think that Trotskyism is a faction of communism—one which makes mistakes, it is true, which does many foolish things, is sometimes even antiSoviet, but which, nevertheless, is a faction of communism. Hence a certain liberalism in the attitude towards the Trotskyists and Trotskyist-minded people. It scarcely needs proof that such a view of Trotskyism is deeply mistaken and harmful. As a matter of fact, Trotskyism has long since ceased to be a faction of communism. As a matter of fact, Trotskyism is the advanced detachment of the counterrevolutionary bourgeoisie, which is fighting against communism, against the Soviet regime, against the building of socialism in the USSR.

Who gave the counterrevolutionary bourgeoisie an ideological weapon against Bolshevism in the shape of the thesis that building socialism in our country is impossible, that the degeneration of the Bolsheviks is inevitable, etc.? Trotskyism gave it that weapon. It is no accident that in their efforts to prove the inevitability of the struggle against the Soviet regime all the antiSoviet groups in the USSR have been referring to the well known Trotskyist thesis that building socialism in our country is impossible, that the degeneration of the Soviet regime is inevitable, that a return to capitalism is probable.

Who gave the counterrevolutionary bourgeoisie in the USSR a tactical weapon in the shape of attempts at open actions against the Soviet regime? The Trotskyists, who tried to organize antiSoviet demonstrations in Moscow and Leningrad on 7 November 1927, gave it that weapon. It is a fact that the antiSoviet actions of the Trotskyists raised the spirits of the bourgeoisie and let loose the wrecking activities of the bourgeois experts.

Who gave the counterrevolutionary bourgeoisie an organizational weapon in the form of attempts at setting up underground antiSoviet organizations? The Trotskyists, who organized their own antiBolshevik illegal group, gave it that weapon. It is a fact that the underground antiSoviet work of the Trotskyists helped the antiSoviet groups in the USSR to assume an organized form.

Trotskyism is the advanced detachment of the counterrevolutionary bourgeoisie.

That is why liberalism in the attitude towards Trotskyism, even though the latter is shattered and camouflaged, is blockheadedness bordering on crime, on treason to the working class.

That is why the attempts at certain "writers" and "historians" to smuggle disguised Trotskyist rubbish into our literature must meet with a determined rebuff from Bolsheviks.

That is why we cannot permit a literary discussion with the Trotskyist smugglers.

It seems to me that "historians" and "writers" of the Trotskyist smuggler category are for the present trying to carry out their smuggling work along two lines.

Firstly, they are trying to prove that in the period before the war Lenin underestimated the danger of Centrism, thereby leaving the inexperienced reader to surmise that, in consequence, Lenin was not yet a real revolutionary at that time; that he became one only after the war, after he had "reequipped" himself with Trotsky's assistance. Slutsky may be regarded as a typical representative of this type of smuggler.

We have seen above that Slutsky and Co. are not worth making much fuss about.

Secondly, they are trying to prove that in the period prior to the war Lenin did not realize the necessity of the growing over of the bourgeois-democratic revolution into a socialist revolution, thereby leaving the inexperienced reader to surmise that, in consequence, Lenin at that time was not yet a real Bolshevik; that he realized the necessity of this growing over only after the war, after he had "reequipped" himself with Trotsky's assistance. Volosevich, author of *A Course in the History of the CPSU(B)*, may be regarded as a typical representative of this type of smuggler.

True, as far back as 1905 Lenin wrote that "*from the democratic revolution we shall at once, and just to the extent of our strength, the strength of the class-conscious and organized proletariat, begin to pass to the socialist revolution*," that "*we stand for uninterrupted revolution*," and "*we shall not stop halfway*." True, a very large number of facts and documents of a similar nature could be found in the works of Lenin. But what do the Voloseviches care about the facts of Lenin's life and work? The Voloseviches write in order, by decking themselves out in Bolshevik colors, to smuggle in their antiLeninist contraband, to utter lies about the Bolsheviks and to falsify the history of the Bolshevik Party.

As you see, the Voloseviches are worthy of the Slutskys.

Such are the "highways and byways" of the Trotskyist smugglers.

You yourselves should realize that it is not the business of the editorial board of *Proletarskaia Revolutsiia* to facilitate the smuggling activities of such "historians" by providing them with a forum for discussion.

The task of the editorial board is, in my opinion, to raise the questions concerning the history of Bolshevism to the proper level, to put the study of the history of our Party on scientific, Bolshevik lines, and to concentrate attention against the Trotskyist and all other falsifiers of the history of our Party, systematically tearing off their masks.

That is all the more necessary since even some of our historians—I am speaking of historians without quotation marks, of *Bolshevik* historians of our Party—are not free from mistakes which bring grist to the mill of the Slutskys and Voloseviches. In this respect, even Comrade Iaroslavsky is not, unfortunately, an exception; his books on the history of the CPSU)B), despite all their merits, contain a number of errors in matters of principle and history.

With Communist greetings,
J. Stalin

Stalin, *Works*, XIII, 86-104.

SOVIET GOVERNMENT GIVES MUTED RESPONSE TO JAPANESE OCCUPATION OF MANCHURIA
14-20 November 1931

On the night of 18-19 September 1931, Japanese military forces occupied Manchuria. One week later lead articles in Pravda and Izvestiia described the invasion and occupation, attributed the action to Japanese domestic economic and political problems, criticized other foreign powers for their pacifism, and claimed that Soviet society was for peace but criticized Japan for its domination of a weaker country. The Japanese Government declared that Japanese forces were inserted into Manchuria to protect the Southern Manchurian Railway and Japanese capital. Japanese forces in Manchuria argued there were Soviet forces in Manchuria, and the Soviets were supporting the Chinese by transporting troops over the Chinese Eastern Railway. The Soviet Commissariat for Foreign Affairs refuted these and other charges to the Japanese ambassador in Moscow. Although Soviet troops were moved up to the Soviet-Manchurian border, the Soviet Government took a neutral stand on the invasion, insisted on noninterference in the Japanese conflict, and called upon Japan to forestall any attack on the Chinese Eastern Railway. The two documents below, notes from Maxim Litvinov to the Japanese ambassador, illustrate the muted response of the Soviet Government to the invasion and its attempt to avoid anything which would embroil the Soviet Union in a military conflict with Japan. The Soviet Government hoped for reaction from the world community and anticipated a Sino-Japanese conflict.

STATEMENT BY LITVINOV TO THE JAPANESE AMBASSADOR IN MOSCOW ON THE SOVIET ATTITUDE TO THE SITUATION IN MANCHURIA
14 November 1931

In the statement handed to you on 29 October of this year by M. Karakhan, Vice-Commissar for Foreign Affairs, the Soviet Government noted the utter absurdity and falseness of the inventions and rumors emanating from irresponsible quarters, concerned, for one reason or another, with the present situation in Manchuria, in spreading provocative rumors.

The Government of the USSR stated with the utmost clarity that it adheres to the policy of strict nonintervention which derives from its traditional and unchanging policy of peace, of respect for the international treaties concluded with China, and of respect for the sovereign rights and independence of other states.

The Soviet Government was entitled to expect that its statement, which was so clear that it left no room whatever for doubt or ambiguity, and which, according to the information you gave to M. Karakhan, Vice-Commissar for Foreign Affairs, was greeted with satisfaction by the Japanese Government, would put an end to the provocative antiSoviet campaign and the inventions about the help said to be given my the Soviet Government to Chinese forces in Manchuria.

It is with the deepest regret that the Soviet Government is compelled to note that interested Japanese military circles are still busily inventing and spreading, through the Japanese press and telegraph agencies, wholly groundless rumors about the help being given by the Soviet Government to some Chinese generals or other.

That these rumors have moreover an official character and source is shown by the official statement made by the representative of the Japanese authorities in Mukden on 12 November, which asserts outright that reinforcements consisting of "Chinese and Korean communists" were transferred from Blagoveschchensk.

Nor can the Soviet Government fail to remark that similar suppositions were made on the same day by Nakano, Japanese Vice-Consul in Harbin, in his interview with the director of the Soviet consulate-general in Harbin.

The Soviet Government draws the attention of the Japanese Government to this unscrupulous antiSoviet campaign, which is being systematically waged by certain military circles in Manchuria with the object of creating difficulties in the relations between Japan and the USSR.

At the same time the Soviet Government considers it appropriate to recall the assurances which the Japanese ambassador gave me, that the interests of the USSR would suffer no loss by the events in Manchuria. It is more necessary to recall this, since there is information that preparations are being made by the Japanese command to cut the Chinese Eastern Railway in the Tsitsihar area, which would paralyze the railway and cause material injury to the USSR. The Soviet Government trusts that the assurances given by the Japanese Government will remain in force and will not be broken.

Degras, II, 514-515.

REPLY BY LITVINOV TO THE JAPANESE AMBASSADOR'S STATEMENT ON THE TRANSPORT OF CHINESE TROOPS ON THE CHINESE EASTERN RAILWAY

20 November 1931

The Soviet Government notes with satisfaction your statement that the Japanese Government does not believe the rumors of the violation of the principle of nonintervention, and of Soviet assistance to the Chinese generals, and that it thus dissociates itself from the irresponsible statements made by Japanese officials, clearly without the sanction of their Government. The Soviet Government could not expect the Japanese Government to have a different attitude to the rumors in question after the perfectly explicit statement by M. Karakhan, made on the instructions of his Government, concerning strict nonintervention in the Japanese-Chinese conflict and the absence of any help given to one side or the other.

Insofar as your statement draws a parallel between the present events in China and the Soviet-Chinese dispute of 1929, I am compelled to point out the incorrectness of the analogy. Although the Chinese authorities indisputably and obviously violated Soviet treaty rights, the Soviet Government did not invade and had no thought of invading Manchuria. Only after repeated attacks by Chinese and Russian White Guard detachments on Soviet territory did Soviet troops cross the Manchurian frontier in order to repel the attackers, disarm them, and put an end to further attacks. There was no question of occupation, even of a temporary character, of Chinese territory by Soviet troops, or of the removal of the existing authorities and the creation of new authorities. Nor was there at the time the remotest possibility of infringing the legitimate rights and interests of Japan. As soon as the Soviet troops had carried out their strictly limited tasks they were withdrawn to Soviet territory. The Soviet Government did not exploit its own military superiority and Chinese weakness to impose any new conditions on China, or to settle questions not directly connected with that particular dispute.

If, Mr. Ambassador, in noting the refusal of the Japanese Government to transport Chinese troops at the time of the 1929 conflict, you refer to the South Manchurian Railway and contrast this with the alleged transport of Chinese troops by the Chinese Eastern Railway during the present Japanese-Chinese conflict, may I make the following explanation. The South Manchurian Railway is under the complete direction and control of Japan and is guarded by Japanese troops, while the Chinese Eastern Railway is under joint Soviet-Chinese administration and is guarded by Chinese troops, under the exclusive control of the Chinese authorities. You are no doubt aware that the Soviet Government voluntarily surrendered the privilege of the Tsarist Government to maintain troops in China and particularly on the Chinese Eastern Railway. It does not regret having done so, for it is convinced that in renouncing the privileges of the Tsarist Government it acted quite correctly. But it follows that conditions on the SMR cannot be identified with conditions on the CER. The Soviet Government is not aware that the Chinese troops guarding the CER were transported by the CER for military operations. There was no necessity for this so long as the sphere of the Japanese-Chinese conflict was confined to South Manchuria. The danger could arise only when the Japanese troops moved up to the line of the CER. When this danger materialized, the Soviet Government took the fact into account and on 12 November instructed the Soviet section of the CER administration to continue to pursue a policy of neutrality and in no circumstances to agree to the transport to the front by the CER of the troops of either of the belligerent parties. And in fact, notwithstanding all the difficulties created by the proximity of the front, the CER as a whole was able to maintain a neutral position. I considered it necessary to make this explanation, Mr. Ambassador, in order to emphasize that I cannot agree with you concerning the responsibility of the CER.

The Soviet Government notes with satisfaction the repeated assurances of the Japanese Government of its anxiety to prevent any damage to the interests of the CER and the USSR, of the absence of any intention on the part of the Japanese armies of paralyzing the work of the CER. But it must be noted that despite the original statement you made to me on the instructions of your Government, of its orders concerning the maximum narrowing down of military operations in Manchuria, these operations have been steadily extended and have gone far beyond their original limits. This fact, which increases the possibility that Soviet interests may be involved, cannot fail to cause grave anxiety to the Soviet Government.

In all its relations with other States the Soviet Government has consistently pursued a strict policy of peace and of peaceful relations. It attaches great importance to the maintenance and consolidation of its present relations with Japan. It adheres to a policy of strict noninterference in the conflicts between other countries. It assumes that the Japanese Government, too, is anxious to maintain the relations between the two countries and that in all its actions and dispositions it will respect the inviolability of Soviet interests.

Degras, II, 515-517.

STALIN REVEALS PERSONAL VIEWS AND PAST WITH GERMAN BIOGRAPHER, EMIL LUDWIG

13 December 1931

In a personal interview with the German author and biographer, Emil Ludwig, Stalin revealed his personal views about Russian history, Marxism, America, and relations with Germany and Poland. He briefly described how he became a Marxist revolutionary, how he was Lenin's pupil, and how he would apply the most ruthless methods against the enemies of the Soviet Union because previous mildness had proven counterproductive.

TALK WITH THE GERMAN AUTHOR EMIL LUDWIG

Ludwig: I am extremely obliged to you for having found it possible to receive me. For over twenty years I have been studying the lives and deeds of outstanding historical personages. I believe I am a good judge of people, but on the other hand I know nothing about social-economic conditions.

Stalin: You are being modest.

Ludwig: No, that is really so, and for that very reason I shall put questions that may seem strange to you. Today, here in the Kremlin, I saw some relics of Peter the Great and the first question I should like to ask you is this: Do you think a parallel can be drawn between yourself and Peter the Great? Do you consider yourself a continuer of the work of Peter the Great?

Stalin: In no way whatever. Historical parallels are always risky. There is no sense in this one.

Ludwig: But after all, Peter the Great did a great deal to develop his country, to bring western culture to Russia.

Stalin: Yes, of course, Peter the Great did much to elevate the landlord class and develop the nascent merchant class. He did very much indeed to create and consolidate the national state of the landlords and merchants. It must be said also that the elevation of the landlord class, the assistance to the nascent merchant class and the consolidation of the national state of these classes took place at the cost of peasant serfs, who were bled white.

As for myself, I am just a pupil of Lenin's, and the aim of my life is to be a worthy pupil of his.

The task to which I have devoted my life is the elevation of a different class—the working class. That task is not the consolidation of some "national" state, but of a socialist state, and that means an international state; and everything that strengthens that state helps to strengthen the entire international working class. If every step I take in my endeavor to elevate the working class were not directed towards strengthening and improving the position of the working class, I should consider my life purposeless.

So you see your parallel does not fit.

As regards Lenin and Peter the Great, the latter was but a drop in the sea, whereas Lenin was a whole ocean.

Ludwig: Marxism denies that the individual plays an outstanding role in history. Do you not see a contradiction between the materialist conception of history and the fact that, after all, you admit the outstanding role played by historical personages?

Stalin: No, there is no contradiction here. Marxism does not at all deny the role played by outstanding individuals or that history is made by people. In Marx' *The Poverty of Philosophy* and in other works of his you will find it stated that it is people who make history. But, of course, people do not make history according to the promptings of their imagination or as some fancy strikes them. Every new generation encounters definite conditions already existing, ready-made when that generation was born. And great people are worth anything at all only to the extent that they are able correctly to understand these conditions, to understand how to change them. If they fail to understand these conditions and want to alter them according to the promptings of their imagination, they will land themselves in the situation of Don Quixote. Thus it is precisely Marx' view that people must not be counterposed to conditions. It is people who make history, but they do so only to the extent that they correctly understand the conditions that they have found ready-made, and only to the extent that they understand how to change those conditions. That, at least, is how we Russian Bolsheviks understand Marx. And we have been studying Marx for a good many years.

Ludwig: Some thirty years ago, when I was at the university, many German professors who considered themselves adherents of the materialist conception of history taught us that Marxism denies the role of heroes, the role of heroic personalities in history.

Stalin: They were vulgarizers of Marxism. Marxism has never denied the role of heroes. On the contrary, it admits that they play a considerable role, but with the reservations I have made.

Ludwig: Sixteen chairs are placed around the table at which we are seated. Abroad people know, on the one hand, that the USSR is a country in which everything must be decided collectively, but they know, on the other hand, that everything is decided by individual persons. Who really does decide?

Stalin: No, individual persons cannot decide. Decisions of individuals are always, or nearly always, one-sided decisions. In every collegium, in every collective body, there are people whose opinion must be reckoned with. In every collegium, in every collective body, there are people who may express wrong opinions. From the experience of three revolutions we know that out of every 100 decisions taken by individual persons without being tested and corrected collectively, approximately 90 are one-sided.

In our leading body, the Central Committee of our Party, which directs all our Soviet and Party organizations, there are about 70 members. Among these 70 members of the Central Committee are our best industrial leaders, our best cooperative leaders, our best managers of supplies, our best military men, our best propagandists and agitators, our best experts on state farms, on collective farms, on individual peasant farms, our best experts on the nations constituting the Soviet Union and on national policy. In this areopagus is concentrated the wisdom of our Party. Each has an opportunity of correcting anyone's individual opinion or proposal. Each has an opportunity of contributing his experience. If this were not the case, if decisions were taken by individual persons, there would be very serious mistakes in our work. But since each has an opportunity of correcting the mistakes of individual persons, and since we pay heed to such corrections, we arrive at decisions that are more or less correct.

Ludwig: You have had decades of experience of illegal work. You have had to transport illegally arms, literature, and so forth. Do you not think that the enemies of the Soviet regime might learn from your experience and fight the Soviet regime with the same methods?

Stalin: That, of course, is quite possible.

Ludwig: Is that not the reason for the severity and ruthlessness of your government in fighting its enemies?

Stalin: No, that is not the chief reason. One could quote certain examples from history. When the Bolsheviks came to power they at first treated their enemies mildly. The Mensheviks continued to exist legally and publish their newspaper. The Socialist-Revolutionaries also continued to exist legally and had their newspaper. Even the Kadets continued to publish their newspaper. When General Krasnov organized his counterrevolutionary campaign against Leningrad and fell into our hands, we could at least have kept him prisoner, according to the rules of war. Indeed, we ought to have shot him. But we released him on his "word of honor". And what happened? It soon became clear that such mildness only helped to undermine the strength of the Soviet Government. We made a mistake in displaying such mildness towards enemies of the working class. To have persisted in that mistake would have been a crime against the working class and a betrayal of its interests. That soon became quite apparent. Very soon it became evident that the milder our attitude towards our enemies, the greater their resistance. Before long the Right Socialist-Revolutionaries—Gotz and others—and the Right Mensheviks were organizing in Leningrad a counterrevolutionary action of the military cadets, as a result of which many of our revolutionary sailors perished. This very Krasnov, whom we had released on his "word of honor", organized the whiteguard Cossacks. He joined forces with Mamontov and for two years waged an armed struggle against the Soviet Government. Very soon it turned out that behind the whiteguard generals stood the agents of the western capitalist states—France, Britain, America—and also Japan. We became convinced that we had made a mistake in displaying mildness. We learned from experience that the only way to deal with such enemies is to apply the most ruthless policy of suppression to them.

Ludwig: It seems to me that a considerable part of the population of the Soviet Union stands in fear and trepidation of Soviet power, and that the stability of the latter rests to a certain extent on that sense of fear. I should like to know what state of mind is produced in you personally by the realization that it is necessary to inspire fear in the interests of strengthening the regime. After all, when you associate with your comrades, your friends, you adopt quite different methods than those of inspiring fear. Yet the population is being inspired with fear.

Stalin: You are mistaken. Incidentally, your mistake is that of many people. Do you really believe that we could have retained power and have had the backing of the vast masses for 14 years by methods of intimidation and terrorization? No, that is impossible. The tsarist government excelled all others in knowing how to intimidate. It had long and vast experience in that sphere. The European bourgeoisie, particularly the French, gave tsarism every assistance in this matter and taught it to terrorize the people. Yet, in spite of that experience and in spite of the European bourgeoisie, the policy of intimidation led to the downfall of tsarism.

Ludwig: But the Romanovs held on for 300 years.

Stalin: Yes, but how many revolts and uprisings there were during those 300 years! There was the uprising of Stepan Razin, the uprising of Iemelian Pugachev, the uprising of the Decembrists, the revolution of 1905, the revolution of February 1917, and the October Revolution. That is apart from the fact that the present conditions of political and cultural life in the country are radically different from those of the old regime, when the ignorance, lack of culture, submissiveness and political downtroddenness of the masses enabled the "rulers" of that time to remain in power for a more or less prolonged period.

As regards the people, the workers and peasants of the USSR, they are not at all so tame, so submissive and intimidated as you imagine. There are many people in Europe whose ideas about the people of the USSR are old-fashioned: They think that the people living in Russia are, firstly, submissive, and, secondly, lazy. That is an antiquated and radically wrong notion. It arose in Europe in those days when the Russian landlords began to flock to Paris, where they squandered the loot they had amassed and spent their days in idleness. These were indeed spineless and worthless people. That gave rise to conclusions about "Russian laziness". But this cannot in the least apply to the Russian workers and peasants, who earned and still earn their living by their own labor. It is indeed strange to consider the Russian peasants and workers submissive and lazy when in a brief period of time they made three revolutions, smashed tsarism and the bourgeoisie, and are now triumphantly building socialism.

Just now you asked me whether everything in our country was decided by one person. Never under any circumstances would our workers now tolerate power in the hands of one person. With us personages of the greatest authority are reduced to nonentities, become mere ciphers, as soon as the masses of the workers lose confidence in them, as soon as they lose contact with the masses of the workers. Plekhanov used to enjoy exceptionally great prestige. And what happened? As soon as he began to stumble politically the workers forgot him. They forsook him and forgot him. Another instance: Trotsky. His prestige too was great, although, of course, it was nothing like Plekhanov's. What happened? As soon as he drifted away from the workers they forgot him.

Ludwig: Entirely forgot him?

Stalin: They remember him sometimes—but with bitterness.

Ludwig: All of them with bitterness?

Stalin: As far as our workers are concerned, they remember Trotsky with bitterness, with exasperation, with hatred.

There is, of course, a certain small section of the population that really does stand in fear of Soviet power, and fights against it. I have in mind the remnants of the moribund classes, which are being eliminated, and primarily that insignificant part of the peasantry, the kulaks. But here it is a matter not merely of a policy of intimidating these groups, a policy that really does exist. Everybody knows that in this case we Bolsheviks do not confine ourselves to intimidation but go further, aiming at the elimination of this bourgeois stratum.

But if you take the laboring population of the USSR, the workers and the laboring peasants, who represent not less than 90 percent of the population, you will find that they are in favor of Soviet power and that the vast majority of them actively support the Soviet regime. They support the Soviet system because that system serves the fundamental interests of the workers and peasants.

That, and not a policy of so-called intimidation, is the basis of the Soviet Government's stability.

Ludwig: I am very grateful to you for that answer. I beg you to forgive me if I ask you a question that may appear to you a strange one. Your biography contains instances of what may be called acts of "highway robbery". Were you ever interested in the personality of Stepan Razin? What is your attitude towards him as an "ideological highwayman"?

Stalin: We Bolsheviks have always taken an interest in such historical personalities as Bolotnikov, Razin, Pugachev, and so on. We regard the deeds of these individuals as a reflection of the spontaneous indignation of the oppressed classes, of the spontaneous rebellion of the peasantry against feudal oppression. The study of the history of these first attempts at such revolt on the part of the peasantry has always been of interest to us. But, of course, no analogy can be drawn here between them and the Bolsheviks. Sporadic peasant uprisings, even when not of the "highway robber" and unorganized type, as in the case of Stepan Razin, cannot lead to anything of importance. Peasant uprisings can be successful only if they are combined with uprisings of the workers and if they are led by the workers. Only a combined uprising headed by the working class can achieve its aim.

Moreover, it must never be forgotten that Razin and Pugachev were tsarists: They came out against the landlords, but were in favor of a "good tsar". That indeed was their slogan.

As you see, it is impossible to draw an analogy here with the Bolsheviks.

Ludwig: Allow me to put a few questions to you concerning your biography. When I went to see Masaryk he told me he was conscious of being a Socialist when only six years old. What made you a Socialist and when was that?

Stalin: I cannot assert that I was already drawn to socialism at the age of six. Not even at the age of ten or twelve. I joined the revolutionary movement when fifteen years old, when I became connected with underground groups of Russian Marxists then living in Transcaucasia. These groups exerted great influence on me and instilled in me a taste for underground Marxist literature.

Ludwig: What impelled you to become an oppositionist? Was it, perhaps, bad treatment by your parents?

Stalin: No. My parents were uneducated, but they did not treat me badly by any means. But it was a different matter at the Orthodox theological seminary which I was then attending. In protest against the outrageous regime and the jesuitical methods prevalent at the seminary,

I was ready to become, and actually did become, a revolutionary, a believer in Marxism as a really revolutionary teaching.

Ludwig: But do you not admit that the Jesuits have good points?

Stalin: Yes, they are systematic and persevering in working to achieve sordid ends. But their principal method is spying, prying, worming their way into people's souls and outraging their feelings. What good can there be in that? For instance, the spying in the hostel. At nine o'clock the bell rings for morning tea, we go to the dining-room, and when we return to our rooms we find that meantime a search has been made and all our chests have been ransacked.... What good point can there be in that?

Ludwig: I notice that in the Soviet Union everything American is held in very high esteem, I might even speak of a worship of everything American, that is, of the Land of the Dollar, the most out-and-out capitalist country. This sentiment exists also in your working class, and applies not only to tractors and automobiles, but also to Americans in general. How do you explain that?

Stalin: You exaggerate. We have no especially high esteem for everything American. But we do respect the efficiency that the Americans display in everything—in industry, in technology, in literature and in life. We never forget that the USA is a capitalist country. But among the Americans there are many people who are mentally and physically healthy, who are healthy in their whole approach to work, to the job on hand. That efficiency, that simplicity, strikes a responsive chord in our hearts. Despite the fact that America is a highly developed capitalist country, the habits prevailing in its industry, the practices existing in productive processes, have an element of democracy about them, which cannot be said of the old European capitalist countries, where the haughty spirit of the feudal aristocracy is still alive.

Ludwig: You do not even suspect how right you are.

Stalin: Maybe I do; who can tell?

In spite of the fact that feudalism as a social order was demolished long ago in Europe, considerable relics survive in manner of life and customs. There are still technicians, specialists, scientists and writers who have sprung from the feudal environment and who carry aristocratic habits into industry, technology, science and literature. Feudal traditions have not been entirely demolished.

That cannot be said of America, which is a country of "free colonists", without landlords and without aristocrats. Hence the sound and comparatively simple habits in American productive life. Our business executives of working-class origin who have visited America at once noted this trait. They relate, not without a certain agreeable surprise, that on a production job in America it is difficult to distinguish an engineer from a worker by outward appearance. That pleases them, of course. But matters are quite different in Europe.

But if we are going to speak of our liking for a particular nation, or rather, for the majority of its citizens, then of course we must not fail to mention our liking for Germans. Our liking for the Americans cannot be compared to that!

Ludwig: Why precisely the German nation?

Stalin: If only for the reason that it gave the world such men as Marx and Engels. It suffices to state the fact as such.

Ludwig: It has recently been noticed that certain German politicians are seriously afraid that the traditional policy of friendship between the USSR and Germany will be pushed into the background. These fears have arisen in connection with the negotiations between the USSR and Poland. Should the recognition of Poland's present frontiers by the USSR become a fact as a result of these negotiations it would spell bitter disappointment for the entire German people, who have hitherto believed that the USSR is fighting the Versailles system and has no intention of recognizing it.

Stalin: I know that a certain dissatisfaction and alarm may be noticed among some German statesmen on the grounds that the Soviet Union, in its negotiations or in some treaty with Poland, may take some step that would imply on the part of the Soviet Union a sanction, a guarantee, for Poland's possessions and frontiers.

In my opinion such fears are mistaken. We have always declared our readiness to conclude a nonaggression pact with any state. We have already concluded such pacts with a number of countries. We have openly declared our readiness to sign such a pact with Poland, too. When we declare that we are ready to sign a pact of nonaggression with Poland, this is not mere rhetoric. It means that we really want to sign such a pact. We are politicians of a special brand, if you like. There are politicians who make a promise or statement one day, and on the next either forget all about it or deny what they stated, and do so without even blushing. We cannot act in that way. Whatever we do abroad inevitably becomes known inside our country, becomes known to all the workers and peasants. If we said one thing and did another, we should forfeit our prestige among the masses of the people. As soon as the Poles declared that they are ready to negotiate a nonaggression pact with us, we naturally agreed and opened negotiations.

What, from the Germans' point of view, is the most dangerous thing that could happen? A change for the worse in our relations with them? But there is no basis whatever for that. We, exactly like the Poles, must declare in the pact that we will not use force or resort to aggression in order to change the frontiers of Poland or the USSR, or violate their independence. Just as we make such a promise to the Poles, so they make the same promise to us. Without such a clause, namely, that we do not intend to go to war for the purpose of violating the independence or integrity of the frontiers of our respective states, no pact can be concluded. Without that a pact is out of the question. That is the most that we can do.

Is this recognition of the Versailles system? No. Or is it, perhaps, a guaranteeing of frontiers? No. We never have been guarantors of Poland and never shall become such, just as Poland has not been and will not be a guarantor of our frontiers. Our friendly relations with Germany will continue as hitherto. That is my firm conviction.

Therefore, the fears you speak of are wholly without foundation. They have arisen on the basis of rumors spread by some Poles and Frenchmen. They will disappear when we publish the pact, if Poland signs it. Everyone will then see that it contains nothing against Germany.

Ludwig: I am very thankful to you for that statement. Allow me to ask you the following question: You speak of "wage equalization", giving the term a distinctly ironical shade of meaning in relation to general equalization. But, surely, general equalization is a socialist ideal.

Stalin: The kind of socialism under which everybody would get the same pay, an equal quantity of meat and an equal quantity of bread, would wear the same clothes and receive the same goods in the same quantities—such a socialism is unknown to Marxism.

All that Marxism says is that until classes have been finally abolished and until labor has been transformed from a means of subsistence into the prime want of man, into voluntary labor for society, people will be paid for their labor according to the work performed. "From each according to his ability, to each according to his work." Such is the Marxist formula of socialism, i.e., the formula of the first stage of communism, the first stage of communist society.

Only at the higher stage of communism, only in its higher phase, will each one, working according to his ability, be recompensed for his work according to his needs: "From each according to his ability, to each according to his needs."

It is quite clear that people's needs vary and will continue to vary under socialism. Socialism has never denied that people differ in their tastes, and in the quantity and quality of their needs. Read how Marx criticized Stirner for his leaning towards egalitarianism; read

Marx' criticism of the Gotha Program of 1875; read the subsequent works of Marx, Engels and Lenin, and you will see how sharply they attack egalitarianism. Egalitarianism owes its origin to the individual peasant type of mentality, the psychology of share and share alike, the psychology of primitive peasant "communism". Egalitarianism has nothing in common with Marxist socialism. Only people who are unacquainted with Marxism can have the primitive notion that the Russian Bolsheviks want to pool all wealth and then share it out equally. That is the notion of people who have nothing in common with Marxism. That is how such people as the primitive "Communists" of the time of Cromwell and the French Revolution pictured communism to themselves. But Marxism and the Russian Bolsheviks have nothing in common with such egalitarian "Communists".

Ludwig: You are smoking a cigarette. Where is your legendary pipe, Mr. Stalin? You once said that words and legends pass, but deeds remain. Now believe me, there are millions of people abroad who do not know about some of your words and deeds, but who do know about your legendary pipe.

Stalin: I left my pipe at home.

Ludwig: I shall now ask you a question that may astonish you greatly.

Stalin: We Russian Bolsheviks have long ceased to be astonished by anything.

Ludwig: Yes, and we in Germany too.

Stalin: Yes, you in Germany will soon stop being astonished.

Ludwig: My question is the following: You have often incurred risks and dangers. You have been persecuted. You have taken part in battles. A number of your close friends have perished. You have survived. How do you explain that? And do you believe in fate?

Stalin: No, I do not. Bolsheviks, Marxists, do not believe in "fate". The very concept of fate, of "Schicksal", is a prejudice, an absurdity, a relic of mythology, like the mythology of the ancient Greeks, for whom a goddess of fate controlled the destinies of men.

Ludwig: That is to say that the fact that you did not perish is an accident?

Stalin: There are internal and external causes, the combined effect of which was that I did not perish. But entirely independent of that, somebody else could have been in my place, for somebody *had* to occupy it. "Fate" is something not governed by natural law, something mystical. I do not believe in mysticism. Of course, there were reasons why danger left me unscathed. But there could have been a number of other fortuitous circumstances, of other causes, which could have led to a directly opposite result. So-called fate has nothing to do with it.

Ludwig: Lenin passed many years in exile abroad. You had occasion to be abroad for only a very short time. Do you consider that this has handicapped you? Who do you believe were of greater benefit to the revolution—those revolutionaries who lived in exile abroad and thus had the opportunity of making a thorough study of Europe, but on the other hand were cut off from direct contact with the people; or those revolutionaries who carried on their work here, knew the moods of the people, but on the other hand knew little of Europe?

Stalin: Lenin must be excluded from this comparison. Very few of those who remained in Russia were as intimately connected with the actual state of affairs there and with the labor movement within the country as Lenin was, although he was a long time abroad. Whenever I went to see him abroad—in 1906, 1907, 1912 and 1913—I saw piles of letters he had received from practical Party workers in Russia, and he was always better informed than those who stayed in Russia. He always considered his stay abroad to be a burden to him.

There are many more comrades in our Party and its leadership who remained in Russia, who did not go abroad, than there are former exiles, and they, of course, were able to be of greater benefit to the revolution than those who were in exile abroad. Actually few former exiles are left in our Party. They may add up to about one or two hundred out of the two million members of the Party. Of the seventy members of the Central Committee scarcely more than three or four lived in exile abroad.

As far as knowledge of Europe, a study of Europe, is concerned, those who wished to make such a study had, of course, more opportunities of doing so while living there. In that respect those of us who did not live long abroad lost something. But living abroad is not at all a decisive factor in making a study of European economics, technique, the cadres of the labor movement and literature of every description, whether belles lettres or scientific. Other things being equal, it is of course easier to study Europe on the spot. But the disadvantage of those who have not lived in Europe is not as much importance. On the contrary, I know many comrades who were abroad twenty years, lived in Charlottenburg or in the Latin Quarter, spent years in cafes drinking beer, and who yet did not manage to acquire a knowledge of Europe and failed to understand it.

Ludwig: Do you not think that among the Germans as a nation love of order is more highly developed than love of freedom?

Stalin: There was a time when people in Germany did indeed show great respect for the law. In 1907, when I happened to spend two or three months in Berlin, we Russian Bolsheviks often used to laugh at some of our German friends on account of their respect for the law. There was, for example, a story in circulation about an occasion when the Berlin Social-Democratic Executive fixed a definite day and hour for a demonstration that was to be attended by the members of all the suburban organizations. A group of about 200 from one of the suburbs arrived in the city punctually at the hour appointed, but failed to appear at the demonstration, the reason being that they had waited two hours on the station platform because the ticket collector at the exit had failed to make his appearance and there had been nobody to give their ticket to. It used to be said in jest that it took a Russian comrade to show the Germans a simple way out of their fix: To leave the platform without giving up their tickets....

But is there anything like that in Germany now? Is there respect for the law in Germany today? What about the National Socialists, who one would think ought to be the first to stand guard over bourgeois legality? Do they not break the law, wreck workers' clubs and assassinate workers with impunity?

I make no mention of the workers, who, it seems to me, long ago lost all respect for bourgeois legality.

Yes, the Germans have changed quite a bit lately.

Ludwig: Under what conditions is it possible to unite the working class finally and completely under the leadership of one party? Why is such a uniting of the working class possible only after the proletarian revolution, as the Communists maintain?

Stalin: Such a uniting of the working class around the Communist Party is most easily accomplished as the result of a victorious proletarian revolution. But it will undoubtedly be achieved in the main even before the revolution.

Ludwig: Does ambition stimulate or hinder a great historical figure in his activities?

Stalin: The part played by ambition differs under different conditions. Ambition may be a stimulus or a hindrance to the activities of a great historical figure. It all depends on circumstances. More often than not it is a hindrance.

Ludwig: Is the October Revolution in any sense the continuation and culmination of the Great French Revolution?

Stalin: The October Revolution is neither the continuation nor the culmination of the Great French Revolution. The purpose of the French Revolution was to abolish feudalism in order to establish capitalism. The purpose of the October Revolution, however, is to abolish capitalism in order to establish socialism.

Stalin, *Works*, XIII, 106-125.

DOCUMENTS BY MAIN TOPICS

COMMUNIST INTERNATIONAL

ECONOMIC POLICIES, INDUSTRY, INDUSTRIAL WORKERS

EDUCATION, CULTURE, ARTS, CULTURAL POLICY

FOREIGN POLICY AND INTERNATIONAL RELATIONS

LAW CODES AND LEGAL ISSUES

MILITARY AFFAIRS

NATIONALITIES

POLITICS AND THE COMMUNIST PARTY

RELIGIOUS ISSUES

GLOSSARY

The glossary is intended to assist those unfamiliar with Russian terminology of the period covered in this volume. Many specific institutions are identified in headnotes to documents in which they are mentioned.

active—see aktiv.
agitprop—Russian acronym for agitation and propaganda. Special organizations established for this purpose were part of many Soviet governmental and party organizations.
aktiv—most active members of a Communist Party organization.
All-Russian—term often used to denote an institution which pertained to the entire RSFSR (Russian republic), such as in "All-Russian Congress of Soviets." Used especially after implementation of constitution creating the RSFSR in 1918.
artel—artisan or agricultural cooperative; a type of collective farm in which the members own implements and farm arable land in common, and each household retains a plot.
AUCCTU (VTsSPS)—All-Union Central Council of Trade Unions.
aul—Turkic word for village in Central Asia and Caucasus.
batrak—hired, day laborer on the farm.
Bund—Jewish socialist party prior to the October Revolution.
CC (TsK)—Central Committee (of the Communist Party).
CCC (TsKK)—Central Control Commission (of the Communist Party).
CEC (TsIK)—Central Executive Committee (executive of the Congress of Soviets). See also VTsIK.

centner—equivalent of 100 kilograms.
CP—Communist Party
CPSU(B)—Communist Party of the Soviet Union (Bolsheviks).
Cheka—The All-Russia Extraordinary Commission to Combat Counter-Revolution and Sabotage; the political police until 1922.
chervonets—unit of currency introduced in 1922 as part of effort to stabilize the currency; coexisted for a period with the ruble.
Comintern—Communist International.
commissar (sometimes commissioner, commissary)—used to denote revolutionary officials in 1917, became the official term for the main government department heads in the Soviet government, used until 1946, as in People's Commissar of for Foreign Affairs." Equivalent of Minister (European) or Secretary (American).
commune—land owned and worked in common, and all animals, implements, and buildings are collectively owned; in many cases, conceived as members' sharing living quarters and preparing and eating food together.
Constituent Assembly—assembly elected by general popular vote with right to determine future of Russia. Elected in November 1917 and dispersed by Bolsheviks following first meeting in January 1918.
Constitutional Democratic Party (Constitutional Democrats, Kadets)—the major Russian liberal party.
CPC—See Council of People's Commissars.
Council for Labor and Defense (STO)—important council of the early Soviet period, responsible especially for coordinating economic and military issues.
Council of People's Commissars (Sovnarkom)—title of government established after the Bolshevik Revolution; in 1946 replaced by the term Council of Ministers.
desiatina—traditional Russian land measurement; one desiatin=2.7 acres or 1.09 hectares.
EKOSO—Economic Council of the Council of People's Commissars of the RSFSR.
ECCI—Executive Committee of the Communist International.
duma—(1) the State Duma, the parliament from 1905-1917 (especially if capitalized); (2) name of city councils before the revolution.
Glavki (sing. Glavk)—central administrative committees or directorates; used especially in economic departments. "Glav" at the beginning of a title usually suggests a central administrative department for that activity and is commonly translated as "chief" or "main."
Glavlit—Main Administration for Affairs of Literature and Publishing.
Goelro—State Commission for the Electrification of Russia.
Gosplan—State Planning Commission.
GPU—State Political Administration. Political Police. Became OGPU (United State Political Administration) in 1923; continued to be called GPU.
guberniia—province, the main administrative subdivision of Russian Empire and of the Soviet State until 1929.
Gubkom—Guberniia committee of the Communist Party.
Izvestiia—without a qualifier refers to the official newspaper of the Soviet government; many local newspapers also tended to be named *Izvestiia*.
IKKI—Executive Committee of the Communist International.
Kadets—See Constitutional Democratic Party.
khozraschet—economic accounting.
kolkhoz—collective farm.
kommuna—see commune.
Komsomol—Communist Youth League.
kulak (pl. kulaki, kulaks)—More prosperous peasant, generally able to hire labor; applied pejoratively by Communists to any peasant opposing their policies.

Left SRs, Left Socialist Revolutionaries—see Socialist Revolutionaries.
Mensheviks—main Russian Marxist party in opposition to Bolsheviks.
Menshevik-Internationalists—left wing of Mensheviks, often cooperated with Bolsheviks in 1917-1918.
MTS—Machine Tractor Station.
Narkompros—People's Commissariat for Education, or alternatively, of Enlightenment (translations vary).
Narodnik (pl. narodniki, narodniks)—Populist(s); agrarian socialist(s).
NEP—The New Economic Policy introduced in 1921; also the era of NEP, i.e., the 1920s.
nomenklatura—system of lists and classifications by which officials are appointed to positions of economic and political authority by the Communist Party.
Nuclei—local party organizations, the lowest level of party organization; party cell.
Obkom—Oblast committee of the Communist Party.
oblast—large administrative subdivision used in some regions instead of guberniia; roughly a province.
obshchina—traditional Russian peasant commune.
OGPU—United State Political Administration. New name for the political police introduced in 1923 along with formation of the Soviet Union.
okrug—large administrative unit, usually subdivision of an oblast, equivalent to an uezd in a guberniia. Certain other types of administrative units also were called okrug, such as some military districts.
Orgburo—The Organizational Bureau of the Central Committee of the Communist Party; a key administrative body of the party.
Party—used with or without capitalization, to mean the Communist Party, as in "the party intends to..."
People's Commissariat—the chief administrative departments of the Soviet government; see commissar, above.
Politburo—Political Bureau of the Central Committee of the Communist Party; effectively the key leadership body.
Politprosvet—Political Educational Committee (of Narkompros).
pood—see pud.
Pravda—central official paper of the Communist Party; some local party papers also used the title.
Proletcult (Proletkult)—Union of Proletarian Cultural-Education Associations.
pud (pood)—Russian measure of weight, equaling 36.11 lbs. or 16.38 kg.
Rabkrin—Workers' and Peasants' Inspectorate.
Rada—lit., Ukrainian equivalent of "soviet." Originally in political sense referred to the Ukrainian Central Rada set up in Kiev during the revolution and which proclaimed itself the government for Ukraine after the Bolshevik Revolution; later part of the Ukrainian language term for the Ukrainian Soviet government and local governments.
Raikom—raion committee of the Communist Party.
raion—smaller administrative subdistrict in some rural areas; also in some larger cities.
Revolutionary Tribunals—special courts set up to expedite revolutionary justice and to deal with important political cases; there also were special tribunals for press and other purposes.
RILU—Red International of Labor Unions.
RKP(b)—Russian Communist Party (Bolsheviks), the party name from the name change of March 1918 to 1925.
RSDRP—Russian Social Democratic Labor Party; without further clarification can refer to either the Bolsheviks or Mensheviks, or, less frequently, to smaller groups.
RSDRP(b)—Russian Social Democratic Labor Party (Bolsheviks), the usual designation for the Bolsheviks before ch ange of party name in 1918.

RSFSR—Russian Socialist Federal Soviet Republic; official name of the new state under constitution of 1918. Later terms were reversed—Russian Soviet Federal Socialist Republic. Middle word translated variously as Federal, Federative or Federated.

RVS(S)—Revolutionary Armed Forces (of the Soviet Union)

Selkom—village committee of the Communist Party.

Smena vekh (Smenovekh, smenavekhov and other forms of the term)—a movement, especially among Russian emigres and former liberal and conservative opponents of the regime, for reconciliation with the Soviet regime on the basis that it was the upholder of Russia's national independence. Used by Communist Party leaders pejoratively. Lit.: "Change of Landmarks."

Smychka—the policy of a close relationship between town and countryside, of workers and peasants.

SNK—Russian initials for Council of People's Commissars (Sovnarkom); used infrequently in translations.

Socialist Revolutionaries—peasant oriented revolutionary party, largest party in 1917 and in Constituent Assembly. The left wing emerged in late 1917 as a virtual separate party, the Left SRs, and cooperated with the Bolsheviks during the first months after the October Revolution.

Soviet—council in Russian. Used both as a short form name of the government (or for reference to its institutions, policies, etc.), and to refer to a variety of other institutions which use that term in their title, i.e., call themselves a council.

Soviet of People's Commissars—alternative translation for Council of People's Commissars (soviet=council).

Sovnarkom—Commonly used abbreviation for Council of People's Commissars, based on first syllable of each word (in Russian). See Council of People's Commissars.

SRs—See Socialist Revolutionaries.

STO—Soviet for Labor and Defense. See Council for Labor and Defense.

subbotnik—special days for voluntary work without pay for the good of society, which later became largely mandatory; lit., "saturdays."

toz (tovarischestvo po obrabotke zemli)—a type of collective farm in which members work some of the land in common, own major machinery collectively, and retain private ownership of animals and implements.

Tsektran—Central Committee for Transportation.

TsIK—Central Executive Committee (executive of the Congress of Soviets).

TsK (CC)—Central Committee (of the Communist Party).

TsKK (CCC)—Central Control Commission (of the Communist Party).

uezd (uyezd)—administrative subdivision of a *guberniia.*

verst (versta)—0.66 mile.

Vesenka—Supreme Council of the National Economy; also called VSNKh and Supreme Economic Council.

volost—rural administrative units within the *uezd.*

VSNKh—Supreme Council of the National Economy; also called *Vesenka* and Supreme Economic Council.

VTsIK—All–Russian Central Executive Committee, although often referred to simply as the Central Executive Committee, TsIK or CC.

White Guards—term used to refer to the Civil War opponents of the Bolsheviks, the "Whites", and at this period used to smear opponents, social groups, or political tendencies.

YCL—see Komsomol.

zemstvo—pre–revolutionary elected local and regional government institutions, especially in rural areas, with limited powers; abolished by Bolsheviks.

Zhenotdel—Women's Department of the Communist Party.

SOURCES CITED

Biulleten' Oppozitsiia. Paris.

Degras, Jane, ed., *Soviet Documents on Foreign Policy*. 3 vols. London: Oxford University Press, 1951-1953.

Fogelevich, L. G., ed., *Osnovnye Direktivy i Zakonodatel'stvo o Pechati*. Moscow: Gosudarstvennoe Izd-vo Sovetskoe Zakonodatel'stvo, 1934.

Goliakov, I. T., ed., *Sbornik Dokumentov po Istorii Ugolovnogo Zakonodatel'stva SSSR i RSFSR, 1917-1952*. Moscow: Gosudarstvennoe Izd-vo Iuridicheskoi Literatury, 1953.

Gsovski, Vladimir, *Soviet Civil Law*, Vol. 2. Ann Arbor: University of Michigan Law School, 1949.

International Press Correspondence. London.

Izvestiia. Moscow.

Kommunist. Moscow

Kommunisticheskaia Partiia Sovetskogo Soiuza v rezoliutsiiakh s"ezdov, konferentsii i plenumov TsK. Vols. 3 and 4, 1924-1931. Moscow: Izd-vo Politicheskoi Literatury, 1970.

KPSS v Vooruzhennykh Silakh. Dokumenty, 1917-1981. Moscow: Voennoe Izd-vo Ministerstva Oborony SSSR, 1981.

KPSS v Vooruzhennykh Silakh. Sbornik Dokumentov, 1917-1958. Moscow: Voennoe Izd-vo Ministerstva Oborony SSSR, 1958.

McNeal, Robert H., ed., *Resolutions and Decisions of the Communist Party of the Soviet Union*. Vol. 2, *The Early Soviet Period: 1917-1929*; Vol 3, *The Stalinist Period: 1930-1953*, ed. by Richard Gregor. Toronto: University of Toronto Press, 1974.

Maiakovsky, Vladimir, *Polnoe Sobranie Sochinenii*. Vol. 12. Moscow: Gosizdat, 1959.

Matthews, Mervyn, ed, *Party, State, and Citizen in the Soviet Union. A Collection of Documents*. Armonk, New York: M.E. Sharpe, 1989.

Polevoi Ustav RKKA (1929). Moscow-Leningrad: Gosudarstvennoe Izd-vo Otdel Voennoi Literatury, 1929.

Pravda. Moscow.

Resheniia Partii i Pravitel'stva po Khoziaistvennym Voprosam, Vol. 2, 1929-1940. Moscow: Izd-vo Politicheskoi Literatury, 1967.

Sbornik Dokumentov i Materialov po Istorii SSSR Sovetskogo Perioda (1917-1958 gg.). Moscow: Izd-vo Moskovskogo Universitata, 1966).

Sobranie Zakonov i Rasporiazhenii Raboche-krestianskogo Pravitel'stva Soiuza Sovetskikh Sotsialisticheskikh Respublik. Moscow.

Sovetsko-Kitaiskie Otnosheniia: Sbornik Dokumentov, 1917-1957. Moscow: Izd-vo Vostochnoi Literatury, 1959.

Soviet Treaty Series. Leonard Schapiro, ed. 2 vols. Washington, D.C.: Georgetown University Press, 1950.

Stalin, Joseph. *Works*. 13 vols. Moscow: Foreign Languages Publishing House, 1952-56.

Statute on the Corrective Labor Camps, USSR. Monograph. Center for International Studies, Massachusetts Institute of Technology, Cambridge, Massachusetts, 7 July 1955.

The Nation. New York.

U.K. Foreign Office. *A Selection of Documents relative to the Labour Legislation in force in the Union of Soviet Socialist Republics, Russia No. 1 (1931)*. London: HMSO, 1931.

U.S. National Archives II. College Park, Maryland.

U.S. Senate, Committee on the Judiciary, *The Church and State Under Communism*, 88th Congress, 2nd Session, 1964, Volume I, Part 1, *The USSR*, Law Library of the Library of Congress, Appendix 2, 12-17.

Wheeler-Bennett, John W., ed, *Documents on International Affairs, 1931*. London: Oxford University Press, 1932.

ACKNOWLEDGEMENTS

The Editor and Publisher wish to thank the following publishers for permission to reproduce copyrighted materials from their publications. The source is given for each document as it appears in the text.

Toronto University Press, for Robert H. McNeal, general series ed., *Resolutions and Decisions of the Communist Party of the Soviet Union*, Volume Two, *The Early Soviet Period: 1917–1929*; Volume Three, *The Stalin Years: 1930–1953*, ed. by Richard Gregor.

PERMISSIONS

INDEXES

The indexes contain page references to the documents and to the headnotes, but not to the Preface or Introduction. They tend to be inclusive rather than exclusive, especially for personal names and geographic places. Some minor persons and places mentioned only in passing, especially foreign ones are omitted. The subject index includes numerous cross references. Although there are headings for subjects and institutions such as Communist Party, Economy, Foreign Policy, such topics in fact pervade the documents and the collection.

INDEX OF PERSONAL NAMES

INDEX OF SUBJECTS

INDEX OF INSTITUTIONS

INDEX OF GEOGRAPHIC AND PLACE NAMES

FROM ACADEMIC INTERNATIONAL PRESS*

THE RUSSIAN SERIES

1 S.F. Platonov **History of Russia** **
2 **The Nicky-Sunny Letters, Correspondence of Nicholas and Alexandra, 1914-1917**
3 Ken Shen Weigh **Russo-Chinese Diplomacy, 1689-1924**
4 Gaston Cahen **Relations of Russia with China...1689-1730**
5 M.N. Pokrovsky **Brief History of Russia**
6 M.N. Pokrovsky **History of Russia from Earliest Times**
7 Robert J. Kerner **Bohemia in the Eighteenth Century**
8 **Memoirs of Prince Adam Czartoryski and His Correspondence with Alexander I**
9 S.F. Platonov **Moscow and the West.**
10 S.F. Platonov **Boris Godunov**
11 Boris Nikolajewsky **Aseff the Spy**
12 Francis Dvornik **Les Legendes de Constantin et de Methode vues de Byzance**
13 Francis Dvornik **Les Slaves, Byzance et Rome au XIe Siecle**
14 A. Leroy-Beaulieu **Un Homme d'Etat Russe (Nicholas Miliutine)...**
15 Nicolas Berdyaev **Leontiev** (In English)
16 V.O. Kliuchevskii **Istoriia soslovii v Rossii**
17 **Tehran Yalta Potsdam. The Soviet Protocols**
18 **The Chronicle of Novgorod**
19 Paul N. Miliukov **Outlines of Russian Culture Vol. III** Pt. 1. The Origins of Ideology
20 P.A. Zaionchkovskii **The Abolition of Serfdom in Russia**
21 V.V. Vinogradov **Russkii iazyk. Grammaticheskoe uchenie o slove**
22 P.A. Zaionchkovsky **The Russian Autocracy under Alexander III**
23 A.E. Presniakov **Emperor Nicholas I of Russia. The Apogee of Autocracy**
24 V.I. Semevskii **Krestianskii vopros v Rossii v XVIII i pervoi polovine XIX veka**
25 S.S. Oldenburg **Last Tsar! Nicholas II, His Reign and His Russia**
26 Carl von Clausewitz **The Campaign of 1812 in Russia**
27 M.K. Liubavskii **Obrazovanie osnovnoi gosudarstvennoi territorii velikorusskoi narodnosti. Zaselenie i obedinenie tsentra**
28 S.F. Platonov **Ivan the Terrible** Paper
29 Paul N. Miliukov **Iz istorii russkoi intelligentsii. Sbornik statei i etiudov**
30 A.E. Presniakov **The Tsardom of Muscovy**
31 M. Gorky, J. Stalin et al., **History of the Civil War in Russia** (Revolution)
32 R.G. Skrynnikov **Ivan the Terrible**
33 P.A. Zaionchkovsky **The Russian Autocracy in Crisis, 1878-1882**
34 Joseph T. Fuhrmann **Tsar Alexis. His Reign and His Russia**
35 R.G. Skrynnikov **Boris Godunov**
36 R.G. Skrynnikov **The Time of Troubles. Russia in Crisis, 1604–1618**
38 V.V. Shulgin **Days of the Russian Revolutions. Memoirs From the Right, 1905– 1907.** Cloth and Paper
39 A.E. Presniakov **The Formation of the Great Russian State.**
40 J.L. Black **"Into the Dustbin of History"! The USSR From August Coup to Commonwealth, 1991. A Documentary Narrative**
41 E.V. Anisimov **Empress Elizabeth. Her Reign and Her Russia, 1741–1761**
42 J.K. Libbey **Russian-American Economic Relations, 1763–1999**
43 Nicholas Zernov **Three Russian Prophets. Khomiakov, Dostoevsky, Soloviev**
44 Paul N. Miliukov **The Russian Revolution** 3 vols.
45 Anton I. Denikin **The White Army**
55 M.V. Rodzianko **The Reign of Rasputin—An Empire's Collapse. Memoirs**
56 **The Memoirs of Alexander Iswolsky**

THE CENTRAL AND EAST EUROPEAN SERIES

1 Louis Eisenmann **Le Compromis Austro-Hongrois de 1867**
3 Francis Dvornik **The Making of Central and Eastern Europe** 2nd edition
4 Feodor F. Zigel **Lectures on Slavonic Law**
10 Doros Alastos **Venizelos—Patriot, Statesman, Revolutionary**
20 Paul Teleki **The Evolution of Hungary and its Place in European History**

FORUM ASIATICA

1 M.I. Sladkovsky **China and Japan—Past and Present**

REFERENCE SERIES

The Modern Encyclopedia of Russian, Soviet and Eurasian History 59 vols.
The Modern Encyclopedia of East Slavic, Baltic and Eurasian Literatures 50 vols.
The Modern Encyclopedia of Religions in Russia and the Soviet Union 30 vols
Russia & Eurasia Military Review Annual
Russia & Eurasia Facts & Figures Annual
Russia & Eurasia Documents Annual
USSR Calendar of Events (1987- 1991) 5 vol. set
USSR Congress of Peoples's Deputies 1989. The Stenographic Record
Documents of Soviet History 12 vols.
Documents of Soviet-American Relations
Gorbachev's Reforms. An Annotated Bibliography of Soviet Writings. Part 1 1985–1987
Military Encyclopedia of Russia and Eurasia 50 vols.
China Facts & Figures Annual
China Documents Annual
Encyclopedia USA. The Encyclopedia of the United States of America Past & Present 50 vols.
Sports Encyclopedia North America 50 vols.
Sports in North America. A Documentary History
Religious Documents North America Annual
The International Military Encyclopedia 50 vols.
Nationalities and Ethnicity Terminologies. An Encyclopedic Dictionary and Research Guide

SPECIAL WORKS

S.M. Soloviev **History of Russia** 50 vols.
SAFRA Papers 1985-

*Request catalogs